INTERCO

Best of

CHINA

Eugene Law

China Intercontinental Press

HISTORY & CULTURE

THE GUIDE

Contents

FOREWORD

I'll never forget my mother's visit to Beijing two years ago. At age 72, she was coming to China for the first time in her life. Soon after entering my downtown apartment, this meticulous woman began to unpack her carefully organized suitcase. Wedged in with her clothes and shoes she had a few items that surprised me: a dozen rolls of toilet paper and a box of laundry detergent.

I couldn't figure out why she would have deemed such items necessary for a trip that would only last two weeks. Then it struck me: except for letters I had sent and conversations we had had about my life in China, her principal source of information about the country was outdated and overly cautious guidebooks written for the most part by short-term visitors.

These books comprised the first generation of China guides. Their authors were pioneering travelers who made their trips in the late 70s, 80s and early 90s when China had just opened to the world after several decades of isolation. Tourists who ventured to China during those years truly did need to worry about finding basic necessities.

At the time, few tourists had seen China – and for that matter, China had seen very few tourists. Because of this, the task of writing guidebooks in those days – guides to lands uncharted in the modern era – fell only to those authors who looked upon hardship as a badge of honor, who sought the glory of being labeled 'pioneers', no matter how many 24-hour hard-seat train rides they'd have to endure in the process. It was all part of the price one paid to go down in modern history as one of the first to set foot in the new China, a country that, to the outside world, had been shrouded in mystery for more than a generation.

A funny thing happened after these books were published: travelers following the routes these popular titles recommended soon created sub-cultures and worlds of their own within China; worlds of foreign travelers and backpacker hotspots in which the primary cultural experiences were foreign: Europeans and Americans running into Australians and Israelis while dining on banana pancakes in restaurants showing Hollywood films on big-screen TVs and playing Eminem on the stereo.

Though these first-generation books are updated every couple of years, it's hard for them to overcome what they are at their core – guides for those seeking a rough-hewn, but frankly clichéd, adventure.

From these pioneering guidebooks my mother came away with out-of-date perceptions of China that were rooted in this earlier generation of China travel. The world she read about was one where a roll of toilet paper would be hard to find, and where even using the tap water to rinse your toothbrush was an invitation to intestinal distress.

Imagine her surprise after arriving in Beijing, when instead of worrying about toilet paper, she was faced with difficult choices like where to dine in this food-lover's paradise. Would it be Peking Duck or Indian, Italian or Japanese cuisine? Or something more familiar from the Outback Steakhouse or TGIFriday's? Consider her shock when rather than encountering the dreaded dearth of washing powder, she was instead confronted by my local market's bulging aisle of cleansing products, their familiar names and screaming colors competing for the attention of discerning shoppers.

Perhaps her biggest misconception was the expectation that Beijing's streets would be clogged with cyclists in Mao suits, rather than the fleets of late model Audis and Buicks that she dodged with care.

As my mother's revelations demonstrate, China is undergoing such rapid change that a guidebook written even a couple of years ago is almost useless. China is no longer the destination for those looking to accumulate hardship tales of scarcity, penury and adversity overcome.

That's the reason a book like the one you're holding in your hands is so crucial. The guidebooks of old – and even some published very recently – have an overly cautious tone and an outsiders' perspective that depicts China as a world not to delve into but to skirt around and approach wearily. This one is different.

Written mostly by native English speakers who are not short-term tourists but long-term China residents, and edited by people who live and work in China, not in New York or London, this book lends a fresh perspective on all things Chinese. It melds foreign and local perspectives into a seamless narrative that allows new light to be cast on China's cities and places of interest.

This guidebook is not meant to be read as a novel. It does not assume the reader needs to be coddled and protected from China. Rather, it contains snapshots of rewarding things to do in and around China's most famous cities. Its compelling mix of cultural insights and practical information is designed to appeal to all readers, foreigners and Chinese, and to whet their appetite for travel in China.

Welcome to the second generation of China guidebooks. Sit back and enjoy.

Michael Wester

Manager of *that's Beijing* Magazine

HISTORY & CULTURE

Brief Introduction to China's History

Over 1.7 million years ago the early ancestors of humans roamed through China.

ARCHEOLOGY & ANCIENT HISTORY

China's culture is one of the oldest in the world. Legend has it that the first rulers of China who are three nobles and five emperors (*sānhuáng wǔdì* 三皇五帝). They're also considered as the ancestors of the Chinese people. Of these legendary figures, some taught the Chinese to build houses, others how to grow grain. All of them were idealized figures during a time when mankind was first learning how to survive in the world. The most famous two of these eight semi-deities were the emperors Yan and Huang. Today the Chinese often refer to themselves as *Yan Huang Zisun* (*Yán Huáng zǐsūn* 炎黄子孙) – descendants of the Yan and Huang emperors.

Despite the lack of written records, through rich archaeological finds, it's possible to build a picture of what life was like in prehistoric China. Fossils of an ancient hominid dating back 1.7 million years were found in Yuanmou County in Yunnan Province. The Yuanmou fossils are the earliest trace of human ancestors in China. Research has shown that during the prehistoric era there were many patches of human inhabitation throughout China. Unearthed jade and pottery show the civilization of that time was technologically advanced.

XIA (22nd – 17th CENTURY BC)

The Xia is the first dynasty recorded in China's history. The dynasty was established by Qi, son of Yu the Great, the legendary hero who tamed the Yellow River and controlled its perennial floods. The Erlitou ruins, discovered in Henan Province, illustrate the advanced technology of Xia culture, particularly the relics of an ancient palace, and point to the rule of one strong figure.

SHANG (17th – 11th CENTURY BC)

According to historical records, the Xia reigned for 471 years and was superseded by the Shang dynasty. The Shang powerbase was in what are now Henan, Hebei and Shandong provinces. Relics of the Shang dynasty, the Yin ruins, were discovered by archaeologists at Xiaotun Village in Henan Province. At the site they unearthed numerous tortoise shells and animal bones inscribed with *jiaguwen* (*jiǎgǔwén* 甲骨文), the precursor to modern Chinese characters. These bones, also called oracle bones, were used in divination ceremonies to help answer such basic questions as what dates would be auspicious for important events, what course of action to take and when to begin harvesting. These bones have given much information about the daily lives of the Shang people.

A significant amount of bronzeware was also excavated, of which the best known is the rectangular *simuwu ding* (*sīmǔwù dàfāngdǐng* 司母戊大方鼎). Named after the characters carved on it, this large vessel is 52 inches (133cm) high and weighs 1,929 pounds (875kg). The *simuwu* is an impressive piece – the technological skill required to cast such pieces was considerable. Much of the Shang bronzeware is inscribed with characters and decorations. The decorations are usually based on animalistic motifs; one that's particularly common is the *taotie* (*tāotiè* 饕餮), a mythical feral animal.

ZHOU (11th CENTURY – 256 BC)

King Zhou (*zhòuwáng* 纣王), the last king of the Shang dynasty and a despotic tyrant, was overthrown by the Zhou (no relation), a tribe from the west. The Zhou dynasty would become the longest ruling dynasty in Chinese history, lasting over 770 years. Initially the Zhou dynasty made its capital in Xi'an, Shaanxi Province, but the capital was later moved east to Luoyang in Henan Province. Historians divide the Zhou dynasty into Western Zhou and Eastern Zhou because of this shift.

The king of the Western Zhou distributed his lands as fiefs to the nobles of his clan. These nobles then established vassal states around the Zhou capital, protecting the ruling authority in the center. The Zhou rulers created an elaborate system of ceremonial rites with every rite matched to music and dance. The Zhou, as a method of control over their subjects, used these rites to explain the nature of the Zhou's supremacy and legitimacy to rule. By performing the rituals, the Zhou believed they maintained the "Mandate of Heaven." As long as the ruling elite continued to have this mandate, their authority to rule remained divinely ordained.

During the rule of King Ping, the capital was moved to Luoyang to escape the threat of the Quanrong, a tribe from the west. This marked the beginning of the Eastern Zhou dynasty. The Eastern Zhou is further subdivided into two periods, the Spring and Autumn period and the Warring States period.

The power of the Zhou kings was slowly whittled away as powerful nobles began to contend for power and only paid nominal homage to the king. Eventually the authority of the Zhou kings only extended to their territories immediately surrounding Luoyang. The most influential Zhou dukes became so powerful they were called "The Five Overlords of the Spring and Autumn Period."

Under a state of constant warfare and expansion, the social system of the Eastern Zhou changed radically. New technologies made their impact felt – the development of iron tools over stone tools coupled with the harnessing of animal power significantly increased agricultural production. With the expansion of agriculture, trade also grew and the first merchants and traders appeared.

The social classes also became more clearly defined into four groups – the scholar (*shì* 士), peasant farmer (*nóng* 农), manual laborer (*gōng* 工) and merchant (*shāng* 商). The social system outgrew the simplistic structure that the Western Zhou rites had established. What was desperately needed was a written code.

Enter Confucius, China's most influential teacher and philosopher who lived from 551 to 479 BC, during one of China's most turbulent periods. This was a transitional

Bronze *ding* vessels were an important part of early Chinese rituals.

time, a period between dynasties when local warlords fought for supremacy – a recurring theme in Chinese history. Confucian theories and teachings would eventually be known simply as Confucianism (*rú jiā* 儒家). His core belief stresses the idea of *ren* (*rén* 仁), which is approximately translated as benevolence, something he felt that society sorely lacked. Confucius traveled extensively, hoping to influence local leaders. On his travels he picked up a large following of students who continued his teachings after his death, thus laying the foundation for the Confucian school of thought, which continues to influence Asia to this day.

Once the Zhou dynasty became nothing but a name, the battle for supremacy intensified. The most powerful of these competing kingdoms are known as the "Seven Overlords." Each competing kingdom sought any advantage it could find over its rivals – this was a dynamic time, replete with reforms and stratagems. It was the Qin kingdom that most successfully reformed and adapted itself politically, economically and technologically to the changing times.

Under the Zhou, the ruling elite held a monopoly on power and were able to define what was culture. With the upheavals of the Warring States period, a new scholarly class (*shì rén* 士人) emerged at the cultural forefront. These scholars formed differing schools of thought, each offering their services as advisors in hopes of gaining influence. Out of this developed the "Hundred Schools of Thought," which promoted the development of systematic learning.

QIN (221 – 206 BC)

In 221 BC, King Ying Zheng (*Yíng Zhèng* 嬴政) established the first unified empire in Chinese history, and named himself Shi Huangdi, which means "First Emperor." He unified the Chinese script, currency and measurement system. His policies were focused on the exploration and stabilization of the Chinese frontier. One of his projects to protect his domains included the renowned Great Wall, which was built on the foundations of older walls. History remembers Qin Shihuang as a tyrant. Severe laws and penalties were enacted as a social control while supreme power lay with the emperor.

Another of the emperor's grandiose projects

A wall carving depicting Confucius' visits to various kingdoms.

included the Terracotta Army. Excavated in Shaanxi Province, this is part of the emperor's massive mausoleum. Tens of thousands of conscripts were sent to construct his tomb. The dynasty's tyrannical reign lasted a mere 16 years. After the emperor's death widespread rebellions broke out. Eventually a rebel army led by Liu Bang, a former local official, established the Han dynasty.

HAN (206 BC – AD 220)

Like the Zhou dynasty, the Han dynasty is divided into two phases, the Western Han and the Eastern Han. The Western Han settled its capital at Xi'an, while the Eastern Han returned it to Luoyang in AD 25. The emperor and his chancellors, having witnessed the sudden collapse of the Qin dynasty, realized that it wasn't feasible to rule a vast kingdom solely on a strict legal system. The monarch relaxed the "legalist system" and allowed the economy, destroyed by war, to recover. Emperor Wudi, one of the early Han emperors, was both ambitious and talented – his reign saw many achievements. By his reign, the Han dynasty was a thriving and powerful empire. One of his most enduring legacies was promoting Confucianism as the official ideology and applying it to the bureaucracy. Ministers were selected based on their knowledge of the Confucian classics, a system that was continued by succeeding dynasties up until the end of the Qing dynasty. He was also able to centralize power, thus removing the threat of powerful nobles rising in rebellion. On the economic side, new trade routes were established between China and Central Asia. Chinese silk was exported along these routes, which would become known as the Silk Road (*sīchóu zhīlù* 丝绸之路).

Under the Eastern Han dynasty, power was further centralized, the economy continued to prosper and cultural achievements reached a peak – this era is considered one of China's golden ages. Paper was also invented during this time. Although samples of paper have been found dating back to the Western Han, it was during the Eastern Han when improved papermaking techniques made it practical to manufacture. With the discovery of paper, the dissemination of information and spread of learning increased China's cultural influence.

The first emperor of a united China, Qin Shihuang.

DISUNION (220 – 589)

From the 3rd to the 6th century, China went through a period of disunity. The disintegration began with the displacement of the Eastern Han by three regimes, the Wei, Shu and Wu. One of China's most famous literary epics, *The Romance of the Three Kingdoms* (*sānguó yǎnyì* 三国演义), which was written by Luo Guanzhong during the Ming dynasty, is a fictionalized account of this period.

Numerous petty kingdoms rose and fell during this time. Groups of northern "barbarians" made inroads into China during this time, establishing a series of kingdoms in the vulnerable north. Eventually the Turgut (*tuòbá* 拓跋) tribe of the Xianbei unified northern China and established the

Northern Wei dynasty.

Xiao Wendi, an emperor of the Northern Wei dynasty, carried out a series of reforms, basing his rule on the Chinese bureaucracy. The Confucian bureaucracy would prove to be one of China's most durable institutions – by adopting it, would-be rulers could gain legitimacy and claim the "Mandate of Heaven," whether they were ethnic Chinese or not. This extended period of northern incursion into Chinese lands saw the intermingling of different ethnic groups and the exchange of knowledge.

It was during the Han dynasty that Buddhism first came to China from India. Temples and stupas, the architecture that people associate with Chinese Buddhism, began to sprout throughout the land. As a sign of devotion, Buddhist cave carvings were begun in northern China. The ones at Yungang and Longmen continue to awe and inspire visitors.

There were mass migrations during this period of upheaval. Some were by people seeking a better future, while others were made up of people forced from their homes. Vast numbers of Han Chinese journeyed south, expanding the cultural boundaries of China. They brought new technologies and Han culture with them as they assimilated among or displaced local populations.

SUI (581 – 618)

The Sui dynasty unified China in AD 581 after more than 400 years of disunity, yet it only lasted 38 years. Much was accomplished during this dynasty's short reign – a population census, reformation of the bloated regional administration system and consolidation of the southern regions. One of the Sui's most important legacies was building the Grand Canal (*dà yùnhé* 大运河) which linked Hangzhou in the south to Beijing in the north. The network of canals aided and enhanced economic and cultural exchange between the south and north and would greatly influence China's development. The downfall of the Sui dynasty came with several military excursions into Korea. These disastrous wars were prohibitively expensive and brought the dynasty to bankruptcy. Peasant rebellions erupted throughout the countryside and Li Yuan, a Sui government minister, ended the Sui dynasty when he founded the Tang dynasty.

An early papermaking workshop.

Heroes from the Three Kingdoms period.

TANG (618 – 907)

The Tang dynasty was one of China's most prosperous and culturally rich periods. Under the rule of the second Tang emperor, Taizong, the economy flourished and the empire experienced an era of stability. Moreover, he was considered an enlightened ruler for his open style of governing.

Not long after Emperor Taizong, Wu Zetian became the only female empress in China's history. She's remembered as a harsh but capable ruler who attracted people of talent to her court.

The Tang dynasty reached its peak under the stewardship of Emperor Xuanzong. His rule heralded a long period of expansion, prosperity and stability, but towards his later years, the dynasty declined. Before long, regional military commanders seized the opportunity to rebel. The greatest peril the dynasty faced was the devastating rebellion of An Lushan, an ethnic Sogdian, who was the adopted son of Xuanzong's favorite concubine, Yang Guifei.

Many of the emperor's closest advisors blamed Yang Guifei, who was nicknamed "the Fat Concubine," for the decline of the empire. The emperor was so enamored by her charms that he ignored state affairs and spent his time frolicking with her instead. Coming from a poor family, Yang Guifei took this opportunity to enrich herself and her family. Eventually the emperor's officials forced the emperor to order his favorite concubine to commit suicide while they were fleeing from An Lushan. After this episode, Xuanzong fell into a deep depression and abdicated the throne. Tang poet Bai Juyi immortalized this fatal love story in his poem *Song of Everlasting Sorrow* (*cháng hèn gē* 长恨歌).

The imperial examination system became highly developed under the Tang. While in theory anyone, even a poor peasant, could take part in the examinations, in practice only those rich enough to afford the years of study could advance through the highly competitive system. Poetry also achieved remarkable heights of artistry during the Tang dynasty. Many of China's most talented poets, such as Li Bai, Du Fu and Bai Juyi, hail from this era.

Under the Tang dynasty China was the largest power in Asia, extending towards Central Asia with its cultural reach playing a key role in the development of Korea and Japan. Numerous envoys and students from foreign countries frequently visited Tang dynasty China. Different ethnic groups that inhabited the periphery of the dynasty allowed for frequent cultural exchanges, making the Tang the most cosmopolitan and open of all China's dynasties.

The Tang legal code and written Chinese characters were some of China's most important exports to Korea and Japan. Thousands of students from both countries arrived in China to study, and Chinese teachers traveled abroad to spread their wisdom. Buddhism continued to spread throughout China, becoming more popular as it became more Chinese in character. An eclectic milieu of religions – Zoroastrianism, Nestorian Christianity, Manichaeism, Judaism and Islam – were brought to China. Technology also traveled along the Silk Road, with Arab traders spreading papermaking techniques. Woodblock printing was invented during the Tang dynasty, with the *Diamond Sutra* (*jīngāng jīng* 金刚经), printed in 868, being the earliest example of a book made using this technique. In late Tang battles, weapons employing gunpowder were used.

Entertainment in a Tang dynasty court.

As the Tang dynasty reeled from An Lushan's rebellion, which lasted for over eight years, increased power was given to military officials to deal with the rebels. But in turn they began to acquire power and carve out kingdoms of their own. In AD 907, the Tang dynasty was overthrown. The dynastic cycle once again began anew. The period following the collapse of the Tang was a time of devastation and turbulence. It was during this period of upheaval that China's economic center shifted from the Chinese heartland of the Yellow River valley in the north to the south. This economic migration south, coupled with frequent invasions from the north, would create a cultural and psychological divide in the Chinese psyche that paralleled the Yangtze River.

SONG (960 – 1279)

In 960, Zhao Kuangyin, a former military official, donned the "Dragon Robe," the symbol of imperial power, and established the Northern Song dynasty. The second Northern Song emperor completed the reunification of the country when he destroyed the remaining opposition. The Song emperors, fully aware that the concentration of power among regional governors led to the downfall of the Tang dynasty, deliberately curbed the powers of the local officials.

While officials had their powers curbed, their numbers increased, and they soon became a severe financial burden on the state coffers. This led to a financial crisis that affected the ability of the dynasty to defend itself militarily. To solve this problem, the scholar-bureaucrats of the Song dynasty launched a series of political reforms. The policies that were proposed by Fan Zhongyan and Wang Anshi are the best known. They were wide ranging and, for the era, considered very liberal.

One characteristic of the Northern Song dynasty was its emphasis on academia and its disdain for the military. The Northern Song developed a complicated administration system and a prosperous

A lively figurine from the Yuan dynasty.

commodity-based economy. Due to the inconvenience of coins for such trade, the first Chinese paper currency, called *jiaozi* (*jiāozǐ* 交子), was developed. Porcelain became a very important export, and commerce flourished. The detailed painting *The Riverside Scene in Pure Brightness* (*qīngmíng shànghé tú* 清明上河图) gives an accurate portrait of bustling city life during this era.

The Jürchen tribe from northern China eventually defeated the Northern Song and established the Jin dynasty. The Song court fled to Hangzhou where they established the Southern Song dynasty, which only controlled south China. The regime was run by a powerful coterie of chancellors increasingly engaged in political infighting. This weakened the dynasty until it was overtaken by the powerful Mongols from the north.

Throughout the 300-year reign of the Song, northern minorities had been a constant threat to its borders. The court was continuously at war or negotiating treaties with these northern groups to secure the Song frontier.

The Song dynasty saw its share of technological breakthroughs. A printer named Bi Sheng invented a method for movable type printing, which made printing far more convenient and accessible. A crude compass, which was first used during the Warring States period, saw continuous development and by the Northern Song would become the predecessor to the modern compass.

YUAN (1206 – 1368)

At the beginning of the 13th century, Genghis Khan (*Chēngjísī hán* 成吉思汗), Tie muzhen (*Tiěmùzhēn* 铁木真) in Chinese, united the feuding Mongolian tribes and created the world's most formidable war machine. Sweeping across Eastern Europe and Asia, he created the largest empire the world has ever seen. Kublai Khan (*hūbìliè* 忽必烈), Genghis's grandson, established the Yuan dynasty after sweeping away the Jin dynasty in China's north and the remnants of the Song to the south. Adopting the Chinese bureaucracy, Kublai Khan officially established the Yuan dynasty in 1271. The Mongolians treated the Han Chinese harshly and rebellions broke out when the dynasty saw the first signs of weakening.

The rule of the Yuan dynasty, though harsh, did see significant cultural exchanges due to the large size of their territory. The Yuan rulers readily embraced new ideas and foreign experts if they could benefit the

A Map of Zheng He's voyage.

empire, regardless of whether those experts wanted to volunteer their services or not. Extensive trade routes were established, and it was during the Yuan dynasty that Marco Polo supposedly visited China.

MING (1368 – 1644)

Zhu Yuanzhang, originally a poor peasant, founded the Ming dynasty after the fall of the turbulent Yuan dynasty. He established a standardized bureaucracy with a strong central authority. His rule was autocratic, heavily censoring his scholars and limiting cultural freedom. Culture enjoyed a liberal revival when the Yongle emperor ascended the Dragon Throne. The *Yongle Canon* (*yǒnglè dàdiǎn* 永乐大典), a massive encyclopedia, was compiled during his reign. To reinforce the frontier defenses in the north, he moved his capital from Nanjing to Beijing, which was also his power base. His reign saw the Ming's greatest expansion – Zheng He's voyages to Southeast Asia, India and Africa were made during this time.

Trade thrived under the Ming, overseas trade expanded and merchants began to form local trade groups – Anhui merchants in the south and Shanxi merchants in the north. During the later Ming, methods of production akin to those of an early capitalist society emerged, particularly in the production of handicraft. As new maritime trade routes were established, European nations increasingly sought trade opportunities in China.

During the late Ming, Western missionaries introduced Christianity and advanced sciences into China. Matteo Ricci, an early Italian Jesuit missionary, became highly influential in the Ming court and a close friend to the emperor.

The closing years of the Ming saw the rise of peasant revolts. The largest of these revolts was led by Li Zicheng. Though he managed to overthrow the Ming, he failed to unify China. Manchu forces from China's northeast had begun to encroach into the Ming's frontier, and in 1644 they defeated Li Zicheng's undisciplined forces in Beijing. Following their victory in Beijing and the establishment of the Qing dynasty, they began a slow conquest of the remaining Ming forces.

QING (1616 – 1911)

The Qing dynasty saw its height of power under three exceptional emperors: Kangxi, Yongzheng and Qianlong. Under their rule, China saw huge advances in literature and

▶▶ Traditional Chinese Medicine

Traditional Chinese medicine (TCM 中医 *zhōngyī*) has developed over thousands of years of practical experience and observation. Unlike Western medicine, which aims at curing a specific illness, TCM aims at healing the body as a whole. Records on m edical studies date back over 2,000 years to the Spring and Autumn period and the Warring States period. During the Han dynasty there were further advances in medical studies and during the Three Kingdoms period, Hua Tuo, a famous doctor, made some of the most significant contributions to the field.

Through careful observation and studies, Hua Tuo was able to discover many medical herbs, even creating an anesthetic mixture that, according to records, allowed him to perform surgeries such as appendicitis. He made use of acupuncture points (*zhēnjiū* 针灸) in order to balance the body's inner *qi*. He was also an early proponent of an active lifestyle, prescribing moderate exercise as a way to stay healthy.

Li Shizhen of the Ming dynasty wrote the *Compendium of Materia Medica* (*běncǎo gāngmù* 本草纲目), which describes the uses for thousands of herbs. This book became a major influence in TCM by explaining the function and nature of each herb and their interaction with each other.

TCM doctors examine patients not by examining the symptoms of illnesses, but by examining the body as a complete system. Diagnoses are made based on the patients pulse, voice and mental state as much as on complaints of physical discomfort.

military technology. Because the Qing rulers weren't ethnic Han Chinese, they imposed tight controls to maintain their rule. However, the Qing had to work closely with Han Chinese scholars and within the Confucian bureaucratic framework to rule their empire effectively. The Qing emperors expanded the frontiers of their empire and consolidated the borders of what would become modern China.

A General of Ming dynasty Zheng Chenggong (Koxinga) expels the Dutch from Taiwan in 1661.

Nevertheless, beneath the aura of splendor cracks emerged in the framework of the empire. Overpopulation and rampant corruption created instability. Population and economic pressures forced many into poverty. With no future, many chose to revolt.

Foreign encroachment from Western powers arrived at a time when the Qing dynasty was on the decline. In the 19th century, Britain began exporting opium to China to reduce a trade imbalance that had arisen with British demand for tea, silk and porcelain. China's wealth was drained as many became addicted to opium. The Qing government's restrictions on the opium trade led to the first Opium War in 1840. The result was that China was forced to face modernity.

MODERN CHINA (1840 – 1949)

Chinese modern history begins with the 1840 Opium War, which was fought between China and Britain. Before the war, the Qing government had already fought a series of battles with Western nations, but it was the Qing defeat in the Opium War that led to the debilitating "Unequal Treaties." Under these treaties, Western nations were able to strip China of its resources and take advantage of its people. In the late 19th century, when capitalism and imperialism fed off each other, Western incursion into China increased. The old Chinese tactic of playing one threat off another was no longer viable because the treaties stipulated a "most favored nation" clause – in effect, whatever concession was given to one nation would be given to all.

As they did in Africa, the imperial powers carved themselves spheres of influence and concession areas where they held extra-territorial powers. In effect, China lost its own sovereignty. For example, Western powers had control of China's customs revenues and could set their own tariffs and taxes for imports.

During this era, China lost control of Macau and Hong Kong, and the Old Summer Palace (*yuánmíng yuán* 圆明园) was burned by Anglo-French forces in 1860.

While foreign countries were eagerly picking apart China, endemic government corruption made any efforts to oppose Western encroachment nearly impossible. After the Opium War, the more farsighted scholars of the ruling class realized that China could strengthen itself by adapting Western science and technology as Japan had done.

Consequently, the scholars actively sought to

The People's Liberation Army enters Beijing in 1949.

reform the military and the antiquated Confucian education system, despite strong opposition from conservative Qing officials. With China's defeat in the Sino-Japanese War of 1895, greater impetus was given to the reformists. In 1898 reformers led by Kang Youwei, Liang Qichao and the near powerless Emperor Guangxu proposed dramatic reforms to the Qing government – they advocated adopting Western-styled political institutions that would have turned the Qing into a constitutional monarchy. Since ultimate power was held by the Empress Dowager Cixi, who was loath to relinquish any of it, the reform movement ended in failure after 100 days.

Popular uprisings, some of which had egalitarian overtones, undermined Qing authority throughout China. Under the leadership of Hong Xiuquan, a failed scholar, the Taiping Rebellion began in 1851. This movement organized and mobilized peasants under a pseudo-Christian banner. In 1899 the Boxer Uprising ignited. The Boxers were originally an underground organization based heavily on superstitious beliefs. The uprising quickly developed into an anti-foreign movement with the aim of expelling Westerners from China.

Some reformers felt that drastic change was necessary to revitalize China. Mere reform of the imperial dynasty was no longer possible – they felt that China required the overthrow of the Qing if it were to survive. In 1911, led by the tireless revolutionary Sun Yat-sen, the Qing dynasty was overthrown. The next year, in 1912, the Republic of China was founded with its capital in Nanjing. The government was based on Sun's "Three Principles of the People."

Three months after the founding of the Republic of China, China fell into the hands of northern warlords led by Yuan Shikai, a former Qing general. Yuan had grandiose plans to crown himself emperor of his own imperial dynasty, but facing universal condemnation, his effort to don the yellow robes of the emperor failed.

Meanwhile, a social revolution was occurring alongside the political revolution. A "New Culture Movement" was launched in 1915. Advocates hoped that democracy and scientific progress could transform China's old culture – they believed that advanced technology from the West and the philosophies of the West's Enlightenment could best guide the course of China's future. During this period, writing in the Chinese vernacular became fully developed – the stiff formal writing of classical Chinese was dropped. Supporters of this new literature included Lu Xun, one of China's most influential writers and social commentators whose works include *The True Story of Ah Q* (*ā Q zhèngzhuàn* 阿Q正传).

In 1919, the May Fourth Movement, spawned by university students protesting China's weakness at the hands of exploitative warlords and Western imperialism, became one of modern China's most pivotal moments. It was one of the earliest manifestations of Chinese nationalism. As people searched for the answers to China's woes, some turned to Marxism, and in 1921, the Chinese Communist Party was established in Shanghai. In 1924, the Nationalists and Communists formally established a united front to combat the rule of the warlords.

In the spring of 1927, the Nationalist government led by Chiang Kai-shek formally returned the seat of national power to Nanjing. This was a time of internal turmoil as the Nationalists and the Communists constantly fought pitched battles. Eventually the Nationalists surrounded the Communist base in the Jiangxi Soviet. In a daring breakout, Communists were forced to embark on a strategic retreat from 1934 to 1936, the epic Long March. The Communists marched 25,000 *li* (a *li* is equal to about three-tenths of a mile, a half kilometer) through swamps and mountains to Yan'an while all the way being pursued by the Nationalists.

The site of the First National Congress of the Chinese Communist Party in Shanghai.

In 1931, the Imperial Japanese Army launched a massive invasion of northeast China. In 1937, the Japanese began a general invasion and all-out war erupted. Faced with a Japanese onslaught, the Nationalists and Communists once again formed a united front against a common enemy. After Japan's defeat in the Second World War, civil war broke out between the Nationalists and Communists. In 1949, the Nationalists were defeated and retreated from the mainland to Taiwan. ■

GREETINGS 问候		
Hello.	nǐhǎo	你好。
How are you today?	nǐhǎo ma	你好吗?
Good morning.	zǎoshàng hǎo	早上好。
Good afternoon.	xiàwǔ hǎo	下午好。
Good evening.	wǎnshàng hǎo	晚上好。
FIRST ENCOUNTERS 初次见面		
My name is···	wǒ de míngzi shì ···	我的名字是 ……
May I ask your name?	nǐ guìxìng	你贵姓?
It's a pleasure to meet you.	hěn gāoxìng rènshi nǐ	很高兴认识你。
It was nice talking to you.	hěn gāoxìng hé nǐ tánhuà	很高兴和你谈话。

General Chronology

Dynasty	Sub-dynasty	Year
Xia 夏		22nd century - 17th century BC
Shang 商		17th century - 11th century BC
Zhou 周	Western Zhou 西周	11th century - 771 BC
	Eastern Zhou 东周	770 - 256 BC
	Spring-Autumn Period 春秋	772 - 481 BC
	Warring States Period 战国	475 - 221 BC
Qin 秦		221 - 206 BC
Han 汉	Western Han 西汉	206 BC - AD 25
	Eastern Han 东汉	25 - 220
Three Kingdoms 三国	Wei 魏	220 - 265
	Shu 蜀	221 - 263
	Wu 吴	222 - 280
Western Jin 西晋		265 - 420
Eastern Jin 东晋		317 - 420
Southern Dynasties 南朝	Song 宋	420 - 479
	Qi 齐	479 - 502
	Liang 梁	502 - 557
	Chen 陈	557 - 589
Northern Dynasties 北朝	Northern Wei 北魏	386 - 534
	Eastern Wei 东魏	534 - 550
	Northern Qi 北齐	550 - 577
	Western Wei 西魏	535 - 556
	Northern Zhou 北周	557 - 581
Sui 隋		581 - 618
Tang 唐		618 - 907
Five Dynasties 五代	Later Liang 后梁	907 - 923
	Later Tang 后唐	923 - 936
	Later Jin 后晋	936 - 947
	Later Han 后汉	947 - 950
	Later Zhou 后周	951 - 960
Song 宋	Northern Song 北宋	960 - 1127
	Southern Song 南宋	1127 - 1279
Yuan 元		1206 - 1368
Ming 明		1368 - 1644
Qing 清		1616 - 1911
Republic of China 中华民国		1912 - 1949
People's Republic of China 中华人民共和国		1949 -

A Western sketch of a Chinese garden.

Chinese Garden Landscaping

As early as the 6th century, Japan had already learn of Chinese garden landscaping. with Europeans first heard learning of the Chinese style through Marco Polo, who visited many Song dynasty gardens in southern China during the Yuan dynasty. In the 17th century, Chinese garden landscaping was introduced to England, from where it then spread to France and the rest of Europe. In the late 18th century, Chinese garden landscaping had a huge influence on the European Romantic Movement, European landscaping moved away from a stiff aristocratic style to the more natural style found in Chinese gardens.

Differences in Western and Eastern garden styles reflect different philosophies of aesthetic beauty. In form, Western landscaping embodies artificial beauty with symmetrical, regular and well-knit layouts. Geometry is ever-present as flowers and plants are pruned upright and square. Chinese garden landscaping doesn't require symmetry or fixed compositions – as plants, trees and decorations are built to a natural form. Whereas Western landscaping theory aims to remedy the defects of nature, Chinese garden landscaping blends plants and buildings into an organic whole and imitates nature by building rocky outcroppings with flowing water to present a quality suggestive of poetry or painting. To fully enjoy the beauty of Chinese gardens, it's important to understand the philosophy implied through the scenery.

The grounds of the Summer Palace were a massive garden for the emperor.

THE ORIGIN & DEVELOPMENT OF CHINESE GARDEN LANDSCAPING

Chinese garden landscaping has a history of more than 4,000 years, with the earliest gardens appearing in 2000 BC during the Shang dynasty. Shang kings used forests and mountains for hunting and as sightseeing destinations. Chinese garden landscaping would develop from this embryonic form of garden.

The first gardens in early Chinese history were status symbols of the kings and aristocrats. Their most distinguishing features were that they covered large areas and had dual purpose, for hunting and for holding sacrificial rites to the gods.

Gradually the appeal of gardens spread beyond the aristocracy to officials, poets, painters and traders who hoped to recreate the scenic spots they saw in the convenience of their hometowns. Early private gardens were small and featured stones piled into mountains; water channels were usually planted with pine and cypress trees and bamboo. These gardens recreated natural scenes and are named "gardens with mountains and water sceneries."

The wealth of the Tang dynasty spurred the building of gardens. The imperial gardens were in Chang'an, present day Xi'an, with the largest being the Forbidden Garden. This "garden" was approximately 8.7 miles (14 km) wide and 7.4 miles (12 km) long and held 24 separate gardens and building complexes. It was the main imperial getaway with scenic spots and different activities like hunting, singing and dancing.

Landscape painting became an independent branch of Chinese art during the Tang dynasty. Mountains, water, trees and villages were popular subjects, and painters sought to embody the harmony between man and nature with their paintings. They not only painted the physical scenes but also expressed their thoughts and emotions with the images. Gardens were built in a similar vein – the garden designer attempted to harmonize architectural beauty with natural beauty so the visitor would see a complete picture.

During the Song dynasty, garden landscaping became even more popular and spread further down the social hierarchy. Owners of teahouses began to build gardens to solicit customers, and common people could now enjoy the beauty of gardens. Landscape painting now had greater influence on garden landscaping than before. For example, the emperor would hire a commercial painter to paint a design, and the garden would be built according to the painting. Great detail was given to the lines, structures and decoration of courtyards, with particular attention paid to the placement of small ornaments.

Chinese garden landscaping reached a golden age in the Ming and Qing dynasties and became an art that blended music, painting, poetry and architecture. Gardens began to influence each other and designers referred to other gardens for inspiration. The number of gardens greatly increased, with many of them private classic examples include the **Humble Administrator's Garden** (*zhuōzhèng yuán* 拙政园), the **Master of Nets Garden** (*wǎngshī yuán* 网师园) and the **Ge Garden** (*gè yuán* 个园). Imperial gardens like the **Old Summer Palace** (*yuánmíng yuán* 圆明园) and the **Summer Palace** (*yíhé yuán* 颐和园) began imitating and copying ideas from private gardens.

CLASSIFICATION OF CHINESE GARDEN LANDSCAPING

Classification by Geographical Location

Northern gardens are large and have grand structures. Because of the climate, northern gardens do not contain a large variety of water areas or evergreen trees and they're not as delicate as their counterparts in southern China. Northern gardens are found mainly in Beijing, Xi'an, Luoyang and Kaifeng, with the gardens in Beijing being the most representative of the northern style.

Guangdong is in a subtropical zone so Cantonese gardens feature more waterscapes and vegetation; and they feature subtropical scenery is typically set off by tall and spacious buildings.

Classification by Owner

Imperial gardens are large and grandiose, and were built using natural mountains and waterways. The most famous ones include the **Imperial Forest Garden** (*shànglín yuán* 上林园) built during the Han dynasty, and the Tang dynasty the **Forbidden Garden** (*cháng'ān jìnyuàn* 长安禁苑) in Xi'an. The current imperial gardens are Qing dynasty creations with **Beihai Park** (*běihǎi gōngyuán* 北海公园), the **Summer Palace** (*yíhé yuán* 颐和园) and the **Old Summer Palace** (*yuánmíng yuán* 圆明园) in Beijing, and the **Imperial Summer Villa** (*chéngdé bìshǔ shānzhuāng* 承德避暑山庄) in Chengde as the finest examples. These gardens highlight

Chinese gardens were similar to nature reserves.

Jiangnan (south of the Yangtze River) gardens cover smaller areas than the ones in the north, but have a variety of waterscapes and evergreen trees. The scenery is delicate and cozy. Southern gardens are found in Nanjing, Shanghai, Wuxi, Suzhou, Hangzhou and Yangzhou, with the gardens in Suzhou considered the best examples. Southern gardens are artistic designs consisting of buildings, mountains, water and plant life. These gardens blend nature, architecture and painting into a unified whole.

scenic spots of China's different regions and blend themes of gods and legends with anecdotes of well-known historical personalities. Particular attention is given to the connection of independent scenes within the garden.

Private gardens were relatively small with small mountains and waterways. Most only measured about 2.5 acres (one hectare), with a few stretching to 10 or 12 acres (4 to 5 hectares). Within such a confined space, particular attention was given to incorporating small buildings, manmade mountains and waterways, and to the placement of vegetation and decorations. The theme of the garden varied according to the taste of the owner. Some showed the owner's upright and outspoken character and others presented the owner's pursuit of a plain and simple life. The private gardens of Suzhou, Yangzhou and Nanjing are considered some of China's most distinguished, with Suzhou being home to the majority of them.

Beautifully painted architecture adds to nature's beauty in many Chinese gardens.

Temple gardens are attached to temples and were built in approximately the same manner as private gardens, but with a greater emphasis on tranquility. Temple gardens are an integral part of the entire building complex and influence the design of the overall structure, thus lending the temples themselves a gardenlike atmosphere.

FEATURES OF CHINESE GARDENS

Although there's a great variety in Chinese gardens, and each garden has its own particular features, there are some common features.

The pursuit of poetic beauty and an artistic ideal closely connects Chinese gardens to poetry and painting. The artistic creation of gardens and paintings are interlinked, with both "in pursuit of poetic meaning," an attempt to recreate a poem or painting in a garden setting. Such characteristics find their expression in the design of the mountains and water. The architectural designs of gardens are very detailed and each garden has its own thematic content. Most gardens are taken from well-known poems and have layouts based on landscape paintings. In general, gardens aim for the harmonization of space and natural scenes according to artistic principles.

Gardens take advantage of scenes to express the designer's emotion and arouse the visitor's associations and imagination. An artistic expression of emotion is a basic theme in art and Chinese gardens are no exception. Because gardens are a recreation of nature in an artificial setting, the process of creating a garden requires imagination and innovation. First, waterways and mountains are created using stones and ditches, and their mutually dependent pairing brings out a striking effect. Second, choosing an auspicious name is an important part of creating associations with the garden and nature. Names are inscribed on stone tablets, gatepost couplets and door boards. These two measures help create a picture for the visitor and set the mood for the garden.

Creating a sense of space within a limited area is important, especially in small private gardens. In order to create more scenes, designers construct mountains, and waterways, plant trees and flowers and breed fish. Fixed scenes are given varied views and perspectives by using contrast, offsetting the point of view and by using winding paths. These measures give a new view at every point throughout the small garden, thus creating a larger sense of spatial freedom. Some methods include making the river banks curved with irregular stones, planting flowers and trees according to different seasons, varying the length of corridors, and using decorative windows and gates. A careful observer will notice in Suzhou gardens that if there's a window facing a white wall, there will also be rocks or vegetation within the frame. The design is meant to create a sense of exploration – the scenes are partly hidden and offer different impressions from different angles.

Gardens borrow and use the scenery of the nearby surroundings. A Chinese garden emphasizes the arrangement of different scenes inside and outside the garden in proper proportions. For example, in the **Ge Garden** (*gè yuán* 个园) in Yangzhou, there's the Summer Mountain, which is topped with a pavilion. From this pavilion the scenery of the **Slender West Lake** (*shòu xīhú* 瘦西湖) can be seen in the distance. In Wuxi, the **Jichang Garden** (*jìchàng yuán* 寄畅园) borrows the pagoda in Xi Shan as a backdrop to set off the scenes in the garden.

The design and landscaping of Chinese gardens has evolved into an independent technique in its own right and it always includes four essential features.

Mountain Scenery

Mountains are the foremost feature in forming garden scenery. During the reign of Emperor Wudi of the Han dynasty laborers shaped a small island from soil they dug out while repairing a pond. This island was an early example of artificial mountains. Later garden designers, instead of duplicating the size of mountains, stressed the important details so artificial mountains closely resembled their real counterparts. From the Tang and Song dynasties, and with the development of landscape painting, landscape gardeners began paying greater attention to construction techniques.

Water Scenery

Waterways are one of the most important scenic features of a garden. Waterscapes in a garden can be static lakes or dynamic waterfalls. There are three ways to construct artificial water scenery.

Coverings

Garden designers often cover the banks of a waterway with a thick growth of grass and construct buildings on the shore. Architectural constructions are usually erected above the water in order to create a sense of flowing water from the base of the structure. Plants and grass along the water will give it an appearance of tranquility and stillness.

Moon arched bridges grace many of China's gardens.

A bridge with an elegantly carved stone railing.

Partitions
Stone bridges, corridors or large stones placed in the water allow visitors to cross the waterway and give the space above the flat water a compartmentalized, layered effect.

Decorations
If the area that water occupies is very small, a winding path along the shore made with irregularly shaped stones or planted vegetation helps to create a spatially open feeling. Fish and water plants in the water also add to the scenic beauty.

Animals and Plants
In order to make the water and mountains look natural, it's necessary to plant vegetation. Plants and flowers are often chosen according to their aesthetic shapes, colors, and fragrance. Landscape gardeners often prefer red maples, green bamboo, colorful roses, and white magnolias, all of which serve as a visual and olfactory ornament in all seasons. The symbolic meaning of each plant is also carefully considered. For example, bamboo is the symbol of uprightness, pine is a symbol of strength and longevity, the lotus is associated with purity and the peony with wealth and rank. Designers use these plants as another method to get across their artistic intention.

Classical Chinese gardens attach considerable importance to animals within the garden. Animals such as goldfishes, mandarin ducks, white cranes, and parrots provide amusement as well as serve as symbols of longevity. Animals allow visitors to feel as if they're in the midst of a truly natural environment.

ARCHITECTURAL CONSTRUCTIONS
Architectural constructions in gardens differ from common buildings since they must embellish the garden as part of the natural scenery while maintaining their practical uses. Halls, pavilions, pleasure boats, corridors, bridges and walls are the various types of a buildings found in gardens.

Halls
Halls are where visitors are served and meetings are held and are the central structure of a garden. The location of the hall influences the disposition of the overall scenery. The hall must be allocated sufficient space as it's usually fairly large, and according to Chinese custom, its entrance should face south. Outside the hall lies the main scenery of the garden.

Buildings
The highest structure in the garden should provide the visitor a panoramic view from all four windowed walls. The building can also be used to store books and paintings.

Pavilions
The sides of a pavilion are open and support a single roof. Pavilions are used as a rest stop or a scenic point. Pavilions vary in shape from three-, six- and eight-sided structures to square or circular. They are usually built next to a scene, next to a pathway or corridor, or adjacent to a wall or edge of a cliff. Famous pavilions include the **Surging Waves Pavilion** (*cānglàng tíng* 沧浪亭) and the **Songfeng Pavilion** (*sōngfēng tíng* 松风亭) in the Humble Administrator's Garden.

Pleasure Boats
These artificial boats are placed along the shore. A good example is the marble boat in the Summer Palace.

Corridors
Corridors are more than passageways; they're also vantage points for sightseeing. Corridors are some of the most creative structures in Chinese gardens; they link the different structures, allowing easy movement within the garden, and provide shelter from the elements. The Long

Corridor in the Summer Place is nearly 800 yards (728 m) long and has more than 14,000 colorful paintings. If a visitor spends only 2 seconds to view each painting, it would take about 8 hours to see them all.

Bridges

Bridges provide vantage points on both sides of the bridge and in the waterscape itself. Garden bridges are straight or twisty, arched or flat and made from stone, bamboo or wood.

THE CONNOTATION OF CHINESE GARDENS

Traditional Chinese thought places humans as a small part of the infinite universe. Each living creature is a part of nature and the intrinsic link between humans and nature can't be broken. Chinese gardens are an effort to imitate nature in the home, to conform to nature without breaking this fundamental connection. Each part of the garden is meant to highlight and remind visitors of the harmony between humans and nature, with the goal of breeding harmony between character and emotion.

Imperial gardens symbolized the supreme power of emperors, but were also places of recreation. Private gardens were places of relaxation and contemplation, a sanctuary to satisfy people's longing for nature. Regardless of geographic location or scale, Chinese gardens represent a tradition of finding harmony within the world by turning to nature. ■

▶▶ Chinese New Year

The most important Chinese holiday is Chinese New Year, which is known in China as **Spring Festival** (*chūn jié* 春节). The festival ushers in the lunar New Year and is the West's Christmas and New Year's Eve rolled into one. From sunup to sundown, this is a time when the whole country throws itself into celebrating and eating.

No one is quite sure exactly when or where the festival originated. Legend has it that once upon a time, there was a monster called *Nian* (*nián* 年) that attacked Chinese villages every spring, eating anything that came its way – people, animals, plants and the odd building. One spring, villagers hung red paper on their doors and threw bamboo on a fire when *Nian* arrived. The monster was so startled by the bright colors and loud crackling noise of the burning bamboo that it turned and fled. Today the word "*nian*" is the Chinese word for year.

Since that day, Chinese people hang red paper signs and lanterns outside their homes and enjoy making loud noises on New Year's Eve. Firecrackers replaced bamboo after gunpowder was invented and the main idea today is the louder and bigger, the better.

In the days leading up to the Spring Festival, every household gets a thorough cleaning. Since sweeping on New Year's Day itself might sweep away the year's good fortune. Breaking dishes or using sharp objects is also seen as potentially unlucky.

The holiday is a time for family celebration and nearly every university student or migrant worker heads home. It'll seem like the whole country is going somewhere at this time, whether on their way home or taking advantage of the long holiday to do some traveling.

On New Year's Eve, once the family has been gathered, food becomes a central consideration. Large numbers of delicacies are prepared and fish is often eaten as the Chinese word for fish (*yú* 鱼) is a homophone for surplus (*yú* 余).

Children particularly enjoy the custom of receiving red envelopes (*hóngbāo* 红包). The envelopes contain gifts of money and are distributed by family elders to young unmarried relatives.

Forthcoming dates of the Spring Festival

Year of the Rat February 7, 2008
Year of the Ox January 26, 2009
Year of the Tiger February 14, 2010

A famous Tang dynasty painting of royal court ladies, *the Beauties Wearing Flowers*.

Chinese Arts

CHINESE PAINTING

Chinese painting originated over 5,000 years ago. Steeped in Chinese history, literature and philosophy, Chinese painting is different from that of the West in its motifs, form and technique.

One basic distinctive feature of Chinese painting is that ideas and motifs are mainly presented in inked lines and dots, rather than through color, proportion and perspective.

Chinese paintings are created using brush pens made of a penholder and a pen head. The penholder is usually made of bamboo or wood, while the pen head is made of animal hair – typically wolf or sheep. The brush heads are soft and flexible, and match well with the style of Chinese paintings. Generally, only black ink is used in Chinese paintings and delicate silk and paper are used as the "canvas" in Chinese paintings.

Chinese paintings fall into three main categories: characters, landscapes and flowers and birds. Of the three traditions, character painting is the oldest, dominating the scene until the end of the Tang dynasty. Landscape paintings were generally of mountains and water, which comes from the Taoist tradition of seeking solitude within nature. Landscape became a favorite subject of artists and would become a dominant subject by the 11th century. Even today, when Chinese say a place is the ideal of natural beauty, they'll say the place has "mountains and water." During the 9th century, a separate genre of flower and bird paintings evolved which included detailed paintings of birds, fruits, insects and flowers. Some of these works are incredibly detailed and lively.

Ancient Chinese painters used paintings as an expression of their sentiments rather than merely reproducing the world on paper. From the 10th century onwards, many painters were also multi-talented poets and calligraphers, who etched poems or descriptive words onto their work. It would be natural that many of the great painters also excelled at calligraphy as it shared many of the brushstroke techniques with Chinese painting. Chinese calligraphy in itself is considered an art that requires years to master.

Chinese paintings are usually presented in scrolls and do not abide by the so-called "Golden Law" – the Western notion of the Law of Proportionality. This law states that two unequal parts of a whole must be in relationship to each other to create a balanced image to the eye. Instead of the "focus perspective" used in Western paintings, Chinese paintings use "spread-point perspective," which offers a delicate sense of proportion. A good example of this can be found in the famous *The Riverside Scene in Pure Brightness* (*qīngmíng shànghé tú* 清明上河图) which measures 9.7 inches by 206 inches (24.8 cm by 528.7 cm). This large scroll painting portrays various aspects of Kaifeng during the Song dynasty. Minutely detailed, the characters and scenes are proportional from any angle.

Another feature of Chinese paintings is that blank spaces are commonly used. The unmarked space is used to evoke the sky. Sometimes they represent water or fog and at other times the blank space is simply nothing – just a sensation of emptiness.

In 1714, the Italian painter Giuseppe Castiglione (*Láng Shìníng* 郎世宁) introduced Western painting methods to China. He taught the artists in the imperial court Western styles and methods, and in turn studied Chinese art. This marked the first fusion of Chinese and Western paintings.

CHINESE SCULPTURE

In ancient China, sculptors were a lowly class who were very rarely mentioned in history books. Chinese sculptures were mainly associated with religion and were commonly found in temples and mausoleums.

Undoubtedly the most famous Chinese sculptures are the Qin dynasty Terracotta Warriors in Xi'an. A total of 8,000 terracotta warriors and horses were unearthed in the 2,200-year-old mausoleum of Qin Shihuang – the first

Chinese sculpting techniques were already highly advanced over 2,000 years ago.

A two-stringed *erhu* is a common instrument in traditional Chinese music.

Emperor of a united China. These terracotta figures of soldiers and horses are set to life-size dimensions. Standing tall, lifelike and mobilized for action, these warriors continue to faithfully guard their monarch, as they have done for over two millennia.

Chinese Buddha sculptures, reflecting Indian and Tibetan influences, initially looked imperious, mysterious and aloof. Gradually, the form evolved to reflect a more nativist Chinese style. Early examples from the 5th to 6th centuries are lean and elegant, and from the 7th to 8th centuries took a form that was plump, round and soft.

Compared with the West, there's a greater emphasis on clothing for Chinese character sculptures. Well-preserved samples of Buddhist-inspired sculptures remain in many temples, especially in the cave carvings of Yungang, Dunhuang, Longmen and Dazu.

TRADITIONAL CHINESE MUSIC

Chinese music goes as far back as Chinese civilization and is highly distinctive from its western counterparts.

Chinese musical instruments can be divided into four basic categories based on the method by which they are played. The first category comprises of stringed instruments such as the *huqin* (*húqín* 胡琴). These are made of wood with a piece of snakeskin stretched over the sound box. They have two strings and the bow is permanently lodged between the strings. The second category is plucked instruments, of which there are three types: dulcimers, lutes and harps. The harp is made of either wood or bamboo with steel strings. In the past, the strings were made of silk. The third category is the woodwind section. These are flutes, pipes and Chinese trumpets, which use double reeds like the oboe but sound like a trumpet. The final category is the percussion section. The main instruments include drums, timpani, gongs and cymbals. For certain melodies, bells, xylophones, tuned gongs and the triangle are used. In traditional Chinese opera, the percussion section is called *wuchang* (*wǔchǎng* 武场), or the martial scene.

TRADITIONAL CHINESE OPERA

Chinese opera has a history dating back some 2,000 years. There are 317 types of opera, of which Peking opera is the most important and well-known.

The practitioner of Peking opera is a master athlete – he must be in top physical shape to accommodate the rigors of this performance art. Most performers begin their training from childhood. A well-known example is kung fu star Jackie Chan, who started training in Peking opera as a child.

Performers wear extensive makeup; their whole faces are painted in bright colors. Colorful masks, inspired from ancient ceremonies and religious symbols, are sometimes don by the actors. The color of each character's face is significant as it represents the character's personality and fate. Understanding the colors will greatly enhance your enjoyment of the opera as it is an intricate part of the story. Red faces represent righteousness; black denotes gallantry and heroism; blue and green signify brawn (not necessarily with brains!) or those held in high regard by commoners; yellow and white are negative colors, often meaning cunning or a tendency to be suspicious; gold denotes deities and silver is reserved for demons or bad spirits. The make-up style indicates if a character is good or evil.

CHINESE POTTERY & PORCELAIN

Pottery and porcelain have over 8,000 years of development in China. Both colored and black pottery were common in ancient times. Terracotta was at its best in the Qing dynasty, and tri-colored pottery (*táng sāncǎi* 唐三彩) reached its zenith at the time of the Tang dynasty. During this period, the glazed porcelains came alive with yellow, green, blue, brown, black and white colors.

Chinese porcelain began flourishing some 3,000 years ago during the Shang dynasty and is one of China's greatest cultural treasures. During the Han dynasty, black and celadon porcelain was mainly produced. Celadon, a type of glaze that resembles the color of jade, saw continued development throughout the dynasties. By the Tang dynasty, celadon porcelain had developed to a high technical standard.

The porcelain wares of the Song dynasty are considered classics. By the Song era, artisans had reached a high level of sophistication in design, firing and glazing. As a result, pieces from this time strike a perfect balance of shape, glaze and artistry.

The capital of porcelain is undoubtedly Jingdezhen, which is located in Jiangxi Province. With over 1,700 years of porcelain production, it continues its seminal role in Chinese porcelain arts and industry.

BRONZE VESSELS

About 5,000 years ago the Chinese began casting bronzeware. During the Shang and Zhou dynasties, aristocrats used bronze vessels for ancestral rituals and for the more mundane tasks of daily life. Ancestral worship was a central belief of this era and bronze vessels played an important role in the ritual offerings. As befitting their important role in society of the time, they were kept in places of honor, such as in ancestral halls and were used during banquets and celebrations.

Common bronze vessels were used for utilitarian purposes such as cooking or to heat millet wine, but large ornate vessels would become symbols of power and status. A *ding* (*dǐng* 鼎), which is a cauldron with three or four legs, was originally used both for cooking and ceremony – but came to symbolize power. *Dings* also had their surfaces etched with details of important political events and memorials to the deceased. These items of intricate and beautiful detail are now important historic markers detailing political alliances and tributes and the lives of those who lived thousands of years ago. Eventually dings came to symbolize power and prestige as they required considerable wealth to commission.

7,000-year-old painted pottery from China.

Bronze work in China developed much faster than in other parts of the world because of extensive use. Technically, Chinese bronzes were unmatched during this period. Early bronze vessels such as *jue* (*jué* 角) and *zhi* (*zhì* 觯) wine goblets, *zun* (*zūn* 樽) wine beakers and *hu* (*hú* 斛) wine goblet beakers were highly sophisticated.

In 1976, archaeologists uncovered a Shang tomb in Anyang in north Henan Province, the former capital of the Shang dynasty. The tomb was the burial chamber of Fuhao, who was Emperor Wuding's consort as well as a top general. The tomb, located at the Yin Palace Ruins Ancestral Worship Temple, remains the only Shang imperial tomb found intact and revealed a rich find of artifacts. Many bronze vessels were found within; some were probably used by Fuhao, while others were funerary objects.

Several famous Shang bronze vessels

currently displayed around the world belong to the legacy of Fuhao's tomb. Most Shang ritual vessels take the form of animals and are decorated with highly stylized animal designs and motifs. One example is the ancient Chinese totem known as the *taotic* (*tāotiè* 饕餮) monster mask – a mythical beast with piercing eyes that is used to express fierceness and strength. This mythical beast is commonly seen in Shang bronzes, as it played a central role in Shang spiritual beliefs. Offerings put into this animal-shaped vessel were symbolically consumed by the *taotie* and transported to the spirit realm. Later, this motif became an artistic motif in itself, signifying the artistry of China's Bronze Age.

Bronze ceremonial vessels display a high level of workmanship.

Chinese Folk Handicrafts

China is home to many different ethnic groups, each with its own unique culture and each with a tradition of handicrafts with their own special style. In such a large country folk customs vary greatly across its broad expanse, as do styles of popular arts and crafts. Travelling in China, you will find that each different place will afford a chance to see local craft items unlike those found elsewhere; the same object will also be made in a different style from one place to the next. Take embroidery for example: the four best known regional styles – China's "Four Great Embroidery Traditions" – are that of Suzhou, the Xiang style from Hunan, the Shu style of Sichuan and the Yue style of Guangdong in the south. There are also well-known styles unique to Beijing, Henan and Shandong. And these are all Han traditions; other ethnic groups in China, the Uighur, Nuosu, Dai, Buyei, Khazaks, Yao, Miao, Bizika, Kachin, Gaeml, Bai, Zhuang, Mongolians and Tibetans also have their own styles of embroidery, which too vary from region to region.

Many of the ethnic groups who live in China's south-west have a special fondness for silver jewellery and ornamentation, with the Bai and Miao people particularly known for this, often adorned from head to toe with silver ornaments. The Bai have traditionally liked their silver jewellery to be thick and bold in style, with carved patterns; whereas the Miao prefer silver ornaments to be delicate and finely worked, winding silver wire into shapes and patterns of great variety.

Sichuan is a province famed for its bamboo and it is home to a unique art-form where hair-fine bamboo strands are plaited around ceramic ware to form an outer covering, encasing the ceramic vessel in a bamboo sheath. The pottery and bamboo seem to be all of a piece, an effect that is quite striking. Moreover each different vessel will be decorated with different patterns in the bamboo weave. The art is found only in Sichuan.

The people of Fengxiang County in Shaanxi are known for the clay figurines they make. The local farmers shape clay into figures of every kind – people, animals, and supernatural characters from folk tales and legends. They make figures representing the twelve animals of the Chinese zodiac and tiger-head plaques to hang on the wall. The figures are painted in bright colours to give them lively expressions and intricately patterned clothes and accessories. The first clay figures were made as toys for children or charms to hang in houses to keep bad luck and evil spirits at bay. As time went on, the forms and decoration grew ever more exaggerated and the colours more eye-catching. The horse and goat zodiac figures were used by China's national post service in one of their commemorative stamp issues.

Folk handicrafts and folk culture are closely

linked. China is the home of shadow puppetry. There were shadow puppet performances right back in the Han dynasty 2,000 years ago, and a millennium ago in the Song dynasty the art was thriving. The then capital (the city that is today Kaifeng in Henan Province) had numerous shadow puppet theatres, always lively with the sounds of the plays being sung and the music and the hubbub of the packed audiences drawn every day to the frequent performances. A number of shadow puppet performers became as famous as today's pop stars, pursued by adoring fans wherever they went. The puppet characters were known as "shadow people." Similar to ancient Egyptian wall art, they were almost always crafted in profile. The puppet makers would use translucent cow or donkey hide and cut it to craft the different characters, with each requiring many hundred of individual cuts to make. Then colour would be added, and the heads, arms, hands, legs and feet would be articulated at the joints allowing them to move very realistically. During performances, the shadows of the puppets would be cast on a white cloth screen using lamp light, with the puppeteers singing the different parts at the same time as they manipulated the puppets. With the arrival of film and television, shadow puppet performances are no longer a common sight but the "shadow people" are still popular and are used as decorative items in the home. This traditional handicraft is still enjoyed as part of everyday life.

The origin of Nuo masks goes right back to the Stone Age many millennia ago. They were worn by priests and shamans in magical and religious rites to play the roles of gods and spirits in dances that mimicked their movements. The power of the god would be evoked to drive away evil spirits and disease. The exaggerated and distorted, often grotesque, features of Nuo masks are typical of much primitive art. The vast array of spirits and gods worshipped in early

Fengxiang mud sculptures.

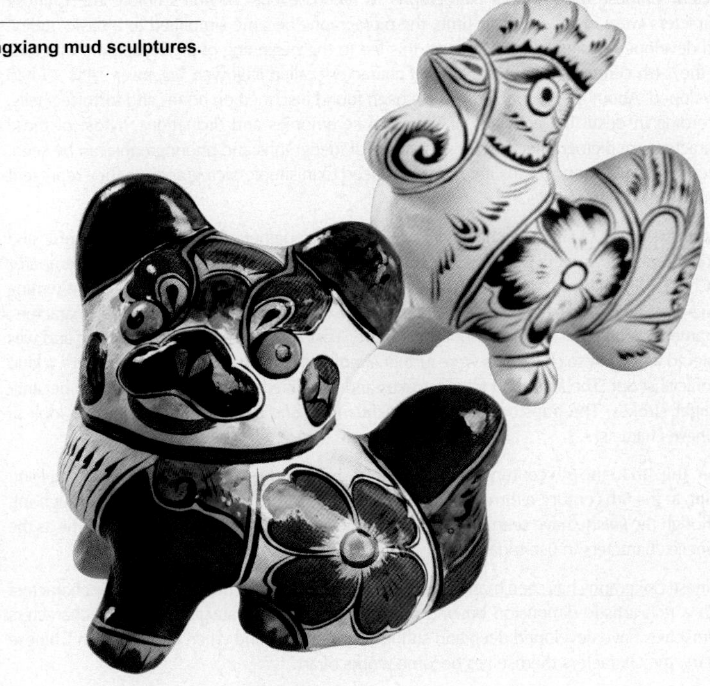

pantheistic cultures mean there are a plethora of different forms of Nuo mask. By the first century CE well over a thousand different gods and spirits featured in Nuo mask dance ceremonies held in the royal courts of the Han dynasty and there were 800 or more different masks to portray them. It was at this time that the masks began to be used not just in religious ceremonies, but also in purely dramatic opera performances. The masks were worn to act out stories and no longer only depicted supernatural beings. Masks representing ordinary people were also made. The tradition of Nuo mask dances has survived to the present day in remoter rural parts of China's south-west in provinces such as Guizhou, Sichuan, Jiangxi and Hunan. These performances, be they ceremonial or theatrical, still have that flavour of ancient mystery and the masks are seen as symbolic of the supernatural world. The masks are now also popular in China as collectible handicraft objects.

Visitors to China are also drawn to her handicrafts and stores selling them can be found in many cities and towns. You can learn more about this rich folk heritage online at www.galleriapangea.com, where you can watch videos of actual manufacturing processes. There are also many different items on sale for you to choose from. ■

▶▶ Chinese Characters

Ancient Egyptian and Babylonian characters were invented over 5,000 years ago and have gone through golden ages of development and use. But among the ancient writing systems, only the Chinese characters have survived the test of time and continue to be used.

Ancient Chinese used simple pictographs to record events or notes before the Chinese characters were invented. Over time, the pictographs became simplified to a basic outline and developed designs and meanings; this led to the beginning of pictographic characters. By the 14th century a mature system of characters called *jiaguwen* (*jiǎgǔwén* 甲骨文) had developed. About 6,000 characters have been found inscribed on bones and tortoise shells, recording in detail the activities of sacrificial ceremonies and divinations. Most of these characters are pictographs, but the beginning of ideographs and phonographs can be seen. Ideographs and phonographs are more advanced than simple pictographs as they represent abstract ideas and sounds.

The abstractness of Chinese characters was further strengthened and more ideographic and phonographic characters were introduced based on *jiaguwen*. After 221 BC, the first emperor of China, Qin Shihuang, took measures to unify and standardize the many different writing styles after he united China. *Xiaozhuan* (*xiǎozhuàn* 小篆), a simplified type of seal characters, became commonly used throughout the empire. *Xiaozhuan* had a simpler structure and was easier to write. These characters were further simplified as *lishu* (*lìshū* 隶书) characters, a kind of official script. The *lishu* had fewer strokes and simplified writing; curved strokes became straight strokes. The transformation of *xiaozhuan* to *lishu* completely changed the look of Chinese characters.

From the 4th to the 6th century, Chinese characters became standardized based on the *lishu* script. In the 6th century, a formal script called *kaishu* (*kǎishū* 楷书) was adopted throughout. Although the *kaishu* have seen minor changes, these characters are basically the same as the Chinese characters in use today.

Chinese calligraphy has seen many artistic and talented giants. They've infused the characters with a rich artistic dimension beyond the meaning of the character itself. The characters themselves have developed deep and subtle connotations, and when coupled with Chinese poetry, the characters themselves become works of art.

Religion in China

Over the ages, many religions have entered China, and at present there are five main religions: Buddhism, Taoism, Islam, Catholicism and Protestantism. Each religion has added its own mark to the cultural history of China.

According to recent surveys, China has over 100 million followers of various religions. Buddhism and Taoism have the largest number of followers, though accurate numbers are hard to come by because Buddhism and Taoism have become a blended faith with many following both religions.

NATURE WORSHIP & ANCESTOR WORSHIP

From ancient times, China has been a multi-ethnic country, with a multitude of religions. According to archeological evidence, between 50,000 and 100,000 years ago, the ancestors of the Chinese first developed systems of religious belief. It was discovered that bodies were buried with their heads in alignment at the site of the "**Upper Caveman**" (*shāndǐngdòng rén* 山顶洞人) unearthed in a mountaintop cave overlooking **Zhoukoudian** (*zhōukǒudiàn* 周口店), on the outskirts of Beijing. The bodies were also buried with spindles, arrowheads and finely made decorations. There's hematite powder scattered around the bodies, which isn't produced in the local area – the closest source is a couple of hundred miles away. From the archeological evidence, it appears this early group attached much importance to burials and archeologists conclude the people believed in the concept of an afterlife, in other words, in the concept of a soul. This is the earliest evidence of a religious belief found in China.

Early society was an agrarian culture and great importance was placed on agricultural production and animal husbandry. Since agrarian cultures are strongly affected by changes in nature, early humans prayed to and worshipped nature.

In this worship of nature, "Heaven" (*tiān* 天) was given precedence over "Earth" (*dì* 地), as were the hosts of heaven such as the mountains and rivers, wind, rain and thunders, and all natural phenomena that had a direct relationship with agricultural production. Worship was also extended to all kinds of natural phenomenon and objects. An abundance of vessels painted with the hosts of heaven have been found in archaeological excavations in recent years. "God," as a word representing "Heaven," has often been found in the remains of ancient books, showing the prevalence of nature worship. The heroic actions of ancient historical figures, often involving battles with natural disasters, led people to worship their ancestors for protection. Nature and ancestor worship became a primitive form of religion for the early Chinese.

Ancestor worship reached a peak during the Shang dynasty, from 1384 to 1111 BC. The excavation of substantial inscriptions on bones or tortoise shells(*jiǎgǔwén* 甲骨文) from the Shang dynasty gives evidence to this. Shang society was very superstitious and frequently asked the gods for advice on

Dragons were once thought to live in the oceans and were the bringers of rain and thunder.

Wenshu Pusa (Manjusri).

any issue, from memorial ceremonies to wars and diseases; the Shang beseeched their gods to guide their actions. Such soothsaying rituals were rigidly controlled by the state up until the Zhou dynasty, which ruled from 1027 to 777 BC. The timing, style and scale of soothsaying rituals were all laid down. The most important of these rituals were presided over by the emperor; junior officials could only preside over lesser rituals.

Ancient Chinese religious beliefs such as the worshipping of Heaven and Earth and the ancestors have continued to this day, influencing Confucianism and all other Chinese religious beliefs.

THE INTRODUCTOIN OF BUDDHISM & THE BIRTH OF TAOISM

Indian prince Siddhartha Gautama founded Buddhism in 556 BC and by AD 2 it had spread to China amongst the imperial family, nobles and scholars. Emperor Mingdi of the Han dynasty was a devout Buddhist and dispatched an embassy to India in a quest for eminent Buddhist teachers. Before arriving in India, his envoys met two distinguished Indian Buddhist missionaries who were invited to meet the emperor. Buddhism spread to the common people once the sutras the two priests were carrying were translated into Chinese. Preaching to the commoners began, and Buddhism expanded. Buddhism influenced Confucianism and Taoism, and was in turn influenced by them.

Buddhism increased in popularity from the 3rd to 6th century and many temples were built across China. In the middle of 3rd century, the first Han Chinese men were initiated into the Buddhist priesthood and the first Han women became nuns in the 4th century. Monk Dao'an established a doctrine that prohibited monks and nuns from eating fish and meat. It was during the Sui and Tang dynasties that Buddhism in China reached its height of influence and splendor.

Xuan Zang, a famous Chinese monk, undertook an epic pilgrimage to India that lasted 17 years. He brought back to China a wealth of sutras and translated them into Chinese, greatly contributing to the development of Buddhism in China: Eventually eight schools of Buddhism developed in China, the Three-Treatises (*sānlùnzōng* 三论宗), Dharmalaksana (*fǎxiàngzōng* 法相宗), Avatamsaka (*huáyánzōng* 华严宗), Vinaya (*lǜzōng* 律宗), Tiantai (*tiāntáizōng* 天台宗), Tantra (*mìzōng* 密宗), Pure Land (*jìngtǔzōng* 净土宗) and Chan (*chánzōng* 禅宗), which is also known by its Japanese name, Zen. Buddhism became thoroughly sinicized, no longer relying on Indian sources and exerting a huge influence on China's politics, economy, culture and society.

Before Buddhism spread into Tibet around the 7th or 8th centuries from central China and Nepal, the Tibetans practiced Bön, a multi-theistic religion. Princess Wenchang became an important figure in spreading Buddhism to Tibet when Tang dynasty Emperor Taizong gave her in marriage to Songtsen Gampo, king of the Tibetan Tubo Kingdom. She brought to Lhasa many Buddhist artifacts and helped convert the Tibetans. Padmasambhava (*Liánhuāshēng* 莲花生), an ancient Indian monk, combined Tantra with the local Bön religion. His Buddhist preaching was popular among Tibetans because he adapted many native Bön rituals and ideas. This developed into Tibetan Buddhism, which is also known as Lamaism because the monks are called lamas.

Ethnic minority groups living in southwest China later adopted Buddhism, and from ancient India, Buddhism spread to Sri Lanka, Burma, Thailand and other Southeast Asian countries.

THE RISE OF TAOISM

Taoism originated in the 2nd century AD as the Eastern Han dynasty began falling apart. As the empire fell into feuding kingdoms, two peasant rebellions broke out in Hebei and Sichuan provinces; one was based on Taiping Taoism and the other on Wudoumi Taoism. They revered Laozi (*Lǎozǐ* 老子), a Chinese philosopher of the Spring and Autumn Period, as the forefather of Taoism. According to the *Tao Te Jing* (*dàodéjīng* 道德经), which is attributed to Laozi, Taoism's core belief is to establish a utopian peace where everyone lives in equality.

The rebellion in Hebei was defeated; however, Wudoumi Taoism in Sichuan and south Shaanxi provinces survived when the rebels surrendered to Cao Cao (*Cáo Cāo* 曹操), a East Han Warlord. After the 3rd century, many scholars and officials began to turn to Wudoumi Taoism, which gradually lost its peasant rebellion origins and became a religion based on the Tao (*dào* 道).

Taoists worship Laozi as their forefather, Zhang Daoling (*Zhāng Dàolíng* 张道陵),

Buddhist monks in Tibet are called Lamas.

▶▶ The Pilgrim's Progress

Xuan Zang (*Xuán Zàng* 玄奘), who lived from AD 602 to 664, was the most famous Buddhist philosopher of the Tang dynasty. His epic journey to India made possible Chinese translations of some of the most important Buddhist texts, as well as providing the inspiration for the famous Chinese novel *Journey to the West* (*xī yóu jì* 西游记) and its stories of a brave pilgrim and mythical Monkey King.

Interested in the life of a Buddhist monk from an early age, Xuan Zang was ordained a priest when he was only 13 years old. He joined a monastery in Chang'an (now Xi'an) that was translating Indian scriptures, but was disappointed by the quality and accuracy of the works available. He decided that an expedition to the home of Buddhism was the best recourse to resolve contradictions he found in the Chinese translations. In AD 627 he set off on foot to India. He was only 26 and would not return for 18 years.

The recently established Tang dynasty refused to give him permission to leave, but with the aid of sympathetic officers – Buddhists themselves – he sweated across the Taklamakan Desert and reached the oasis city of Turpan. The Great Khan of Western Turks, who controlled an area stretching from modern day Afghanistan to China's Xinjiang Uyghur Autonomous Region, took a liking to the adventurous monk and tried to force him to stay. Xuan Zang refused and threatened a hunger strike. His unswerving devotion to his mission convinced the Khan to release him and he was sent on his way.

His first five years in India were spent learning Sanskrit and studying at the Nalanda Monastery under the many masters there. During the 14th and 15th centuries Nalanda was the largest Buddhist "university" in the world, attracting Buddhists from as far as Mongolia, Korea and Japan.

For the next six years he traveled around India and consulted erudite Buddhist dharmas in over more than 100 different regions of the subcontinent. He began to give lectures himself and the charisma that had charmed the Great Khan won him large audiences, which helped spread a new and intensely abstract school of meditation called Yogacara.

On his return to China, he was given a hero's welcome by the same Tang emperor who had made his outbound journey so difficult years before. The 600 scriptures HE brought back were translated into Chinese and are still used in many monasteries throughout China. His legacy in spreading Buddhist knowledge throughout China cannot be understated.

Xuan Zang's epic journey became the basis for Wu Cheng'en's Ming dynasty novel *Journey to the West*. Xuan Zang's journey is fictionalized and embellished with adventures with his intrepid guide and protector, the playful Monkey King and Zhu Bajie, a happy-go-lucky pig.

founder of Wudoumi Taoism, as the Celestial Master(*tiānshī* 天师)and take the *Tao Te Jing* as their bible. In the book, "Tao" is the origin of the universe and the creator of all living beings. Taoism adopted nature and ancestor worship from earlier Chinese beliefs. Taoists also believed men could attain immortality and become celestial beings by living an austere life.

The emperors of past dynasties bestowed the title Celestial Master on the descendents of Zhang Daoling in order to canonize Taoism, which became known as "*tianshi dao*" or "*zhengyi dao*." In the middle of the 12th century, the Taoist Wang Chongyang laid the foundations for the Quanzhen School of Taoism by proposing that Taoists should also adhere to tenets of Buddhism and Confucianism; that Taoists should remain celibate, only live with other Taoists, become vegetarians and adopt other austerities. Taoism then became divided into two schools, Quanzhen and Zhengyi.

ISLAM ARRIVES WITH CULTURAL EXCHANGE & MIGRATION

Trade and cultural exchange between China and Arabia was becoming increasingly frequent by the 7th century. Many Arabian merchants became integrated into central China and settled along the Silk Road as a result of business or intermarriage. The traders and their descendants would become the earliest Muslims in China.

Trade on the Silk Road all but ceased during the Song dynasty due to wars; this led to the creation of the Maritime Silk Road, which flowed from China's coastal cities down to the coast of Southeast Asia then into Arabia. Many mosques built in the Song dynasty still survive in Guangzhou, Quanzhou, Hangzhou and Yangzhou.

Ethnic immigration is another factor that contributed to the introduction of Islam to China. A major wave of immigration took place during the An Lushan and Shi Siming rebellions during the Tang dynasty. The Tang emperor had to recruit soldiers from Arabia in order to crush the revolt, and after the war, many of the Muslim soldiers settled in China. Another mass influx occurred after Genghis Khan established his enormous empire across Asia and Europe. He encouraged a large number of people from Central and Western Asia to immigrate to China, most of whom were Muslims. This later migration formed the basis of the Hui nationality and today the Hui continue to practice Islam with their own unique traditions.

After the 10th century, ethnic minorities in China's northwest began turning to Islam. In the late 15th century, it spread to the Uyghurs living in Xinjiang and it became the dominant religion in the region by the 17th century with the majority of Chinese Muslims following the Sunni branch.

THE INTERRUPTIONS & RE-ENTRY OF CHRISTIANITY

The earliest version of Christianity in China was called *Jingjiao* – Nestorian Christianity, which diverged from the Eastern Orthodox Church and spoke of Christ as one person (prosopon) with two natures (physis), human and divine. Olopen, a clergyman from Rome, arrived at Chang'an, the capital of the Tang dynasty, and was welcomed by Emperor Taizong in 635. In 638 Olopen was allowed to build a church, the Daqin Temple (*dàqín sì* 大秦寺) for the emperor. During the reign of the Emperor Gaozong, Nestorian churches sprang up all over China, but 250 years later, the religion became prohibited. Nonetheless, groups in northwest China continued in their faith and practice of Nestorian Christianity. Not until the Yuan dynasty in the 13th century did Nestorian Christianity spread again to central China, and four bishoprics were established in Datong, Beijing, Zhangye and Kashgar.

The first Catholic priest to visit China was Giovanni da Montecorvino, who was sent in 1294 by the Vatican to Dadu, the capital of the Yuan dynasty at present day Beijing. He was received by the emperor and allowed to build a church and preach in Dadu. A bishopric was set up in Dadu in 1307 with da Montecorvino as bishop until his death in 1328.

The Franciscan priest Marignolli was dispatched by the Vatican to become the bishop in Dadu in 1342. However, Catholicism was only prevalent among the Mongolian ruling class, and once the Ming dynasty overthrew the Yuan dynasty, Catholicism and Nestorian Christianity were banished from central China along with the Mongolians.

A Catholic church on Beijing's busy Wangfujing pedestrian street.

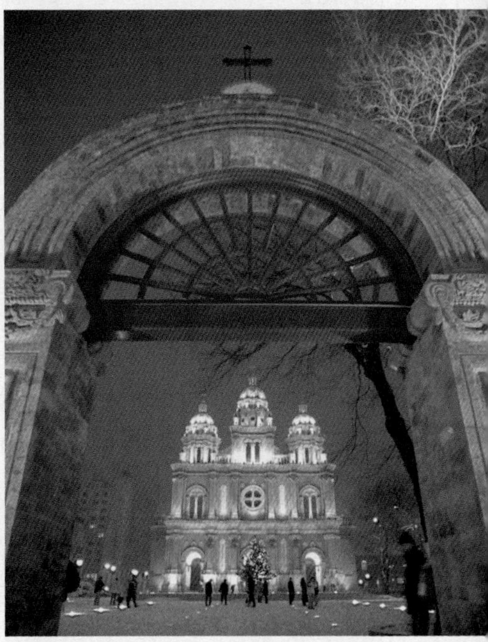

The second influx of Christianity to China was the arrival of the Italian Jesuit Matteo Ricci in Macau. He built churches in Guangdong and developed a local priesthood numbering about 80. Ricci and his followers worked within the framework of Chinese culture and etiquette and introduced advanced Western science to China. He was given the position of court astronomer and served both the Ming and Qing dynasty, gaining the trust of emperors and court officials. Catholicism developed rapidly and had about 300,000 followers and 250 churches around China; however, the Franciscans and the Order of Preachers condemned the Jesuits. Their disagreement triggered the Rites Controversy and in 1704, the Vatican issued a ban on Chinese customs such as ancestor worship, which the Jesuits had argued wasn't incompatible with Catholic teachings. This irritated Emperor Kangxi and he ordered the expulsion of all missionaries who sought to convert the Chinese from their customs. This initiated a 100-year-long ban on Catholicism and the end of the second stage of missionary activity in China.

In 1807, Robert Morrison, from the London Missionary Society, arrived in Guangzhou. He not only preached the gospel but also translated the New and Old Testaments into Chinese. He was the first to preach Protestantism, but his mission didn't go well and by 1814, he had only one follower. The third entry of Catholicism to China came in 1840 after the Opium War. The war had turned China into a half-colonial state and foreign missionaries secured a series of privileges, including the right to proselytize. This did little to win over the Chinese who continued to view Christianity as a "foreign religion." ■

ACCOMMODATION 住宿		
Where's the··· Hotel?	··· bīnguǎn zài nǎr	···宾馆在哪儿?
Are there any vacant rooms?	yǒu fángjiān ma	有房间吗?
I'd like a ···.	wǒ yào yījiān ···	我要一间···
single room	dānrén fáng	单人房
double room	shuāngrén fáng	双人房
economy room	pǔtōng fáng	普通房
standard room	biāozhǔn fáng	标准房
deluxe suite	háohuá tàofáng	豪华套房
How much for a room?	duōshǎo qián yītiān	多少钱一天?
I'd like to see the room?	wǒ néng kànkan fángjiān ma	我能看看房间吗?
I'll take this room.	zhège fángjiān wǒ yàole	这个房间我要了。
Is there a laundry service?	yǒu xǐyī fúwù ma	有洗衣服务吗?
Is my laundry ready?	wǒde yīfu xǐ hǎole ma	我的衣服洗好了吗?
Can I deposit my valuables here?	kěyǐ cúnfàng guìzhòng wùpǐn ma	可以存放贵重物品吗?
How do I make an international call?	guójì chángtú zěnme dǎ	国际长途怎么打?
Please give me a wakeup call at ··· tomorrow morning.	qǐng zài míngzǎo ··· diǎn jiàoxǐng wǒ	请在明早···点叫醒我。
I am ready to checkout.	wǒ xiǎng tuìfáng	我想退房。
Please give me the bill.	qǐng jiézhàng	请结账。
Can I pay by traveler's cheque?	kěyǐ fù lǚxíng zhīpiào ma	可以付旅行支票吗?

Food in China

China's cuisine has evolved into one of the great cuisines of the world. For more than 5,000 years, food has played an auspicious role in nearly all aspects of Chinese society, from health and medicine to business and celebration, and it is no less important today. The overall importance of food in China can't be understated; upon greeting, Westerners will inquire about your health; the Chinese will ask if you've eaten.

Rich in scenic beauty, China's geography spans a wide spectrum from fertile plains to high mountains. Its climate is also extremely broad in scope, ranging from sub-arctic to subtropical with everything in between. This combination of varied geography, climate and sheer land size produces an extraordinary cornucopia of fruit, vegetables, meats and seafood, and has evolved into one of the most interesting, creative and widely enjoyed cuisines of the world.

Emphasis on the freshness, flavor and texture of ingredients is key to fine Chinese cooking. To get the most out of even simple ingredients, a variety of techniques is used to highlight and accent food qualities. Quick cooking with a wok and deep-frying are universal to most styles of cooking in China. You'll also find other cooking methods such as steaming, roasting, barbecuing, stewing, poaching and braising used extensively.

Many of the coastal and border regions of China have adopted outside influences into their cuisine. In general, the farther south you travel the more tropical the weather, affording better growing conditions, and the lighter and more refined the food tends to be. With harsh winters and short growing conditions, northern and western regions tend to offer much heartier cuisine. Traders, missionaries and invading peoples have all had their influence in how gastronomy has evolved in various regions. New World foods such as tomatoes and corn are now common ingredients throughout China; in Hong Kong you'll find the use of mayonnaise; and chilies have directly influenced an entire genre of food from Sichuan. In ancient times and even today, those living in the remote areas didn't travel extensively and there have been few outside influences from other cultures. The foods they eat and their cooking, essentially their entire way of life, has been insulated and has remained the same for countless generations. If you visit these remote places, you'll have a fascinating

An ancient Chinese drinking party.

opportunity to have a taste of ancient history.

One note for those who don't eat pork – if a dish has an unnamed meat, that meat is usually pork. Strict vegetarians and vegans will find it hard to avoid meat or meat products altogether. Some restaurants will simply pick out the most obvious pieces of meat from their dishes or may use lard in their cooking. The best way to avoid meat is to tell the service staff you're allergic to meat or Buddhist. Here are two helpful phrases "I don't eat meat" (*wǒ bù chī hūn de* 我不吃荤的) or "I only eat vegetables" (*wǒ zhǐ chī sù de* 我只吃素的). Monosodium glutamate (MSG) is also widely used, but you can always ask for none (*bú yào wèijīng* 不要味精).

NORTHERN CHINA

The cuisine of northern China centers on Beijing and includes the provinces of Shandong, Hebei, Shanxi, Inner Mongolia and the northeast, which is collectively known as dongbei in Chinese. The harsh northern climate consists of blistering hot summers and cold dry winters matching the strong, bold and salty flavors of this region.

A traditional Beijing style charcoal fueled hot pot.

Stir-frying, stewing, and deep-frying are typical ways of cooking fairly basic ingredients such as chicken, mutton, fish and tofu. There tends to be an emphasis on meats, with vegetables taking a back seat. Common condiments include bean pastes, dark soy sauces, vinegar and sugar, resulting in dishes with rich brown sauces. Pungent, aromatic and forceful flavors from garlic, ginger and spring onion dominate as well.

Wheat is the staple grain that grows well here and you'll find an abundance of wheat products in the form of buns, noodles, dumplings and pancakes. Look for hand-pulled noodles being made to order – an exciting and artful demonstration of skill. A master noodle puller can create strands of noodles so fine they're called "dragon's whiskers" (*lóngxūmiàn* 龙须面). Also, look for "hand shaved"(*dāoxiāomiàn* 刀削面) noodles made to order served with flavorful soups or dumplings (*jiǎozi* 饺子), which are a universal simple pleasure served with vinegar and hot chili oil for dipping. Try dumplings with pork and cabbage, egg and chives or pork and black mushroom fillings, which are standard combinations available in most dumpling houses.

There's also a strong Muslim influence introduced by Central Asian traders who made their way along the Silk Road. You can taste their influence in the form of barbecued lamb skewers (*yángròu chuànr* 羊肉串儿) flavored with cumin seed or lamb stir-fried with vegetables. Mongolian hotpot (*huǒguō* 火锅) is a year-round specialty that is especially welcome in the winter. Set in the middle of your dining table is a simmering pot of flavorful broth, spiced with hot oil if you like, in which you cook paper-thin slices of lamb, beef or pork, chunks of chicken and seafood as well as vegetables; a sesame paste dipping sauce spiced to your liking accompanies this. Nearly anything can be found cooking in a hotpot – for the adventurous, try ordering cubes of duck blood.

Lakes and rivers are a reliable source of freshwater fish. Look for "squirrel fish" (*sōngshǔ guìyú* 松鼠桂鱼), a dish made with mandarin fish, a type of freshwater bass. Ask to see it before it's cooked to ensure that it is "swimming fresh." Most restaurants expect patrons to ask, and it'll be ceremoniously brought directly to the table for your inspection. The fish is carefully filleted, then deep fried and artfully served with a sweet and sour tomato sauce. This is a favorite in Beijing, as the Chinese pronunciation is a homonym for "expensive."

Peking duck (*běijīng kǎoyā* 北京烤鸭) is the most famous dish of Beijing. Your best bet is to find it at restaurants that specialize in it. After it is roasted in a wood-fired oven, watch a master chef carve the duck, skillfully slicing it with a thin bladed cleaver. The delicacy you are after is the crispy duck skin, paired with scallion, cucumber and sweet bean sauce all wrapped in thin flour pancakes. If there's one dish to seek out when in Beijing, the duck is it.

The imperial court was probably the largest influence on diversity within northern Chinese cuisine. The standards and demands of this elaborate cuisine are no longer practiced in its full indulgence, but the skills and flavors are of great influence on the standards used for banquets and celebrations today. For the truly indulgent, take part in an imperial banquet. Recipes are based on those that once graced the tables of emperors.

Ten Representative Northern Dishes:

Beef with spring onions (*qīngcōng chǎo niúròu* 青葱炒牛肉) – a dish of beef and spring onions that is flavored with soy sauce, sugar and sesame oil.

Cabbage rolls with mustard oil (*jièmò báicài* 芥末白菜) – Chinese cabbage brushed with mustard oil, rolled up and steamed, a simple dish that reflects its humble northern roots.

Earthen jar pork (*guànròu* 罐肉) – fatty pork belly, the same cut as bacon, is cooked slowly in a clay jar, creating a very rich brown sauce and succulent pork.

Hand pulled noodles in soup (*chēn miàn* 抻面) – literally pulled by hand, this soup is "flavored" with such various ingredients as red-stewed beef or pork, pickled vegetables, or with shredded chicken and a big dollop of chili sauce.

Mongolian hotpot (*huǒ guō* 火锅) – thought to be first practiced by Mongolian soldiers using their helmets to prepare meals, hotpot today uses simmering cauldrons of soup over charcoal, within which are cooked all manner of meat, fish, seafood and vegetables. Soup may be spicy hot, depending on personal taste.

Mu shu pork (*mùxū ròu* 木须肉) – despite being listed on a variety of menus everywhere, this is actually a northern dish originating from Beijing. Pork cut into shreds is combined with black mushrooms, wood ear fungus, and cabbage and accompanied by pancakes and hoisin sauce.

Boiled mutton is popular in the cold north.

Peking duck (*běijīng kǎoyā* 北京烤鸭) – the most famous dish from Beijing, a multi-step preparation that results in succulent crisp skin eaten with scallion, cucumber and a sweet brown sauce, wrapped in a thin wheat pancake.

Stir-fried eggs and tomatoes (*fānqié chǎodàn* 番茄炒蛋)– this simple dish is relatively modern in that tomatoes are a New World ingredient, yet today has become a staple dish in the north.

Shandong sweet and sour carp (*shāndōng tángcù yú* 山东糖醋鱼) – deep fried carp with a sauce based on sugar and vinegar.

Stewed sea cucumber with crab eggs (*shāndōng xièhuáng hǎishēn* 山东蟹黄海参) – a Shandong specialty, sea cucumber, also known as sea slug, readily absorbs flavors and has an almost crunchy texture. The crab eggs lend a rich subtle flavor to the otherwise bland sea cucumber.

EASTERN CHINA

The cuisine of eastern China tends to revolve around Shanghai and the surrounding provinces of Zhejiang, Jiangxi, Anhui and Jiangsu. Although Shanghai cuisine is often spoken of, it's hard to define because it's derived from the surrounding areas. The fertile plains of the Yangtze River offer a rich variety of fish and produce. The style of cooking tends to be lighter than in the west and north. Relatively refined soups, braised and stir-fried dishes flavored with ginger, dark soy sauce, Shaoxing wine and rice vinegar are balanced by using sugar. Look for "red-stewed" (*hóngshāo* 红烧) foods, especially red-stewed pork (*hóngshāo ròu* 红烧肉), a specialty of the region.

Seafood and fish are important components in eastern cuisine. Try shrimp cooked with tea leaves and garnished with vinegar, frog stewed with mushrooms, clams stir-fried with scallions, or crab coated with salted egg yolk and deep fried. Steamed freshwater hairy crab from Yangcheng Lake is a much sought after specialty that's in peak season in October and November. The rich, creamy and intensely flavored roe of the crab is the most luxurious part, though be prepared to get your hands messy extracting the meat.

A must try are Shanghai steamed dumplings (*xiǎolóng bāo* 小笼包) served with vinegar for dipping. They are often found in street market food stalls as well as in restaurants. This Shanghai standard is sometimes elevated to luxury status with the addition of crabmeat or hairy crab roe.

A local eastern Chinese delicacy.

Ten Representative Eastern Dishes:

Beggar's chicken (*jiàohuā jī* 叫化鸡) – traditionally a whole chicken flavored with Shaoxing wine, it is first wrapped in lotus leaves then with clay and cooked in a fire.

Dongpo pork (*dōngpō ròu* 东坡肉) – named after the distinguished poet Su Dongpo of the 11th century, this is a red-stewed, braised pork dish, succulent and rich, usually cooked in an earthenware vessel.

Dragon Well tea prawns (*lóngjǐng xiā* 龙井虾) – prawns cooked with fresh Dragon Well tea leaves, a specialty in the Hangzhou region.

Hot and sour soup (*suānlà tāng* 酸辣汤) – deliciously spicy with a tinge of vinegar, this soup is filled with slivers of meat, tofu, bamboo shoots and egg.

Lion's head meatballs (*shīzi tóu* 狮子头) – these meatballs are said to resemble a "lion's head" accompanied by a "mane" of bok choy, made with pork, deep fried and braised in a rich brown sauce.

Red-stewed pork (*hóngshāo ròu* 红烧肉) – braised pork leg dish made with Shaoxing rice wine, dark soy sauce, five-spice powder and rock sugar.

Sweet and sour pork (*gǔlǎo ròu* 古老肉) – deliciously deep fried pieces of pork are drenched in a sweet and sour sauce with chunks of pineapples.

West Lake beef soup (*xīhú niúròu gēng* 西湖牛肉羹) – this famous soup is named after West Lake of Hangzhou and made with beef, peas and eggs.

West Lake poached fish (*xīhú cùyú* 西湖醋鱼) – originally from Hangzhou, the fish is first marinated with ginger, soy sauce, sugar and black vinegar, poached whole, then sauced with the marinade.

Yangzhou fried rice (*yángzhōu chǎofàn* 扬州炒饭) – this well-known fried rice dish uses shrimp, peas, and scrambled eggs. It is distinctly flavored with chicken stock, Shoaxing wine, thin soy sauce and sesame oil.

SOUTHERN CHINA

Rich and prosperous southern Chinese cuisine is dominated by Guangdong Province and is best characterized by fresh flavors and textures using cooking techniques that preserve the integrity of ingredients. As a gateway to the New World, all manner of food products from the rest of China – fresh and preserved – flowed through Guangdong. Expect many foods to be lightly seasoned with simple flavors and literally all cooking techniques used – don't be surprised to see salt, clay or lotus leaves wrapped around something tasty to eat. The subtropical climate provides an abundance of fresh vegetables and fruits, a profusion of fish and seafood (fresh and all manner of dried), as well as poultry and pork. If you want to see a veritable zoo, you only need visit a local market; the Cantonese are known to pretty much eat anything in the name of eating well. Common exotics include dogs, cats, and frogs – you've been warned.

Fresh seafood in southern China is perhaps the best available in China. Nearly all restaurants have swimmingly fresh fish and seafood, which is the standard. Look for the live tanks filled with incredible varieties of fish, clams, crab, abalone and lobster – pretty much anything that swims. You can go to the live tanks and just point your finger at anything you want. Try clams or crab stir-fried with ginger and spring onion; nearly any seafood can be done this way. Whole fish steamed until just cooked and seasoned with light soy sauce and sprinkled with scallions is a classic dish. If you love seafood, southern China is the place to be.

"*Yum cha,*" or literally "drink tea," is perhaps the most social of all dining traditions in China and is a must especially when in Hong Kong or Guangzhou. From morning to mid-afternoon, small snacks or tidbits called dim sum, or "touch of the heart," are served with bottomless pots of hot tea. It's a time to socialize and catch up with friends and family or just read the morning paper while snacking on a variety of savory and sweet items that are steamed, fried or baked. There are perhaps thousands of different dim sum items to choose from but it couldn't be any easier to order. Just point at anything you like on the dim sum cart that is wheeled about and you are served immediately.

Fresh vegetables are abundant in southern China and are usually cooked with reverence – usually very simply to retain color, flavor and texture. They're typically stir-fried with a bit of garlic and a minimum of oil or cooked "in soup." Try Chinese broccoli with oyster sauce, or pea shoots stir-fried with garlic. Pea shoots are the tender young tendrils of the pea vine; they taste a bit like fresh peas. Most vegetables are cooked with some crunch and texture remaining, and seasoned very lightly with soy sauce, oyster sauce, or a chicken-stock-based sauce.

Cantonese-style roast ducks hang for hungry buyers to select.

The world's original deli is perhaps the famous Cantonese roast or barbecued meats. Pork and duck are favorites and can't be missed – you can find them prominently displayed in shop windows. Try crispy roast pork, barbecued duck or salt baked chicken cut to order with a side of rice to make a quick lunch.

When visiting southern China, remember that the Cantonese people live to eat.

Ten Representative Southern Dishes:

Chinese broccoli with oyster sauce (*háoyóu jièlán* 蚝油芥兰) – a very simple classic preparation for Chinese broccoli or other vegetables such as lettuce, using oyster sauce which makes the dish. Premium oyster sauce starts with about 10 gallons (40 liters) of oysters to yield 1 quart (1 liter) of sauce.

Clay pot chicken (*hǎinán jīfàn* 海南鸡饭) – chicken, long grain rice, sweet pork sausage and black mushrooms are cooked in a clay pot and served with a soy, rice wine, sugar and sesame-oil based sauce.

Drunken prawns steamed with rice wine (*zuì xiā* 醉虾)– live shrimp are first " drowned" by letting them swim in Shaoxing wine, or other rice-based wine, then steamed.

Barbeque pork (*mìzhī chāshāo* 蜜汁叉烧) – usually dark red on the outside and juicy and succulent on the inside, barbecue pork is often served as a side dish or on top of rice or noodles.

Pepper and salt fried shrimp (*jiāoyán xiā* 椒盐虾) – seasoned with pepper and salt, the shrimp are cooked very crisp, resulting in shrimp shells that are crunchy and edible; if cooked whole the heads may be eaten as well.

Pig knuckle stew (*báiyún zhūshǒu* 白云猪手) – a pig knuckle is first boiled, then slowly stewed in a mixture of vinegar, sugar and salt. This dish has a sweet tangy zest.

Roast duck Cantonese style (*guǎngdōng kǎoyā* 广东烤鸭) – this roast duck does not have the crispy skin of Peking duck, but is more flavorful. It's marinated with five spice powder, soy and sugar or honey, and typically some marinade is poured into the duck's cavity before roasting.

Roast pigeon (*kǎo gē* 烤鸽) – best when plain roasted and accompanied by pepper and salt for dipping, the rich succulent flavor of pigeon is not masked by anything – typical of Cantonese cuisine.

Salt baked chicken (*yán kǎo jī* 盐烤鸡) – a whole chicken is buried in salt and cooked in a large wok, creating an "oven" that produces amazingly succulent chicken.

Whole steamed fish (*qīngzhēng quányū* 清蒸全鱼) – nearly any variety can be used, and so this is more of a universal Cantonese technique than a dish. It often uses slivers of scallion and ginger, thin soy sauce and a quick dousing of smoking hot oil, and the whole fish is steamed until just cooked.

WESTERN CHINA

Western Chinese cuisine includes influences from Sichuan, Hunan, Guangxi and the Xinjiang regions. The fertile plains and terraced hills of the western Chinese heartland fed by the Yangtze River and its tributaries, offer a garden of produce. Flavors are characteristically spicy and pungent – most often associated with chilies, though chilies are not indigenous to China. In fact, chilies were originally brought to the region by Portuguese traders and missionaries, and for the last several hundred years have been used quite extensively. One word of warning – genuine Sichuan food will be absolutely the hottest food you've ever eaten.

Though highly prominent, chilies aren't the only ingredient used in western Chinese cooking. Typical flavors also come from vinegar, garlic, onions, ginger, sesame oil and a very curious spice called Sichuan peppercorn, also known as prickly ash. Sichuan peppercorns have a very strong numbing effect (*má là* 麻辣) on the mouth when eaten. You'll know it if you're eating an authentic version of mapo tofu (*mápó dòufu* 麻婆豆腐) – your tongue will hang out of your mouth, a casualty of the dish's extraordinary level of Sichuan peppercorns and chilies. Not to be left out, the Sichuan version of hotpot also has a fiery level of chili.

Pork, freshwater fish, eggplant, soybeans and legumes such as peanuts are prominent ingredients, as are bamboo shoots, mushrooms and rice from the mountains. Typical cooking methods include frying, frying without oil called dry frying, pickling and braising as well as stir-frying. Fish-flavored shredded pork (*yúxiāng ròusī* 鱼香肉丝) gets its curious flavor from liberal use of ginger, garlic, vinegar, chili and spring onion but no fish.

There is a strong ethnic minority presence in this area of China and the use of goat's milk for cheese is an example of their influence. Muslim influences also show up in goat meat and dried beef dishes, reflecting a historically nomadic lifestyle. Try the slightly sweet-cured Yunnan ham (*xuānwēi huǒtuǐ* 宣威火腿), and crossing-the-bridge noodles soup (*guòqiáo mǐxiàn* 过桥米线).

The Xinjiang influence in western China is very much Arabic in origin, strong in lamb and mutton, with a distinct flavor. In fact, you'll find authentic Arabic flat bread (*náng* 馕), baked in ovens very similar to the Indian tandoor. Mutton kebabs seasoned with toasted cumin are very popular and tasty and should not be missed. Fruit as well has an Arabic influence featuring fresh melons, grapes, apricots and raisins.

Ten Representative Western Dishes:

Ants climbing up a tree (*mǎyǐ shàngshù* 蚂蚁上树) – a spicy dish of bean thread noodles and pork that resemble ants climbing trees.

Bang bang chicken (*bàngbang jī* 棒棒鸡) – a classic Sichuanese cold platter made with chicken, cucumber and bean thread noodles, dressed with a sesame based sauce.

Crispy shredded beef (*dēngyǐng niúròu* 灯影牛肉) – thought to originate from Sichuan or Hunan, with carrots, spring onion, garlic and chili, sauced with sugar, vinegar and soy.

Dan dan noodles (*dāndan miàn* 担担面) – noodles with a spicy sauce made with hot chilies and ground pork.

Dry fried green beans (*gānbiān sìjìdòu* 干煸四季豆) – sometimes yard long beans are used, though always cut into bite-size pieces; They are first deep fried, then stir-fried with ground pork and Sichuan peppercorns.

Kung pao chicken (*gōngbǎo jīdīng* 宫保鸡丁) – this classic dish from Sichuan is made with chicken, chili and peanuts.

Mapo tofu (*mápó dòufu* 麻婆豆腐) – a classic Sichuan dish literally meaning "pockmarked grandmother tofu" using tofu, ground pork, copious quantities of red chilies and Sichuan peppercorns; it's named after an old woman thought to have first made this dish in her restaurant.

Mouth watering beef (*shuǐzhǔ niúròu* 水煮牛肉) – named because this dish is so good it "makes your mouth water with anticipation," beef is cooked with a very large quantity of chili-laced oil. This dish can be made with fish or lamb as well.

Smoked fish (*xūn yú* 熏鱼) – originating from Guangxi, this fish dish is not smoked, but takes on a smoky quality from first being marinated with five spices, ginger, Shaoxing wine, and sugar, deep fried then marinated again.

Twice cooked pork (*huíguō ròu* 回锅肉) – pork is first boiled, then stir-fried with peppers, chili and soy.

BASIC DINING ETIQUETTE & CUSTOMS IN CHINA

Dining etiquette in China can be quite intricate and daunting at first. You'll

Mutton is a staple in northwest China.

probably make a few faux pas, but with a little basic understanding and the realization that most practices are intended to make the guests feel comfortable and honored, you'll soon be able enjoy China's cuisine without worry.

One of the first things you will do at the table is drink tea. Be sure to pour tea for those around you first and your own teacup last – it's considered bad form to fill yours first or even worse, just fill your own. Even if the teacups of those around you are full, you should dribble a little anyway, this is considered polite. One reoccurring theme, which is mainly directed at the host, is to make sure your guests always have a full plate and cup.

When using chopsticks, never point them directly at people and never stick them standing upright in your rice bowl – this is a reminder of the incense burned at funerals. To serve yourself or others use a clean spoon solely for taking food from communal plates, though it is perfectly acceptable to either take food directly with your own chopsticks at informal settings. If you serve someone with your own chopsticks, use the blunt ends that don't go into your mouth.

If you're invited to be a guest at a meal, your host will want to ensure that there's more than enough food for everyone. If your host miscalculates (usually not often), don't be surprised if he orders more food to "save face" and prove his generosity and graciousness. Along this same theme, don't be surprised to find your host serving you choice morsels of food whether you ask for it or not. This is another sign of generosity – be sure to accept gracefully.

If you are a particularly important guest, fish will likely be served and the host may serve you the fish's head (which is considered a very choice part of the fish). If you aren't particularly fond of fish heads, just graciously accept, be brave and tuck in. It may embarrass (make him lose face) or even insult your host to return or refuse the fish's head. A better tactic would be to serve your host the fish's head first as a gesture of thanks for being so generous. Be gracious if at anytime you feel the need to decline a serving.

It's assumed that each person will pay their own share, unless it's been specifically stated that one person is treating. In Chinese custom, unless amongst friends or in an informal setting, it's the inviter that pays for the meal. It's polite to make an effort to pay, but expect strong resistance. It's a common sight in many Chinese restaurants to see two people loudly arguing after a meal – they're fighting for the right to pay.

When in doubt, do as your host does or simply ask – just remember that your host ultimately wants you to have a good time and feel welcome. ■

Emperor Tongzhi's old eating utensils.

THE GUIDE

Practical Information

WEATHER

China is vast and conditions can be extreme. Depending on the season and region, there are many pleasant times to travel. Inner Mongolia and Heilongjiang, in the north and northeast, can reach temperatures of -22°F (-30°C) during the winter, but have moderate rainfall and highs in the 70s°and low 80s°F (20s°C) in the summer. Shanghai, which is on China's central eastern seaboard, has a long humid summer, a short winter and a moderate, but chilly spring and autumn. The south has hot humid summers that last from April to September with temperatures in the high 90s°F or even higher (high 30s°C). Late summers also include a rainy season, so beware of typhoons. Springs and autumns are pleasant with temperatures in the low 70s°F (low 20s°C), but evenings can be damp and chilly. Tibet is bitterly cold and windy during the winters. The summers can be very hot, with daytime temperatures above 95°F (high 30s°C), but summer nights can practically turn into winter until the sun rises again. The northwest has hot but dry summers. Xinjiang, in the far northwest, is just as cold as the rest of northern China during the winters.

ENGLISH AT YOUR SERVICE

Higher-end hotels have English-speaking staff. Western food establishments, large shopping centers and a few small vendors will be able to execute transactions in English. Most bars and high-end Chinese restaurants near hotels have English-language menus and a staff with basic English knowledge. Taxi drivers are beginning to learn English, though most know very little beyond "hello" and "goodbye." Try to exercise patience when encountering someone who doesn't speak English and hope they'll do the same if you don't speak Chinese. Since the 70s, the students start learning English in middle school. When you need to find someone who can speak English, young Chinese in their early 20s will have a better chance understanding you.

EMBASSIES & CONSULATES

Log on to www.embassyworld.com for a comprehensive listing of Chinese embassies and consulates around the world and foreign embassies and consulates in China. Beijing, as the capital, is home to foreign embassies, and a number of countries have consulates in cities such as Shanghai, Chengdu, Hong Kong, Chongqing and Shenyang, among others.

VISA REQUIREMENTS

A visa is required for foreigners to enter the People's Republic of China. Foreign travelers to China can easily obtain Tourist/Family Visit Visas or "L" Visas. Applicants can opt for single or double entry. "L" Visas allow for a stay of 30 days, and are valid for 3 months upon issue; the count begins when you enter China. Stays of up to 90 and 180 days are also possible. Visa applications can be obtained through your regional Chinese embassy or consulate or through travel agencies. It's best to ask your local People's Republic of China representative office for up-to-date information for visa requirements. Application processes usually take 3 to 5 business days but expedited same day or next day service is usually available for a fee.

Visa extensions in China are handled at the local Public Security Bureau's (*gōng'ān jú* 公安局) Foreign Affairs Department. One month extensions may be granted at the discretion of the issuing officer. Hong Kong is a good place to get new visas into China without going too far away.

Be aware that some travel destinations will require special travel permits – destinations that require these are mentioned in the individual articles.

CUSTOMS

There are restrictions on the type of things you can bring into and take from China. These limits include the amount of cigarettes (400) and wine or spirits (2 bottles) that can be imported. Cash amounts that exceed US $5,000 must be declared at customs upon entering China. Importing perishable goods is prohibited. Jewelry, cultural relics, gold and silver items and handicrafts bought in China are required to be shown to customs when departing. Customs reserves the right to confiscate articles deemed "cultural treasures," which are items dated earlier than 1795. Make sure you keep the receipt when you buy jewelry, art, and antiques. You might need to present the receipt to the custom officials when you leave China.

CURRENCY & EXCHANGE

Most major currencies can be exchanged into Chinese currency, which is called *renminbi* (RMB 人民币 *rénmínbi* or "people's money.") The basic unit is the *yuan* (*yuán* 元) or colloquially known as the *kuai* (*kuài* 块). One *yuan* is divided into 10 *jiao* (*jiǎo* 角), which is also called a *mao* (*máo* 毛). One is further divided into 10 *fen* (*fēn* 分). Foreign currency can be exchanged at airports, border crossings, tourist hotels, some large shopping centers and major branches of Bank of China (*zhōngguó yínháng* 中国银行). Exchange rates are subject to change, so it's best to check your local bank or the many websites that offer conversion information.

TRAVELERS CHEQUES

Hotels in China accept travelers checks from their guests and the exchange rate is slightly higher than cash. Large Bank of China branches also accept them, though it's convenient to exchange them at the airport upon arrival. You'll need to keep exchange receipts if you plan on exchanging back into the original currency. If your checks are issued from a major company, there shouldn't be a problem in cashing them. If you are uncertain, check with the hotel beforehand.

CREDIT CARDS

Credit cards are becoming more widely accepted in China but are still the domain of upscale venues. Some places advertise with the Visa logo but only accept Chinese cards; ask if they accept international cards. Cash advances are also possible but only at major Bank of China locations where a commission and a minimum amount is usually stipulated.

ATMS

Automated Teller Machines (ATMs) are found throughout large cities like Beijing, Shanghai, Guangzhou and Shenzhen, though more are appearing elsewhere. Airports, large banks and some hotels have ATMs that issue RMB directly. There is a maximum daily withdrawal limit. Cirrus, Mastercard, Visa and American Express are among the accepted credit cards and Hong Kong and Macau have a number of others. It's not a good idea to completely rely on ATMs, as they are prone to disrepair.

TIPS, SERVICE CHARGES & TAX

Tips are not expected for most services. Many mid-range and high-end restaurants and hotels include a service fee in the bill, so tipping is not expected and may even be refused if you try. Exceptions to this rule include hotel porters and tour guides, who gladly appreciate them. Taxes are included in the stated prices.

DRIVING LICENSES & RESTRICTIONS

Foreigners who want to drive in China require an International Driving Permit; this can be arranged at the local PSB. However, there are extensive restrictions on inter-city driving. Cars can be rented in Hong Kong and Macau relatively hassle free. If you're renting a car in Beijing or Shanghai, you'll be restricted within the city limits. Information on drivers-for-hire can be found in ex-pat entertainment magazines.

PHONE & COMMUNICATIONS

Police: 110
Fire: 119
Ambulance: 120, 999

PHONE CARDS & LONG-DISTANCE CALLING

Internet Phone cards (IP 卡) are very common in China. They can be found in hotels, news kiosks, airports and many stores. These cards can be used for domestic long distance and international calls. International rates run from RMB 2.5 to 3.5 per minute. Conventional phone cards are twice the price and are found only in hotels and telecommunication shops. Dialing direct and calling collect are more expensive options.

For local calls, a mobile phone isn't a necessity since there are many card-operated phone booths in the city – one can purchase the necessary "IC" phone cards (IC 卡) in mom-and-pop shops, newsstands and phone stores. Furthermore, many small shops prominently display (usually red) phones that customers can use for a fee.

MOBILE PHONES

Having a mobile phone during your stay in China can be extremely practical, especially if you're traveling on business. China has both GSM and CDMA networks, though the former is far more popular. You can bring your tri-band phone from home and it'll work with the Chinese networks, though any calls you make will be considered long-distance. A cheaper option, and one that is especially attractive to people who visit frequently, is to acquire a local telephone number. To do so, simply buy a SIM card (SIM 卡), which is a telephone number, at any mobile phone store and insert it into your phone – don't forget to replace it with your original card when you go home. (Incidentally, cell phone numbers which contain lucky digits, like "8," which sounds like "wealth" in Chinese, are more expensive than those with unlucky ones, like "4," which sounds like "death.") Once you have a local number, purchase a prepaid calling card (*chōngzhí kǎ* 充值卡)– they come in denominations of RMB 30, 50, 100, 300 and 500 – add it to your SIM card and start dialing. Prepaid cards are sold in cell phone shops, convenience stores and newsstands. Replace as needed.

INTERNET

Internet café are a booming business in China and you should have no trouble finding one in cities, big or small. Besides internet bars (*wǎngbā* 网吧), tourist hotels, universities and libraries should be connected. Connection speed for foreign websites might be slow due to the bandwidth bottleneck between China and the West.

MEDIA

Four- and five-star hotels may have ESPN, CNN or BBC. The state-run Chinese Central Television (CCTV) has an English language channel, CCTV 9. This broadcast runs international news, business reports and Chinese cultural programs for foreigners.

ENGLISH PUBLICATIONS

Newsstands in China generally don't stock foreign newspapers and magazines, but most four- and five- star hotels sell publications like *The International Herald Tribune, USA Today, the Asian Wall Street Journal, The Financial Times, The Economist, Newsweek* and *Time*.

If you want to know what's happening in China, your best bet is to consult a locally published English-language newspaper or magazine. *China Daily*, a broadsheet often offered for free in hotels and sold for RMB 1 in newsstands, is a trove of information about China. Its Tuesday insert, *Business Weekly*, provides in-depth coverage of business and finance, and its weekend section focuses on travel and entertainment.

Large cities like Shanghai and Beijing offer expat-authored English language entertainment guides. Here you can find the latest specific information on nightlife, services, resources, and entertainment acts in your locale. A major ex-pat guide is the *that's* series which has a Beijing, Shanghai, PRD (Pearl River Delta) and national edition.

Large bookstores usually have a foreign language section with some translated Chinese literature and Western classics.

Major cities have large foreign language bookstores (*wàiwén shūdiàn* 外文书店). It's also a good place to stock up on phrasebooks and anything related to Chinese culture or history.

You may find it helpful to have a good map (*dìtú* 地图) to complement those found in this book. Basic maps are widely available: hotels give them to guests; hawkers sell them outside tourist sites.

CHINESE WEIGHTS & MEASURES

The metric system is used in China, though Chinese weights are still common. The Chinese *jin* (*jīn* 斤), which is equal to half a kilogram or 1.1 pounds (*gōngjīn* 公斤), is used by street venders – but not in supermarkets. The Chinese word for kilometer (.62 mile) is *gongli* (*gōnglǐ* 公里), and is used on taxi meters and road signs. Another useful word is *mi* (*mǐ* 米), which is Chinese for meter.

TIME DIFFERENCES

Time in all of China is officially set to Beijing time, which is eight hours ahead of GMT. However, since China is spread across several lines of longitude, people in the western regions of Xinjiang and Tibet adjust their schedules a couple hours earlier according to the sun. The following are some examples of time differences with other major cities in the world.

Noon in Beijing means it's:

2pm in Sydney
1pm in Tokyo
7am in Moscow
6am in Johannesburg
5am in Berlin
4am in London
11pm in New York (previous day)
8pm in Vancouver (previous day)

BUSINESS HOURS

Government and business offices follow a Monday through Friday work week, though some are open on Saturday as well. The workday is roughly 8:30am to 5pm or 6pm with a one- or two-hour lunch break at midday. Many museums are open on the weekend and pick two weekdays to close.

Most businesses, including travel agencies and banks, keep similar hours – but they don't close for lunch and are open throughout the weekend. Zoos and public parks also operate on similar schedules.

Chinese restaurants may close in the late afternoon before the dinner rush. Some restaurants and most bars stay open until late at night. There are an increasing number of 24-hour fast-food outlets and convenience stores.

CALENDAR

Traditionally the Chinese used the lunar calendar and many Chinese holidays are based on lunar dates; therefore, the dates jump around on the Western calendar. Nowadays, folks use the Western calendar in everyday life.

MAJOR HOLIDAYS

Here's a list of major holidays:

New Year's Day 元旦
January 1

Spring Festival (Chinese New Year) 春节
late-January or early-February

Lantern Festival 元宵节
early February

Tomb Sweeping Day (Qing Ming Festival) 清明节
early April

International Labor Day 劳动节
May 1

Dragon Boat Festival 端午节
falls in June

Mid-Autumn Festival 中秋节
falls in September

National Day 国庆节
October 1

The different origins of celebrations mean varying degrees of enthusiasm for a given holiday. Christmas and New Year's Day has begun to draw widespread celebration.

WATER & FOOD

Only drink water that has been boiled, purified or bottled. Be careful not to consume food that has been sitting out for a long period of time. Hot, steaming food is most likely safe – heat kills germs. Most popular or well-established restaurants should be sanitary.

ALCOHOL & TOBACOO

Domestic beer, popular Chinese spirits such as *baijiu* (*báijiǔ* 白酒), wine and cigarettes are widely available. There is a nationwide anti-smoking campaign, which is severely cutting back on young peoples' smoking habits.

TOILETS

Squatting toilets are abundant in China. If you're out and about and nature calls, look for a "WC" sign – these are public toilets. Public toilets can be found in commercial areas and are usually well-marked. A useful word to know is *cesuo* (*cèsuǒ* 厕所), which is Chinese for toilet. Some public toilets require a small fee, others are free. Most public toilets don't supply toilet paper (*wèishēng zhǐ* 卫生纸), but have it for sale. Still, it's advisable to carry some tissue paper with you at all times. If you can't seem to find a washroom, try heading into a McDonalds or Kentucky Fried Chicken outlet; most fast-food places will have a relatively clean washroom.

SAFETY PRECAUTIONS

China is generally safe for foreigners, though there are some things travelers should be aware of. Crimes against travelers are usually petty thefts rather than violent crimes. It's best not to leave valuables in your hotel room while you're gone. Take advantage of the hotel's safe if it offers one. General safety precautions and common sense should be used.

When you are taking a metered taxi, the driver should push down the flag at the start of the ride – this engages the meter. If your driver should fail to engage it, remind him to use the meter (*dǎ biǎo* 打表). At the end of the ride, pay the amount shown on the meter – the only surcharge may be highway toll fees. Taxi drivers don't expect tips. You can ask for your receipt (*fāpiào* 发票), which will list the driver's identification and company telephone number. These are useful numbers to have if you've left something in the cab or wish to lodge a complaint.

HEALTH

It's a good idea to bring whatever medication you'll need, prescription and brand name drugs. Large cities have well-stocked pharmacies, but it's better to bring your own medication for basic illnesses such as headaches and diarrhea – you don't want to be stuck with an upset stomach while trying to figure out what medicine to buy in a foreign language. Depending on where you go, mosquito repellent is a good idea.

ELECTRICITY

Voltage is 220v in China. Most outlets fit two-pronged parallel or three-pronged triangular plugs. Converters of 110V to 240V may be hard to find.

SHOPPING

Street market vendors and smaller shopping centers expect price bargaining. They will attempt to overcharge foreigners, but a skilled bargainer can drop a price to near the Chinese one. Hotels, restaurants and large shopping centers with clearly marked prices usually will not bargain. Exchanges are possible if you hold on to receipts. Be cautious when buying expensive antiques unless you're knowledgeable about them. Genuine antiques have a red seal at the bottom indicating they're authentic and can be exported from China, though be weary of fake seals. Antiques dated before 1795 can't leave the country. Finally, keep your receipts, since you may have to show them when departing China. ■

BEIJING

Beijing, the Cultural Soul of China

Area Code 010

Heritage: Forbidden City, Temple of Heaven, Summer Palace, Great Wall, Ming Tombs, Peking Man Site at Zhoukoudian

The political and cultural heart of China, **Beijing** has a rich history that's mirrored in its spectacular palaces, temples and parks. However, this doesn't mean that it's shackled to the past. Quite the contrary, Beijing is a vibrant international capital that's moving toward the future at hyper-speed. Thanks to its roaring economy, skyscrapers crowd the skyline, cars jam the roads and residents flock to spend at a frenetic pace.

Beijing is a city of contrasts, vast neon-lit avenues coexist with narrow *hutongs* (alleys) and futuristic structures of titanium and glass cast their shadow over ancient palaces. Friendly and hardworking, the city's population of about 15 million is also diverse. Wizened men with pet songbirds share the streets with laptop-toting executives and foreign investors with migrants from the countryside. Along with its people, historical sights and vibrancy, Beijing's drawing cards include its mouth-watering cuisine, fabulous shopping and thriving nightlife. In short, a thrilling and unforgettable experience awaits visitors in Beijing.

A BRIEF HISTORY

Local history begins some 500,000 years ago at a time when the north China plain, which encompasses Beijing, was covered in semi-tropical forest and dotted with lakes. Anthropologists digging at Zhoukoudian, a village near modern Beijing, discovered in 1929 the area was inhabited by a previously unknown human ancestor soon dubbed Peking Man. This hominid, the famous dig revealed, had mastered fire and used stone tools.

Modern human beings began to settle in the area around 3000 BC, surviving on rudimentary agriculture and animal husbandry. During the Zhou dynasty, a military and administrative center was established near present-day Beijing to protect China's northeastern border and oversee trade between Chinese farmers and the nomadic ancestors of the Mongols and Koreans.

However, neither the presence of troops nor the construction of the Great Wall by Beijing, which began in the 4th century BC, would permanently repel northern attacks. Indeed, incursions from the north would

A bird's-eye view of the Forbidden City.

become a recurring feature of Beijing's history. During the Song dynasty, a tribe from the Mongolian steppes called the Qidan swept down into north China and founded the Liao dynasty, eventually making their capital, called Yanjing, at what is now Beijing. The name Yanjing survives today as a brand of a popular local beer.

Proving the adage "those who live by the sword, die by the sword," the Liao were in turn defeated in 1125 by invaders from Manchuria – the Jürchen. The latter founded the Jin dynasty and ruled much of north China from their capital, Zhongdu, which also stood in present-day Beijing. Graced with handsome palaces, Zhongdu had over a million residents – roughly the population size of ancient Rome at its peak in the 1st century AD.

Unfortunately, little remains of Zhongdu since it was burnt to the ground by the armies of Genghis Khan in 1215. Genghis's grandson, Kublai Khan, completed the Mongol conquest of China, crowning himself emperor in 1260 and founding the Yuan dynasty in 1271. Kublai built his capital, Dadu, on the ruins of Zhongdu. It was the first time that all of China was governed from the city that would become Beijing.

Distrustful of local officials and lacking the administrative know-how and personnel to govern their vast empire, the Mongol rulers never won over the hearts of their Han Chinese subjects. When their grip on power began to weaken, revolts broke out throughout China.

In 1368, a former peasant and rebel leader named Zhu Yuanzhang overthrew the Yuan dynasty, took Dadu and established the Ming dynasty. He renamed the city Beiping, meaning Northern Peace, and set up his court in Nanjing, which means Southern Capital. The power struggle that broke out after his death in 1398 was resolved in favor of a usurper, the fourth of his 36 sons. A vigorous and capable leader, this son ruled as the Yongle emperor.

Emperor Yongle officially moved the Ming capital back to Beijing in 1421 because his power base was in the north and as the usurper, he felt insecure in the south. The emperor would have a huge impact on Beijing: he gave the city its current name, which means Northern Capital, and rebuilt it on a chessboard pattern that survives to

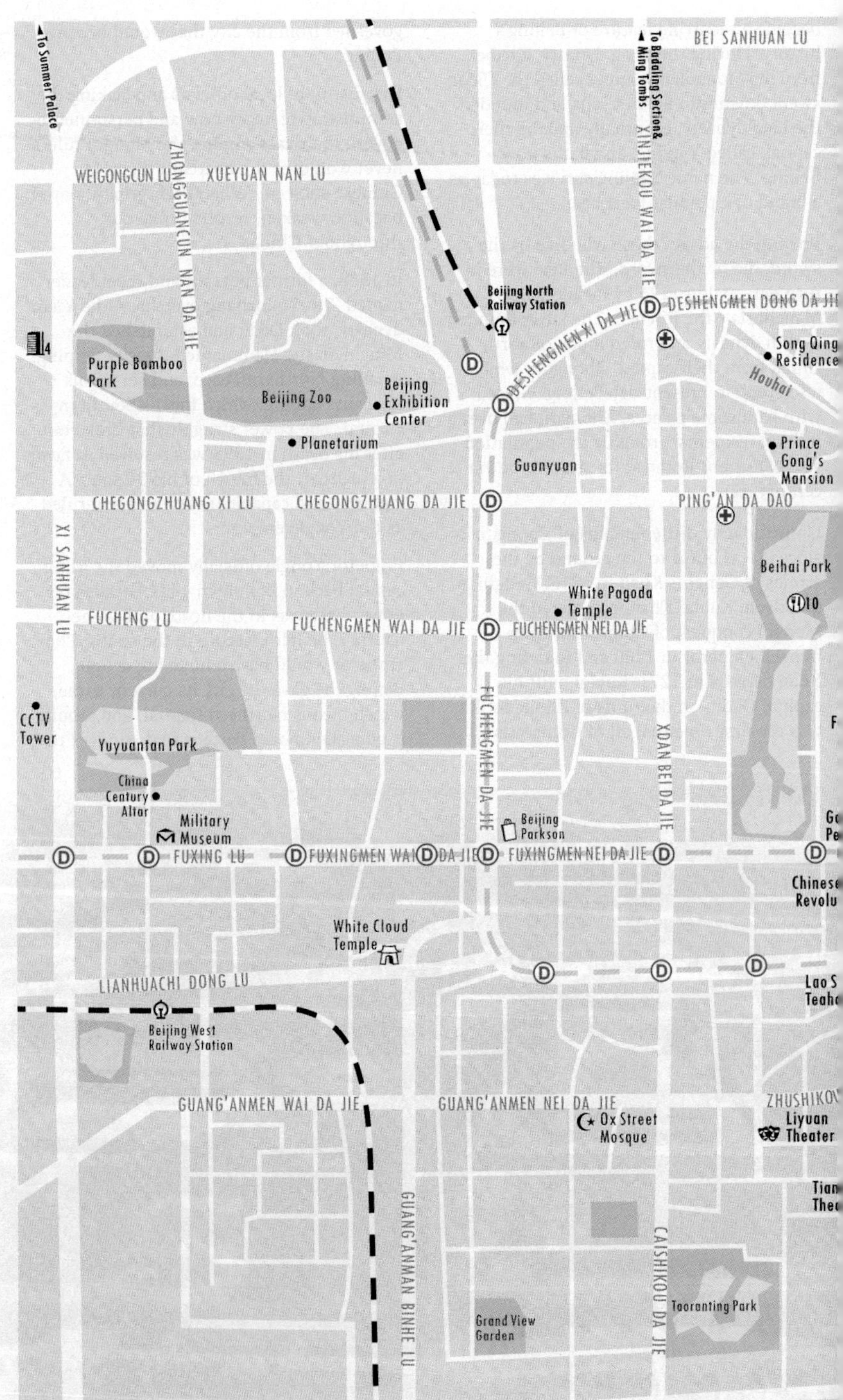
To Summer Palace
BEI SANHUAN LU
To Badaling Section & Ming Tombs
WEIGONGCUN LU
XUEYUAN NAN LU
ZHONGGUANCUN NAN DA JIE
XINJIEKOU WAI DA JIE
Beijing North Railway Station
DESHENGMEN DONG DA JIE
DESHENGMEN XI DA JIE
Song Qing Residence
Houhai
Purple Bamboo Park
Beijing Zoo
Beijing Exhibition Center
Planetarium
Guanyuan
Prince Gong's Mansion
CHEGONGZHUANG XI LU
CHEGONGZHUANG DA JIE
PING'AN DA DAO
XI SANHUAN LU
Beihai Park
White Pagoda Temple
FUCHENG LU
FUCHENGMEN WAI DA JIE
FUCHENGMEN NEI DA JIE
CCTV Tower
Yuyuantan Park
FUCHENGMEN DA JIE
XDAN BEI DA JIE
China Century Altar
Military Museum
Beijing Parkson
FUXING LU
FUXINGMEN WAI DA JIE
FUXINGMEN NEI DA JIE
White Cloud Temple
LIANHUACHI DONG LU
Beijing West Railway Station
GUANG'ANMEN WAI DA JIE
GUANG'ANMEN NEI DA JIE
Ox Street Mosque
Liyuan Theater
GUANG'ANMAN BINHE LU
CAISHIKOU DA JIE
Taoranting Park
Grand View Garden

To Beijing Capital International Airport
ANDINGMEN WAI DA JIE
HEPINGLI XI JIE
HEPINGLI DONG JIE
Temple of Earth
ANDINGMEN DONG DA JIE
Temple of Confucius
Lama Temple
Lufthansa Center
11
2
DONGZHIMEN WAI DA JIE
DONGZHIMEN DA JIE
Chaoyang Park
Poly Theater
Yaxiu Clothing Market
Sanlitun Bar Area
GONGRENTIYUCHANG BEI LU
NONGZHANGUAN NAN LU
12
8
5
Workers' Stadium
15
ational Art
useum of China
DONG SANHUAN LU
CHAOYANGMEN DA JIE
DONGDAN BEI DA JIE
Donghuamen Night Market
7
3
Foreign
anguages
Bookstore
Wangfujing
16
13
Ritan Park
Embassy Area
Chang'an Grand Theater
Friendship Store
Beijing Hotel
Oriental Plaza
14
1
JIANGUOMEN NEI DA JIE
JIANGUOMEN WAI DA JIE
JIANGUO LU
17
Ancient Observatory
6
Beijing Railway Station
MEN DONG DA JIE
CHONGWENMEN DONG DA JIE
HIKOU DONG DA JIE
GUANGQUMEN NEI DA JIE
GUANGQUMEN WAI DA JIE
GUANGQU LU
Hongqiao Market
eum of
ral History
Temple of Heaven
Longtan Lake Park
Beijing Amusement Park
Panjiayuan Flea Market

The imperial seal of the emperor.

this day. His building program for Beijing began in 1406 and included the construction of such architectural masterpieces as the Forbidden City, the Bell Tower and the Temple of Heaven. Surrounding the palace was a web of alleyways and gray-hued quadrangle courtyard homes. It should be noted that the Beijing of today, with the imperial gilded roofs and the maze-like neighborhoods are mainly Ming and Qing creations.

Additionally, he chose a beautiful site north of Beijing for a royal cemetery, an area now known as the Ming Tombs. His successors broadened the city; they built moats, canals and a massive city wall to protect the capital against attackers from the north. A similar motive was behind their decision to restore and lengthen sections of the Great Wall near Beijing.

These safeguards were ultimately in vain. Weakened by revolts, corruption and banditry, the Ming proved no match for the force from Manchuria, part of northeastern China today. In 1644, the Manchus conquered Beijing. By adopting the Ming administrative system, embracing Confucian values and maintaining a strong army, the Manchus were able to co-opt the scholarly gentry class and remain in power until 1911.

The Qing expanded Beijing's alley-laced *hutong* neighborhoods and commissioned suburban palaces set in luxuriant gardens, the most famous of which was the Old Summer Palace. This pleasure dome was looted and razed by French and British troops during the Second Opium War in 1860. The crippling "Unequal Treaties" imposed by western powers after the Opium Wars coupled with Chinese ferment for political change led to the downfall of the Qing and the foundation by Sun Yat-sen of the Republic of China in 1912.

During much of the 1911 to 1949 Republican period, de facto power resided with powerful warlords who fought for control of the city and country. In 1928, the capital was moved to Nanjing and Beijing was once again renamed Beiping, a name that it held until 1949. During this period, Beijing was the scene of much political upheaval. The Versailles Treaty signed after the First World War, under which the Allied powers gave Germany's possessions in China (Qingdao for example) to Japan rather than to China galvanized Beijing's students into organizing a march on May 4, 1919. Their protests – against imperialism and the warlords, would spawn the "May Fourth Movement." In this intellectual atmosphere,

Emperor Kangxi of the Qing dynasty.

an erstwhile librarian's assistant at Peking University named Mao Zedong would become a founding member of the Chinese Communist Party (CCP) in 1921.

In 1937, after overcoming Chinese troops at the Marco Polo Bridge (*lúgōu qiáo* 卢沟桥) on the outskirts of Beijing, the Japanese army occupied the city and began a general invasion of China. The end of the Second World War was followed by a civil war in which the Communist Party would triumph. On January 31, 1949, the victorious People's Liberation Army entered the city and in Tian'anmen Square on October 1, 1949, Mao Zedong proclaimed the founding of the People's Republic of China. "We the Chinese people have stood up and our future is infinitely bright," Mao told a crowd of 300,000.

In Beijing, the new leaders soon embarked on a building program of their own. The old city walls were torn down in 1964 to make way for the roadway that would become today's Second Ring Road. Tian'anmen Square was dramatically expanded and two modern buildings were erected on its flanks: the Great Hall of the People (home to China's parliament) and the Chinese History and Revolution Museum. The 1950's saw the construction of apartment blocks, factories and Beijing's first subway line.

The economic reforms initiated by Deng Xiaoping in 1978 set the stage for Beijing's ongoing development boom. Rapid economic growth combined with preparations for events like the 1990 Asian Games and the 50th anniversary of the People's Republic of China in 1999 fuelled countless construction and infrastructure projects. Avenues were broadened, highways were built, new neighborhoods were created, and towers of steel and glass were erected seemingly overnight. Under Deng and his successors Jiang Zemin and Hu Jintao, foreign investment and new ideas were welcomed, ensuring that Beijing became increasingly outward-looking, technological and prosperous.

LOOKING AHEAD TO 2008 & BEYOND

So what does the future hold for Beijing? One thing is clear: development will continue at a dizzying pace as it gets ready to host the 2008 Summer Olympic Games. By one estimate, government and private sources will spend US $3.4 billion on preparations for the Beijing Olympics.

The organizing committee has revealed that 28 million square meters of city property will be redeveloped in the 2002 to 2008 period. The most visible project is the Olympic Park in north Beijing that will house 14 competition venues including the Olympic stadium, the Athletes' Village and the International Broadcasting Center. The city

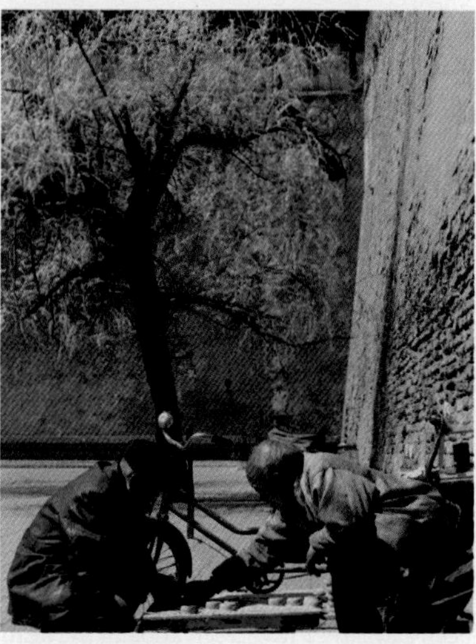

Playing chess by the Forbidden City's formidable walls.

expects to raise its number of star-rated hotel rooms from 80,000 in 2000 to 130,000 in 2008, a year when some 8.3 million foreign tourists are expected, compared with 3.1 million in 2002. Concurrently, Beijing will step up the development of commercial zones like the Central Business District, the Zhongguancun High-Tech Zone and the Banking and Finance District.

To improve transportation, blueprints call for the expansion of the inner and outer-city expressway systems along with the subway and light rail networks. To lessen the incidences of dust storms and soil erosion, Beijing will build a "Green Great Wall" by planting large bands of trees and grass. Air pollution will be alleviated by forcing

The Beijing National Stadium will be the main track and field stadium for the 2008 Summer Olympics.

polluting factories to reduce emissions or move out. Faced with a serious water shortage, Beijing will enhance sewage systems and waste treatment facilities and promote water-conservation. Planners have also earmarked US $3.6 billion to upgrade the capital's fiber optic and cellular networks, and build a digital cable TV infrastructure capable of high definition TV transmissions from all Olympic venues.

In short, the next few years promise nothing less than an enormous overhaul of Beijing. Fortunately for history enthusiasts, an area measuring 2.16 square miles (5.6 km^2) has been earmarked for preservation in the heart of the city. The conservation effort aims to preserve some traditional *hutongs* (alleyways), restore ancient sites and monuments and convert the most attractive of them into public museums, thereby expanding the historical areas open to visitors.

BEIJING CULTURE: AN EMBARRASSMENT OF RICHES

For centuries Beijing has been a magnet for scholars, merchants and artists who have given it a cultural life unrivalled in China. Beijing culture is a fusion of indigenous and imported traditions since the populace has always included provincials and ethnic minorities. Another factor to consider is the impact of the city's intellectuals on local culture. The capital has more colleges and universities than any other city in China, a reflection of its past as a center of Confucian scholarship in imperial times. This concentration of thinkers has created an enthusiastic audience for literature, painting and the performing arts. As a result, the city has many museums, galleries, theaters and music halls.

Beijing's culture comes in many forms, from food to music, and from architecture to handicrafts. Eat Peking duck, visit the Temple of Heaven, meander in the old *hutongs* or check out a contemporary art show and you'll discover a unique milieu of new and old that is Beijing culture.

Perhaps the most original expression of local culture is Peking opera (*jīng jù* 京剧). A multidimensional art, Peking opera blends singing, music, dancing and acrobatics. Performers wear elaborate costumes and makeup that identify their roles from peasant to emperor, and character traits from selfless to selfish. The singers are accompanied by orchestras made up of traditional Chinese instruments, including two-stringed fiddles, the *erhu* (*èrhú* 二胡) and *jinghu* (*jīnghú* 京胡), lutes, drums and gongs. Plot lines are based on famous myths, well-known stories and historical events.

Since the action can be hard for foreigners to follow, some theaters now provide English subtitles during the shows and offer abridged versions of operas. Several Beijing teahouses also stage scenes from famous operas interspersed with other traditional acts like magic shows, puppetry, and "cross-talk" (comic dialogues reminiscent of Abbott and Costello). Viewing such performances over tea and snacks is a classic Beijing experience. Many visitors likewise enjoy displays of Chinese martial arts and acrobatics, which are regularly held in local theaters.

If you want to witness local culture on a mass scale, nothing beats Beijing's temple fairs. These are held in temples, parks and streets during the Spring Festival (Chinese New Year). Dating back to the Liao dynasty, the fairs mix the spiritual and the temporal. Families come in droves not only to burn incense and pray for good fortune, but also for the carnival atmosphere and performances. The temple fairs are gathering spots for acrobats, singers and dancers. They also attract artisans and merchants who sell an assortment of handicrafts and goods. Some fairs also offer rides and games of chance for those to try their new year's luck. For some visitors, the best reason to come is the myriad stalls serving up savory snacks from around China. Beijing's most popular temple fairs are held in Temple of Earth (*dìtán gōngyuán* 地坛公园), White Cloud Temple (*báiyún guàn* 白云观), and Changdian (*chǎngdiàn* 厂甸) in the Liulichang antiques district.

SPLENDORS OF BEIJING

TIAN'ANMEN SQUARE

Tian'anmen Square (*tiān'ānmén guǎngchǎng* 天安门广场) is the spiritual heart of the world's most populous country. It earned this distinction by serving as the stage for momentous historical events, like the demonstrations on May 4th 1919 that inspired young Chinese to fight imperialists and warlords, and build a strong independent country. Among those swept up in the ferment of the "May Fourth Movement" was Mao Zedong who would help found the Communist Party of China two years later.

On October 1st, 1949, Mao climbed atop the "Gate of Heavenly Peace", which gives the square its name, to proclaim the foundation of the People's Republic of China.

In 1949, Tian'anmen Square was a narrow walled plaza, but it was expanded in the 1950's to its present size of 99 acres, or 4,300,000 square feet (400,000 m^2). The site of major parades, the square has also played host to impromptu celebrations as when Beijing was awarded the 2008 Olympic Games in July 2001.

The sun begins to rise over Tian'anmen, the Gate of Heavenly Peace.

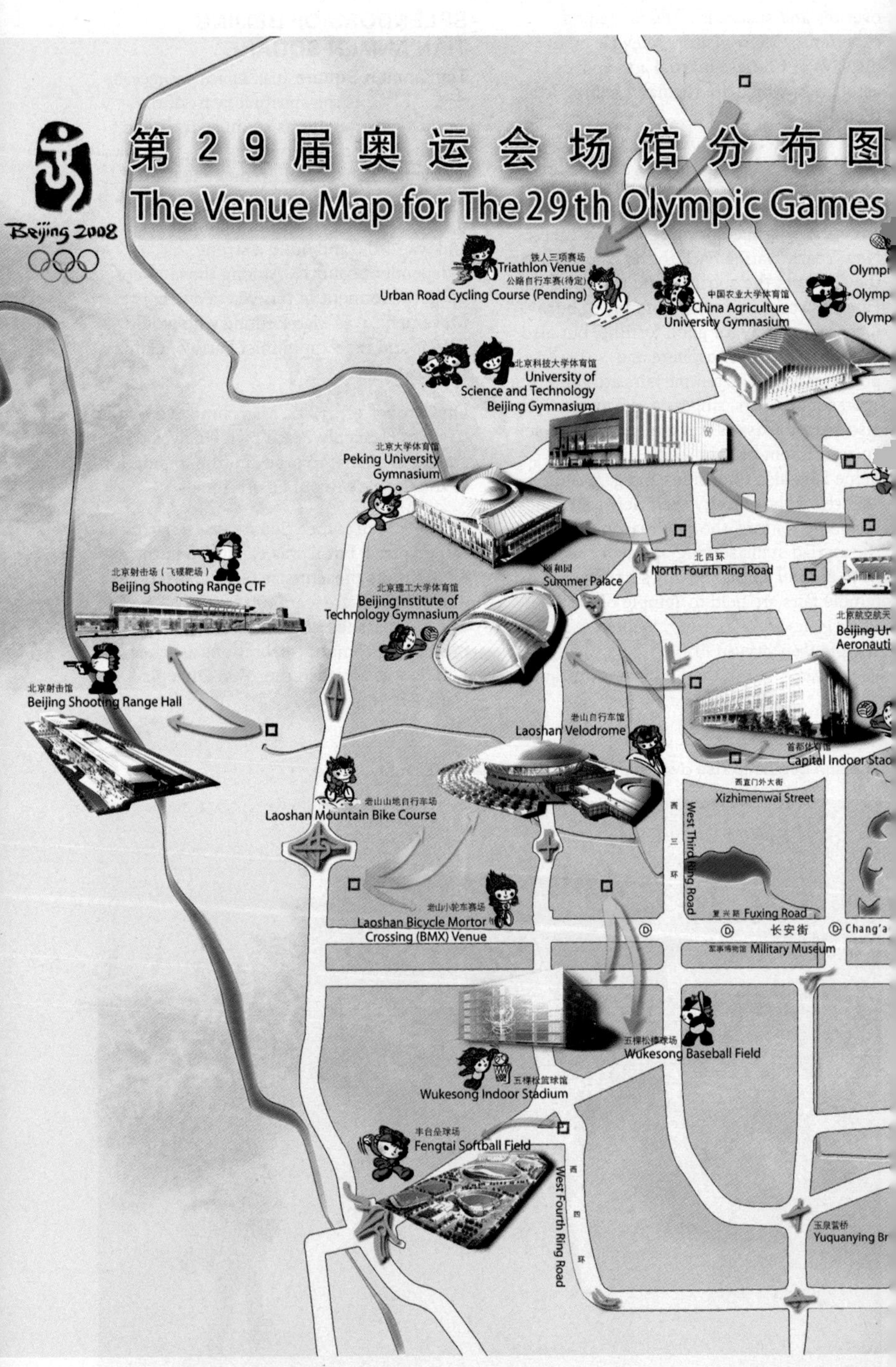

第29届奥运会场馆分布图
The Venue Map for The 29th Olympic Games
Beijing 2008
铁人三项赛场
Triathlon Venue
公路自行车赛(待定)
Urban Road Cycling Course (Pending)
中国农业大学体育馆
China Agriculture University Gymnasium
北京科技大学体育馆
University of Science and Technology Beijing Gymnasium
北京大学体育馆
Peking University Gymnasium
北京射击场（飞碟靶场）
Beijing Shooting Range CTF
北京理工大学体育馆
Beijing Institute of Technology Gymnasium
颐和园
Summer Palace
北四环
North Fourth Ring Road
北京射击馆
Beijing Shooting Range Hall
老山自行车馆
Laoshan Velodrome
首都体育馆
Capital Indoor Stad
老山山地自行车场
Laoshan Mountain Bike Course
西直门外大街
Xizhimenwai Street
西三环
West Third Ring Road
复兴路 Fuxing Road
老山小轮车赛场
Laoshan Bicycle Mortor Crossing (BMX) Venue
长安街
Chang'a
军事博物馆 Military Museum
五棵松棒球场
Wukesong Baseball Field
五棵松篮球馆
Wukesong Indoor Stadium
丰台垒球场
Fengtai Softball Field
西四环
West Fourth Ring Road
玉泉营桥
Yuquanying Br
北京航空航天
Beijing Ur
Aeronauti
Olymp

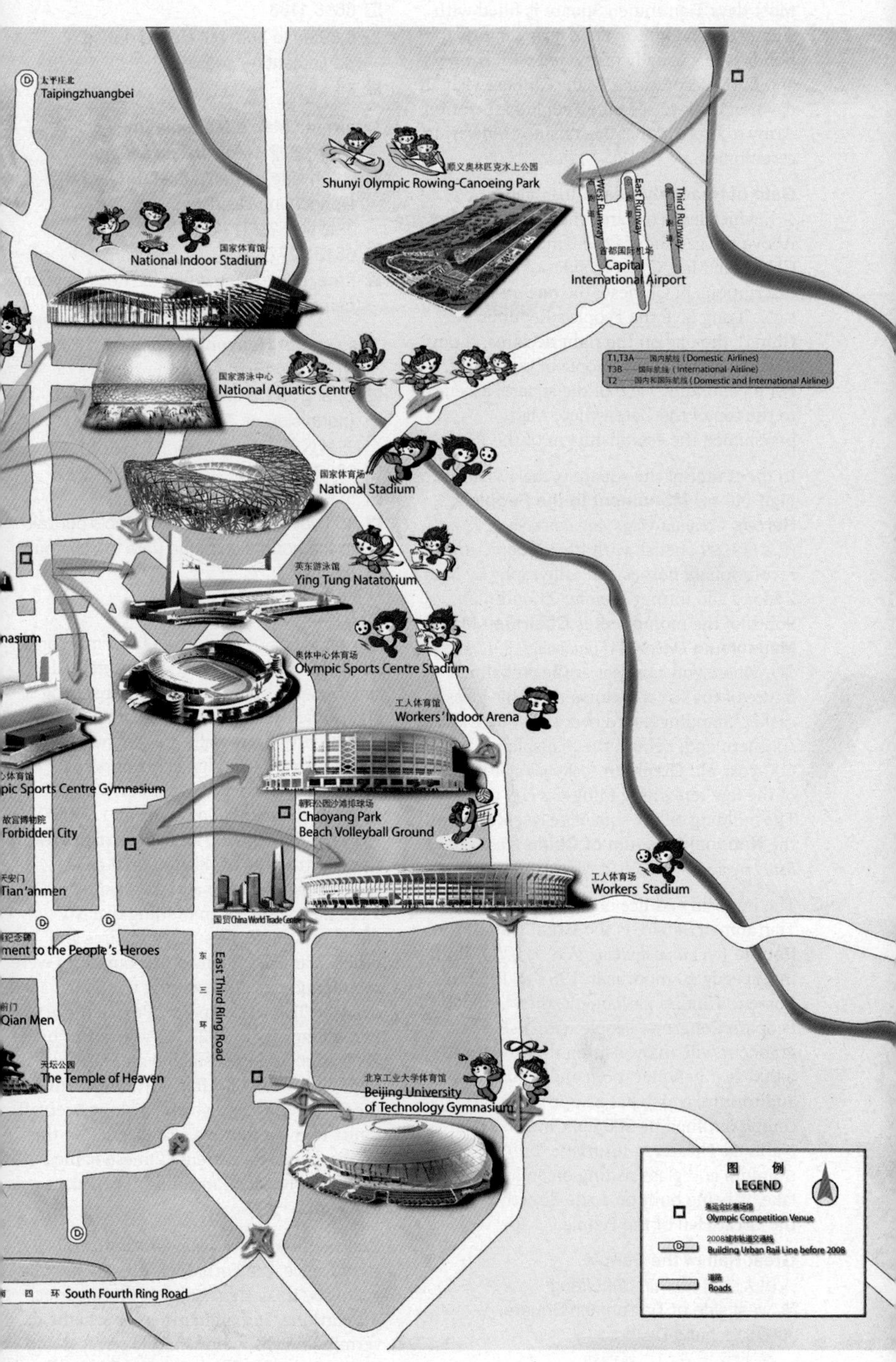

太平庄北
Taipingzhuangbei
顺义奥林匹克水上公园
Shunyi Olympic Rowing-Canoeing Park
West Runway
East Runway
Third Runway
首都国际机场
Capital International Airport
国家体育馆
National Indoor Stadium
国家游泳中心
National Aquatics Centre
T1,T3A——国内航线（Domestic Airlines）
T3B——国际航线（International Airline）
T2——国内和国际航线（Domestic and International Airline）
国家体育场
National Stadium
英东游泳馆
Ying Tung Natatorium
奥体中心体育场
Olympic Sports Centre Stadium
工人体育馆
Workers' Indoor Arena
pic Sports Centre Gymnasium
朝阳公园沙滩排球场
Chaoyang Park
Beach Volleyball Ground
故宫博物院
Forbidden City
天安门
Tian'anmen
工人体育场
Workers Stadium
国贸China World Trade Centre
ment to the People's Heroes
东三环
East Third Ring Road
Qian Men
天坛公园
The Temple of Heaven
北京工业大学体育馆
Beijing University
of Technology Gymnasium
四环 South Fourth Ring Road
图例
LEGEND
奥运会比赛场馆
Olympic Competition Venue
2008城市轨道交通线
Building Urban Rail Line before 2008
道路
Roads

Most days Tian'anmen Square is filled with sightseers and kite-flyers. During national holidays, it's usually festooned with banners and floral decorations. Many Chinese visit at dawn or dusk to see elite People's Liberation Army troops conduct flag raising or lowering ceremonies.

Gate of Heavenly Peace (*tiān'ānmén* 天安门), which leads towards the Forbidden City. Above the gate hangs the famous portrait of Chairman Mao. On both sides of the gate are inscriptions in Chinese: the one on the left says, "Long Live the People's Republic of China"; the one on the right declares, "Long Live the Unity of the People of the World." For a panoramic view of the square, ascend to the top of the Gate, where Mao proclaimed the establishment of the PRC.

In the center of the square is the 131-foot-high (40-m) **Monument to the People's Heroes** (*rénmín yīngxióng jìniànbēi* 人民英雄纪念碑), an obelisk with friezes depicting revolutionary heroes and calligraphy by Mao Zedong and former Premier Zhou Enlai. South of the monument is **Chairman Mao's Mausoleum** (*Máozhǔxí jìniàntáng* 毛主席纪念堂), where you can peer at the embalmed figure of the Great Helmsman in his glass casket. Standing guard over the square's southern end, behind the mausoleum, is 600-year-old **Qianmen** (*qiánmén* 前门), one of the few remaining Ming-era city gates. The building on the square's east side houses the **National Museum of China** (*zhōngguó lìshǐ bówùguǎn* 中国历史博物馆).

The imposing edifice on the west side of Tian'anmen Square is the **Great Hall of the People** (*rénmín dàhuìtáng* 人民大会堂). Built in a speedy 10 months in 1958 to 1959, it's home to China's parliament, the National People's Congress. People with a sense of grandeur will enjoy visiting the Great Hall's 5,000-seat banquet room and 10,000-seat auditorium, which has a large red star on the ceiling outlined by 500 light bulbs. The National Theater, a futuristic "bubble" of titanium and glass resting on an artificial lake, is being built on a site directly west of the Great Hall of the People.

Great Hall of the People
人民大会堂 *rénmín dàhuìtáng*
✉ west side of Tian'anmen Square, Dongcheng District
东城区天安门广场西边
☎ 6608 1188
🕒 8:30am to 3pm but closed during parliamentary sessions
¥ 15

Chairman Mao's Mausoleum
毛主席纪念堂 *Máozhǔxí jìniàntáng*
✉ south side of Tian'anmen Square, Dongcheng District
东城区天安门广场南边
☎ 6513 2277
¥ Free, but you must pay to check-in your camera(s) and bag(s)

The Gate of Heavenly Peace
天安门 *tiān'ānmén*
✉ Chang'an Da Jie Dongcheng District (north side of Tian'anmen Square)
东城区长安大街(天安门广场北边)
☎ 6309 5718
🕒 8:30am to 5pm
¥ 15 (walk under Chairman Mao's portrait to the north side of the gate to buy your ticket)

FORBIDDEN CITY

The abode of 24 Ming and Qing emperors of the Celestial Empire, the **Forbidden City** (*gùgōng* 故宫) is a fittingly awe-inspiring sight. Enclosed behind its moat and 32.5-foot-high (9.9-m) walls are 980 buildings, vast courtyards and long corridors that occupy a total area of 178 acres (720,000 m^2). It's alleged that as many as 1,000,000 workers and 100,000 artisans participated in the construction of this imperial palace, which began in 1406 and was completed in 1420 during the reign of Ming dynasty emperor Yongle. Destroyed by fires and other calamities, many of the buildings were rebuilt and expanded during the Qing dynasty. The last emperor, Puyi, left the Forbidden City in 1924, 11 years after his abdication and the establishment of the Republic of China. After Puyi's departure, the Forbidden City, which had long been off-limits to most mortals, was opened to the public, hence its current Chinese name, *gugong bowuyuan*, meaning "The Palace Museum."

Besides its massive scale and historical significance, the Forbidden City strikes any visitor by its design. Its clear lines, perfect proportions, and dramatic color scheme of vermilion walls, white marble terraces and staircases and brilliant yellow-tiled roofs create one of the world's most beautiful architectural complexes. It was built along a meridian line: from the Dragon's throne, an axis can be drawn directly south through the many gates, right through to Qianmen. From his northern seat, the emperor could symbolically survey his entire kingdom.

Taking all this in requires time, at least 3 hours, and a comfortable pair of shoes. The English audio tour is highly insightful and features the suave voice of Roger Moore of James Bond fame. Readers interested in the Forbidden City's past grandeur should watch *The Last Emperor* by Bernardo Bertolucci, a film that was largely shot on location.

The main entry point for the Forbidden City is the **Meridian Gate** (*wǔmén* 午门) which is a ten-minute walk due north from Tian'anmen Square. Don't confuse Meridian Gate with the Gate of Heavenly Peace, above which hangs Mao's portrait. The "Son of Heaven," as the emperor was called, would come to the Meridian Gate to review armies and announce the new calendar. As you walk through Meridian Gate, keep in mind that in imperial times you would have been guilty of a capital offense – only the emperor could use this central archway. Officials and royal family members had to employ the side passageways.

Beyond the Meridian Gate is a courtyard bisected by a canal in the shape of a bow that's spanned by five marble bridges. On the far side of the canal is the **Gate of Supreme Harmony** (*tàihé mén* 太和门), which opens up to a second gigantic courtyard that held audiences of 100,000. On the north end of that courtyard is the first of three great ceremonial halls, the **Hall of Supreme Harmony** (*tàihé diàn* 太和殿). This is where the Emperor read important edicts, celebrated his birthday and appointed military leaders. Inside the hall is an elaborately decorated throne flanked by cloisonné cranes (symbolizing longevity) and gorgeous columns carved with dragons.

The second ceremonial hall, called the **Hall of Middle Harmony** (*zhōnghé diàn* 中和殿), was used by the emperor and his ministers as a staging area to prepare for official ceremonies. Directly behind it is the **Hall of Preserving Harmony** (*bǎohé diàn* 保和殿)

One of the elegant watchtowers that continue to guard the Forbidden City.

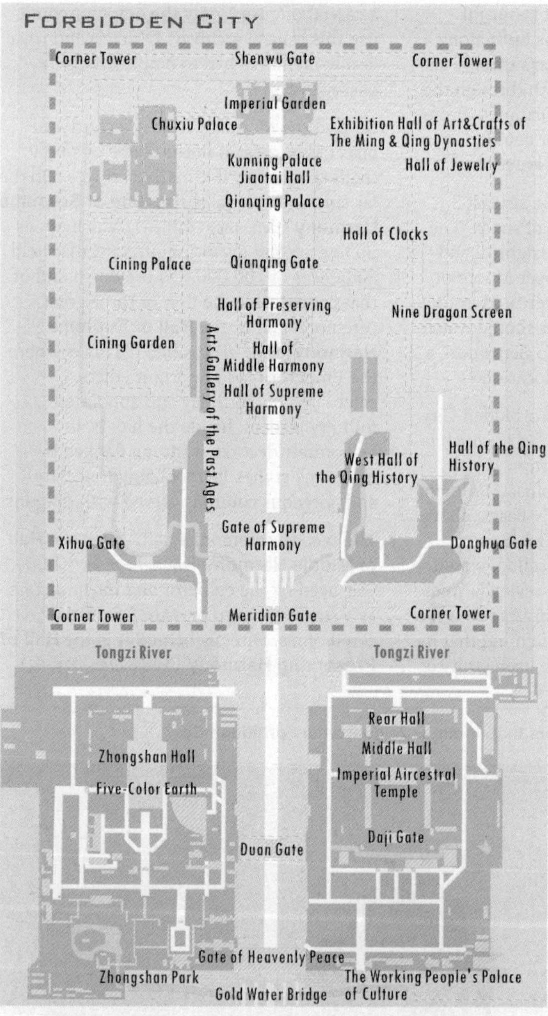

(*zhēnbǎo guǎn* 珍宝馆), where antiques are exhibited.

Due north of the Hall of Preserving Harmony is the Inner Palace, a series of elegant buildings and courtyards where the emperor lived with his family and concubines. In addition to a throne room and nuptial chamber, the buildings include libraries, temples and a theater. At the northern end of the compound is the **Imperial Garden** (*yùhuāyuán* 御花园) with gnarled cypresses, scholars' rocks and pavilions. Reflecting their separate purposes, the Garden and the Inner Palace were built on a far more human scale than the grandiose ceremonial halls: the former were designed for the emperor's private life, the latter for his public persona as the embodiment of the state and Son of Heaven. The garden is also the only place in the palace grounds that has trees because of the importance of symbolism to the emperor. The palace grounds are in the shape of a square – think of them as a box. If the box has the Chinese character for tree inside, it becomes the character meaning imprisoned (*kùn* 困), not exactly an auspicious symbol for the emperor.

where Qing dynasty New Year's Eve banquets were held. This edifice was also used as an imperial examination hall for top scholars seeking official positions.

After passing the Hall of Preserving Harmony, some visitors pause over a cappuccino at the Forbidden City's Starbucks while others meander eastward in an area that served as the quarters for imperial attendants, including, at one point, an estimated 70,000 eunuchs. There are signs pointing towards the **Hall of Clocks** (*zhōngbiǎo guǎn* 钟表馆) and **Hall of Jewelry**

To the north of the garden is the exit via the north gate. Be sure to take in the spectacular view of the Forbidden City's moat, outer wall and corner guard towers. If you want an even better view, cross Jingshan Qian Jie and climb to the top of **Coal Hill** (*jǐng shān* 景山).

✉ North of Tian'anmen Square, Dongcheng District 东城区天安门广场北侧
☎ 6513 2255
🕒 8:30am to 5pm

¥ 60 peak-season
40 off-season
30 for audio tour, plus 300 for deposit

BEIHAI PARK

Beijing's most elegant park is built around the *bei hai* (North Lake). The lakes in Beijing are often mistakenly referred to as seas because the Mongolian word for lake sounds like "*hai*," a homophone for the Chinese character for sea, which is also the character used in their names. Once exclusively restricted to the emperor and his court, **Beihai Park's** (*běihǎi gōngyuán* 北海公园) charms include pavilions, gardens and a stunning Tibetan-style pagoda.

Beihai Park's imperial connection began in the 13th century, when Kublai Khan chose the site for his palace, a marvelous structure according to Marco Polo. Little has survived of the Khan's pleasure dome except an enormous green jade jar that was given to him in 1265 and was purportedly used to store his wine. You'll find this 3.5-ton jar displayed in the **Round City** (*tuán chéng* 团城), a former royal barracks near the park's main (southeast) entrance. The main structure in the Round City is the **Hall of Receiving Light** (*chéngguāng diàn* 承光殿), so named because the emperor would come here to watch fireworks. A Buddha given by Burma to the Empress Dowager Cixi is now exhibited there. The statue is carved of white jade and wears a crown and garment of gold sheet.

Jade Isle (*qiónghuá dǎo* 琼华岛) lies across the bridge from the Round City. In summer, lotus flowers bloom in the channel to the east of the bridge and this flowery motif is echoed on the bridge itself, which is decorated with carved lotus flowers and petals. At the foot of the manmade hill that dominates Jade Isle is the pleasant **Yong'an Temple** (*yǒng'ān sì* 永安寺).

Far more dramatic than the temple is the **White Dagoba** (*báitǎ* 白塔) that stands on top of the hill. Erected in 1651 in honor of a visiting Dalai Lama, it was flattened by an earthquake and later rebuilt. From a tiered base, it rises approximately 118 feet (36 m) towards the sky and is said to contain Buddhist scriptures, robes and other sacred objects. Though visitors aren't allowed inside the dagoba, they can inspect the Tibetan sutras that are carved inside its front gate. The views of the city from atop the hill are dazzling.

Ringing the northwest shore of Jade Isle is the **Painted Gallery** (*qióngdǎo chūnyīn bēi* 琼岛春荫碑), a double-tiered covered veranda. Midway along the length of the gallery, near the boat dock, is the **Hall of Rippling Waters** (*yīlántáng* 漪澜堂) that's home to the famous **Fangshan Restaurant** (*fǎngshàn fànzhuāng* 仿膳饭庄) and its elaborate imperial banquets.

You can reach the north side of Beihai by

The intricate and colorful Nine Dragon Screen in Beihai Park.

taking a boat to **Five Dragon Pavilion** (*wǔlóng tíng* 五龙亭) or walking around the park via the isle's east bridge. Sticking out from the northwest shoreline, the Five Dragon Pavilion was built on 1543 for a Ming dynasty emperor who wanted a nice spot to fish and admire the moon. **Neighboring Minor Western Heaven** (*xiǎoxītiān* 小西天) is a square-shaped temple dedicated to Guanyin, the Buddhist Goddess of Mercy, which Emperor Qianlong built for his mother. Don't miss the delightful botanical gardens in the park's northwest corner that features a greenhouse and lotus-filled pools. By the northern exit is the **Nine Dragon Screen** (*jiǔlóng bì* 九龙壁), an 89-foot-long (27-m) structure covered in tiled dragons that was designed to ward off evil spirits; it was built in 1756.

It should be noted that historic monuments are only half the fun of visiting the park. Like all parks in Beijing, Beihai is a hive of fascinating human activity, especially in the morning when it's overrun with kung fu masters wielding swords, couples waltzing, calligraphers writing poems on the pavement with water, choirs of senior citizens, badminton players and Peking opera singers who exercise their voice by screaming across the lake. What's more, you can rent paddleboats when weather permits.

An evening cruise on one of Beijing's many waterways.

✉ 1 Wenjin Jie, Xicheng District
西城区文津街1号

☎ 6403 1102

🕒 9am to 9pm (though some buildings close earlier)

¥ 10 peak-season
5 off-season

TEMPLE OF HEAVEN

The **Temple of Heaven** (*tiāntán* 天坛) served Ming and Qing dynasty emperors as a vast sacred space to perform ceremonial rites on behalf of the Chinese nation. Prior to the winter solstice, the emperor would lead a solemn procession, which commoners were forbidden to witness, from the Forbidden City to the Temple of Heaven. At first light on the winter solstice, after a night of fasting and ritual cleansing, the emperor would offer ritual sacrifices and make a report to heaven. He would also visit on the 15th day of the first lunar month to pray for a good harvest. The temple was vitally important to the imperial universe as it was the link between the emperor and Heaven.

The Temple of Heaven includes a large verdant park that's worth visiting on its own, especially in the early morning when limber septuagenarians practice calisthenics. The Temple of Heaven incorporates several religious structures, the crown jewel of which is the **Hall for the Prayer of Good Harvests** (*qǐnián diàn* 祈年殿). The layout of the compound reflects its religious purpose and so adheres to geomantic precepts. For instance, the northern end of the park is curved while the southern end is square, reflecting the traditional Chinese conception of heaven as round and the earth as square. Likewise, the park gates are located at the four cardinal points.

The **Circular Altar** (*huánqiū* 圜丘) is the three-tiered structure closest to the southern gate. Built in 1530, the Circular Altar was where the emperor, facing north, gave heaven his report. It was acoustically designed to help the emperor's words reach the cosmos. Indeed, the altar magnifies the

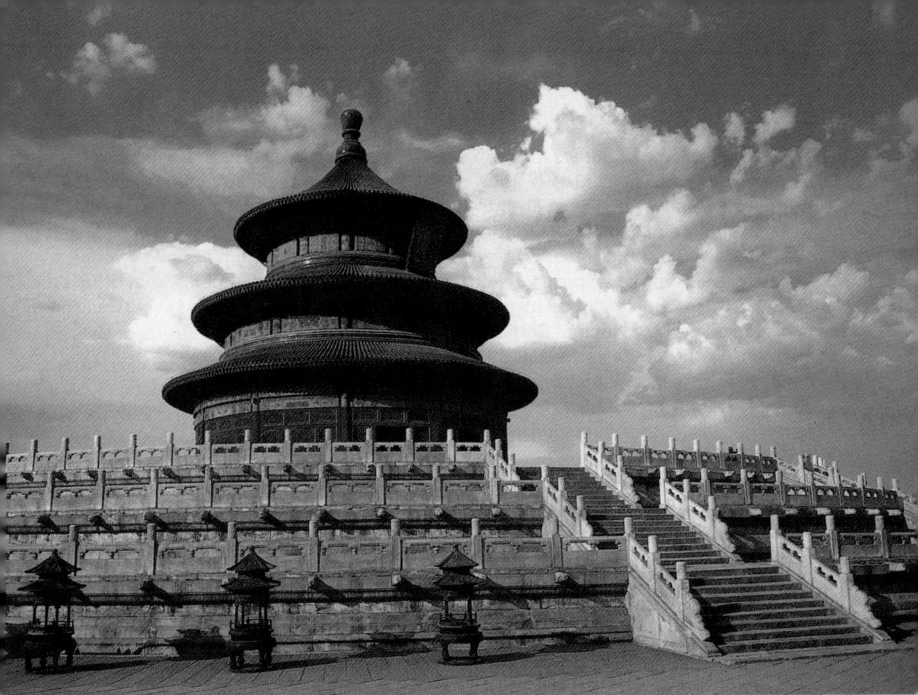

One of Beijing's most famous landmarks, the Temple of Heaven.

voice of a speaker standing in its center, though only the speaker will hear this magnification, as sound waves bounce off the balustrades. Another interesting feature of the altar is that it was built with rows of marble slabs in multiples of the number 9, which was considered the most auspicious number. The first row has 9 slabs, the second 18, and so on.

Moving northward, the next compound is the **Imperial Vault of Heaven** (*huángqióngyǔ* 皇穹宇), which contained tablets of the emperor's ancestors that were used in the solstice ceremony. The vault is surrounded by the **Echo Wall** (*huíyīn bì* 回音壁), which has marvelous acoustic properties. Its curvature acts as a parabola allowing two people to converse in quiet voices at a great distance from each other. However, on a crowded day when every visitor attempts this experience, all you may hear is a cacophonous muddle. The designers of the temple grounds incorporated numerous unique acoustic properties to the layout of the complex as there are many spots where sounds are amplified, echoed or redirected.

Circle around the outside of the vault after exiting and proceed north through a gate to the elevated walkway. As you walk, the Hall for the Prayer of Good Harvests will rise into view. This is where the emperor prayed to heaven on behalf of his subjects. This wooden tower was erected without a single nail, it's held in place by an ingenious system of supporting beams and massive pillars. The design is also rich in symbolism. Topped by a golden orb, its cascading roof is blue, representing the color of heaven. The four central pillars represent the seasons, the 12 inner pillars symbolize the months, and the 12 outer pillars symbolize the 12 watches of the day. Inside the hall, on the ceiling, is a single golden dragon representing the emperor. Initially constructed in 1420, the Hall was set ablaze by a bolt of lightning in 1889 and was faithfully rebuilt with lumber imported from Oregon.

✉ Tiantan South Gate, Chongwen District
崇文区天坛南门

☎ 6702 8866

🕒 8am to 5pm for the buildings
6am to 9pm for the park

¥ 35 peak-season, 30 off-season for full access
15 peak-season, 10 off-season for the park only

SUMMER PALACE

With its handsome buildings, pretty scenery and tumultuous history, the **Summer Palace** (*yíhé yuán* 颐和园) is a wonderful place to explore. As long ago as the Yuan dynasty, officials set up their private gardens in the scenic area, but the Summer Palace didn't take on its present appearance until the reign of Emperor Qianlong of the Qing dynasty. He deepened the park's manmade lake and added buildings to serve as a "country home" for his mother, though it would be the Empress Dowager Cixi who would have the biggest impact on the palace's appearance.

During the Second Opium War in 1860, the Summer Palace was looted and partially destroyed by French and British forces. In 1886, Cixi diverted funds earmarked to build a modern Chinese navy and spent the money on endowing the Summer Palace with a marble boat-shaped pavilion and other extravagances throughout the palace. She also gave the palace its current name, *yiheyuan*, which means the "Garden for Cultivating Harmony," an ill-fitting name as the Summer Palace would inspire little harmony. China soon paid for her imperial lavishness when a modern Japanese fleet destroyed its navy in 1895.

In 1900, Western armies again inharmoniously sacked the Summer Palace, this time in retaliation for the Boxer Rebellion. Undeterred, Cixi again rebuilt this pleasure dome which had become her fulltime residence. She died in 1908, but the imprint of this cunning and powerful woman, who ruled China from behind the scenes for years, remains very strong on the buildings today.

Most of the major sights are concentrated in the northern part of the compound. Near the East Palace Gate, the entry point for most tourists is the **Hall of Benevolent Longevity** (*rénshòu diàn* 仁寿殿), where Cixi held court on her hardwood throne. A short walk away, on the shore of **Kunming Lake** (*kūnmíng hú* 昆明湖), is the **Hall of Jade Ripples** (*yùlán táng* 玉澜堂) where Emperor Guangxu, Cixi's nephew, was held under house arrest on Cixi's orders for daring to undermine her authority. The **Hall for Cultivating Happiness** (*déhé yuán* 德和园) is the name of Cixi's delightful private theater that was built for her 60th birthday. Nearby is a display that includes a Mercedes Benz, the first car imported into China. The Empress Dowager lived in the **Hall of Happiness and Longevity** (*lèshòu táng* 乐寿堂), which is decorated with many period pieces.

These private apartments open up to the most arresting construction in the Summer

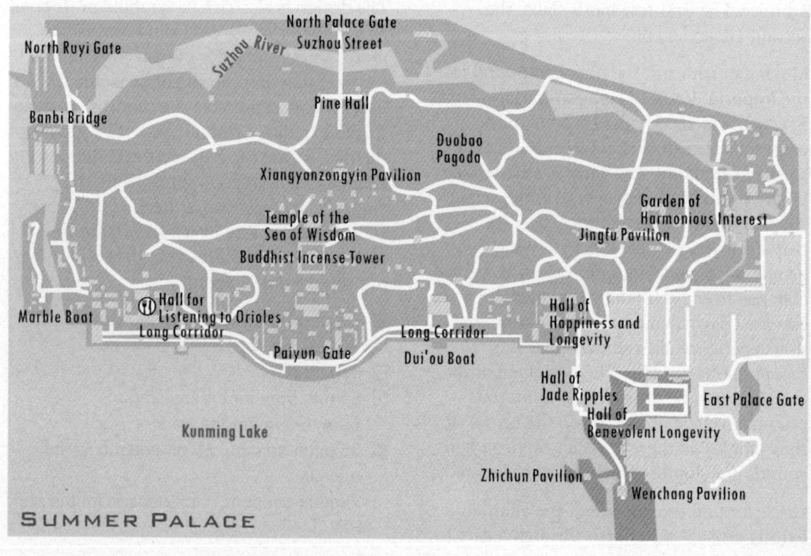

Palace, the **Long Corridor** (*chángláng* 长廊). More than 765 yards (700 m) long and ending at the **Marble Boat** (*shífǎng* 石舫), this shaded walkway is decorated with some 10,000 painted scenes, each one different. Paths lead off from the Long Corridor to the temple complex atop **Longevity Hill** (*wànshòu shān* 万寿山), which includes the **Buddhist Incense Tower** (*fóxiāng gé* 佛香阁) and the tiled **Temple of the Sea of Wisdom** (*zhìhuì hǎi* 智慧海). The climb will be rewarded with sweeping views of the Summer Palace and the **Fragrant Hills** (*xiāng shān* 香山)

The vast Summer Palace compound centers on Kunming Lake. In summer, visitors can explore the lake on boat, and skate across its frozen expanse in the winter. The highly photogenic **17 Arch Bridge** (*shíqīkǒng qiáo* 十七孔桥) links the lake's eastern shore to South Lake Island. The most pleasurable way to escape the crowds is to take a leisurely stroll on the willow-shaded paths and arched bridges that encircle the lake – bring your camera and a picnic.

✉ Haidian District 海淀区
☎ 6288 1144
🕒 6:30am to 6pm, peak-season
7am to 5pm, off-season
7am to 9pm, national holidays
¥ 50 peak-season, 40 off-season, for full access
30 peak-season, 20 off-season, for the park only

Top: A colorful performance of Peking opera.

LAMA TEMPLE

The **Lama Temple** (*yōnghé gōng* 雍和宫) is an island of Buddhism in the heart of the concrete jungle. Monks in wine-colored robes live, study and pray in its pleasant gardens and halls. Decorated with delicate scrolls and massive icons, its buildings are a hybrid of Tibetan, Mongolian and Han architectural styles. The Lama Temple is a tranquil spot, except during the Spring Festival (Chinese New Year) when it seems all of China's Buddhists throng its altars to burn bushels of incense and pray for good fortune.

This compound was originally built for Count Yin Zhen who resided here until 1723 when he moved to the Forbidden City to become Emperor Yongzheng. After his death, his devout son, Emperor Qianlong, converted the site into a Buddhist lamasery of the Yellow Hat sect, a sect that's mainly associated with Tibet.

A walkway leads from the ticket booth

through the garden and several archways to the temple grounds. After passing through the gateway at the end of the garden, visitors will notice a small Bell Tower on the right, and Drum Tower on the left. Ahead is the first of five worship halls, the **Hall of Heavenly Kings** (*tiānwáng diàn* 天王殿) that contains a large statue of Maitreiya, the Future Buddha with the four Heavenly Kings on the side. In the courtyard behind the hall is a pond with a bronze mandala depicting the Buddhist paradise. Next is the **Hall of Harmony** (*dàxióng bǎodiàn* 大雄宝殿), which is filled with prayer wheels and Buddhas of the Past, Present and Future, flanked by statues of 18 arhats, Buddhist "saints" who have reached Nirvana but have returned to help others. Formerly the emperor-to-be's living room, the **Hall of Eternal Blessing** (*yǒngyòu diàn* 永佑殿) houses statues of the Buddha of Longevity and Buddha of Medicine, to who believers appeal for long lives and good health.

The fourth hall, the **Hall of the Wheel of Law** (*fǎlún diàn* 法轮殿) is where the monks study scripture and pray in the presence of a 12m-tall bronze statue of Tsong Khapa, the founder of the Yellow Hat sect. Behind this statue is a sculpture of a hill on which stand 500 arhats made of gold, silver, copper, iron and tin. Elegant frescos illustrating the life of the Buddha adorn the east and west walls and there's a rare sand mandala preserved under glass on the west side of the building. The Lama Temple's crown awaits in the **Pavilion of 10,000 Blessings** (*wànfú gé* 万福阁), the last and tallest worship hall. Inside is an extraordinary statue of Buddha standing 59 feet (18 m) tall, with an additional 26 feet (8 m) underground, which was carved from a single Tibetan sandalwood tree. Satin prayer scarves flow from his giant hands.

As you retrace your steps to the entrance, pop into the minor halls that flank the courtyards, some of which contain Tibetan Buddhist deities covered in scarves to conceal their passionate embraces. From the main entrance, it is but a short walk to the **Temple of Confucius** (*kǒng miào* 孔庙).

✉ 12 Yonghegong Da Jie, Dongcheng District 东城区雍和宫大街 12 号

☎ 6404 4499

🕒 9am to 4:30pm

¥ 25

The Marble Boat floating on Kunming Lake in the Summer Palace.

A Buddhist dance in the Lama Temple.

GREAT WALL

The **Great Wall** (*wànlǐ chángchéng* 万里长城) snakes its way across northern China, from the Yellow Sea and past the Gobi Desert, for some 3,700 miles (6,000 km). While it's not visible from the moon as has been claimed, it's still a remarkable piece of engineering and is the most famous symbol of China.

The genesis of the Great Wall dates to the Warring States period from 475 to 221 BC, when Chinese feudal kingdoms built earthen ramparts to defend against nomadic invaders. It was under the fierce emperor Qin Shihuang, who unified China in 221 BC that the Great Wall really began to take shape. He conscripted some 300,000 laborers to work for ten years on joining the various pre-existing sections into a single fortified wall. The suffering of the workers who toiled in freezing winters and scorching summers became legendary. As the dynasty came into being and passed into history, the Great Wall was continuously repaired and extended.

The sections of the Great Wall near Beijing were renovated during the Ming dynasty, whose leaders spent a century strengthening and extending the Wall to the Yellow Sea. The previous ramparts, which were made of stones, packed earth and wood, were covered by Ming builders with bricks. They built crenellations to protect archers, widened the Wall so it could accommodate five horses abreast, and added many watchtowers. A system of beacons lit from tower to tower ensured that enemy troop movements were swiftly relayed to headquarters.

Despite such defensive features, the Great Wall failed in its purpose of keeping out invaders. It was breached several times, notably by the armies of Genghis Khan in 1215 and by Manchu troops in 1644. Conversely, the Great Wall was a tremendous success in forging a sense of nationhood since it marked the physical boundary between China and abroad, and the psychological boundary between civilization and chaos. Scaling forbidding landscapes of mountains and deserts, the Great Wall was also a triumph of the emperor's will over nature.

There are three major sections of the Great Wall open to tourists near Beijing: **Badaling**

The Great Wall winds its way across China like a giant dragon.

(*bādálǐng* 八达岭), **Mutianyu** (*mùtián yù* 慕田峪) and **Simatai** (*sīmǎtái* 司马台). All three are built on steep terrain so it's a good idea to wear comfortable shoes and bring water. This advice holds especially true when going to the Simatai section or to the "Wild Wall" sections that haven't been restored. Many expats enjoy hiking along the "Wild Wall" but it's not for the faint of heart: climbing conditions can be arduous and there are no signposts, so hikers will need a good map or a guide.

Whatever section you choose to visit, the simplest way to get there is to hire a car and driver for the day. Depending on the type of vehicle and the distance to be covered, expect to pay anywhere from RMB 500 to 1,000 (plus an additional RMB 400 for an English-speaking guide). Another option is to join a guided tour, these cost around RMB 250 to 400 per person. Both private cars and tour bus reservations can be booked through hotels and travel agencies like CITS, CYTS and BTG.

Badaling Section
八达岭长城 *bādálǐng chángchéng*
Only 43 miles (70 km) away by superhighway, Badaling is the closest section of the Great Wall to Beijing and can be visited in half a day. Moreover, its proximity to the Ming Tombs means both sites can be seen in a single outing. Badaling was completely restored after 1957. It has a chairlift and fast food restaurants and can be very crowded with hawkers and tourists, but all that fades away once you leave the parking area and begin to walk along the Wall.

✉ Yanqing County 延庆县
☎ 6912 1235, 6912 1737
🕒 6am to 6pm

Quotes

"I tell friends to go to the Lama Temple since it's the only Tibetan Lamaist temple you can visit in Northern China and has an enormous collection of Buddhist art."

"In the summer you should go eat spicy crayfish and drink beer in one of the restaurants on Ghost Street (Guijie 簋街)."

"An underrated historic site that I particularly enjoy is the Bell Tower (behind the Drum Tower). Usually there are no other visitors and you have this wonderful old building to yourself. It's a very peaceful place from which to contemplate the nearby hutongs, the bustling modern city in the distance, and the contrast between them."

¥ 45 peak-season
40 off-season

Mutianyu Section
慕田峪长城 *mùtiányù chángchéng*
Mutianyu is located some 56 miles (90 km) north of Beijing, and like Badaling, is a recently renovated section that's very popular. Mutianyu lies in rugged territory and reaching the Wall from the main gate involves a strenuous climb up a steep stairway, but fortunately there's a chairlift. Once on top, the views of the Wall undulating down wooded canyons and up mountain ridges are breathtaking.

✉ Huairou County 怀柔县.
☎ 6162 6873
⏲ 7am to 6pm
¥ 35

Simatai Section
司马台长城 *sīmǎtái chángchéng*
The Simatai section is a dramatic testimony to Ming engineering skills with one section as steep as 85 degrees. Only partially restored, Simatai allows athletic visitors who climb past the first watchtowers to see the Wall in its wild, crumbling state. Less intrepid visitors can take a gondola. Simatai is 68 miles (110 km) northwest of Beijing.

✉ Gubeikou Town, Miyun County
密云县古北口镇
☎ 6903 1051
⏲ 8am to 9pm
¥ 30

MING TOMBS

The tombs of 13 Ming dynasty emperors and their consorts are scattered in a gorgeous valley 28 miles (45 km) northwest of Beijing. All but three of the Ming emperors are buried here. The first Ming emperor lies in Nanjing, the tomb of the second emperor remains unknown as he had his throne usurped by his uncle and another emperor was considered illegitimate and wasn't given the honor of an imperial tomb.

The site for the **Ming Tombs** (*shísān líng* 十三陵) was carefully chosen as the imperial cemetery by *fengshui* masters after careful examination of the surrounding area on orders from the indefatigable Emperor Yongle, who also commissioned the Forbidden City and Temple of Heaven. Once a year, sitting emperors would come here to perform extravagant rituals for their ancestors in order to keep their spirits placated.

For the history-conscious and family-centered Chinese, filial piety, in life and in death, was of utter importance – to show disrespect to your father was a capital crime. Entrenched by Confucian values and the belief that ancestors require the occasional sign of deference, lest they cause trouble in the living world, ancestor worship became one of the central tenets of Chinese religious practices.

The Ming Tombs are an example of the importance laid upon showing proper filial piety and the self-grandeur of the emperors, many of whom began construction of their tombs as soon as they ascended the throne, with construction ending only when they moved in.

The **Memorial Arch** (*páifāng* 牌坊), built in 1540, marks the entrance to the valley. At 39 feet (12 m) high, 102 feet (31 m) wide and sporting six intricately carved arches, this is the first indicator that no expense was spared when the emperors constructed their final self-monuments. Continuing along the path leads to the **Grand Red Gate** (*dà hóngmén* 大红门), which was built in 1426. At this point all worshippers had to dismount from their horses and carriages and walk the rest of the way. Further behind this gate is a **Stele Pavilion** (*bēi tíng* 碑亭) that's held up by four large ornate columns. Inside this pavilion stands China's largest stele, which is carved with the names of past Ming emperors. Exquisitely carved, this stele was completed in 1435 and is held up by mythical turtles, a symbol of longevity.

Once past the pavilion is the mythical **Spirit Way** (*shéndào* 神道). The path is lined with animals and mystical beasts like the *qilin* (*qílín* 麒麟) with horned heads and scaly bodies, seers of wisdom, and the *xiezhi* (*xièzhi* 獬豸) with lion heads and horse bodies, seers of justice. There are also four statues each of military, civilian and imperial officials, who serve the emperor in his afterlife.

Of the 13 tombs, two are open for viewing, **Changling** (*chánglíng* 长陵) and **Dingling** (*dìnglíng* 定陵). The tombs were built with symbolism in mind. In front of the tombs are square courtyards representing earth. This is where the aboveground buildings are and it was in these buildings where the memorial rituals were performed. Behind the courtyards are the circular tomb mounds representing heaven.

The Dingling Tomb is the burial site of the Wanli emperor, the 13th Ming emperor, who ruled for 48 years until his death in 1620. Two of his empresses are also buried here along with him. The extremely well-built tomb took over 600,000 laborers six years to complete. Excavation of the tomb occurred from 1956 to 1958. The underground chamber was discovered through sheer luck when archeologists discovered a stone tablet left by the original builders. The stone tablet gave instructions on how to find the tomb – this was necessary when the tomb was re-opened for the burial of the emperor. Opening the tomb doors was also exceedingly difficult: the designers created an ingenious door-locking mechanism that sealed the doors behind them. Around the Dingling Tomb are exhibition halls displaying various artifacts founds in the tomb, and the underground burial chamber itself is open for public viewing.

The Yongle emperor and his empress are buried in the Changling Tomb. This tomb was the first and largest of the Ming tombs. Completed in 1427, this complex took 28 years to complete. Exquisitely built, this tomb features one of the largest halls in China. Huge columns and architecture along the same lines as the grandiose Forbidden City allow the aboveground portions of this tomb to cast the emperor's long shadow even in death.

✉ Changping District 昌平区
☏ 6076 1423
◷ 8am to 6pm, peak-season
8:30am to 5pm, off-season
¥ 30 peak-season, 20 off-season for the Spirit Way
60 peak-season, 40 off-season for Dingling Tomb
45 peak-season, 30 off-season for Changling Tomb

SIGHTSEEING: HUTONG WALKS

Alleyways (*hútóng* 胡同) and **courtyard homes** (*sìhéyuàn* 四合院) have been the signature features of Beijing's urban landscape since the Ming dynasty. These homes traditionally comprised buildings built around an enclosed courtyard, but many have been subdivided in modern times. The narrowness of the alleyways and of many courtyard homes discourages heavy traffic and encourages residents to live their lives on the street, fostering a strong sense of community. The pace of life in these neighborhoods is less hurried than on Beijing's broad modern avenues the noises less grating. The *hutongs* are like villages within the megalopolis. As you wander through them, you may feel as though you have stepped back in time.

Many *hutongs* have disappeared in the past decade to make way for modern apartment buildings and wider roads. Fortunately, some historic neighborhoods are being preserved, as you'll discover if you take the walks described below. Besides winding you along some of Beijing's most beautiful *hutongs*, these walks will take you to some of the capital's best sights. We suggest going on foot since this will allow you to soak in the atmosphere, move at your own pace and observe the small details that make *hutongs* unique.

Renting a bicycle is also a good option this way you can cover more ground. Bikes for rent can be found at several prominent places in the Qianhai/Houhai areas. You'll have to leave a deposit, but the hourly fees are very reasonable. Tandem bicycles are also available. If you're not into biking, you can hire a pedi-cab. One reputable pedi-cab company that operates tours in the Qianhai and Houhai areas is **Hutong Pedi-cab Tours** (*běijīng hútòng yóu* 北京胡同游, ☎ 6615 9097 or 6400 2787). Tours cost RMB 180 per person and leave every day at 9am and 2pm; the tours last 2.5 to 3 hours. They start on Qianhai Xi Jie just across the street from the north gate of Baihai Park; the company's riders wear distinctive orange vests and badges.

LAKESIDE HUTONG STROLL

The charming *hutongs* around Houhai and Qianhai lakes meander through quiet neighborhoods and parks along the lakeshore. The *hutongs*, despite being a tourist attraction, are living communities enclosed within a warren-like maze of narrow lanes. You can see residents chatting over a pot of tea on whicker chairs while their songbirds chitter their musical tunes.

Typical traditional architecture.

Strolling through the Houhai and Qianhai areas will take you by grand homes, hip café and the centuries old Bell and Drum Towers. A thorough exploration of the area will take about 3 hours, though 2 hours will be more than enough time to get a good look and feel for life in a *hutong*. While you're there, it's hard to get lost, just walk in any direction and you'll come across a major landmark. There are numerous café along the way drop into any one of them for a drink or a bite to eat. The area across from the north gate of Beihai Park, and where Qianhai Lake meets Houhai Lake, has lots of eating and drinking options. Any of them make perfect rest stops.

Drum Tower 鼓楼 *gǔlóu*
Bell Tower 钟楼 *zhōnglóu*

The impressive Drum Tower was initially built in AD 1272 during the reign of Kublai Khan. Its drums were beaten at fixed hours to mark the time. Climb up to the top floor for a great bird's-eye view of the surrounding *hutongs* and the urban sprawl beyond. Inside is a collection of enormous Chinese drums on the 2nd floor and a shop selling Tibetan curios on the 1st floor. Good views are also on offer at the striking Bell Tower, which boasts a 63-ton bell that's rung on important occasions like Chinese New Year.

✉ Di'anmen Da Jie, Dongcheng District
东城区地安门大街
🕒 9am to 5pm
¥ 20 for the Drum Tower
10 for the Bell Tower

Prince Gong's Mansion
恭王府 *gōngwángfǔ*

It was good to be the Prince. Built in 1777 by a venal official, this 15 acre (60,000 m²) compound was the home of Prince Gong, the last emperor's father. Landscaped with ponds, arched bridges, rock gardens and pavilions, it offers a glimpse into the lifestyles of the rich and famous during the Qing dynasty. In summer, extracts from Peking Operas are occasionally performed outdoors or in the large hall.

✉ 17 Qianhai Xi Jie, Xicheng District
西城区前海西街 17 号
☎ 6616 8149
🕒 8:30am to 5pm
¥ 20

ANTIQUE MARKETS HUTONG WALK

The *hutongs* of Liulichang and Dazhalan lie in commercial areas. Poking around the old shops in Liulichang and Dazhalan is one of this area's many attractions. If you decide to buy something, be sure to do some comparative shopping in nearby stores before pulling out your wallet.

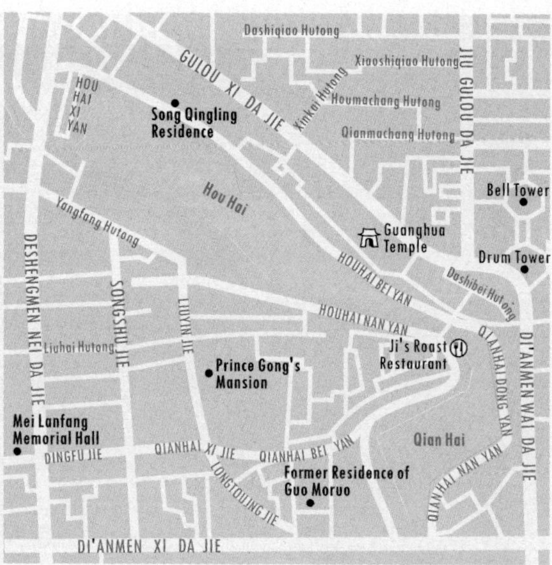

The **Liulichang** (*liúlíchǎng* 琉璃厂) neighborhood spreads across both sides of Nanxinhua Jie. Scholars and artists have frequented Liulichang's art shops and bookstores for centuries. Impoverished students from the provinces would sell their books and paintings here to finance their journey home. Nowadays, local merchants also cater to tourists, selling antiques, reproductions and souvenirs. Like the objects for sale, the neighborhood itself evokes the past since it has been restored to its early-20th-century appearance.

Walking along Liulichang Xi Jie is like strolling through a living museum, the *hutong* filled with shops selling antiques and antique reproductions, kites, drums, posters from the 1930's, Mao memorabilia, contemporary paintings and more. The most famous emporium is **Rongbaozhai** (*róngbǎozhāi* 荣宝斋, 19 Liulichang Xi Jie 琉璃厂西街 19 号), which for years has specialized in supplies for the scholar, gentleman and artist. These includes ink stones – shallow basins in which ink blocks are mixed with water – calligraphy brushes, seals, paper and scrolls. The shop's brush sets, lacquer containers and paintings might make good gifts for the folks back home.

A branch of the famous **Cathay Bookshop** (*zhōngguó shūdiàn* 中国书店) can be found here (57 Liulichang Xi Jie 琉璃厂西街 57 号). On the ground floor is an exhibit of photographs of pre-Revolutionary Beijing, ancient maps, old books and more.

The Liulichang Dong Jie *hutong* runs east to west and is lined with a myriad of antique and imitation antique shops. On offer, running the spectrum from kitsch to truly collectible, are shadow puppets, ceramics, Peking opera masks, Buddha statues, paper lanterns, cloisonné swords, opium pipes, paintings and more. It's hard to recommend one store over another but **Jiguge** (*jígǔ gé* 汲古阁, 136 Liulichang Dong Jie 琉璃厂东街 136 号) has a good reputation. If you need a break from antiques, step into the **Tian Fu Teashop** (65 Liulichang Dong Jie 琉璃厂东街 65 号, ☎ 6304 8671), where you'll undoubtedly be offered a complimentary cup.

Nestled in the Tiaozhou hutong is the tiny **Tiaozhou Hutong Mosque** (*tiáozhou hútòng qīngzhēnsi* 笤帚胡同清真寺). This quaint mosque is not open to non-Muslims but you may be able to pop your head in for a quick peek. South of the mosque, at the intersection, is a Muslim bakery.

East of Liulichang is **Dazhalan** (*dàshílànr* 大栅栏), a wide pedestrian mall that's bustling with activity. Also known as Dashilanr (pronounced *da-shi-lar*), this is Beijing's oldest commercial street and is crowded with long-established shops selling clothing, fabric, shoes, Chinese medicine and more. The neighboring *hutongs* are also worth exploring. Look up while you stroll: some of the buildings on Dazhalan have turn-of-the-century gables and other architectural accents.

The impressive building with sloping Chinese roofs and two statues of mythical beasts (*qílín* 麒麟) outside its entrance is **Tongrentang** (*tóngréntáng* 同仁堂, 24

Dazhalan Jie 大栅栏街 24 号, ☎ 6303 1155). Established in 1669, Tongrentang is China's most famous purveyor of traditional Chinese medicine. On the 2nd floor are pharmaceutical ingredients like deer antler and ginseng, the latter often imported from the US. (One package of "President" brand ginseng features a portrait of George Washington.) The 3rd floor sells imported medicine and vitamins.

Towards the east end, on the north side of Dazhalan, is **Ruifuxiang** (*ruìfúxiáng* 瑞蚨祥, 5 Dazhalan Jie 大栅栏街 5 号, ☎ 6303 5313), which has been selling silk here since 1893. The fashions are a little stodgy, but the building, with its carved panels of flowers and cranes, is worth admiring. Next door is the gaudy green façade of Yichengzhou Department Store.

Before Liberation, **Zhubaoshi Jie** (*zhūbǎoshì jiē* 珠宝市街), in the east end of Dazhanlan, was Beijing's major theater district. Today, it's lined with small retailers stocking clothes, shoes, glasses and toys.

In a peppermint-green-and-white building at 5 Zhubaoshi Jie is the **Qianxiangyi** (*qiānxiángyì sīchóu yǒuxiàn zérèn gōngsī* 谦祥益丝绸有限责任公司, ☎ 6301 6658). Established in 1840, it's one of the most reputable silk shops in Beijing. The ground floor has a huge selection of bolts that are sold by the meter, while the 2nd floor has shirts, negligees, pajamas and gorgeous tapestries.

SIGHTSEEING: MUSEUMS & GALLERIES, CULTURAL SIGHTS

MUSEUMS & GALLERIES

An easy way to find out about current and upcoming exhibitions is to consult the numerous free English-language magazines.

Hailing a taxi in the *hutongs* is relatively easy.

Beijing Tokyo Art Projects 北京东京艺术工程 *běijīng dōngjīng yìshù gōngchéng*

This gallery hosts exhibits of Japanese and Chinese artists that have drawn rave reviews. It is located in the now-fashionable 798 District in Dashanzi, an area of reconverted factories which, like New York's SOHO, is full of new galleries, bars and restaurants.

✉ 4 Jiuxianqiao Lu, Dashanzi Art District, Chaoyang District

Memorable Experiences

Taking a shortcut across the frozen Kunming Lake in the Summer Palace and admiring the snow-covered scenery from the top of Longevity Hill.

Spending the day exploring every passageway in the Forbidden City then climbing to the top of the Coal Hill for a panorama view of the Forbidden City and downtown Bejing.

Renting a tandem bike and getting lost in the maze of *hutongs* around the Houhai and Qianhai areas.

Finally getting up to that distant watchtower on the wild Great Wall on a warm spring day with clear blue skies and absolute silence.

朝阳区大山子艺术区酒仙桥路 4 号
☎ 8457 3245
🕒 10am to 6:30pm Tuesday to Sunday
¥ Free
@ www.tokyo-gallery.com

China Millenium Monument Art Museum
中华世纪坛艺术馆 *zhōnghuá shìjìtán yìshùguǎn*
Underneath the China Millenium Monument (the large sundial), this gallery holds a potpourri of interesting exhibits running the gamut from Jingdezhen pottery to modern art.

✉ 9A Fuxing Lu, Haidian District
海淀区复兴路甲 9 号
☎ 6851 3322
🕒 8:30am to 5:30pm
¥ 30
@ www.bj2000.org.cn

CourtYard Gallery
四合院画廊 *sìhéyuàn huàláng*
Located in the basement of a pricey fusion restaurant, this gallery hosts shows of prominent contemporary Chinese artists.

✉ Basement, 95 Donghuamen Da Jie, Dongcheng District, (near the East Gate of the Forbidden City) 东城区东华门大街 95 号地下一层,故宫东门附近
☎ 6526 8882
🕒 11am to 7pm Monday to Saturday
12pm to 7pm on Sunday
(If you're eating in the restaurant, you can poke in after hours)
¥ Free
@ www.courtyard-gallery.com

Children and adult can all find something interesting at the market.

National Art Museum of China
中国美术馆 *zhōngguó měishùguǎn*
Recently refurbished, the National Museum of China has a vast permanent collection of modern art from China and abroad.

✉ 1 Wusi Da Jie, Dongcheng District (near the northern end of Wangfujing)
东城区五四大街 1 号,王府井北端
☎ 6401 7076
🕒 9am to 4pm
¥ 20

The Red Gate Gallery
红门画廊 *hóngmén huàláng*
Occupying the 1st and 4th floors of a Ming dynasty watchtower, the Red Gate is one of the coolest exhibition spaces in the world. Curator Brian Wallace organizes cutting edge contemporary art shows. After your visit, walk west along the old city walls or go north to the Ancient Observatory.

✉ Dongbianmen Watchtower, Chongwenmen Dong Da Jie, Chongwen District 崇文区崇文门东大街东便门角楼
☎ 6525 1005
🕒 10am to 5pm
¥ Free
@ www.redgategallery.com

CULTURAL SIGHTS

Ancient Observatory
古观象台 *gǔ guānxiàng tái*
This observatory was built in 1446 on a watchtower that was part of the city wall. The wall has vanished and today this Ming dynasty relic is surrounded by gleaming skyscrapers and busy highways creating a photo-friendly architectural contrast. The observatory has displays of rare stargazing instruments including some given to the emperor by Jesuit monks in the 17th century.

✉ 2 Dongbiaobei Hutong, Jianguomenwai, Dongcheng District
东城区建国门外东裱褙胡同 2 号
☎ 6512 8923
🕒 9am to 5pm, peak-season

9am to 4pm, off-season
¥ 10

Coal Hill 景山公园 *jǐngshān gōngyuán*
Made from earth excavated to create the Forbidden City's moat, Coal Hill is the centerpiece of a pleasant park. Aligned directly north of the Forbidden City, Coal Hill, it was believed, would protect the palace from evil spirits. Despite such *fengshui*, the last Ming emperor was unable to halt the disintegration of his dynasty and hung himself on a cypress tree at the foot of the hill as Beijing fell to a rebel army in 1644. Coal Hill's top drawing card is the panorama visible from Wanshou Pavilion atop the hill, notably the spectacular views of the Forbidden City.

✉ Jingshan Qian Jie, Dongcheng District (directly north of the Forbidden City) 东城区景山前街,故宫北门外
☎ 6404 4071
🕒 6am to 10pm, peak-season
6:30am to 7pm, off-season
¥ 2

Eastern Qing Tombs 清东陵 *qīng dōng líng*
One of two royal cemeteries of the Qing dynasty, these stately tombs hold the remains of five emperors, 15 empresses and assorted nobility and concubines. The Spirit Way and the tombs of Emperor Qianlong and Empress Dowager Cixi are the most memorable sights. The Eastern Qing Tombs are some 3 hours away from Beijing by car.

✉ Zunhua, Hebei Province 河北省遵化
☎ 0315 – 694 5471
🕒 8am to 5pm, peak-season
9am to 4pm, off-season
¥ 80

Fragrant Hills Park
香山公园 *xiāng shān gōngyuán*
Beijing Botanical Gardens
北京植物园 *běijīng zhíwù yuán*
Fragrant Hills Park and Beijing Botanical Gardens can easily be visited in a single excursion. On the grounds of Fragrant Hills Park, a former imperial hunting reserve, are pavilions, pagodas and lakes, connected by winding, tree-lined paths. The park is best visited during the spring or autumn. The Beijing Botanical Gardens are near Fragrant Hills Park on the road to Beijing. Recently expanded, they're a delightful spot for a stroll and a picnic, notably in spring when the magnolia and cheery trees are in bloom.

Fragrant Hills Park
香山公园 *xiāngshān gōngyuán*
✉ Xiang Shan 香山
☎ 8259 0297
🕒 6am to 7pm
¥ 10 peak-season, 5 off-season for the park
10 for the Azure Cloud Temple
50 for the chairlift, two-way (may be closed in winter)

Beijing Botanical Gardens
北京植物园 *běijīng zhíwù yuán*
✉ Xiangyi Lu, Xiang Shan 香山香颐路
☎ 6259 1283
🕒 6am to 7pm
¥ 5 for the park only
15 includes the Sleeping Buddha Temple and the other two sites

Old Summer Palace 圆明园 *yuánmíng yuán*
Like the Summer Palace, the Old Summer Palace was an imperial retreat that was razed by the French and British troops during the Second Opium War in 1860. The compound's 145 buildings, some of them European-looking palaces designed by Jesuit priests, were never rebuilt and the ruins stand as reminders of the ravages of imperialism. But don't let that stop you from coming: this huge park contains several lotus-filled lakes, a maze and canals that are great fun to explore.

✉ 28 Qinghua Xi Lu, Haidian District (near the west gate of Qinghua University)

The Azure Cloud Temple lies in the lush Fragrant Hills.

Hints of European architecture in the Old Summer Palace.

海淀区清华西路 28 号,清华大学西门附近

☎ 6255 1488, 6262 8501

🕒 7am to 7pm

¥ 10 for the park only
25 for full access

Ox Street Mosque

牛街清真寺 *niújiē qīngzhēnsì*

The spiritual heart of Beijing's 200,000 strong Muslim community, the Ox Street Mosque was built by the son of an Arab imam in AD 966. Architecturally, it is a fascinating hybrid of Arab and Chinese styles: the exterior looks like a Chinese temple with a typical curved roof, but its pillars are decorated with verses from the Koran and there's a minaret at the back. Though you can peer in, the handsome prayer hall is off limits to non-Muslims. All visitors must wear long pants or skirts to enter this religious sanctuary.

✉ 88 Niu Jie, Xuanwu District
宣武区牛街 88 号

☎ 6353 2564

🕒 8am to 7pm (but closed to non-Muslims during services)

¥ 10 (Muslims can enter for free)

Song Qingling Residence

宋庆龄故居 *Sòng Qìnglíng gùjū*

The home of a rich aristocrat during the Qing dynasty, this lush compound with pavilions and waterways is a window onto China's past, when only imperial courtiers were allowed to build homes on the shores of Houhai Lake. The renovated buildings, decorated in vintage 1960's style, are preserved as a museum honoring Song Qingling, who lived there from 1963 to 1981. Educated in the US, Song married Dr. Sun Yat-sen, the founder of the Republic of China, and she herself became vice-president of the People's Republic of China.

✉ 46 Houhai Bei Yan, Xicheng District
西城区后海北沿 46 号

☎ 6404 4205

🕒 9am to 4:30pm, peak-season
9am to 4pm, off-season

¥ 20

Temple of Confucius 孔庙 *kǒng miào*

Built in AD 1302, this underrated temple exudes a wonderful ambiance. In addition to the temple building, there's a statue of the Sage, aged cypress trees and a small museum of Beijing history. On the grounds are 198 stone tablets that record the names, ranks and hometowns of scholars who passed the formidable jinshi examination, the highest civil service test given during the dynastic era.

✉ 13 Guozijian Jie, Dongcheng District (a street running west across from the Lama Temple's main gate)
东城区国子监街 13 号,雍和宫正门西侧

☎ 6401 2799

🕒 8:30am to 5pm

¥ 10

Quotes

"I really like the 798 art district in Dashanzi, where factories have been converted into art galleries, restaurants and café. It's different from any other place in Beijing: the atmosphere is laid back and creative and there are no crowds!"

"If you come to Beijing, you simply have to try Peking duck. My favorite duck restaurants are Da Dong Roast Duck (☎ 6463 2783) and Li Qun Roast Duck Restaurant (☎ 6705 5578 - it's located in a *hutong* so call for directions)."

Making Your Trip Easy

Practical Tips

Spring and autumn are the best times to come to Beijing, but beware that during national holidays the city's hotels and sights will be packed. Autumns are dry with strong winds and winters can dip down to 5°F (-15°C). Summers are hot but dry and temperatures average around the high 90s °F (30s °C). Beijing was once infamous for its pollution, but things have cleared up considerably in preparation for the 2008 Summer Olympics.

The city has lots of cars and trucks clogging the streets and traffic is bad at all times, so don't even think about getting anywhere fast during rush hour by car. The subway will generally get you to your destination faster than car if you don't mind the crowds during peak hours.

Most young people in Beijing know enough English to help a lost tourist or point the way to the nearest toilet.

Tours & Travel Groups

Most four and five star hotels can make domestic and international airplane, train and bus reservations for their guests. Furthermore, they can organize guided sightseeing tours of Beijing for individuals or groups.

Alternatively, you can buy tickets or book Beijing tours on your own by calling one of the following English-speaking agencies. Dealing with the agencies directly should be cheaper, but it'll be more time consuming than depending on a hotel.

Beijing Youth Travel Service Co. LTD 北京青年旅行社股份有限公司
běijīng qīngnián lǚxíngshè gǔfèn yǒuxiàn gōngsī
Offers one day city tour in Beijing: Great Wall – Ming Tombs, departs at everyday, RMB 160 per person; Forbidden City – Temple of Heaven – Summer Palace, departs at each Tuesday, Thursday and Saturday, RMB 260 per person. Both includes entrance fee, air-conditioned bus, English-speaking guide and lunch. Books one day in advance.
☎ 6507 7723

BTG International Travel & Tours 北京神舟国际旅行社集团有限公司
běijīng shénzhōu guójì lǚxíngshè jítuán yǒuxiàn gōngsī
BTG offers tours of Beijing.
✉ Beijing Tourism Building, 28 Jianguomenwai Da Jie, Chaoyang District 朝阳区建国门外大街28号北京旅游大厦
☎ 6515 7515
@ info@btg-tours.com

China International Travel Service
中国国际旅行社 *zhōngguó guójì lǚxíngshè*
CITS can arrange air, train, boat, and hotel reservations in China, and organizes half and full day guided tours of Beijing.
✉ 103 Fuxingmennei Da Jie, Xicheng District 西城区复兴门内大街103号

Striking a pose in front of Tian'anmen.

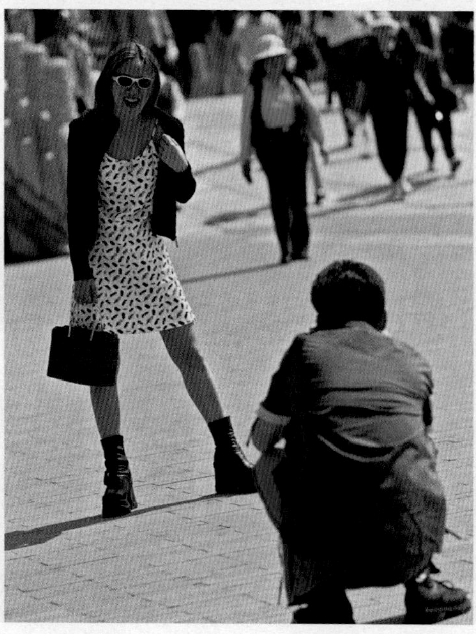

☎ 6601 1122
@ webmaster@cits.net
ⓔ www.cits.net

CYTS 中青旅控股股份有限公司
zhōngqīnglǚ kònggǔ gǔfèn yǒuxiàn gōngsī
CYTS provides sightseeing tours of Beijing and can book flights and hotels throughout China.

✉ 17/F, AVIC Tower, 2 Dongsanhuan Nan Lu, Chaoyang District
朝阳区东三环南路 2 号艾维克大厦 17 层
☎ 6567 9900
@ webs@cytsonline.com
ⓔ english.cytsonline.com

Kingdom Travel
中侨国际旅行社 *zhōngqiáo guójì lǚxíngshè*
This friendly boutique agency provides good rates on domestic and international flights and package tours.

✉ Room 06B, Unit 1, Tower B, Global Trade Mansion, Chaoyang District
朝阳区世贸国际公寓 B 座 1 单元 06B 室
☎ 6502 5588
@ kdtravel@163bj.com

Tourism Complaint Hotline
☎ 6513 0828 ext2

Maps

Detailed maps show all of Beijing's streets, including its narrow *hutongs*, and provide the names of roads and major sites in Chinese characters, pinyin and English. They can be bought for RMB 10 to 30, depending on size and quality, in the Foreign Language Bookstore as well as some hotel gift shops.

Newspapers, Magazines & Bookstores

Beijing has several free English magazines, notably *that's Beijing* and *City Weekend*, which contain reviews and detailed listings of restaurants, clubs, concerts, art exhibits, fashion emporiums and more. Copies of these magazines can be found in businesses

A bird's-eye view of Beijing's Chang'an Jie.

catering to foreigners, bars, restaurants and imported food stores.

Hotels are good places to buy English books and you'll find an even wider selection of books in English at the following stores:

The Foreign Languages Bookstore
北京外文书店 *běijīng wàiwén shūdiàn*
This cavernous shop sells fiction, art books, magazines, dictionaries, novels and more.
✉ 235 Wangfujing Da Jie, Dongcheng District 东城区王府井大街 235 号
☎ 6512 6927
@ www.bpiec.com.cn

The Friendship Store
友谊商店 *yǒuyì shāngdiàn*
The 1st floor bookshop in this department store sells a wide range of imported magazines (titles like *Elle* and *National Geographic*), novels and books about Beijing and China.
✉ 17 Jianguomenwai Da Jie, Chaoyang District 朝阳区建国门外大街 17 号
☎ 6500 3311

Transportation

Beijing is a major transportation hub with daily connections by air and rail to thousands of destinations in China and beyond. Transportation options within the city are likewise plentiful. Buying tickets to other destinations in China during national holidays can be difficult, so be sure to plan ahead.

AIRPORT

The Beijing Capital International Airport (*běijīng shǒudū jīchǎng* 北京首都机场) is China's busiest airport, with over 1200 domestic air routes and flights to many international destinations. After a highly successful facelift completed in 2005, the airport is modern and efficient. To prepare for the surge of visitors expected for the 2008 Olympics, a third terminal and two new runways will be built.

All departing passengers must pay an airport tax before they check-in. The tax is collected at booths in the main departure hall. Passengers must keep their tax vouchers

with them since these are collected after the security check. At present the tax on domestic flights is RMB 50 and RMB 90 on international ones.

✉ Jichang Lu, Chaoyang District
朝阳区机场路
☎ 6454 1100 ext 2
@ www.bcia.com.cn/en

Getting to/from the airport: The Beijing Capital International Airport is about 17 miles (28 km) from the city center and depending on traffic, it takes anywhere from 25 to 40 minutes to drive from the airport to downtown via the airport expressway.

A taxi ride from the airport to the city center should cost RMB 70 to 100, including RMB 10 added to the meter for the expressway toll. To avoid being overcharged, don't accept a ride from a tout whose taxi could be unlicensed. The line for licensed taxis at the airport is clearly marked.

Many upscale hotels can arrange for private cars or limousines to pick up and drop off guests. This service should cost RMB 120 to 300. Hotels also commonly operate airport shuttle buses. Be sure to reserve your private car or seat on a shuttle bus prior to your arrival or departure.

Airport shuttle buses leave the airport every 10 to 30 minutes between 7am and 10pm for several destinations in the city, like the National Art Gallery (near Wangfujing) and Zhongguancun (Beijing's "Silicon Valley" in the northwest Haidian District). While these buses are cheap (RMB 16 per trip), they're difficult to use if you don't speak Chinese. Moreover, you may have to take a taxi to get from the bus stop to your final destination.

At the moment, there is no train or subway that connects the city with the airport, but a light rail link is planned and should be operational when the Games begin in 2008.

BICYCLE

Biking is a great way to get around, it's faster than walking and lets you see a lot more sights. There are many places in Beijing where you can rent a bike. Some hotels offer them for free to their guests; others charge up to RMB 20 per hour. You can always get a good deal by renting from a bicycle shop. Bike shops usually ask that you leave a refundable deposit, between RMB 200 and 500, when renting a bike. Inspect the bike and check the brakes before setting off on your adventure. A lock will normally be provided. In the unlikely event of mechanical trouble or a flat tire, there are curbside bike repairmen all over Beijing.

Beijing Jiuhe Weiye Bicycles
北京九河伟业自行车商场
běijīng jiǔhé wěiyè zìxíngchē shāngchǎng
This reputable shop rents sturdy bikes for RMB 40 per day.

Quotes

"One of my favorite places to visit in Beijing is Liuyin Park, near Andingmenwai Da Jie. It's not well known, but it's really picturesque with willow trees and waterways filled with lotuses and ducks. There's an outdoor teahouse on the island where you can buy drinks and snacks and relax in the shade. Coming here is like stepping into a Chinese landscape painting."

"If there's one thing you absolutely should do while in Beijing it is to visit a park at 6:30am. At that hour the parks are filled with tango-dancers, wrestlers, martial arts practitioners and people whose form of exercise is to scream at trees. It's a completely unique experience. My favorite park is the Temple of Heaven."

"In underrated historic site that I particularly enjoy is the Bell Tower (behind the Drum Tower). Usually there are no other visitors and you have this wonderful old building to yourself. It's a very peaceful place from which to contemplate the nearby *hutongs*, the bustling modern city in the distance, and the contrast between them."

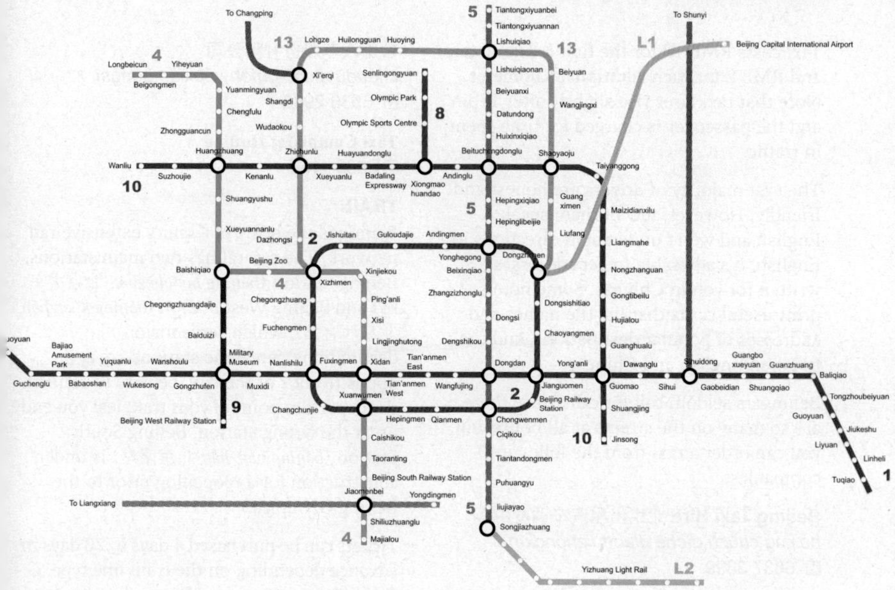

🖂 121 Beiheyan Da Jie, Dongcheng District, (north of Donghuamen, near Wangfujing)
东城区北河沿大街 121 号，王府井附近，东华门北侧
☎ 6523 8721

Di'anmen Supermarket Bicycle Shop
地安门商场自行车部 *dì'ānmén shāngchǎng zìxíngchē bù*
Located in the Houhai Lake neighborhood, which is a great place for a leisurely ride, this shop rents bikes for RMB 20 per hour. Tandem and three-person bikes are also available.
🖂 31 Di'anmen Da Jie, Xicheng District (at the rear of the supermarket on the north side beside the lake)
西城区地安门大街 31 号
☎ 6404 1336 ext 2414

Beijing Bike Rental
北京贝科蓝图自行车租赁 *běijīng bèikē lántú zìxíngchē zūlìn*
There are over 10 branches inside Beijing. RMB 5 per hour, RMB 10 per half day, RMB 400 for deposit.
☎ 96156, 400 896 5917, 800 810 5917

PUBLIC TRANSPORTATION

Beijing has an extensive bus system. You can reach almost every corner of the city by bus. You can deposit a refundable RMB 20 to get a Beijing Bus IC card. With the card, most bus rides only cost 0.4 yuan (only about 6 cents U.S.), and no messy small bills any more. The city's subway and light rail cars are easier for foreigners to use since notices are translated into English and stations signs are written in *pinyin*.

At present, there are three subway lines: the first runs east to west along Chang'an Jie, the second is a loop line that goes under the second ring road, the two lines connect at two stations; also from Beijing CBD area to Tongzhou (the east suburb) through the Batong light rail line. Beijing's elevated light rail line goes from Xizhimen subway station to Dongzhimen subway station through the northern suburbs. Work on new lines, including a subway that will link the Olympic Park with the city center, is underway and should be completed before the opening ceremony in 2008.

Subway and light rail tickets cost RMB 2.

TAXI

Taxies in Beijing are readily available. Most the taxies are Hyundai and VW sedans painted in Yellow with blue or white stripes. Licensed taxies have signs on their roofs and a laminated card on the dashboard with the driver's photograph, service number and name. When cabs are for hire, a red illuminated medallion will be visible in the front window. Don't accept a ride in a car that lacks any of these identifying signs.

Taxi costs RMB 10 for the first 3 Kilometers and RMB 2 for each additional Kilometer. Note that taxi fares rise slightly after 11pm and the passenger is charged for time spent in traffic.

The vast majority of drivers are honest and friendly. However, few of them speak English and won't understand directions in English. It's advisable to get addresses written for you in Chinese. Some hotels print useful cards that list the names and addresses of popular destinations, and the hotel, in English and Chinese.

Beijingers seldom call for cabs since there are so many on the streets at all hours, but you can order a taxi from the following companies:

Beijing Taxi Hire 北京出租汽车调度中心
běijīng chūzū qìchē diàodù zhōngxīn
☎ 6837 3399

Beijing Yinjian Taxi Company
北京银建出租汽车公司
běijīng yínjiàn chūzū qìchē gōngsī
☎ 96103

Capital Taxi Company
首都汽车股份有限公司
shǒudū qìchē gǔfèn yǒuxiàn gōngsī
☎ 6530 2988

Taxi Complaint Hotline
☎ 6835 1150

TRAIN

Beijing is the heart of China's extensive rail network. The capital has two main stations, Beijing Station (*běijīng huǒchēzhàn* 北京火车站) and Beijing West Station (*běijīng xīkèzhàn* 北京西客站), which serve major destinations. Since the stations are at opposite ends of the city, be sure to confirm the departure point of your train lest you end up at the wrong station. Beijing South Station (*běijīng nánzhàn* 北京南站) is under construction for a reopening prior to the Beijing Olympics.

Tickets can be purchased 4 days to 20 days in advance depending on the train line type. Train lines start with a "D" are the new Chinese high speed bullet trains; lines with a "Z" initial are the one stop trains. Foreigners can purchase at the foreigners' railway ticket office in the central hall of Beijing Station. Tickets on local trains or

A Chinese bride and her foreign groom celebrate in traditional style.

commuter trains to nearby Tianjin can be bought at the station before departure. The most convenient way to grab some tickets is through a travel agent or your hotel concierge.

Taxis, subways and buses serve both major stations.

Beijing South Station
北京南站 *běijīng nánzhàn*
✉ Xuanwu District 宣武区

Beijing Station
北京火车站 *běijīng huǒchēzhàn*
✉ Jianguomennei Da Jie, Dongcheng District 东城区建国门内大街
☎ 5101 9999

Beijing West Station
北京西客站 *běijīng xīkèzhàn*
✉ Lianhuachi Dong Lu, Fengtai District 丰台区莲花池东路
☎ 5182 6253

Hotels

China World Hotel
中国大饭店 *zhōngguó dàfàndiàn* ★★★★★
✉ 1 Jianguomenwai Da Jie, Chaoyang District 朝阳区建外大街 1 号❶
☎ 6505 2266
¥ 2,822 – double room, peak-season
1,693 – double room, off-season
@ www.shangri-La.com

Great Wall Sheraton Hotel Beijing
长城饭店 *chángchéng fàndiàn* ★★★★★
✉ 10 Dongsanhuan Bei Lu, Chaoyang District (near Lufuthansa Center) 朝阳区东三环北路 10 号,燕莎中心附近❷
☎ 6590 5566
¥ 1,992 – double room, peak-season
955 – double room, off-season
@ www.Sheraton.com/beijing

Peninsula Palace
王府饭店 *wángfǔ fàndiàn* ★★★★★
✉ 8 Jinyu Hutong, Dongcheng District 东城区金鱼胡同 8 号❸
☎ 6512 8899
¥ 1,536 – double room, peak-season
1,203 – double room, off-season
@ www.perinsula.com

Shangri-La Hotel Beijing
香格里拉饭店 *xiānggélǐlā fàndiàn* ★★★★★
✉ 29 Zizhuyuan Lu, Haidian District 海淀区紫竹院路 29 号❹
☎ 6841 2211
¥ 1,826 – double room
@ www.shangri-La.com

Swiss Hotel Beijing 港澳中心瑞士酒店
gǎng'ào zhōngxīn ruìshì jiǔdiàn ★★★★★
✉ 2 Chaoyangmen Bei Da Jie, Dongcheng District 东城区朝阳门北大街 2 号❺
☎ 6553 2288
¥ 1,909 – double room, peak-season
902 – double room, off-season
@ www.swisshotel.com

Gloria Plaza Hotel
凯莱大酒店 *kǎilái dàjiǔdiàn* ★★★★
✉ 2 Jianguomenwai Nan Da Jie,Chaoyang District 朝阳区建外南大街 2 号❻
☎ 6515 8855
¥ 700 – double room
@ www.gphbeijing.com

Holiday Inn Lido Hotel
丽都假日饭店 *lìdū jiàrì fàndiàn* ★★★★
✉ intersection of Jiangtai Lu and Jichang Lu, Chaoyang District 朝阳区机场路将台路口
☎ 6437 6688
¥ 788 – double room
@ www.holiday-inn.com

Peace Hotel
和平宾馆 *hépíng bīnguǎn* ★★★★
✉ 3 Jinyu Hutong, Dongcheng District 东城区金鱼胡同 3 号❼
☎ 6512 8833
¥ 844 – double room, peak-season
764 – double room, off-season
@ www.accorhotels-asia.com

Food & Restaurants

In 2003, enthusiastic eaters could choose from among 40,000 registered restaurants, a 5,000% increase from 1976. These restaurants range from cheap noodle shops to luxury banquet halls, and thanks to rising incomes, curiosity about new flavors and the influx of migrants from other parts of China and beyond, Beijing's restaurants offer a nearly endless variety of local, regional and international cuisines. In short, Beijing is one of the gourmet capitals of the world.

Beijing's signature dish is Peking duck (*běijīng kǎoyā* 北京烤鸭). After a short life of hearty feedings, the fowl is killed, plucked, inflated (to separate the skin from the meat) and basted in honey and vinegar. Once it has been air-dried, it's roasted in an oven heated by a fire made of fragrant wood or roasted over an open flame. A waiter presents the cooked duck to the table and then uses a sharp cleaver to slice little morsels of skin and meat. These tasty tidbits are eaten rolled up in steamed pancakes along with scallions, cucumbers and a sweet brown sauce. A soup made from the duck's bones follows the main course.

Tea is still China's favorite drink.

One of the great pleasures of visiting Beijing is that, in addition to local dishes like Peking duck, you can eat succulent specialties from around China.

Listed below are some of Beijing's best Chinese and foreign restaurants. You'll find far more restaurant reviews in local English-language magazines. Most Chinese restaurants don't have English menus, so bring a Mandarin phrasebook or glance at what your neighbors are eating and order the same.

Most restaurants take reservations, but credits cards aren't commonly accepted except in higher-end restaurants.

CHINESE RESTAURANTS

Bai Zhou Xiang 百粥乡

Rice porridge in all its many forms, supplements the congee collection with a variety of homestyle snake.

✉ 1F Bldg A, Donghuan Guangchang, 9 Dongzhong Jie, Dongcheng District
东城区东中街 9 号，东环广场 A 座一层

☎ 6418 5681

🕒 24 hours

Chenghuangmiao Xiaochi 城隍庙小吃

Over twenty locations around town.Good for Shanghai fast food any time of the day. Daily 24 hours.

✉ 51 Beisanhuan Xilu, Haidian District
海淀区北三环西路 51 号

☎ 6255 9446

Beijing Roast Duck Restaurant 大董烤鸭店

A good location near Sanlitun and possibly the best Peking duck (RMB 98 each) in the city explain this restaurant's enormous popularity, so call ahead to make a reservation. The seafood and vegetable dishes are also tasty. Photographs in the menus make ordering a cinch.

✉ Building 3, Tuanjiehu Beikou, Chaoyang District (across Sanhuan Lu from the Zhaolong Hotel)
朝阳区团结湖北口 3 号楼，兆龙饭店对面❽

☎ 6582 2892

🕒 11am to 9:30pm

Bellagio 鹿港小镇

This Taiwan-style restaurant boasts chic, minimalist décor, solicitous service and good prices. More importantly, the food is superb and brings together dishes from throughout the Chinese diaspora. Favorites include three-cup chicken (*sān bēi jī* 三杯鸡), beef and fried dough (*yóutiáo niúròu* 油条牛肉) and Singapore-style noodles (*xīnjiāpō chǎomiàn* 新加坡炒面).

✉ 35 Xiaoyunlu, Chaoyang District (near the Hilton Hotel)
朝阳区霄云路 35 号，希尔顿饭店附近

☎ 8451 9988, 8448 0520

🕒 11am to 4am

Donghuamen Night Market 东华门夜市

Every evening at 6pm, an entire block of this avenue is closed off and filled with food carts manned by cheerful chefs serving a galaxy of inexpensive Chinese snacks like dumplings, red bean soup and succulent burrito-like rolls. More exotic offerings include the scorpions, deep fried silkworms and sparrows on a stick. Good times guaranteed.

✉ north of the Wangfujing pedestrian street
王府井步行街北

East Ocean Seafood 东海海鲜酒家

The numerous Hong Kong natives who flock to this fancy Cantonese restaurant attest to the authenticity, consistency and quality of its dishes. The tea is fragrant and the seafood is swimming in gleaming tanks minutes before it's on your table. Dim sum is served daily.

✉ 39 Maizidian Jie, Chaoyang District (near the Lufthansa Center)
朝阳区麦子店街 39 号,燕莎商城附近
☎ 6508 3482
◷ 11am to 11pm

Fangshan Restaurant 仿膳饭庄
Opened in 1925, Fangshan reproduces the dishes of the imperial kitchen during the Qing dynasty. The well-appointed banquet rooms, the solicitous costumed staff, and the gorgeous location on Beihai Lake create a lovely setting for a meal. You can eat a la carte, but most patrons select set meals since these feature a well-balanced combination of different tastes. If you really want to feel like an emperor, order the 20-course meal that features such exotica as bird's nest soup with deer tendon and turtle with Chinese herbs. Simpler fare is available. Reservations are recommended.

✉ East Gate of Beihai Park, Xicheng District (on Jade Isle inside Beihai Park – enter through the east gate and cross the bridge to the island)
西城区北海公园东门内琼华岛上⑩
☎ 6401 1889
◷ 11am to 1:30pm, 5pm to 7:30pm

Pazi Hotpot 爬子火锅城
Unless you can truly stand Sichuan's five-alarm spices, order a *yuan-yang huoguo* (鸳鸯火锅), a pot split into two halves, one containing a mild broth, the other a fiery soup. Select your ingredients and your dipping sauce, then cook everything in the pot. Top it all off with a draft beer.

✉ 13 Xinyuan Li, Chaoyang District (near Capital Mansion)
朝阳区新源里 13 号,京城大厦附近⑪
☎ 8451 0505
◷ 24 hours

Quanjude Roast Duck Restaurant
全聚德烤鸭店
The most famous duck restaurant in the city, Quanjude has been serving up fowl since 1864. Crowds of tourists and locals come here for the Peking duck which are RMB 168 each. The duck is roasted in a fragrant fire of date, peach and pear tree wood. If you're feeling adventurous, try the duck tongue or duck feet appetizers.

✉ 32 Qianmen Da Jie, Chongwen District
崇文区前门大街 32 号⑨
☎ 6511 2418
◷ 10:30am to 2pm, 4:30pm to 8:30pm

The Red Capital Club 新红资俱乐部
A meal at the Red Capital Club is an unforgettable experience. The restaurant is housed inside an exquisitely renovated courtyard home that lies on a sleepy hutong (look for the old Red Flag limousine that's often parked in front). Inside, you'll find a comfy bar decorated entirely in vintage Communist memorabilia from the 50's to the 70's. You can dine either under the stars in the courtyard or in a second room that features classical Chinese art. Containing entertaining descriptions of each dish, the menu features a mix of imperial cuisine and the hearty favorites of China's early communist leaders. Other draws are the extensive wine list and cigars.

✉ 66 Dongsi Jiutiao, Dongcheng District
东城区东四九条 66 号
☎ 6402 7150
◷ 6pm to 11pm
@ www.redcapitalclub.com.cn

South Beauty 俏江南
With several other branches in the city, South Beauty has clearly found the right formula. Tasty Sichuan food, elegant dècor and good service produce happy, repeat customers. If you're in the mood for something spicy, try the *lazi ji* (辣子鸡) – pieces of fried chicken swimming in hot peppers.

✉ 3/F, Pacific Century Place, Gongti Bei Lu, Chaoyang District
朝阳区工体北路太平洋百货三层⑫
☎ 6539 3502
◷ 11am to 11pm

Xihe Yaju 羲和雅居
This delightful restaurant abutting leafy Ritan Park draws a clientele of journalists, executives and diplomats who come for its extensive menu of dishes from all over China. The outdoor courtyard is idyllic in the spring and autumn – at other times you can eat in the comfortable indoor rooms. The service is good and the menu is bilingual.

✉ northeast corner of Ritan Park, Chaoyang District 朝阳区日坛公园东北角⑬
☎ 8561 7643
◷ 11am to 2pm, 5pm to 10pm

FOREIGN RESTAURANTS

Craving a taste of home? You can get your fix at the following restaurants.

Danieli's 丹尼艾丽意大利餐厅

Danieli's swish surroundings, attentive service, long wine list, homemade pasta and lovely meat and fish dishes may transport you, in spirit, to sunny Italy. Such gastronomic exultation doesn't come cheap, but the restaurant frequently offers business lunch specials.

✉ 2/F, St. Regis Hotel, 21 Jianguomenwai Da Jie, Chaoyang District 朝阳区建国门外大街 21 号国际俱乐部饭店二层 ⓮

☎ 6460 6688 ext 2441

🕒 11:30am to 2pm, 6pm to 10pm

Flo 福楼

The large number of French tourists who make the pilgrimage to Flo attest to this brasserie's authenticity. They come for the warm ambiance, oysters imported from France, the steak, the sauerkraut and the wines.

✉ 2/F, Rainbow Plaza, 16 Dongsanhuan Lu, Chaoyang District 朝阳区东三环路 16 号隆博广场二层⓯

☎ 6595 5139

🕒 11am to 3 pm, 6pm to 11pm

Hatsune 隐泉日本料理

Sleek décor, the freshest ingredients and a creative chef make Hatsune a marvelous dining experience. Everything is good here, especially the rolls (the "butterfly roll" is heavenly). Hatsune attracts droves of Japanese executives and ex-pat hipsters so do make a reservation. At the time of writing, Hatsune's owner was planning to open a Japanese barbecue restaurant in the building's basement.

✉ 2/F Heqiao Dasha, 8A Guanghua Lu, Chaoyang District, (east of Sanhuan Lu, near Kelun Dasha) 朝阳区光华路甲 8 号和乔大厦 C 座二层(三环外科伦大厦附近)

☎ 6581 3939

🕒 11:30am to 2pm, 5:30pm to 10pm

Jing 京

This restaurant's funky open plan layout allows you to watch the chefs in action as they whip up sumptuous concoctions that fuse Asian and European culinary influences. Jing was included in Conde Nast Traveler's 100 "Hot Tables" list in 2003.

✉ Basement, Peninsula Palace Hotel, 8 Jinyu Hutong, Wangfujing, Dongcheng District 东城区王府井街金鱼胡同 8 号王府饭店地下一层

☎ 6559 2888 ext 7561

🕒 5:30am to 11:30pm

Schindler's Filling Station 申德勒加油站

Need to unwind? Then come to this relaxed restaurant for great sausages, grilled meat, potatoes, sauerkraut and more washed down with imported German beer. Prices are moderate, and the outdoor terrace lies in Ritan Park. Enormously satisfying.

✉ A15 Guanghua Lu, Chaoyang District, about 220 yards (200 m) east of the south gate of Ritan Park 朝阳区光华路甲 15 号,日坛南门东 200 米

☎ 8562 6439

🕒 11am to 11pm

Nights Out in Beijing

A visit to Beijing isn't complete without sampling its vibrant nightlife. After two decades of breakneck economic growth, the city is experiencing a cultural renaissance. Actors, musicians and artists from all over the country come to the capital seeking ideas, camaraderie and the "big break." Beijing's theaters, concert halls, galleries and underground rock clubs attract eager crowds, as do bars and café. With so many entertainment options, Beijing surely has something to offer every visitor.

Listed below are some of Beijing's best entertainment venues. You'll find information about upcoming events in the free English magazines. These publications are bursting with information about anything you'll need to know on how and where to have fun. Be warned though, many bars and clubs come and go, so it's always best to check in one those free magazines and see if the bar you're planning on going to tonight is still around.

BARS & CAFES

TThere are several Beijing neighborhoods where numerous bars are clustered together. These include Sanlitun, Chaoyang Park and Houhai.

Most establishments serve coffee and alcohol, some serve snacks and meals.

ARIA 阿丽雅

Aria blends elegant surroundings,

Drinking outdoors on a hot summer night.

sophisticated cocktails, and a long wine list. If you're hungry, head upstairs to the restaurant that serves refined continental and fusion fare.

✉ 2/F China World Hotel, 1 Jianguomenwai Da Jie, Chaoyang District
朝阳区建外大街 1 号中国大饭店二层

☎ 6505 2266 ext. 36

🕒 11am to midnight

Durty Nellies 爱尔兰酒吧

Beijing's favorite Irish pub has Guinness on tap, hearty Irish stew, a pool table and friendly staff. On Friday nights, when the cover band takes the stage, this is not a place for a quiet conversation.

✉ 1/B Liangmaqiao Flower Market, Chaoyang District
朝阳区亮马桥花卉市场地下一层

☎ 6593 5050

🕒 11:00am to 1:30am

First Café 第一咖啡

A small upscale joint without bells or whistles: Just a place to slide up to, grab a quality cocktail and have a conversation. Mandopop-inspired jazz, candlelight and a dark and heavy color scheme combined with large picture windows on the second floor room allow sippers to contemplate Bar Street in solitude.

✉ Nansanlitun Lu, Chaoyang District
朝阳区南三里屯路

☎ 6501 8812

🕒 6pm to 2am

Frank's Place 万龙

Frank's Place has kept its all-American image going since the late 80's. Beijing's unofficial 19th hole, it draws a faithful crowd of golf aficionados and ex-pat business types who come for imported beer on tap and Beijing's best burgers.

✉ Gongti Dong Lu, 200m south of the City Hotel , Chaoyang District 朝阳区工体东路，城市宾馆南 200 米处

☎ 6507 2617

🕒 11:00am to midnight

Goose and Duck Pub 鹅和鸭

British pub grub like bangers-and-mash and fish'n'chips, imported beer, pool tables, darts and nonstop sports on the big-screen TV's make the Goose and Duck Beijing's most popular sports bar.

✉ 1 Bihuju Nan Lu, opposite the west gate of Chaoyang Park, Chaoyang District
朝阳区碧湖居南路 1 号朝阳公园西门对面

☎ 6538 1691
🕒 24 hours

Hutong Bar 胡同写意
A small but airy courtyard house with open-concept rooms – one of the few bars in the hood that has paid more attention to the space between its walls than space beside the lake.
✉ 8 Houhai Nangyan, Xicheng
☎ 6615 8691
🕒 2:00am to 2pm

No Name Bar 无名酒吧
The birth of the cool, this nameless bar was the first to set up in the now-thriving Houhai area. A great place in which to spend a mellow afternoon or evening, the bar's interior is a study in wood, rattan and tropical greenery. On the stereo is muted acid jazz and world music. If this place is full, you can visit one of its many imitators in the area. Next door is Nuage, a funky Vietnamese restaurant.
✉ 3 Qianhai Dong Yan, Xicheng District (next to Kao Rou Ji Restaurant)
西城区前海东沿 3 号,烤肉季隔壁
☎ 6401 8541
🕒 noon to late

Starbucks 星巴克咖啡厅
Starbucks is immensely popular with Beijing's young professionals. New outlets seem to open all the time–they can be found nearly everywhere.
✉ 2/F, China World Trade Center, 1 Jianguomenwai Da Jie, Chaoyang District
朝阳区建国门外大街 1 号, 国贸大厦二层
☎ 6505 2288 ext 8122

CLUB Entrance
The 88 Club
Most bars on "Super Bar Street" share a problem: the surrounding bar infestation. But the area's greatest attraction is the man-made lake beside which Club Entrance has set up shop. Club Entrance specializes in house music, has a free pool table and expects to open their second floor patio soon.
✉ 18 Xingba lu, Nüren Jie, Chaoyang District
☎ 6465 2284
🕒 6pm to 2am

The Den 敦煌
The granddaddy of Beijing's club scene, this establishment still draws an international crowd to its second-story dance floor where DJs spin a mix of pop, house and R&B. On the ground there's a lounge/restaurant where you can grab a pizza, lasagna – or even breakfast if you're still grooving at 6am.
✉ 4 Gongti Bei Lu, Chaoyang District (beside the City Hotel)
朝阳区工体北路 4 号, 城市宾馆附近
☎ 6592 6290
🕒 9am to 3am Sunday to Thursday, 10:30am to 6am Friday to Saturday

Lotus Cafe 莲花
A spruced-up storefront with an assortment of delicious cocktails (RMB15 – 40). Their namesake, available in sweet, sour and bitter, is a must. A couple of couches can hold a party of six, and a small rooftop terrace houses additional seats.
✉ 29 Yandai Xiejie, Xicheng District
西城区烟袋斜街 29 号
☎ 6407 7857
🕒 2pm to midnight

Rock & Roll 滚石
IIn-house go-go girls put on regular performances to the mix of Cantonese techno and NRG beats. There's a karaoke bar off to the side where patrons can belt out the hits. This club is very popular with Beijing's nouveau riche.
✉ Yard 4, Gongti Bei Lu, Chaoyang District (behind The Loft, in the area near Pacific Century Place) 朝阳区工体北路 4 号院,藏酷后边,太平洋百货附近
☎ 6592 9856, 6503 4301
🕒 8pm to 5am

Vic's 威克斯
With its cheap cover and inexpensive drinks, Vic's draws a loyal, hormonally charged crowd. The pool table, summer beer garden and the sofa chill-out area offer a respite from the hot, smoky dance floor. Depending on the night, DJs will play R&B, pop, soul, reggae or hip-hop.
✉ inside the North Gate of Worker's Stadium, Chaoyang District
朝阳区工人体育场北门内
☎ 6593 6215

THEATERS
Located inside the Exhibition Center complex, this theater stages Chinese and Western plays, operas and ballets.

Beijing Exhibition Theater
北京展览馆剧场 *běijīng zhǎnlǎnguǎn jùchǎng*
✉ 135 Xizhimenwai Da Jie, Xicheng District (near the zoo) 西城区西直门外大街 135 号, 北京动物园附近
☎ 6835 4455, 6835 1383

Capital Theater 首都剧场 *shǒudū jùchǎng*
Beijing's most prestigious theater, the Capital stages big Chinese productions and the occasional foreign show.
✉ 22 Wangfujing Da Jie, Dongcheng District 东城区王府井大街 22 号
☎ 6524 9847

Lao She Teahouse
老舍茶馆 *lǎoshě cháguǎn*
Named after a famous Beijing writer, this teahouse stages shows that incorporate several traditional Chinese performing arts like magic shows, puppetry, and"cross talk." It also includes scenes of Peking opera. Tea and snacks are served during the show. You don't have to speak Chinese to enjoy the performances.
✉ 3 Qianmen Xi Da Jie, Xuanwu District (south of Tian'anmen Square) 宣武区前门西大街 3 号, 天安门广场往南
☎ 6303 6830, 6304 6334
@ www.laosheteahouse.com

Poly Theater 保利剧院 *bǎolì jùyuàn*
One of Beijing's top performance venues, Poly Theater hosts big production plays and musicals, symphonies, European operas and dances.
✉ 1/F Poly Plaza, 14 Dongzhimen Nan Da Jie, Dongcheng District 东城区东直门南大街 14 号保利大厦 1 层
☎ 6500 1188 ext 5126
@ www.polyhotel.com

Tianqiao Theater 天桥剧场 *tiānqiáo jùchǎng*
Features a variety of Beijing-style cabaret acts, such as singing, magic shows, fire-eating and "cross talk." The Tianqiao also stages touring productions of musicals and plays from abroad. When it's not staging variety shows, the Tianqiao hosts overseas productions of musicals and opera.
✉ 30 Beiwei Lu, Xuanwu District (west of the Temple of Heaven) 宣武区北纬路 30 号,天坛公园西侧
☎ 8315 6300, 8315 9893
@ www.cpaa.com.cn

ACROBATICS & MARTIAL ARTS

Universal Theater 天地剧场 *tiāndì jùchǎng*
IIt's also called Heaven and Earth Theater. The acrobats here spin plates on bamboo poles, jump through hoops, pile onto bicycles by the dozen and contort into pretzels.
✉ 10 Dongzhimen Nan Da Jie, Dongcheng District (50m north of Poly Plaza) 东城区东直门南大街 10 号, 保利大厦往北 50 米
☎ 6416 2649, 6502 2649
🕒 7:15pm to 8:45pm

Wansheng Theater
万胜剧院 *wànshèng jùyuàn*
The award winning nightly show by the Beijing Acrobatic Troupe features impressive feats of strength and agility. Performers juggle and tumble while balancing towering beams.
✉ 95 Tianqiao Shichang Jie, Xuanwu District (east end of Beiwei Lu near the Tianqiao Teahouse) 宣武区北纬路东口天桥市场街 95 号,天桥茶馆附近
☎ 6303 7449
🕒 7:15pm to 9pm

MUSIC

ROCK, JAZZ & FOLK

Cross Club 法雨 *fǎyǔ*
The kind of bar British diplomats frequented in colonial Southeast Asia. Opulent Oriental chic, salon couches draped with fox pelts, a walk-in humidor, cognac, and an abundance of thick candles and antiques. Membership nets access to the basement and third floor – the hoi polloi are relegated to floor two, where a stage hosts live jazz.
✉ 78 Sanlitun Nanlu, Chaoyang District 朝阳区三里屯南路 78 号
☎ 6586 5020

Jazz-Ya 爵士 *juéshì*
This comfortable bar and restaurant maintains the look and feel of a Japanese diner, complete with the clientele and Japanese pop music (interspersed with some great jazz). The main room has a bar and large wooden tables, while off to the side is a smaller restaurant area where they serve everything form Tokyo noodles to spaghetti carbonara and tasty Long Island ice teas.
✉ 18 Sanlitun Beilu(North Bar Street),

Chaoyang District
朝阳区三里屯北路 18 号(北酒吧街)
☎ 6415 1227
🕒 11:30am to 2am

The Star Live 星光现场 *xīngguang xiànchǎng*
The only real medium-sized live music venue in Beijing. Hosts local pop and international acts. Spread over two floors, the VIP section is upstairs while the open space on the ground floor is satisfyingly close to the stage.
✉ 3/F, Tango, 79 Heping Xijie, Dongcheng District 东城区和平西街 79 号糖果三层
☎ 6425 5166, 6426 4436

CLASSICAL

Forbidden City Concert Hall
中山音乐堂 *zhōngshān yīnyuè táng*
Visiting and local symphony orchestras regularly give performances in this hall.
✉ inside Zhongshan Park, Xi Chang'an Jie, Xicheng District (entrance is just west of Gate of Heavenly Peace)西城区西长安街中山公园内,天安门城楼西侧
☎ 6601 6364, 6559 8285

Poly Theater 保利剧院 *bǎolì jùyuàn*
✉ 1/F Poly Plaza, 14 Dongzhimen Nan Da Jie, Dongcheng District
东城区东直门南大街 14 号保利大厦 1 层
☎ 6500 1188 ext 5126
🌐 www.polyhotel.com

PEKING OPERA

Chang'an Grand Theater
长安大戏院 *cháng'ān dàxìyuàn*
The Chang'an Grand Theater offers full Peking operas on weekend evenings.
✉ 7 Jianguomennei Da Jie, Dongcheng District 东城区建国门内大街 7 号
☎ 6510 1309, 6510 1310

Lao She Teahouse
老舍茶馆 *lǎoshě cháguǎn*
✉ 3 Qianmen Xi Da Jie, Xuanwu District
宣武区前门西大街 3 号, 天安门广场往南
☎ 6303 6830, 6304 6334
🌐 www.laosheteahouse.com

Beijing's seniors practice their operatic skills in the Temple of Heaven Park.

Liyuan Theater 梨园剧场 *líyuán jùchǎng*
Action-packed excerpts of Peking operas are staged at the Liyuan making it a good place for first-timers to discover this ancient art.

✉ 1/F, Qianmen Hotel, 175 Yong'an Lu, Xuanwu District
宣武区永安路 175 号前门饭店一层
☎ 6301 6688 ext 8860 or 8864

Tianqiao Theater 天桥剧场 *tiānqiáo jùchǎng*
✉ 30 Beiwei Lu, Xuanwu District (west of the Temple of Heaven)
宣武区北纬路 30 号,天坛公园西侧
☎ 8315 6300, 8315 9893
🌐 www.cpaa.com.cn

Souvenirs

Shopping in Beijing is tremendously rewarding. Visitors will find the best products that China has to offer in the capital's stores while exploring a wide variety of interesting shopping venues like outdoor markets, small boutiques and luxury malls.

Prices in Beijing are generally very competitive, but that can depend on your bargaining skills. In places like department stores, prices are clearly marked and generally non-negotiable. Conversely, in markets, bazaars and shops where prices are not indicated, haggling is expected.

Potentially worse than paying too much is buying something that's mislabeled. Many of the pieces in markets like Liulichang and Panjiayuan are antique reproductions, not genuine antiques. A well-made antique reproduction can make a lovely purchase, so long as you don't pay an exorbitant sum to acquire it. Bear in mind that genuine antiques should have a red seal at the bottom indicating that they're authentic and can be exported from China. However, antiques dated before 1795 can't leave the country. Goods made after 1949 aren't considered antiques and won't have a seal. Be sure to keep your receipts since you may have to show them when departing China.

Beijing's contemporary art scene is among the most exciting in the world, and commands international attention. Fortunately, paintings and prints by Chinese artists are far more affordable in China than they are overseas. Moreover, they are among the most original purchases you can make in the city and, if history is any guide, their value can appreciate significantly.

Among Beijing's best buys are art, antiques and reproductions, carpets, clothes, handicrafts, jewelry, silk and tea. You can acquire these goods and more at the following locations, listed in alphabetical order. Please note that the prices quoted below may be subject to change. You can also visit www.GalleriaPangea.com for authentic Chinese art and handicrafts.

Aduowei 阿多韦 *āduōwéi*
This boutique features clothes, jewelry and accessories inspired by the designs of southwestern China's Miao ethnic minority. The most eye-catching and expensive item during a recent visit was a green qipao (Chinese dress) made out of the traditional cloud-patterned brocade once worn by emperors (RMB 18,800). A white business suit with a traditional collar is a more affordable RMB 1,200. Coral and amber necklaces cost RMB 100 to 580, while handbags with floral embroidery cost RMB 680.

✉ Room 2010, Ritan Office Building, 15A Guanghua Lu, Chaoyang District
朝阳区光华路甲 15 号日坛商务楼 2010 房间
☎ 8859 8525
🕒 10am to 8pm

Antique Carpets 古董地毯 *gǔdǒng ditǎn*
This store sells genuine handcrafted antique carpets from all over China. The most stunning rugs come from Muslim oasis towns, like Khotan (Hetian) and Yarkand (Shache), in China's Xinjiang Uyghur Autonomous Region. Though prices here are high, starting at several thousand RMB, consider that a well-made antique rug is an investment that could outlive you by decades. Factors that determine the value of a carpet include its age, the quality of its knitting, the purity of its wool and dyes, and the manner in which it was made (i.e. by hand or machine).

✉ A6 Gongti Donglu, Chaoyang District (in the cluster of shops near the City Hotel, due east of the Workers' Stadium)
朝阳区工体东路甲 6 号,城市宾馆附近
☎ 6463 1669

Chaowai Furniture Warehouse

北京兆佳朝外古典家具市场 *běijīng zhàojiā cháowài gǔdiǎn jiājù shìchǎng*

An ex-pat favorite, Chaowai is a four-storey building crammed wall-to-wall with stalls selling furniture and decorative items like vases, statuettes (RMB 70 for a Buddha head) and bird cages (RMB 200 and up). Most of the pieces are reproductions, but they look great and are reasonably priced. If you buy something that's too big to fit in your suitcase, the vendors can arrange to ship it home. One of the better-known firms that has a showroom in Chaowai is Wanyou (Showroom 47, ☎ 6771 0087). You can combine visits to Chaowai and nearby the Panjiayuan.

✉ 43 Huawei Bei Li, Dongsanhuan Bei Lu, Chaoyang District
朝阳区东三环北路华威北里 43 号

☏ 6770 6402

China World Trade Center

国贸购物中心 *guómào gòuwù zhōngxīn*

Known by expats as Guomao, this shopping center is extremely fashionable thanks to stores like Mocchino, Louis Vuitton, Prada and Shanghai Tang. More affordable offerings are found in such shops as Max & Co., BCBG, Esprit and Red Earth makeup. You'll also find an artsy bookstore, children's shops, a CRC (foreign grocery) supermarket, a wine shop, Starbucks, Baskin Robbins and several restaurants, including Aria (in the China World Hotel). There's even an ice rink in the basement.

✉ China World Trade Center，1 Jianguomenwai Da Jie, Chaoyang District
朝阳区建国门外大街 1 号国贸购物中心

☏ 6505 2288

Friendship Store 友谊商店 *yǒuyì shāngdiàn*

This government-run department store aimed at tourists sells imported goods, groceries, English books and magazines, and a wealth of Chinese arts and crafts. This is a good one-stop destination for souvenirs like silks, porcelain, carpets, paintings, cloisonné, embroidery, antiques and jewelry. Though prices here are higher than at the markets, quality is guaranteed and there's a shipping department to handle bulky purchases.

✉ 17 Jianguomenwai Da Jie, Chaoyang District 朝阳区建国门外大街 17 号

☏ 6500 3311

Gold Finger Jewellery Design Workshop

金枫阁首饰铭刻工作室 *jīnfēnggé shǒushì míngkè gōngzuòshì*

This workshop can engrave all kinds of characters inside the wedding rings.

✉ A1006 Yuanyang Deyi Commercial Garden, Guangqumen, Chongwen District
崇文区广渠门远洋德邑商务花园 A1006 室

☏ 8775 7177

@ ring@fashion.cn

Hongqiao Market—The Pearl Market

红桥市场 *hóngqiáo shìchǎng*

Hongqiao is a shopping Mecca with individual stall holders selling clothes, suitcases, shoes, jewelry, cloisonné, old watches, vintage cameras, porcelain, jade, teapots, Cultural Revolution memorabilia and more. Hongqiao is most famous for its cultured pearls, which are much cheaper than they are in the West. When buying pearls, consider their luster, surface, shape and size. Real pearls should feel cooler and more grainy than fakes. If you want to design your own necklace, most shops can accommodate you in less than 24 hours. A " Jackie Kennedy" style necklace with three strands of pearls should cost RMB 500, but baby pearl necklaces are as cheap as RMB 20 each.

✉ Tiantan Dong Lu, Chongwen District (across from the east gate of the Temple of Heaven)
崇文区天坛东路天坛公园东门对面

☏ 6711 7429

Iris Tea Street

马连道茶叶街 *mǎliándào cháyèjiē*

This nearly mile-long (1,500 m) thoroughfare contains eight wholesale tea markets and more than 600 teashops selling over 500 kinds of tea. Average tea prices, which are around 30% to 50% cheaper than in other locales, hover around RMB 30 per jin (half kilo, or about 1.1 pounds). Top teas, like Dragon Well Tea from Hangzhou, cost RMB 200 per jin. Ceramic and cloisonné, teapot-and-cup sets average RMB 60.

✉ Malian Dao, Xuanwu District 宣武区马连道

Liangma Antique Market 亮马收藏品市场 *liàngmǎ shōucángpǐn shìchǎng*
The vendors in this indoor market sell porcelain, jade, paintings, calligraphy, Chinese lamps, furniture, Buddhist statues, and curios like snuff bottles. Some of the goods are reproductions and some are genuine antiques. The shop owners are less pushy than in other markets, but you should still bargain over the price. A favorite is the store run by the English-speaking Mr. Cui Zhiqian (Stall A112, ☎ 136 5103 2336). He sells antique and contemporary rugs from Tibet, Xinjiang, Inner Mongolia and eastern China. His prices for antique carpets range from RMB 2,300 for a small Tibetan prayer rug to RMB 9,500 for a handsome Muslim-style carpet from Ningxia in western China.
✉ 27 Liangma Lu, Chaoyang District
朝阳区亮马路 27 号
☎ 6467 9664

Liulichang 琉璃厂 *liúlíchǎng*
Spreading across both sides of Nanxinhua Jie, the Liulichang neighborhood is filled with stores selling art, antiques, antique reproductions and handicrafts. These include shadow puppets, ceramics, seals, opium pipes, paper lanterns, cloisonné and Buddha statues. The area's most famous store is Rongbaozhai (荣宝斋 19 Liulichang Xi Jie 琉璃厂西街 19 号), which stocks supplies for the scholar, gentleman and artist, like ink stones – shallow basins in which ink blocks are mixed with water – calligraphy brushes, seals, paper and scrolls as well as lacquer boxes and paintings. Other stores worth visiting are the Cathay Bookshop (中国书店 115 Nanxinhua Jie 南新华街 115 号) and Jiguge (汲古阁 136 Liulichang Dong Jie 琉璃厂东街 136 号).
✉ the intersection of Liulichang Xi Jie and Nanxinhua Jie, one block south of Qianmen Xi Da Jie
琉璃厂西街和南新华街交叉路口

Lizhi 励智 *lìzhì*
Lizhi stocks an excellent assortment of porcelain lamps and silk "palace" lanterns for RMB 150 and up. Nearby stores sell planters, vases and other chinoiserie.
✉ 12 Liangma Flower Market, Chaoyang District (on the south bank of the Liangma River, across from the Lufthansa Center)
朝阳区亮马花卉市场 12 号，亮马河南岸，燕莎商城旁边
☎ 6586 8551

Lufthansa Center
燕莎商城 *yànshā shāngchéng*
The Lufthansa Center was the first Western-style department store built in Beijing. As its name implies, the shopping experience here is similar to an airport. You'll find tourist trinkets, perfume, books and expensive brand-name goods. That said, with so much under one roof, the Lufthansa is a very practical place to shop.
✉ 50 Liangmaqiao Lu, Chaoyang District
朝阳区亮马桥路 50 号
☎ 6465 1188, 6465 3388

Panjiayuan Flea Market
潘家园旧货市场 *pānjiāyuán jiùhuò shìchǎng*
If you only shop in one place in Beijing, let it be Panjiayuan. This recently remodeled market is home to over 3,000 dealers who scour China's countryside in search of antiques, family heirlooms and curios. Many of them arrive in Beijing on early Saturday mornings and head straight to Panjiayuan. Since they are eager to make their first sales, Beijing's best bargains are offered early on weekend mornings – between 6:30am and 8:30am. After that, more shoppers arrive and prices go up. During weekdays, the market is a shadow of its weekend self.

Some dealers have stalls, others have actual shops and the remainder sell their goods outside Panjiayuan's east wall. On offer is a galaxy of attractive items, most of which were made in the last 80 years. There are Qing dynasty antiques but these are rare and may be hard for the untrained eye to distinguish.

Prices here are lower than anywhere else in Beijing. Popular items include china plates for RMB 15 and up; carved wood such as brush holders RMB 60 each, statues of Guanyin for RMB 250; pottery vases for RMB 40, opium pipes for RMB 80, carpets at RMB 400, calligraphy brushes for RMB 30, calligraphy scrolls at RMB 50, embroidered pillow cases for RMB 50, old Chinese jackets around RMB 100. You'll also find lots of jewelry and jade, though real jade can be hard to identify – it should be cool and harder than glass (try to scratch a piece of glass with it).

✉ Panjiayuan Qiao, Chaoyang District, (just inside the southeast Third Ring Road) 朝阳区潘家园桥

☎ 6775 2405

Peninsula Palace Hotel Shopping Arcade 王府饭店地下商场 *wángfǔ fàndiàn dìxià shāngchǎng*

This Versailles of fashion is home to such royalty as Dior, Chanel, Gucci, Hermes and Versace. And if shoes, clothes and handbags don't sate your appetite for luxury, the hotel's Cartier and Tiffany outlets can drape you in gold and diamonds. Prices tags shouldn't be read by the faint of heart.

✉ Peninsula Palace Hotel, 8 Jinyu Hutong, Wangfujing, Dongcheng District 东城区王府井金鱼胡同 8 号王府饭店地下

☎ 6559 2888

Qianxiangyi 谦祥益丝绸有限责任公司 *qiānxiángyì sīchóu yǒuxiàn zérèn gōngsī*

Established in 1840, this is one of the most reputable silk shops in Beijing. The ground floor has a huge selection of silk bolts that are RMB 40 to 120 per meter. The 2nd floor has shirts, dresses, negligees, pajamas and gorgeous tapestries. The tapestries can cost as much as RMB 10,000 each. The store's tailors can custom-fit or design traditional *qipaos* (旗袍, Chinese dresses).

✉ 5 Zhubaoshi Jie, Xuanwu District (southwest of Qianmen) 宣武区珠宝市街 5 号,前门西南

☎ 6301 6658

Red Phoenix 红凤凰 *hóng fènghuáng*

This boutique sells exquisite clothes that update traditional designs with modern colors to a clientele of pop stars, business leaders and visiting dignitaries like Hillary Clinton. Gu Lin, the designer, creates her own fabrics by using traditional techniques like blowing smoke on silk. She's fastidious about the quality of the stitching and knows how to have fun: buttons are plush velvet swirls; cuffs are scallop-shaped. You can buy off-the-rack or, if you can wait ten days or so, have something custom-tailored for you. Prices of *qipao* dresses average RMB 1,000 to 4,000.

✉ North 30 Building, Sanlitun Lu, Chaoyang District (northern end of the Sanlitun strip near Dongzhimen) 朝阳区三里屯北 30 楼

☎ 6417 3591

Tibet Shop 爱尔屋 *ài'ěr wū*

This small shop specializes in colorful hand-woven Tibetan rugs. Their narrowness reflects their original function as portable, single occupancy, bedding for the nomadic Tibetans. They're commonly decorated with religious medallions, dragons and tigers to ward off evil spirits. Most carpets here are reproductions and cost RMB 500 and up. The shop also stocks attractive Tibetan necklaces designed by the friendly English-speaking owner, You Tao, made of bone, amber, agate and crystal are RMB 50 and up. Rice paper lamps make great and inexpensive gifts at RMB 20.

✉ South Building 37, Flat 1, Room 2, North Sanlitun, Chaoyang District 朝阳区北三里屯南 37 楼 1 单元 2 号

☎ 6417 5963

Wangfujing 王府井 *wángfǔjǐng*

Beijing's most famous shopping district is this pedestrian only street in the center of town. It's girded on its northern and southern ends by two mega malls: Sun Dong'an Plaza and Oriental Plaza. There are several souvenir shops on Wangfujing as well as Beijing's largest children's store. In the evening, a lively food market sets up on nearby Donghuamen Da Jie (the avenue that crosses Wangfujing near Sun Dong'an Plaza) where you can feast on a multitude of inexpensive Chinese snacks. Even if you don't buy anything, Wangfujing is a great place to stroll and people-watch. Some visitors are approached by English-speaking "art students" trying to interest them in paintings that, it often turns out, are grossly overpriced.

✉ Wangfujing, Dongcheng District 东城区王府井

Yaxiu Clothing Market 雅秀服装市场 *yǎxiù fúzhuāng shìchǎng*

Very popular with foreigners for its "real name-brand" clothes and accessories (e.g. jeans for RMB 100, jackets for RMB 280), Yaxiu market also sells souvenir T-shirts for RMB 40, antique-style pillowcases are RMB 25, cloisonné kites (RMB 25), porcelain

Dressing up as his imperial highness and consort.

sculptures (six small horses for RMB 90), jade (rings for RMB 60), sports equipment and more. There are many silk shops on the third floor including Ruifuxiang (瑞蚨祥). These sell bolts as well as ties for RMB 10, suits and traditional Chinese garments (RMB 250 and up for a *qipao*). There are tailors on-site who can custom make items for you.

✉ 58 Gongti Bei Lu, Chaoyang District
朝阳区工体北路 58 号

☎ 6413 2722, 6415 4548

Health

WESTERN MEDICINE

The following medical institutions are staffed by qualified, English-speaking foreign and foreign-trained doctors and nurses. They serve the foreign community and offer a level of basic care that's comparable to the West. Moreover, these institutions all have onsite pharmacies stocked with a full range of western medicine.

With the exception of state-run Peking Union Medical Hospital, the prices charged by these private institutions are also on par with fees in the West (e.g. US $100 for a 20-minute consultation). Therefore, visitors are strongly recommended to have medical insurance. Most medical institutions in Beijing require payment up-front, in cash or by credit card, and the patient must subsequently apply to their insurance company for reimbursement.

Though appointments aren't necessary to see a general practitioner, they can save you a long wait. Appointments will be necessary if you need to see a specialist.

Bayley & Jackson Medical Center
庇利积臣医疗中心 *bìlìjīchén yīliáo zhōngxīn*
✉ 7 Ritan Dong Lu, Chaoyang District
朝阳区日坛东路 7 号
☎ 8562 9998
🌐 www.bjhealthcare.com

Beijing International SOS Clinic
北京国际紧急 SOS 救援中心
běijīng guójì jǐnjí SOS jiùyuán zhōngxīn
✉ Building C, BITIC Leasing Center, Xingfu SanCun,1 BeiJie, Chaoyang District (just north of the Spanish embassy)
朝阳区幸福三村北街 1 号北信租赁中心 C 座 (西班牙大使馆北面)
☎ 6462 9112
@ China.inquiries@internationalsos.com
🌐 www.internationalsos.com

Beijing United Family Hospital
北京和睦家医院 *běijīng hémùjiā yīyuàn*
✉ 2 Jiangtai Lu, Chaoyang District
朝阳区将台路 2 号
☎ 6433 3960
@ bjunited@bjunited.com.cn
🌐 www.bjunited.com.cn

International Medical Center 北京国际医疗中心 *běijīng guójì yīliáo zhōngxīn*
✉ Room 106, Lufthansa Center, 50 Liangmaqiao Lu, Chaoyang District 朝阳区亮马桥路 50 号燕莎中心办公楼 106 室
☎ 6465 1561

Peking Union Medical Hospital
协和医院 *xiéhé yīyuàn*
✉ 53 Dongdan Bei Da Jie, Dongcheng District, 东城区东单北大街 53 号⑯
☎ 6529 5284
🌐 pumch.salu.net

BODY & FOOT MASSAGE

After a long day spent climbing the Great Wall or negotiating a hard deal, a body or foot massage is heavenly.

Aibosen 爱博森盲人按摩医院 *àibósēn mángrén ànmó yīyuàn*
Like many of China's top massage artists, the masseurs here are blind. A body massage costs RMB 88 for 50 minutes, while a foot massage costs RMB 88 for 70 minutes. Fresh coffee and an English-speaking manager complement the experience.
✉ 11 Liufang Bei Li, Chaoyang District
朝阳区柳芳北里 11 号
☎ 6466 1247, 6465 2044
✉ Building 11, Area 2, Anzhen Xi Li, Chaoyang District
朝阳区安贞西里 2 区 11 号楼
☎ 6445 2015, 6445 2016
🕒 1pm to 1am

Beijing Magic Foot Massage 北京妙手健身中心 *běijīng miàoshǒu jiànshēn zhōngxīn*
Soothe your aching feet here, RMB 88 for a 90-minute massage.
✉ 6/F, 1 Xiagongfu, Gangmei Dasha, Dongcheng District (behind the Beijing Hotel) 东城区港美大厦霞公府 1 号 6 楼，北京饭店后面
☎ 6512 0868

Heping Keep-fit Massage Center
和平盲人保健按摩中心 *hépíng mángrén bǎojiàn ànmó zhōngxīn*
The rubdowns are performed by traditional Chinese medicine practitioners and cost RMB 150 per hour for body massages and RMB 100 per hour for foot massages.
✉ 6 Fangyuan Xi Lu, Chaoyang District
朝阳区芳圆西路 6 号
☎ 6436 7370
🕒 noon to 1am

Oriental Health Land
东方康乐园 *dōngfāng kānglèyuán*
This Japanese owned establishment has single-sex baths along with Chinese and Japanese-style traditional massage.
✉ Dongzhimenwai Xie Jie, Chaoyang District 朝阳区东直门外斜街

☎ 6466 1302
☎ 6466 1301 (Fax)
🕒 24 hours

BEAUTY SALONS

The following salons will leave you looking fa-bu-lous. Please note that many hotels also have in-house hair stylists.

Atlantis Beauty Club 艾伦台丝 *àilún táisī*

This fancy day spa offers facials, body waxing, manicures and pedicures.

✉ 6 Guanghua Lu, Chaoyang District (near the Kelun building)
朝阳区光华路 6 号, 科伦大厦附近
☎ 6583 0382

Clarins
娇韵诗美容院 *jiāoyùnshī měiróngyuàn*

This salon purportedly offers Beijing's most luxurious beauty treatments, using only Clarins products.

✉ Basement, Peninsula Palace Hotel, 8 Jinyu Hutong, Wangfujing, Dongcheng District 东城区王府井金鱼胡同 8 号王府饭店地下一层
☎ 8516 2888 ext 3564

Eric's of Paris
爱丽克美发中心 *àilìkè měifà zhōngxīn*

Opened by a French stylist, this is the fanciest hair salon in the city. Depending on who does it, a haircut can cost upwards of RMB 400, while a full coloring job cost RMB 840.

✉ Kerry Center, 1 Guanghua Lu, Chaoyang District 朝阳区光华路 1 号嘉里中心
☎ 8529 9423

Toni & Guy

This is the Beijing outpost of the famous British hair salon chain. Haircuts cost RMB 120 to 420, depending on the stylist, while perms and colorings cost RMB 300. Cheaper cuts start at missing text (missing in book also) Toni & Guy hair care products are sold here.

✉ 9 Guanghua Xi Lu near Dongdaqiao
光华西路 9 号，东大桥附近
☎ 6586 4315

Other Information

POST OFFICES

Asian Game Village Post Office 亚运村邮局

✉ Asian Game Village 亚运村
☎ 6491 0050

Beijing Customer Service Center
北京邮政客户服务中心

Offers a variety of services such as postal code search, postal complaints and plane and performance ticket reservations.

☎ 185, then 4 to reach an operator

Ganshiqiao Post Office 甘石桥邮局

✉ 100 Xidan Bei Da Jie 西单北大街 100 号
☎ 6602 2403

Jiannei Da Jie Post Office 建内大街邮局

✉ 1 Jianguomen Nei Da Jie
建国门内大街 1 号 ⑰
☎ 6519 6644

Qianmen Da Jie Post Office 前门大街邮局

✉ 90 Qianmen Da Jie 前门大街 90 号
☎ 6702 0669

Wanfujing Post Office 王府井邮局

✉ 45 Dong'anmen Da Jie 东安门大街 45 号
☎ 6512 9645

Zhongguancun Post Office 中关村邮局

✉ 9 Zhongguancun Da Jie 中关村大街 9 号
☎ 6265 3813

MOBILE PHONES

You can rent a cell phone or SIM card while in Beijing from one of the following companies:

Phonerent

Cell phones cost RMB 120 per day, inclusive of all local calls. On top of this, expect to pay an RMB 1,000 prepayment for long distance calls and an RMB 1,800 refundable deposit for the phone itself. If you already have a GSM phone, you can simply rent a local SIM card. Reservations online.

✉ Jinzhiqiao Dasha (near China World), A1 Jianwai Da Jie, Chaoyang District
朝阳区建国门外大街甲 1 号金之桥大厦(中国大饭店附近)
☎ 6586 6669
@ www.phonerent.com

Tourfone

Order your cell phone online or by fax. Rates vary but begin at US $10, which includes 5 days, with subsequent days at US $2 per day.

2/F, 216 Chaoyangmennei Da Jie, Dongcheng District
东城区朝阳门内大街 216 号 2 层
6528 9495
www.tourfone.com

EMBASSIES

Most embassies are clustered in two Beijing neighborhoods, Sanlitun (三里屯) and Jianguomenwai (建国门外). At the time of writing, some nations were planning to move their embassies to a new diplomatic district near the Lufthansa Center outside the northwest Third Ring Road. Therefore, it might be wise to call ahead before visiting your embassy.

Another reason to phone in advance is that most embassies' consular, commercial and visa sections are only open a few hours each day. Emergency assistance, on the other hand, is generally available 24 hours a day. Please note that visitors must show a valid passport to enter most embassies. If you don't find your embassy below, check one of the free local English magazines or a quick search online should get you their contact information.

Australia 澳大利亚
21 Dongzhimenwai Da Jie, Chaoyang District 朝阳区东直门外大街 21 号
6532 2331
6532 4349 (Fax)
www.austemb.org.cn

Canada 加拿大
19 Dongzhimenwai Da Jie, Chaoyang District 朝阳区东直门外大街 19 号
6532 3536
6532 4072 (Fax)
www.beijing.gc.ca

France 法国
3 Dong San Jie, Sanlitun, Chaoyang District 朝阳区三里屯东三街 3 号
6532 1331
6532 4841 (Fax)
www.ambafrance-cn.org

Germany 德国
17 Dongzhimenwai Da Jie, Sanlitun, Chaoyang District
朝阳区三里屯东直门外大街 17 号
6532 2161
6532 5336 (Fax)
www.deutschebotschaft-china.org

Ireland 爱尔兰
3, Ritan Dong Lu, Jianguomenwai, Chaoyang District
朝阳区建国门外日坛东路 3 号
6532 2691
6532 6857 (Fax)
www.ireland-china.com.cn

New Zealand 新西兰
1, 21 Jie, Ritan Dong Lu, Jianguomenwai, Chaoyang District
朝阳区建国门外日坛东路 21 街 1 号
6532 2731
6532 4317 (Fax)
www.nzembassy.com/china

United Kingdom of Great Britain and Northern Ireland 英国
11 Guanghua Lu, Jianguomenwai, Chaoyang District
朝阳区建国门外光华路 11 号
6532 1961
6532 1937 (Fax)
ww.britishembassy.org.cn

United States of America 美国
3 Xiushui Bei Jie, Jianguomenwai, Chaoyang District
朝阳区建国门外秀水北街 3 号
6532 3831
6532 5141 (Fax)
www.usembassy-china.org.cn

NORTHEAST CHINA

Harbin's Frozen Beauty

Area Code 0451

IIn the winter **Harbin** comes alive-sculptures and buildings rise up out of the ice that grips the city. Snow, ice castles and a frozen river – it's a glittering spectacle that's well worth the risk of a little frostbite.

If you tell a Chinese person you're going to Harbin, they'll most likely shudder and encourage you to alter your plans: "Too cold," they'll say. Despite that, it's not too cold for the three million people who live in this city perched up in far northeastern Heilongjiang Province. Tradition has it that China is shaped like a rooster, Heilongjiang being the head and Harbin the eye and the city retains important unique features and a peculiar charm that you won't find anywhere else in the country.

Harbin was just a tiny town in China's northeast for hundreds of years – until at the end of the 19th century the Russians decided they wanted to build a railway from Moscow to Vladivostok. The railway was laid in 1896 when the Chinese government was forced to grant Russia a concession at Harbin, which quickly grew to dwarf the old Chinese town. After the Russian Revolution in 1917, thousands of White Russian refugees crossed the **Black Dragon River**, better known in the west as the Amur River. At one stage around 160,000 foreigners from 33 countries were living in the city and they set up well over 1,000 companies, including China's first beer brewery in 1900. The city soon became known as the "Moscow of the East," and at only seven days train journey from Paris was proud to know the latest fashions well before Shanghai or Hong Kong.

Snow sculptures at Sun Island Park.

Much of the Russian architecture remains standing today and one of the prime attractions of the city is a walk along the **Central Street** (*zhōngyāng dàjiē* 中央大街). There are buildings of most European early twentieth-century styles along the length of this cobbled street, which remains today the most popular shopping area of the city. While McDonalds, KFC, and Western stores have redecorated most of the interiors, there are some buildings that have survived that kind of unfortunate modernization and still look and feel quite European.

Central Street is found in **Daoli District**, which was where the majority of the foreigners settled. It is now the center of the municipal government offices and the site of most of the best sightseeing opportunities in Harbin. Strolling around the area you will find a little Russian chocolate shop, Russian gift-stores, coffee shops and some of the most expensive restaurants in town.

To the east of the Central Street, surrounded on all sides by modern department stores, you will find the **Church of St. Sophia** (*shèng suǒfēiyà jiàotáng* 圣索菲亚教堂), a lovely Orthodox church that is Harbin's most famous landmark. It was badly

A Russian-style house overlooks the frigid Songhua River.

damaged during the cultural revolution but later restored to its original 1907 splendor. Inside there is a little photographic exhibition tracing some of Harbin's history, but most people report being disappointed with what they get to see for their RMB 10. There are a number of other Orthodox churches you will find around the city center that are worth a few minute's look, though none are as impressive as St. Sophia's.

Walking along the river is entertaining any time of the year and whether you're watching the locals paddle rented boats in summer or trying to remember how to ice-skate in the winter, there's plenty to do to occupy a few hours. There's the odd toboggan for hire if you're feeling brave. A more sedate pursuit is to wait for the old woman with scissors to find you – for just RMB 1 or 2 she'll cut a perfect profile of you in some colored paper. For those with antifreeze for blood, you can speak to local guides about finding a hole in the ice for swimming – but there are no saunas here to run into after your dip, so it is fairly likely you will catch severe hypothermia. In case you were thinking that it was a tradition, then be assured that the locals think the winter swimmers are all *feng le* – crazy.

Across the river, taking either the ferry or a taxi, you'll find **Sun Island Park** (*tàiyáng dǎo gōngyuán* 太阳岛公园), which was once the retreat of choice for Harbin residents in the hot summer. A huge park with plenty of green to counteract the gray palette of the city's apartment blocks, it's pleasant to stroll around when sunny, though it really comes into its own when snow falls and the yearly sculpture exhibition moves in. This is the artistic high point of the winter season, with the snow sculptures (ice covered with compressed snow) being crafted by artists from around the world. From small figures to 30-foot-wide panoramas, the artists try to out do each other year after year. There are also a number of "ice-games" you can play in the park, and for a few RMB you can hire sleds drawn by huskies.

If animals are indeed your thing, then you might want to take a look at the **Siberian**

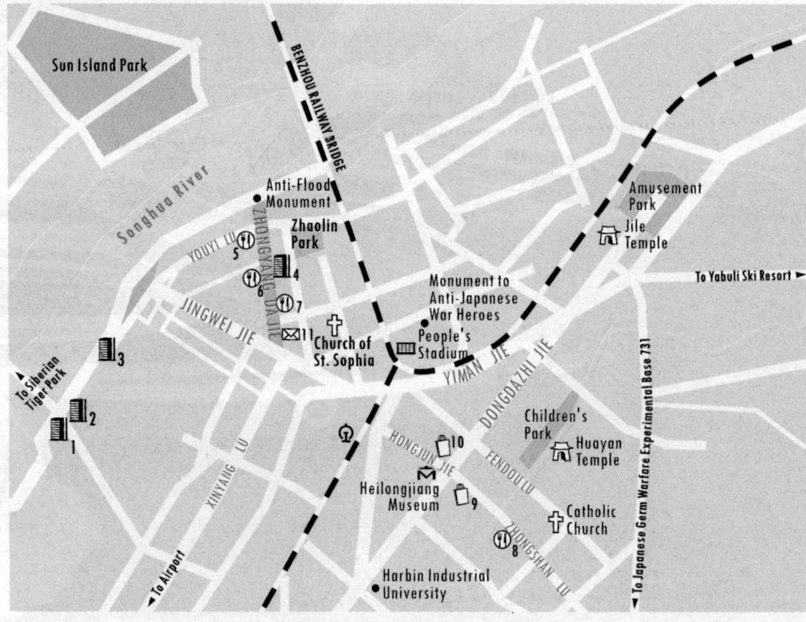

Tiger Park (*dōngběihǔ línyuán* 东北虎林园). A little more than 9 miles (15 km) further north than Sun Island Park. Here you can find about three hundred Siberian tigers, lions and other big cats. There are only an estimated 700 Siberian tigers left in the wild, so Harbin's park is an important breeding base, though rather unusual in that it allows visitors to purchase the food that's thrown to the cats. You can buy a chicken, bits of beef or even a whole deer and in a circling and shaky bus, watch the tigers enjoy their meal. Critics argue that this practice associates tourists with feeding-time.

A very important but highly unpleasant site for the people of Harbin is the **Japanese Germ Warfare Experimental Base 731** (*rìběn xìjūn shíyàn jīdì 731 bùduì* 日本细菌试验基地 731 部队). Harbin and the rest of northeast China made up part of the Japanese puppet state Manchukuo after the Japanese invasion in 1931 and in 1939, Division 731 constructed a top-secret base to study germ warfare. Prisoners of war and anyone who had the misfortune of being captured were used as living subjects for horrific medical "experiments." Over 40,000 people were tortured then killed in ways as savage and cruel as vivisection and roasting to death. Anger remains about Japan's record during the Second World War and old chemical weapons continue to be dug up. Base 731 can be reached 12.4 miles (20 km) south of Harbin and the small exhibition displays some of the implements used in the tortures. The base was only discovered in the 1980's.

Memorable Experiences

Wandering down Central Street and stopping at a Russian café for a coffee and croissant.

Watching everyone walking on the frozen Songhua River, flying kites, skating, having horse rides and buying an ice cream from an open box laid on the street.

On approaching the Ice Lantern Festival, realizing that the castle you can see is made entirely out of ice, and big enough that you can enter it.

The **Ice Lantern Festival** (*bīngdēng jié* 冰灯节) is the fun highlight of the year in Harbin. Held in **Zhaolin Park** (*zhàolín gōngyuán* 兆麟公园) in Daoli district, teams of workers transport large chunks of ice taken from further north along the Songhua River (thanks to global warming, increasingly further) and carve it into shapes or whole buildings. Neon tubes are inserted inside the ice, and then the whole thing is lit up in luminescent blues, pinks, green and yellows. It's like a frozen Disneyworld and they often build replicas of famous buildings from around the world: Big Ben; the Eiffel Tower; the Taj Mahal; and, of course, a stretch of the Great Wall. There are also a few vertiginously high ice slides you can slide down, an ice maze, and an "ice forest," where the trees are covered with a spider's web of icicles. It is all wonderfully surreal, and there are endless photos to take, if your camera does not freeze. ■

Making Your Trip Easy

Practical Tips

Winters in Harbin are extremely cold, regularly going down to -22°F (-30°C), but January to March is also the best time to visit the city. The Ski Festival is on December 26 and the International Ice Festival takes place annually on January 5. Remember to pack thermal underwear and as many layers of clothing as you can. Gloves, hats, scarves, shoe-insulators – are all widely available on the streets and you'll need to wear them all. The good news is that buildings are well heated. Harbin is a little cooler than most other cities in China if you come during the summer, though it still reaches 90°F (32°C) on hot days.

Transportation

Airport – The airport is approximately 19 miles (30 km) outside of town. There are airport shuttle buses to the city, a taxi should cost about RMB 120, which includes a RMB 20 highway toll. The ride into town will take 30 to 45 minutes. The city has many domestic connections and some international flights to, among other cities, Seoul and Vladivostok.

Taxi – Most taxi rides around Harbin will cost about RMB 20. Motorcycle taxis charge around RMB 6 per trip. Full-size taxis are RMB 8 at flag-fall and compact taxis are RMB 7. The smaller taxis are slightly cheaper per kilometer.

The Best of Harbin

Church of St. Sophia
圣索菲亚教堂 *shèng suǒfēiyà jiàotáng*
✉ Zhaolin Jie 兆麟街
🕒 9:30am to 5:30pm
¥ 25 to enter the small exhibition inside

Siberian Tiger Park 黑龙江东北虎林园
hēilóngjiāng dōngběihǔ línyuán
✉ 88 Songbei Jie, Daowai District
道外区松北街 88 号

Over 40 years of Ice Festivals have been celebrated at Harbin.

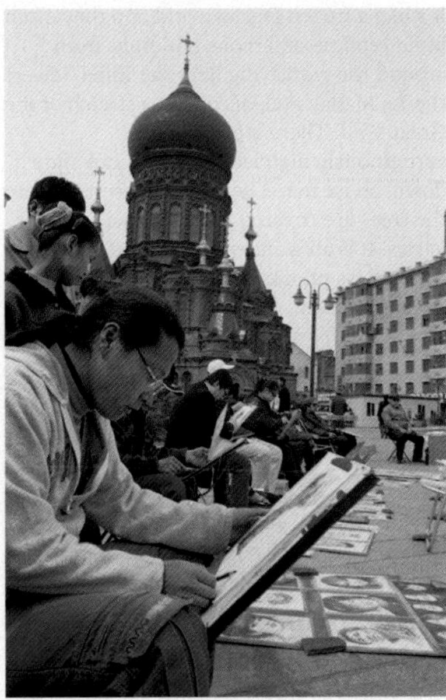

Church of St. Sophia inspires local artists.

☎ 8808 0098
⏲ 9am to 4pm during the winter
8:30am to 6pm during the summer
¥ 50

Sun Island Park
太阳岛公园 *tàiyángdǎo gōngyuán*
✉ eastern end of Sun Island 太阳岛东区
☎ 8819 1181
⏲ 8am to 9pm
¥ 50

Hotels

Shangri-La Hotel Harbin
哈尔滨香格里拉大饭店 *hā'ěrbīn xiānggélǐlā dàfàndiàn* ★★★★★
✉ 555 Youyi Lu, Daoli District
道里区友谊路 555 号❷
☎ 8485 8888, 8462 1333
¥ 880 – double room, peak-season
580 – double room, off-season
@ www.shangri-La.com

Singapore Hotel
新加坡大酒店 *xīnjiāpō dàjiǔdiàn* ★★★★★
✉ 68 Ganshui Lu, Xiangfang District
香坊区赣水路 68 号
☎ 8233 6888, 8233 1668
¥ 688 – double room, peak-season
669 – double room, off-season
@ www.harbinsingaporehtl.com

Press Plaza
报业大厦 *bàoyè dàshà* ★★★★
✉ 399 Youyi Lu, Daoli District
道里区友谊路 399 号❸
☎ 8489 0888, 8489 0757
¥ 400 – double room

Rongfu Conifer Hotel 融府康年酒店 *róngfǔ kāngnián jiǔdiàn* ★★★★
✉ 88 Heqing Jie, Daoli District
道里区河清街 88 号❶
☎ 8483 6888, 8483 1066
¥ 688 – double room, peak-season
388 – double room, off-season
@ rongfu@publk.hr.hl.cn

Modern Hotel
马迭尔宾馆 *mǎdié'ěr bīnguǎn* ★★★
✉ 89 Zhongyang Dajie, Daoli District
道里区中央大街 89 号❹
☎ 8461 5846, 8488 4099
¥ 464 – double room,peak-season
348 – double room,off-season
@ www.modern.com.cn

Food & Restaurants

Harbin's fare is suited to the people who live there: simple, solid and warming. There are plenty of meat-on-sticks (*ròu chuànr* 肉串) restaurants, as well as Mongolian lamb hotpot (*huǒguō* 火锅) from their north-western neighbors. Dumplings (*jiǎozi* 饺子)

Quotes

"I didn't think people could live in this kind of cold, but they do, and they seem to be proud of the fact!"

"The monuments made out of ice were one of the strangest and amazing things I have ever seen. They were more colorful than I imagined and great fun to slip and slide around in."

are also hugely popular and there are a number of chains around the city serving them up with countless imaginative fillings. But unique to China, it's the foreign cuisine that's best sampled in Harbin. Russian and Russian influenced Western restaurants will lead you to the most surprising tastes. A side of European-style smoked pork sausages (*ròulián hóngcháng* 肉联红肠) washed down with Harbin Beer (*hā'ěrbīn píjiǔ* 哈尔滨啤酒 or *hāpí* 哈啤) or even some chilled vodka is a great way to fill up and keep warm. For beer enthusiasts, there's *qiulin damianbao* (秋林大面包), a gigantic circular bread baked with a crispy crust. It uses beer yeast, which gives it a slight beer flavor. The number of lanterns outside restaurants indicates quality – the more the better. Blue lanterns indicate Muslim food.

Who cares if it's -22°F (-30°C).

RESTAURANTS

Dafengshou 大丰收
✉ 283 Yiman Jie, Nangang District 南岗区一曼街 283 号❺
☎ 5364 6824

Daquan BBQ 大全烧烤
✉ Jiaoyuyuan Xiaoqu, Caoshi Jie, Daowai District 道外区草市街北兴教育园小区
☎ 8834 8888

Huamei Xi Canting 华梅西餐厅
Established in 1925, it's the most famous Russian-influenced Western restaurant in the city. Its signature fish dish is *kao naizhi guiyu* (烤奶汁桂鱼).
✉ 112 Zhongyang Dajie 中央大街 112 号❻
☎ 8461 9818
🕒 11am to 9pm

Lao Duyichu 老都一处
Established in 1929, specializes in dumplings, and has over 26 kinds of fillings on offer.
✉ 25 Xi Shisandao Jie, Daoli District 道里区西十三道街 25 号❼
☎ 8461 5895
🕒 10am to 9pm

Maomao Chunbing 毛毛春饼
✉ 161 Guogeli Dajie, Nangang District ❽
☎ 8264 8814

Poterman Western Restaurant 波曼西餐厅
✉ 12 Xidazhi Jie, Nangang District 南岗区西大直街 12 号
☎ 5362 5888

Xiangcun Dayuan 乡村大院酒店
Specializes in northern farm style dishes such as a fish-head dish called *jinguo yutou* (金锅鱼头) and spareribs called *fengshou paigu* (丰收排骨).
✉ 13 Dashun Jie, Nangang District 南岗区大顺街 13 号
☎ 8234 0258
🕒 9am to 12pm

Souvenirs

The best things to buy in Harbin are, not surprisingly, Russian in origin. From fur hats to Russian dolls, anything and everything that hails from the north can be found in stores throughout the city. Having dealt with Russian traders for years, the vendors in Harbin are shrewd traders and expect to bargain – disregard all price tags except at the very up-market department stores. Harbin has a reputation in China for being a cheap city and it's true that you can pick up some very good bargains on fans or calligraphy if you haggle. If you have a week or so in the city, you could go to the Silk

Market near Heilongjiang University (*hēilóngjiāng dàxué* 黑龙江大学) and get a custom-made *qipao* (旗袍) for a third of the price they charge in Beijing. Otherwise, try the Russian stores on Central Street or go to the indoor Russian market near Hongbo Square (*hóngbó guǎngchǎng* 红博广场). The most expensive stores can be found around Hongbo Square and at the northern end of Central Street, but you'll pay Western prices for things you could get much cheaper if you ventured into the markets. Perhaps the most appropriate souvenir you could bring home from Harbin would be one of the green ex-military overcoats that the locals all wear in winter – very good at keeping you warm. Rustic souvenirs made from straw and shells make great gifts. Look for these knick-knacks at the Zhongwai Minmao Market (*zhōngwài mínmào shìchǎng* 中外民贸市场❾, ☎ 5367 2347) on Jianshe Lu – many of the small stores along this street carry Russian items. The Guomao Cheng (国贸城❿) is an interesting shopping venue. Built in a former bomb-shelter, this huge complex houses many small shops and makes for good shopping (Dongdazhi Jie 东大直街 underground tunnel, ☎ 5365 7621).

Other Information

POST OFFICES

Daoli Post Office 道里邮局

✉ 48 Xi Shisidao Jie, Daoli District
道里区西十四道街 48 号⓫

☎ 8461 4464

Fashion with a northern twist.

Nangang Post Office 南岗邮局
✉ 51 Jianshe Jie Nangang District
南岗区建设街 51 号
☏ 5363 3137

HOSPITALS

Harbin Second Medical School Hospital
哈尔滨医科大学第二附属医院
✉ 148 Baojian Lu, Nangang District
南岗区保健路 148 号
☏ 8666 2961

COMPLAINT HOTLINES
☏ General: 8620 0315
☏ Taxi: 8632 3 900

CHINESE TYPICAL DISHES 中国特色菜		
Peking duck	běijīng kǎoyā	北京烤鸭
hotpot	huǒguō	火锅
kung pao chicken	gōngbǎo jīdīng	宫保鸡丁
stir-fried marinated chicken breasts in a salty sauce	jiàngbào jīdīng	酱爆鸡丁
diced pork with chili	làzi ròudīng	辣子肉丁
red-stewed pork	hóngshāo ròu	红烧肉
twice-cooked pork	huíguō ròu	回锅肉
lion's head meatballs	shīzi tóu	狮子头
sweet and sour spare ribs	tángcù páigǔ	糖醋排骨
fish-flavored pork	yúxiāng ròusī	鱼香肉丝
red-stewed fish	hóngshāo yú	红烧鱼
steamed fish	qīngzhēng yú	清蒸鱼
sweet-and-sour fish	tángcù yú	糖醋鱼
braised eggplant	shāo qiézi	烧茄子
red-cooked bean curd	hóngshāo dòufu	红烧豆腐
mapo tofu	mápó dòufu	麻婆豆腐
stir-fried mixed vegetables	chǎo shíjǐn shūcài	炒什锦蔬菜
stir-fried tomatoes and eggs	xīhóngshì chǎo jīdàn	西红柿炒鸡蛋
hot and sour soup	suānlà tāng	酸辣汤
chicken soup	jī tāng	鸡汤
egg and tomato soup	xīhóngshì jīdàn tāng	西红柿鸡蛋汤
Sichuan pickled vegetable soup	zhàcài tāng	榨菜汤
CHINESE TRADITIONAL FOOD 中国传统食品		
steamed buns	bāozi	包子
congee	xīfàn /zhōu	稀饭/粥
dumplings	jiǎozi	饺子
noodles	miàntiáo	面条
rice noodles	mǐxiàn	米线
fried rice	chǎofàn	炒饭
soup	tāng	汤

Changbai Shan, Nature's Heavenly Lake

Area Code 0433

Inactive volcanoes, crystal-clear lakes and looming trees – the unspoiled natural beauty of **Changbai Shan** rewards the intrepid travelers who make their way out to this northern diamond.

For nature buffs, Changbai Shan is a piece of heaven, and it certainly lives up to its name, which means "Ever-White Mountain." Budding naturalists will be in a proverbial paradise as they explore the explosion of animal, insect and plant life on this dormant volcano, which is also China's largest nature reserve. Those 810 square miles (210,000 ha) on the border of China's Jilin Province and the Democratic People's Republic of Korea (DPRK, or North Korea). Created in 1961, the nature reserve is home to one of the most diverse mountain-forest ecosystems in Asia. Evergreen species like Korean pines and Japanese yews share the slopes with Mongolian oaks, dwarf birch and other deciduous trees.

A steeple rises high above the Songhua River.

The variation in plant and animal life is due to the changing altitudes. From the foot of the mountain up to 3,300 feet (1,000 m) are mixed coniferous and broad-leaved trees. Hardy and valuable coniferous trees like dragon spruce and fir can be found from 3,300 to 5,900 feet (1,000 to 1,800 m). Above 6,600 feet (2,000 m), only lichen survives. Within this treasure trove thrives over 300 medicinal plants such as the winter daphne and wild ginseng.

Changbai Shan Nature Reserve (*chángbái shān zirán bǎohù qū* 长白山自然保护区), designated by UNESCO as a nature reserve in 1979, is a vital wildlife zone. Though predators such as Siberian tigers, leopards, lynx, and brown bears prowl the forests, there's no reason to shun the mountain. The lucky hiker might even catch a glimpse of elusive animals such as the shy deer, gorals, wild pigs, otters and dozens of other mammal species. Rare, endangered birds like hazel grouse, black storks, mandarin ducks and oriental storks also abound.

Sitting pretty atop Changbai Shan is the stunning **Lake of Heaven** (*tiānchí* 天池). This feather on Changbai Shan's cap was formed centuries ago by volcanic eruptions. Over time, water filled the vent and eventually formed an oval lake about 8 miles (13 km) in circumference and 650 to 980 feet (200 m to 300 m) deep. Sixteen mountain peaks surround the Lake of Heaven like sentries guarding the watery

A snow covered cottage remains cozy throughout the winter.

gates of heaven. No birds, animals or flora distract one from its tranquil beauty. The highest peak, **White Cloud Peak** (*báiyún fēng* 白云峰), soars some 9,000 feet (2,744 m) above sea level. When the fair skies fill with fluffy clouds, their reflection in the crystal-clear water, framed by jagged peaks, makes a heavenly composition.

Rough hiking trails aside, there are guaranteed views of babbling brooks, waterfalls and thermal springs. Just beside the Lake of Heaven is **Changbai Lake** (*chángbái hú* 长白湖), also known as Little Lake of Heaven. Water from the Lake of Heaven careens into a roaring waterfall some 200 feet (60 m) high, nourishing the Yalu (*yālù jiāng* 鸭绿江) and Songhua rivers (*sōnghuā jiāng* 松花江), two of northeast China's most important rivers.

Naturally, Changbai Shan has its fair share of fables. One myth is about the origins of the Manchu ethnic group, who are said to have sprung from the waters of the Lake of Heaven. Three celestial maidens visited the lake for a quick, albeit chilly dip. A magic magpie dropped an enchanted berry and one of the heavenly ladies picked it up, and when she ate the berry, she became pregnant. The baby boy she bore founded the warrior Manchu dynasty.

From 1677, this region was considered by the Manchu as their sacred homeland. No one was allowed to enter and log trees for over 200 years. Today, Manchus share the intoxicating Changbai Shan region with a large ethnic Korean population. By dress, the latter are indistinguishable from their Manchu counterparts, but they still retain some of their traditional practices and festivals. Friendly and hospitable, most ethnic Korean locals live north and northeast of **Erdao Baihe Town** (*èrdào báihé zhèn* 二道白河镇) in the area known as the Yanbian Korean Autonomous Prefecture.

SCALING SIGHTS

Traipsing through Changbai Shan's wilderness can be adventurous or tame, but first get oriented. If your objective is the famous Lake of Heaven, the safest route is via the **Northern Pass** (*běi pō* 北坡) from

The crystal expanse of Lake of Heaven during the winter.

Erdao Baihe, a small town some 12.4 miles (20 km) south of the nature reserve's southern entrance. You can also head to the lake via **Tianchi Passage** (*tiānchí chánglán g* 天池长廊). This route costs RMB 25, but it's also relatively safe – the other routes occasionally have rockslides. Alternatively, you can hop onto a jeep at the Athlete's Village parking lot. They'll take you up to the Lake of Heaven for RMB 80; this includes the admission price for the lake.

Day trippers can hop onto a jeep and arrive without breaking a sweat at the 8,758-foot-high (2,670 m) **Tianwen Peak** (*tiānwén fēng* 天文峰), otherwise known as **Main Peak** (*zhǔ fēng* 主峰). From the parking lot near Main Peak Road, there's another 2.5 miles (4 km) to go before you hear the roar of the stunning **Changbai Waterfall** (*chángbái pùbù* 长白瀑布). If you're game for a bit of trekking, the path to the Main Peak is a brief 15 minute hike from the left of the parking lot. There are 13 spectacular geysers around Changbai Waterfall.

If you are feeling slightly more adventurous, once you reach the waterfall, look around for a steep path that brings you to the top of the waterfall. If you follow this path for about an hour, you eventually reach Lake of Heaven. Getting off the main access road is not a good idea, unless you are an experienced hiker. The narrow, difficult 1.9-mile (3 km) trail pointing downwards heads to the **Underground Forest** (*dìxià sēnlín* 地下森林).

Hiking enthusiasts will enjoy a rockier version of Changbai Shan. Look out for a trail that branches off the road heading to Changbai Waterfall. This hour-long trail will take you through lush greenery towards **Black Wind Pass** (*hēifēng kǒu* 黑风口),

Memorable Experiences

Having refreshments by a glade after a long hard climb.

Chancing upon adventurous souls - very few, along the trails and sharing our travel stories.

Admiring our own sweaty faces in the mirror-like waters of Lake of Heaven.

where it can get extremely windy. The pavilion here offers fantastic views of the gushing Changbai Waterfall. Several hot springs bubble at 140°F to 176°F (60°C to 80°C) at the bottom of the pass. Choose a spot where people are not busy boiling eggs, and take a soothing bath – these hot springs are reputed to have healing properties. Re-energized, you may be able to reach Main Peak in 3 hours.

That was just appetizer; now for the main course. The first leg of a tough hike entails scaling past a perilous gorge onto a grassy slope – continue trudging up this slope for at least 2 hours. Once past Main Peak, look out for **Huagai Peak** (*huágài fēng* 华盖峰), just 2 hours from the DPRK border. Once you've reached this peak, then you've already navigated a quarter of the circumference of the Lake of Heaven. Take time to admire the geological treasures peculiar to Changbai Shan. In winter, skiing is an option on Changbai Shan.

If you follow a tiny trail off the main road, near the parking lot, you arrive at **Little Lake of Heaven** (*xiǎo tiānchí* 小天池). Pushing on, you hit the awe-inspiring **Dragon Gate Peak** (*lóngmén fēng* 龙门峰) and after a challenging ascent, **White Cloud Peak** (*báiyún fēng* 白云峰). Beyond this Peak is the Western Pass. The ascending hike between Little Lake of Heaven and White Cloud Peak takes about 6 hours, and it takes half that time to descend. Between Little Lake of Heaven and Western Pass is 10 hours of upward trekking, and 8 hours of descent.

If you visit via the Western Pass, you get to see the **Changbai Shan Gorge** (*chángbái shān dàxiágǔ* 长白山大峡谷), which is a frightful 80m deep valley formed from molten lava. Look carefully around you. Along this path is a tree that is in fact three different tree-species entwined as one. Past the end of the 6.2 mile (10 km) road is a flight of gravelly stairs that offers a panoramic view of the pass. An easy hour-long route leads you down to the Lake of Heaven. Just beneath the pass begins a strenuous trek to White Cloud Peak and Southern Pass. ■

Making Your Trip Easy

Practical Tips

Getting to Changbai Shan is itself an adventure that requires grit. Buses and hired cars will drop you off at the main parking lot in the scenic area. Traipsing through Changbai Shan's wilderness can be adventurous or tame, but be sure to bring hiking gear, a first-aid kit, food and enough water. The sun on the mountain can be very strong; make sure you bring plenty of sun block and your sunglasses.

Weather is unpredictable because of the high altitude. A fine day can suddenly turn cloudy and chilly. Waterproof jackets can be bought from the hawkers waiting at Tianchi bus stop. Be sure to bring enough layers, you can always add or remove them as you climb. The best time to visit the lake is from June to late-September when the lake and the road from Erdao Baihe to the nature reserve aren't frozen over. If snow and skiing are on your mind, any other time is good.

Be sure not to cross the border into the

Ethnic Koreans performing a traditional dance.

Quotes

"Being exhausted from the climb, I rested beside a tree. Then I saw one of the prettiest birds ever. Don't know the name though!"

"The lake was really a heavenly sight."

"No city noises, no pollution, no one - perfect."

DPRK when trekking around the lake – pay attention to the signs.

From late June to mid-July the western slope of the mountain holds an annual wildflower festival. The annual Changbai Snow Festival begins in mid-December and lasts until late-February.

Transportation

Airport – The closest airport to Changbai Shan is the Yanji International Airport. Yanji is about 3 miles (5 km) away from the airport and it takes about 10 minutes to reach by car.

Bus – From Yanji to Changbai Shan is a RMB 55 bus ride from the long distance bus station.

Taxi – Taxies here don't have meters – since Yanji is rather small, it only costs RMB 5 to get anywhere within the city. This goes for any of the small towns around the mountain.

Train – The train station is in Erdao Baihe Town, about 15.5 miles (25 km) south of the nature reserve. From here you can catch a bumpy minibus into Changbai Shan between 6am and 12pm. Tickets cost about RMB 50. For greater flexibility, especially if you want more time to trek, consider hiring a driver with car for RMB 300.

The Best of Changbai Shan

Changbai Shan Scenic Area
长白山风景区 *chángbái shān fēngjǐng qū*
✉ Erdao Baihe Town, Antu County
安图县二道白河镇
☎ 571 0888, 571 0985
¥ 100, includes RMB 5 insurance, and the charges of other spots as Changbai Shan Underground Forest and Changbai Shan Waterfall

Changbai Shan Underground Forest
长白山地下森林 *chángbái shān dìxià sēnlín*
✉ inside the Changbai Shan Scenic Area
长白山风景区内

Changbai Waterfall
长白山瀑布 *chángbái shān pùbù*
✉ inside the Changbai Shan Scenic Area
长白山风景区内

Lake of Heaven
长白山天池 *chángbái shān tiānchí*
✉ inside the Changbai Shan Scenic Area
长白山风景区内
¥ 25 if via Tianchi Passage

Hotels

Yanbian Baishan Hotel 延边白山大厦
yánbiān báishān dàshà ★★★★
✉ 2 Youyi Lu, Yanji 延吉市友谊路 2 号
☎ 251 5956
¥ 580 – per person, peak-season
380 – per person, off-season

Changbai Shan Dayu Hotel 长白山大宇饭店
chángbái shān dàyǔ fàndiàn ★★★
✉ Erdaohe Town, Changbai Shan
长白山二道河镇
☎ 574 6011, 574 6015
¥ 700 – per person, peak-season
320 – per person, off-season

Baishan Binguan
白山宾馆 *báishān bīnguǎn* ★★
✉ 42 An Jie, Mingyue Town, Antu County
安图县明月镇安街 42 号
☎ 852 4450
¥ 160 – double room

Baishan Hotel
白山大酒店 *báishān dàjiǔdiàn* ★★
✉ 5km from Changbai Shan's entrance
长白山山门外 5 公里
☎ 571 8777
¥ 280 – double room, peak-season
140 – double room, off-season

Food & Restaurants

Food in Yanji is a mixture of different ethnic Manchurian and Korean styles. The emphasis here is on freshness and nutritional value. Cold noodles (*lěngmiàn* 冷

A cascading waterfall turns into a wall of ice in the winter.

面) are one of the better-known dishes. Being so close to the border of the DPRK, it's natural that Korean food abounds. Try the sticky cake (*dǎgāo* 打糕); it's a traditional Korean dish eaten during the New Year. Kimchi (*cháoxiǎn pàocài* 朝鲜泡菜), a spicy pickled cabbage, is a tasty side dish that can be eaten on its own or added to dishes. Don't forget to try the traditional Dongbei sausage (*báiròu xuěcháng* 白肉雪肠).

Several mini-guesthouses offer village fare in the Changbai Shan region. The proprietors are easygoing and the mood relaxed.

RESTAURANTS

Jindalai Restaurant 金达莱饭店

Offers Yanji cuisine, also known for its Korean dishes.

✉ 388 Hailan Lu, Yanji 延吉市海兰路 388 号

☎ 251 1740

🕒 9am to11pm

Yanji Meishi Jie 延吉美食街

One street packed with food vendors.

✉ Hailan Lu, Yanji 延吉市海兰路

🕒 9am to 11pm

Souvenirs

In Yanji check out the Antu Fuman Shengtai Cheng Shopping Center (安图福满生态城旅游购物中心) or the International Exhibition Center (延边国际会展中心) for your shopping needs. The exhibition center also features ethnic Korean performances.

While on the mountain, resist plucking forest tokens for souvenirs and don't scrape your initials on the rocks. Beyond that, the Changbai Shan area offers quite a few unique souvenirs. The "three northeast treasures," ginseng, fur and deer antlers, can be found here and are renowned throughout China.

Other Information

HOSPITALS

Yanbian Hospital 延边医院

✉ Renmin Lu, Yanji 延吉人民路

☎ 266 0163

COMPLAINT HOTLINES

☎ General: 571 0778

☎ Taxi: 582 3036

Dalian, Jewel of the Northeast

Area Code 0411

Dalian, on China's far northeast coast, is popular with domestic travelers but is yet to be discovered by international tourists. This refreshing coastal city is the perfect antidote for those aching to get away from the congestion and pollution of China's big cities.

Dalian is a relatively new city by Chinese standards and has grown rapidly by virtue of having an excellent natural harbor – which made it prime real-estate for the imperialist ambitions of Russia and Japan. Much of Dalian's recent history reflects the 20th century conflicts of China. Today Dalian is a major center for shipping, logistics and fishing. The proximity to good t ransportation and its special economic stimulus policies have attracted a rapidly growing pool of high-tech industries. Prosperous, clean, jolly, and vibrant, it offers a stark contrast to the often gritty realities of other northeastern cities. Even in a country where local pride runs strong, the people of Dalian stand out with a fierce pride in their city.

There are some worthwhile things to do here. Some of the beaches are nice, and its high latitude and ocean breezes help it escape some of the worst of steamy Chinese summers – that's why the Chinese come here. There are some fine examples of classic Russian and Japanese architecture here, and

Modern buildings overlook one of Dalian's many spacious parks.

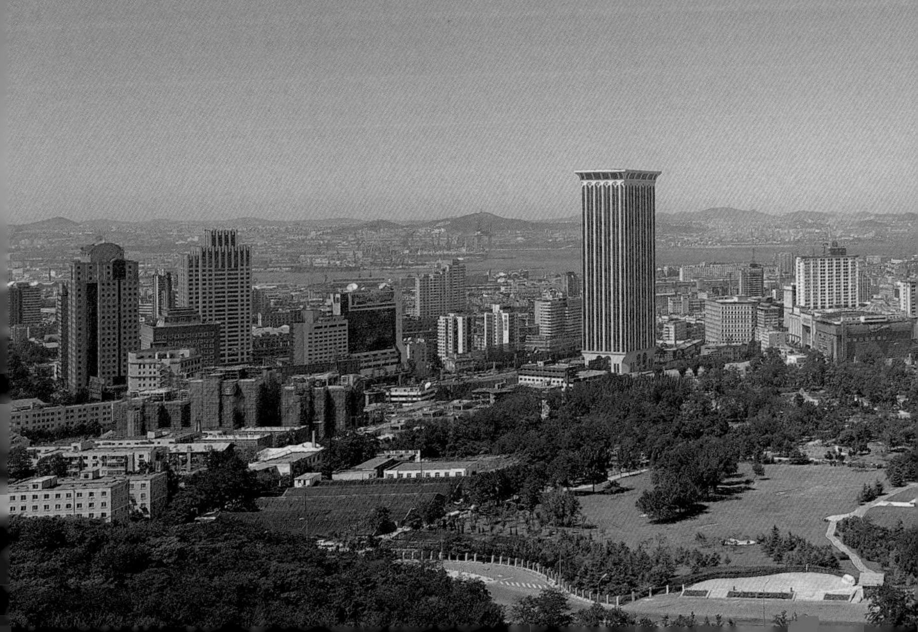

the seafood is excellent. Moreover, it's just a pleasant place to be.

Beneath their hardhats-and-forklifts, workday look, the people of Dalian harbor a surprising fondness for fashion, and the city is a major center of the fashion industry in China. The Dalian International Fashion Exhibition, held in mid-September, ranks as one of the largest fashion shows in Asia. High fashion is a large part of the daily lives of the ordinary people. Small shows are held year-round in shopping centers and parks, and they attract huge and enthusiastic crowds.

A SUMMER HAVEN

Dalian's greatest appeal to domestic tourists comes from its beaches and relatively mild summers. Most famous of these is **Tiger Beach** (*lǎohǔ tān* 老虎滩), which offers stunning views of the seaside cliffs. Inside the Tiger Beach area are hundreds of birds at the **Niaoyu Lin** (*niǎoyǔlín* 鸟语林). Just be careful at the bird show – the birds like to pluck money from your hands. The **Golden Pebble Beach National Resort** (*jīnshí tān guójiā lǚyóu dùjiàqū* 金石滩国家旅游度假区) has an eclectic selection of activities ranging from golf to paintballing. Scuba diving is also a popular pastime; the clear waters off Dalian make for a good excursion during the summers. Dolphins are also a local resident in the waters; you might be able to catch a glimpse of them if you're lucky. Both beaches are located northeast of the city near the booming Economic Development Zone. Swimming and other typical touristy

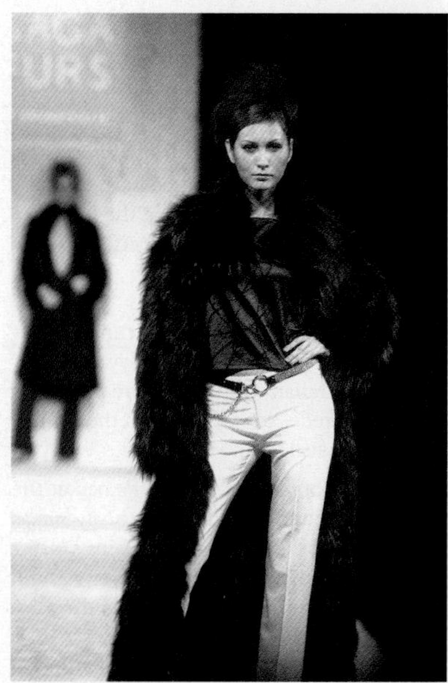

Saga Design Centre's models strut down the runway during the Fashion Festival.

entertainments during the warm seasons are on offer, but due to the crowds, the parks may actually be most pleasant during the off-season when you can spend some time beside the ocean without the jostling.

Other oceanfront areas can be hard to find for non-locals. They don't have the lovely sands and the facilities of the better-developed beaches, but they can also be a pleasant experience and provide opportunities for fishing. Unfortunately, it's impossible to get to the ocean anywhere near downtown Dalian – the harbor areas are very tightly secured – so is Lüshun to the south, which is a naval base.

There is an interesting time to be had at the **Sun-Asia Ocean World** (*shèngyà hǎiyáng shìjiè* 圣亚海洋世界), it's one of China's larger aquariums with a see-through walkway built under the ocean. Another choice is the **Forest Zoo** (*sēnlín gōngyuán* 森林公园). Located in the thickly wooded hills around the city, the main zoo section is pretty small and mundane. They do have some pandas, but be warned that pandas in Chinese zoos prefer to sleep rather than frolic. More interesting are the raccoon-like Lesser Pandas, Siberian White Tigers and other tiger species, Père David's Deer and a few other truly unusual zoo offerings. On the other side of the zoo is a safari ride. The best part of the Forest Zoo is the enormous cable car system that offers a dazzling view of Dalian and the natural setting in which the zoo is built. Perhaps the zoo should really be named the "Mountain Zoo" – traversing it is a moderately arduous hike through some striking forests and hills. The Forest Zoo also has an aquarium, but in this seafood-loving city restaurants and markets offer a better assortment of live ocean life than the commercial aquariums.

Some nice places to hang out include **Xinghai Park** (*xīnghǎi gōngyuán* 星海公园), located seaside and on the edge of the city, and **Zhongshan Square** (*zhōngshān guǎngchǎng* 中山广场), located in the heart of downtown. Zhongshan Square has a Jumbotron TV often playing movies or soccer matches or, for a really surreal experience, old Woody Woodpecker or Tom and Jerry cartoons dubbed into Mandarin. It's not uncommon to see folk musicians, dancers, fashion shows or other entertainers here. It's a very pleasant place to chill out and people watch, which is precisely what the locals do here. Also look for the mounted police: Dalian's the only city in China that has police that serve and protect on horseback, and they're all women. ■

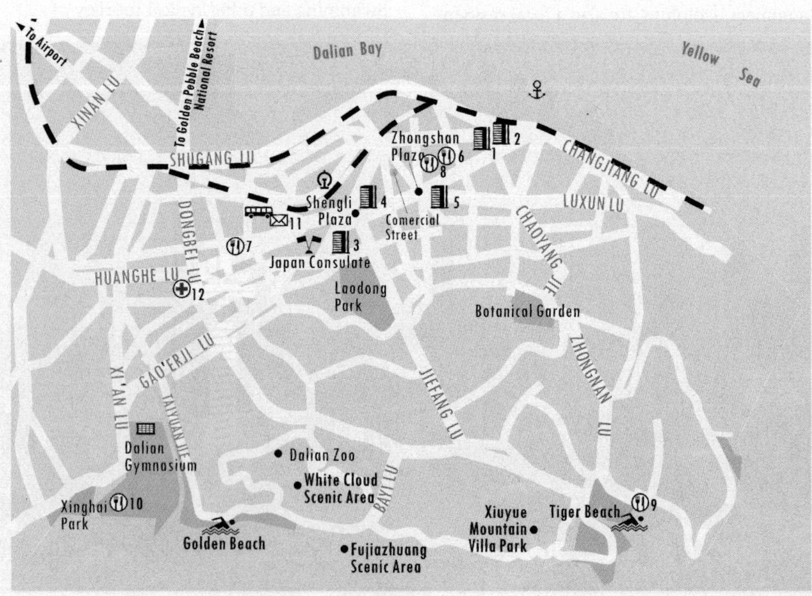

Soccer is Dalian's lifeblood.

Making Your Trip Easy

Practical Tips

The best time to visit Dalian is from September to October. The weather is wonderful, the local fruit harvests are coming in, and the city seems particularly invigorated. Springtime is also a nice season to visit Dalian although it's a little more prone to rain. The ocean tends to moderate Dalian's extreme seasonal weather somewhat. Summers are usually uncomfortably hot during the days in July and August. Fortunately, there are frequent ocean breezes that cool the city around sundown. Winters can be very cold and wet here, but not nearly as bad as those seen in nearby cities further inland such as in Shenyang. Summers are great for swimming; the best beaches are at Golden Pebble Beach, Fujiazhuang (*fùjiāzhuāng* 付家庄) and Xinghai Park. These beaches are great for some sunbathing and swimming; just be careful though, the water becomes very deep rapidly. Every September there's an International Fashion Festival that features fashion shows and exhibitions. You'll be hard pressed to miss any of it: models sashay down the runway on every street. Hotel prices will rise during this time and rooms will be hard to find.

Transportation

Airport – Dalian has a small international airport that's located to the northwest of the city. The airport has international flights to Japan and the Republic of Korea(South Korea). Domestic direct flights to most major cities in China are readily available. It takes about 15 to 30 minutes from the airport to the city center by shuttle bus or taxi.

Ship – There are passenger boats available for connection to Inchon in the Republic of Korea as well as to other Chinese ports. There are numerous daily ferries to Yantai in Shandong Province. Landlubbers beware –

Memorable Experiences

Singing with the folk musicians in Zhongshan Square, far more entertaining than the typical karaoke session.

Combing the beach for interesting stones and aquatic life while the sea breeze blows against our faces.

Riding the Forest Zoo cable cars and looking down at all the gorgeous scenery surrounding us.

choppy seas, big crowds and locked passenger compartments can make for an uncomfortable trip.

Streetcar – One of the things that make Dalian so livable is its excellent and quaint streetcar line. The line is limited from Xinggong Jie to Heshi Jiao, but it is very convenient. The fare is RMB 1 to RMB 2 depending on the distance traveled. The streetcars run from 6am to 8pm.

Taxi – Taxis are RMB 8 at flag-fall. Within downtown Dalian most places can be reached for under RMB 30; however, be advised that taxi travel to the Economic Development Zone or the public beaches can be lengthy and expensive.

The Best of Dalian

Golden Pebble Beach National Resort
金石滩国家旅游度假区 *jīnshítān guójiā lǚyóu dùjiàqū*
✉ inside the Golden Pebble Beach National Resort 金石滩国家旅游度假区内
☎ 8790 0241
🕒 24 hours
¥ 66

Polar Aquarium 极地馆 *jídì guǎn*
✉ inside the Tiger Beach Ocean Park 老虎滩海洋公园内
☎ 8289 3111
🕒 8am to 6pm, peak-season
9am to 4pm, off-season
¥ 100

Sun-Asia Ocean World 圣亚海洋世界 *shèngyà hǎiyáng shìjiè*
✉ Xinghai Park, Shahekou District 沙河口区星海公园内
☎ 8468 5136
🕒 9am to 4pm,peak-season
8am to 5pm,off-season
¥ 100

Hotels

Furama Hotel
富丽华大酒店 *fùlìhuá dàjiǔdiàn* ★★★★★
✉ 60 Renmin Lu, Zhongshan District
中山区人民路 60 号❶
☎ 8263 0888
¥ 1200 – double room
@ www.furama.com.cn

Shangri-La Hotel 香格里拉大饭店 *xiānggélǐlā dàfàndiàn* ★★★★★
✉ 66 Renmin Lu, Zhongshan District
中山区人民路 66 号❷
☎ 8252 5000
¥ 822 – double room, peak-season
681 – double room, off-season
@ www.shangri-La.com

Swiss Ôtel Dalian
瑞士酒店 *ruìshì jiǔdiàn* ★★★★★
✉ 21 Wuhui Lu, Zhongshan District
中山区五惠路 21 号❸
☎ 8230 3388
¥ 711 – double room, peak-season
638 – double room, off-season
@ www.swissotel-dalian.com

Ramada Hotel Dalian 九州华美达酒店 *jiǔzhōu huáměidá jiǔdiàn* ★★★★
✉ 18 Shengli Square, Zhongshan District
中山区胜利广场 18 号❹
☎ 8280 8888
¥ 398 – double room
@ www.ramada.com

Dalian Hotel 大连宾馆 *dàlián bīnguǎn* ★★★
✉ 4 Zhongshan Square, Zhongshan District
中山区中山广场 4 号❺
☎ 8263 3111
¥ 450 – double room, peak-season
400 – double room, off-season

Food & Restaurants

Seafood dominates Dalian's local cuisine. There's a bewildering profusion of saltwater fish, as well as fresh shrimp, lobster, crabs, scallops, squid, abalone, and much more. An interesting local seafood favorite is the sea slug or the very slug-like sea cucumber; to most Western palates these foods are about as appealing as they sound. Seafood prices are good and the quality is unparalleled. It's hard to find a bad seafood restaurant here – find a place with lots of aquariums. Freshness is important and you can't get a dish fresher than one that goes straight from the water tank to the wok. Walk in, point to some specimens you fancy, then wait – you won't be disappointed. One standout restaurant is the local TTYG chain. It stands for *tiantian yugang* (天天渔港), which translates to something like the "every day fish company." They work in partnership with the local fisheries and are renowned for their seafood in a town where seafood is a cherished way of life. Otherwise, Dalian's food is very much in the northeastern mode: hearty meals featuring strong flavors, wheat noodles, cabbage, potatoes, and dumplings. Dalian is also famous for fresh fruit – the surrounding areas produce peaches, strawberries and apples.

RESTAURANTS

Dadi Chunbing Restaurant 大地春饼店

✉ 696 Huanghe Lu, Shahekou District 沙河口区黄河路 696 号❿

☎ 8461 1688

Pinhai Lou 品海楼

Very famous for local seafood.

✉ 46 Beidou Jie, Zhongshan District 中山区北斗街 46 号

☎ 8271 9688

🕒 9am to 11pm

Shuangsheng Yuan Restaurant 双盛园饭店

Very good salted fish.

✉ 1 Anle Jie, Zhongshan District 中山区安乐街 1 号❻

☎ 8264 7800

🕒 9am to 10pm

Tiantian Yugang 天天渔港

Famous for local seafood, dinner will go from RMB 50 to 200 per person, shrimp with spicy cabbage (*xiārén làbáicài* 虾仁辣白菜) is a must.

✉ 72 Tianjin Jie, Zhongshan District 中山区天津街 72 号❽

☎ 8263 3898

🕒 10:30am to 10pm

Wanbao Seafood Restaurant 万宝海鲜舫

✉ 108 Jiefang Lu, Zhongshan District 中山区解放路 108 号❾

☎ 8881 28888

Xindongfang Yurenmatou 新东方渔人码头

Specializes in seafood and Cantonese cuisine.

✉ 3 Gangwan Guangchang, Zhongshan District 中山区港湾广场 3 号

☎ 8270 6999

🕒 11am to 2:30pm, 5pm to 9:30

Zhuangjiayuan Restaurant 庄稼院食府

Specializes in northeast home-style cooking, known for pickled vegetables with clam in a claypot (*suāncài hǎilìguō* 酸菜海蛎锅), pork and noodle stew (*zhūròu dùn fěntiáo* 猪肉炖粉条) and chicken and mushroom stew (*xiǎojī dùn mógu* 小鸡炖蘑菇).

✉ 1-2/F, Waijingmaowei Dalou, Huanghe Lu 黄河路外经贸委大楼 1-2F ❼

☎ 8378 0016

🕒 10am to 10:30pm

Dalian's landscape is dotted with expansive plazas.

Dalian's Bangchui Island is a popular spot for sun-worshippers.

Quotes

"I love it here. This is the best city in China to live in, and it might just be the best city in Asia."

"The people here are the best. Not just nice, there's a cocky self-assurance to their friendliness that I have come to love. I can always tell if a person comes from Dalian."

Souvenirs

Sculptures and other works utilizing local seashells abound in this seaside town. There is a local arts community, although many of the same crafts and souvenirs are available throughout China. *Cuiyan douhua* (崔岩豆画) is a kind of drawing made from colorful beans. Subjects include folklore legends and modern landscapes. One popular subject is the "*Eight Immortals Crossing the Ocean*" (*bāxiān guòhǎi* 八仙过海), a well-known legend of the eight Taoist Immortals. These pieces of bean art cost about RMB 20. Shells with intricate carvings on them (*bèidiāo* 贝雕) go for RMB 5 to over RMB 10.

Dalian has some excellent shopping for a city of its size. Qingniwa (*qīngníwā shāngquān* 青泥洼商圈) is a popular shopping area with clusters of stores and small vendors. Shengli Square (*shènglì guǎngchǎng* 胜利广场) is a modern mall with good restaurants. Tianjin Jie Shangquan (天津街商圈) is a pedestrian street lined with shops, and a good place to go for a window-shopping stroll. The Friendship Store (*yǒuyì shāngchéng* 友谊商城) stocks all kinds of name brand products and stands beside Zhongshan Square . Most stores are open from 9am to 9pm.

Other Information

POST OFFICES

Zhanqian Post Office 站前邮政局

✉ west side of the train station
火车站前西侧⓫

☎ 8364 2116

HOSPITALS

The First Chinese Medical University Hospital 中国医科大学附属第一医院

✉ Zhongshan Lu, Xigang District
西岗区中山路⓬

☎ 8363 5963

Traditional Chinese Medicine Hospital 中医院

✉ Jiefang Lu, Zhongshan District
中山区解放路

☎ 8268 1738

CONSULATES

Japan

✉ 3/F, Senmao Dasha, Xigang District
西岗区森茂大厦 3 楼

☎ 8370 4077

COMPLAINT HOTLINES

☎ General: 362 7127

☎ Taxi: 8363 8119

NORTH CHINA

Tianjin's modern cityscape.

Tianjin's modern cityscape

Area Code 022

Antiques markets and scrumptious snacks make **Tianjin** a nice getaway destination. Spend a few days exploring the city's narrow alleys, browsing its antiques markets and sampling its famous snacks.

Over 600 years old, Tianjin, the largest port city in north China, lies on the coast of the Bohai Sea. The city continues a legacy that's both ancient and modern, Chinese and Western. Most of all, the city is known among Chinese cities for its colonial buildings in the former concession areas that still retain a European air of elegance.

There are over 1,000 concession-era buildings in Tianjin, the construction of which began in 1858 when the Qing court was forced to sign the Treaty of Tianjin, allowing for the establishment of concessions in the city. Britain, France, Japan, Germany, Russia, Belgium, Italy and Austria divvied up Tianjin, and each nation created its own self-sustaining walled enclave, where its citizens could forget they were far from their native soil.

Walking down **Fifth Avenue** or **Chifeng Lu** is like strolling through an old black and white movie. There are more than 230 buildings of English, French and Italian styles on Fifth Avenue alone. French buildings stand out among the crowd, especially on Chifeng Lu, which was the heart of the French zone. From **Central Park**, which used to be a French garden, six lanes branch out into downtown shopping areas.

Fifth Avenue was once a seedy den of traitors and intrigue. Before 1949, the street was known as The Governors' Street, named for the many warlords and politicians who made this street their refuge after being deposed or run out of office in the mercurial world of Chinese politics. Many Chinese celebrities also made their home in this stylish area in an effort to escape the chaos of the era.

Transformed from high treason to high fashion, Chifeng Lu now forms the core of Tianjin's fashion scene. The street, home to rows of hip clothing shops with funky names like Bomb Plastic, Bubbly Disco and Rome Holiday, draw the young and fashionable who swarm to this area for the latest in haute couture.

Not only did the foreign residents build charming homes, they also left many places of worship in the city. Among them, the **Wanghai Lou Cathedral** (*wànghǎi lóu jiàotáng* 望海楼教堂) has experienced dramatic ups and downs, emblematic of China's turbulent past with the West. The cathedral, located by the **Shizi Lin Bridge** (*shīzi lín qiáo* 狮子林桥), north of the Haihe River, was first built in 1869 by French Catholics. Over the years it was destroyed and rebuilt several times and is now once again an active place of worship.

Unlike many Chinese cities, Buddhist temples don't dominate the places of worship in Tianjin. The largest and best-maintained temple is the **Grand Mercy Temple** (*dàbēi chánsì* 大悲禅寺) beside the Jingang Bridge in the Hebei District. More than 300 years old, it's home to some outstanding bronze, stone and wooden statues dating back several centuries.

The streets in Tianjin tend to be twisty mazes. Once you step off the main boulevard, it's easy to get lost in the labyrinth of old concession era and Chinese style buildings. The small streets are great for those looking for a cozy *hutong* adventure through the narrow alleyways. A great way to get about the city's narrow streets is to rent a bike for the day.

Although Tianjin has over a century of Western influence, the city has produced

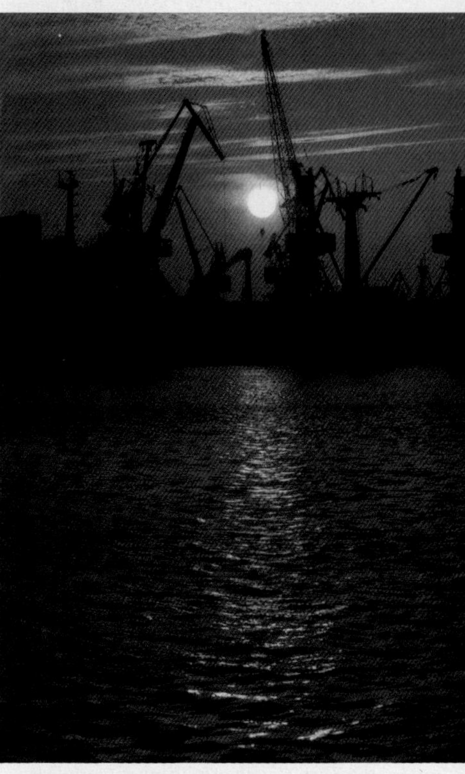

Tianjin's port connects China to the world.

Quotes

"Although it has the misfortune of being shadowed by the capital city of Beijing, Tianjin is a treasure trove for those who are interested in both traditional Chinese folk art and Western culture."

"It's a major city but has the leisure of a small town. Watching grannies doing *tai chi* in the early morning is a lot of fun."

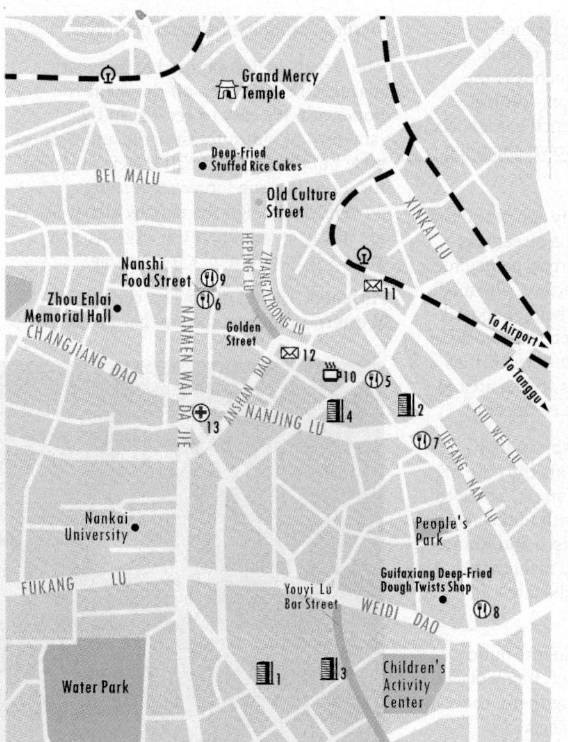

some of China's best folk artists. The **Old Culture Street** (*gǔwénhuà jiē* 古文化街), a reconstructed antiques marketplace in the Nankai District, is a good place to scour for traditional Chinese art and souvenirs. Most of the items here, knick-knacks like meditation balls, stone seals and jade (or faux-jade) jewelry, are aimed directly at tourists. There's also a marvelous array of less common items such as traditional kites and clay figurines of mythological figures and opera characters available at many shops. These figurines (*ní rén* 泥人) are famous in Tianjin, especially those made by the Zhang family. Unlike the colorful clay figures from other parts of China, the works by the Zhangs are a reflection on life – the eyes of these small mud men express sorrow, happiness, joy and frustration. The Zhang's shop and other shops selling these figurines can be found on the Old Culture Street.

During the **Spring Festival** (Chinese New Year), the marketplace is clogged with vendors selling paintings and calligraphy that are hung on doorways and windows for good luck in the New Year. A handful of shops sell these decorations all year around and they make for interesting gifts. During Spring Festival, the whole city is outfitted in red, and entire windows are plastered with red paper cuttings (*jiǎn zhǐ* 剪纸) of flowers and good luck symbols. The normal drab gray of northern Chinese cities suddenly turns scarlet as any available piece of frontage is pasted with these festive decorations.

People in Tianjin are also known as great talkers; they can yak on and on, which also makes them great arguers. Many of China's most famous cross-talkers, comedians who give hilarious pun-filled monologues and dialogues, hail from Tianjin. Even if you're not fluent in Chinese, just observing the animated conversations of the locals will convince you that they've been given the gift of gab. ■

Memorable Experiences

Sampling food of various flavors at the Nanshi Food Street and then soaking up local culture at local arts and crafts stalls on the Old Culture Street.

Strolling through the former concession areas and getting a feel of what life must have been like 100 years ago.

Making Your Trip Easy

Practical Tips

Tianjin enjoys temperate weather and four distinct seasons a year, with spring and autumn being the best time to visit. Autumn is especially nice when the leaves change color and the weather hasn't yet turned too cold. It's the coldest in January and hottest in July. Bring a sweater or jacket if you come in spring or autumn and a very warm coat in winter. It's also pretty wet during the spring and summer, so bring rain gear.

A week of college boat races on Haihe River begin on October 2. Students race dragon boats and perform variety shows. For ten days during the Ocean Fair (*tiānjīn hǎihuì* 天津海会), which is held in late June, there's more aquatic entertainment such as heading out to sea to do some fishing then eating your catch with a fishing family. The Ocean Fair is held at Tanggu (塘沽).

Transportation

Airport – The Tianjin Binhai International Airport is located 8 miles (13 km) from the downtown area. Taking a taxi will cost about RMB 50, shuttle buses cost around RMB 10 (☎ 2330 1543). There's also a shuttle bus service to Beijing's international airport for RMB 70; it operates from 6am to 5:30pm with buses leaving every 45 minutes.

Bus – The Beijing-Tianjin-Tanggu Expressway connects Tianjin to Beijing. It's only a 1.5-hour drive to Beijing on the highway. Numerous buses shuttle back and forth between Tianjin and Beijing and they leave about every 30 minutes. The number of buses thins out during the evening.

Ferry – From Tianjin's port there are three domestic routes, to Dalian, Yantai and Longkou. International routes go to Inchon in the Republic of Korea and Kobe in Japan. Tickets can be arranged through your hotel or at the ferry's ticket office (1 Pukou Dao, Hexi District, 河西区浦口道 1 号, ☎ 2339 9573).

Taxi – Most cabs are small compacts and flag-fall is RMB 8.

Train – There are dozens of trains between Beijing and Tianjin. The double-decked "K"

Yangliuqing wood block prints date back to the 17th century.

Souvenir hunting among Qing-style buildings in the Old Culture Street.

series depart about every hour or so and the trip takes around 2 hours. You can also buy your return ticket from attendants on the train. Tianjin has four stations, with Tianjin Station being the largest.

The Best of Tianjin

Grand Mercy Temple
大悲禅寺 *dàbēi chánsì*
✉ 40 Tianwei Lu, Hebei District
河北区天纬路 40 号
☎ 2635 5534
🕒 9am to 4pm
¥ 10

Nanshi Food Street
南市食品街 *nánshì shípǐnjiē*
✉ Nanshi Qinghe Jie, Heping District
和平区南市清和街
☎ 2727 1761
🕒 6am to midnight

Old Cultural Street
古文化街 *gǔwénhuà jiē*
✉ Tongbei Lu, Nankai District 南开区通北路
☎ 2735 6666
🕒 9am to 6pm

Hotels

Sheraton Tianjin Hotel
天津喜来登大酒店
tiānjīn xǐláidēng dàjiǔdiàn ★★★★★
✉ Zijinshan Lu, Hexi District
河西区紫金山路❶
☎ 2334 3388
¥ 1,100 – double room, peak-season
848 – double room, off-season
@ www.sheraton.com

Crystal Palace Hotel 水晶宫饭店
shuǐjīnggōng fàndiàn ★★★★
✉ 28 Binshui Dao, Youyi Lu, Hexi District
河西区友谊路宾水道 28 号❸
☎ 2835 6888
¥ 500 – double room
@ www.tcph.cn

Hyatt Regency Tianjin
天津凯悦饭店 *tiānjīn kǎiyuè fàndiàn* ★★★★
✉ 219 Jiefang Bei Lu, Heping District
和平区解放北路 219 号❷
☎ 2330 1234
¥ 690 – double room, peak-season
590 – double room, off-season
@ tianjin.regency.hyatt.com

Friendship Hotel
友谊宾馆 *yǒuyì bīnguǎn* ★★★
✉ 94 Nanjing Lu, Heping District
和平区南京路 94 号❹
☎ 2331 0372
¥ 480 – double room, peak-season
360 – double room, off-season

Victory Hotel
胜利宾馆 *shènglì bīnguǎn* ★★★
✉ 11 Jintang Gonglu, Tanggu District
塘沽区津塘公路 11 号
☎ 2534 5833
¥ 329 – double room
@ www.victoryhotel.com

Food & Restaurants

Most of Beijing's cuisine derives from Tianjin and Beijingers make a point of going to Tianjin for the cheap eats and the great snacks. Tianjin's most famous contribution to the Chinese menu are *goubuli* meat buns (*gǒubùlǐ bāozi* 狗不理包子). Goubuli literally translates as "dog doesn't care." The story has it that the inventor of these meat buns had the humble name of "Dog." His meat buns became so popular and sold so fast that he didn't have time to greet his customers, so when his regulars felt ignored, they said that" Dog doesn't care about us." Another story goes that he was so ugly that even dogs wouldn't pay any attention to him.

Tianjin is crammed with cheap restaurants that offer a wide range of food. For those who are craving something different, Tianjin offers an abundance of choices. Tea soup (*chá tāng* 茶汤) is a sweet drink that's made on the spot. The cha tang master mixes rice flour, sugar and minced nuts in a bowl and then fills the bowl with boiling water from a huge bronze teapot. Crispy deep-fried dough twists (*má huā* 麻花) made from wheat mixed with sesame seeds, sugar and preserved fruits and nuts make for tasty snacks. Local specialties include chewy deep-fried stuffed rice cakes (*ěrduoyǎnr zhágāo* 耳朵眼儿炸糕), mutton soup (*yángròu tāng* 羊肉汤) and *jianbing guozi* (煎饼果子). Jianbing guozi is a thin pancake made from green bean flour. When it's being grilled, an egg is broken and spread over top of the pancake, then a sweet soy sauce and a hot sauce is spread over the pancake. The pancake is then wrapped around a Chinese donut (*yóu tiáo* 油条).

There are some snacks that are only for the brave of stomach. In fall, grasshoppers aren't seen only in the grass but also on plates. When the leaves change color, peddlers set up stalls along the roads and fry up some grasshoppers.

For those who are hungry to dip their chopsticks into Chinese dishes of various flavors, the Nanshi Food Street (*nánshì shípǐn jiē* 南市食品街) provides some of the country's best choices. It's particularly known for its seafood, culled from the port area of Tanggu. In typical Chinese custom, the fish is brought live to your table for your pre-cooking approval before being prepared.

Most of the bars are on Youyi Lu in Hexi District. Lots of them feature an international cast that spans the globe.

RESTAURANTS

Goubuli Baozi Dian 狗不理包子店
Specializes in the tasty meat buns.
✉ 322 Heping Lu, Heping District
和平区和平路 322 号❺
☎ 2303 1115
🕒 10am to 9pm

Hongqishun Fanzhuang 鸿起顺饭庄
Offers Muslim cuisine.
✉ 668 Dagu Nan Lu, Hexi District
河西区大沽南路 668 号❽
☎ 2832 7956
🕒 10am to 9pm

Nanshi Food Street 南市食品街
The street is packed with restaurants and snack shops.
✉ NanShi Qinghe Jie, Heping District
和平区南市清和街
☎ 2727 1761
🕒 10am to 9pm

Qishilin Xicanting 起士林西餐厅
One of the oldest European restaurants in the city.
✉ 27 Zhejiang Lu, Heping District
和平区浙江路 27 号❼
☎ 2332 2247
🕒 10am to 9pm

Tianjin Caiguan 天津菜馆
Delicious Tianjin cuisine, especially recommended are the stir-fried crab eggs (*qīngchǎo xiārén* 清炒虾仁) and *cengbeng liyu* (蹭蹦鲤鱼), a fish that's been de-boned.
✉ 20 Nanshi Shipin Jie Siqu
南市食品街四区 20 号❾
☎ 2735 2115
🕒 10am to 9pm

Tianjinwei 1928 天津卫 1928
Guangdong and Tianjin cuisine.
✉ 1/F Nüren Jie, 5 Nanmenwai Dajie, Heping District 和平区南门外大街 5 号女人街 1 层❻
☎ 2728 1928

Souvenirs

The Quanyechang Bazaar (*quànyè chǎng* 劝业场) has stood at the juncture of Binjiang Lu and Heping Lu for more than 70 years and remains a favorite shopping area for locals. Head over to Xiangzhong Lu (厢中路), where there's a pedestrian street to explore, and do some souvenir hunting.

Carpets and rugs are Tianjin specialties; they can be pricey if they're handmade since

All of Tianjin's snacks can be found at the Nanshi Food Street.

they're very labor intensive. Tongqingli Shopping Street (*tōngqìnglǐ lǚyóu gòuwù jiē* 通庆里旅游购物街), in the Old Culture Street area, has souvenirs galore and is housed inside a complex of ten old courtyard homes.

If you're looking for some modernity, then head over to Golden Street (*jīn jiē* 金街), where the city's upscale shopping district is located. With malls and plazas lining the streets, Tianjin is just as fashionable as Beijing and offers much better prices.

The village of Yangliuqing is 20 kilometers west of Tianjin City. The village is famous for its wood block prints with vibrant colors. The prints, also known as Nian Hua (yearly painting), have been used for door decoration for the Chinese New Years for over 600 years. The paintings mostly features gate guardians, babies, and other lucky charms.

Other Information

POST OFFICES

Heping Lu Post Office 和平路邮政局

✉ 123 Heping Lu, Heping District
和平区和平路 123 号⓬

☎ 2730 5959

🕒 8:30am to 6:30pm

Tianjin Station Post Office 天津站邮政局

✉ 86 Haihe Dong Lu, Hedong District
河东区海河东路 86 号⓫

☎ 2401 3070

🕒 24 hours

HOSPITALS

Tianjin Medical University General Hospital 天津市医科大学总医院

✉ 154 Anshan Dao, Heping District
和平区鞍山道 154 号⓭

☎ 6036 2255

COMPLAINT HOTLINES

☎ General: 2835 9093

☎ Taxi: 2354 9000

Entertainment

Tianjin Grand Plaza 天津大舞台

A large entertainment complex with an opera house, western restaurants, bars, and KTV.

✉ 44 Guangrong Lu, Hongqiao District
红桥区光荣路 44 号

☎ 2668 8888

🕒 1pm to 3am

Tianjin Mingliu Teahouse 天津名流茶馆

Local folk performances while sipping tea and munching on snacks.

✉ 177 Xinhua Lu, Heping District
和平区新华路 177 号⓾

☎ 2711 6382

🕒 2pm to 6pm, Variety shows
7:45pm to 10:30pm, Comic dialogues

¥ 5, Variety shows
10, Comic dialogues

Chengde, the Emperor's Summer Getaway

Area Code 0314

Heritage: Imperial Summer Villa, Eight Outer Temples

Lush forests, bleak rock formations and unique temples make a trip to **Chengde** an outdoor adventure and cultural tour.

If you thought the Summer Palace was a nice place to escape the city swelter, then you should head further north to Chengde, a town that boasts the largest imperial summer retreat complex in China. Known as the **Imperial Summer Villa** (*bishǔ shānzhuāng* 避暑山庄), or "escape the heat mountain villa," the park has been Chengde's main attraction since 1703. Set in a mountain valley and surrounded by an ancient wall, the parkland includes its own lake, pine forests, hunting ground and pavilions.

The town of Chengde itself sprung up only to support the imperial entourage that set up camp there every summer, and it has never lost the feel of a tourist destination. Radiating from the southern gate of the Imperial Summer Villa, modern Chengde is small, but has a lively street scene with vendors and markets and pleasant tree-lined lanes. Crossing the **Wulie River** on the only bridge into town, you'll find Chengde is a relaxed town far from the din and bustle of Beijing. These days travelers don't come just to escape the summer heat, but also for Chengde's clean mountain air.

When the weather is still warm, people of all

One of the Imperial Summer Villa's quiet pavilions.

ages come to hang out in the **Town Square**, flying kites and playing badminton well past dusk. The square on Nanyingzi Da Jie is the heart of the town and a fine place to sit and people-watch. Further north along the road is a towering statue of Qing emperor Kangxi on horseback guarding the city's largest traffic circle. Close to the statue is Lizhengmen Da Jie, which curves close to the Imperial Summer Villa wall with grassy spaces that make for pleasant walks past the two main gates of the park. The eastern edge of town is bound by the Wulie River, a broad gentle waterway with views across to the hills that tumble right down to its banks. Along much of the length of the river is a waterfront park with winding paths, pine trees and rocks sculpture – another fine place for a stroll. If it's hot, you might try the public swimming area just upstream from the city's main bridge.

Besides the famed Imperial Summer Villa, Chengde also boasts the **Eight Outer Temples** (*wàibāmiào* 外八庙), built during the reigns of Emperor Kangxi and his grandson Qianlong. There were once 12 temples, but today only eight remain open to visitors. In its heyday, the temples had imperial patronage, and supported a large and vibrant spiritual community. The eight temples are all set in the hills north of the town center where the mountain scenery alone makes it worth the trip, not to mention the amazing Buddhist art.

One of the highlights of the eight temples is the enchanting golden statue of Guanyin, the Bodhisattva of Mercy, at **Temple of Universal Tranquility** (*pǔníng sì* 普宁寺). At 72 feet (22 m) tall and with 42 arms, her figure is one that's not easily forgotten. Climb a ladder to get a closer look at the Bodhisattva, one of the most stunning statues of its kind. The temple was built by Emperor Qianlong to commemorate his victory over Mongolian tribes and mixes Han Chinese and Tibetan ethnic styles.

And if you don't have time to swing through Tibet during your stay in China, you should check out **Putuozongcheng Zhi Miao** (*pǔtuózōngchéng zhī miào* 普陀宗乘之庙), a replica of Lhasa's Potala Palace, set against a backdrop of piney hills just to the north of the Imperial Summer Villa park. The temple was built for visiting heads of various

The largest of the Eight Outer Temples, a replica of the Potala Palace in Tibet.

Tibetan and Mongolian tribes who came to celebrate Emperor Qianlong's 60th birthday; it was hoped they would feel more at home with a familiar sight. When you enter the first gate you can smell the whiff of incense, and heading up the stairs you're slowly transported to Lhasa. The Potala is one of the finest architectural gems around, even if only in imitation. Spin the old brass prayer wheels for good luck – but make sure to spin them clockwise. Also make sure to look for

the numerous artifacts exhibited within. The view from the top of the temple is stunning.

Also incorporating Tibetan architecture is the **Temple of Happiness and Longevity** (*xūmífúshòu zhī miào* 须弥福寿之庙), built to honor the sixth Panchen Lama who visited Chengde in 1780 for Qianlong's birthday celebrations. On sunny days, the roof of the main hall is spellbinding. The hall's double-tiered roof is made of copper and is gilded with 1,100 pounds (500 kg) of gold, and each eave sports two dragons, each made from about a ton of gold. This and Putuozongcheng are typical Lamaist structures as the Qing emperors were fervent followers of Lamaist Buddhism. The **Temple of Universal Happiness** (*pǔlè sì* 普乐寺) was built in 1766 for visiting dignitaries from minority groups.

Beyond the outer temples, the dry mountains of northern Hebei Province recede into the haze. The sandstone formations here are truly spectacular; they're vaguely reminiscent of the American Southwest. A few of the more fantastic rock forms have been given names, the most notable being **Hammer Mountain** (*bàngchui shān* 棒槌山), which looks like a giant hammer with its handle up, and **Frog Rock** (*háma shí* 蛤蟆石), which looks like a frog about

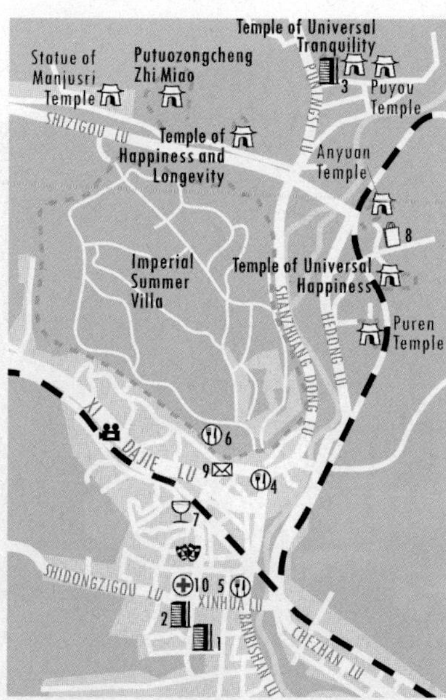

to jump. These two unusual formations are just uphill from the Temple of Universal Happiness, so it's easy to do both in one excursion. More-intrepid travelers might want to explore the trails heading off southeast that connect with peasant tracks and can be followed to more distant mountains and ridges, all without entrance fees.

For those looking to make a complete circuit of the sites outside the town, buses leave from many of the large hotels every morning and taxis are abundant. The temples aren't too far away from town and going by bike is an excellent way to see the sights.

IMPERIAL SUMMER VILLA

While first established by Emperor Kangxi, the renowned mountain resort reached its prime in the 1790's during the reign of Emperor Qianlong – one of the most famous Qing emperors. They each ordered the construction of 36 scenic spots, from moon gazing pavilions to rocks carved with Tang calligraphy. Today many of the 72 originals are no more – lost in the layers of time or destroyed by war. But in this a park of nearly 2.3 square miles (590 ha), there are still plenty of delightful old buildings tucked into meadows or glens. The entire parkland is closed in by a wall along the dramatic ridge at the northern edge and abuts the town along the south, adding to the feeling of separation from regular life. Tasteful trails cross the various creeks and hills and the wall itself can be walked in its entirety. While the surrounding countryside has long since been logged of its big trees, inside the park is a mature forest of pines and cypress, a rare treat in China. It's easy to imagine royalty roaming this imperial playground on lazy summer days, perhaps stopping to write a poem when the mood struck.

As for the famous spots, many are worth mentioning. The first and grandest is the **Front Palace** (*zhèng gōng* 正宫). The throne hall is an impressive structure, worthy of seating any emperor, and the **Hall of Simplicity and Sincerity** (*dànbó jìngchéng diàn* 澹泊敬诚殿) is notable for the fragrant wood, nanmu, from which it's constructed. Just beyond the palace is a large lake crisscrossed by bridges and islands and dotted with 18th century buildings. This area is the most beautiful in the park and meets expectations for a traditional Chinese landscape. Be sure to visit **Ruyi Island** (*rúyì zhōu* 如意洲) and the **Misty Rain Tower** (*yānyǔ lóu* 烟雨楼), the former imperial study. Beyond the lake is the **Wenjin Chamber** (*wénjīn gé* 文津阁), which housed a set of anthologies commissioned by Emperor Qianlong. The anthologies took 10 years to compile. Sadly, of the original four sets, three have been lost and the remaining one is now in Beijing. Further on down the path is the **Yongyou Temple Pagoda** (*yǒngyòusì tǎ* 永佑寺塔), proudly standing over a grassy meadow and the remnants of a temple.

Quotes

"If I had known this was a hunting-ground I would've brought my bow and found my own dinner."

"Our family takes a trip to a different famous temple in China every summer, but this time we got to see eight, all in four days!"

After you've had your fill of historic sites, roaming the hills in search of solitude and birdsong is a pleasure in itself. Who knows, you might find one of the missing 72 scenic spots. The back of the park was originally the imperial hunting grounds, chosen for its varied terrain. Now, instead of going on horseback, there are hourly tour bus trips up the hills that stop at the scenic points where tourists still look for deer or joke about tigers and wolves. If you make it up to the top ridge the views are indeed superb and many of the other local sights are visible, including Hammer Mountain to the east and the Putuozongcheng Zhi Miao to the north. ■

Making Your Trip Easy

Practical Tips

While emperors came here to escape the summer heat, Chengde isn't really much cooler than Beijing. However, it's much less humid and sticky. Bring sunscreen and lip protection for the dry air. If you go in the winter, it's cold and often there's snow, but it's just as scenic. Also, by visiting in the winter, you can escape the summer crowds. Chengde is a great place for walking, so bring a sturdy pair of shoes.

Transportation

Bus – Taking a bus is also a viable option. The big advantage is that you can get off at the Jinshanling Great Wall (*jīnshānlǐng chángchéng* 金山岭长城), which is about half way from Beijing to Chengde near the border of Hebei Province. Air-conditioned buses leave for Beijing every 30 minutes and tickets are RMB 45. The bus station is just off the entrance of the Beijing-Chengde highway.

Taxi – Taking a taxi within the city will cost about RMB 5, and RMB 10 to the surrounding area. Most drivers won't use the meters, so you'll have to agree on a price before setting off.

Train – The most comfortable and convenient way to Chengde is by train from Beijing. The Chengde express from Beijing takes about 5 hours and is a "soft seat" train. One-way tickets cost RMB 61. From the Chengde train station it's only a 15-minute taxi ride into the city center.

The Best of Chengde

Imperial Summer Villa
避暑山庄 *bìshǔ shānzhuāng*
✉ Shanzhuang Lu 山庄路
☎ 216 0513
🕒 8am to 5pm
¥ 90, peak-season
72, off-season

Putuozongcheng Zhi Miao
普陀宗乘之庙 *pǔtuózōngchéng zhī miào*
✉ Shizigou Lu 狮子沟路
☎ 216 3072
🕒 8am to 5pm
¥ 50, peak-season
40, off-season

Temple of Universal Tranquility
普宁寺 *pǔníng sì*
✉ Puning Lu, Bei Xinglong Jie
北兴隆街普宁路
☎ 205 8882
🕒 8am to 5pm
¥ 50, peak-season
40, off-season

Puning Temple's monks performing their religious ceremonies.

The 120-ton, 72-foot-tall (22 m) wood statue of Guanyin and her 42 arms.

Hotels

Jintai Hotel 金泰饭店 *jīntài fàndiàn* ★★★
✉ A1, Cuiqiao Lu, Shuangqiao District
双桥区翠桥路甲 1 号❷
☎ 206 9870, 227 8200
¥ 400 – double room, peak-season
240 – double room, off-season
@ www.cncdt.com/lvhotel/fl/jintai.htl

Lolo Hotel 露露大酒店 *lùlù dàjiǔdiàn* ★★★
✉ Nan 6, Cuiqiao Lu 翠桥路南 6 号❶
☎ 206 8888 ext 2007 or 2088
¥ 450 – double room, peak-season
260 – double room, off-season
@ www.lolohotel.com

Shangketang Hotel
普宁寺上客堂 *pǔníngsì shàngkètáng* ★★★
✉ west side of Temple of Universal Tranquility 普宁寺西侧❸
☎ 205 8886, 205 8888
¥ 350 – double room, peak-season
250 – double room, off-season
@ www.cncdt.com/lvhotel/fl/shangkt.htl

Food & Restaurants

Chengde is full of small street-side stalls and hole-in-the-wall restaurants. A good pick is *rou jia mo* (肉夹馍), which is a bread pocket stuffed with pork and cilantro. Not to be missed are the great Chengde hand-tossed noodles, straight from a big black pot sizzling with peppers, eggs and greens. Corn on the cob, a local specialty, is tasty and sold everywhere. Chengde's cuisine is typical northeast fare – hearty and warming. Some of the local specials include rice rolls with a sweet bean stuffing (*lǘ dǎ gǔn* 驴打滚) and *boyu mian* (拨御面) a snow-white noodle that's served in a chicken stock. In some restaurants you can also find local wild game like deer or pheasant, fresh and lightly seasoned.

RESTAURANTS

Dongpo Fanzhuang 东坡饭庄
✉ Xiaonanmen 南小门❼
☎ 210 6315

Qiwang Lou Restaurant 绮望楼宾馆餐厅
✉ Bifengmen Lu 碧峰门路❻
☎ 202 2196

Saiwai Jiujia 塞外酒家

Memorable Experiences

Sitting outside for dinner at a short table with short stools, eating kabobs of various local meats, from tasty rabbit to spicy lamb, and drinking beers with some locals.

Watching the nightly procession of dancers and music-makers walk from the Statue of Kangxi southeast into town, beating gongs and cymbals all the way.

Hiking up to Hammer Mountain - there was a nice breeze that day and the views were superb.

✉ West of Imperial Summer Villa's Dehui Gate 避暑山庄德惠门西侧❹

Xin Qianlong Restaurant
新乾隆酒楼
✉ inside Dijingyuan Dasha 帝景园大厦内❺
☎ 207 2222

Souvenirs

In the center of town there are shaded avenues, winding alleys and markets. The markets are filled with street vendors and food stands, and locals bargaining for their daily veggies or household goods. People sell everything from Tibetan tiger claws, (though highly illegal), to pots and pans. These streets are good for wandering - just head any old way and eventually you'll come out at the river or on Nanyingzi Da Jie.

Some items unique to Chengde include Fengning cloth paintings (*fēngníng bùhúhuà* 丰宁布糊画) or little knick-knacks made from nutshells (*hépí gōngyìpǐn* 核皮工艺品).

You can do most of the souvenir shopping at Kangqian Tourist Shopping City (kāngqián lǚyóu shāngpǐnchéng 康乾旅游商品城❽, ☎ 295 7000) at B1B Rongji Garden, Puning Lu (普宁路容基花园 B1B 座), which is open from 7am to 7pm.

Other Informaiton

POST OFFICES

Huoshen Miao Post Office 火神庙邮局
✉ Huoshen Miao 火神庙❾
☎ 203 0673

HOSPITALS

Chengde Medical School Hospital
承德市医学院附属医院
✉ Nanyingzi Da Jie 南营子大街❿
☎ 206 4747

COMPLAINT HOTLINES

☎ General: 202 4548
☎ Taxi: 216 0073

TOURISM INFORMATION WEBSITE

www.cncdt.com

AT THE POST OFFICE 在邮局			
How much will it cost to mail this to…?		jì dào … duōshǎo qián	寄到…多少钱?
I'd like to buy a(n)….		wǒ xiǎng mǎi …	我想买…
	envelope	xìnfēng	信封
	airmail envelope	hángkōng xìnfēng	航空信封
	postcard	míngxìnpiàn	明信片
	stamp	yóupiào	邮票
I'd like to mail it by ….		wǒ xiǎng jì	我想寄…
	airmail	hángkōng	航空
	express mail	tèkuài zhuāndì	特快专递
	registered mail	guàhào	挂号
	surface mail	píngxìn	平信

Beidaihe & Shanhaiguan; Sun, Sand and the Great Wall

Area Code 0335

The seaside resort town of **Beidaihe** is famous for its beaches, while in neighboring Shanhaiguan you'll find relics of the past in this ancient military stronghold.

While children build imperial sand castles on the beach, parents lounge around in their swimsuits and buy ice cream from one of the many street vendors. Along the beach, streets are lined with outdoor seafood restaurants, shell shops and hawkers selling their wares. In the summer months, the seaside resort town of Beidaihe, about 175 miles (280 km) from Beijing, comes alive with wealthy Chinese families taking a break from city life. Most people come here for the beach, the sunshine and the fresh air. But there's a lot more to Beidaihe than sun and sand – away from the beach, you'll find ancient temples and mountain parks.

At the turn of the 19th century, Beidaihe was transformed from a tiny fishing village into a summer resort for European diplomats, missionaries and businessmen from Beijing and Tianjin. Today it has opened up to local and international tourists alike, who flock here in droves during the hottest summer months.

A tower sits on top of the city walls with a tablet proclaiming "The First Pass Under Heaven."

Beidaihe's sandy beaches stretch for some 6 miles (10 km) along the Bohai Sea. Though the beaches are jam-packed in July and August, it's still possible to find a few quiet coves where you can escape the crowds. The coastline is divided into three main beaches: Middle Beach (*zhōng hǎitān* 中海滩), East Mountain (*dōng shān* 东山) and West Beach (*xī hǎitān* 西海滩). Of the three beaches, Middle Beach (which is made up of many small beaches, separated by rocky outcrops) is the most popular and it's easy to find drinks, snacks and souvenirs – and be bombarded by hackers pushing bracelets and shells. West Beach is similar, though a little quieter. East Mountain features long stretches of beach where you can bask in some hard-to-find privacy. **Tiger Rocks** (*lǎohǔ shí* 老虎石), in the central beach area, is a popular spot for locals to gather and fish, fly kites and unwind. From a distance, the rocks look like a group of tigers bathing in the sea. **Pigeon's Nest** (*gēzi wō* 鸽子窝) over at East Mountain is a good spot to catch the sunrise as it slowly peers over the sea's horizon.

Lianfeng Mountain (*liánfēng shān* 联峰山) stands 500 feet (153 m) above sea level and is covered in pines and cypress trees. This small mountain has two adjoining peaks and backs onto the beach, and features pavilions, walking paths and winding bridges. The **Sea-Viewing Pavilion** (*wànghǎi tíng* 望海亭) has great views of the Bohai Sea. At the base of the mountain is **Lotus Stone Park** (*liánhuāshí gōngyuán* 莲花石公园), named

Red-roofed buildings at Beidaihe's seashore.

after several upright rocks in the shape of a lotus flower. In the northern end of the park is the **Guanyin Temple** (*guānyīn sì* 观音寺). It's close to downtown Beidaihe and most local hotels offer direct shuttles to the park.

Because of Beidaihe's relative fame and the crowds it draws, the beaches have become overcrowded. **Nandaihe**, to the south, is also a well-developed tourist destination, offering, among other activities, sand sledding – with some runs ending in the water.

While the best beaches are in Beidaihe, the best historical sites are in neighboring **Shanhaiguan**, a small, sleepy town with a bloody past. Situated between the Bohai Sea and the Yanshan Mountains, Shanhaiguan was a military stronghold during the Ming dynasty and served as a major pass in the eastern section of the Great Wall. It was considered a key location for the defense of the ancient capitals of Beijing and Xi'an from northern invaders. You can still get a sense of the town's history with its old city walls, small hutongs and views of the Great Wall winding its way up the Yanshan Mountains or in the opposite direction, plunging into the Bohai Sea.

The First Pass Under Heaven (*tiānxià dìyī guān* 天下第一关), also known as the Eastern Gate or Shanhai Pass, was once the final barrier preventing the northern tribes from encroaching into Beijing. An inscription over the arched gate reads "The First Pass Under Heaven" in bold Chinese characters 5 feet (1.6 m) high, left behind by Ming calligraphist Xiao Xian. The gate features a 40-foot-high (12 m) wall and a two-story, double-roofed tower built in 1381. The tower features 68 archery slots facing north, east and south, giving archers a clear line of sight to shoot any invaders. The gate also features an exhibition of weaponry, military uniforms and traditional costumes.

Memorable Experiences

Watching the sunrise at Yingjiao Pavilion on the northwest beach – one of China's nine famous sunrise-watching spots.

Eating at one of Shanhaiguan's hole-in-the-wall restaurants, choosing my dinner from a pail of live sea creatures.

Riding a bicycle-built-for-two around Beidaihe's quiet, tree-lined streets, checking out the bizarre and tacky resort villas with their shady gardens.

Sitting on a deserted stretch of beach late at night, watching the stars and listening to the waves.

Beidaihe's busy summer beach.

Just outside of town is **Old Dragon's Head** (*lǎo lóngtóu* 老龙头), where the Great Wall meets the sea. This is the easternmost point of the Great Wall, where a stone-carved dragon head once faced the sea. The original wall was badly damaged by the Eight-Power Allied Forces in 1900, but the area was restored to its former glory in 1987. Now it's a major tourist site, complete with a restored city, pagodas, towers and small museum – even a maze. Old Dragon's Head, which stretches 87 feet (23 m) into the sea, is surrounded by pretty beaches, which are only accessible if you pay the admission price to the site. It's easily reached by bus or taxi, but it's more interesting to ride a bike or go for a bumpy jaunt in an auto-rickshaw. ■

Making Your Trip Easy

Practical Tips

The best time to travel to Beidaihe and Shanhaiguan is from May to September when the temperature holds steady around 77°F (25°C). However, July and August are when vacationing Beijingers hit the beaches and it can be noisy and crowded. Tickets and hotel prices also soar during the peak-season. If you don't like crowds, avoid visiting on the weekends. In June, there's a festival on the Great Wall that involves fireworks, races up the wall and performances by actors dressed in Ming dynasty costumes. This is a great time to visit despite being packed with tourists.

Transportation

Airport – There is a small airport located 12.5 miles (20 km) to Qinhuangdao offering flights to major cities in the region.

Bicycle – Bikes are also a good option and can be rented at most hotels.

Taxi – Flag-fall is RMB 5 and taxis can be rented for the day from RMB 150 to 200.

Train – There are train stations in Qinhuangdao, Beidaihe and Shanhaiguan, but not all trains stop at every station, so be sure to check before buying a ticket. During the summer months, trains depart daily from most major cities in the region. It's 3 hours to Beijing and 4 hours to Tianjin.

The Best of Beidaihe & Shanhaiguan

The First Pass Under Heaven

天下第一关景区 *tiānxià dìyīguān jǐngqū*

The inviting waters of Nandaihe disgorges its catch.

✉ 1 Dong Da Jie, Shanhaiguan District
山海关区东大街 1 号
☎ 505 1106
🕒 7am to 6:30pm, peak-season
7:30am to 5pm, off-season

Nandaihe International Recreation Center
南戴河国际娱乐中心 *nándàihé guójì yúlè zhōngxīn*
✉ 999 Yanhai Lu, Nandaihe, Funing County
抚宁县南戴河旅游渡假区沿海路 999 号
🕒 7am to 7pm, peak-season
8am to 4:30pm, off-season
¥ 60

Old Dragon's Head 老龙头 *lǎo lóngtóu*
✉ Nanhai Xi Lu, Shanhaiguan
山海关区南海西路
☎ 515 2996
🕒 7am to 6pm,peak-season
7:30am to 5pm,off-season
¥ 50

Hotels

Great Wall Hotel 秦皇岛长城酒店
qínhuángdǎo chángchéng jiǔdiàn ★★★★
✉ 202 Yanshan Da Jie 燕山大街 202 号
☎ 306 1666, 364 4555
¥ 434 – double room

International Hotel 秦皇岛国际饭店
qínhuángdǎo guójì fàndiàn ★★★★
✉ 303 Wenhua Lu 文化路 303 号
☎ 308 3083
¥ 420 – double room
@ www.qhdih.com

Yangcheng Hotel
羊城大酒店 *yángchéng dàjiǔdiàn* ★★★
✉ 132 Yingbin Lu 迎宾路 132 号
☎ 360 4466
¥ 380 – double room, peak-season
198 – double room, off-season
@ www.ychotel.com

Beijing TV Journalism Training Center
北京电视台记者培训中心 *běijīng diànshìtái jìzhě péixùn zhōngxīn*
✉ Sanwei Lu, Golden Beach, Changli County 昌黎县黄金海岸三纬路
☎ 228 8999, 228 9911
¥ 780 – double room, peak-season
272 – double room, off-season

Food & Restaurants

As one might guess from its close proximity

Quotes

"The food was marvelous! Seafood, seafood and more seafood. We had barbeque every night we were there - small fish, crab, corn on the cob, spicy beef and chicken. Outdoor seafood barbeque is a specialty of the area."

"Beidaihe was a great place to get away and relax under a blue sky. I sat on an empty beach all day and read a book, enjoying the sea breeze - and no noise but the waves hitting the shore."

to the sea, Beidaihe is known for its wide variety of fresh seafood. You don't need to speak Chinese to order – just point at your entrée swimming around in a bucket of water. Beidaihe is best known for its shellfish, especially crab, lobster, cuttlefish and scallops. The prawns, battered or slathered in garlic, are a must. The best places to go are along the beachfront, where endless stalls and outdoor restaurants serve up grilled seafood and spicy kebabs. In Shanhaiguan, the best restaurants can be found along Nan Da Jie while in Beidaihe head over to Bao Er Lu.

RESTAURANTS

Haitian Yise Jiudian 海天一色酒店

Specializes in seafood.

✉ 56 Nanshan Jie, Haigang District
海港区南山街 56 号

☎ 342 7788

🕒 10am to midnight

Haixian Ju 海鲜居

✉ Hongqi Lu, Qinhuangdao 秦皇岛红旗路

☎ 323 0432

🕒 10am to 10pm

Xicheng BBQ 熙成烤肉城

✉ Hebei Dajie, Haigang District
海港区河北大街

☎ 806 8138

Xinya Chuanbing 新雅春饼

✉ 86 Gangcheng Dajie, Haigang District
海港区港城大街 86 号

☎ 364 06666

Souvenirs

Once you bypass the tacky plastic trinkets and gaudy shell statues, you can find some real treasures in Beidaihe; particularly if it's a set of pearls you're after. Beidaihe has a huge indoor market at Shitang Lu that stretches for at least two city blocks and is 2 stories high. Here you'll find everything from pearls, shells and wooden carvings to seafood and spices (not to mention stuffed turtles and life-size shell sculptures). It's similar to the Pearl Market in Beijing, but prices are much better. Still, be prepared to bargain. There are hundreds of vendors selling pearl necklaces, bracelets and earrings, but be on the lookout for fakes. Fake pearls have a coating that can be scratched off with your fingernail – most vendors will let you scratch away at their wares to check for authenticity. There is also a night market by the wharf where you can buy shells and local handicrafts. In Shanhaiguan, you can also find pearls and handicrafts. Check out the street market on Nan Da Jie or the clothing market.

Other Information

POST OFFICES

Hebei Da Jie Post Office 河北大街邮局

✉ Hebei Da Jie 河北大街

☎ 304 0161

HOSPITALS

The First Qinhuangdao People's Hospital
秦皇岛市第一人民医院

✉ 22 Wenhua Lu, Haigang District
海港区文化路 22 号

☎ 303 4187

COMPLAINT HOTLINES

☎ General: 307 6564

☎ Taxi: 362 7305

TOURISM INFORMATION WEBSITE

ⓔ www.beidaihe.com.cn

Life on Inner Mongolia's vast grasslands.

Hohhot, the Green Pastures of the North

Area Code 0471

Inner Mongolia has the lure of open grassy plains, herds of horses and sheep roaming freely while nomadic herdsmen watch over their flock, and a stretch of blue sky that eventually touches the green plains far off in the horizon.

Hohhot, the capital of the Inner Mongolia Autonomous Region, may not immediately stir images of a rough and ready frontier, but what this cosmopolitan city does offer is a gateway to the majesty of the grasslands which lie just beyond the city. The sights within the city shouldn't be dismissed either. Once a political and cultural center, the relics of the past are strewn throughout. More than 36 ethnic groups live in Hohhot's confines, with Mongolians making up about 9% of the population.

Bone fragments of early humans who lived in the area as early as 500,000 years ago have been found; these early ancestors are thought to be contemporaries of Peking Man. The first permanent establishment began about 2,300 years ago during the

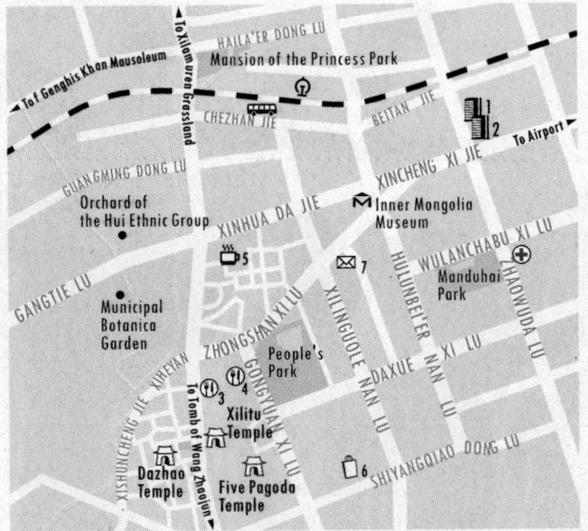

Warring States Period when the King of Zhao built the city of Yunzhong in the area. The merger of a 16th century Mongolian settlement and a city founded by Ming emperor Wanli has become present-day Hohhot.

Though no longer apparent, the city was once a center of Buddhism with over 50 temples, although many are now in ruins. The **Dazhao Temple** (*dàzhāo* 大召) – "*zhao*" means "temple" in Mongolian – was built in 1580 and is home to a 8.2-foot-tall (2.5 m) tall silver Buddha which the 3rd Dalai Lama came to personally bless in 1586. The 7.4-acre (30,000m2) complex is an interesting mix of Tibetan and Han architectural traditions.

The **Xilitu Temple** (*xílìtú zhāo* 席力图召), only a few hundred feet (100 m) away from the Dazhao Temple, is the largest and prettiest temple. It was built from 1567 to 1619 and has seen continual expansion. The 4th Dalai Lama's teacher was the former abbot of this Lama temple, and upon the accession of the 4th Dalai Lama, the temple was greatly expanded in honor of his teacher. The temple complex is mostly of traditional Han Chinese design, but the **Dajing Hall** (*dàjīng táng* 大经堂) features Tibetan styling. In the southeast corner is a 50-foot (15 m) high tower. During the regularly held Buddhist festivals, colorful dancers wear intricate Tibetan style masks.

Just north of the Dazhao Temple is the **Five Pagoda Temple** (*wǔtǎ sì* 五塔寺). This site

Horse taming is still an important skill.

was originally part of Cideng Temple (*cídēng sì* 慈灯寺), which had five pagodas. Only one pagoda remains in this smallish garden; the rest of the pagodas were unable to stand the test of time. The remaining pagoda stands a tall 52.5 feet (16 m) and is topped with five smaller pagodas. Carved into the bottom of the pagoda are Buddhist scriptures in Tibetan, Mongolian and Han script. On the upper-tiers of the pagoda are more than a thousand gold plated Buddha figurines. On the northern wall, there's a 57-inch-long (1.45 m) astronomical map in Mongolian, the only one of its kind.

About 5.6 miles (9 km) south of Hohhot is the 98-foot-high (30 m) **Tomb of Wang Zhaojun** (*zhāojūn mù* 昭君墓). Wang Zhaojun was a maid in waiting during the Western Han dynasty who was renowned for her exceptional beauty and intelligence. Wang Zhaojun wasn't an actual concubine; rather she was one of the many women who were concubine candidates. These women would live uneventful lives in the palace, waiting for the emperor to choose them to grace his imperial bedchamber. When a northern Xiongnu chief asked for a Han princess to marry, the emperor decided to betroth Wang Zhaojun. At the wedding banquet the emperor was chagrined to discover her amazing beauty and exceptional wit. He later discovered that the court painter had purposely painted her ugly because the upright maiden refused to offer him a bribe. The able bride was now freed from the stifling palace and played an important role in keeping the peace between the Han dynasty and the northern tribes. Her burial mound, which is covered with trees and grass, is nicknamed the "Green Tomb" (*qīng zhǒng* 青冢) because, supposedly, the grass on the small mound remains green when all others wither with the arrival of cold weather.

One cannot mention Mongolia without referring to one of the world's most famous

Genghis Khan carved out the world's largest empire.

and feared figures of all time, Genghis Khan. From humble beginnings, the Great Khan united the feuding Mongolian tribes into an unstoppable war-machine that created an empire spreading from the Pacific Ocean to the doors of Western Europe. Genghis Khan conquered all within his path and was known for integrating new ideas and foreign personnel if they were useful. His mounted warriors were so feared in Europe that their coming was considered the coming of the Apocalypse.

Genghis died in 1227 battling the Western Xia in China's northwest. According to Mongolian tradition of the time, nobles would be buried at a place of their own choosing and Genghis's chosen site has yet to be discovered. According to legend, after he was buried, horses were herded over his tomb and once the grass had returned, the 2,000 laborers who built his tomb were killed by 800 soldiers, who in turn were executed to keep the location a secret.

The **Genghis Khan Mausoleum** (*chéngjísīhán líng* 成吉思汗陵) isn't close to Hohhot, but it deserves special mention. The

Quotes

"The grassland is amazing. Coming from a big city, I've ever seen such vast expanses before. It's like a green carpet that never ends."

"The people here are great. They're friendly and all smiles. It's hard to imagine them nearly overrunning Europe centuries ago."

Memorable Experiences

Riding on a galloping horse as he decides to ignore my instructions and takes off on his own volition, leaving me to sit on the saddle and hope he knows where he's going.

Spending a night in a yurt while eating and drinking with a voluble Mongolian family.

mausoleum is best reached by long-distance bus; the closest cities are Baotou and Dongsheng. You will see the towering blue-roofed domes of the three yurt-like structures rising above the plain long before you actually arrive. A massive 16-foot-tall (5 m) tall statue of the Khan on horseback gazes out over the grasslands he once roamed and ruled. Though his remains aren't actually housed in the mausoleum, there are enough artifacts here to keep any would-be world conqueror occupied. Weapons, saddles and numerous other artifacts including replicas of his, his wives' and brothers' coffins are displayed throughout the mausoleum.

The mausoleum is an important pilgrimage destination for ethnic Mongolians and chances are you'll meet groups of Mongolians who've come here to pay their respects to their most famous kin.

About 56 miles (90 km) away from Hohhot is **Xilamuren**(*xīlāmùrén* 希拉穆仁), where the Great Wall runs across Inner Mongolia. Here one can experience life on the grasslands and in a yurt, a traditional Mongolian tent-like structure made from sheep's hide. The setting isn't completely authentic – it's a spot set aside for tours, after all, and the rough living of nomadic life has been toned down in favor of comfort and convenience. However horseback riding, performances by traditional dancers and singers as well as treks into the hinterland are all available. The more adventurous might want to try some camel riding or even going head-to-head with a Mongolian wrestler.

Visiting a Mongolian family inside their yurts offers an interesting glimpse into a rapidly changing lifestyle. Mongolians are famous for their hospitality (despite what you may think of Genghis) and many tour packages include a stay with a family. A small gift – tea is always welcomed – is a great ice-breaker.

A great time to visit Inner Mongolia is during **Nadaam Festival** (*nàdámù* 那达慕) when traditional Mongolian competitions such as wrestling, archery and horse and camel races occur. The festival is the high point for the Mongolians and every year families from throughout the region congregate around Hohhot in a makeshift campground. The festival's date depends on the Mongolian lunar calendar, but usually falls between mid-July and mid-August. ■

Making Your Trip Easy

Practical Tips

The best travel time is from July to September. The weather is mild and the animals most active.

Transportation

Airport – Baita Airport is east of Hohhot, about 5.6 miles (9 km) from downtown. It takes 15 minutes by taxi or 30 minutes by airport shuttle bus from the airport to downtown.

Taxi – The meter stars at RMB 6.

The Best of Hohhot

Dazhao Temple 大召 *dàzhāo*

✉ Dazhao Qian Jie, Yuquan District 玉泉区大召前街

☎ 630 3154

🕒 8am to 6pm

¥ 20

Tomb of Wang Zhaojun 昭君墓 *zhāojūn mù*

✉ 3.7 miles (6 km) south of Hohhot 呼和浩特市南 6 公里处

☎ 515 0201
🕒 8am to 6pm
¥ 40

Hotels

Inner Mongolia Hotel 内蒙古饭店 *nèiměnggǔ fàndiàn* ★★★★★
✉ Wulanchabu Xi Lu 乌兰察布西路
☎ 693 8888
¥ 788 – double room
@ www.nmghotel.com

Phoenix Hotel 内蒙古国航大厦 *nèiměnggǔ guóháng dàshà* ★★★★
✉ Xincheng Bei Jie 新城北街❶
☎ 660 8888
¥ 450 – double room
@ www.ni-phoenix.com.cn

Yitai Hotel 内蒙古伊泰大酒店 *nèiměnggǔ yītài dàjiǔdiàn* ★★★★
✉ 69 Dongying Nan Jie, Saihan Lu 赛罕路东影南街 69 号
☎ 223 3388
¥ 638 – double room, peak-season
346 – double room, off- season
@ www.yt-hotel.com

Pearl Inner Mongolia Hotel 草原明珠大酒店 *cǎoyuán míngzhū dàjiǔdiàn* ★★★
✉ 2 Xincheng Bei Jie 新城北街 2 号❷
☎ 660 8800
¥ 580 – double room, peak-season
280 – double room, off-season
@ www.pearl-hotel.com

Zhaojun Hotel
昭君大酒店 *zhāojūn dàjiǔdiàn* ★★★
✉ 53 Xinhua Da Jie 新华大街 53 号
☎ 696 2211
¥ 600 – double room, peak-season
260 – double room, off-season

Food & Restaurants

The food of Hohhot is a mixture of northern Chinese and ethnic Mongolian. Traditional Mongolian dishes include roasted whole sheep (*kǎoquányáng* 烤全羊), milk tea (*nǎichá* 奶茶) and oat flour noodles (*yóumiàn* 莜面). The roasted sheep is daubed with salt, then coated with a mixture of chopped ginger, scallions and pepper. It's then roasted in an oven for about an hour, until it turns golden brown. Milk tea is a traditional favorite of the Mongolians. It's made with hot tea and fresh milk; some like to add a little salt, butter or cooked millet. *Shoupa rou* (手扒肉) is a popular traditional dish that has been enjoyed for thousands of years. Mutton is simply boiled and when it's cooked, diners help themselves using their hands or small knives. *Shao mei* (稍美) is a kind of steamed dumpling that's a local delicacy, with an irresistible aroma.

Visiting a traditional yurt and having a down-home traditional Mongolian meal is one of the most genuine experiences of visiting Inner Mongolia. While eating mutton in Mongolia, there are some important traditions to follow if you're the guests of a Mongolian. Guests shouldn't help themselves to the meat; let the host select which cuts of meat you eat. Depending on seniority and whether the guest is a man or woman, different parts are served.

RESTAURANTS

Banmudi Youmian Dawang 半亩地莜面大王
Specializes in local home-style dishes and is famous for oat flour noodle feast (*yóumiàn yàn* 莜面宴).
✉ Jiwei Ganxiao, Tuanjie Xiaoqu 团结小区计委干校
☎ 466 2286

Caoyuan Cheng 草原城
Specializes in roasted sheep, roasted sheep back, *shoupa rou* and milk tea; also offers traditional singing and dancing.
✉ south of 5303 Factory, Xinganbei Lu 兴安北路 5303 工厂南
☎ 658 7899

Maixiangcun Jiulou 麦香村酒楼
Good for traditional dishes and renowned for

The Mausoleum of Genghis Khan honors the ethnic Mongolian's most revered ancestor.

Mongolian wrestling during the Nadaam Festival.

its delicious *shao mei*.

✉ 44 Da Bei Jie 大北街 44 号❸

☎ 631 5068

Menggu Daying 蒙古大营

Favorites include roasted sheep, roasted sheep back and milk tea, make reservations at least 6 hours ahead if you feel like downing a roasted sheep.

✉ Menggu Daying, Saima Chang, Hulunbeier Bei Lu
呼伦贝尔北路赛马场蒙古大营

☎ 651 6868

Xiao Feiyang 小肥羊

Authentic hotpot.

✉ Wulanchabu Dong Lu 乌兰察布东路❹

☎ 490 1998

TEAHOUSES

Humin Chacheng 呼敏茶城

✉ 2/F, Tongdao Nanjie, Huimin District 回民区通道南街

☎ 631 0771

Heavenly Pool Tea 天池茶艺

✉ inside the Inner Mongolia Stadium, 14 Xinhua Da Jie
新华大街 14 号内蒙古体育馆院内❺

☎ 639 6599

Souvenirs

Mongolian knives (*měnggǔ dāo* 蒙古刀), clothes, silver jewelry, leather products and rugs (*guàtǎn* 挂毯) are great souvenirs to grab while in Hohhot. The Mongolian knife is both an ornamental and a practical tool for everyday use – most locals carry one on their belts. Bowls (*yínwǎn* 银碗) made of pure silver, silver alloys or wood have unique designs carved into them. If you're looking for a unique beer mug, get a *jiemeng bei* (结盟杯), which are cups made from horns and decorated with silver. These cups were used by neighboring tribes: they would share a drink to seal an alliance or as a mark of friendship.

Head over to Wutasi Dong Jie (五塔寺东街) and check out the Foreign Trade Arts and Crafts Factory of Inner Mongolia (*nèiměnggǔ wàimào gōngyìpǐn chǎng* 内蒙古外贸工艺品厂 ❻, ☎ 597 3591) for your souvenir needs. About 1,000 feet (300 m) west of Huagong Lu (化工路) is the Mengliang Arts and Crafts Factory (*měngliàng gōngyìpǐn chǎng* 蒙亮工艺品厂, ☎ 396 7681), which produces Mongolian souvenirs.

Other Information

POST OFFICES

Zhongshan Lu Post Office 中山路邮局

✉ 3 Zhongshan Dong Lu 中山东路 3 号❼

☎ 692 5579

HOSPITALS

Inner Mongolia Hospital 内蒙古医院

✉ 20 Zhaowuda Lu 昭乌达路 20 号❽

☎ 662 0000

Inner Mongolia Medical University Hospital 内蒙古医学院附属医院

✉ 1 Tongdao Bei Jie 通道北街 1 号

☎ 696 5931

COMPLAINT HOTLINES

☎ General: 466 9766

☎ Taxi: 396 5296

Entertainment

Erdos Wedding Ceremony Performance 鄂尔多斯婚礼表演

Performs traditional Mongolian weddings dances.

✉ Mongolian Custom Garden 蒙古风情园

☎ 496 9993

Zhama Feast 诈马宴

A huge feast with Yuan era dancing and singing, and dishes that trace back to the imperial cuisine of the dynasty.

✉ Mongolian Custom Garden 蒙古风情园

☎ 496 9993

Wutai Shan, the Five Peaks of Serenity

Area Code 0350

Once a remote outpost reached only by the most pious of pilgrims who traveled for months with wills steeled by devotion, **Wutai Shan** remains a hidden treasure for those seeking true contemplation.

Wutai Shan's name means "five terraces," which accurately describes the five flat peaks of this sacred spot – north, east, south, west and central peak. In the quiet valleys between the peaks lie a smattering of ancient temples, twisting trails and awe-inspiring views.

The major sights at Wutai Shan are rather spread out, forcing one to indulge in the gorgeous scenery that surrounds the five terraces. This also means that no one sight is overwhelmed with tour groups. Wutai Shan's temples are an eclectic mix of Han Buddhist and Tibetan and Mongolian Lamaist traditions, making the mountain one of the best places in China to view Buddhist architecture.

The shrines on Wutai Shan date back to the Eastern Han dynasty, and the second Buddhist temple in China was built here at a time when Taoism dominated the area. A legend goes that a Buddhist monk beseeched the emperor to construct the **Xiantong Temple** (*xiǎntōng sì* 显通寺) on the mountain and suggested that a Taoist and Buddhist scroll each be put into a fire to test which religion was true. When the Taoist scroll was burned to ashes, but miraculously the Buddhist scroll remained undamaged, the temple was built. Later, Wutai Shan became a popular pilgrimage destination as more monasteries and temples were built in succeeding dynasties.

During the Sui and Tang dynasties, when Buddhism held imperial favor, over 360

Wutai Shan is one of China's most important centers of Buddhism.

Memorable Experiences

Walking on the cobbled paths in the town, serenaded by the tinkling of bells from the temples under the starlight.

Wandering between temples and viewing in awe the snow-capped peaks.

temples were built. The mountain also became an international destination point for Buddhists from other countries as they were drawn to the many temples as centers of learning. Lama Buddhists began to settle on the mountain during the Qing dynasty. Today there are 47 temples and monasteries and they continue to draw devotees and curious sightseers.

Most of the temples are located around **Taihuai**, a small town nestling in valley 5,576 feet (1,700 m) above sea level. The temples on Wutai Shan are dedicated to **Wenshu Pusa** (Manjusri), the Bodhisattva of Wisdom and Virtue. A visiting Indian monk had a vision of Wenshu in the 1st century AD and concluded Wutai Shan to be the mystical abode of Buddha's most important assistant. Numerous legends speak of how apparitions of Wenshu riding on the back of a blue lion have been sighted high above the monasteries.

ours normally begin at Taihuai; one daylong trip south of town allows you to visit several stylistically different temples. All temples share a transcendental aura, so if you're looking to get away from the drab, mundane concerns of urban life, any temple will do.

Intricate paper cuts of two female Beijing opera characters.

108 carved granite steps (the same as the number of beads on a Buddhist rosary) lead to **Dailuo Ding** (*dàiluó dǐng* 黛螺顶), the temple that houses statues of five different forms of Wenshu Pusa, each of whom supposedly lives on a different peak. Legend has it that a young monk suggested statues representing the five incarnations of Wenshu be built here to save visiting emperors from a grueling trek. For those who want to visit the bodhisattvas but don't have the time to make a house call, this is the place to ask Wutai Shan's guardians for a blessing. To make things even easier, there's now a cable car from the foot of Wutai Shan to the temple. Piety with convenience – if only the early pilgrims had it this easy.

Xiantong Temple is the largest and oldest temple on the mountain and is also conveniently located in the heart of town. It houses the amazing **Beamless Pavilion** (*wúliáng diàn* 无梁殿), which contains no beams and is supported through a complex set of interlocking pins. The impressive **Bronze Pavilion** (*tóng diàn* 铜殿) is made from 110,000 pounds (50,000 kg) of bronze; it's a perfect replica of a wooden pavilion, and the interior houses thousands of tiny Buddhas. Continuing on the bronze theme, the **Youming Bell** (*yōumíng zhōng* 幽冥钟) cast in 1620, is the largest bronze bell in the region: it's 8.2 feet (2.5 m) high, 5.25 feet (1.6 m) across, and weighs 9999.5 *jin*, or 11,000 pounds (5,000 kg). A Buddhist sutra of over 10,000 Chinese characters decorates the body of the bell.

Behind the Xiantong Temple is the largest Lama temple on the mountain, the **Pusa Ding** (*púsà dǐng* 菩萨顶). Climb the 108 stairs to this temple and gaze out on the expansive views of Taihuai and the surrounding countryside. Tibetan and Mongolian Lamas stayed here during the Ming and Qing dynasties, believing that Wenshu Pusa once lived in the same place. The Wenshu Pavilion has an interesting feature: water is stored on

Tayuan Temple is famous for the White Pagoda.

the roof when it rains and on sunny days it drips down the roof.

The 164-foot-high (50 m) high Tibetan styled **White Pagoda** (*bái tǎ* 白塔), designed by a Nepali in 1301, has become a symbol of Wutai Shan. It stands on the grounds of **Tayuan Temple** (*tǎyuàn sì* 塔院寺), also in Taihuai. A marketplace forms around it with vendors selling incense, prayer beads, Buddhist booklets and bronze Buddhas.

Just 10 minutes away from Tayuan Temple is **Shuxiang Temple** (*shūxiàng sì* 殊像寺), which features a 20-foot-tall (6 m) statue of Wenshu riding a lion. The temple itself was last rebuilt in 1487. Take a short 10 minute walk southwest and the **Puhua Temple** (*pǔhuá sì* 普华寺) will come into view. The buildings here feature intricate carvings. About 2 miles (3 km) southwest is the **South Mountain Temple** (*nánshān sì* 南山寺) where 18 Ming dynasty statues of arhats (beings who have reached Nirvana) reside.

Follow a packed earth trail down the hill for about 3 miles (5 km) and you'll arrive at the **Dragon Fountain Temple** (*lóngquán sì* 龙泉寺), where 108 steps lead to an elaborate marble entrance with carvings of Buddhas, bodhisattvas, dragons and flowers. In the main hall is an exquisitely carved **Puji Dagoba** (*pǔjì chánshī tǎ* 普济禅师塔) with a laughing Buddha looking out from each cardinal direction. In the courtyard hundreds of small chimes tinkle in the wind.

Not far from the Tayuan Temple is the **Luohou Temple** (*luóhóu sì* 罗睺寺); the present structures date from 1492. The temple features a unique circle altar where a lotus opens up to reveal a Buddha carved inside. The statue was made from a tree where an emperor saw a divine light. When the tree died during the Qing dynasty, it was carved into this lotus – a mechanism underground allows the lotus petals to be raised and lowered. ■

Quotes

"The temples are very beautiful and solemn. It's very quiet at night. I can feel the spirits floating in the air."

"Perhaps nowhere else in all of China can one view so clearly the traditional ways and the superb temple architecture of old China."

Making Your Trip Easy

Practical Tips

Wutai Shan averages more than 3,280 feet (1,000 m) above sea level and at such a high elevations, the mountain can be rather chilly. The northern terrace, at 10,030 feet (3,058 m), is the highest point in north China. It's best to visit during the summer, from June to September. This is when the temperature averages around 68°F (20°C), but be aware that the weather varies at different altitudes. It begins to snow in September, and continues until April, so bring warm clothes. The temperature starts to warm up in April and rain gear will be necessary in the summer. The temperature drops significantly at night, so be prepared.

Allow for at least three days if you're really into temples and want to soak up the atmosphere. Avoid the weekends when the tourists swarm to the mountain, especially during the summer when guesthouses double their prices. Admission to Wutai Shan is RMB 90. RMB 15 for insurance is optional. The admissions to the temples range between RMB 5 to 10. During Wenshu Pusa's birthday, the 14th day of the 6th lunar month, celebrations are held throughout the temples.

From the 18th day of the last lunar month to the 18th day of the first lunar month (usually around February) is the *fosu minhuai nian* (佛俗民怀年), a celebration that's held in Taihuai Town. Traditional Spring Festival (Chinese New Year) celebrations take over the town; people paste red paper cuttings on their windows, families spend the cold days making dumplings and the nights are punctured with the cascading lights of fireworks and deafening bangs of firecrackers. Visiting the temples during this time is spectacular. Take part in the bell-ringing ceremonies that bring in the Chinese New Year and dig into tasty vegetarian meals.

Keep in mind that Wutai Shan is a place of worship. This means showing proper respect while in the temples and towards the monks.

Transportation

Airport – Wusu Airport is 10.5 miles (17 km) southeast of downtown Taiyuan. It takes about 2 hours from Taiyuan City to the Wutai Shan Scenic Area.

Bus – There are buses from Taihuai to Beijing, Datong and Taiyuan. Taking the bus from Taiyuan to Wutai Shan costs RMB 43. From the Wutai Shan Railway Station to the mountain is 30 miles (48 km) and costs RMB 20.

Taxi – A taxi from Taiyuan to Wutai Shan will be about RMB 200. Taxis around the mountain should cost RMB 10. A taxi tour from the east terrace to the south terrace is RMB 30 per person for a round trip. Another route that goes from the middle terrace to the west terrace then finally to the north terrace is RMB 35 per person for a round trip. Another route that covers ten temples is RMB 40 per person (☎ 654 5844, 654 6150).

Train – Taihuai Town is well serviced by trains. The small train station is about an hour away from the mountain.

The Best of Wutai Shan

Pusa Ding 菩萨顶 *púsà dǐng*
✉ Taihuai Town 台怀镇
☎ 654 5499
¥ 5

Xiantong Temple 显通寺 *xiǎntōng sì*
✉ Taihuai Town 台怀镇
☎ 654 5414
🕒 7:30am to 7pm, peak-season
8am to 5pm, off-season
¥ 10

Ten Thousand Buddha Pavilion
万佛阁 *wàn fó gé*
✉ Taihuai Town 台怀镇
☎ 654 5428
🕒 5:30am to 8pm, peak-season
6am to 6pm, off-season
¥ Free

Hotels

Jin Xiu Villa
锦绣山庄 *jǐnxiù shānzhuāng* ★★★★
✉ Dachegou Village, Taihuai Town, Wutai County 五台县台怀镇大车沟村
☎ 654 8758, 654 8081

The monks of Wutai Shan performing their religious rites.

¥ 688 – double room, peak-season
588 – double room, off-season

Wu Feng Hotel 五台山五峰宾馆 *wǔtái shān wǔfēng bīnguǎn* ★★★
✉ next to Dragon Fountain Temple, Taihuai Town, Wutai County 五台县台怀镇龙泉寺旁
☎ 654 8988, 654 5998
¥ 380 – double room, peak-season
304 – double room, off-season
@ www.wutaishan.com.cn/wfeng/index.htm

Yin Du Hotel
银都山庄 *yíndū shānzhuāng* ★★★
✉ Dachegou Village, Taihuai Town, Wutai County 五台县台怀镇大车沟村
☎ 654 8888, 654 8898
¥ 480 – double room, peak-season
240 – double room, off-season

Yin Hai Hotel
银海山庄 *yínhǎi shānzhuāng* ★★★
✉ Yangbaiyu, Taihuai Town, Wutai County
五台县台怀镇杨柏峪
☎ 654 2676, 654 2949
¥ 630 – double room, peak-season
430 – double room, off-season
@ zwf168@163.net

Yunfeng Hotel
云峰宾馆 *yúnfēng bīnguǎn* ★★
✉ Yangbaiyu, Taihuai Town, Wutai County
五台县台怀镇杨柏峪
☎ 654 8131, 654 8566
¥ 480 – double room, peak-season
280 – double room, off-season
@ www.sx.wts.xq.com

Food & Restaurants

Flour is the basis of most dishes in Shanxi and chefs here are known for their variously shaped noodles. The noodles get their unique names from how they're made or the odd shapes the chef molds them into. The most common variety is *la mian* (拉面),

which are hand-pulled noodles served up with a variety of sauces. Watching the chef pull and twist the lump of dough into long thin noodles is as entertaining as the noodles are tempting. There's an assortment of thicker noodles cut from lumps of dough then boiled or stir-fried; these types include *daoxiao mian* (刀削面), which come in large flat pieces. Don't be put off by cat's ear noodles (*māo'ěrduo* 猫耳朵) – they're called that because they're shaped like cat's ears.

Many roadside restaurants offer simple noodles with their own homemade sauce. A specialty in Wutai Shan is *tai mo* (台蘑), a mushroom dish that can cost up to RMB 80 a plate. The fat, juicy mushrooms only grow in the area around Wutai Shan and are considered to have medicinal properties that help miscellaneous ailments like arthritis. *Wanjuansu* (万卷酥), a very delicate cookie, was an imperial favorite. Lotus flower beans make good snacks: beans are first boiled then deep fried until they turn into the shape of a lotus flower.

Good spots to try out these tasty treats are found at the morning and evening markets. There's one at Jinjie Temple (*jīnjiè sì* 金界寺) at the top of Dailuo Ding (黛螺顶), and in Taihuai's travel area's parking lot.

RESTAURANTS

Minsu Fengqingyuan 民俗风情园

✉ Taihuai Jie 台怀街

☎ 654 5505

Taishan Huibinlou 台山汇宾楼

✉ Inside Huibinlou Hotel, Mingqing Jie, Taihuai County 台怀镇明清街汇宾楼宾馆内

☎ 654 5888

Souvenirs

Local special souvenirs include paper cuttings (*jiǎn zhǐ* 剪纸), lacquerware, inkstands, mushrooms and ginseng. In Taihuai, the shopping district, brimming with souvenir shops, is centered on Yanglin Lu. If you feel like brushing up on your calligraphy, then buy a *chengni yan* (澄泥砚) ink stone. These were popular during the Tang dynasty and modern ones cost RMB 50 to 80. For the ink stone connoisseur, *tai yan* (台砚) is a great gift, they can cost over RMB 200. Exquisite multi-colored wood bowls (*mùwǎn* 木碗) go for around RMB 10. Walking sticks (*xiánglóngmù shǒuzhàng* 降龙木手杖) are an elaborate souvenir and are handy when climbing the mountain; they go for around RMB 10. As in most places, bargaining is a must. If you want to go the source of these goodies, head to the Industrial Arts Factory of Wutai County (五台县工艺美术厂, ☎ 654 5263). It's about .3 mile (500 m) east of Da Baita in the Tayuan Temple on Wutai Shan.

Other Information

POST OFFICES

Wutai Shan Post Office 五台山邮政局

✉ Yanglin Jie, Taihuai Town, Wutai County 五台县台怀镇杨林街

☎ 654 5051

HOSPITALS

First Aid Center of Wutai Shan Hospital 五台山医院急救中心

✉ opposite the Taihuaizhen Binguan, Taihuai Town, Wutai County 五台县台怀镇台怀镇宾馆对面

☎ 654 5349

Wutai Shan Hospital 五台山医院

✉ Yangbaiyu Village, Taihuai Town, Wutai County 五台县台怀镇杨柏峪村

☎ 654 2526

COMPLAINT HOTLINES

☎ General: 654 3133

☎ Taxi: 654 5844, 654 2880

TOURISM INFORMATION WEBSITE

@ www.wutaishan.com

LANGUAGE DIFFICULTIES 语言困难		
I don't speak Chinese.	wǒ búhuì jiǎng zhōngwén	我不会讲中文。
Do you speak English?	nǐ huì shuō yīngyǔ ma	你会说英语吗?
Please say that again.	qǐng zàishuō yībiàn	请再说一遍。
Please speak more slowly.	néng shuō màndiǎnr ma	能说慢点儿吗?
What does this mean?	zhè shì shénme yìsi	这是什么意思?

Pingyao, the Walled City of Antiquity

Area Code 0354

Heritage: the Ancient City of Pingyao

The past is alive in **Pingyao**. Whereas other cities have embraced modernity often at the expense of their historical heritage, Pingyao tenaciously holds onto its past.

When dawn breaks and the morning sun bathes Pingyao's gray city walls in warm tones, you find yourself flung back in time as your eyes behold a Ming dynasty fortress in all its imposing glory. Watchtowers, cast iron cannons, intimidating wooden gates and sturdy walls impart a sense of invulnerability to the scene. And then the city wakes up. Narrow alleys that coil around time-honored courtyard homes fill up with its 480,000 denizens. Shops open their doors to reveal modern cash registers perched on antique tabletops. Bustling about are bicycles, rickshaws and scooters. Here in Pingyao, modernity lives with centuries old relics.

The old walled city is an architectural treasure trove. Civic buildings, private homes and streets are well preserved in Ming and Qing styles. Few buildings rise above two stories. Several are adorned with splendid eaved roofs, intricately latticed windows, hand-painted glass lanterns and ornate wood.

Such exquisite handiwork didn't come cheap, but then again, Pingyao was China's premier banking center during the two dynasties. Its wealthy residents were

Built in 1370, one of the six city gates that continues to guard Pingyao.

Memorable Experiences

Watching the city folk play card games and hang out at the Temple of the City God gates.

Sampling the street snacks: sugarcane, nuts, candied and dried fruit.

Enjoying tea with the locals, who spend lazy afternoons in the street-side teahouses.

Listening to the sounds of the city below while perched atop the Town Tower.

Observing how millet wine is made at a wine shop called Changsheng Yuan, next to the Town Tower.

merchants and businessmen who set about constructing sprawling mansions as expertly as they built up their business and trade. Of the many banks in Pingyao, Rishengchang Exchange Shop is the most famous. Originally established in 1643, it still has records of its earliest days in business.

One reason for the city's prosperity was its location. It lay at the heart of Shanxi Province between the central plain and the northern desert. Han Chinese merchants occupying the central plains could communicate easily with the northern tribes and set up trade links with the rest of China.

A three-storey Town Tower stands over South Street.

The stoic city walls also did their part to shield Pingyao from marauding enemies from the 14th to 19th centuries, allowing the city to flourish. The walls were first erected in the Zhou dynasty and last rebuilt during the Ming. After the Song army set the earthen walls on fire in AD 960, the walls were covered with bricks.

The fortifications are sophisticated - the square perimeter is 39 feet (12 m) high and 16 feet (5 m) thick and there are platforms every 165 feet (50 m) with 3,000 crenellations on the outer wall, 72 watchtowers, and a water drainage system reinforced with bricks at the top. The wall is surrounded by moats roughly 10 feet (3 m) wide and deep and six suspension bridges once fronted each city gate. You can walk all the way around the walls in 2 hours.

By the 19th century, the once dynamic town fell into provincial obscurity and the walls became a psychological prison. When modernization fever swept through China in the 1980's, town officials laid plans to demolish the ancient city and rebuild the town to accommodate what was hoped to be a future economic boom.

As the city planners dreamt of a modernized city and Pingyao's economic revival, people on the ground struggled to rescue the ancient city. Professor Ruan Yisan, who specialized in urban planning at Tongji University in Shanghai, worked tirelessly to make officials aware of the cultural value of Pingyao. His efforts paid off, and modernization was left outside the ancient wall. In 1986, Pingyao was declared a national historical city and protected it from demolition. The town was flush with funds, accelerating its conservation efforts. In 1997,

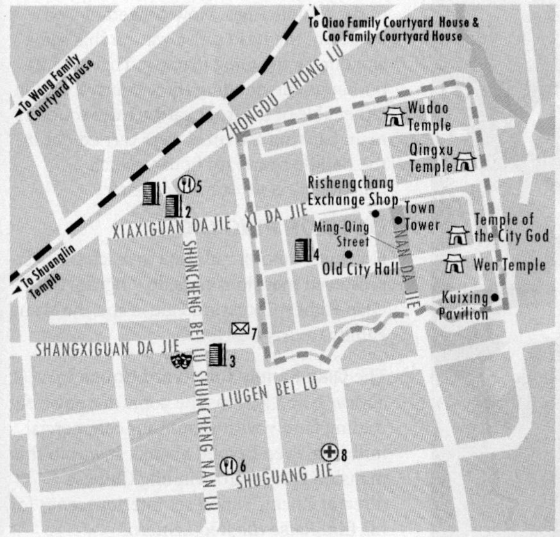

There are so many mansions, temples, museums, inns and shops – where do you start exploring? Chances are that you will put up at a hotel near **Ming Qing Jie** (*míngqīng jiē* 明清街) also known as Nan Da Jie, the main downtown thoroughfare. This street has undergone major restoration and its attractions now include hotels offering traditional brick-oven beds (*kàng* 炕), restaurants serving Pingyao's famous beef and shops hawking an astonishing array of art wares such as antiques, furniture, ancient coins, Chinese paintings, jadeware, lacquerware and traditional folk clothing. In the old days, over 700 shops peppered this same street and several remain exactly as they have for centuries. On this lively street, just shouting to be climbed, is the 60.7-foot-high (18.5 m) high **Town Tower** (*shìlóu* 市楼) – the tallest structure in town. Don't start your ascent without your camera: you'll want to catch the view of the tiled roofs flowing over the entire city when you reach the top.

You can find many notable museums along Ming Qing Street. **Tongxinggong Armed Escort Company Museum** (*tóngxīnggōng biāojú* 同兴公镖局) offers an eye-opening insight into the significant role played by armed escorts in promoting commerce. The economic boom under the two dynasties meant a lot of cash moving from one area to the next. To thwart thieving hands, Pingyao's ever-resourceful and pragmatic merchants left their cash in the professional hands of security escorts. Wang Zhenqing, a martial arts exponent, set up the first armed escort firm to provide this crucial service, which was instrumental to the speedy development of Chinese trade.

Temple of the City God (*chénghuáng miào* 城隍庙) on Nan Da Jie hails from the Northern Song dynasty. Visitors enter through a double-eave, triple-gate wooden archway. It has a theater hall, where one can catch operatic shows during the annual temple fair

Pingyao made it to the list of UNESCO's World Heritage Sites, and thus a silver lining finally revealed itself.

The city is also known as **Turtle City** (*guī chéng* 龟城). The south and north gates represent a turtle's head and tail, and the four gates on the east and west represent four legs; the two wells just beyond southern gate are the eyes. A web of alleys links the main streets in such a way that even the layout of the town resembles the markings on a turtle shell.

Slipping into the city, you feel as if you're entering the movie set of an elaborate Chinese period drama production. Elegant Ming and Qing architecture line the quaint streets. Like in the good old days, there are no cars in Pingyao's winding alleys; pedestrians and bicycles crowd the lanes, and a rickshaw rider scurries past. You might want to hop on for fun, but going slow on foot can be a visually rewarding feast. The ancient abodes of the commoners are fascinating cultural relics. Most of the compounds are arranged in quadrangles (*sìhéyuàn* 四合院), where the houses are built around a square courtyard. There are 3,797 such residences, with over 400 in immaculate condition. They're in such pristine condition partly because of Shanxi's arid climate and also because they weren't destroyed by wars.

A parade of Shanxi culture.

on May 27, with six large urns positioned to amplify the performer's voices.

On the eastern end of Xi Da Jie is **Rishengchang** (*rìshēngchāng piàohào* 日昇昌票号), meaning "sunrise prosperity," China's first bank. What started out as a single businessman's efforts to safely manage the accounts of his widely spread company became a private banking enterprise that caught on like wildfire – a similar phenomenon occurred in Europe at the end of the Middle Ages. Now converted into a museum, the head office was on this same site during the Qing dynasty. There are 21 buildings surrounding three courtyards. On either side of the front yard are the counters, main banking activities were carried out in the middle courtyard house, which functioned as an exchange center.

OUTSIDE PINGYAO

Hop onto a motorcycle taxi to reach the best-preserved mansions outside Pingyao, the Qiao Family Courtyard House and the Wang Family Courtyard House.

The **Qiao Family Courtyard House** (*qiáojiā dàyuàn* 乔家大院) was the home of a powerful trading family with significant commercial influence even beyond Shanxi. It was in this mansion that award-winning Chinese director Zhang Yimou set interior scenes for his film *Raise the Red Lantern*.

Located some 12 miles (20 km) north of Pingyao, the compound is fortified behind a 33-foot-high (10 m) wall with battlements. A watchtower perches from each of the four corners. The main entrance opens east into a spacious compound that covers 2.16 acres (8,724m^2), with 313 rooms, six major courtyards and 20 smaller ones. An 87-yard (80 m) passageway divides the complex into half. The inner courtyards and corridors follow the Chinese character for the words "double happiness" (*shuāng xǐ* 双喜). The roof styles are varied, from dramatically sloping to curved or terraced eaves. In classical Qing style, roof ridges are decorated with floral and fauna patterns. There are some 140 chimneys, each carrying a distinctive design. The Ancestral Temple of the Qiao Family (*qiáojiā cítáng* 乔家祠堂) is found at the western end.

Quotes

"Not just for the back-packer, but anyone who appreciates old stuff. This place is steeped in culture!"

"Architecture here is excellently preserved. You remember why big cities can be so off-putting when you get such an inspiring visual treat."

"The locals comprise mainly Han Chinese whose families have lived here for a few generations. People here have sunk long roots. They love their homes."

"Definitely a house-proud bunch of folks. Admirable efforts of restoration!"

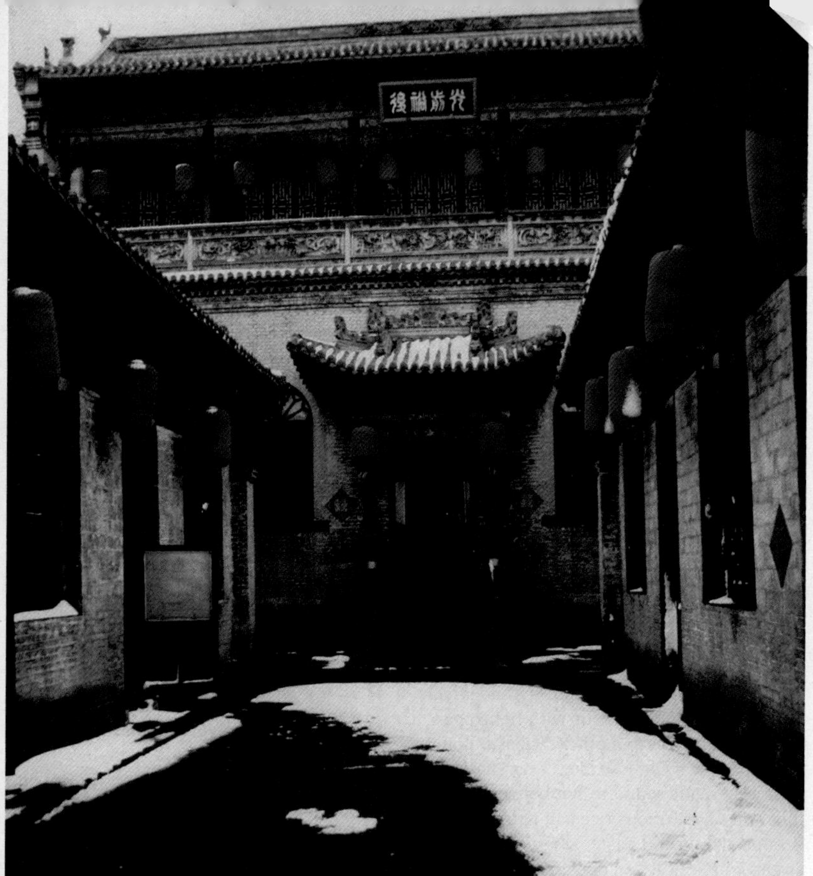

With 313 rooms the Qiao Family Courtyard House offers many examples of typical northern Chinese architecture.

The original name of the manor was Zhai Zhong Tang, which roughly translates as being fair in all dealings. "The Qiao family's" philosophy, "Descendants be righteous, brothers show mutual care so the family may prosper," is inscribed on each side of the main door. Besieged by invading forces, Empress Dowager Cixi passed through the manor while escaping Beijing for Xi'an. The Qiao family gave her money and as a token of her appreciation, Empress Cixi issued an imperial edict to send the Qiaos an inscription, which now hangs above the main gate. Beyond the gate is a screen wall on which is carved Chinese characters evoking the theme of longevity. In 1937, when Japanese troops invaded China, the Qiao family fled this residence forever.

The **Wang Family Courtyard House** (*wángjiā dàyuàn* 王家大院) was the Wang clan's private residence and is four times larger than Qiao's, with 54 courtyards and 1,052 rooms. The mansion took more than half a century to build and is located on a hilly area. This rambling complex was home to the first Wang family in 1312. The Wangs had a rags-to-riches story, starting out as farmers and bean curd sellers, before entering business and politics. Some 300 family members later became officials.

The interior is divided into three complexes, the **East Courtyards** (*gāojiā yá* 高家崖) is spread over terraces on the mountain terrain and includes 13 cave dwellings; the **Red Gate Castle** (*hóngmén bǎo* 红门堡) has only one gate, the door of which is painted red; and **Ancestral Temples** (*wángjiā cítáng* 王家祠堂). The streets in the compound form a pattern similar to the Chinese character "Wang" for the family name. The buildings of Wang compound have an eye-popping array of sculptures and carvings on wood, brick and stone.

After 600 years, the family fortunes started to decline, and several residences within the compound were sold outside the family. When the Japanese forces came, the owner Wang Yirang sold off all the family shops and moved out. Since then, several houses in the compound have been lived in by non-Wangs or converted into showpieces.

Shuanglin Temple (*shuānglín sì* 双林寺), a musty monastery 4.3 miles (7 km) south of Pingyao, has traditional paintings and some 2,000 terracotta figurines dating back to the Song and Yuan dynasties. Other temples include **Zhenguo Temple** (*zhènguó sì* 镇国寺) 9.3 miles (15 km) north of Pingyao, which features Buddha figures and **Dacheng Hall** (*dàchéng diàn* 大成殿), located southeast of Pingyao. It's the only Confucian temple built during the Song dynasty and has an 800-year history. ■

Making Your Trip Easy

Practical Tips

If you visit during the Lantern Festival, 15 days after the Chinese New Year, there's an annual parade on Liugen Lu. The streets are dolled up with pretty red lanterns, and street performers awe the crowds with tightrope walks, lion dances and other displays. You get to sample a Chinese New Year snack of *yuanxiao*, made round to symbolize the moon. It's a glutinous rice ball with sweet sesame and walnut paste inside, served in a sweet soup. But if you don't like crowds, avoid the May and October national holidays.

Transportation

Airport – The closet airport is in Taiyuan, about 56 miles (90 km) away.

Bus – Getting to Pingyao from Taiyuan by bus will take about an hour; tickets are about RMB 10. The Taiyuan bus station is next to the train station on Yingze Da Jie. The bus station in Pingyao is also beside the train station.

Pedi-cab – RMB 2 to 5 for distances up to 2km, if you're going further than 2km (1.24 mi), you'll have to discuss a price with the driver.

Taxi – Compact taxis are RMB 6, full-sized taxis are RMB 12.

Train – Pingyao is well-connected by trains. Trains also go to the Qiao Family Courtyard House in Qi County.

The Best of Pingyao

The Ancient City of Pingyao
平遥古城 *píngyáo gǔchéng*

✉ inside Pingyao 平遥县城内
☎ 568 7805, 568 1544
🕒 7:30am to 7:30pm, peak-season
8am to 6pm, off-season
¥ 120, for access to all sights within Pingyao

Qiao Family Courtyard House
乔家大院 *qiáojiā dàyuàn*

✉ Qiaojia Bao, Dongguan Town, Qi County, 40km from Taiyuan and 20km from Pingyao 祁县东观镇乔家堡
☎ 532 1045
🕒 8am to 5:30pm
¥ 40

Shuanglin Temple 双林寺 *shuānglín sì*

✉ Qiaotou Village, Zhongdu Town, 6km west of Pingyao 中都乡桥头村
☎ 577 9023
🕒 8am to 6pm, peak-season
9am to 5pm, off-season
¥ 25

Hotels

Shihua Hotel 石化宾馆 *shíhuà bīnguǎn* ★★

✉ 29 Shuncheng Lu 顺城路 29 号❷
☎ 567 1718, 567 2499
¥ 360 – double room, peak-season
260 – double room, off-season
@ www.pingyao.com.cn

Zhongdu Hotel
中都宾馆 *zhōngdū bīnguǎn* ★★

✉ 1 Shuncheng Lu 顺城路 1 号❶
☎ 567 2858, 567 2618
¥ 280 – double room, peak-season
120 – double room, off-season
@ www.pyzhdu.com

Pingyao Hotel 平遥宾馆 *píngyáo bīnguǎn*
✉ 23 Shaxiang 沙巷 23 号❹
☎ 568 3782, 568 3038
¥ 200 – double room, peak-season
120 – double room, off-season

Yunfeng Hotel 云峰宾馆 *yúnfēng bīnguǎn*
✉ 190 Shuncheng Lu 顺城路 190 号❸
☎ 563 2183, 563 2188
¥ 380 – double room, peak-season
288 – double room, off-season

Food & Restaurants

Pingyao offers traditional northern China cuisine and specializes in various noodle dishes and pastries. Locals will tell you they have over 108 kinds of noodles and pastries – try *wantuoze*(碗脱则), a famous noodle dish. Also sink your teeth into Pingyao's beefy dishes. Pingyao's stewed beef is slow cooked in its own gravy and mouthwatering tender – it's known throughout China. The street food menu includes fried pork-stuffed buns called *shui jianbao* (水煎包), pancakes topped with string beans called *doumianjianbao* (豆面煎包) and steaming bowls of dumpling called *kaolao* (栲栳). Pingyao doesn't have ritzy high-end restaurants; the food here is rustic and homey. All the restaurants here are open from 8am to 9:30pm. For beverages, try yellow millet wine.

RESTAURANTS

Changxinglong 昌兴隆
✉ 29 Longmiao Jie 隆庙街 29 号
☎ 568 4188

Dejuyuan Kezhan 德居源客栈
✉ 43 Xi Da Jie 西大街 43 号
☎ 568 5266

Guifu Restaurant 桂馥饭店
✉ 3 Shuguang Lu 曙光路 3 号❻
☎ 562 0849

Juguang Ju 居广居
✉ 20 Shuncheng Lu 顺城路 20 号❺
☎ 567 3031

Tianyuankui Kezhan 天元奎客栈
✉ 73 Nan Da Jie 南大街 73 号
☎ 568 0069

Laohuaishu Kezhan 老槐树客栈
✉ 6 Zhaobinanjie 照壁南街 6 号
☎ 568 6188

Yuantaichang 源泰昌
✉ 54 Xi Da Jie 西大街 54 号
☎ 568 6188

Yunjincheng 云锦成
✉ 29 Nan Da Jie 南大街 29 号
☎ 568 0944

Souvenirs

Lacquerware is the local specialty with lacquer jewelry boxes, which cost around RMB 200, being the local hot item. Check out the traditional paper cuttings, complex patterns are cut into the paper using scissors. Try on a pair of handmade cloth shoes. They're very comfy and only cost RMB 30 to 50. Old coins, antique furniture, jade jewelry and other goodies are available. Lots of shops along Ming Qing Street offer similar wares, so take your time browsing.

Other Information

POST OFFICES

Pingyao County Post Office 平遥县邮局
✉ 43 Shang Xi Guan Jie 上西关街 43 号❼
☎ 562 0177

HOSPITALS

Pingyao County People's Hospital
平遥县人民医院
✉ 61 Shuguang Lu 曙光路 61 号❽
☎ 562 3177

COMPLAINT HOTLINES

☎ General: 567 2110, 562 4333
☎ Taxi: 567 0270, 567 1804

TOURISM INFORMATION WEBSITES

@ www.pingyao.com.cn

GOODBYE 再见		
Goodbye.	zài jiàn	再见。
Goodnight.	wǎn ān	晚安。
See you tomorrow.	míngtiān jiàn	明天见。
See you soon.	huítóu jiàn	回头见。
I have to go now.	wǒ děi zǒule	我得走了。

Yungang Caves, a Mountain of Buddhas

Area Code 0352

Heritage: Yungang Caves

From thumb-sized figurines to a 56-foot (17 m) colossus, the Buddhist carvings at Yungang are one of the most spectacular holy sites in China.

Clustered in groups, the **Yungang Caves** (*yúngǎng shíkū* 云冈石窟) are meant to be viewed as a whole. This endeavor will take a few hours, but considering the carvings took almost half a century and 40,000 laborers to complete, the few hours spent exploring these majestic caves is time well-spent. Of the numerous artistic masterpieces that Buddhism has germinated in China in the past 2,000 years, the caves at Yungang are among the most profound.

The caves are located 10 miles (16 km) west of **Datong** in northern Shanxi Province. A notch south of Inner Mongolia, this strategic location was once a cultural crossroad, with influences from India, Central Asia and Mongolia. In AD 368 a group called the Tangut (*tuòbá* 拓跋) made Datong the capital of their Northern Wei dynasty. The Tanguts were fervent Buddhists and began work on the caves in 453, ending around 494 when the Northern Wei moved their capital to Luoyang and continued their devotional work at the Longmen Caves.

Over the centuries, the region's fortunes have wavered. Datong is now an industrial city and an important coal production center. Situated on the Loess Plateau, the old capital is sometimes referred to as the "Sea of Coal." Convoys of coal-laden trucks and swarms of bicycles clog the flat road to the mountain.

Once out of the city the traffic begins to thin out and the Wuzhou Hills ripple into view. Stone watch towers that have guarded China's northern border for thousands of years are silhouetted against the horizon. Amid such sparse surroundings, caves full of Buddhas in fanciful poses come into view. Though the caves are famous for their

Carved in the 5th century AD, seven standing Buddhas in Cave 11 wearing colorful clothing.

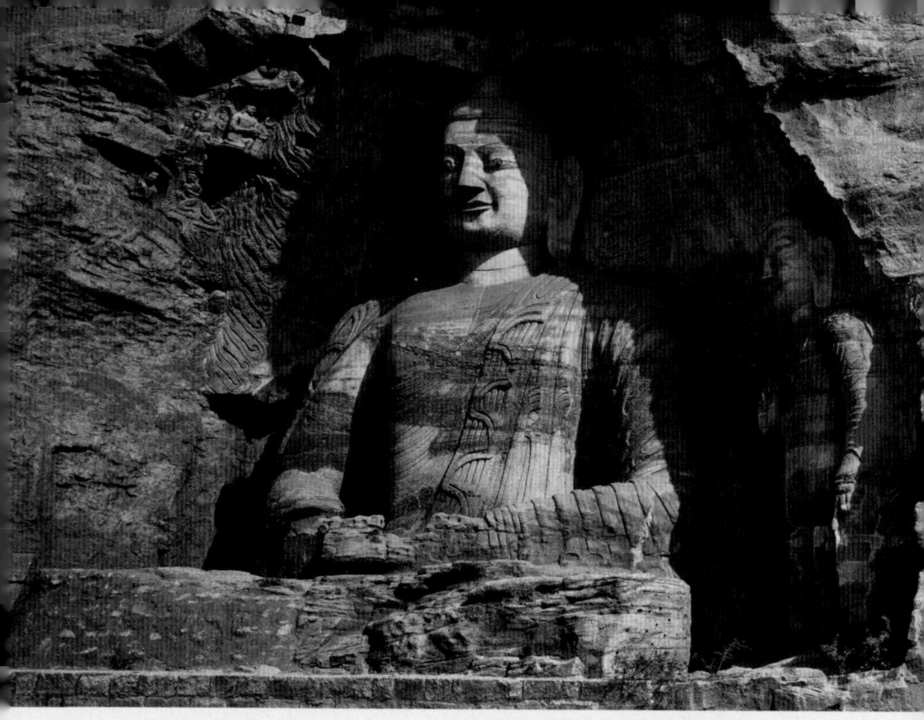

Cave 20's Buddha is representative of the skilled craftsmanship found throughout the site.

depictions of the Buddha, other celestial beings are also represented. There are minutely detailed bodhisattvas and apsaras. Some caves are guarded by stone soldiers and others are covered with exuberant designs painted onto walls and ceilings.

The caves extend about six-tenths of a mile (1 km) from east to west and are divided into three major clusters. The grouping of the caves is seemingly haphazard, but it's possible to follow stylistic changes in the carvings as influences ebbed and flowed. Persian, Indian, even Greek and Byzantine influences can be seen in the rock carvings from the weapons, music instruments and clothing displayed.

Tours normally begin at **Caves 5** to **13**. Located centrally, they were built from AD 462 to 495 and contain some of the best artistic works at Yungang. Meandering from one cave to the next, the high level of artistry within the caves is readily apparent. In **Cave 5** is an awe-inspiring 56-foot-high (17 m) high seated Buddha. This pudgy Buddha would be barely able to fit his thumbs into the cave entrance if he could stand and move around. Resembling a dimly lit cathedral, at either side of the cave is an arched door with fine relief sculptures of flying apsaras at the top. The walls of the cave are festooned with a tightly knit honeycomb of smaller Buddhist figures, some retaining their ancient colorings thanks to recent restoration efforts, while others remain stark and stunning in sandstone hues. Pale light filters down from what seems like an open window which was actually the original entrance for workmen to hollow out the massive chamber.

Large or small, most Yungang statues have square faces, thick lips, high noses, wide shoulders and broad chests – stylistically representative of the Northern Wei, but traces of other cultural influences are also present. **Cave 8** features multi-headed statues of Indian origins which demonstrate the successful mixing of differing artistic traditions and the eclectic influences of the era. There is a five-headed, six-armed statue of the Hindu God Shiva sitting on a giant bird. Beside Shiva is the three-headed Vishnu sitting on a bull.

For art students studying this era, caves 9 to 13 are an important resource. **Caves 9** and **10** are of a square design consisting of an outer and inner room. The outer pillars of

The Hanging Temple clings to the side of Heng Shan in Shanxi Province.

each cave are carved with intricate figures bearing musical instruments. The eastern and western walls of the outer rooms and the door lintels of the inner room are finely carved with plant designs.

Cave 12 is known as the musical cave. Walking into the cave, you are greeted by a carved bank of celestial musicians holding different musical instruments demonstrating the vibrant cultural exchange of the time. Such instruments as the *konghou* (箜篌), *pipa* (琵琶) and waist-drums were introduced from Central Asia while panpipes and zithers originated from China. The cave is an invaluable resource for researchers on ancient China's music and dance.

Neatly arranged rows upon rows of tiny seated Buddha carved into the walls greet you upon entering Cave 15. There are more than 10,000 miniature Buddha carvings in this cave, thus the name **Cave of Ten Thousand Buddha** (*wànfó dòng* 万佛洞)

Royal stories are behind **Caves 16** to **20**, the oldest caves in Yungang. Each of the statues in the five caves symbolizes an emperor from the Northern Wei dynasty, reflecting their belief that the emperor is a living embodiment of Buddha. The caves, collectively known as "Five Cloudy and Luminary Caves" (*tányào wǔkū* 昙曜五窟), were created in AD 453 to 462. According to the legend, one emperor was convinced by an adviser to renounce Buddhism. To the adviser's misfortune, the emperor followed his suggestion then immediately fell ill. After executing his non-believing adviser, the wayward emperor returned to the faith and quickly recovered from his illness. The succeeding emperor began construction of these caves as a sign of piety in hopes of avoiding his predecessor's fate. The Buddhas

Memorable Experiences

Strolling outside the caves as braziers launch fragrant aromas into the air while the musky smoke from incense wafts from the caves, chimes from temple bells sail through the air as monks, dressed in their traditional garb stroll back and forth.

At night, the Da Xi Jie in the commercial district of Datong is filled with peddlers of local food and souvenirs. The cool air is filled with the aroma of various spices.

here are clad in robes with their palms pressed together in front of their chests, a gesture of devotion.

Most of the caves were dug during the Northern Wei dynasty; however, **Cave 3**, the largest of the Yungang caves, was created by later artists during the Sui and Tang dynasties. The face of the cliff into which it was carved is about 79 feet (24 m) high; on the upper central part are 12 rectangular holes that were used to hold beams that supported a monastery. The cave is divided into inner and outer chambers. There is now only one Buddha statue and two bodhisattvas in the west end of the inner chamber. The faces of these images are full and smooth, the figures full-bodied. Because this cave was carved at a later period, the sculptural style here differs from that in the other caves.

Yungang Caves are famous for their depictions of the Buddha, but other celestial beings are also represented. There are minutely detailed bodhisattvas, disciples who have elected to forego nirvana in order to save others. Some caves are guarded by stone soldiers and others are covered with exuberant designs painted onto walls and ceilings. The mingling of different cultures in ancient Datong is vividly reflected in the cave art.

Unfortunately, pollution from this industrialized valley has had a profound effect on the statues. Soot has covered the exposed areas of many of the carvings, while their undersides, which are normally hidden in shadow, appear bright in contrast.

Besides the caves, there are many other sites of interest within driving distance. One interesting sight is the 1,500-year-old **Hanging Temple** (*xuánkōng sì* 悬空寺). The temple is a Northern Wei dynasty structure that clings precariously to the side of the Heng Shan mountain range. Caves carved into the cliffs or along natural contours make up the rooms and walkways, and bridges connect the different halls. Rain or shine, a few dozen slender beams acrobatically balance the temple and visitors walking on top of the narrow squeaky walkways.

Back to the city, Datong itself is dotted with its own assortment of ancient landmarks, such as the **Drum Tower** (*gǔ lóu* 鼓楼), **Nine Dragon Screen** (*jiǔlóng bì* 九龙壁), and **Huayan Monastery** (*huáyán sì* 华严寺). The Drum Tower is located in the downtown area, rising above the shorter buildings of the city and making itself a key point of reference. The Nine Dragon Screen, a preserved Ming dynasty wall section, is 26 feet (8 m) high, 148 feet (45 m) long and 6.6 feet (2m) thick, about four times larger and 350 years older than a similar one in Beijing's Beihai Park (*běihǎi gōngyuán* 北海公园). There are a few other minor dragon walls in Datong. The Huayan Monastery is unusual in that it faces east whereas most temples in China face south. It's one of China's few remaining wooden Buddhist temples. ■

Making Your Trip Easy

Practical Tips

This area is located on the Loess Plateau, more than 3,600 feet (1,100 m) above sea level. Often affected by the Siberian cold front, the annual temperature averages between 41°F and 45°F (5°C and 7°C). Summers are cool, but in winter the temperature can drop to around 8°F (-13°C). It's hottest in July and coldest in January.

Datong China International Travel Service (540 2265 / 2165) can arrange tours to the Yungang Caves and Hanging Temple for RMB 100. Most tours depart at 9am and finish around 6pm. They can also help buy train tickets.

The ten-day Yungang International Travel Festival is held annually in August. The festival features various exhibitions on folk customs and a multitude of variety shows.

Transportation

Bus – The long distance bus station is located on Xinjian Nan Lu. There are daily buses from Datong to Beijing.

Taxi – Taxis are RMB 5 at flag-fall for full-sized cabs.

A young boy greets visitors during the Chinese New Year.

Train – Daily trains from Datong to Beijing are about 5 hours. Trains to Xi'an take about 16 hours.

The Best of Datong

Hanging Temple 悬空寺 *xuánkōng sì*
- ✉ Hunyuan County 浑源县
- ☎ 832 7795, 832 7300
- 🕒 6am to 7pm, peak-season
  8am to 5pm, off-season
- ¥ 60

Huayan Monastery
上下华严寺 *shàngxià huáyán sì*
- ✉ Huayan Jie 华严街
- ☎ 206 1480, 242 7185
- 🕒 8am to 6pm, peak-season
  8:30am to 5pm, off-season
- ¥ 45

Yungang Caves 云冈石窟 *yúngǎng shíkū*
- ✉ 1 Dong Jie, Yungang Town; 16km west of Datong
  大同市城西 16 公里处，云冈镇东街 1 号
- ☎ 302 6230
- 🕒 8am to 5:30pm, peak-season
  8:30am to 5pm, off-season
- ¥ 60

Hotels

Datong Hotel
大同宾馆 *dàtóng bīnguǎn* ★★★★
- ✉ 37 Yingbin Xi Lu 迎宾西路 37 号
- ☎ 586 8666
- ¥ 380 – double room
- @ www.datonghotel.com

Hong'an International Hotel
宏安国际酒店 *hóng'ān guójì jiǔdiàn* ★★★★
- ✉ 28 Yingbin Xi Lu 迎宾西路 28 号
- ☎ 586 6655
- ¥ 360– double room

Jingyuan Hotel
京原迎宾馆 *jīngyuán yíngbīnguǎn* ★★★★
- ✉ 3A Yongjun Nan Lu 拥军南路甲 3 号
- ☎ 288 0988
- ¥ 280 – double room
- @ www.jingyuanhotel.com

Yungang Hotel
云冈宾馆 *yúngǎng bīnguǎn* ★★★
- ✉ 21 Yingbin Dong Lu 迎宾东路 21 号
- ☎ 502 1601
- ¥ 400 – double room, peak-season
  260 – double room, off-season

Yungang International Hotel
云冈国际酒店 *yúngǎng guójì jiǔdiàn*
- ✉ 38 Daxi Jie 大西街 38 号
- ☎ 586 2002
- ¥ 390 – double room

Food & Restaurants

Cuisine here is based on flour and the generous use of vinegar; Shanxi's famous vinegar is mild with a tinge of sweetness. With over 2,500 years of development, Shanxi people love their vinegar. Local flour based creations range from pastries to noodles and come in a variety of shapes. Cat's ear noodles (*māo'ěr miàn* 猫耳面) are served with a tomato and egg sauce or a meat sauce, but don't worry, no cats will be harmed in the making of this dish. It's a popular fill-me-up and can be found on most menus for about RMB 5 a bowl. Try the fried cake (*yóuzhá gāo* 油炸糕), a Chinese version

Quotes

"Yungang Caves are the best of the stone carvings art in China."

"The sight of thousands of Buddhas on a mountain is a real thrill. No other place can be compared to Yungang Caves."

of a doughnut, fatty but very delicious. Another local delicacy is *youmian tuntun* (莜面饨饨), a kind of wonton where the shell is made of oat and filled with vegetables.

RESTAURANTS

Chengxin Waipoqiao Jiudian 丞鑫外婆桥酒店
Specializes in hot pot, Cantonese, Sichuan, Hunan and Shandong, cuisines.
✉ 29 Chaochangcheng Jie 操场城街 29 号
☎ 602 1891

Daziran Jiulou 大自然酒楼
Specializes in hot pot, Cantonese, Sichuan, Hunan and Shandong, cuisines.
✉ Xinkai Xi'erlu, Zhenhua Nanjie 振华南街新开西二路
☎ 201 0866

Hongqi Restaurant 红旗大饭店
Specializes in Sichuan, Shandong, Cantonese and Shanghai dishes.
✉ 11 Zhanqian Jie, Railway Station Square 火车站广场站前街 11 号
☎ 536 6566
🕒 7am to 2am

Jindadu Restaurant 金大都酒家有限公司
✉ 1 Yingbin Xi Lu 迎宾西路 1 号
☎ 502 8535

Lao Datong Restaurant 老大同饭店
Specializes in hot pot, Cantonese, Sichuan, Hunan and Shandong, cuisines.
✉ No. 3 Bus Station, Zhenhua Bei Jie 振华北街 3 路汽车总站
☎ 210 3270

Lüyuan Restaurant 绿园饭店
✉ Yingbin Xilu 迎宾西路
☎ 518 6818

Yonghe Shifu 永和食府
✉ No.1 Shanhuasi Lu 善化寺路 1 号
☎ 204 7999

Souvenirs

There are many art and antique shops around the caves where you can buy jade and bronze Buddhist statues at low prices. You can get them at 60% of the offered price if you enjoy bargaining.

Since the area around Datong is an important coal-mining center, Jinhua coal sculptures (*jìnhuá méidiāo* 晋华煤雕) make for a unique souvenir. Depending on the complexity and size, prices can range from RMB 10 to 1,000. You can head over to the Jinhua Mine (*jìnhuá gōngkuàng* 晋华宫矿) and browse the Jinhua Mine Handicrafts Gallery (*jìnhuá gōngkuàng jìnhuá gōngyì měishùchǎng* 晋华宫矿晋华工艺美术厂, ☎ 708 6754) and check out the artisans making their works of art.

The Yinxing Jindian (银星金店) on 8 Da Dong Jie (大东街 8 号) specializes in gold and sliver jewelry. Also try Datong Jiayi Lipin Store (大同市佳艺礼品商场) on 328 Xinkai Nan Lu (新开南路 328 号) for your souvenir needs. If you want some upscale shopping you'll need to get back to Datong. West Street (*dà xī jiē* 大西街) and South Street (*xiǎo nán jiē* 小南街) are the main higher-end shopping areas.

Other Information

POST OFFICES

Guangchang Post Office 广场分局
✉ Post Office Square 邮政局广场
☎ 202 3937, 202 3751

HOSPITALS

The Third Datong Municipal People's Hospital 大同市第三人民医院
✉ 1 Yiwei Jie 医卫街 1 号
☎ 502 1001

COMPLAINT HOTLINES

☎ General: 202 0315
☎ Taxi: 202 2322

TOURISM INORMATION WEBSITE

@ www.yungang.org

FEELINGS 感受		
I'm (very)···	wǒ (fēicháng) ···	我(非常)···
angry	shēngqì	生气
happy	gāoxìng	高兴
cold	lěng	冷
hot	rè	热
hungry	è	饿
thirsty	kě	渴
sleepy	kùn	困
tired	lèi	累

SHOPPING 购物			
Where can I buy…?		nǎr néng mǎidào …	哪儿能买到…?
Where's the nearest…?		zuìjìnde … zài nǎr	最近的…在哪儿?
	bank	yínháng	银行
	bookstore	shūdiàn	书店
	camera store	shèyǐng qìcái diàn	摄影器材店
	department store	bǎihuò shāngdiàn	百货商店
	market	shìchǎng	市场
	music store	yīnxiàngdiàn	音像店
	newsstand	bàokāntíng	报刊亭
	pharmacy	yàodiàn	药店
	shopping center	gòuwù zhōngxīn	购物中心
	supermarket	chāoshì	超市
	travel agency	lǚxíngshè	旅行社
I'd like to buy….		wǒ xiǎng mǎi …	我想买…
I'd like to see it.		gěi wǒ kànkan	给我看看。
Do you have any others?		yǒu biéde mā	有别的吗?
I want something of better quality.		wǒ xiǎngyào zhìliàng hǎo diǎnr de	我想要质量好点儿的。
I want something like this.		wǒ yào zhèyàng de	我要这样的。
No, thanks!		wǒ bùyào zhègè	我不要这个!
Can you show me another one?		huàn yījiàn	换一件。
I'll take it.		wǒ mǎi le	我买了。
Please wrap it up for me.		qǐng bāng wǒ bāo shàng	请帮我包上。
How much does this cost?		zhège duōshǎo qián	这个多少钱?
Can you write down the price?		néng bǎ jiàgé xiě xiàlái mā	能把价格写下来吗?
Can I pay by credit card?		néng shuākǎ mā	能刷卡吗?
Do you accept US dollars?		kěyǐ fù měijīn mā	可以付美金吗?
Can I try this on?		wǒ kěyǐ shìshi mā	我可以试试吗?
Where's the dressing room?		shìyījiān zài nǎr	试衣间在哪儿?
It's too….		tài … le	太…了。
	big	dà	大
	small	xiǎo	小
	long	cháng	长
	short	duǎn	短
I want ... color.		wǒ yào ... yánsè	我要...颜色。
	black	hēi	黑
	red	hóng	红

NORTHWEST CHINA

Yinchuan, Temples and Tombs

Area Code 0951

Yinchuan, the capital of the **Ningxia Hui Autonomous Region**, is an often-overlooked city that is irrigated by the mighty Yellow River amidst the arid landscape of China's dry northwest.

The thin Ningxia Hui Autonomous Region in China's stark northwest is surrounded by Gansu in the south and Inner Mongolia to the north. 20% of China's Hui Muslim minority lives in this region, giving Ningxia the nickname "the Muslim Region." The Hui minority trace their origins to the Silk Road, which brought Central Asian traders to China during the Tang dynasty. Succeeding waves of migration enriched and enlarged this population.

Recently Yinchuan has been divided into three quarters linked by a 15.5 miles (25 km) road, though locals refer to the city as if it's divided into two. The western section is the new city while the eastern quarter is the old city. The new city is where the train station is located, but the majority of sights and hotels are located in the old city in the east. Though most people use Yinchuan as a transit point for further adventures into Inner Mongolia, the city has enough personality and interesting sights to hold its own.

Making up 28% of the city's population, the Hui influence throughout the city is obvious. Whether it's the Arabic domes of the city mosque rising above the low skyline or the smell of roasted lamb wafting through the market stalls, there's no mistake that Yinchuan's heritage is as much Central Asian as Chinese. The old city still manages to retain a sleepy pace with old men wearing their white skullcaps, and sporting long wispy beards sipping tea along the sides of the road.

The laidback city with its tree-lined streets,

One of the Western Xia Imperial Tombs.

Traditional irrigation wheels are still in use after hundreds of years.

its melding of Hui and Han ethnic culture, belies the chaotic history of the region. Once a region of various feuding kingdoms offering nominal loyalty to the Tang then Song dynasties, the area came under the powerful rule of the Western Xia kingdom from AD 1032 to 1227. Led by Li Yuanhao, an ethnic Turgut (*tuòbá* 拓跋), he established the Western Xia as a regional power in the northwest that developed its own distinct writing and culture. Unfortunately Genghis Khan, who initially sought the kingdom as an ally, didn't take rejection with grace. To his chagrin, his attempts at invasion were repelled six times, with the final campaign proving fatal. He did survive long enough to give the final order to raze the kingdom.

Despite his orders, sights still abound in and around the city. The **Chengtian Temple** (*chéngtiān sì* 承天寺) is located in the southwest part of town. Inside the temple ground resides the **Chengtian Si Pagoda** (*chéngtiānsì tǎ* 承天寺塔), or known locally as the **Western Pagoda** (*xī tǎ* 西塔). This pagoda was built by the widow of Li Yuanhao. After his death, the empress had this Buddhist tower in hopes of ensuring a long life for their year old son. Perhaps because Genghis Khan's underlings carried out his final order to destroy the Western Xia with such zeal, this is the only pagoda that retains any surviving records of its construction. The octagonal pagoda is 211.6 feet (64.5 m) high and was built in AD 1050. Climb up the pagoda for a good view of Yinchuan and of the nearby **Helan Shan** (*hèlán shān* 贺兰山). The temple originally had two courtyards; one of them is now occupied by the **Ningxia Museum** (*níngxià bówùguǎn* 宁夏博物馆), which has 4 exhibition halls detailing the Western Xia, Hui culture and history, Ningxia history and the prehistoric paintings at Helan Shan.

In the old section of town is the **Nanguan Mosque** (*nánguān qīngzhēn sì* 南关清真寺), which was originally built at the end of the Ming dynasty and rebuilt in 1981. The Arabic styled domes can be clearly seen rising above the city's low skyline – an unusual sight since the majority of mosques

Traditional goat skin rafts are used to cross the Yellow River in Ningxia.

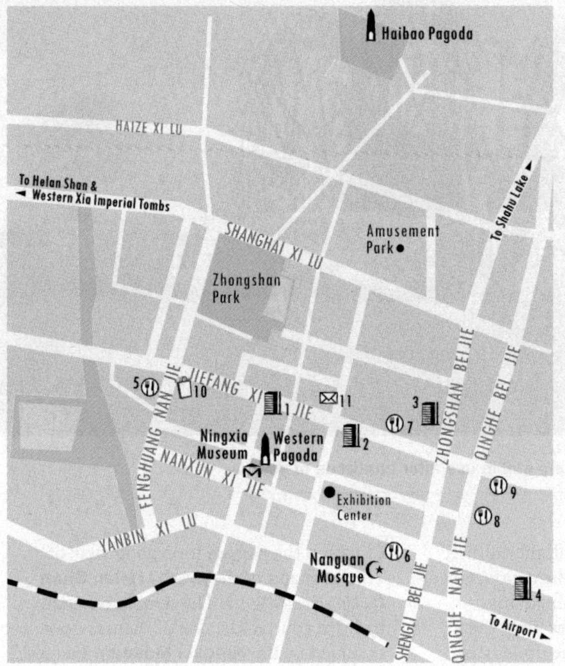

1739 and the current one dates from 1771. The pagoda itself is uniquely constructed with outcropping niches that make it appear multi-sided. Climbing to the top rewards you with a spectacular view of the countryside, the nearby mountains and the Yellow River. A 23-foot (7 m) Buddha relaxes in one of the halls on the temple grounds.

Nineteen miles (30 km) from Yinchuan is the **Western Xia Imperial Tombs** (*xīxià wánglíng* 西夏王陵). Measuring 19 square miles (50 km²), 9 large tombs hold the remains of Western Xia emperors plus 140 accompanying tombs for their courtiers, some of whom may not have actually been dead when buried along with their emperor. Many of the tombs were destroyed by the Mongols, with grave robbers finishing the area off, though archeologists still make the occasional find. Unique to China, the burial mounds are shaped as pyramids.

About 31 miles (50 km) northwest of Yinchuan is Helan Shan. Some 3,000 to 10,000 years ago, the people who lived in the area immortalized themselves by painting various scenes of their lives and their beliefs into the rock face. Over 1,000 petroglyphs have been discovered at the **Helan Shan Yanhua** (*hèlán shān yánhuà* 贺兰山岩画) site. At Helan Kou is a valley that penetrates through the desolate mountain. Most of the

in China adopt Sinicized archi-tectural styles that are hard for the untrained eye to distinguish. The two-story main hall has the prayer hall on the second level; if you're here on a Friday, the Islamic holy day, the area will appear deluged in a sea of white as the pious don their white skullcaps and kneel in prayer. The prayer hall can hold up to 1,300 devout worshippers. There's also an exhibition hall displaying Muslim texts from the Koran. The mosque also welcomes non-believers, though one must observe proper etiquette and dress modestly.

The **Haibao Pagoda** (*hǎibǎo tǎ* 海宝塔) stands on the foundations of a 5th century pagoda in northern Yinchuan. The original pagoda was destroyed in an earthquake in

Memorable Experiences

Strolling through the pyramid-shaped burial mounds at the Western Xia Imperial Tombs. The tombs are eerie when there's no one around and the wind begins to blow, sweeping sand around the desolate site.

Climbing Helan Shan for a spectacular view of the surrounding desert. The sand dunes, the eroded rock formations and the ancient petroglyphs all add to the beauty and historical significance of the area.

Helan Shan's ancient prehistoric paintings.

paintings are on both sides of this valley, running for three-eighths of a mile (600 m). The ancient artists left vivid depictions of hunting, herding, battles, dancing and religious ceremonies with many of the human figures painted in an abstract style. Halfway up the mountain is an impressive painting of what's believed to be a sun deity, which is definitely worth the hike. The Western Xia also added their legacy to the rock face by carving intricate calligraphy over the ancient petroglyphs. If the cliff paintings don't grab your interest, the stunning mountains and views will. ■

Quotes

"The rock paintings at Helan Shan are amazing. To see something that has survived for so many years, just imagining someone was standing here thousands of years ago boggles the mind."

Making Your Trip Easy

Practical Tips

Summers and autumns are the best time to visit Yinchuan. Be aware that the temperature can drop dramatically at night, so dress appropriately.

Transportation

Airport – The airport is about 12 miles (20 km) east from the city. It'll take about 20 minutes to the airport by taxi.

Taxi – Flag-fall is RMB 5.

The Best of Yinchuan

Helan Shan Yanhua
贺兰山岩画 *hèlán shān yánhuà*
✉ Jinshan Village, Helan County
贺兰山中段贺兰县金山乡
☎ 410 8346
¥ 25

Nanguan Mosque
南关清真寺 *nánguān qīngzhēn sì*
✉ Xingqing District 兴庆区

Taking a relaxed camel ride around the Sand Lake.

☎ 410 6714
¥ 12

Western Xia Imperial Tombs
西夏王陵 *xīxià wánglíng*
✉ Helan Shan, 35km west of Yinchuan
银川西部约 35 公里贺兰山东麓中段
☎ 602 2127
¥ 40

Hotels

Kaida Hotel
凯达大酒店 *kǎidá dàjiǔdiàn* ★★★★
✉ 256 Qinghe Nan Jie, Xingqing District
兴庆区清和南街 256 ❹
☎ 602 1698
¥ 328 – double room, peak-season
263 – double room, off-season

Rainbow Bridge Hotel
虹桥大酒店 *hóngqiáo dàjiǔdiàn* ★★★★
✉ 38 Jiefang Xi Jie, Xingqing District
兴庆区解放西街 38 号❶
☎ 691 8888
¥ 339 – double room

West Garden Holiday Hotel
西部花园 *xībù huāyuán* ★★★★
✉ the north point of Renmin Square, Jinfeng District 金凤区人民广场北端
☎ 306 8999
¥ 298 – double room, peak-season
239 – double room, off-season
@ www.nxwestgarden.com.cn

Era Mansion 世纪大厦 *shìjì dàshà* ★★★
✉ 24 Yuhuangge Bei Jie, Xingqing District
兴庆区玉皇阁北街 24 号❸
☎ 608 0688
¥ 266 – double room
@ www.era-nx.com

Ningfeng Hotel
宁丰宾馆 *níngfēng bīnguǎn* ★★★
✉ 6 Jiefang Dong Jie, Xingqing District
兴庆区解放东街 6 号❷
☎ 602 8898
¥ 230 – double room, peak-season
184 – double room, off-season

Food & Restaurants

Yinchuan cuisine is predominantly Muslim fare centered around beef and mutton. Chicken, duck and fish are also popular. Food here makes use of fresh ingredients, retaining the food's delicate flavors with a touch of sugar. If you're not afraid to get your hands dirty then try the *shouzhua yangrou* (手抓羊肉), a mutton dish that's eaten with your hands. Noodles with mutton (*yángròu cuōmiàn* 羊肉搓面) are a common sight in eateries throughout the area. Braised mutton (*huì yángzásui* 烩羊杂碎) is cooked with chili and caraway seeds giving it a tasty kick. Sweet and sour Yellow River carp (*tángcù huánghé lǐyú* 糖醋黄河鲤鱼), a local specialty that swims with flavor. During festivals and fairs, fried dough is a popular snack (*sǎnzi* 馓子).

RESTAURANTS

Delonglou Qingzhen Restaurant
德隆楼清真餐厅
Tasty Muslim fare.
✉ 91 Jiefang Dong Jie, Xingqing District 兴庆区解放东街 91 号❼
☎ 602 2073
🕒 10:30am to11pm

Guangdong Xuehua Dajiulou
广东雪花大酒楼
Cantonese food.
✉ 14 Zhongshan Bei Jie, Xingqing District 兴庆区中山北街 14 号❾
☎ 602 9888
🕒 10:30am to 11pm

Xianhe Lou 仙鹤楼
✉ 204 Xinhua Jie, Xingqing District 兴庆区新华街 204 号❽
☎ 609 1844, 6017542

Ningxia Laomao Shouzhua Meishilou
宁夏老毛手抓美食楼
✉ West of Nanguan Mosque, Xingqing District 兴庆区南关清真寺西侧❺
☎ 411 2817
🕒 10:30am to 11pm

Yangzhou Seafood World 洋洲海鲜大世界
✉ 412 Jiefang Xi Jie, Xingqing District 兴庆区解放西街 412 号❻
☎ 502 8797
🕒 10:30am to 11pm

Souvenirs

Medlar (*gǒuqǐ* 枸杞) is an ingredient used in traditional Chinese medicine and Ningxia has been cultivating it for over 480 years. Helan Stone (*hèlánshí* 贺兰石), which comes from Helan Shan, is often carved into ink stones. It's a very hard stone with a glossy finish and a tinge of purple coloring. Items made from lamb's wool (*tānyáng èrmáopí* 滩羊二毛皮) are abundant; they're soft and warm. The West Pagoda Culture Market (*xītǎ wénhuà shichǎng* 西塔文化市场) is a good place to browse for antiques, stoneware and assorted souvenirs; look for it over on Liqun Xi Jie (利群西街, ☎ 502 8237). If you're interested in jewelry then the Ningxia Gem City (*níngxià zhūbǎo chéng* 宁夏珠宝城❿) is your store-it specializes in gold and silver jewelry, and precious stones. It's on 164 Jiefang Xi Jie, Xingqing District (兴庆区解放西街 164 号, 504 5822).

Other Information

POST OFFICES

Yinchuan City Post Office 银川市邮政局
✉ 2 Minzu Bei Jie 民族北街 2 号⓫
☎ 602 9969

HOSPITALS

Ningxia Hui Autonomous Region People's Hospital 宁夏回族自治区人民医院
✉ 148 Huaiyuan Xi Lu, Xixia District 西夏区怀远西路 148 号
☎ 206 3081

COMPLAINT HOTLINES
☎ General: 603 1138
☎ Taxi: 603 1915

REQUEST 请人帮忙		
Please help me. / Can you do me a favor?	qǐng nǐ bānggèmáng	请你帮个忙。
Mind helping me take a picture.	néng bāng wǒ pāizhào ma	能帮我拍照吗?
Mind if I take a picture with you?	kěyǐ hé nǐ pāizhào ma	可以和你拍照吗?
Excuse me···.	láojià, ···	劳驾,···
Excuse me, may I take your picture?	láojià, gěi nǐ pāizhào xíng ma	劳驾,给你拍照行吗?

Xi'an, the Museum City

Area Code 029

Heritage: The Mausoleum of the First Qin Emperor & Terracotta Warriors

Xi'an is a museum city dotted with the historic relics of past dynasties, from the restored city walls to the majesty of the Terracotta Warriors. Xi'an will delight travelers today, as it did centuries ago as the starting point of the famed Silk Road.

Xi'an, the capital of **Shaanxi** Province, has over 3,000 years of recorded history, with human habitation present here as early as the Neolithic times, as discovered at the **Banpo Village**. Xi'an has been the capital of 12 dynasties, though it has been known as various names, most notably as Chang'an. It was also the starting point of the Silk Road, where camels were loaded for their long and perilous journey to Central Asia. Xi'an's links to Central Asia goes beyond trade as Islam continues to have an influence on the local flavor through the Muslim Hui minority.

Dynasty after dynasty added their own mark to Xi'an, and the relics of old palaces, temples and tombs abound throughout the city and surrounding countryside. The tyrannical Qin dynasty emperor Qin Shihuang, with his capital at Xianyang, close to present day Xi'an, left his indelible mark through the famed Terracotta Warriors.

The Tang dynasty is considered one of China's golden ages for its unmatched cultural achievements. Trade reached Central Asia and Europe, thousands of students from Japan and Korea arrived in Xi'an to study in acknowledgement of Tang cultural pre-eminence and Chinese monks traveled to India to copy Buddhist sutras. At its zenith during the Tang dynasty, Xi'an was the world's largest and most cosmopolitan city, stretching over 32.5 square miles (84.1 km^2) and holding over one million residents.

Part of a Tang dynasty painting of noblewomen taking a trip in spring.

Though Xi'an was large, it was not affected by the incomprehensible twisting and turning lanes of similar cities of the era. As the first planned city in China, it was organized into a neat grid layout, highly symbolic in geomancy. Xi'an's city layout would influence other cities such as Beijing and Kyoto.

With the influx of foreign traders and students, and the self-confidence of the powerful and cosmopolitan

The Terracotta Warriors stand prepared for battle.

Tang dynasty, Xi'an became not only a trading center but also a nexus of cultures, religions, artistic endeavor and learning.

Today the city's charm lies in its historic atmosphere. There's a palpable sense of past glories, and vestiges of its history are ever present. One can easily imagine the sights and sounds of Xi'an at the height of its glory when wandering along the city walls or strolling through the old Muslim quarter.

Xi'an has recently become an important center for the central government's drive to develop western China. As an economic center for the region, Xi'an is in a natural position for further development; aviation is already an important industry for the city.

INNER CITY

Xi'an's gray **city walls** (*chéngqiáng* 城墙) are imposing and built to keep out bandits and barbarians. The massive walls measure 39 feet (12 m) high and 52.5 feet (16 m) wide at the base, tapering to between 39 feet and 46 feet (12 to 14 m); they are 8.5 miles (13.74 km) in circumference. Towers at each corner of the walls have defensive towers jutting out along the length of the walls. The surviving walls, built on Tang dynasty foundations, date to the Ming dynasty and were built during the 14th century. Parts of the wall have been destroyed and the wall is incomplete but many sections remain or have been rebuilt. You can get up on the walls at any gate at the compass points. The scenery at the south gate is the best.

South of the city walls is the brick **Big Wild Goose Pagoda** (*dàyàn tǎ* 大雁塔) in the **Temple of Great Maternal Grace** (*cí'ēn sì* 慈恩寺) complex. The temple was built in AD 648 by Tang emperor Gaozong as an act of filial piety to honor his mother. The temple was destroyed after the fall of the Tang dynasty and the present buildings, mainly from the Qing dynasty, have been recently renovated.

The Big Wild Goose Pagoda is regarded by many as a symbol of the city. Built in AD 652, the pagoda has a 16.4-foot-high (5 m) square base and reaches 212 feet (64.5 m) in height. It was built to house and protect Buddhist scriptures collected by a Chinese monk, Xuan Zang, who spent an epic 17 years traveling to India and back gathering them and an equal amount of time translating them. His journey has been immortalized in the novel Journey to the West, one of China's most important literary works.

Located in Muslim district along **Huajue Lane** (*huàjué xiàng* 化觉巷), the **Great Mosque** (*dà qīngzhēn sì* 大清真寺) is a short walk from the **Drum Tower** (*gǔ lóu* 鼓楼) and the **Bell Tower** (*zhōng lóu* 钟楼) at the center of town. The mosque, which is still an active place of worship, was established by the Tang dynasty in AD 742 for Muslim traders from Central Asia who settled in Xi'an.

Inside the Great Mosque compound it is difficult to tell that the buildings are Islamic because it was built according to traditional Chinese architectural forms and many of the Islamic symbols are Sinicized. Unlike typical Chinese temples, which are built on a north-south axis, the mosque is built east-west with the prayer hall at the far west end in accordance to the Islamic regulation of facing Mecca for prayer. Although originally built during the Tang dynasty, it has been extensively renovated with many of the present buildings hailing from the Qing dynasty. The mosque and the surrounding buildings take up an area of some 3.2 acres (13,000 m^2), though not all areas, such as the prayer hall, are accessible to non-Muslims.

The mosque grounds are quiet, giving it an aura of religious sanctity and there's a large wooden gateway dating from the reign of the emperor of the Qing dynasty, Kangxi, who reigned from AD 1662 to 1723. The gateway features the calligraphy by **Mi Fu**, a famous Northern Song dynasty calligrapher and painter. The Introspection Minaret, though doesn't look like an Arabic minaret, is where the cleric preaches to his congregation on an upraised platform.

The area surrounding the mosque is called

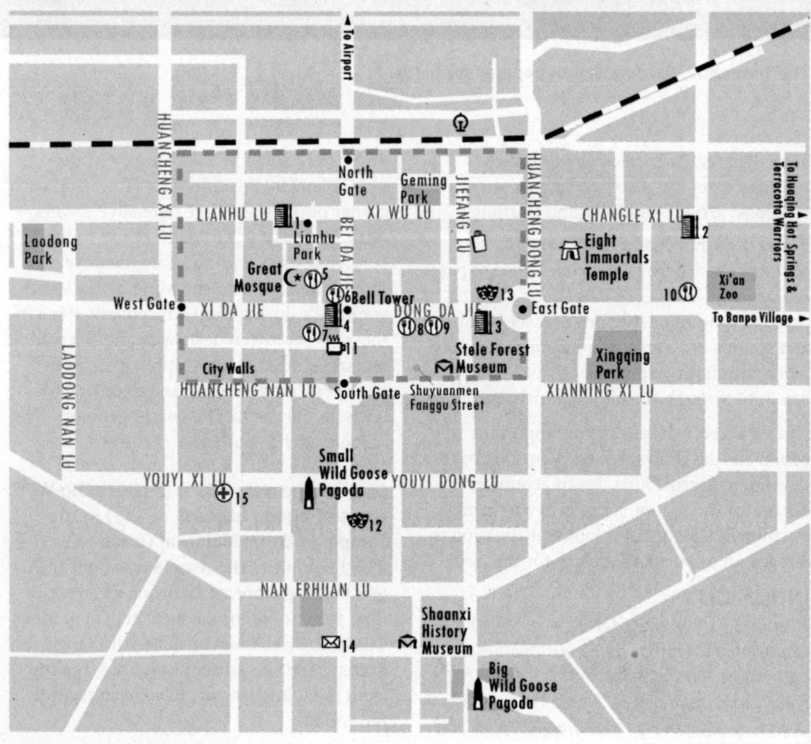

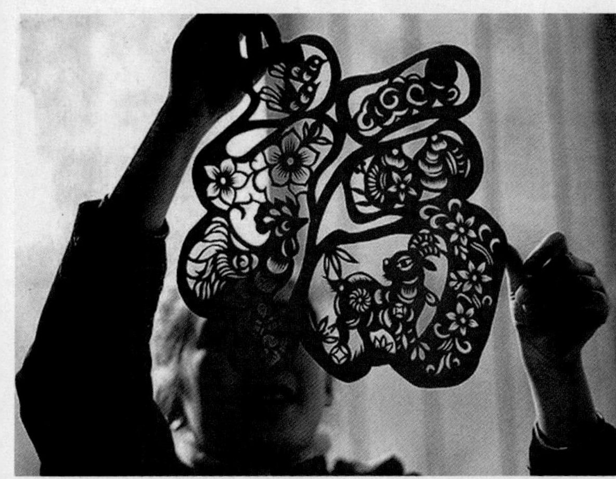

Shaanxi's elaborate paper cuttings are usually pasted onto windows during Chinese New Year.

Huifang and has a distinct Muslim atmosphere, with small tree lined lanes crowded with restaurants and shops that are alive with activity.

To the south of the city walls, northwest of the Big Wild Goose Pagoda, is the **Shaanxi History Museum** (*shǎnxī lìshǐ bówùguǎn* 陕西历史博物馆) which opened in 1991. It is the largest comprehensive museum in the province. The museum exhibits over 3,000 historical relics, a small fraction of their collection, ranging from 115,000-year-old prehistoric artifacts to items from the Opium Wars of the 1840's.

The museum, although built in a traditional Tang dynasty architectural style, is modern and well designed. The main attraction of the museum is the magnificent collection of Tang dynasty artifacts. Of special significance are the bronze pieces and the Tang gold and silverware, the terracotta pieces and murals from Tang dynasty tombs.

EASTERN TRAVEL ROUTE

The **Huaqing Hot Springs** (*huáqīng chí* 华清池), nearly 19 miles (30 km) east of Xi'an, was once the playground of Tang dynasty emperors, though there have been buildings there as early as the Western Zhou, with later additions built during the Qin and Sui dynasties. The hot springs are famous because of Yang Guifei, a regular guest and the central character in one of China's most enduring legends of ill-fated love.

Yang Guifei, also known as the fat concubine – well-proportioned women were considered the epitome of beauty during the Tang dynasty – was a girl of humble origins but of exceptional beauty. She attracted the attention of Tang dynasty emperor Xuanzong, who became so enamored by her beauty, he ignored his imperial duties. As the empire began to crumble from rebellion, the emperor was forced to flee Xi'an. While on the run, the emperor's courtiers, blaming Yang Guifei for the ruin of the empire, forced the emperor to order her to hang herself. The emperor, literally sick with grief, abdicated the throne to one of his sons.

The natural springs are considered to have beneficial minerals and there are several places to bathe. The Hot Springs Bathhouse offers private baths, but communal bath-houses have more of the local atmosphere and are inexpensive. Entry to the Huaqing Hot Springs is RMB 30 and is open from 8am to 7pm.

Banpo Village(*bànpō bówùguǎn* 半坡博物馆), inhabited long before the glories of the various empires that made Xi'an home, was discovered in 1953. The village is the earliest example of the Neolithic Yangshao culture that's renowned for its colorful ceramics that feature etchings that are possibly an early

Quotes

"It's amazing how Xi'an history envelops you. There's always a constant reminder of its past."

Locals hang out at the Bell Tower at night.

form of writing. The site itself is made up of divided into three separate areas: a residential area, a manufacturing area, and a cemetery. Remaining are 45 houses and buildings, 250 adult graves, 73 children's burial urns, and six pottery kilns. The villagers cultivated various crops, domesticated pigs and dogs, fished in the nearby Wei River and manufactured ceramics.

Some archeologists have argued that Banpo represents a matriarchal society, though the supporting evidence remains vague. The site has been a treasure trove of artifacts though, with over 8,000 pieces unearthed. Some of the most interesting artifacts are the children's burial urns. Children weren't buried with the adults, but placed in urns which were buried close to homes. The lids on the urns have a hole in the top in order for the spirits of the deceased to travel to the afterworld.

The Banpo site holds two attractions: the Neolithic Village and theme park-esque Matriarchal Village.

THE TERRACOTTA WARRIORS

In 221 BC, for the first time in its history, China was united under one emperor, Qin Shihuang of the Qin dynasty. The Qin emperor's influence far outlived his short dynasty. His most important achievement was unifying the various warring kingdoms and integrating standardized writing, money, weights and measures into one centralized bureaucracy. Like many autocrats, Qin Shihuang had an early start on his own mausoleum; construction began when he was only 14 and continued for 36 years.

The emperor's tomb complex is a massive memorial to a man that history remembers as both brilliant and brutal. Many parts of his rich tomb remain unexplored because current archeological technology isn't advanced enough to preserve the priceless artifacts held within.

The tomb complex of the Qin emperor, at 21.7 square miles (56.25 km^2), is best described as an underground palace with stables and an inner and outer city. Han dynasty historian Sima Qian detailed the construction effort, he wrote of the vast effort required to build the emperor's final resting place. Over 700,000 conscript and slave laborers built the tomb to hold the numerous treasures within, rivers of

▶▶ Qin Shihuang

Qin Shihuang, who lived from 259 to 210 BC, was the cunning first Emperor of a unified China. His brilliant military victories and political stratagems ended the Warring States period, a time of disunity and upheaval. To consolidate his power, he embarked on construction projects of astonishing size and grandeur – the Terracotta Warriors and the Great Wall are all linked to him.

He became King of Qin when he was only 13 years old, but it wasn't until he was in his thirties that he finally managed to defeat six other rival states and bring China under centralized control. He divided his new kingdom into 36 counties which were subdivided into prefectures. The local military and administrative leaders were all personally appointed by him.

Deciding his own achievements had surpassed those of previous rulers, he renamed himself Shi Huangdi. Shi means first, and Huang and Di were titles of earlier kings – together it came to mean "the First Emperor." Today he's known as Qin Shihuang.

One important way for him to exert his control was to unify the various different standards that developed in each warring kingdom. He set to work standardizing weights and measurements, formed one national currency using the Qin standard (round copper coins with square holes in their center), and standardized the exact form of the written characters. New roads were built to link his capital in Xianyang (close to present day Xi'an) with his newly conquered domains.

There was, however, the vexing problem of nomadic tribes to the north of the empire. A number of walls had been built by individual states and Qin Shihuang had them repaired, enlarged, and extended, then linked them together to form the Great Wall. He also launched a military campaign against the tribes, but this would prove inconclusive and China would continue to be vulnerable to these mounted nomads throughout its history.

Qin Shihuang's rule is often remembered for its ruthlessness. The Great Wall was constructed by 500,000 laborers, most of whom were prisoners of war, and it's believed that up to 70% of them died from exhaustion or starvation. In 212 BC, when some intellectuals attempted to reinstate the systems of the Zhou dynasty, the emperor ordered the burning of any books not about medicine, divination or agriculture. This infamous book burning would destroy many of China's earliest classics. A year later he buried alive 460 Confucian scholars who criticized his policies.

Work began on his mausoleum when he was only 14. Over 70,000 of his subjects constructed replica palaces, pavilions, ships and the famous Terracotta Warriors on a site covering over 19 square miles (50km^2) of land near Xi'an. The whole complex would only be completed a few years after his death.

In 1974 some peasants discovered the long forgotten site by accident while digging a well. Excavations have been slowly uncovering the area over the last 30 years, but the underground palace, the central part of the mausoleum, remains a mystery. Archeologists predict that it might take 200 years to unearth it all, and no one is quite sure what they'll find - the artisans and craftsmen who built it were rumored to have been entombed inside to ensure they never revealed the emperor's secrets.

mercury, constellations of pearls and gems embedded into the ceiling, plus an assortment of valuables the emperor would require in his afterlife, including live soldiers, concubines and servants – plus the artisans who worked on the mausoleum lest they reveal its secrets.

Today Qin Shihuang's unopened vault, 0.9 miles (1.5 km) from the Terracotta Warriors, still guards its secrets. The nondescript grassy mound above the vault is surrounded by trees. On peaceful sunny days, the wind blows yellow earth across the countryside, what may lie underneath belies the humble

Memorable Experiences

Wandering through the Muslim quarter and experiencing the sights and sounds of Xi'an's Hui minority.

Biking atop the old city wall and enjoying a great view of the city.

Eating the various local specialties at the food market.

surroundings and tantalizes the imagination.

The Terracotta Warriors (*bīngmǎ yǒng* 兵马俑) form only a part of the Qin emperor's tomb complex. They may have remained forgotten had it not been for the fortuitous discovery by local peasants drilling a well in 1974. What they found would excite the archeology world.

In a vault of approximately 3 acres (12,000 m^2), lying some 16 feet (5 m) underground, stood some 8,000 terracotta infantry soldiers, archers, cavalrymen and chariots arranged in battle formation, ready to defend their emperor's immortal soul. Each soldier is approximately 71 inches (1.8 m) tall, with higher-ranking soldiers being taller, and made of 3-inch-thick (7.6 cm) clay. Each part of the hollow body was made separately. While the trunk, limbs and hands were mass-produced, the heads were individually constructed and the face of each warrior is distinct. It has been theorized the faces were sculpted from the likeness of the soldiers and artisans. The terracotta sculptures show a high level of artistry with individualized facial expressions, hairstyles and clothing and were once brightly painted with black armor, colorful red scarves and green pants, though the colors have long faded. As warriors, they each held weapons: bronze swords, spears, axes and halberds – which were still sharp when discovered – and longbows and crossbows.

Three pits containing warriors are open; a nearby fourth pit was found empty. The pits are still being excavated and in many, warriors lay toppled as if they fell in combat. Shattered and headless statues give the eerie sense of viewing the carnage of an ancient battlefield. Though a daunting task, archeologists continue to piece together the broken remains of those warriors who lost their battle against time.

Pit 1 is the largest and contains about 6,000 warriors with war chariots and horses. Housed in a gigantic building that resembles an airplane hangar, the warriors are protected from the elements and tourists who view them from elevated walkways. The warriors are lined in 38 trenches, facing eastwards to the emperor's tomb.

The warriors in Pit 2 are mostly hidden and excavation continues with most of the area closed off. This pit show signs of fire damage, the wooden roof structure was burned when the mausoleum was looted by Xiang Yu, one of the warlords who battled for supremacy after the fall of the Qin dynasty. While the first pit contains mostly foot soldiers, the second pit is the mobile arm of the army with chariots, cavalry and archers. A tall statue, thought to be a general, was also found in this pit.

The third pit is the command center for the ghostly army, with 68 statues of officers around a war chariot. The clothing of the officers differs from common soldiers: the officers wear fine robes and are much taller.

There's a display hall with two bronze chariots unearthed near the base of the emperor's tomb. These elaborate half-sized chariots are intricately detailed, with drivers and horses sporting decorated plumes and gold and silver inlaid harnesses. These richly decorated chariots feature working parts such as windows that open and close and turning handles. There are also exhibitions featuring artifacts from the pits, allowing a closer look at the intricate workmanship.

Outside the gates of the Terracotta Warriors, present-day market warriors will give a shrill battle cry as you approach. They're armed with different wares, from ubiquitous replica terracotta warriors to postcards – the best defense is a good offense and that means bargaining. ■

Making Your Trip Easy

Practical Tips

Be aware that taking photos inside the pits at the Terracotta Warriors is officially prohibited.

Xi'an is famed for its annual festivals; one of the livelier ones is the Silk Road International Tourism Festival. Every September people gather in downtown Xi'an for this event. Fireworks, folk music and dance performances, talent shows, cultural exhibitions are all part of the itinerary.

Transportation

Airport – The Xianyang International Airport is in Xiangyang Beiyuan, about 25.5 miles (41 km) from the city center; it's about an hour away by highway. There are hourly airport shuttle buses connecting Xishaomen to the airport from 5am to 6pm.

Taxi – Taxis in Xi'an are RMB 6 at flag-fall (8323 5863).

The Best of Xi'an

Big Wild Goose Pagoda 大雁塔 *dàyàn tǎ*
✉ Nanduan, Yanta Lu 雁塔路南段
☎ 8552 7958
🕒 8am to 5pm
¥ 25, (RMB 15 for the pagoda)

Terracotta Warriors 兵马俑 *bīngmǎ yǒng*
✉ Lintong District 临潼区
☎ 8139 9001
🕒 8am to 6pm
¥ 90

Shaanxi History Museum
陕西历史博物馆 *shǎnxī lìshǐ bówùguǎn*
✉ Xiaozhai Dong Lu 小寨东路
🕒 8:30am to 6pm, peak-season
9am to 5:30pm, off-season
¥ 35

Hotels

Hyatt Regency Hotel
西安凯悦（阿房宫）饭店 *xī'ān kǎiyuè (ēfáng gōng) fàndiàn* ★★★★★
✉ 158 Dong Da Jie 东大街 158 号❸
☎ 8723 1234
¥ 1,000 – double room
@ www.xian.regency.hyatt.com

Shangri-La Golden Flower Hotel
西安香格里拉金花饭店
xī'ān xiānggélǐlā jīnhuā fàndiàn ★★★★★
✉ 8 Changle Xi Lu 长乐西路 8 号❷
☎ 8323 2981
¥ 680 – single room
800 – double room
@ www.shangri-la.com

Bell Tower Hotel Xi'an 西安钟楼饭店 *xī'ān zhōnglóu fàndiàn* ★★★★
✉ 110 Nan Da Jie 南大街 110 号❹
☎ 8760 0000
¥ 458 – double room
@ www.belltowerhtl.com

Grand New World Hotel 西安古都新世界大酒店 *xī'ān gǔdū xīnshìjiè dàjiǔdiàn* ★★★★
✉ 172 Lianhu Lu 莲湖路 172 号❶
☎ 8721 6868
¥ 955 – double room, peak-season
450 – double room, off-season
@ www.gnwhxian.com

Food & Restaurants

Xi'an cuisine is simple and hearty; you won't

Terracotta warriors that have just been released from their earthly prison reveal traces of their once vivid colors.

leave the table hungry. Noodles and dumplings are predominant and these are always filling. Due to the large Hui community, Muslim food is common. Nanshi Jie, by Dong Da Jie has a lively food market. Try local delicacies at the Beiyuanmen Hui Snack Street (*běiyuànmén huímín xiǎochī yītiáojiē* 北院门回民小吃一条街) where traditional Chinese buildings line the street and offer a smorgasbord of Muslim fare.

Shredded pancakes in a mutton or beef soup (*yángròu pàomó* 羊肉泡馍) are a local Muslim delicacy that warms the stomach. The table etiquette is an art in itself as the diner breaks up a flatbread that's mixed into the soup. Dumplings (*jiǎozi* 饺子) are a northern specialty in China and Xi'an is famous for its dumpling feasts. Introduced in 1984 by the Xi'an Dumpling Feast Restaurant, the banquet features a selection of 108 dumplings that differ in shape and filling. *Jiasan guantang baozi* (贾三灌汤包子) is a unique Muslim dumpling treat. A filling of ground beef and chopped vegetables is mixed with gravy before the paper-thin dumpling skin is sealed, making these dumplings delightfully juicy. Buckwheat noodles (*héle miàn* 饸饹面) can be served hot or cold and are delicious with different vegetable toppings and sauces.

Bars and coffee shops are clustered around Defu Xiang, west of Nan Da Jie near the Bell Tower. Most of these are set in quiet neighborhoods and make a great setting to grab a cold beer or a cup of java.

Shaanxi History Museum.

RESTAURANTS

Defachang Jiaozi Guan 德发长饺子馆
Dumplings and more dumplings, dumpling banquets at RMB 60 to 200 per person.
✉ 3 Xi Da Jie, Zhonggulou Square 西大街 3 号，钟鼓楼广场❻
☎ 8721 4065
🕒 10am to 2pm, 5pm to 9pm

Fanjia Lazhi Rou Pu 樊家腊汁肉铺
Sandwiches stuffed with delicious meats RMB 2.5 to 10 per person.
✉ 53 Zhubashi 竹笆市 53 号❼
☎ 8727 3917
🕒 8am to 9pm

Jiasan Guantang Baozi 贾三灌汤包子
Tasty Muslim cuisine.
✉ 93 Beiyuanmen, Huimin Jie, Lianhu District 莲湖区回民街北院门 93 号❺
☎ 8727 9114, 8725 7507
🕒 7:30am to 9pm

King Coffee K 咖啡
✉ 52 Nandajie, Beilin District 碑林区南大街 52 号⓫
☎ 5545 5655

Laosunjia Niuyangrou Paomo 老孙家牛羊肉泡馍

Beef and lamb *paomo* (泡馍) for RMB 20.8 a bowl.
✉ 364 Dong Da Jie 东大街 364 号❽
☎ 8721 4438, 8721 2835
🕒 6:30am to 10:30pm

Qinchao Waguan 秦朝瓦罐
Experience what a banquet 2,000 years would've been like.
✉ 6 Jinhua Bei Lu 金花北路 6 号❿
☎ 8322 5388
🕒 10:30am to 9:30pm

Xi'an Fanzhuang 西安饭庄
Offers the best of traditional Shaanxi snacks. RMB 30 to 200 per person.
✉ 298 Dong Da Jie 东大街 298 号❾
☎ 8768 0618
🕒 10am to 2pm; 5pm to 9pm

Souvenirs

Xi'an is a great place to shop for cultural items. Jiefang Lu is a thriving shopping area and offers great window-shopping. Just south of the Drum Tower is Dong Da Jie and Xi Da Jie. This street runs east to west through the city and is lined with many stores. In the Muslim quarter just outside the Great Mosque is the Dajue Xiang Market (*dàjué xiàng shìchǎng* 大觉巷市场). Here you'll find a little of everything – antiques, musical instruments and Mao memorabilia. Don't expect genuine antiques though.

Shuyuanmen Street (*shūyuànmén fǎnggǔ yītiáojiē* 书院门仿古一条街), located east of Nanmenli, offers good knick-knack hunting opportunities amongst replica Ming and Qing dynasties' architecture – anything and everything related to Chinese culture can be found here. Wenbao zhai (文宝斋) over at 5 Zhongduan, Yanta Lu (雁塔路中段 5 号, ☎ 8551 2020) is a good place to pick up some local folk art. For the serious antique collector, Zhongtian Ge (中天阁) is a good stop. Located at 65 Shuyuan Men (书院门 65 号, ☎ 8725 2939), this store has fine collectables with export certificates.

Xi'an is known for its Tang dynasty tri-colored porcelain (*táng sāncǎi* 唐三彩). The subjects of this pottery are bold and life-like, and the glazed colors are diverse and expressive, though be wary of any shops that claim their wares are "old." As a storehouse of ancient culture, books featuring the calligraphy of famous calligraphers are popular items. Paper cutting (*jiǎnzhǐ* 剪纸) is a popular folk art in Shaanxi, on holidays and weddings, villagers decorate their homes with bright (mostly red) paper cuttings that are rich and varied and always feature symbols of good luck. Cashing in on Xi'an's main attraction, replicas of Terracotta Warriors (*bīngmǎyǒng* 兵马俑) are everywhere; they range from a few inches tall to life-size, with prices of up to several thousand US dollars.

Also check out the colorful clay sculptures of Fengxiang. Originally toys for children during the farming off-season. The long history and unique artistic style have made the sculptures very famous in China. And the Chinese zodiac animal designs have been frequently featured on Chinese stamps.

Other Information

POST OFFICES

Xiaozhai Post Office 小寨邮局
✉ 3 Xiaozhai Xi Lu 小寨西路 3 号⓮
☎ 8525 2484

HOSPITALS

Shaanxi Provincial People's Hospital 陕西省人民医院
✉ 256 Youyi Xi Lu 友谊西路 256 号⓯
☎ 8524 9640

COMPLAINT HOTLINES

☎ General: 8763 0166
☎ Taxi: 8420 6801

TOURISM INFORMATION WEBSITE

@ www.xian-tourism.com

Entertainment

Dihao Theater 帝豪歌剧院
A comprehensive entertainment center with a theater, karaoke and a nightclub.
✉ 12/F, Xinli Guomao Dasha, 119 Dong Da Jie 东大街 119 号新立国贸大厦 12 楼⓭
☎ 8741 8000, 8741 9000
🕒 8am to 2am

Tangyue Gong 唐乐宫
A feast for the senses as delicious cuisine is served alongside Tang song and dance performances – a veritable Tang dynasty extravaganza.
✉ 75 Chang'an Bei Lu 长安北路 75 号⓬
☎ 8526 1633
🕒 6:30pm to 9:40pm
¥ 410 includes dinner
200 just the show

Hua Shan, a Painting Springs to Life

Area Code 0913

As the minibus ascends the winding road to **Hua Shan**, the jagged scenery unfolds like a captivating piece of Chinese calligraphic art. Overhanging rock and distant precipices wink from above, and clumps of vegetation peek out from mysterious crevices. Hua Shan's awe-inspiring peaks will take your breath away. Located some 74 miles (120 km) from the ancient capital Xi'an in Shaanxi Province, Hua Shan is the result of dramatic tectonic movements millions of years ago, and is one of China's most perilous mountain areas. Although covering an area of just 58 square miles (150 km²), Hua Shan is inundated with over 70 peaks and ridges.

This ridge on Hua Shan's West Peak is imaginatively likened to a carp's back.

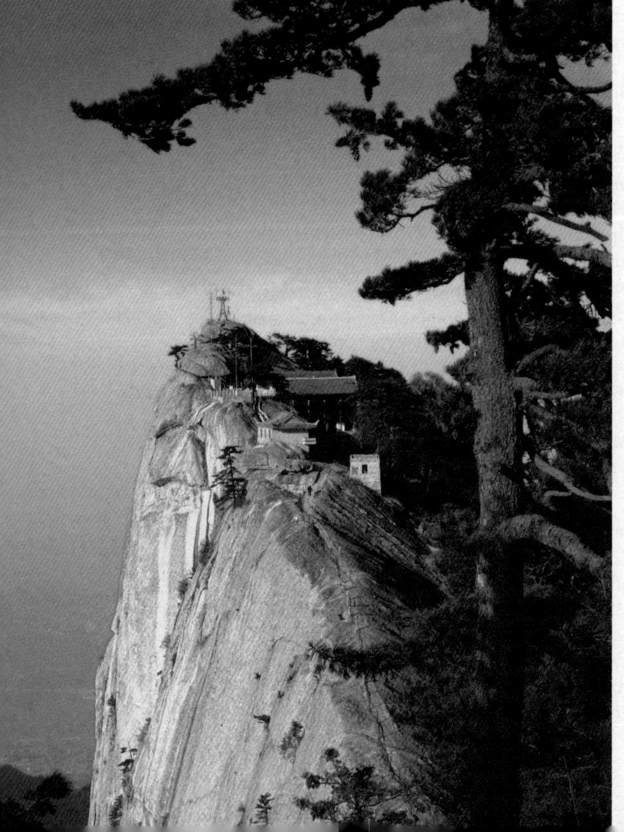

The most outstanding peaks are North, South, East, West and Central – they stand like the petals of a lotus flower reaching for the heavens. These five imperious peaks gaze over the Wei and Yellow Rivers in the north and embrace the Qinling Mountains in the south.

At 7,085 feet (2,160 m), **South Peak** (*nán fēng* 南峰) tops the lot. Her closest rivals are **East Peak** (*dōng fēng* 东峰) and **West Peak** (*xī fēng* 西峰). The **Central Peak** (*zhōng fēng* 中峰), also called **Jade Maiden Peak** (*yùnǚ fēng* 玉女峰) and the **North Peak** (*běi fēng* 北峰) are slightly less statuesque but equally beautiful. In the early mornings and late evenings, cushions of mist dramatically swirl around these granite peaks, lending a romantic and mythic air.

All five peaks are accessible by foot, and for even the most lethargic – by cable car. The Austrian built cable car has its terminus at the "base" of Hua Shan and ferries visitors to the North Peak.

From the North Peak, you can step your way to the other four peaks and scenic spots. Hua Shan has inspired much lyrical poetry through the ages, some of which is carved onto the rock outcroppings. Poets and their paramours have strolled beneath its granite arches, lovers have stolen kisses beneath the dipping willows and under the privacy of peak-top pavilions made from stone. Heroes have visited, hermits have sought serenity and legends have flourished at these rocky walls.

The mountain has electrified the imaginations of generations of visitors, testified by the interesting names given to the nooks and crevices atop Hua Shan – lovely titles like **Lotus Flower Cave** or **Waterfall Cave**. Ridges have names like **Blue Dragon**, **Flying Fish**, **Lion and Black Tiger**. Mountain terraces are christened Peach Woods and Wild Ginger for the particular fruit and flora that grace the warmer seasons.

There are nine cliffs: **Looking onto the Wei River** (*fǔwèi yá* 俯渭崖), **Touching Ear** (*cā'ěr yá* 擦耳崖), **Thrusting into the Clouds** (*chōngxiāo yá* 冲霄崖), **Sacrificing Oneself** (*shěshēn yá* 舍身崖), **Escaping the Imperial Edict** (*bìzhào yá* 避诏崖), **Bright Star** (*míngxīng yá* 明星崖), **Sun and Moon** (*rìyuè yá* 日月崖) and **Immortal's Palm** (*xiānzhǎng yá* 仙掌崖). There are also eight viewing platforms with colorful names like the **Three Emperors** (*sānhuáng tái* 三皇台), **Immortals Gathering** (*jùxiān tái* 聚仙台) and **Purple Vapor** (*zǐqì tái* 紫气台). They are built in traditional styles in harmony with the area's natural beauty. The view from any angle is pretty neat.

Mountain rivulets meander along the many twists and turns of metamorphic rock. The water is funneled into a dramatic **Qingke Waterfall** (*qīngkē píng* 青柯坪), about 6.2 miles (10 km) from the mouth of the valley.

CLIMBING NORTH PEAK

Visiting Hua Shan can be a day-trip, a two-day or even a three-day affair. There are two ways up Hua Shan. The cable car reaches the top of North Peak in 10 to 15 minutes or you can follow the stairs that lead up North Peak.

To see as many peaks as you can in one day, but to save time and energy, it's best to take the cable car up the North Peak and from there make your way to the other peaks. The five peaks are about an hour's walk from each other, but if you have a bit more time on your hands and are ready to get that heart pumping, read on for the sights you'd have missed if you took the quick and easy route.

North Peak is also referred to as **Clouds Stand Peak** (*yúntái fēng* 云台峰) because of the three cliffs surrounding it. Only one narrow road leads southwards to Touching Ear Precipice.

The climb up the 5,293-foot-high (1,614 m) North Peak starts off gradually enough, but you've just begun a 3.7 mile (6 km) trek that includes over 3,000 steps. Most of the steps are in good condition and though some are horizontal incisions trying to pass off as steps, chained railings help the ascent. At a leisurely pace, it takes an average 2 to 3 hours. The route presents several opportunities to test your mettle: **Heavenward Ladder** (*shàngtiān tī* 上天梯), **Sun and Moon Precipice** and the sinewy dragon-shaped ridge in front of West Peak, called **Dark-green Dragon Ridge** (*cānglóng lǐng* 苍龙岭).

After the first 500 steps, there's a platform – fortunately one of several, where you can rest and soak in the tranquility. On a sunlit day, the sun's rays cast dramatic light and shadows against the rocky surfaces. Endless steps snake through trees, boulders, lush greenery, and over rippling brooks. You've been transported into the underbelly of a heaving canyon.

With each step, even more captivating scenery unfolds. The skyscrapers of New York or Shanghai are chopsticks when compared to the towering beauty of Hua Shan.

As you walk your thousandth step, your legs will begin to seriously protest the vigorous step-ups you've inflicted on them, but ignore the mocking hum of cable cars overhead. Concentrate instead on the spellbinding view. Cavernous cliffs loll like waves into bushy valleys and depending on the season, you might run into a little waterfall where you can take a dip and chill out.

You know you have almost reached the halfway point when you arrive at a refreshment stand manned by a plump villager. There are little stools and tables where you can sit and catch your breath without having to purchase anything. Keep in mind refreshment items get pricier the higher up the mountain you go.

The villagers at these shops climb up and down North Peak daily. As you lament your exhausted physical state, they console you that you're much better off climbing up rather than down the mountain, because your knees would then hurt twice as much.

Rest well because what's around the corner is rather frightful. There are three different flights of steps ahead, each more harrowing than the next. All are inclined at an uncomfortably steep gradient, so it will be difficult for you to rest and take a sip of water or stretch your legs midway. Whichever your choice, put your faith in the rusty railings by the side of the steps and go up on all fours, if need be.

Although you're at the halfway point of North Peak, that last set of steep steps was only the aperitif. A longer 1,500-step stairway, **Huangfu Col** path, awaits you on a huge mound, called **Turtle Carrying Stone** (*guī bēi shí* 龟背石) by the locals. Tigers and black bears once prowled the southern slopes. The shy and elusive denizens of Hua Shan include mountain goats, snakes, squirrels and on the West Peak, monkeys.

Once over the Turtle Carrying Stone hurdle, the peak-end of the cable car terminus looms into view. It gleams like a champion's trophy. People hover at the foot and mountaintop of Hua Shan. Human prattle soon replaces the chirping of birds. The hum of the cable car gets louder and drowns out the trickling sound of running water.

At Hua Shan, nature makes the best companion. Between pinnacle and valley is a restful calm. No wonder many Confucian scholars and Taoist religious masters came to Hua Shan to meditate and refine their teachings.

The sun sets just as splendidly from the North or the West Peaks. After such strenuous exertion, reward yourself with a sumptuous dinner at the North Peak Hotel.

Energetic waist drummers, a traditional Shaanxi way to celebrate important occasions.

PEAK-A-BOO

The saying, "the early bird gets the worm," is definitely true on Hua Shan. If you sleep in, you'll lose out on a gorgeously sensual sunrise. At around 6am, the warm rays of the sun caress your skin, cool from the fresh morning breeze. You thaw slowly, as if just waking up from hibernation. Your sore muscles may take a bit more persuasion to work the morning after your "Hua Shan-scalathon." East Peak, sometimes called **Sun Facing Peak** (*cháoyáng fēng* 朝阳峰), even has a viewing platform for sun-lovers.

Quotes

"One-third of the way up, I wished I'd taken the cable car. The climb was so strenuous! But I felt like skipping for joy when I reached the top – can't believe I did it!"

"Whether you visit Hua Shan in winter or summer, it's always so pretty. The rocks capture my imagination."

Get a move on early if you want to visit the rest of the four peaks, not to mention the many ridges, caves, pavilions, sculptures, engravings, Buddhist and Taoist temples, such as the **Yuquan Yuan** (*yùquán yuàn* 玉泉院) and **Xiyue Temple** (*xīyuè miào* 西岳庙).

Hua Shan's highest point is South Peak or **Dropping Goose Peak** (*luòyàn fēng* 落雁峰). Along it is a planked route lined with iron chains, which guide the very adventurous, or foolish, up a nerve-racking path. Waves of clouds drift above a fantastic horizon of mountain ranges and distant river waters.

On West Peak in front of **Cuiyun Temple** (*cuìyún gōng* 翠云宫), sits a massive lotus-shaped rock called **Lotus Peak** (*liánhuā fēng* 莲花峰). Beside the temple is another deeply scarred crack called **Axe-Splitting Rock** (*fǔpī shí* 斧劈石). Legend goes that a filial youth by the name of Chen Xiang used a giant axe to crack apart the mountain to rescue his mother. The northwest face of West Peak drops so steeply it appears to be cleaved by a sharp sword, hence its name, **Fatal Cliff**. The eastern face is lush with dense forest. ■

Making Your Trip Easy

Practical Tips

Before you start, leave behind everything you don't need – best to be mobile; at some point, you'll need both hands to cling onto railings for support. A pair of cotton gloves might be useful to keep blisters at bay – they cost about RMB 2. Maps of Hua Shan are handy to identify scenic spots; they're about RMB 1 to 2 each. Bring adequate water, sun-protection gear (cap, sunscreen, sunglasses) in hotter months and adequate winter gear in the colder season. Proper shoes are indispensable. If you decide to climb up at night be sure to bring a flashlight, and it's advised to go in a group. Pay attention to your surroundings as some places during the climb are rather narrow and dangerous. Check with your hotel: some offer day-trip packages to Hua Shan, at RMB 220 per person, including transport and admission costs.

April to May and October are the busiest months – not all visitors necessarily stay overnight on Hua Shan – while September is the most beautiful time to visit. During the winter months Hua Shan remains open to tourists. The main paths are cleared of snow, but it's more hazardous to visit then.

Accommodations on top of the mountain tend to be basic. It's a place to commune with nature, so time is best spent outdoors anyways.

Transportation

Airport – The closet airport is the Xianyang International Airport about 25 miles (41 km) away from Xi'an and 87 miles (140 km) away from Hua Shan. From the airport, you can take a taxi or tour bus to Hua Shan, about 2 hours away.

Bus – From the chaotic bus station at Xi'an, touts will be clawing you to get on their minibus. The ride will take about 3 to 4 hours and several buses leave for Hua Shan. It won't be first class and be warned that the bus may not leave until full, contrary to promises. One-way bus fare from the Xi'an Bus station to Hua Shan is RMB 35. Once you're there, the entrance fee to Hua Shan is

All of Hua Shan's goods are carried up the mountain one step at a time.

RMB 60 while the fee to enter the Hua Shan scenic area is RMB 20. To get back to Xi'an, there'll be minibuses parked at the foot of Hua Shan that head for a small town about 20 minutes away. From here, look for another bus (like a chartered bus) to take you back to Xi'an. Alternatively, make arrangements at your Xi'an hotel for private two-way transport. It's more comfortable and a lot less time is wasted on the waiting game.

Cable Car – The cable car at Hua Shan costs RMB 60 one-way and RMB 110 for a two-way ticket. It's open from 7am to 7pm during the summer and 9am to 5pm during the winter.

Taxi – Taxis normally cost around RMB 5 to 15. Most taxis at Hua Shan don't have a meter so you'll need to bargain for a price beforehand.

The Best of Hua Shan

Hua Shan Western Route
华山西路 *huàshān xī lù*
The Route Recommended

This route used to be the only path up the mountain and because of that, it is lined with most historic sights.
¥ 100

Xiyue Temple 西岳庙 *xīyuè miào*
☎ 461 2521
🕒 8am to 5pm
¥ 30

Hotels

Hua Shan Financial Hotel 陕西华山金融宾馆 *shǎnxī huàshān jīnróng bīnguǎn* ★★★
✉ Zhongduan, Yuquan Lu, Huayin City 华阴市玉泉路中段
☎ 436 3121
¥ 320 – double room

Shaanxi Hua Shan Lotus Hotel
陕西华山莲花山庄
shǎnxī huàshān liánhuā shānzhuāng ★★★
✉ within the Hua Shan Scenic Spot 华山风景区内
☎ 436 8000
¥ 280 – double room
@ www.lfhoTel.com

Hua Shan Jinsui Hotel
华山金穗宾馆 *huàshān jīnsuì bīnguǎn* ★★
✉ Yuquan Lu, Huayin City 华阴市玉泉路
☎ 436 6000
¥ 180 – double room

Food & Restaurants

Over the years Hua Shan has become more tourist-friendly. A little village has sprouted at the foot of Hua Shan with over 25 stalls

Memorable Experiences

Watching the rosy sunrise and sunset.

Having a delicious, well-deserved dinner under the stars, away from city noises.

Reaching the top and getting looks of admiration from cop-outs who took the cable car.

Chatting with refreshment sellers at rest stations along the path, and listening to their stories.

offering refreshments and local dishes. Some Hua Shan specialties include: wheat pastry with vegetables (*huàyīn máshí* 华阴麻食); *qiaomai liangfen* (荞麦凉粉), a type of cold noodle that looks like a thick flat vermicelli but is usually made with potato powder; buckwheat noodles (*qiáo miàn* 荞面); and a sweet steamed pumpkin filled with rice, raisins, plums, peanuts, lotus and walnuts called *babao nangua* (八宝南瓜).

If you're up on the mountain, any hotel will whip up a delicious meal, but be prepared to pay up to four times more. Try chicken cooked with sweet sauce and peppers, stir-fried beef with capsicum, leafy vegetables with mushrooms topped with oyster sauce at the Hua Shan North Peak Hotel.

Many small restaurants can also be found in Yuquan Lu (玉泉路).

Souvenirs

Many of the small shops are cramped with souvenirs like fake rhinoceros horns and jade pieces, Hua Shan rocks and "friendship locks." Others tout more useful items like caps, sunglasses, binoculars and scarlet good-luck ribbons – apparently protection for a potentially "hazardous" climb ahead.

Hua county is the birthplace for Chinese Shadow Plays, an ancient art form combining opera singing, light, and silhouette. The shadow puppets are made with cowhide with movable joints and often carved with intricate decorations and patterns. Most souvenir shops sell the leather puppets, but it takes a bit of searching to find a genuine one.

You can get all your souvenir needs at the cable car's gift shop (*huàshān suǒdào lǚyóu jìniànpǐn shāngdiàn* 华山索道旅游纪念品商店) at the Wayougou stop. For a genuine Hua Shan souvenir, buy some famed Hua Shan glossy ganoderma – a rare traditional Chinese medicine ingredient which reputedly has anti-tumor properties and is good for the circulatory system. They go for RMB 30 to 300, or pick up a hand-made leather silhouette puppet for RMB 50 to 100.

The best souvenirs are the ones you take with your camera. Don't start chiseling away at the granite and leaving your names behind as souvenirs – you'll be back for another climb and the peaks will still be there, waiting.

A leather cutting of Zhong Kui, the Chinese Ghost Buster.

Other Information

POST OFFICES

Hua Shan Post Office 华山邮政支局

✉ Zhongduan, Yuquan Lu, Huayin City 华阴市玉泉路中段

☎ 436 2001

HOSPITALS

Rongkang Hospital 荣康医院

✉ Kangfu Lu, Hua Shan; inside Hua Shan Scenic Spot 华山康复路，华山景区内

☎ 436 3975

Xiehe Hospital 协和医院

✉ located in Hua Shan Scenic Spot 华山景区内

☎ 435 2815

COMPLAINT HOTLINES

☎ General: 436 2661, 436 2691, 436 2692

TOURISM INFORMATION WEBSITE

@ www.huashan-china.com

Xining, China's Wild West

Area Code 0971

Situated on the edge of the Qinghai-Tibet Plateau and heavily populated by minority groups, **Xining** has earned a reputation as one of the more mysterious and diverse cities in China.

Situated on the edge of an inhospitable wilderness, Xining was a historic military garrison town. Those venturing beyond Xining into the frozen Qinghai-Tibet Plateau or the scorching deserts of Xinjiang were virtually guaranteed to never be seen or heard from again. This harsh remoteness made Xining and the surrounding areas perfectly suitable to serve as China's Siberia. The result is a diverse, open, slightly adventurous local population of Han Chinese as well as a large minority of Muslims and Tibetans.

First impressions upon arrival in Xining will likely be of the stark valley landscape and colorful people. The 30-minute trip from the airport into town takes visitors through a handful of small Muslim villages and one begins to realize that this is a part of China that has remained untouched by the mighty hand of commercial tourism. The village

Butter lamps light up the Kumbum Monastery in Xining.

homes are made of mud-bricks and wood, and horse drawn carts carrying people or goods are more prevalent than cars. As you get closer to the city you begin to see more urban development and soon enough, you've entered Xining. At first glance it appears to be a fairly typical developing Chinese city but scratch the surface, and you'll discover a thriving center of cultural diversity not found anywhere else in China.

Located on Dongguan Da Jie, near the center of the city, lies the **Great Mosque** (*qīngzhēn dà sì* 清真大寺), the largest mosque in Xining and one of the largest in China. There are many mosques in Xining but this is by far the largest and most impressive. Make it a point to visit on Friday, the Muslim holy day, around 1pm to get an idea of just how large and active the local Muslim population is. Generally, the locals will be glad to show male visitors around, just dress and act respectfully.

Just a few blocks west on Nan Da Jie you'll find the city's only practicing Buddhist monastery. While it pales in comparison to nearby Kumbum Monastery, it does give a taste of the Tibetan Buddhist religion and is worth a visit if you have the time. The monks are friendly and will do their best to introduce you to the place.

A pilgrim gives the prayer wheels a spin.

Another temple worth a visit is the Taoist **North Mountain Temple** (*běishān sì* 北山寺) located on Changjiang Lu. There are some interesting caves, pavilions and pagodas, but hiking in the surrounding hills is what makes the trip really worthwhile. There are great views of the city just a short walk up the hills from the temple.

▶▶ The Tibetan Antelope

Prized for their fine wool, the Tibetan antelope population was ravaged in the 20th century by overhunting and poaching. The Chinese government is urgently trying to stop the poaching – and numbers are slowly rising.

Pantholops hodgsoni is found only on the Qinghai-Tibet Plateau, "the roof of the world." These graceful animals are 4 feet (1.2 m) tall and the males have 20-inch (50 cm) horns giving them a similar appearance to a gazelle. The antelope grazes 14,760 feet (4,500 m) above sea level and sports a coat that has evolved to deal with the extreme cold.

However, their coat is also their curse. The fiber is a fifth of the thickness of human hair and was named "shahtoosh," or "king of wools" by Persians, and "ring shawls" made from the wool have been popular for over a century.

Shahtoosh's popularity led to the wholesale slaughter of the antelope and numbers dropped from around a million at the turn of the century to less than 75,000 in the mid-1990's when environmental activists lobbied governments to enforce an international trade ban on the material. Unfortunately, the animals are still poached and skinned in Tibetan areas and then smuggled into the politically unstable Kashmir region for manufacture. Until governments are able to cooperate and jointly tackle the issue of poaching and smuggling, the best that can be done is preventing international shipments.

Scientists have been working on breeding other animals with similarly fine wool and recent reports suggest the genes of a goat from Ngari Prefecture in Tibet may be the antelope's salvation.

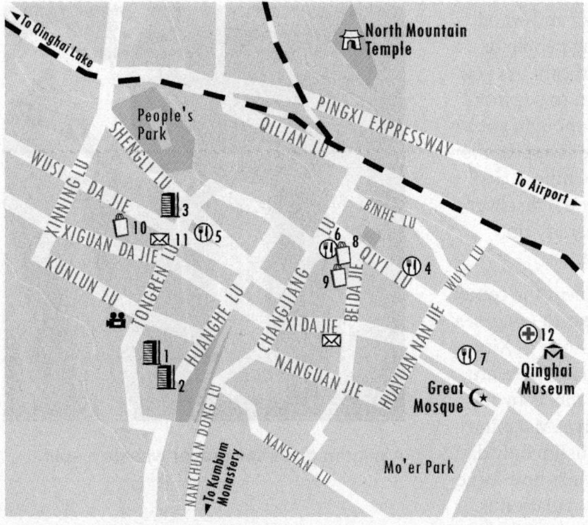

Heading west from Xining, the road immediately begins climbing as you ascend the Qinghai-Tibet Plateau. The road to the lake winds its way through stark and tranquil valley scenery while surrounded by terraced fields of rapeseed and wheat. About an hour and a half from Xining is the **Sun Moon Pass** (*rì yuè shān* 日月山). It offers splendid views of the grasslands and is a great spot to snap a few pictures. Continuing from there, the scenery is of classic plateau grasslands and the lake soon appears as a watery, albeit salty, blue oasis. A couple hours and possibly a stop for lunch at the Tibetan tents later you arrive at **Bird Island** (*niǎo dǎo* 鸟岛).

While the scenery and cultural experience around the lake are worth the trip alone, most visitors come to see the main attraction, Bird Island. From March through June every year, this island becomes a breeding ground for tens of thousands of rare migrating birds. The trip costs RMB 120 and usually includes stops at all the sites of interest along the way. Entrance to the park is RMB 35. Usually the tour is booked as a day trip, but you also can arrange overnight accommodation through a travel agent.

The Qinghai Lake trip generally includes a stop at Xining's other gem, **Kumbum Monastery** (*tǎ'ěr sì* 塔尔寺). Located just 19 miles (30 km) from Xining, this monastery is one of the most important Yellow Hat sect monasteries in the world. Construction of

QINGHAI LAKE & KUMBUM MONASTERY

Every region in China has at least one or two don't miss destinations, and **Qinghai Lake** (*qīnghǎi hú* 青海湖) and Kumbum Monastery fit the bill for Xining. While not actually in the city, both can be reached conveniently with local transportation or the help of a travel agent and can both be seen in one long day trip.

Qinghai Lake, the largest saltwater lake in China, is truly a spectacular sight. At an elevation of approximately 11,800 feet (3,600 m), it's surrounded by seemingly endless rolling grasslands that make up the Qinghai-Tibet Plateau. Ethnic Tibetan nomads living in tents can be seen scattered about in the summer when they come down from higher elevations to graze their yaks on the lush green grass surrounding the lake. If you're looking for an authentic Tibetan experience, this is a great place to find it.

Quotes

"I never in my wildest dreams imagined I'd find a place as culturally diverse as Xining in China."

"One day I had breakfast with my Han tour group leader, sipped yak butter tea in the afternoon with Tibetan monks and ate roast lamb in the evening in a Muslim tent."

"I came to see the sites but ended up falling in love with the people."

The intricate and beautiful yak butter sculptures of the Kumbum Monastery.

this building began in 1577 at the birthplace of Tsong Khapa, founder of the Yellow Hat sect of Tibetan Buddhism. The monastery offers an authentic glimpse of the Tibetan Buddhist religious tradition, a mere 45 minutes from Xining. It presently houses several thousand monks and hosts a number of important religious festivals each year. Don't miss the assorted yak butter sculptures in the **Hall of Butter Sculpture** (*sūyóuhuā yuàn* 酥油花院), a Tibetan art specialty. The monks are quite friendly and regularly invite tourists in for a cup of yak butter tea or a bowl of tsamba (*zānbā* 糌粑) crushed roasted barley. Taking a hike up the valley towards the back of the monastery reveals magnificent views of the temples and surrounding scenery. The small shops outside the monastery are a great place to pick up Tibetan jewelry and other trinkets but be aware that bargaining is a must. Entrance to the monastery is RMB 35 and English speaking guides are available for a little extra. ■

Making Your Trip Easy

Practical Tips

Summers are pleasant but the winters are very cold and dry. The best time to visit is spring and summer as the weather is comfortable and scenery at its most impressive.

There's not much of an English speaking population so communication can be a bit of a problem. It's advisable to bring a Chinese phrasebook to help you communicate.

You might need a day or two to get acclimatized to the lower levels of oxygen due to Qinghai's high elevation. It's not as serious as going to Tibet, but take it easy for the first few days. The climate here can be rough, with a strong sun, gusty winds, dry air and dramatic changes in temperature – be prepared.

Memorable Experiences

Eating lamb kebabs, flat bread, and drinking salt tea late at night on the streets of Xining in Muslim food tents.

Drinking yak butter tea and chatting with monks at Kumbum Monastery.

Sipping tea while enjoying the sunset view.

Be sensitive of local customs while in Qinghai. The ethnic Tibetans have their own etiquette; some of their rules include not eating dog, horse or donkey meat. It's considered polite to accept a toast from a Tibetan, but if you don't drink, then it's best to decline politely. If you're offered a *Hada* (哈达), a long white silk scarf, it's considered good form to place it around your neck using two hands. Local Muslims don't eat pork, horse or dog meat; they don't smoke or drink either.

Transportation

Airport – The airport is about 19 miles (30 km) east of the city. It takes about 40 minutes to get to the airport by taxi.

Taxi – Compact taxis are RMB 6 at flag-fall while full-sized taxis are RMB 7. Full-sized taxis are slightly more expensive than their compact brethren.

The Best of Xining

Great Mosque 清真大寺 *qīngzhēn dàsì*
- ✉ 31 Dongguan Da Jie 东关大街 31 号
- ☎ 817 0489
- 🕒 8:00am to noon, 2pm to 6pm
- ¥ 10

Young boys are often excellent horse riders in Xining.

Qinghai Lake 青海湖 *qīnghǎi hú*
- ✉ Niannaisuoma Village, Gangcha County, Haibei Tibetan Autonomous Prefecture 海北藏族自治州刚察县年乃索玛村
- ☎ 0970 – 865 5058
- 🕒 8:30am to 5:00pm
- ¥ 58

Kumbum Monastery 塔尔寺 *tǎ'ěr sì*
- ✉ 25km from Xining, Lusha'er Town, Huangzhong County 湟中县鲁沙尔镇，距西宁 25 公里
- ☎ 223 2357
- 🕒 8:30am to 5:30pm
- ¥ 80

Hotels

Qinghai Hotel
青海宾馆 *qīnghǎi bīnguǎn* ★★★★
- ✉ 158 Huanghe Lu, north of the Children's Park 黄河路 158 号，儿童公园北侧❶
- ☎ 614 4888
- ¥ 465 – double room, peak-season
  282 – double room, off-season

Qinghai Victory Hotel
胜利宾馆 *shènglì bīnguǎn* ★★★★
- ✉ 160 Huanghe Lu, north of the Children's Park 黄河路 160 号，儿童公园北侧❷
- ☎ 614 4365
- ¥ 465 – double room, peak-season
  282 – double room, off-season

Qinghai Beifu Hotel
北浮宾馆 *běifú bīnguǎn* ★★★
- ✉ 40 Wusi Da Jie 五四大街 40 号❸
- ☎ 615 5666
- ¥ 220 – double room, peak-season
  145 – double room, off-season
- 🌐 www.bei-fu.com

Qinghai Huade Hotel
华德宾馆 *huádé bīnguǎn* ★★★
- ✉ 97 Qilian Lu 祁连路 97 号
- ☎ 812 1898
- ¥ 268 – double room, peak-season
  140 – double room, off-season

Eight Buddhist stupas stand in a row at Kumbum Monastery.

Zhongfayuan Hotel 中发源饭店
zhōngfāyuán fàndiàn ★★★
✉ 1 Shulin Xiang 树林巷 1 号
☎ 817 1888
¥ 332 – double room, peak-season
200 – double room, off-season
@ www.zfy-hotel.com

Food & Restaurants

Xining is an exceptionally diverse city with a population comprised of several different minority groups, so it's natural that you'll find a similar level of diversity in your dining experience. You'll find all of the great culinary traditions of China represented here, but the local flavor reflects a marked Muslim influence with a wide selection of noodles, mutton dishes and various flatbreads.

Try *mian pian* (面片) while in Xining – these square flat noodles are delicious. Noodles in a beef broth (*niúròu miàn* 牛肉面) are great on a cold day. Xining boasts many excellent lamb dishes, but perhaps the most famous are *shouzhua yangrou* (手抓羊肉), a boiled mutton that you eat with your hands and *huangmen yangrou* (黄焖羊肉), a spicy mutton fried with potatoes and vegetables. For a good snack try the mutton kebabs (*kǎo yángròu* 烤羊肉); stalls selling these can be found everywhere. Don't forget to try the local yogurt (*suān nǎi* 酸奶), its got bite.

RESTAURANTS

Laochufang Sifangcai 老厨房私房菜
Dishes up Muslim cuisine.
✉ inside Xining Hotel, Qiyi Lu 七一路西宁宾馆院内
☎ 545 4184, 845 4785

Mazhong Shifu 马忠食府
✉ 22 Nandajie 南大街 22 号

Qinghai Restaurant 青海饭店
✉ 334 Qiyi Lu, Chengzhong District 城中区七一路 934 号❹
☎ 845 8179

Qingsongling Restaurant 青松岭酒店
✉ 11 Shengli Lu 胜利路 11 号❺
☎ 611 5999

Shalihai Meishicheng 沙力海美食城
✉ 491 Qiyi Lu 七一路 491 号
☎ 821 5426

Wangzai Xiang Caiguan 旺仔湘菜馆
Spicy Hunan cuisine for those who like it hot.
✉ 59 Xiguan Da Jie 西关大街 59 号
☎ 612 5032

Some monks catch a lift on the back of a truck while a young boy uses a more traditional method to get around.

Xiaoyuanmen Restaurant 小园门
🖂 186 Dongguan Dajie 东关大街 186 号❻
☎ 812 5529

Yinlong Dajiudian 银龙大酒店
🖂 38 Huanghe Lu 黄河路 38 号❼
☎ 616 6666

Souvenirs

Xining isn't generally considered a major shopping center but this can be a benefit as the prices tend to be a bit lower and the experience more enjoyable. There are definitely treasures to be had in the form of Tibetan jewelry, knives and swords, antiques, clothes and other trinkets and religious paraphernalia. The best place to shop for Tibetan goods is the Tibetan market across from the main bus station on Jianguo Lu and the small shops outside the Kumbum Monastery.

Another specialty unique to Xining and Qinghai Province are handmade Tibetan and Muslim carpets. There are a number of places to browse and buy carpets, but the widest selection can be found at the No. 2 Factory located on Bayi Lu. While it may seem inconvenient to transport a rug all the way back home, most shops are willing to assist with the shipping process. It's also a lot cheaper to buy a carpet directly from the factory rather than back at home.

For more guaranteed quality but sometimes significantly higher prices, you can find most local handicrafts in hotel gift shops. Some other places to check out are the Textile Products Building (*fǎngzhīpǐn dàlóu* 纺织品大楼❿) on Xiguan Da Jie, the Qinghai Traveling Products Company (*qīnghǎi lǚyóu chǎnpǐn gōngyìng gōngsī* 青海旅游产品供应公司❽) and the Qinghai Antique Shop (*qīnghǎishěng wénwù shāngdiàn* 青海省文物商店❾) across from the Xining Hotel.

Qinghai also offers a good selection of hard to find ingredients for traditional Chinese medicine such as the *dongchong xiacao* (冬虫夏草), which is thought to be good for respiratory ailments and *xuelian* (雪莲), which is particularly helpful for women.

Other Information

POST OFFICES

Wusi Da Jie Post Office 五四大街邮局
🖂 78 Wusi Dajie 五四大街 78 号⓫
☎ 614 6106

HOSPITALS

Qinghai People's First Hospital
青海省第一人民医院
🖂 2 Gonghe Lu 共和路 2 号⓬
☎ 806 6200

COMPLAINT HOTLINES

☎ General:610 0110
☎ Taxi:631 6110

A beautiful mural of a flying apsaras at the Mogao Caves.

Dunhuang's Buddhist Oasis

Area Code 0937

Heritage: Mogao Caves

Set on the edge of the Gobi Desert, **Dunhuang** may seem like an unlikely place to find an oasis of Buddhist art. With towering sand dunes in the background, the caves here reflect the power of divine inspiration.

One summer day in 1900, Wang Yuanlu, an unassuming Taoist priest who lived nearby, stumbled into a cave that had been covered by a rockslide. His accidental discovery would lead to one of the most significant collection of Buddhist artifacts ever uncovered.

Inside the cave were artifacts dating from the 4th to 14th century, a complete collection spanning approximately a thousand years tracing the development of Buddhism from its initial arrival in China. A cornucopia of treatises on subjects ranging from history to politics to the military and science, Buddhist sutras and even personal documents such as tax receipts were discovered preserved within a dry dark cave. In fact, so much material has been found that the discovery has led to a new branch of academic study called Dunhuang Studies.

Unfortunately most of the documents are now in museums and collections scattered across the world; the invaluable *Diamond Sutra*, for example, the earliest printed book, is now held in the British Library. While the documents may have been dispersed, the caves still hold a treasure trove of statues and wall paintings.

Today Dunhuang is a relaxed town in Gansu Province with the **Mogao Caves** (*mògāo kū* 莫高窟), where the famed carvings are located, 15.5 miles (25 km) to the southeast. Once an important oasis town on the Silk Road, Dunhuang lies close to the border of Qinghai, Tibet and Xinjiang. In 111 BC, under the Han dynasty, the Great Wall was extended here.

Mogao Caves.

From the present-day city it's hard to picture the importance of ancient Dunhuang. Its strategic position meant that it was an important transit point for the spreading of Buddhism, which entered China during the 3rd century AD. As Buddhism developed, so did the city. During the 4th century, Dunhuang was the last stop for Chinese Buddhist pilgrims on the road to India and the first stop for arriving missionaries.

In AD 366, Le Zun, a Chinese monk on his way to India, had a divine vision of Buddha, which led him to believe he was on holy ground. In his fervor, he began carving out the first caves in the mile-long (1.6 km) sandstone cliff face. Development continued through 10 dynasties and reached a peak during the Sui and Tang dynasties. Though the Sui dynasty lasted a short 38 years, Emperor Wendi was a fervent Buddhist and during his reign 101 caves were carved, over twice as many as in the previous 180 years.

It was during the Tang dynasty, China's golden age of economic prosperity and openness, when the caves were the most active. A community of monks, craftsmen and artists lived at the caves, getting their water from the mountain fed Daquan River that flows in front of the cliff. The highly international dynasty saw the introduction of Greek, Hindu and Central and Western Asian cultural influences. Of the over 1,000 Tang era caves, 232 have survived, about half the remaining 492 surviving caves. Most importantly, the Tang dynasty caves are considered the most artistically developed.

Of the 492 caves, 60 are open to visitors, though others maybe opened for a high fee. About 484,000 square feet (45,000 m²) of wall paintings and over 2,400 Buddhist sculptures have been preserved in this dry desert climate. The paintings themselves are a priceless resource documenting the changes in lifestyle, religion and culture over a thousand-year period. In 1987 the caves were added to the UNESCO list of World Heritage Sites.

Reflecting the convergence of influences in this area, the architecture in the caves is a mixture of Chinese, Central Asian and Indian styles, which is more apparent in the earlier pre-Tang caves. After the Tang

Quotes

"The caves are amazing. The Buddhas definitely add a divine aura to the place. It's hard to imagine people actually lived here and created all these."

"Definitely try the sand surfing; it sounded more fun than getting buried up to my neck."

dynasty there wasn't any space left to carve new caves, forcing artisans to re-work older caves. Some stylistic differences to look for are: the older statues tend to be stiffer and appear stronger with the lines are much more defined. Tang sculptures tend to be fluid, with flowing lines – this is especially clear when looking at the robes of the statues. Whereas earlier statues have severe and dour faces, Tang statues are lively and expressive.

Cave 328 is an example of the melding of two different styles. The sculptures in this cave date to the Tang dynasty, but the ceiling and wall paintings are from the Song dynasty. Inside are three statues of Sakyamuni flanked by two disciples. The artisans who worked on the sculptures, to emphasize that Sakyamuni wasn't Chinese, painted a "typical" Central Asian face on the statue. Take a close look at his mustache. To the right of the somber Sakyamuni is a proud

▶▶ The Silk Road

Silk was first cultivated in China around 2600 BC, but it would take two and a half millennia for it to spread west. The Romans first encountered the material while battling the Parthians in 53 BC and were told it came from a mysterious tribe in the east. Roman agents were dispatched, commodities bartered and the "Silk Road" established.

The Chinese had known about trade routes going west across the Taklamakan Desert for centuries. However, these routes only became important when Emperor Wudi of the Han dynasty formed alliances with western tribes against the northern nomads, China's old enemy.

In 138 BC, Zhang Qian, a court official, was sent west to negotiate with the Yuezhi tribe. Unfortunately, he was captured and imprisoned for over ten years by the northern nomads. When he eventually escaped, he discovered the Yuezhi had resettled in northern India and had adopted a nonviolent way of life. Zhang Qian compensated for his diplomatic failure by returning with invaluable information about the areas to the west of the empire and the intrigued emperor launched more exploratory missions.

Trade quickly grew from these diplomatic missions and the Silk Road was established. It would eventually become a vast conduit for exchanging goods and information, stretching between three continents and thousands of kilometers from Chang'an (the Han dynasty capital) to Dunhuang, through Turpan, Kashgar and into modern Afghanistan, Iran and Syria with further branches connecting to the Roman Empire and the Black Sea. Most caravans only traveled a fraction of the route; goods passed through a chain of middlemen from China through Central Asia to Europe.

However, more important than the exchanging of goods was the exchanging of ideas. Buddhism came to China from India over the Karakorum Pass and was spread by Silk Road merchants. The Eastern Han emperor showed signs of interest in this new faith, but it was during the Northern Wei dynasty when the government adopted it as the state religion. Many of the local ethnic groups living along the Silk Road adopted Buddhism and the particularly devout carved grand monuments along the route.

It was during the Tang dynasty when the Silk Road reached its apex; the monk Xuan Zang made his epic journey to India in search of Buddhist scriptures; Chang'an, the cosmopolitan capital, had over 5,000 foreign traders and each year tons of silk and spices passed through the city gates. However, when the Tang dynasty fell, so did trade. The Silk Road finally passed out of use in the 10th century with the discovery of faster and more convenient sea routes.

The 19th century saw a revived interest in the ancient Silk Road and it was at this time when the name was first coined. Treasure hunters and archeologists stormed the Silk Road, taking with them whatever treasures they could carry. These relics now fill museums across the world while countless treasures still lie buried in the sand, maintaining the mystique and romance of the Silk Road.

Surrounded by Mingsha Shan, the tiny Crescent Moon Lake shines like a diamond in the sand.

looking Ah Nan, one of Sakyamuni's favorites. Standing to Sakyamuni's left is a skinny Jia Ye, his face showing the lines of a hard life. **Caves 98** and **100** are also clear examples of two different styles in a single cave.

For architecture aficionados, **Cave 96** is a highlight. This is one of the largest caves and has a 113-foot-tall (34.5 m) tall Tang dynasty statue of Maitreya, the Buddha of the Future. There's also a pagoda outside that's the same height as the cliff. Only the core of the Buddha is rock – the rock in this area is extremely soft and unsuitable for carving. The craftsman and artisans had to use a terracotta-like plaster pasted over the rock, from which they would mould and carve the intricate details. Smaller statues used a wooden skeleton that was then covered in wheat husks, reeds, hemp and mud before being smeared with plaster. Once carved, painters would paint them with lively colors bringing them to life. Not many of the Tang dynasty sculptures that were made this way have survived, making the remaining ones highly valuable and a focus of preservation efforts.

The wall paintings are definitely the big draw at the caves. If the paintings were lined up end to end they would measure 15.5 miles (25 km). The paintings are so important as a historic record that scholars have dubbed them a "mounted library." Some paintings are Buddhist scriptures and sutras, while others illustrate the different ethnicities that passed through Dunhuang. Social hierarchies, traditions, clothing, even music and dancing have been the subject of ancient painters. The different traditions and how they've evolved have been clearly recorded, from important life events such as marriages to mundane activities like farming and business transactions. **Caves 47**, **112** and **220** have better examples of these paintings.

The area surrounding the caves also makes for an interesting diversion. Climbing to the top of the cliff offers a majestic view of the surrounding desert, mountain and oasis. West of the caves and south of Dunhuang is **Mingsha Shan** (*míngshā shān* 鸣沙山), which means "singing sand mountain," though it's not really a mountain, but a giant sand dune. If you're looking for some excitement after the solemn caves, this is the place to be. The Buddhist pilgrims of old never had it this good. Sand-surfing, camel rides and therapeutic sand baths (imagine being buried up to your neck) are available activities. In the same area is the shallow spring fed **Crescent Moon Lake** (*yuèyá quán* 月牙泉), which forms an oasis at the desert's edge. A peculiar natural phenomenon occurs when standing on top of the sand dune. If it's a windless day, a sound similar to a flute can be heard, but if there are many people descending the dune at once it becomes a thunderclap. The corresponding legend goes that a horrific sandstorm buried an army that rested at this oasis and the sounds heard are those of the buried men trying to claw their way to freedom. It's best to go there in the late afternoon when it's a lot cooler.

The Han dynasty **Jade Gate Pass** (*yùmén guān* 玉门关) is 61 miles (98 km) northwest

Memorable Experiences

Going for a bumpy camel ride around the Crescent Moon Lake and Mingsha Shan.

Quietly going from cave to cave and seeing the exquisite artistry that the devout pilgrims of the past instilled into the barren site.

of Dunhuang. Here was the ancient equivalent of the last gas station before a long stretch of road, the Silk Road to India that is. There's a preserved section of the **Silk Road** (*sīchóu gǔdào* 丝绸古道) here.

Further north of Dunhuang, in the Gobi Desert, is a section of the Han dynasty Great Wall that originally stretched for 93 miles (150 km). In one of the beacon towers, which were used as signaling stations, Han dynasty writings on bamboo, thought to be letters, official documents and the ancient equivalent of wanted posters were found amongst the ashes.

Mirages can also be seen on extremely hot days when out in the desert. Just be sure not to be lured away by them – the admission price may be quite costly. ■

A camel caravan makes its dusty way through Mingsha Shan.

Making Your Trip Easy

Practical Tips

The best time to visit Dunhuang is from April to October. In the summer the sun is very strong so sunscreen is essential. In winter it's very cold so bring plenty of warm clothes.

Many traditional customs continue to thrive in Dunhuang. Usually in early-May the Dragon Boast Festival (*duānwǔ jié* 端午节) is held. During this time, glutinous rice wrapped with lotus leaves (*zòngzi* 粽子) is eaten in honor of an upright official who committed suicide after his kingdom fell. On the 8th day of the 12th lunar month *laba zhou* (腊八粥), rice porridge with nuts and dried fruits, is eaten.

Transportation

Airport – The airport is about 8 miles (13 km) east of the city. It's a 20-minute taxi from the city.

Bicycle – Bicycles can be rented for RMB 1 per hour from the Fengwei Restaurant (风味餐馆, ☎ 883 3039) on the north side of Dunhuang's Labor Union Building (市总工会北侧). They can also be rented from the Dunhuang Liaolidian (敦煌料理店, ☎ 388 8162) on the south side of the Labor Union Building (市总工会南侧).

Taxi – Dunhuang is a relatively small city so taxi fare should be about RMB 5 to anywhere within the city limits.

The Best of Dunhuang

Mingsha Shan, Crescent Moon Lake
鸣沙山月牙泉 *míngshā shān yuèyá quán*

- 3 miles (5 km) south of Dunhuang 敦煌市区南 5 公里处
- 888 2074 ext 8001
- 24 hours
- 80

Mogao Caves 莫高窟 *mògāo kū*

- 15.5 miles (25 km) southeast of Dunhuang 敦煌市区东南 25 公里处
- 886 9060
- 8am to 6pm
- 100

Yangguan Pass 阳关 *yángguān*

- 43 miles (70 km) west of Dunhuang 敦煌市区西 70 公里处
- 882 4914
- 8am to 9pm
- 40

Hotels

Dunhuang Hotel
敦煌宾馆 *dūnhuáng bīnguǎn* ★★★★

- 14 Yangguan Dong Lu 阳关东路 14 号
- 885 9128
- 280 – double room

Taiyang Dajiudian
太阳大酒店 *tàiyáng dàjiǔdiàn* ★★★★

- 5 Shazhou Bei Lu 沙洲北路 5 号
- 882 9998, 882 2168
- 688 – double room, peak-season
  280 – double room, off-season
- www.dhsuntravel.com

Dunhuang Shanzhuang
敦煌山庄 *dūnhuáng shānzhuāng* ★★★

- west of Dunyue Lu 敦月路西侧

The Jade Gate Pass has stood guard over the desolate desert since the Han dynasty.

☎ 888 2088, 888 2086
¥ 688 – double room, peak-season
480 – double room, off-season
@ www.the-silk-road.com

Food & Restaurants

Like most cuisines in west China, the food here is spicy. Locals like to serve guests a special wheat noodle called *saozi mian* (敦煌臊子面) – it's very tasty. *Dunhuang huangmian* (敦煌黄面) is another delectable noodle dish; the thin long noodles are added to a broth then topped with vegetables. The Dunhuang Hotel offers *pao'er yougao* (泡儿油糕) a delicious cake snack. Dunhuang banquets (*dūnhuáng yàn* 敦煌宴) offer great food and rousing entertainment.

The weather here is also good for growing fruit; plump grapes, plums and juicy melons abound.

RESTAURANTS

Daji Lürou Huangmian Guan
达记驴肉黄面馆
Specializes in *lürou Huangmian* (驴肉黄面), thin noodles with donkey meat.
✉ West Entrance of the Market, Dunhuang 农贸市场西口
🕒 10am to 10pm

Dunhuang Hotel's Chinese Restaurant
敦煌宾馆中餐厅
One of the classiest restaurants in the city; specializes in Dunhuang banquets that go from RMB 400 to RMB1,000.
✉ 14 Yangguan Zhong Lu 阳关中路 14 号
☎ 885 9128
🕒 8am to 10pm

Dunhuang Yeshi Mingyou Xiaochi Guangchang 敦煌夜市名优小吃广场
Specializes in snacks from around China.
✉ east of the city center
市中心东侧敦煌沙洲夜市
☎ 884 0151
🕒 8am to midnight, during summer
10am to 10pm, during winter

Dunhuang Shanzhuang Canting
敦煌山庄餐厅
House specials include *silu feng* (丝路风), *pipa duxing* (琵琶独行) and *yinyang xianbao* (阴阳献宝).
✉ Dunyue Lu 敦月公路西侧
☎ 888 2088
🕒 8am to 10pm

Making some noodles, the beginning of a delicious meal.

Dunhuang Taiyang Da Jiudian's Restaurant 敦煌太阳大酒店餐厅
Specializes in *jinqian xianggao yangrou* (金钱香羔羊肉), a mutton dish and *xiang huangjin zunyu* (香黄金鳟鱼), a kind of fish.
✉ 5 Shazhou Bei Lu 沙洲北路 5 号
☎ 882 9998
🕒 8am to 10 pm

Feitian Canting 飞天宾馆餐厅
Specializes in baked baby pork (*kǎo rǔzhū* 烤乳猪), goat's tail with honeydew (*mìzhī yángwěi* 蜜汁羊尾) and camel's paw (*xuěshān tuózhǎng* 雪山驼掌).
✉ 22 Mingshan Lu 鸣山路 22 号
☎ 882 2726
🕒 8am to 10pm

Feitian Dumpling Restaurant 飞天饺子馆
A restaurant set in a traditional venue, offers 20 kinds of dumplings.
✉ inside the Nongmao Market 农贸市场内
🕒 8am to 10pm

Shazhou Canting 沙洲大酒店餐厅
Upscale dining with a variety of dishes, can arrange Chinese and Western cocktail parties and receptions.
✉ 13 Yangguan Zhong Lu 阳关中路 13 号
☎ 882 5031
🕒 8am to 10pm

BARS

Baimeigui Yezonghui 白玫瑰夜总会

✉ 16 Mingsha Lu 鸣沙路 16 号

☎ 885 2998

Yangguang Yezonghui 阳光夜总会

✉ 1/BF, Dunhuang Dajiudian, 16 Yangguan Zhonglu 阳关中路敦煌大酒店地下 1 层

☎ 883 4211

Souvenirs

The best souvenirs in Dunhuang are the replicas of murals (*fǎngzhēn dūnhuáng nízhìhuà* 仿真敦煌泥质画), paintings and calligraphy (*dūnhuáng shūhuà* 敦煌书画) found at the caves. Prices range from a few hundred to a few thousand RMB. Dunhuang rugs (*dūnhuáng dìtǎn* 敦煌地毯) are colorful and durable, and they make great gifts. Replica statues made from clay (*dūnhuáng táoyì* 敦煌陶艺) cost RMB 30 to 800. For something truly unique, try a stuffed cloth camel (*dūnhuáng bùluòtuo* 敦煌布骆驼), they're RMB 20 to 100.

Other Information

POST OFFICES

Dunhuang City Post Office 敦煌市邮政局

✉ 1 Yangguan Zhong Lu 阳关中路 1 号

☎ 882 4084

HOSPITALS

Dunhuang City Hospital 敦煌市医院

✉ 20 Yangguan Dong Lu 阳关东路 20 号

☎ 885 9168

COMPLAINT HOTLINES

☎ General: 882 1303

☎ Taxi: 882 1303

Entertainment

"Summer of Dunhuang"

"敦煌之夏"敦煌乐舞表演

Dancing and singing performance.

✉ Entertainment Palace south of the Dunhuang Hotel 敦煌宾馆南楼乐舞宫

☎ 885 9269

🕒 8pm and 9:10pm

¥ 160

FINDING YOUR WAY 问路		
Can you tell me where I am?	néng gàosu wǒ wǒ zàinǎr ma	能告诉我我在哪儿吗?
How do I get to…?	qù … zěnme zǒu	去…怎么走?
Excuse me, is this the right direction to…?	láojià, qù … zhège fāngxiàng duì ma	劳驾，去…这个方向对吗?
I'm lost.	wǒ mílù le	我迷路了。
Where's the…?	… zài nǎr	…在哪儿?
airport	jīchǎng	机场
art gallery	měishùguǎn	美术馆
bank	yínháng	银行
bus stop	gōnggòng qìchē zhàn	公共汽车站
church	jiàotáng	教堂
embassy	dàshǐguǎn	大使馆
hotel	bīnguǎn	宾馆
market	shìchǎng	市场
museum	bówùguǎn	博物馆
post office	yóujú	邮局
public toilet	gōnggòng cèsuǒ	公共厕所
subway station	dìtiě zhàn	地铁站

Turpan's Grape Oasis

Area Code 0995

Turpan is famous for its bountiful harvest of grapes.

An ancient Silk Road trading post, the **Turpan** oasis is surrounded by desert and mountains, ruined cities and Buddhist caves.

It's often said that when hanging clothes out during the summer in Turpan, it'll have dried before you're finished. Enjoying numerous consecutive days over 104°F (40°C), the dry heat of Turpan's summer days infuses the city with a languid torpor relegating daytime activities to consist mainly of drinking tea and sleeping.

Such is oasis life. With mountains to the north and west, and arid desert to the south, Turpan lies in the Turpan Depression, 505 feet (154 m) below sea level at its lowest point, and is surrounded by the Gobi Desert. It was an important center of commerce and culture on the Silk Road and served as a key staging post on the north silk route. The momentous wash of religious influences over the past 2,000 years – Shamanist, Buddhist and Islam – have given the people a sense of tolerance and hospitality that contrasts vibrantly with its harsh desert surroundings. With a population of about 70% Uyghur and the remaining 30% comprised of other ethnicities, Turpan maintains the Silk Road's romantic identity as a cultural crossroads.

The lush scenery of Xinjiang.

City life centers around the bazaar with its numerous food stalls and goods for sale, and the **public square**, which deserted in the daytime, becomes a riot of colors, scents and sounds by night. Though the heat of day can make even the hardiest of travelers nearly comatose, many of Turpan's streets are covered with grape trellises providing welcome shade. Turpan has long been famous for its grapes and was once renowned throughout all of Asia for its wine. Now, most local families have a hand in the grape industry, either in the growing or selling them as they are or as raisins.

Because the Uyghurs are Muslims, there are many interesting mosques around Turpan. The most active is the **City Mosque** (*qīngzhēn si* 清真寺), located 1.9 miles (3 km) out of town on the city's western outskirts. As goes for visiting mosques anywhere, shorts are considered disrespectful and women should cover up. Also, it's a place of worship so loud or disruptive behavior is not appreciated.

Aesthetically more impressive is the 131-foot-tall (40 m) tall, 18th century **Emin Minaret** (*émǐn tǎ* 额敏塔). Built in an understated Islamic style in 1778 by local ruler Emin Hoja, its sun-dried brown bricks are layered in different patterns all the way to its rounded top. There is an adjacent temple, used for services on Fridays and Saturdays, built around an open, shaded space. Only 1.2 miles (2 km) southeast of the city, it's reachable by foot or by bike.

Another interesting option for exploring Turpan and the immediate surrounding countryside is to hire a donkey cart for a morning or evening tour. Leaving the city, dusty roads soon give way to traditional mud-brick homes, irrigation canals winding through poplar trees that sway in the desert breeze and hordes of smiling children playing in the streets.

TURPAN DESERT TOUR

Most of Turpan's most dramatic and impressive sights dot the desert surrounding the city. Over its 2,000-year history, the focus of commercial and cultural activity has shifted several times, often following the shifting courses of the melting snows of the Tian Shan. These sites are best taken in by hiring a minibus. They often wait outside the hotels and tourist café, offering their services. While the ride itself is cheap, usually around RMB 40 per person for the day, most of the sites have their own prices for admission.

To avoid the midday heat, most tours start out at the crack of dawn. The first stop is usually the **Gaochang Ruins** (*gāochāng gùchéng* 高昌故城), 29.5 miles (46 km) east of Turpan. Dating back to the 7th century during the Tang dynasty, Gaochang, once the capital of a local ruler, hold remnants of the Uyghur's pre-Islamic past. A large Buddhist

Quotes

"Turpan is everything I dreamed off; the romance of the old Silk Road and the vibrancies of a culture kept alive to this day."

"That an oasis could be this rich and this tranquil when surrounded by the inhospitable desert is true homage to the spirit of man."

monastery stands above the southwestern corner of the walled city. Most people walk or hire donkey carts to ride around the crumbling mud-brick structures where the whispering desert wind evokes a sense of endless time.

Located nearby are the **Astana Graves** (*āsītǎnà gǔmùqún* 阿斯塔那古墓群) where Gaochang ancestors are buried. The history of the graves are somewhat shrouded in mystery – archeologists have discovered many of those buried here are Han Chinese and Uyghur. Three of these tombs are open to tourists and are approached through narrow staircases descending to cool, damp burial chambers nearly 20 feet (6m) below ground. Paintings on the walls, many depicting birds, indicate the belief in an afterlife. The paintings were meant to honor the dead and reflect hopes for their repose. One tomb contains two well-preserved corpses; a third was relocated to Turpan's museum. Artifacts dating back to the Jin dynasty, from the 3rd to 5th centuries AD, were uncovered here, including sashes containing important records and documents.

Leaving the graves, the ride takes in the **Flaming Mountains** (*huǒyàn shān* 火焰山), a great photo opportunity. Made famous by the ancient Chinese classic novel *Journey to the West* (*xīyóu jì* 西游记), the surfaces of these desiccated mountains have been whipped into the shape of flames by howling desert winds. Under the relentless heat of the midday sun, the mountains radiate heat and with a dash of imagination, may appear to be on fire.

The next major stop is the **Bezeklik Thousand Buddha Caves** (*bózīkèlǐkè qiānfó dòng* 柏孜克里克千佛洞). Though they pale in comparison to the cave art of Dunhuang, it's still possible to sense the importance of Buddhism to Silk Road travelers, many of whom stopped here to pray for a successful journey. Most of the relics here were carted off by German explorer Albert Von Le Qoc and subsequently destroyed in the Allied bombing of Berlin. Dug into a mountainside beneath sweeping sand dunes and overlooking a roaring stream, the location is beautiful and haunting. Even if you don't go into the actual caves, the site is well worth seeing.

To escape the noon sun's onslaught, all tours stop for lunch at the **Grape Valley** (*pútáo gōu* 葡萄沟). Though it's a bit of a tourist trap, the beautifully trellised valley provides a needed respite from the heat. Dug into the Gobi Desert with the Flaming Mountains on either side, the valley is a lush stripe of green in the barren desert surroundings. At the valley's core is a flume of fast moving icy cold water traveling from the Tian Shan to Turpan City. The food in the valley is good and it's also a good chance to shop for souvenirs and dried fruits. Those with excessive energy can climb the Flaming Mountains for great views of the valley, the Tian Shan and the Gobi.

One of the most interesting stops on the tour is a **Karez Irrigation Site** (*kǎnr jǐng* 坎儿井). It's the site the locals are most proud of, and rightfully so – the irrigation method is probably their greatest contribution to desert dwellers and has been employed as far

A traditional Xinjiang dance.

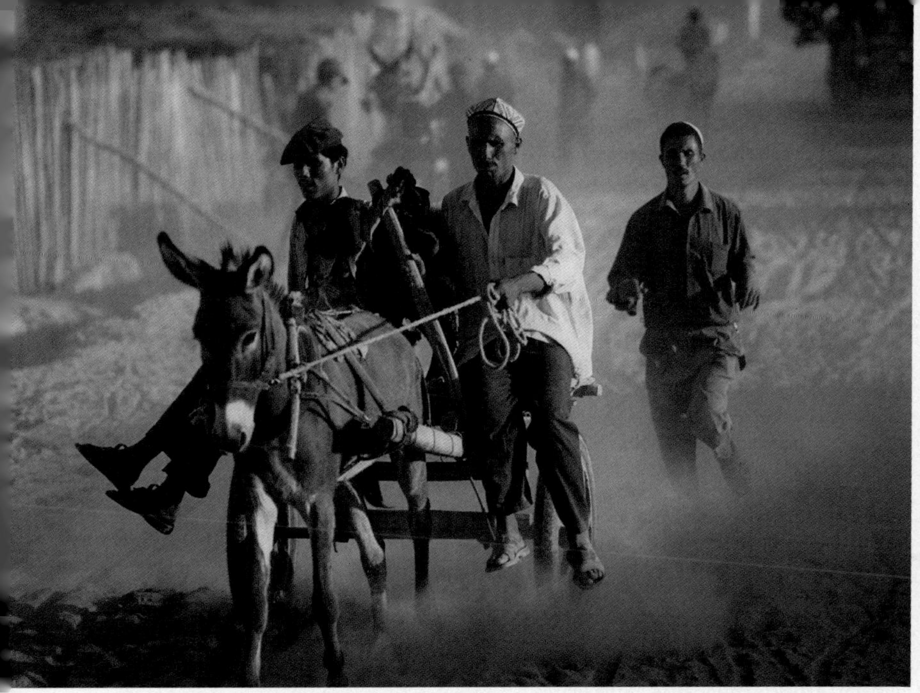

Turpan locals going for a spin on their donkey cart.

away as Afghanistan and Iran. More than 2,000 years ago, it was developed as a way to bring the snowmelt waters of the Tian Shan to the city through a series of wells dug into underground water channels. By transporting the water underground, they were able to prevent evaporation and to keep dust and dirt out of their water supply. The Karez Irrigation Site is like a museum explaining how the wells are built and maintained and even includes a sample channel and well that you can explore.

As the sun descends and the tour nears its end, the last stop is the **Jiaohe Ruins** (*jiāohé gǔchéng* 交河古城). Built during the Han dynasty as a Chinese garrison town to defend the borderlands, it's less romantic but better preserved than Gaochang. Although the town was razed by Genghis Khan and his Mongol army, many structures maintain some semblance of their original form. Roads lead clearly through the town and a monastery with statues of the Buddha still stands. The town was built on an island at the confluence of two rivers. As the tours usually stop here in the late afternoon, the sunlight turns the stone almost golden and shutterbugs can have a field day.

If your driver's done a good job, tips are always appreciated though never expected. The minibus will usually drop you off back at your hotel where, covered in dirt and dust, you'll almost certainly make a long shower becomes the order of the day. ■

Making Your Trip Easy

Practical Tips

Though summer is blisteringly hot with temperatures going up to 118°F (48°C), it's also the peak travel time and when the town moves into full swing to cater to tourists. Though spring may be cooler, there are often sandstorms that are much harder to deal with than the heat. Fall is probably the ideal time to be here though the winter can come on fast, bringing with it the biting cold of the desert. Every August 25 there's the annual Silk Road Turpan Grape Festival at the

Memorable Experiences

Walking through the Gaochang Ruins in the morning as the sun comes out from the clouds.

Hiking on the Flaming Mountains followed by swimming in the cool, fast stream at the Grape Valley.

Eating kebabs in the night market while Uyghur music and dance videos blare from the vendors.

Turpan Travel and Culture Square.

Chinese isn't widely spoken here limiting the usefulness of your Chinese phrasebook. Learning a few phrases of Uyghur isn't only convenient but also does wonders to break the ice.

Though grapevines and fruit trees are ever-present, the fruit isn't free. Don't pick fruit from the trellises – they're the life-blood of the farmers who grow them, if that isn't enough to stop you, the large fines that are given for illegally picking fruit will.

Transportation

Airport – The nearest airport is in Urumqi. From downtown Urumqi there are frequent buses to Turpan which is 112 miles (180 km) away; buses will make the trip in about 4 hours. Alternatively, at the airport you can hire a taxi for about RMB 100 for the 2-hour ride to Turpan.

Bus – This is the most convenient way to reach Turpan. There's regular service from Urumqi as well as daily service from Hami, Korla, and other points in the Xinjiang.

Taxi – Flag-fall is RMB 5 in the city and RMB 10 in the outskirts. Going from the city to the Grape Valley will cost from RMB 15 to 20. From Turpan's train station into town will be about RMB 20.

Train – The nearest train station is located in Daheyan, some 35 miles (56 km) north of Turpan and has trains servicing destinations in Xinjiang and Gansu. Minibuses leave Turpan for Daheyan every 30 minutes from 7am to 6pm. A taxi will cost about RMB 70. Train tickets for Daheyan can be bought in Turpan.

The Best of Turpan

Grape Valley 葡萄沟 *pútáo gōu*
✉ Turpan 吐鲁番
☎ 853 5615
🕒 24 hours in summer
closed in winter
¥ 60

Jiaohe Ruins 交河古城 *jiāohé gǔchéng*
✉ Ya'er Town 亚尔乡
☎ 866 7028
🕒 9am to 6pm
¥ 40

Sugong Mosque 苏公塔 *sūgōng tǎ*
✉ Muna'er Village, Ya'er Town
亚尔乡木纳尔村
☎ 856 7047
🕒 9am to 6pm
¥ 30

Hotels

Grand Turpan Hotel
吐鲁番大饭店 *tǔlǔfān dàfàndiàn* ★★★
✉ 20 Gaochang Lu 高昌路 20 号
☎ 855 3918
¥ 280 – double room, peak-season
140 – double room, off-season
@ www.hoitakhotel.com

Oasis Hotel Turpan 吐鲁番丝路绿洲宾馆
tǔlǔfān sīlù lǜzhōu bīnguǎn ★★★
✉ 41 Qingnian Lu 青年路 41 号
☎ 852 2491
¥ 360 – double room, peak-season
180 – double room, off-season

Shanshan Jintian Hotel 鄯善金田大酒店
shànshàn jīntián dàjiǔdiàn ★★★
✉ Jiefang Nan Lu, Train Station, Shanshan County 鄯善县火车站解放南路
☎ 831 2998
¥ 198 – double room

Turpan Hotel
吐鲁番宾馆 *tǔlǔfān bīnguǎn* ★★★
✉ 2 Qingnian Lu 青年路 2 号
☎ 852 2025, 852 2301
¥ 380 – double room, peak-season

The once thriving Han dynasty city of Jiaohe is today nothing more than windswept ancient ruins.

280 – double room, off-season

Turpan Post Hongyuan Hotel
吐鲁番邮政鸿远酒店 *tǔlǔfān yóuzhèng hóngyuǎn jiǔdiàn* ★★★
✉ Gaochang Lu 高昌路
☎ 857 8199
¥ 160 – double room, peak-season
100 – double room, off-season

Food & Restaurants

Wheat is the staple grain and mutton the most common meat in Xinjiang. Noodles (*lā miàn* 拉面), served in soup or stir fried, are plentiful. Cold noodles are a welcome treat in the summer. The night market on Gaochang Lu near Wenhua Lu is full of vendors selling everything from kebabs of meat and liver to whole roast sheep. Xinjiang's specialty pilau rice, cooked with carrots and chunks of meat is widely available. Restaurants generally offer *dapan ji* (大盘鸡), chopped chicken simmered with potatoes, onions and bell peppers. Try *shouzhua fan* (手抓饭), a rice and mutton dish eaten with your hands. This comes in two types: one which is a little sweet with eggs, radishes, currants, dried apricots and peanuts; the other variety contains beef or mutton and onions.

On Laocheng Lu, near the bus station, is a bazaar that specializes in baked pockets of pastry stuffed with spiced mutton that serves as a hearty breakfast or lunch. One real treat here is the homemade ice cream shaved from a block of ice mixed with yogurt and sweetened with rice wine. It's also a great place to sample Turpan's famous raisins and other dried fruits or nuts.

RESTAURANTS

A Taichi Restaurant 阿太赤餐厅
Specializes in local cuisine.
✉ Minmao Dasha, Laocheng Lu 老城路民贸大厦
☎ 852 9775
🕒 24 hours

Grape Mountain Villa 葡萄山庄
Specializes in local dishes.
✉ Grape Valley 葡萄沟
☎ 855 9361
🕒 24 hours

Huozhou Hotel 火洲大酒店
House specialty is Inner Mongolian lamb.
✉ Gaochang Lu 高昌路
☎ 856 2000
🕒 24 hours

Oasis Hotel Turpan 丝路绿洲宾馆

Specializes in both Chinese and Western food.

✉ 41 Qingnian Lu 青年路 41 号
☎ 855 3227
🕒 24 hours

Souvenirs

Though Turpan still maintains its traditional bazaar, it pales in comparison to the ones in Kashgar. Once known for its hand-woven, naturally dyed carpets, these are no longer easy to find here. More commonly available are brightly decorated locally produced knives and traditional hats worn by Uyghur men and women. Locally produced boots and clothing are also available as are synthetic fabrics commonly made into clothing by Turpan's residents. The most distinctive locally produced goods are the sweet green raisins, in great abundance here, and other dried goods like walnuts, almonds, dates and figs.

The bazaar on Laocheng Lu is a great place to shop for souvenirs or just while away a few hours. If you have trouble finding it, just say "bazaar" to any local and they'll point you in the right direction. The night market on the corner of Gaochang and Wenhua Lu has an assorted selection of knick-knacks. Another market of note is the Turpan Dabazha Market (*tǔlǔfān dàbāzhā shìchǎng* 吐鲁番大巴扎市场) which is at Laocheng Lu. If you're looking for department store shopping, then go check out the Turpan Department Store (*tǔlǔfān bǎihuò dàlóu* 吐鲁番百货大楼) over at Gaochang Lu.

Other Information

POST OFFICES

Turpan Post Office 吐鲁番邮政大楼
✉ Gaochang Lu 高昌路
☎ 857 8066

HOSPITALS

Turpan City People's Hospital
吐鲁番市人民医院
✉ Gaochang Lu 高昌路
☎ 852 2461

Turpan Regional Hospital
吐鲁番地区医院
✉ 23 Lüzhou Zhong Lu 绿洲中路 23 号
☎ 856 4689

COMPLAINT HOTLINES

☎ General: 852 3216
☎ Taxi: 856 1977

TOURISM INFORMATION WEBSITE

@ www.turpantours.com

BUYING TICKETS 买票					
Where's the ticket counter?		shòupiàochù zài nǎr		售票处在哪儿?	
Are there any tickets to….		yǒu dào … de piào ma		有到…的票吗?	
I want to book a ticket to….		dìng yīzhāng qù … de piào		订一张去…的票。	
I want to book a return ticket to….		dìng yīzhāng qù … de wǎngfǎn piào		订一张去…的往返票。	
I want a… seat.		wǒ xiǎng mǎi …		我想买… 。	
	first class		tóuděngcāng		头等舱
	business class		shāngwùcāng		商务舱
	economy		jīngjìcāng		经济舱
I want a… ticket.		wǒ xiǎng mǎi …		我想买… 。	
	hard-seat		yìngzuò		硬座
	hard-sleeper		yìngwò		硬卧
	soft-seat		ruǎnzuò		软座
	soft-sleeper		ruǎnwò		软卧
How much is it?		duōshǎo qián		多少钱?	
I'd like to upgrade my ticket.		wǒ yào bǔpiào		我要补票。	

Kashgar's Desert Gem

Area Code 0998

Stepping into **Kashgar** is like being transported into one of the thousand and one nights of The Arabian Tales.

This far-flung city in the **Xinjiang Uyghur Autonomous Region** is a must-see for its beautiful scenery and intoxicating culture. Miraculously, modern China peels away to reveal the arresting sights, sounds, fragrance and atmosphere of a 2,000-year-old Middle Eastern town. Open air markets hum with squawking livestock and the buzz of locals. Every so often, old mosques peep out from a labyrinth of well-worn, humble homes and rouse the neighborhood with calls to prayer.

Perched on the western rim of the world's largest inland basin, the Tarim Basin, and nestled beside the desolate **Taklamakan Desert**, which ominously means: "those going in never return," Kashgar is an oasis carved of sand and stone.

Located in a little cul-de-sac, framed by desert dunes, and rolling mountains, Kashgar was once a last stop outfitting station and trading post for travelers and merchants plying the ancient Silk Road that linked China, India, Pakistan and the great Roman Empire. Today, trade continues to weave its timeless magic.

Colorfully dressed locals cooling off with some frozen treats.

In the ancient enclave called the **Old Town** (*gǔchéng* 古城), sinuous dirt paths barely two-mules wide are lined with age-old shops. Generous legs of lamb, succulent mutton strips, leather, pots of all shapes and sizes or caps for every occasion hang from rickety wooden beams – the same as it's been for centuries. Newer shops announce their service on signboards in three languages: Uyghur, Chinese and English for the adventurous foreigner.

This mesmerizing Muslim city tucked away in China's westernmost frontier brims with color and contrasts. Fridays and Saturdays may be quiet prayer days but when Sunday comes around, watch the city thrive with life. The entire community and visitors by the thousands throng Kashgar's famed Sunday Market.

Kashgar is miles from nowhere, but the items that turn up at its markets are varied. At the weekly **Animal Bazaar**, fowl and various four-legged animals are scrutinized, prodded and traded. One or two donkeys may even be taken for a test drive.

Observe the traders closely for their bargaining is an ancient art form; the sellers and buyers indicate their asking price and counter-price by scripting it into each other's palms all the while shaking each other's hand.

The people of the region give Kashgar its unique vitality and charm. Over a dozen of China's ethnic groups live in Xinjiang and the majority can be found in Kashgar, several belong to nomadic tribes from nearby mountain villages. Uyghurs, mostly Sunni Muslims, form the largest ethnic group. Be prepared for a melting pot of Central Asian faces that mingle harmoniously in street corners and in the maze of roadside stalls and teahouses.

An extremely relaxed bunch, the locals spend the sizzling summers lounging in

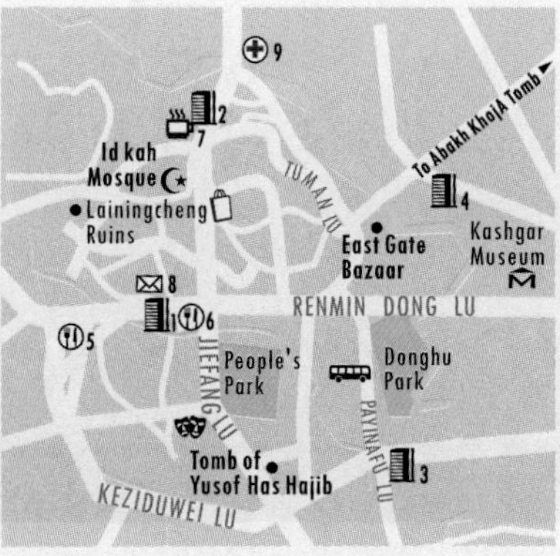

ubiquitous snack shops. They chat, smoke and sip salty milk tea. Attire is comfortable and diverse. The older men sport Abraham Lincoln beards and doppi (skullcaps), which are fur lined in winter. The younger men wear neat shirts, with sleeves rolled to the elbows and long pants. Women's fashion is more varied, a few are in head-to-toe burkhas and some sport headscarves; many are in rainbow-hued dresses and long skirts. Sandals are very popular in summer and children can be seen pattering about barefoot.

BIKING IN KASHGAR

Getting around Kashgar is a piece of cake – simply rent a bicycle from any bicycle shop dotting the streets.

A quick ride from new to old district shows that urban planning is rather haphazard. Traditional homes are dwarfed by convenience stores and new blockish apartment buildings. Only sections of the outer walls of the old town, some 500 years old, remain standing. Most parts have been demolished to make way for new living quarters.

The visual treats are mostly in the Uyghur **Old Town**, north of the town center. The main square is a good starting point for

Quotes

"In Kashgar, I am transported back in time. Goodbye modern world. Hello time warp!"

"It's rugged, heady; sometimes too hot, sometimes too cold. It's breathtaking."

"Bring lots of film because you will want to photograph everything."

The Muslim faithful flock to their mosque answering the call to prayer.

touring the city. It has a large clock tower that most definitely won't reflect the time on your watch. Far away from the capital, people in Kashgar follow their own time zone. Kashgar's time is set back 2 hours from Beijing's, so don't be overly surprised to find out you've just entered town in time for breakfast rather than lunch. The square is almost always a hub of activity. By day, fruit vendors, cobblers, and bike repairmen occupy the square. Barbershops are everywhere. Heads are given a thorough shave or a robust massage, though few beards seem to go under the razor. At night, the same square is transformed to a shoppers' atrium. A different product is up for sale each night. The flavor of the night could be electronic goods, footwear or an array of fascinating bric-a-brac piled sky-high.

At every corner, whiffs of cumin and pepper, the aroma of grilled kebabs and baking bread will entice you to stop for a bite. Resistance is futile. Hop off your bike and sample the flavor of the street. Move out of the main thoroughfare and explore the backstreets and you'll find yourself in a rabbit-warren of earthen-walled houses. Occasionally, toothy old folks can be found chatting in Uyghur by the wayside. You may also become a magnet for the neighborhood kids. They're very friendly and will be happy to show you the rest of the street or pose for a picture.

DIVINE TOMBS

Id Kah Mosque (*àitígă'ěr qīngzhēn sì* 艾提尕尔清真寺) is in the center of the city and is China's largest mosque. Built in 1442 by Kashgar's ruler Shakessimirzha in what was then the outskirts of the town, the beautiful yellow-tiled mosque has undergone much restoration. The central dome is flanked by minarets more commonly seen in the Middle East. Its exquisite Islamic architecture sets it apart from Chinese-style mosques and its grandness has grown with its increasing stature. Today it's the key place of worship for China's Muslims and each year, tens of thousands of worshippers enter its gates for Friday prayers alone. During Ramadan, worshippers number around 100,000. From a tower above the delicately carved entrance gate, the imam calls Muslims to prayers. A pond in the tree-lined courtyard languidly beckons worshippers to cleanse themselves before entering the main hall. Steps lead up to an enshrined throne, which is cast majestically into the central wall. Remember to be appropriately attired – women will have to don headscarves – and remove your

Memorable Experiences

Chilling out with ice-blended doh – a refreshing concoction of shaved ice, rich vanilla ice cream and thick syrup served in a big soup bowl.

An impromptu bike tour with youths Mohamed Yassin and Ali John, who enthusiastically translated Kashgar's mysterious charms into English. @ uyghurguide80@yahoo.com

Learning more about the old town's history from retiree Arenhan, who used to work as a Uyghur-Chinese translator.

shoes when entering the mosque. To avoid the crowd, visit early in the morning.

Nearby, along Tiyu Lu, is the **Tomb of Yusof Has Hajib** (*yùsùfǔ hāsī hājífǔ língmù* 玉素甫・哈斯・哈吉甫陵墓), a revered Muslim philosopher whose teachings are widely practiced by the Uyghur community. The tomb has a blue tiled dome, framed by blue topped minarets and the tiles on the walls are decorated with blue flower patterns.

Pushing on a little further, you will arrive at another religious site some 3 miles (5 km) northeast of the city center. The **Abakh Khoja Tomb** (*ābā huòjiā mù* 阿巴霍加墓) is the family tomb of Abakh Khoja, a powerful 17th century Kashgar ruler. Built in 1640, this tomb holds five generations of his family. The tomb is an architectural masterpiece and one of Xinjiang's holiest places. During the **Korban Festival**, Muslim pilgrims from all over Xinjiang visit this tomb. The first generation buried here was the family of Yusof Khoja, a revered Islamic missionary and upon his death, his eldest son Abakh Khoja continued his work. When Abakh Kohja passed away in 1693, his reputation had far exceeded his father's and the tomb was renamed after him. On the outset, you'll see a pretty gate tower decorated with colorful paintings and beautiful brick carvings. Not far is a lovely pond framed by swaying trees, lending the place a feeling of tranquility.

The tomb complex is comprised of several magnificent buildings, with the **Tombs Hall** as the central structure. It's easily identified from the outside by its huge dome, which is covered in green-glazed tiles and measures some 56 feet (17 m) across. The dome and its four minarets seem like a mini replica of the India's Taj Mahal.

Inside the 85-foot-high (26 m), 128-foot-long (39 m) Tombs Hall are several tombs, each covered by a different colored cloth. Built with glazed bricks, the tombs are decorated with beautiful flower patterns set against a white background. The larger-sized tombs house the males, while the females occupy smaller-sized tombs.

To the west of Tombs Hall is the Great Hall of Prayer – a spacious enclosure framed by wooden balustrades. The walls are adorned by handiwork of ancient craftsmen. The other major building is the **Doctrine-Hall of Teaching** (*jiǎngjīng táng* 讲经堂).

Another important tomb is the **Xiangfei Mu** (*xiāngfēi mù* 香妃墓), which belongs to Abakh Khoja's granddaughter, Iparhan. Legend goes that Iparhan, known as Xiangfei in Chinese, was taken to the capital to be the imperial consort of the Qing emperor

Fruits and nuts abound in Kashgar's markets.

The tomb of Xiangfei, one of the most revered concubines of the emperor.

Qianlong, who fell desperately in love with her. She spent 28 years in the Forbidden City and never saw her family again. There's a tomb belonging to her in the Eastern Qing Mausoleum, where the rest of Emperor Qianlong's concubines are buried, but the final resting place of her mortal remains continues to be a point of contention.

OVERNIGHT TRIP TO KARAKUL LAKE

Hire a four wheeler in the early morning and hit the **Karakoram Highway** (*zhōngbā gōnglù* 中巴公路) before the heat gets to you. You'll be on the road for 4 to 5 hours, give and take the several stops for compulsory picture taking. Hiking around the lake's rugged terrain takes about 5 hours during which you'll see a Kyrgyz village and graveyard cast against a backdrop of snow-capped mountains. You get to sleep in tents called yurts at an altitude of 11,800 feet (3,600 m). It's beautiful, but gets quite chilly at night. ■

Making Your Trip Easy

Practical Tips

Be generous with sunscreen during the summer when temperatures can soar above 104°F (40 °C). Alternately, dress sensibly in the winter when temperatures can drop to -13°F (-25 °C). All of China is tuned to Beijing time, but for practical purposes, operating hours in Kashgar are about 2 hours behind the shown time. For example, stores will open at 11am instead of 9am and dinner will be eaten at 8pm rather than 6pm.

Some important festivals in Kashgar are the Korban Festival (*gǔ'ěrbāng jié* 古尔邦节) and the Rozi Festival (*ròuzī jié* 肉孜节). The Korban Festival, also known as the *zaisheng jie* (宰牲节), is one of the liveliest times to be in Kashgar. Preparations for this festival take place days beforehand with families cleaning their homes and preparing a feast. The men, wearing their best clothes, head to the Id Kah Mosque for a prayer ceremony then return home to prepare a slaughtered lamb or calf. Later, the men return to the mosque and perform the religious Sa Ma Dance(*sàmǎ wǔ* 萨玛舞). The festivities last for three days with thousands of people filling the squares in an ocean of celebration.

Ramadan (*zhāiyuè* 斋月) is Islam's most important religious observance; this is when Muslims believe the Holy Quran was given to Muhammad from Allah. It's a time of contemplation and reflection. During the month long observance, Muslims are forbidden to eat or drink during the daylight hours, only breaking their fast at night. During the evenings they also visit friends and family and attend special prayers at their mosque.

The beginning of the Islamic month, Shawwal, marks the end of Ramadan and the beginning of a three-day celebration called Eid al-Fitr (*kāizhāi jié* 开斋节). The ending of the fast is a time of great festivities marked by feasting and giving of gifts.

If you're lucky, you might catch daring acrobats doing tightrope walks called *dawaz* (*dáwǎzī* 达瓦孜). The performers do more than walk across the rope; they also perform different death defying stunts high above the ground without any safety nets. Goat fighting is another popular pastime in the villages. Two goats head butt each other in a show of strength.

Transportation

Airport – The Kashgar International Airport is about 9 miles (15 km) east of the city. It's about 20 minutes from the airport to the city center by taxi and 30 minutes by bus. The airport shuttle bus costs RMB 3.

Taxi – Taxis are readily available. RMB 5 per trip will be enough to get you anywhere within the city.

The Best of Kashgar

Abakh Khoja Tomb
阿巴霍加墓 *ābā huòjiā mù*
✉ Aizi Laiti Lu 艾孜来提路
☎ 265 0630
🕒 10am to 7pm
¥ 40

Id Kah Mosque
艾提尕尔清真寺 *àitígǎ'ěr qīngzhēn sì*
✉ center of Kashgar City 位于市中心
☎ 282 7113
🕒 9am to 5pm
¥ 30

The Stone City 石头城 *shítóu chéng*
✉ Tashiku'ergan County 塔什库尔干县
🕒 11am to 8pm
¥ 30

Hotels

Qinbag Hotel
其尼瓦克宾馆 *qíníwǎkè bīnguǎn* ★★★
✉ 144 Seman Lu 色满路 144 号❷
☎ 298 0617
¥ 300 – per person, peak-season
¥ 200 – per person, off-season

Wenzhou Dasha
温州大厦 *wēnzhōu dàshà* ★★★
✉ 17 Renmin Xi Lu 人民西路 17 号❶
☎ 280 8889
¥ 220 – per person, peak-season
180 – per person, off-season

Xinlong Da Jiudian
新隆大酒店 *xīnlóng dàjiǔdiàn* ★★★

Naan bread is the local staple and can be found everywhere.

✉ Binhe Lu 滨河路❸
☎ 261 7998, 261 7688
¥ 200 – per person, peak-season
168 – per person, off-season

Kashgar Hotel
喀什噶尔宾馆 *kāshígá'ěr bīnguǎn* ★★
✉ 57 Tawuguzi Lu 塔吾古孜路 57 号❹
☎ 265 4954, 265 2363
¥ 180 – per person, peak-season

100 – per person, off-season

Seman Hotel 色满宾馆 *sèmǎn bīnguǎn* ★★
✉ 337 Seman Lu 色满路 337 号
☎ 258 2150, 258 2129
¥ 160 – per person, peak-season
120 – per person, off-season

Food & Restaurants

Tuck into delicious meat pies called daman or gosh girde (*kǎo bāozī* 烤包子) in Uyghur. It's a Kashgar specialty and is great for breakfast. Pilau, rice with lamb and yellow peppers (*yángròu zhuāfàn* 羊肉抓饭) and shashlik kebabs (*ròu chuànr* 肉串儿) are perfect for lunch. Hot-from-the-oven Uyghur naan flatbreads (kǎo náng 烤馕), which has over 50 varieties, sprinkled with sesame seed are made for tea. Finish off the day with laghman (*lā tiáozi* 拉条子) – wheat noodles in a thick spicy soup of chopped mutton, peppers and tomatoes for dinner.

That's just the menu for the first day. There are endless bagels, baked envelopes of meat called samsas and suoman (square noodles) to sample. The locals rely on mutton for protein and wheat as their staple. Strong Turkish influences are apparent in the ingredients and cooking methods. Check out the food stalls near the Id Kah Mosque just off Jiefang Bei Lu.

Kashgar is also a city of mouthwatering fruits. Countless varieties of nuts are found at the street stalls. Melons, apricots, peaches, figs, cherries, raisins and grapes are sold everywhere.

RESTAURANTS

Baijin Restaurant 白金快餐
Serves up yummy local cuisine.
✉ 50 Jiefang Nan Lu 解放南路 50 号❻
☎ 282 8888
🕒 10am to 10pm

Caravan Café 凯瑞咖啡
A European café managed with sandwiches, cakes and pizza.
✉ 30m from Qinbag Hotel
其尼瓦克宾馆大门旁 30 米处❼
🕒 10am to 10:30pm

Chayuan 茶园
One of the best restaurants in Kashgar for local food.
✉ 244 Renmin Xi Lu 人民西路 244 号❺
☎ 284 2002, 2824 4671
🕒 8am to midnight

Souvenirs

You can't miss the Yekshenba Bazaar, also known as the Sunday Bazaar (*xīngqīrì shìchǎng* 星期日市场), at Aizilaiti Lu. It's the mother of all bazaars. Farmers from out of town will congregate by their donkey carts just to hawk their wares at the famed Sunday bazaar. The visual spectacle of people, animals and items of every imaginable shape, size and function will send your cameras into overdrive.

If you miss the Sunday bazaar, the daily bazaars are still the focus of much activity. Centuries before, caravans would roll into Kashgar with Chinese silk, exquisite porcelain and exotic spices. Farmers and herdsmen continue this age-old tradition, selling anything from leather ware, Turkish teapots to and beautifully woven carpets. Some stalls sell a little of everything. Others offer specialty goods. Kashgar is famous for its hats and knives; handmade hats can cost up to RMB 8 to RMB 300.

Located in the eastern suburb of Kashgar, the East Gate Bazaar (*dōngmén dàbāzhā* 东门大巴扎) is another souvenir hunter's paradise. Look for handmade doppa hats (*wéiwú'ěr huāmào* 维吾尔花帽) and exquisitely made Yengsar knives (*yīngjíshā xiǎodāo* 英吉沙小刀).

If you have energy left, head for the animal market. Rows and rows of cattle, mules, camels and exotic songbirds are looking for new owners. You might want to try your luck at bargaining for a horse; then you could ride back to your hotel in style.

Other Information

HOSPITALS

Kashgar People's Hospital
喀什地区人民医院
✉ 66 Jichang Lu 机场路 66 号❾
☎ 296 2911

POST OFFICES

Kashgar Post Office 喀什地区邮政局
✉ 40 Renmin Xi Lu 人民西路 40 号❽
☎ 282 7336

COMPLAINT HOTLINES

☎ General: 282 2173
☎ Taxi: 296 4817

EAST CHINA

The Oriental Pearl TV Tower and the Jin Mao Tower dominate Pudong's skyline.

Shanghai, China's Star

Area Code 021

When **Shanghai** was first founded, it was far from obvious that the world would one day hear its roar. Since its humble beginnings, though, Shanghai has seen dramatic changes, spinning along the edge of Fortune's wheel.

The financial capital of China, Shanghai, which means "go to the sea" in Chinese, is a city of 16 million that remembers its turbulent history. Divided in half by the Huangpu River into Puxi (west of the Huangpu) and Pudong (east of the Huangpu), Shanghai's story is one of millions made and mirages lost. Pried open by British guns in the First Opium War, this once sleepy fishing and weaving village gained notoriety as the "Paris of the East" – a colonial city of commerce, vice, money and political intrigue. More recently, Shanghai has benefited from China's economic reforms, rapidly rising as the shining "Pearl of the Orient."

Dynamic is the best word to describe today's Shanghai. Since the 1990 opening of the Pudong Special Economic Zone (SEZ), the city has found itself with building cranes whose numbers rival those of North America. Towers of glass and steel sprout up amidst ivy covered colonial villas and old Chinese homes. Displaying all the contrasts of modern China, teeming neighborhoods and birch trees are woven together by elevated highways and modern skyscrapers. Worldly travelers brush elbows with migrant workers; students and artists mingle as they pursue their dreams of wealth.

A BRIEF HISTORY

Earliest settlement in the region dates back to 5900 BC. Shanghai became a key cotton exporter under the Song dynasty. The silting of the Wusong River shifted the regional capital to Shanghai in the 13th century. Growing richer, the town needed to defend itself against marauding Japanese pirates. A 3.7-mile-long (6 km) wall with six gates and 20 archers' towers was erected in 1553 during the Ming dynasty. Although meteoric development would later engulf this area, it continues to stand as the Old Chinese City. To increase trade, a customs house was erected in 1685 to sell silk and tea. The city's population swelled to 50,000, among whom were many noted Chinese scholars. One particularly important resident was Xu Guangqi (*Xú Guāngqǐ* 徐光启), friend and pupil of the Jesuit missionary and early Western explorer, Matteo Ricci. However, despite such promising international beginnings, in the end, it was by far less friendly persuasion that Shanghai was finally opened up to the West.

Before the colonial period, Chinese silk, porcelain and tea were in high demand in Britain. But China would trade them only for gold. A massive trade deficit built up and the British sought a product they could sell to the Chinese to restore the balance. Seizing on opium, produced cheaply in colonial India, Britain entered the Chinese market with narcotics. Though illegal, many Chinese couldn't resist the forbidden pleasure and the Qing dynasty soon faced a crisis as drugs began flowing in and silver flowed out.

When China finally moved to stop the importation of opium, it was too late. The result of the First Opium War was the 1842 Treaty of Nanjing, first of the many "Unequal Treaties." The treaty granted the opening of five ports: Shanghai, Ningbo, Fuzhou, Xiamen and Guangzhou.

America would ride Britain's coattails into Shanghai with the Treaty of Wangxia, giving them the same rights as the British. Unwilling to miss a good party, France joined in and secured a similar deal, giving France a large concession in the southern half of Shanghai.

As the Taiping Rebellion swept through the surrounding countryside in the 1850's, peasants fled en masse to Shanghai. Arriving

Shanghai in 1873.

by rafts on the Suzhou Creek, opportunistic businessmen seized the chance to fleece naive peasants. The wealthy purchased large tracts of land and erected tenement housing overnight. They rented these tiny rooms to displaced farmers at grossly inflated rates. Thus began the birth of urban Shanghai.

Trade, with opium at the helm, drew some of the world's largest trading vessels. Clippers and steamers began to clog the Huangpu River's sprawling port. It would be a tough market for the British to hold onto as more traders moved in, making Shanghai a truly international city.

The 1863 formation of the Municipal Council gave Britain, France and America a free hand in administering and governing Shanghai. That same year, America and Britain solidified their partnership by the formation of the International Settlement, jointly ruling with their own brand of colonial law and order. Meanwhile France continued to develop its own concession.

Legal vagaries gave Shanghai a reputation as a city of adventurers. Missionaries, mercenaries, merchants, grafters, gadflies and gangsters of all stripes flocked here. The population increased from 50,000 to a million by 1900, a mushrooming growth rate of 2,000%.

Meanwhile large foreign trading houses began to diversify their interests into textiles, insurance, real estate and shipping. Architects erected imposing buildings, along the Bund, including the green-tower-capped Cathay Hotel, the domed Hong Kong and Shanghai Bank and the clocktower crowned Customs House.

The alleys of Shanghai retain a historical feel.

The ball continued for ex-pats who made Shanghai their home. Film houses began making movies in Shanghai and actors like Charlie Chaplin arrived. Christopher Isherwood, Bernard Shaw and Andre Malraux came to relish its vibrancy for their writing. Jazz wailed and flappers danced. The streets were clogged by rickshaws pulled by men in rags and loaded with tuxedoed men and gowned debutantes. Aldous Huxley said of the city in 1926, "Life itself··· dense, rank, richly clotted··· nothing more intensely living can be imagined."

Amidst the chaos of drugs, civil strife and colonialism, the young intellectuals of China began to search for the solutions to China's rampant poverty and subservience to the West. Many looked to Marxism and the victorious Russian Revolution. Several Chinese Marxist groups met in Shanghai and founded the Chinese Communist Party (CCP) in 1921; among them was future CCP Chairman, Mao Zedong (*Máo Zédōng* 毛泽东).

Following the power vacuum that ensued after the death of revolutionary hero Sun Yat-sen (*Sūn Zhōngshān* 孙中山) in 1925, Chiang Kai-shek (*Jiǎng Jièshí* 蒋介石) stepped into the political fore with the secret backing of the Green Gang, Shanghai's powerful underground. Under the banner of the Nationalist Party, Chiang began the ambitious Northern Expedition in 1926 to quell the warlords and unite a fractured nation. For the time being, the Nationalists and the Communists cooperated under the aegis of a united front, which would spectacularly rupture in Shanghai.

As Chiang's Nationalist forces approached Shanghai in 1927, the CCP organized a general strike as a sign of support and solidarity, but once Chiang entered Shanghai, the strike was brutally crushed. Strike organizers were rounded up and executed in the streets and over 5,000 strikers and students were killed. It was the beginning of a ruthless campaign to crush the Communists, one that accelerated when Chiang captured Beijing in 1928 and

Some of the 2008 Beijing Olympic soccer qualifying matches will be held at Shanghai's new soccer stadium.

successfully completed his Northern Expedition.

Though Chiang nominally united China, Japanese imperialism was a constant threat. When Japan invaded northeast China in 1931, the Shanghainese responded by boycotting Japanese shops and goods. Five years later Japan began a general invasion of China and Imperial Japanese planes and warships bombed Shanghai while European and American ex-pats stood on the roof of their exclusive clubs watching the bombardment.

China ended the Second World War as a member of the victorious Allied powers and many flocked back to Shanghai hoping to return to the status quo of easy living and easier profits. But as quickly as one conflict ended, the civil war between the Nationalists and Communists swiftly resumed. Shanghai, once an economic bastion, was reduced to financial ruins as Chiang and his cronies mismanaged the nation's treasury and siphoned away public funds into their private accounts.

The 1949 liberation of the city by the CCP marked the beginning of a new era for Shanghai. The brothels and opium dens were shut down with the addicts receiving rehabilitation and the prostitutes job training. Child labor was banned, slums eliminated and inflation slowed.

SHANGHAI & THE FUTURE

Deng Xiaoping's sweeping economic reforms of the early 1980's sought to open China and bring wealth back into the nation. With Deng's successors continuing his policies of economic development, Shanghai continues to experience massive growth. The city has been propelled so far forward that it doesn't even have the time to look back.

While many point to Shenzhen's meteoric rise from fishing village to metropolis, Pudong's rise is just as spectacular. Facing the Bund across the Huangpu River, it was once a nearly uninhabitable marshland better known as Shanghai's vegetable

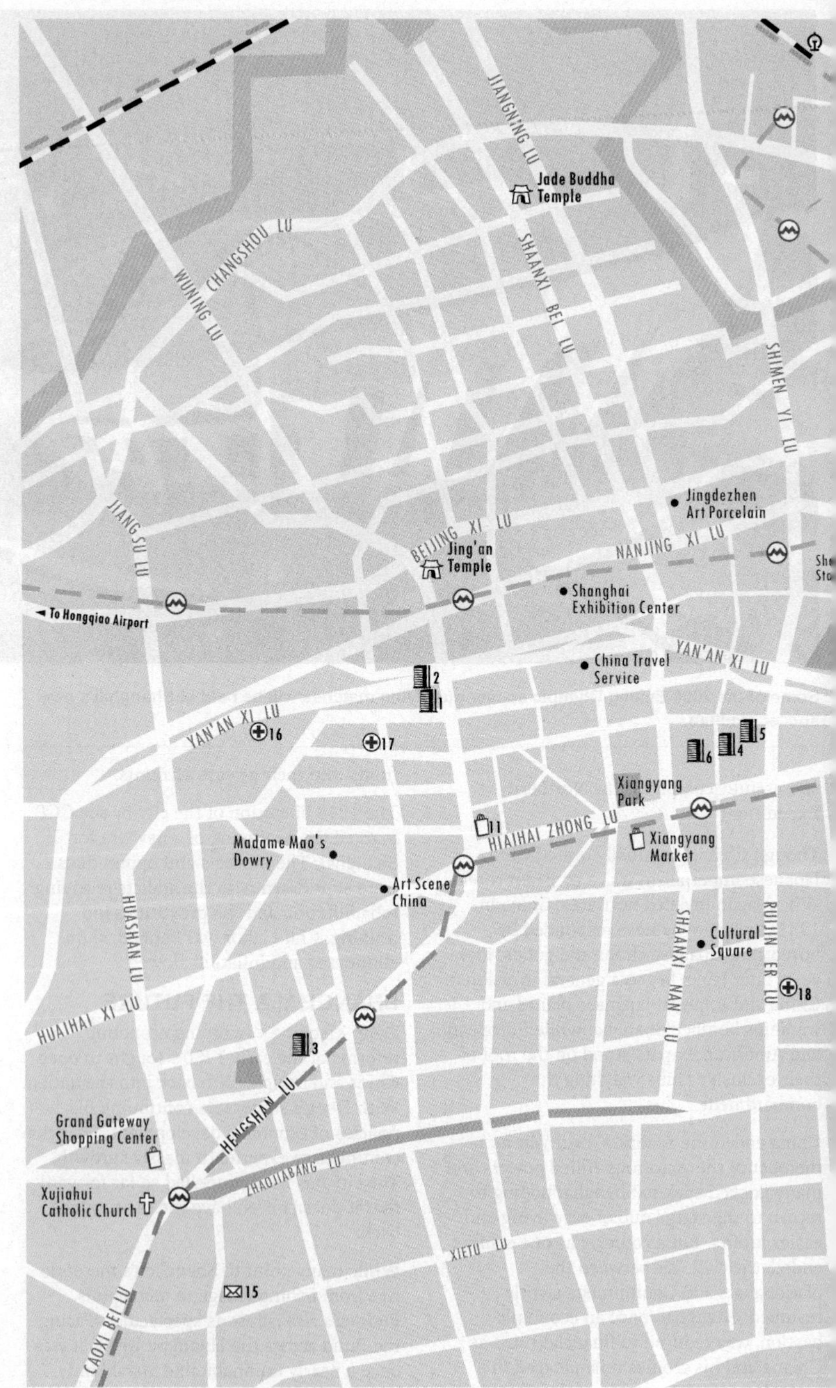

JIANGNING LU
Jade Buddha Temple
CHANGSHOU LU
WUNING LU
SHAANXI BEI LU
SHIMEN YI LU
JIANGSU LU
Jingdezhen Art Porcelain
BEIJING XI LU
Jing'an Temple
NANJING XI LU
Shanghai Exhibition Center
To Hongqiao Airport
China Travel Service
YAN'AN XI LU
2
1
YAN'AN XI LU
16
17
5
4
6
Xiangyang Park
11
HUAIHAI ZHONG LU
Xiangyang Market
Madame Mao's Dowry
Art Scene China
HUASHAN LU
SHAANXI NAN LU
Cultural Square
RUIJIN ER LU
18
HUAIHAI XI LU
3
HENGSHAN LU
Grand Gateway Shopping Center
ZHAOJIABANG LU
Xujiahui Catholic Church
XIETU LU
15
CAOXI BEI LU

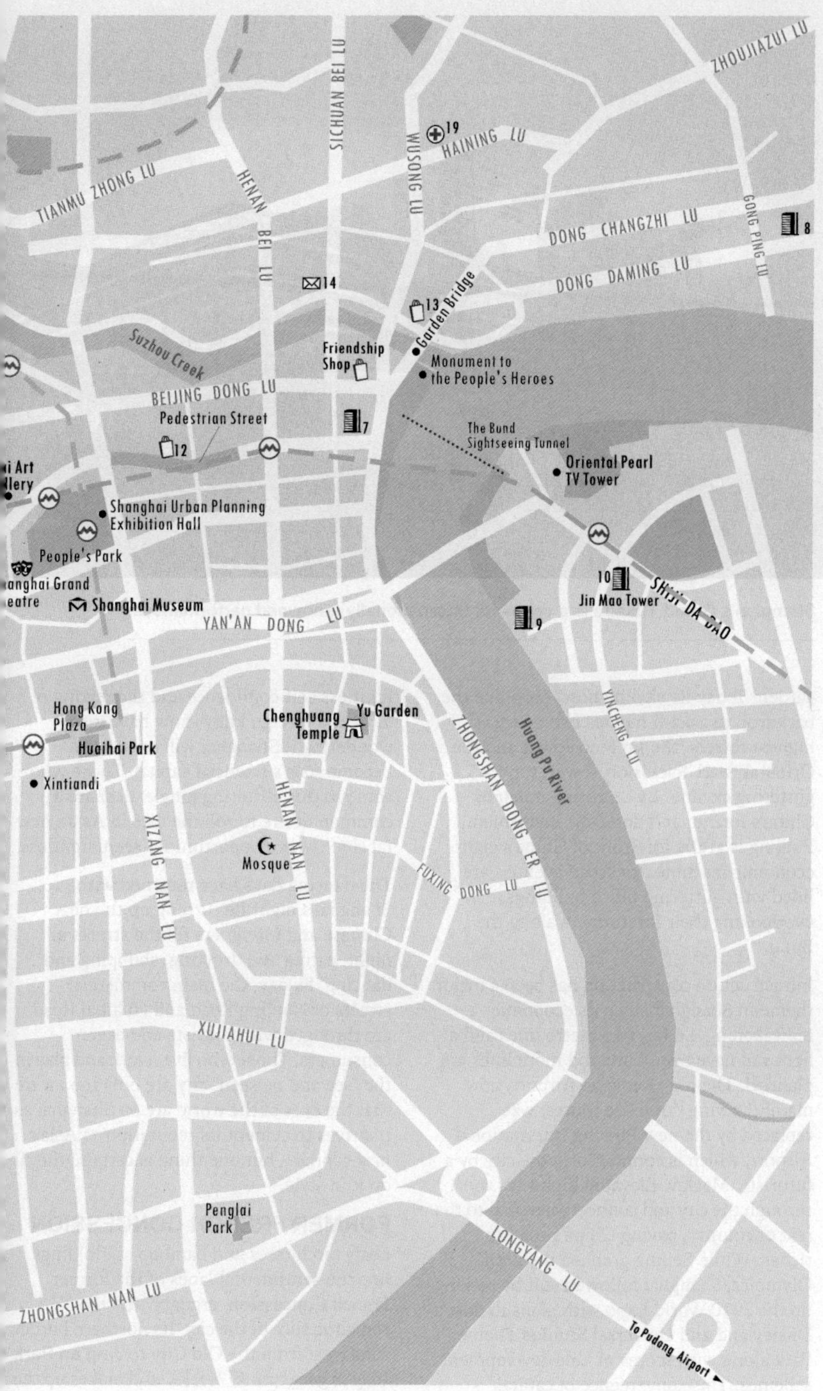
ZHOUJIAZUI LU
SICHUAN BEI LU
WUSONG LU
19
HAINING LU
TIANMU ZHONG LU
HENAN BEI LU
GONG PING LU
DONG CHANGZHI LU
8
DONG DAMING LU
14
13
Garden Bridge
Suzhou Creek
Friendship Shop
Monument to the People's Heroes
BEIJING DONG LU
Pedestrian Street
7
The Bund Sightseeing Tunnel
12
Oriental Pearl TV Tower
Shanghai Urban Planning Exhibition Hall
People's Park
10
Jin Mao Tower
SHIJI DA DAO
Shanghai Museum
YAN'AN DONG LU
9
Hong Kong Plaza
Huaihai Park
Xintiandi
Chenghuang Temple
Yu Garden
ZHONGSHAN DONG ER LU
Huang Pu River
YINCHENG LU
HENAN NAN LU
XIZANG NAN LU
Mosque
FUXING DONG LU
XUJIAHUI LU
Penglai Park
LONGYANG LU
ZHONGSHAN NAN LU
To Pudong Airport

Shanghai's Grand Theatre is a venue for internationally renowned performances.

garden. Today its skyline now looks like the backdrop to a sci-fi movie. Two of Asia's highest towers, the Jin Mao Tower and the Oriental Pearl Television Tower, top its glittering skyline. By capturing much of China's foreign and domestic investment, Pudong is at the forefront of China's giant economic machine. Its broad avenues are lined with glittering office buildings overlooking their forerunners along the Bund.

Infrastructure construction has been a major theme in Shanghai since its economic reawakening. So far, two metro lines and a light rail have been built and more lines are planned. The old Hongqiao Airport, now mainly serving domestic routes, was replaced by the new Pudong International Airport, which is connected to the city by a futuristic Maglev. Elevated highways run through the city and connect Shanghai to the rest of country, paving China's road to riches. While Beijing grabbed the 2008 Olympics, Shanghai followed suit by picking up the 2010 World Expo with plans to host a Disneyland and Universal Studios Theme Park along with scores of new development schemes. This convergence of capital, limitless self-confidence and the mixing of local and foreign know-how have many wondering if Shanghai will once again become Asia's financial capital. Those who come to this glittering jungle all share a common desire to roll the dice in Asia's new fat city – where opportunities seem limitless.

The dancing days have returned with Shanghai's nightlife turning up the heat. Chinese and foreigners fill the streets at night, eating and drinking, shopping and dancing. By day, the main commercial streets of Nanjing Road and Huaihai Road are thronged with tourists and eager consumers. Those who live, work and play in the "see and be seen" city are only too aware that the eyes of the world are on Shanghai as it strives to cement its reputation as Asia's new capital – but one thing is certain, they'll do it in style.

FORMER FRENCH CONCESSION

Leafy birch trees and bamboo scaffoldings line the sentimental lanes of the former French Concession, arguably the most romantic slice of the city. Its northern border runs west from the Old City to **Jing'an Park** (*jìng'ān gōngyuán* 静安公园) and makes up the area south of Yan'an Road. There remains much to see around this colonial quarter, from the French dog track to the former revolutionary residencies of Sun Yat-sen and Zhou Enlai to the glitz of modern Xintiandi. Its heady history and glamorous present promise to grab your attention.

The easiest way to reach the classical arteries of the former French Concession is from People's Square. From **People's Square**, take metro line 1 to Huangpi South Road Station. Take Exit 3 up to the bustling Madang Road. Turn right (south) and you'll find yourself at the intersection of Huaihai Road (the former Avenue Joffre). Don't be lured away by the glass towers at the **Hong Kong Plaza** (*xiānggǎng guǎngchǎng* 香港广场) shopping mall. Avoid the pull of shopping for now and head one block south on Madang Road to the trendiest place in town: **Xintiandi** (*xīntiāndì* 新天地). Until the mid-1990's, this ultra-chic neighborhood for Shanghai's partying elite was inhabited by old warehouses. Redecorated and gentrified, the area now sports immaculately reconstructed buildings updated with a modern twist. Swanky bars and discos burst with revelers and posh restaurants dish up cuisine as beautiful as the venue itself. Standing in front of the Starbucks on the corner of Taicang Road and Madang Road, it's hard to fathom that this is just a stone's throw from where the Chinese Communist Party was founded. Follow the broad cobblestone lanes and wander behind Xintiandi to the back alleys to spot refurbished tenement homes with doors framed with large stones (*shíkù mén* 石库门). Follow the signs on Xingye Road to the **1st National Congress of the Chinese Communist Party**, a Marxist exhibit of heroic red and gold proportions.

From the corner of Madang Road and Huaihai Road head west on Huaihai Road,

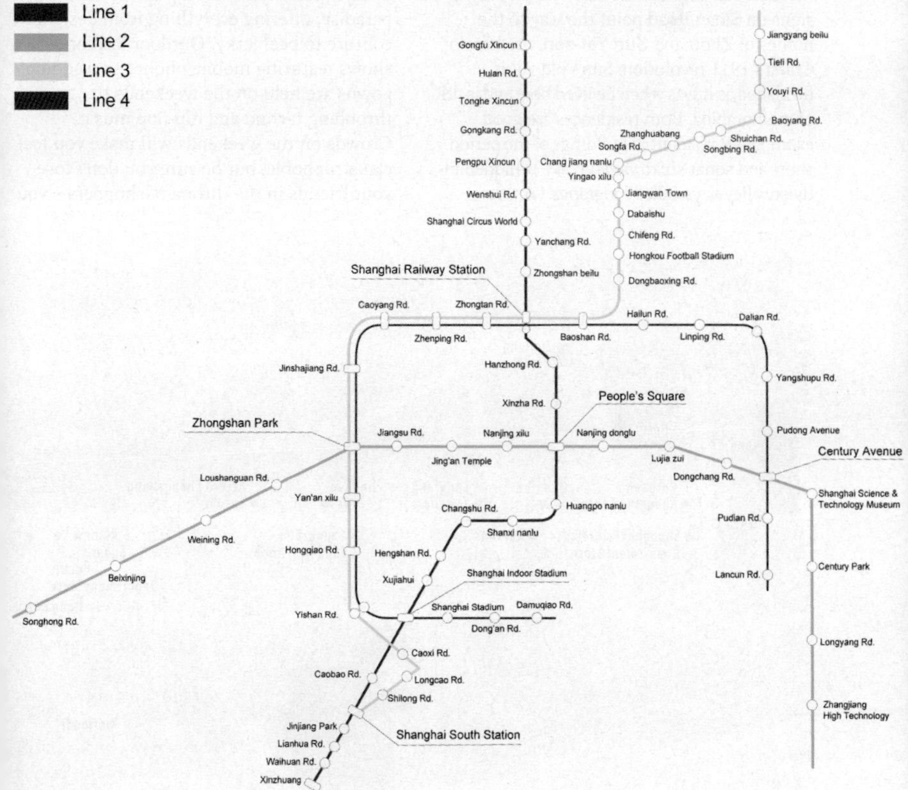

go under the elevated highways, until you reach Yandang Road. This pedestrian street hosts charming teahouses, bars and restaurants and takes you to the mouth of the lush **Fuxing Park** (*fùxīng gōngyuán* 复兴公园), formerly known as French Park. The shady paths of Fuxing Park are a godsend during Shanghai's hot and humid summers. Abutting this quiet park is the uber-hip Park 97 nightclub that sets the park into party-mode during the weekends.

From the park head into the bottleneck alley of Gaolan Road and look for the Ashanti Dome, a French restaurant in the former Russian Orthodox **St. Nicholas Church**. This 1930's era church features classical frescoes in homage to Tsar Nicholas II. Following the Russian Revolution, thousands of White Russian refugees flooded the French Concession and made part of it into a little Moscow: black bread and vodka abounded. Just a few blocks away on Sinan Road is the **Old Residence of Zhou Enlai**, a key leader of the Chinese Communist Party. Giant brown signs on Sinan Road point the way to the homes of Zhou and **Sun Yat-sen**, the hero of China's 1911 revolution. Sun's old flat is furnished as it was when he lived here and is full of memorabilia. Both residences are good examples of residential buildings of the period – short and squat *shikumens*(石库门) hidden in twisty alleyways called *longtangs* (弄堂).

A few blocks west from Sinan Road is Maoming Road. While Xintiandi is for the posh, the strip of clubs on Maoming Nan Road is where the all-night-spill-onto-the-street parties take place. North along this street leads to the area's most fashionable shops and boutiques offering chic clothing, fine art and classy furniture. On Maoming Road, just north Huaihai Road, is the historic Jinjiang Hotel, a one-time hot spot from the "Roaring Twenties." Ballroom dances, exclusive clubs and champagne fantasies were all lived out here by the rich and those aspiring to make their fortune. One block west on Huaihai Road, at the corner of Shaanxi South Road, are two massive shopping malls, Parksons and Printemps – upscale fashion and everyday goods can be bought here. Small café also dot this area, making it a good place to grab an iced-coffee in the summer and a hot tea in winters.

Running from east to west, Huaihai Road is a major commercial artery and a consumer's paradise, offering everything from designer couture to beef jerky. Outdoor fashion shows featuring mobile phones to wedding gowns are held on the weekends to throbbing techno and hip-hop music. Crowds on the weekends will make you feel claustrophobic, but be sure you don't lose your friends in the throng of shoppers – you

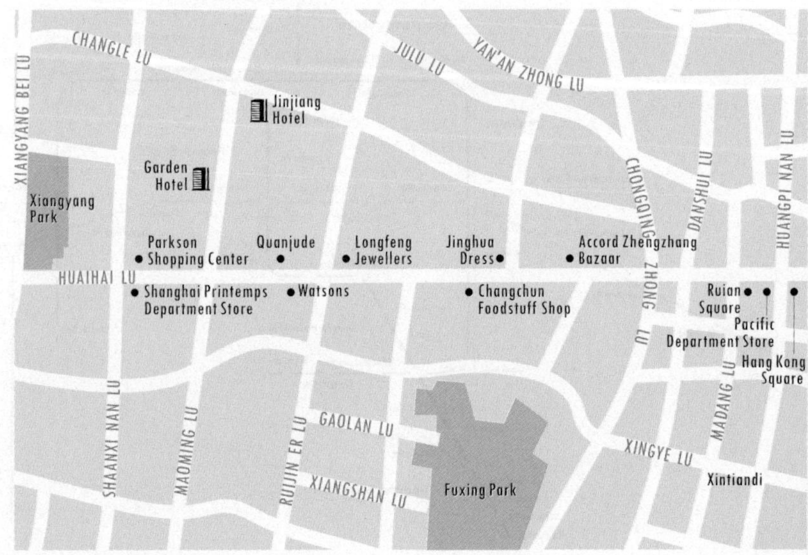

There's never a dull moment on the Nanjing Road pedestrian street.

may never seen them again. Several line 1 metro stations follow the road and give easy access to the shops.

Just west of Shaanxi South Road is the sprawling **Xiangyang Market** (*xiāngyánglù shìchǎng* 襄阳路市场). Expect to be accosted by all manner of watch, purse and clothing vendors who will lead you into twisting back alleys for copies of international brands. In Xiangyang Market itself, there are hundreds of open-air clothing, jewelry and trinket stalls. If you're after bazaar-style street bargaining then this is the place to come. The vendors will shove a calculator in front of you with a price entered. Punch in 20% of the opening price and bargain accordingly – haggling is essential so don't be timid: great deals await the skillful bargainer. One final tip – buying in quantity will get the vendors into the mood to slash prices, so it's a good place to stock up on gifts for the folks back home. An eclectic blend of restaurants and open-air café also line the streets in this area. Everything from noodles to donuts is available for the tired shopper.

Along Ruijin Er Road is the cozy Ruijin Guesthouse. This lovely compound of trees and brick buildings is also home to the trendy Face bar and the fashionable restaurant Colours. The Ruijin Guesthouses were built by media mogul Mohawk Morris of the *North China News* and later used as the seat of the Shanghai government following liberation in 1949.

At the end of Maoming Road, where it meets Yongjia Road, is a large alleyway that leads into the **Maoming Flower Market** where all sorts of orchids and ferns are sold wholesale. The flower market is planted in the **Cultural Square** (*wénhuà guǎngchǎng* 文化广场), which used to be the site of the old French dog track. Its heyday of franc-fisted fights and celebratory champagne toasts over bets on the hounds are long over. Now the area boasts quaint tree-lined streets where early risers do their exercises and vendors sell the morning's breakfast of *youtiao* (*yóutiáo* 油条) and steamed buns.

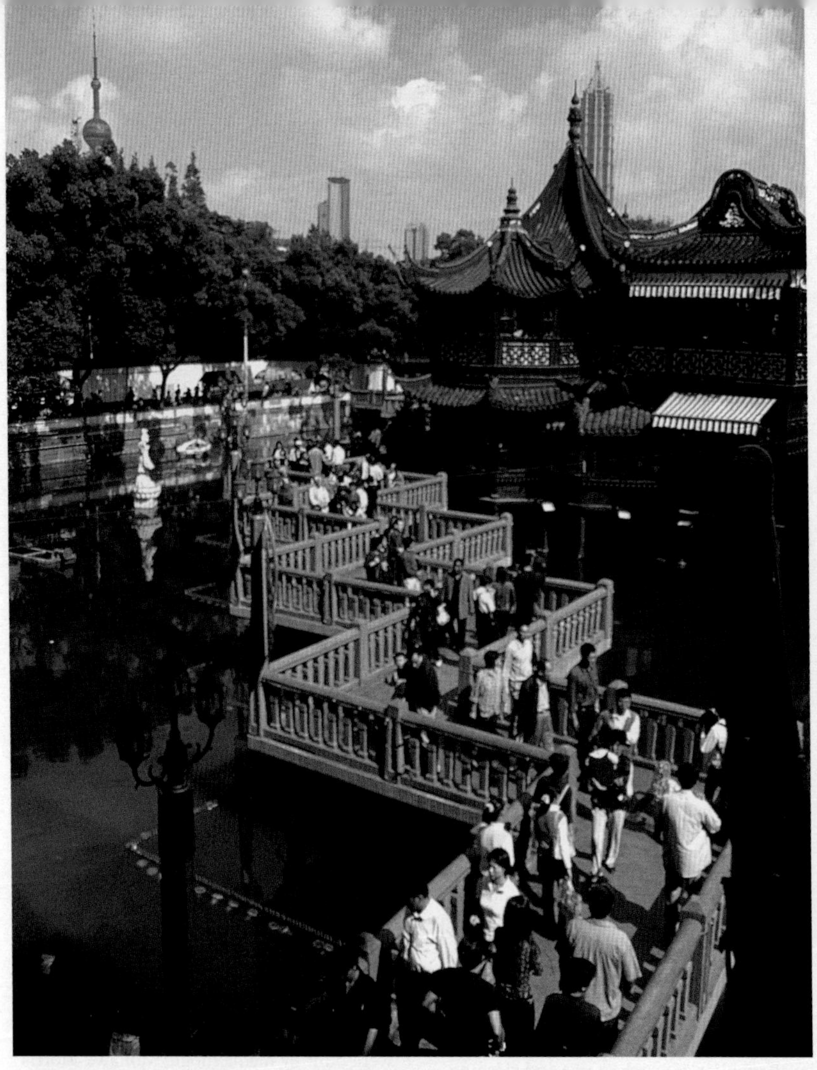

The famous Nine-Bend Bridge in Shanghai's buzzing Yu Garden.

OLD TOWN & YU GARDEN

Made into a rounded walled city in 1553 to fend off Japanese pirates, the **Old Town** (*nánshì* 南市) displays the richness of Ming and Qing architecture and the vibrancy of traditional Shanghai street life. Some call this Shanghai's "Chinatown" because of the traditional atmosphere, though the bright visages of Colonel Sanders and neon lights lining the narrow alleys add a modern touch. Considered unhealthily overcrowded, dirty and smelly by foreigners during the concession era, this was the one place that the Chinese could call their own in Shanghai.

Today the Old City is one of the few historic tourist highlights in a city that's all about modernity. One of the best ways to enter this area is through the northern gate from Renmin Road and Lishui Road. Walk south on Lishui past the new park underneath a massive gate straddling the road.

Some streets in the Old City are more understated than others. Explore the sidewalk shops and lanes for quiet shopping opportunities. Small niches filled with clay kettles, glazed teacups and assorted trinkets line the walls in small stores, and antiques and antique replicas lure collectors and those stumped for souvenirs. Posters of 1930's era beauties to simple peasant art vie for your attention and cash. Parts of this area remain residential, and it's easy to get lost in the maze of *longtangs* while walking past residents washing vegetables at outdoor sinks, toddlers playing hide and seek, and old men hunched over a game of Chinese chess.

Head down Chenxiangge Road and walk west down a tight alley to the mustard yellow walls of **Chenxiangge Temple** (*chénxiāng gé* 沉香阁). Tourists come to take a peek into this tiny temple that was once part of the larger estate that held the Yu Garden. The dainty temple continues to serve the people of this neighborhood. Narrow streets are framed with tiny two-story abodes with doorways that lead to an apparent maze of cluttered corridors.

A block south is the intersection of Fuyou Road and the start of Old Jiaochang Road, it's marked with jutting traditional Chinese roof peaks and roadside vendors. Large department stores selling high-end items such as gold, pearls, massive Buddhas, silk embroidery, sandalwood fans, jade chopsticks and an assortment of teas and alcohol are housed in the buildings that circle the Yu Garden. The kitschy atmosphere of traditional architecture spiced up with modern pop music and garish lights attract tourists like moths to a flame.

Traditional Chinese medicine shops are also abundant – you'll smell them before you see them. The fragrant aromas of curious plants and dried animals will tell your nose how to reach them. Ginseng is a big seller here – the tiny roots, which are eerily human shaped, can sell for thousands of RMB and are highly valued for their therapeutic properties.

To enter the main nerve of Old Town and visit the Ming era **Yu Garden** (*yùyuán* 豫园), look for one of the many small entrances that lead into the central garden area. The dark narrow lanes are towered over by a mish-mash of Chinese architecture and modern styling. Commercialism is the word of the day; it's a modern version of an old bustling market – with the added kick the Shanghainese throw into making money.

Different snacks and trinkets are available. Tasty goodies include sweet sticky rice candies, grilled sausages and assorted fried kebabs (check out the fried swallows). Shanghai is known for its steamed meat dumplings (*xiǎolóng bāo* 小笼包) and the most famous in Shanghai are found in the Yu Garden shopping complex. Just off the central pond, this vendor is hard to miss – just look for the long line of salivating people. The dumplings are made on the spot and steamed to juicy perfection in a few minutes.

Like a green aquatic gem ensconced in a shell, the lake in the center of the market complex features a nine-bend bridge where locals and tourists alike all compete for the best photo opportunity. Fat fish swim lazily underneath the bridge, but come alive in a feeding frenzy whenever people throw in some food.

Across the bridge is the famed Huxinting Teahouse (*húxīntíng chálóu* 湖心亭茶楼) with its massive upturned eaves. This huge structure dominates the Yu Garden skyline. Originally built in 1784, became a teahouse just before the turn of the 19th century. The restaurant inside the five-sided structure is as famous as the dignitaries that have poked their chopsticks into the restaurant's rice bowls. Pictures of Jiang Zemin, Queen

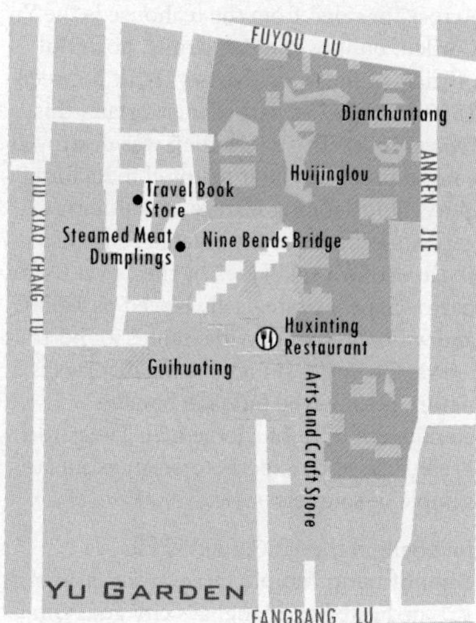

Yu Garden continues to bustle with activity as it did a century ago.

Elizabeth II and the Clintons mingling with the staff hang on the walls.

Across the pond from the teahouse is the Yu Garden, built by the Pan family, powerful officials of the Ming dynasty. Built between 1559 and 1577 as part of their estate, this typical southern-style garden was destroyed several times and later restored to its former glory. One defining feature of southern gardens is the carefully created sense of space within a small area by the clever use of narrow lanes, strategically placed partitions and windows that provide frames for portrait views. One of its more alluring displays is a naturally hollowed out jade boulder standing in front of a large hall. The garden is considered by experts to be an exquisite sample of southern style.

Just behind the Yu Garden is the **Chenghuang Temple** (*chénghuáng miào* 城隍庙), dedicated to Shanghai's city god, Qin Yubo. Each Chinese city used to have a city god chosen from the Taoist pantheon of Chinese deities and they were worshipped in these colorful temples. Loud, crowded and full of eager worshippers, these temples were rambunctious places where people would gather and pray for health and wealth, perhaps more for wealth here, this being Shanghai. Originally the Jinshan Temple, it was rebuilt during the reign of Emperor Yongle of the Ming dynasty in the 13th century. The temple was refurbished again in 1926 and today, still drenched in incense smoke, it continues to attract worshippers. In the front hall is a statue of a Han dynasty general while in the back hall stands Qin Yubo.

Arriving at the Yu Garden in the afternoon then spending the day shopping and eating is a perfect way to spend a lazy day. As night falls over the city, the old buildings light up and the crowds thin out allowing visitors to explore the old city in relative peace. The night vista of the upturned eaves falling from tiled roofs juxtaposed against the Herculean metallic towers of light from nearby Pudong nicely sums up Shanghai's past and present.

Opera performances can be seen at the Yuyuan Stage Theater. Other "must-sees" in the Old City includes the colorful antiques and bird market a few blocks west of Yu Garden on Tibet South Road. The lane is full of ceramic and glass curios as well as chirping chickadees. Make sure to take in the buildings in this area – it's highly probable that they'll be redeveloped into skyscrapers within the next few years.

Chenghuang Temple
城隍庙 *chénghuáng miào*
✉ 249 Fangbang Middle Road
方浜中路 249 号
☎ 6386 8649, 6386 5700

Chenxiangge Temple 沉香阁 *chénxiāng gé*
✉ 29 Chenxiangge Road 沉香阁路 29 号
☎ 6320 0400
¥ 5

Yu Garden Stage 豫园古戏台 *yùyuán gǔxìtái*
Chinese opera and sublime tea tasting. Performances start at 7pm, tickets are RMB 200.
✉ 3/F, 10 Wenchang Road 文昌路 10 号 3 层
☎ 6215 9190

THE BUND

Of all the sights evocative of the splendor and decadence of old Shanghai, none is singularly more impressive then **the Bund** (*wàitān* 外滩). Getting its name from an Anglo-Indian word meaning "muddy embankment," the Bund rolls down a million dollar mile along the west bank of Shanghai's most essential waterway, the **Huangpu River** (*huángpŭ jiāng* 黄浦江). It's on this swampy riverbank where Shanghai's previous *taipans* (heads of trading houses) erected their monuments to wealth. The Bund still remains Shanghai's number one tourist site, and even with all the things to see in Shanghai, this is the one that can't be missed. Running the length of the Bund is Zhongshan East Road, a major thoroughfare that can be crossed via tunnels or pedestrian bridges.

During the 1920's and 30's, the Bund served as the focal point for the thriving city's financial and social life. The great edifices built here held great symbolic importance. When junks and cargo ships reached Shanghai, this promenade along Shanghai's waterfront was the first sight they would see. If any doubted the economic prowess Shanghai enjoyed during those times, the buildings along the Bund quickly disposed of any notions that the city was a pretender. From their windows overlooking the teeming Huangpu, Shanghai's wealthy could watch with bated breath as their cargoes of opium, gold and silver bullion, tea and spices were loaded on and off their ships.

Built of marble and stone, the buildings of the Bund are emblematic of foreign interest and business anchored in Shanghai's staying power. They also served to assure Shanghai's foreign residents and visitors as to who was in control. By night, away from the brothels and opium dens lining the Bund's side streets, Shanghai's richest met in the British and French Clubs to quaff whiskey sours while their countrymen sampled Shanghai's endless illicit pleasures.

Although things are different now, the Bund retains much of its previous grandeur. To prevent flooding from the Huangpu and **Suzhou Creek** (*sūzhōu hé* 苏州河), the promenade was raised from a simple street to an elevated, cement walkway. As one of Shanghai's few free tourist attractions, it's regularly thronged with both domestic and international tourists. Hawkers sell glow sticks and light-up toys by night while photographers offer to capture your magic moment backlit by either Pudong's futuristic skyline or the Bund's colonial massif. The best place to view the Bund is from the walkway along the river's edge; from here you can take in the view of the old masterpieces and the new wonders across the river.

Today's Bund both evolves Shanghai's yesteryears and hints at the city's tomorrow. The once teeming wharves have been moved further downstream, though the Bund is still a great place to view the Huangpu River's ship traffic. When the foreigners left, control of the buildings was assumed by the state though very few continued to perform their original functions. The Peace Hotel, the AIA Building and the Shanghai Customs House, though no longer holding the eminent prestige of the past, have persisted throughout the march of time. M on the Bund, one of the city's classiest restaurants, serves martinis and haute cuisine while providing stunning views of the Huangpu and Pudong.

Lanterns light up the Chenghuang Temple during Chinese New Year.

The northern end of the Bund begins just south of the **Garden Bridge** (*wàibáidù qiáo* 外白渡桥). Despite being north of the bridge, the **Park Hotel** (*shànghǎi guójì fàndiàn* 上海国际饭店), the **Astor House Hotel** (*pǔjiāng fàndiàn* 浦江饭店) and the **Russian Consulate** (*éluósī lǐngshìguǎn* 俄罗斯领事馆) are worth visiting. Still sporting a Bayer neon sign at its apex, today's Park Hotel is where pharmaceutical giant Bayer began distilling opium into morphine. On the other side of the street stands the Astor House Hotel, now the Pujiang Hotel; it dates back to 1860 and was Shanghai's first hotel. Once the darling of Shanghai and host to luminaries such as Albert Einstein, Bertrand Russel and Charlie Chaplin, it's now Shanghai's number one choice for backpackers. Directly across the old Astor House stands the Russian Consulate in its austere gray.

A wooden toll bridge, built by an English businessman in 1856, originally crossed the Suzhou Creek along the Bund, but because its arch wasn't high enough to accommodate the increasing number of tall ships, it was replaced by the Garden Bridge, an iron span built in 1906. Boats still pass under the Garden Bridge because Suzhou Creek remains an important waterway linking Shanghai with inland China.

At the Bund's northern end stands the **Monument to the People's Heroes** (*rénmín yīngxióng jìniàn tǎ* 人民英雄纪念塔). This granite obelisk, erected in 1993, honors those (post-1949) who fought for the new China and is flanked by walls carved with their names. At its base is the **Bund History Museum** (*wàitān lìshǐ bówùguǎn* 外滩历史博物馆) where visitors can gaze at a collection of photos from Shanghai's old days.

Heading south from the north end of the Bund, one of the first architectural monuments to catch the visitor's eye is the Friendship Store Curios Branch (*yǒuyì shāngdiàn* 友谊商店), a branch of the Friendship Store that specializes in art and antiques. Continuing south is the former **Banque de l'Indo-Chine** (28 Zhongshan East Road 中山东路 28 号) Built in 1914, this classical French building features baroque arches and Greek columns. Next to this building is the stylistically eclectic **Glen Line Building** (29 Zhongshan East Road 中山东路 29 号). Built in 1922, the Glen Line was once Shanghai's largest German bank.

Today's Shanghai Foreign Trade Bureau (*wàimào dàshà* 外贸大厦) is the former home of **Jardine Matheson and Co.**, once the largest and most powerful trading house in Shanghai. Their prominent position on the Bund reflects the importance of this firm – the company was instrumental, both politically and financially, in Shanghai's early development and corruption. This massive English Renaissance structure was constructed in 1920 with Roman arches, huge blocks of stone and giant pillars.

The **Peace Hotel** (*hépíng fàndiàn* 和平饭店) was built in 1929 as the private residence and office of Victor Sassoon. Then known as the **Cathay Hotel**, it still stands in all its art deco glory at the intersection of Nanjing Road and the Bund as a Shanghai cornerstone. Its green pyramid roof, once Victor Sassoon's penthouse apartment, is illuminated at night and in the Peace Hotel's bar, jazz musicians still jam to the tunes of years gone by. If you're looking for a building that evokes the Bund's past glamour – suave gentlemen in tuxedos with debutantes preening in their glittering dresses – this is the place to go.

South of the Peace Hotel stands the former **Palace Hotel** (now the south wing of the Peace Hotel), which sports an eye-catching exterior of red and white brickwork. Built in 1906, the edifice features an English-style exterior punctuated with baroque windows. The **former Chartered Bank of America, India, and China** (18 Zhongshan East Road 中山东路 18 号), featuring Renaissance architecture, was built in 1922. Beside this structure is the **former North Daily News Building** (17 Zhongshan East Road 中山东路 17 号), which was built in 1921 and is now the AIA Building. These two buildings share the block with the Palace Hotel and are slated for restoration. The next block features the **former Russo-Chinese Bank Building** (15 Zhongshan East Road 中山东路 15 号). This squat building was built in 1901 and features six carved columns. Also on the same block is the **former Bank of Communications Building** (14 Zhongshan East Road 中山东路 14 号). Designed with all the modernity of 1940, this streamlined building looks like it came straight out of Batman's Gotham City.

One of the few buildings on the Bund to have changed owners but not purpose is the **Shanghai Customs House** (13 Zhongshan East Road 中山东路 13 号). Built in 1927 and distinguished by its four colossal Roman granite columns, the Customs House is topped with a bell tower and a clock face visible up and down the river, reminding ships that it would soon be time to pay. The bell now rings to "The East is Red," though it's hard to hear above the noise of the street and boat noise.

Designed by G. L. Wilson, the **former Hong Kong and Shanghai Bank** (12 Zhongshan East Road 中山东路 12 号) was the second largest bank in the world when it was completed in 1923 and is still one of the largest buildings on the Bund. It has been extensively restored and the lobby approaches its former 1920's splendor. A dome stands above its exterior columns and archways and is decorated with panels saluting the financial capitals of their day. Many consider this building to be icing on the Bund's architectural cake.

Now the Bangkok Bank and Thai Consulate, the **Hospital of the Shanghai Navigation Company** (7 Zhongshan East Road 中山东路 7 号), built in 1907, is one of the oldest buildings on the Bund and is next to the even older **China Merchants Bank** (6 Zhongshan East Road 中山东路 6 号), which was built in 1897 and once served as the British Municipal City Hall. Built in an English Gothic style with baroque pillars, it's one of the more poignant relics of the colonial period, a reminder of the contradiction of Shanghai's past.

South of Guangdong Road stands another of the Bund's most important buildings. The Dong Feng Hotel is the **former Shanghai Club** (2 Zhongshan East Road 中山东路 2 号), which was built in 1910 and was once the city's most lavish private club. A haunt of

The Jin Mao Tower is a famous Shanghai landmark.

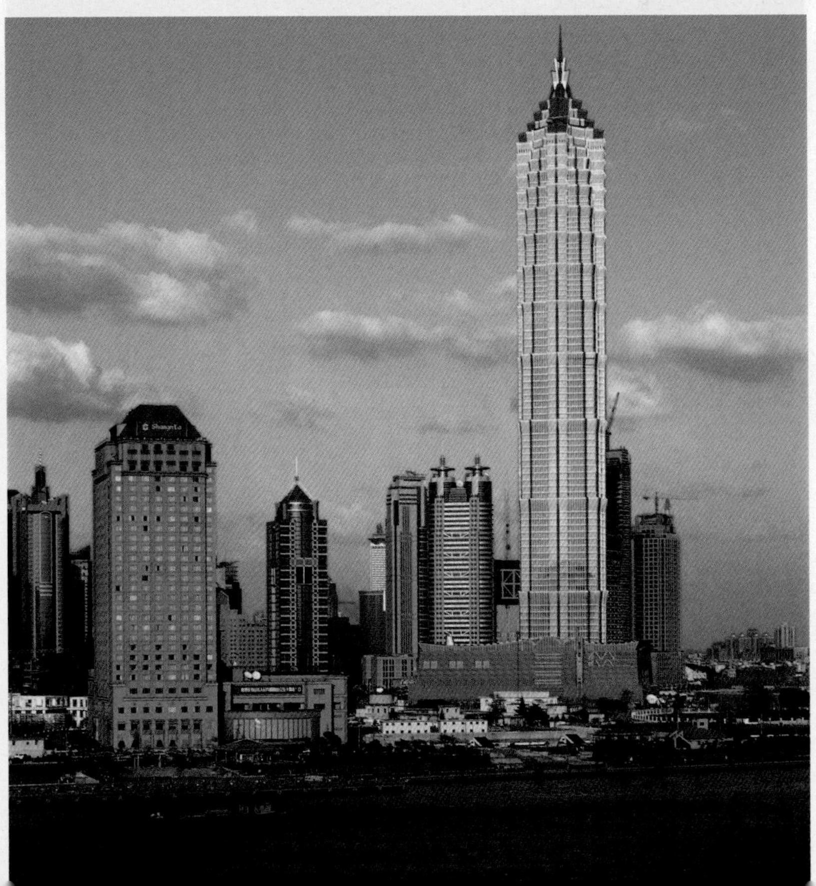

British and American bankers and merchants, it was rivaled only by the marble fronted French Club further south down the Bund. The Shanghai Club was once the home to the world-renowned black and white granite "Long Bar," measuring over 100 feet and, at the time, the longest in the world.

From here, it's possible to continue south into what was once the French Concession's part of the Bund or cross over Zhongshan East Road to the elevated walkway. From this position you can take in all the buildings you've just visited as they stand facing the Huangpu like giant stone sentinels. At Nanjing Road and the Bund there's a psychedelic **tourist tunnel** (*wàitān guānguāng suìdào* 外滩观光隧道) to Pudong – be prepared to be perplexed by the short kitschy ride. There are also pedestrian tunnels at Fuzhou Road going underneath Zhongshan East Road towards the banks of the river.

Bund History Museum 外滩历史博物馆
wàitān lìshǐ bówùguǎn
✉ north end of the Bund 外滩北端
🕒 9am to 5pm
¥ 10

NANJING ROAD

Shanghai's most famous thoroughfare, Nanjing Road spills from its eastern terminus on **the Bund** and past the **People's Square** to its western extreme by the newly remodeled **Jing'an Temple** (*jìng'ān sì* 静安寺). Divided into East, Middle and West

The lights of the Bund continue to shine into the 21st century.

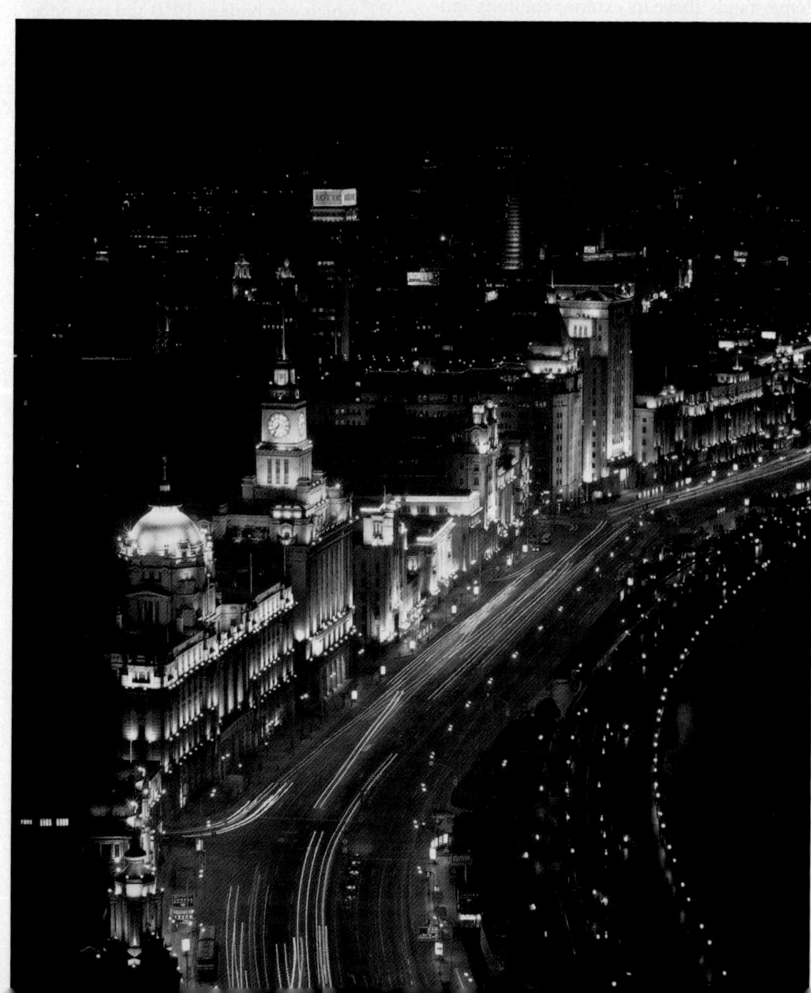

sections, it's at times a pedestrian shopping street, a winding tree-lined road, and a modern thoroughfare cutting between some of Shanghai's most posh hotels.

Once known as the premier shopping street in China and Asia, colonial Nanjing Road stood in stark contrast to the rest of agrarian China. The hottest fashions from Italy were imported regularly and the road was full of shops selling some of China's finest silks. Massive department stores were built, the most famous being the **Great World** and **Wing-On**, where shopping was only one of the activities enjoyed amongst gambling and sing-song halls, game parlors, bars and freak shows.

Originally named Bubbling Well Road after a small stream that once ran beneath it, Nanjing Road became China's most famous strip and may now regain this crown. Modern department stores, though not as elegant as the old ones, still line the street and exert a tremendous tourist draw over Chinese and foreign visitors alike. During holidays, it's common to see people jostling to have their photo taken in front of the Nanjing Road sculpture at the two ends of the pedestrian street.

Beginning at the Jing'an Temple metro station, the redesigned **Jing'an Park** (*jìng'ān gōngyuán* 静安公园) features upscale restaurants and charming teahouses. By morning, Shanghai's elderly flock there to practice Tai Chi as the young stumble home from the bars. All day long people while away the day taking in the scenery or chat on its numerous benches.

Directly across the street stands the Jing'an Temple. Dating back to the 19th century, it was once one of Shanghai's richest and most frequently visited temples. Located on the busy intersection of Huashan Road and Nanjing West Road, this small temple manages to filter out the cacophony of the street and creates a small niche of tranquility.

Continuing west is the **Shanghai Center** (*shànghǎi shāngchéng* 上海商城), home to the **Portman Ritz-Carlton**, and one of Shanghai's masterpieces of modern architecture. Featuring three towers, it fully utilizes its space yet provides numerous

Shanghai is China's trend setting city.

vistas that dramatically change with your line of sight. Home to numerous upscale shops and restaurants, it has one of Shanghai's first Western-style supermarkets, a Western medical clinic and a branch of the **HSBC Bank**.

Built in 1955 with help from the Soviet Union, the **Shanghai Exhibition Center** (*shànghǎi zhǎnlǎn zhōngxīn* 上海展览中心) received a facelift over the past few years and now stands as an ornate sandblasted monument to Sino-Soviet friendship. Once home to the Hardoon Gardens, which was built by a Persian millionaire, the Shanghai Exhibition Center is as prime as Shanghai real estate gets.

Continuing east, the shopping malls and hotels of modern Shanghai's commercial greatness arise. **Plaza 66, CITIC Center, Meilong Zhen, the Hilton Hotel**, and **the J.W. Marriot**, none budget options, provide numerous choices for dining and shopping – look for big names, from Louis Vuitton to Kenny Roger's Roasters. For a taste of traditional China, try the Shanghai Jingdezhen Porcelain Artware store on the corner of Nanjing and Shaanxi Road. A wide array of pottery and porcelain is for sale, much of it originating in Jingdezhen, one of

China's traditional pottery centers.

Stretching from Maoming Road to the Shanghai Television Station, slightly south of Nanjing Road is the **Wujiang Food Street** (*wújiānglù shípǐnjiē* 吴江路食品街), a nighttime hotspot filled with shops, food stalls, trinket stands and restaurants. The **Shanghai Broadcasting and Television International News Exchange Center** (*shànghǎi diànshìtái* 上海电视台) stands at the street's eastern terminus.

At this point Nanjing West Road becomes Nanjing Middle Road and skirts the northern perimeter of People's Square and People's Park. Under the square is Shanghai's largest metro station; it's also the transfer station

Shanghai's busy streets are a mixture of old and new.

between metro lines 1 and 2. Across the park and square is the **Shanghai Arts and Crafts Shopping Center** (*shànghǎi gōngyì měishù shāngshà* 上海工艺美术商厦), a fascinating market filled with small shops selling everything from birdcages and picture frames to strangely shaped rocks and plants.

From the Tibet Road overpass to the Henan Road metro station, a sprawling street closed to vehicular traffic winds between numerous shops, restaurants, hotels and department stores. The **Nanjing Road Pedestrian Mall** (*nánjīng lù bùxíng jiē* 南京路步行街), while it is usually flush with tourists and shoppers, makes for easy walking and provides numerous places to sit down and people-watch.

On the eastern end of the pedestrian mall is the east building of the **Number 1 Department Store** (*xīnshìjiè bǎihuò* 新世界百货). Formerly known as the Sun, it was one of Nanjing Road's four anchor department stores. Opening its doors back in 1934, it was designed by Chinese architects and was the first building in China to use an escalator. At its pre-liberation peak, it attracted more than 150,000 shoppers daily.

Two other Nanjing Road shopping anchors were the world famous Wing-On and the Great World. Old descriptions of these shopping centers call up images closer to three-ring circuses than modern department stores. The former Wing-On stands at the southwest corner of an expansive square now replete with a giant television monitor and numerous vendors. This square, at the mid-point of the pedestrian street, occasionally has weekend performances and during the early morning it's used by seniors practicing Tai Chi or women doing traditional dances for exercise.

Before reaching the Henan Middle Road metro station, you'll pass by Shanghai's City of Books and the old Sincere Department Store, another of the famed "big four" department stores. Past the metro station, the pedestrian street ends and Nanjing Road resumes its bustling traffic of cars, trucks and buses heading towards or away from the Bund. Two blocks further east and the road ends by the riverside. If your legs are tired, the metro station is your best option for a quick escape. Tourist trolleys can be ridden the entire pedestrian section of Nanjing Road for RMB 1.

Jing'an Park 静安公园 *jìng'ān gōngyuán*
✉ Adjacent to Jing'an Metro Station
靠近静安寺地铁站
🕒 Open 24 hours
¥ Free

Jing'an Temple 静安寺 *jìng'ān sì*
✉ 1686 Nanjing West Road, Jing'an District
静安区南京西路 1686 号
☎ 6248 6366
🕒 9am to 5pm
¥ 5

Shanghai Exhibition Center
上海展览中心 *shànghǎi zhǎnlǎn zhōngxīn*

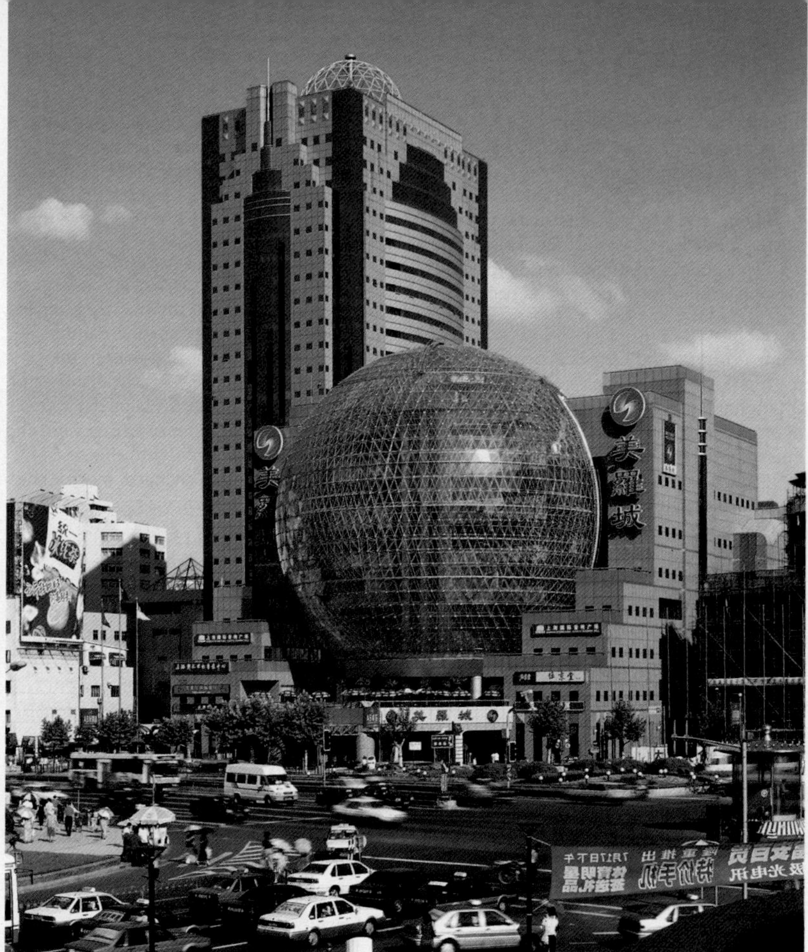

Metro City in Xujiahui.

- 1000 Yan'an Middle Road
  延安中路 1000 号
- 9am to 5pm
- Free to visit but special exhibitions may have a charge

PEOPLE'S SQUARE

Shanghai's **People's Square** (*rénmín guǎngchǎng* 人民广场) occupies a large portion of the geographic city center and is home to Shanghai's city hall. Underneath the square is the city's largest metro station and the only station to transfer between metro lines one and two. Linking the two lines are elongated shopping arcades while above ground is the People's Park, the Shanghai Museum, the Shanghai Art Museum, the Grand Theatre and the Urban Planning Hall.

The lawns and plazas making up People's Square hint at the old racetrack that once occupied the grounds. Of all the Western extravagances throughout old Shanghai, none was more celebrated by the wealthy than the horse races, which were held twice annually. The rich imported horses from Arabia and Mongolia and trained them throughout the year in preparation. On the big day, schools and businesses went on holiday and all social life focused on the outcomes of the races and the surrounding festivities. After 1949, the racetrack was converted into the People's Park to offer festivities all could enjoy.

People's Square is now mainly used for transit, and the addition of several cultural centers has increased tourism. Expansion of the park and open spaces gives locals a pleasant place to enjoy Shanghai's balmy springs and crisp autumns. The square remains quite crowded, especially during rush hour, and ongoing construction only seems to exacerbate congestion. However, it's also a good place to fly kites, enjoy an evening stroll or read a book and people-watch.

From a cultural and historical perspective, the highlight of the People's Square is the **Shanghai Museum** (*shànghǎi bówùguǎn* 上海博物馆). Often ranked as China's best museum, the new building was completed in 1996 at a cost of RMB 570 million and is a modern and well-kept facility. The museum was designed by Shanghai architect Xing Tonghe to evoke the image of a *ding*, an ancient Chinese vessel, and architecturally, it's a harmonious fusion of ancient and contemporary styles. The entrance, flanked by six stone lions and two stone *bixi*, mythical ancient Chinese beasts, opens onto a wide plaza with benches for sitting and music at night.

Inside, China's greatest display of art and artifacts awaits the visitor. Though museums in Beijing and Xi'an have larger collections, nowhere are they better exhibited. Its 14 galleries house collections of bronzes, sculptures, ceramics, paintings, calligraphy, seals, jades, coins, furniture and ethnic minority art. Whereas most major Chinese museums are arranged chronologically by dynasties, the exhibits in the Shanghai Museum are arranged by theme, allowing the visitor to observe the progression of aesthetics and style.

Signs introducing the objects are in English as well as Chinese and the track lighting is focused and bright. For anyone visiting Shanghai, or China for that matter, the museum is a must see. Chinese history and culture buffs will likely find one day too short to take in the extensive collection, and with over 120,000 artifacts to choose from, the displays are often changed, making the museum worth a return visit.

Now housed in the old Race Club Building, the **Shanghai Art Gallery** (*shànghǎi měishùguǎn* 上海美术馆) has steadily improved its collection to provide visitors with greater access to Chinese and foreign masterpieces. In 2002, the museum hosted a blown glass exhibition featuring colored glass blown into traditional and modern shapes. Much of the collection has since found its way into high-priced boutiques on Nanjing and Huaihai Road. With a focus on modern Chinese art, the museum still strives to feature works of ethnic artists and Renaissance masters.

Another highlight found in People's Square is **People's Park** (*rénmín gōngyuán* 人民公园),

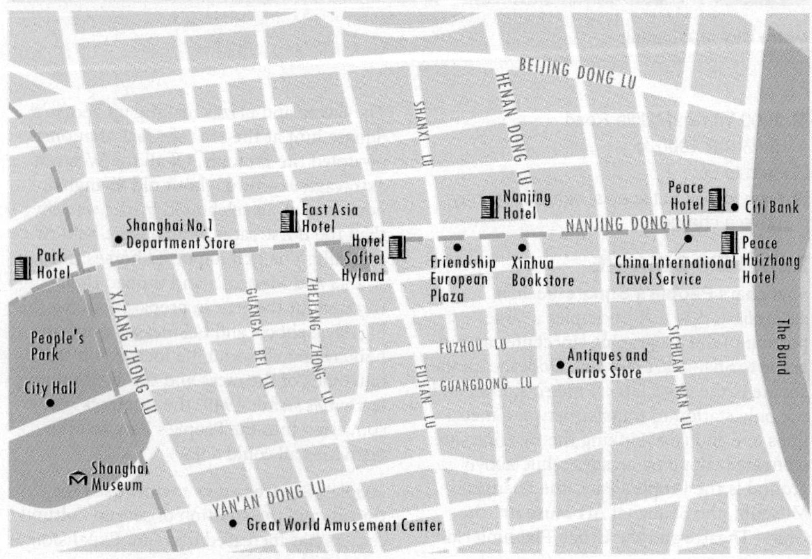

The Shanghai Museum's design is based on ancient Chinese bronze vessels.

a welcome respite from the crowds. Tree-lined lanes wind through pools and over gentle rises topped with small pavilions. It's one of the few places in Shanghai where visitors can sit on the grass and this park is rarely crowded despite its central location. Vendors sell drinks and snacks outside the entrance.

Located near the west-end of People's Park is Shanghai's premier venue for truly big name entertainment, the **Shanghai Grand Theatre** (*shànghǎi dàjùyuàn* 上海大剧院). The highlights of its early days may have been limited to Chinese symphonies and visiting orchestras and ballet troops from Russia, but the theater's billing has grown rapidly in recent years. A one-month engagement in 2002 of Les Miserables featured the original Broadway cast, and in early 2003 it hosted the Broadway cast of Cats. Featuring the largest stage in the world, Shanghai Grand Theatre is comprised of three different theatres, the largest seating 1,800. Its space-age design somehow resembles a giant Chinese pagoda.

To the east is Shanghai's city hall, the Municipal Government Building. This structure resembles most other government buildings in China – imposing and boxy. To its east is the more interesting and accessible **Shanghai Urban Planning Exhibition Hall** (*shànghǎi chéngshì guīhuà zhǎnshì guǎn* 上海城市规划展示馆). This hall is open to visitors and has numerous scale models detailing the history and future of Shanghai's development. It's a good place to get some perspective on the changes sweeping through the city. One highlight worth viewing is the latest scale model of the planned development in preparation for Shanghai's 2010 World Expo. Shanghai is a city that's growing in leaps and bounds and in a blink of an eye, much of the city has already changed.

People's Park 人民公园 *rénmín gōngyuán*

✉ 213 Nanjing West Road, Huangpu District 黄浦区南京西路 213 号

🕒 6am to 8pm

¥ 5

Shanghai Art Museum

上海美术馆 *shànghǎi měishùguǎn*

Zhongyin Mansion in Lujiazui.

225 Nanjing West Road 南京西路 225 号
6327 2829
9am to 4pm
20

Shanghai Grand Theatre
上海大剧院 *shànghǎi dàjùyuàn*
300 Renmin Dadao, People's Square
人民广场，人民大道 300 号
6372 8701
9am to 1pm
50

Shanghai Museum
上海博物馆 *shànghǎi bówùguǎn*
201 Renmin Dadao, near People's Square metro station
人民大道 201 号，靠近人民广场地铁站
6372 3500
9am to 5pm
20

LUJIAZUI

It's hard to imagine that just over a decade ago this area was defined by farmhouses and small warehouses hemmed in by rice paddies and the muddy Huangpu. In 1990, this area was dubbed the Pudong New Area and made into a Special Economic Zone. This kick started Shanghai's second rising and construction began on some of China's tallest buildings. A modern Wall Street-style financial district complete with world-class convention centers have been built alongside expansive avenues, plush shopping malls and grandiose apartments.

To appreciate its rapid ascent into the upper regions of advanced capitalism, one should start under the sea at the **Shanghai Ocean Aquarium** (*shànghǎi hǎiyáng shuǐzú guǎn* 上海海洋水族馆). The best way to reach this liquid marvel is to take metro line 2 to Lujiazui station just across from the Huangpu River. Take exit 1 and walk straight towards the Oriental Pearl TV Tower, a thought-provoking building that looks like a rocket with enormous pink bubbles that most people either love or hate. The aquarium is a large triangle shaped concrete building decorated with striking blue and green lines that form the outlines of fish. The Shanghai Ocean Aquarium is a state of the art facility featuring every marine eco-system representing nearly every continent, with hairy spider crabs, sleek penguins, stealthy sharks, and neon fish of every hue. Escalators and moving floors allow visitors to rest as they take in the large collections and elaborate displays of sea life. The aquarium features Asia's longest underwater glass tunnel and visitors glide under sweeping manta rays, happy turtles and tunas that get nervous when sharks come too close.

Head back to the **Oriental Pearl TV Tower** (*dōngfāng míngzhū diànshì tǎ* 东方明珠电视塔) and queue up for a sci-fi architectural exploration. Most visitors will rush towards the elevators to see the city in all its expanse, chaos and splendor. However, before heading up to see what Shanghai is becoming, take some time to wander through the basement history museum. This catacomb of excellent historical displays takes you from Shanghai's early days as a walled fort under the Ming dynasty to the beginning of European colonialism and up to the Japanese invasion. Several of the displays are interactive and the museum is worthy of a half-day visit. It certainly adds a few layers of meaning when you step into the elevator and rocket up 10 feet (3 m) per second to the mid-level bubble to gaze at the bustling city below. An additional elevator will take you to the heady top pod – over 1,122 feet (342 m) above the ground. From this top module, there's a chairman style desk flanked by a flag of China where visitors can sit and have their picture taken and imagine being a captain of capitalism, going where no one has gone before. If the view from even this vantage point leaves you wanting more, take the series of breathtaking elevator descents and head over to the **Jin Mao Tower** (*jīnmào dàshà* 金茂大厦). Rising 1,379 feet (420.5 m) off the ground, it's the tallest building in China and hard to miss.

Constructed by the same team that built the Sears Tower in Chicago, the building symbolizes wealth and prosperity with Buddhist symbolism gone post-modern. It has 88 floors (8 is a lucky number in Chinese) and 13 bands, which is symbolic in Buddhism. Its name carries several meanings from "economy and trade" to "gold and prosperity." Whatever the backers had in mind, one thing is for sure, it's doing everything they wanted. Fortune 500 firms and joint ventures all share the same office space in this giant monolith. The floors are well guarded and only two areas are open to the public: the **observation floor** on the 88th floor and the restaurant and bar in the **Shanghai Grand Hyatt Hotel**(*shànghǎi jīnmào jūnyuè dàjiǔdiàn* 上海金茂君悦大酒店). The entrance to the high-speed elevators are in the high-tech basement and for those who aren't drunk from the view, there's the Cloud 9 bar on the 87th floor. Head into the Grand Hyatt Hotel and signs will point you the way. There's also a restaurant and café in the Grand Hyatt that offers great views if the haze isn't too bad. Be sure to check out the main lounge and try not to fall over when looking up at the gigantic open atrium.

Head back to earth and back towards the Pearl Tower. Pass the behemoth Super Brand Shopping Mall and follow the sound of ship

The Nanpu Bridge crosses the Huangpu River, connecting Puxi with the newly developed Pudong.

Oriental Pearl Tower in Pudong.

horns, and you'll soon find yourself overlooking the old Bund. There are numerous restaurants and café on the walkways and vendors selling souvenirs, sodas and teas. Outdoor seating allows visitors to sit in the sun and drink in the river view. It's best to come here just before dusk and get a good table. That way you can drink and eat to your heart's content while watching the old buildings on the Bund light up at sunset. It's a nice way to close a fine day in the Pudong or begin a wild Shanghai night.

Along metro line 2 is **Century Park** (*shìjì gōngyuán* 世纪公园) and the **Shanghai Science and Technology Museum** (*shànghǎi kējì guǎn* 上海科技馆). Both are good places to visit if you happen to be farther out in Pudong. Century Park has large tracts of grass and a sizeable lake. The science museum features many interactive displays and an IMAX theater that'll please children who don't appreciate architecture and history.

Jin Mao Tower 金茂大厦 *jīnmào dàshà*
✉ 88 Century Boulevard, Pudong
浦东世纪大道 88 号
☎ 5049 1234
🕒 8:30am to 9pm
¥ 50 for adults,
25 for children to the observation deck

Oriental Pearl TV Tower
东方明珠电视塔 *dōngfāng míngzhū diànshìtǎ*
✉ 1 Century Boulevard, Pudong
浦东世纪大道 1 号
☎ 5879 1888
🕒 8:30am to 9pm
¥ 100 for adults for access to all levels,
75 for children

Shanghai Ocean Aquarium 上海海洋水族馆 *shànghǎi hǎiyáng shuǐzú guǎn*
✉ 158 Yincheng North Road, Pudong
浦东银城北路 158 号
☎ 5877 9988
🕒 9am to 8:30pm
¥ 110 for adults, 70 for children

JADE BUDDHA TEMPLE

Located in the northwest part of Shanghai and tucked away amidst a jumble of charming turn of the century two-story cottages and small glass office buildings, the **Jade Buddha Temple** (*yùfó sì* 玉佛寺) is a spiritual oasis in the midst of a booming city.

The heavily renovated temple was built with Song dynasty architecture in 1918 to house two legendary jade Buddhas. Its mustard yellow outer walls are shrouded with bamboo scaffolding and lined with queues of tourists and worshippers alike. Devotees carry clusters of burning joss sticks and bow in front of the **Hall of Heavenly Kings** (*tiānwáng diàn* 天王殿), a giant cavern that holds humbling statues of various golden and bearded arhats that tower over those who enter. Wander past the **Grand Hall** towards the back of the compound and follow the signs to the Abbott Room, where the jade Buddhas resides.

The two Buddhas in the Abbot room were once part a magnificent five-piece jade collection brought to China from Myanmar by a Chinese monk. The larger of the two Buddhas is encrusted in jewels. It was hand-chiseled and polished from white jade and stands 6.2 feet (1.9 m) tall. On each side of this statue is a famous collection of Buddhists texts printed from woodblocks in 1890. At 35 inches (90 cm), the other Buddha is smaller, but is just as impressive with light glinting off its elegant jade body as it reclines languidly. A gnarled sandalwood trunk with carved Chinese characters and displays of late-Qing handicrafts add to the charm of this building. On the first floor outside the Abbot room are several gift shops selling everything from paper prints to traditional Chinese paintings to sandalwood fans and Buddha figurines carved from pure jade.

Crossing the courtyard back to the entrance to the Abbot room is a corridor that takes visitors to a splendid traditional Chinese teashop. The temple entrance fee includes a ticket to sample different sets of tea that can remedy everything from headaches to indigestion. There's a polite sales pitch included, but all of the proceeds go to the temple.

Across the hall from the tearoom is a vegetarian restaurant that serves all manner of lunch dishes, many of which are fashioned into mouthwatering faux-meat entrees. Enclosed in a walled courtyard is a Buddhist research library that has some English books. The bald monks and jade Buddhas provide a visual and spiritual break from Shanghai's frenetic drive to buy, eat and spend.

Jade Buddha Temple 玉佛寺 *yùfó sì*
✉ 170 Anyuan Road 安远路 170 号
☎ 6266 2668
🕒 8:30am to 5pm
¥ 10, 5 to see the jade Buddhas

A jade Buddha in the Jade Buddha Temple.

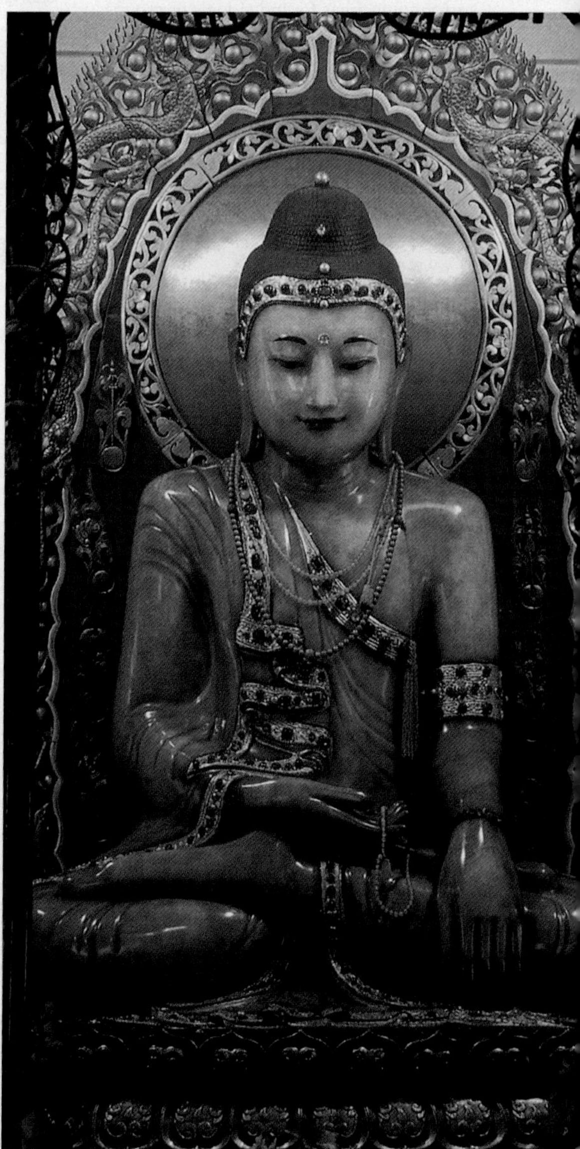

Making Your Trip Easy

Tours & Travel Groups

Most four and five star hotels can make domestic and international airplane, train and bus reservations for their guests. Furthermore, they can organize guided sightseeing tours of Shanghai and the surrounding areas for individuals or groups.

Alternatively, you can buy tickets or book Shanghai tours on your own by calling one of the following agencies.

China International Travel Service Shanghai Branch 中国国际旅行社上海分社 *zhōngguó guójì lǚxíngshè shànghǎi fēnshè*

1277 Beijing West Road 北京西路 1277 号

6289 8899

www.scits.com

China Travel Service Shanghai Branch 中国旅行社上海分社 *zhōngguó lǚxíngshè shànghǎi fēnshè*

881 Yan'an Middle Road 延安中路 881 号

6247 8888

Shanghai Airlines International Travel Service Co., Ltd. 上海航空国际旅游公司 *shànghǎi hángkōng guójì lǚyóu gōngsī*

3/F, 599 Jiangsu Road 江苏路 599 号 3 楼

6252 4466

satim@online.sh.cn

Tourism Complaint

2525 Zhongshan West Road 中山西路 2525 号

6439 0630, 6439 3615

9am to 5pm

Maps

A good map of Shanghai will be a helpful complement to the one in this book. Given the massive construction craze going on in

Pudong's City Hall.

the city, it's impossible to find an accurate map detailing all of the narrow *longtangs* (alleyways), but good maps can be found that provide the names of roads and major sites in Chinese characters, *pinyin* and English. The best local maps are found at Shanghai Foreign Languages Bookshop; detailed maps can also be found in most hotel gift shops as well.

Newspapers, Magazines & Bookstores

Newstands in Shanghai only feature two daily English newspapers, *China Daily* and *Shanghai Daily* and the weekly *Shanghai Star*. For international newspapers or magazines such as the *Asian Wall Street Journal*, *International Tribune*, *Time* or *The Economist*, head to the five star hotels. *that's Shanghai*, *Metrozine*, *Quo* and *Whenever Shanghai* (Japanese) are monthly magazines that provide detailed listings of ongoing events and hot spots. They can be found in most venues that attract a large crowd of foreigners such as the main hotels, Starbucks and at most restaurants in Xintiandi.

Fuzhou Road is the main nerve for bookshops in Shanghai. Here you can buy everything from basic Mandarin phrase books to fashion magazines to the latest novels.

Old China Hand Reading Room
汉源书店 *hànyuán shūdiàn*
This cozy little bookstore is tucked in a quiet tree-lined street in the former French Concession. The interior is furnished with an eclectic collection of antiques and knick-knacks from Shanghai's past.
✉ 27 Shaoxing Road 绍兴路 27 号
☎ 6473 2526
@ www.han-yuan.com

Scholar Books 思考乐书局 *sīkǎolè shūjú*
Cozy bookstore adjacent to a Starbucks with a modest but good selection of foreign and language books on the 3rd floor.
✉ 567 Fuzhou Road 福州路 567 号
☎ 6322 3770

Shanghai Foreign Languages Bookshop
上海外文书店 *shànghǎi wàiwén shūdiàn*
Features mostly Chinese-English language books on the first floor and has an impressive collection of foreign books on the 4th floor.
✉ 390 Fuzhou Road 福州路 390 号

The newly constructed Pudong International Airport is the first sight most visitors see.

☎ 6468 7249

Shanghai's City of Books
上海书城 *shànghǎi shūchéng*
Mammoth building clogged with avid readers; visit the 7th floor for the collection of foreign books.
✉ 465 Fuzhou Road 福州路 465 号
☎ 6352 2222

Transportation

Shanghai is a key hub with daily connections by air and rail to thousands of destinations in China and beyond. Transportation options within the city itself are plentiful. Though most international flights are now through Pudong International Airport, some are still operated from Hongqiao Airport, so be sure which airport you need to go to.

AIRPORT

Hongqiao Airport 虹桥机场
Hongqiao Airport is located on the eastern edge of central Shanghai and is easily reached by private hotel shuttles and taxis. This airport handles all domestic flights throughout mainland China and Hainan Island and some international flights. The departure tax is RMB 50, and international

Shanghai's public works department paints the city's public spaces to keep things looking neat and clean.

tax is RMB 90.
✉ 2550 Hongqiao Road 虹桥路 2550 号
☎ 6268 8918

Getting to/from the airport: Taxis from this relatively central location to most places in Shanghai should be around RMB 30 to 50. A RMB 15 toll is added to whatever is on the meter.

Shanghai Pudong International Airport
上海浦东国际机场
Located roughly 22 miles (35 km) from the heart of the city, this newly opened airport is Shanghai's door to the world. Departures are on the upper floor and arrivals on the bottom floor. Departing passengers on international flights must fill a departure card and pay the airport fee before heading to the security check. Because these procedures, in addition to check-in time, can be time consuming, airlines advise international passengers to show up at the airport 2.5 hours before departure.
✉ 100 Jiangzhenwei First Road, Pudong New District 浦东新区江镇纬一路 100 号
☎ 6834 1000, 3848 4500

Getting to/from the airport: Taxis are available outside the airport. A taxi to Pudong will cost around RMB 100 to 150; to Puxi it'll cost from RMB 130 to 160. If there's no traffic, the trip should be about 1 hour; if there is traffic, be prepared to wait.

Many upscale hotels can arrange for private cars or limousines to pick up and drop off guests. This service should cost RMB 120 to 300. Hotels also commonly operate airport shuttle buses. Be sure to reserve your private car or seat on a shuttle bus prior to your arrival or departure.

Also available are airport shuttle buses, but unless you know where to get off, it's probably better to take a cab.

For those who have somewhere to go quickly, the newly opened Maglev, which goes about 186 mph (300 kmh) per hour, runs from the airport to Pudong for RMB 50.

BICYCLE

You'd have to be a little bit crazy to brave the mind-boggling traffic of Puxi, but Pudong with its wide boulevards and parks are good for cycling enthusiasts. Though the roads in Shanghai aren't exactly great for biking, interesting daytrips can be made into the outlying areas.

Shenhuan Rickshaw Company
申环力车有限公司
Handles basic rentals from street to mountain bikes and offers repairs and equipment.

Quotes

"People say the Shanghainese have a certain attitude, and that's totally true. It's a mixture of boundless optimism and confidence that makes it so fun to party here."

"Try the hairy crabs when they're in season in early autumn. They're absolutely amazing, indescribably delicious."

✉ 456 Huaxia East Road, Pudong District
浦东区华夏东路 456 号
☎ 5857 9532, 5857 0440

Wolf's Bike Club 上海单车运动联合会
Caters to everything from custom-made bikes to extreme mountain bikes. Repairs, accessories and single and tandem bike rentals are also available. They also offer regular bike trips.

✉ Room103, No.12, Lane 2986, Hongqiao Road, Minhang District
闵行区虹梅路 2986 弄 12 号 103 室
☎ 700 210 140140, 6401 0632, 13801953000 (Mr. Wang)
www.shanghaicycling.org
@ Wolfsbike@hotmail.com

PUBLIC TRANSPORTATION

Shanghai has a highly efficient and clean subway system with two underground lines and an elevated light rail. The station announcements are in Chinese and English and signs are posted in pinyin, making the subway a convenient mode of transportation for foreigners. Avoid rush hour unless you want to know how sardines feel – expect a lot of jostling and be prepared to push and be pushed. Several more subway lines are under construction and are slated to open in 2006.

Subway lines 1 and 2 connect at People's Square, while the above ground line 3 connects at various stations. The subway maps are easy to understand and the exits are clearly marked and include English. The cost of tickets depends on distance traveled, with most costing between RMB 2 and 4.

While buses are mostly clean and comfortable, they may be hard for you to manage unless you understand Chinese, though most have screens or announcements that broadcast in English. Buses charge a fixed fare, usually RMB 1 for regular buses and RMB 2 for air-conditioned buses, or fares that depend on the distant traveled.

TAXI

Shanghai has some of the best taxis in China; the ubiquitous Volkswagen Santana and newer sports utility vehicles and vans are also starting to appear. All certified taxis have a white placard with the driver's picture, license number and stars, which designate rank. Flag-fall is RMB 10, most rides in Puxi will cost RMB 15 to 30, going to or from Pudong will cost more. It's best to have your destination written in Chinese, since most taxi drivers know very little or no English. Make sure to get the receipt (*fāpiào* 发票) which has the company's phone number and taxi number – you can complain about the service or call in if you've left something in the taxi. Taxis are everywhere and available at all hours. Companies are color-coded; the better companies tend to have taxis in better condition.

Dazhong Taxi Company 大众出租汽车公司
These taxis are light metallic blue.
☎ 6258 1688

Shanghai Qiangsheng Taxi
上海强生出租汽车公司
These taxis have a brownish-yellow paint scheme.
☎ 6258 0000

Shanghai's speedy subway.

Shanghai Youyi Taxi Company
上海友谊出租汽车公司
☎ 6258 4584

Taxi Complaint Hotline
☎ 6323 2150

TRAIN

Nearly all trains coming into and leaving Shanghai go through the Shanghai Train Station (*shànghǎi zhàn* 上海站) located in the northern part of the city. Some trains, however, operate from the South Train Station (*shànghǎi nánzhàn* 上海南站). Shanghai is well-connected to the rest of China. Comfortable trains go to Suzhou and

Hangzhou. Tickets can be bought at the station, but it's far more convenient to go through your hotel or travel agent.

Hotels

Garden Hotel Shanghai 上海花园饭店 *shànghǎi huāyuán fàndiàn* ★★★★★
✉ 58 Maoming South Road 茂名南路 58 号❻
☎ 6415 1111
¥ 1,490 – double room
@ www.gardenhotelshanghai.com

Grand Hyatt Shanghai
上海金茂君悦大酒店 *shànghǎi jīnmào jūnyuè dàjiǔdiàn* ★★★★★
✉ 88 Century Boulerard, Pudong 浦东世纪大道 88 号❿
☎ 5047 1234, 5047 1111
¥ 2,367 – double room
@ www.hyatt.com

Hilton Hotel Shanghai
上海静安希尔顿大酒店 *shànghǎi jìng'ān xī'ěrdùn dàjiǔdiàn* ★★★★★
✉ 250 Huashan Road 华山路 250 号❶
☎ 6248 0000, 6248 3848
¥ 1,100 – double room
@ www.shhilton.com

Huating Hotel
华亭宾馆 *huátíng bīnguǎn* ★★★★★
✉ 1200 Caoxi North Road 漕溪北路 1200 号
☎ 6439 1000, 6255 0830
¥ 768 – double room
@ www.huating-hotel.com

Inter Continental Pudong Shanghai
浦东新亚汤臣洲际大酒店 *pǔdōng xīnyà tāngchén zhōujì dàjiǔdiàn* ★★★★★
✉ 777 Zhangyang Road, Pudong New District 浦东新区张扬路 777 号
☎ 5831 8888, 583 1777
¥ 1,167 – double room
@ www.intercontinental.com

Jinjiang Hotel
锦江饭店 *jǐnjiāng fàndiàn* ★★★★★
✉ 59 Maoming South Road 茂名南路 59 号❹
☎ 6258 2582, 6472 5588
¥ 1,050 – double room
@ www.jinjianghotelshanghai.com

Jinjiang Tower 新锦江大酒店 *xīn jǐnjiāng dàjiǔdiàn* ★★★★★
✉ 161 Changle Road 长乐路 161 号❺
☎ 6415 1188, 6415 0048
¥ 1,243 – double room
@ www.jjtcn.com

Peace Hotel
和平饭店 *hépíng fàndiàn* ★★★★★
✉ 20 Nanjing East Road 南京东路 20 号❼
☎ 6321 6888, 6329 0300
¥ 1,100 – double room
@ www.shanghaipeacehotel.com

Pudong Shangri-La Hotel
浦东香格里拉大酒店 *pǔdōng xiānggélǐlā dàjiǔdiàn* ★★★★★
✉ 33 Fucheng Road, Pudong District 浦东富城路 33 号❾
☎ 6882 8888, 6882 6688
¥ 1,909 – double room
@ www.shanghai-la.com

Regal International East Asia Hotel
富豪环球东亚酒店 *fùháo huánqiú dōngyà jiǔdiàn* ★★★★★
✉ 516 Hengshan Road 衡山路 516 号❸
☎ 6415 5588 6445 8899
¥ 1,200 – double room
@ www.regal-eastaisa.com

Shanghai Marriott Hotel Hongqiao
上海万豪虹桥大酒店 *shànghǎi wànháo hóngqiáo dàjiǔdiàn* ★★★★★
✉ 2270 Hongqiao Road 虹桥路 2270 号
☎ 6237 6000, 6237 6222
¥ 1,432 – double room
@ www.marriot.com

Sheraton Grand Tai Ping Yang Shanghai Hotel 喜来登豪达太平洋大酒店 *xǐláidēng háodá tàipíngyáng dàjiǔdiàn* ★★★★★
✉ 5 Zunyi South Road 遵义南路 5 号
☎ 6275 8888, 6275 5420
¥ 1,173 – double room
@ www.westin-shanghai.com

Hotel Equatarial Shanghai 国际贵都大酒店 *guójì guìdū dàjiǔdiàn* ★★★★
✉ 65 Yan'an West Road 延安西路 65 号❷
☎ 6248 1688, 6248 1773
¥ 865 – double room
@ www.equatarial.com

Ocean Hotel
远洋宾馆 *yuǎnyáng bīnguǎn* ★★★★
✉ 1171 Dong Daming Road 东大名路 1171 号❽

Modern teahouses are popular with the young in Shanghai.

☎ 6545 8888
¥ 498 – double room
@ www.oceanhotel-sh.com

Food & Restaurants

Shanghai's restaurant business is fiercely competitive, forcing owners to continually push expectations higher. As more foreigners and Chinese continue to pour into Shanghai, expect to see Chinese food get more experimental and your choices of Western and Asian food expand. Like bars and nightclubs, new restaurants open and close here by the day. For the latest hotspots, it's always wise to consult the local English publications.

Throughout China, Shanghainese cuisine is known for being sweet and oily. For a true Shanghai specialty, try the hairy crab, a fresh water crab that becomes mature in fall – the crab roe is delectable. Another popular dish is the drunken shrimp – live shrimp are marinated in an alcohol-based marinade. They're a bit hard to eat because they squirm and jump in your hands, but they're delicious. A variation on this is drunken crab, where raw pieces of crab are marinated in a similar sauce. For street food, Shanghai's most famous contributions are the steamed buns (*xiǎolóng bāo* 小笼包) or fried meat dumplings (*shēngjiān bāo* 生煎包). Dining options are numerous in Shanghai. Because of Shanghai's large expat community, cuisines from all over the world are available, from delicate Japanese sushi to tender Brazilian barbeque. Choices are unlimited and so are the prices.

Most restaurants take reservations, and they are advised, as the Shanghainese love to eat out.

CHINESE RESTAURANTS

1221

Chic and quiet, 1221 is a favorite restaurant for romantic meals and large get-togethers. The spacey orange and white interior sets the pace for unearthly dining. The drunken crab appetizer is a local delight. All major credit cards are accepted.

✉ 1221 Yan'an West Road 延安西路 1221 号
☎ 6213 6585
🕒 11am to 2pm, 5pm to 11am

Bao Luo Restaurant 保罗酒楼

This place is packed almost anytime, day or night, but it's also deceptively large with spacious dining rooms and numerous private rooms tucked into the old building's nooks and crannies. For some Shanghainese favorites, try the red dates stuffed with sticky rice, the crabmeat tofu soup or the incredibly rich and tender *dongpo* meat. The service

Quotes

"Shanghai is probably the most glamorous city in China. Just head down to Xintiandi on Saturday night and you'll see all the snazziest people in this town partying it up."

"The Shanghai Museum is great. We spent the better part of the day there going through all the exhibition halls - the best part is there's actually English explanations that make sense. Afterwards we went down the Nanjing Road pedestrian street and checked out the small restaurants that branch from it. Walking down the Bund in the evening was a great way to end the day."

staff is competent and fast and large parties, often drinking Shaoxing wine, give the restaurant a heady, frenetic atmosphere.

✉ 271 Fumin Road, Luwan District
卢湾区富民路 271 号
☎ 5403 7239
🕒 10am to 6am

Meilongzhen 梅陇镇
lished in 1938, the colonial flare is maintained with its classic decor of marble furniture and paneled walls. Sichuan influences run throughout many of the dishes. Try the Sichuan duck or the Meilongzhen Special Chicken for a real treat. All major credit cards are accepted.

✉ No. 22, Lane 1081, Nanjing West Road, Jing'an District
静安区南京西路 1081 弄 22 号
☎ 6253 5353
🕒 11am to 1:30pm, 4pm to 10pm daily

Nanxiang Steamed Bun Restaurant
南翔馒头店
If there is a Shanghai institution for snack food and traditional local fare, this place is it. Not only is it located in the beautiful and historic Yu Garden, it's widely known throughout the city as the place to go for steamed dumplings. The restaurant complex actually consists of three separate dining rooms with prices increasing as you ascend. In the two upstairs dining rooms, traditional Shanghainese dishes and Cantonese dim sum abound. It fills up fast and waiting for a table is not uncommon. Even with the crowds and noise, if you want a taste of old Shanghai, don't miss the place. Look for the lines.

✉ 85 Yu Garden Road, Nanshi District
南市区豫园路 85 号
☎ 6326 5265
🕒 7am to 10pm

Shanghai Dexing Guan 上海德兴馆
✉ 29 Dongmen Road, Huangpu District
黄浦区东门路 29 号
☎ 6374 3772
🕒 6:30am to 8:30pm

Shanghai Laofandian 上海老饭店
✉ 242 Fuyou Road, Huangpu District
黄浦区福佑路 242 号
☎ 6311 1777
🕒 11:30am to 2:30pm, 5pm to 8:30pm

Summer Pavilion 夏苑
Aiming to be Shanghai's premier Cantonese restaurant, the Summer Pavilion is elegant and refined and the food is top notch. The menu ranges from Bird's Nest, Shark's Fin and Abalone to the more pedestrian dishes of Crispy Pigeon and Roast Duck. All major credit cards are accepted.

✉ Portman Ritz-Carlton, 1376 Nanjing West Road 南京西路 1376 号波特曼丽嘉酒店内
☎ 6279 8888 ext 4700
🕒 11:30am to 2:30pm, 5:30pm to 10:30pm

Yang's Kitchen 杨家厨房
Long renowned as one of the best restaurants for traditional Shanghainese fare, Yang's is set back in a charming lane off the leafy, ambling Hengshan Road. The atmosphere at Yang's is decidedly reserved and elegant but that doesn't mean the food is boring. The stewed eggplant pork mince (*ròumò qiéguā jiābǐng* 肉末茄瓜夹饼), rolled up into small pancakes, is outstanding. Yang's long tradition of quality cuisine and polite dining continues to draw both locals

and guests throughout the years. All major credit cards are accepted.

✉ No. 3, Lane 9 Hengshan Road, Xuhui District 徐汇区衡山路 9 弄 3 号

☎ 6445 8418

🕒 11am to 2pm, 5pm to 11pm

FOREIGN RESTAURANTS

Da Marco 大马可

Though quality Italian Restaurants continue to open both on their own and within fine hotels, Da Marco has true Shanghai staying power. A favorite with Italians living in Shanghai and with diners searching for true European ambiance, Da Marco offers fine Italian cuisine and a wide selection of wines. The squid ink pasta is an adventurous dish while the pizzas always please. All major credit cards are accepted.

✉ 103 Dongzhu Anbang Road, Jing'an District 静安区东诸安浜路 103 号

☎ 6210 4495

🕒 12pm to 11:30pm

Malone's 马龙

Originally opened by a Canadian chain, Malone's is Shanghai's premier American-style sports bar and grill. It easily makes the best burgers in town and its fries are crispy and light. Big screen televisions make it an ideal place to take in large sporting events and by night, live bands often whip the crowd into a frenzy. All major credit cards are accepted.

✉ 255 Tongren Street, Jing'an District 静安区铜仁路 255 号

☎ 6247 2400

🕒 11am to 2am

M on the Bund 米氏西餐厅

This may be Shanghai's most distinctive place for fine dining and classy drinks. Located on the 7th floor of the Huaxia Building on the Bund it offers magnificent views of both Pudong and of the Bund's colonial masterpieces. Even if you don't want to eat there, the sprawling terrace is the perfect place for a few drinks after work or before a night out on the town. M on the Bund has helped Shanghai win international acclaim as a city for haute cuisine. The menu is continental and European chefs prepare dishes with imagination and flair. The wine list is extensive and the bakery competent. If you're still not convinced, try the set lunch at

Century Boulevard leading to Century Park in Pudong.

RMB 98 or the Sunday brunch for RMB 188. All major credit cards are accepted.

✉ 7/F, 20 Guangdong Road, Huangpu District 黄浦区广东路 20 号 7 楼
☎ 6350 9988
🕒 11:30am to 2:30pm, 6:15pm to 12am

Sasha's 萨莎

Encamped in the palatial old Song Family Estate, Sasha's serves up continental fare with knowledge and expertise. Sit in the large, oak-paneled dining room where Chiang Kai-shek used to eat or in the ambling garden. Large fans resembling palm leaves sweep across the room in the summer recalling a scene out of Burmese Days.

Sasha's is probably best known for their Sunday brunch serving up incomparable Eggs Benedict and Eggs Florentine. Their food is always fresh and in recent years, summertime sees a large barbecue set up in the gardens. Choose from several different English beers on tap or browse through the extensive lists of wine and cordials. Sasha's is an ideal place to try and recapture Shanghai's colonial elegance. All major credit cards are accepted.

✉ House 11, 9 Dongping Road, Xuhui District 徐汇区东平路 9 号 11 幢
☎ 6474 6628
🕒 11am to 11pm

A couple taking a rest in front of the St. Ignatius Cathedral in Xujiahui.

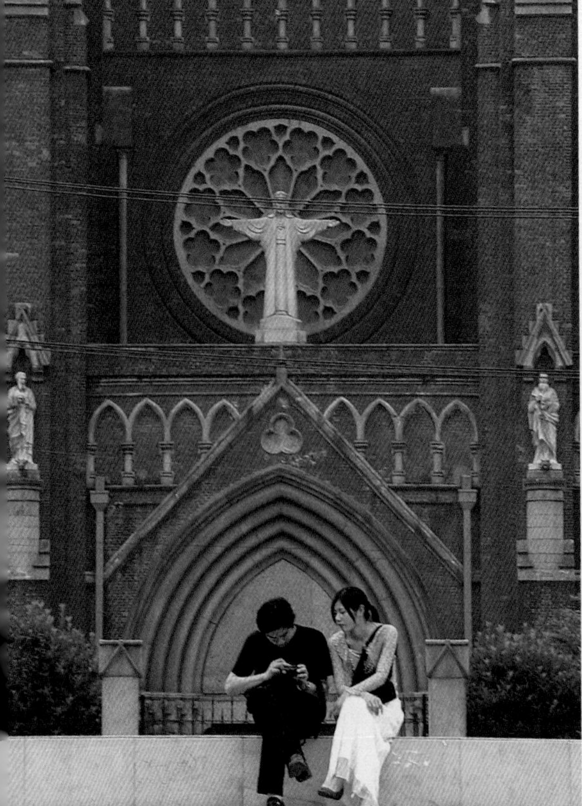

Nights Out in Shanghai

Shanghai didn't earn the nickname "Paris of the Orient" without good reason. Among the Chinese, its reputation, like New York City's, is one of endless nights. It's not far from the truth, as many bars stay open until 4am and later. Xintiandi and favorite bar streets Maoming Road and Julu Road are often packed till dawn while the clubs continue thumping away throughout the early mornings.

Like restaurants, nightlife in Shanghai is fast and furious with places opening up and closing down nearly daily. If you plan on staying in Shanghai for some time, it's worth looking into which bars and clubs have drink specials on which nights. Although it is still China, going out in Shanghai is often far from cheap.

For live entertainment and special engagements, check the local magazines to keep up to date. DJ's from all over Asia and the world come to spin and Shanghai is becoming increasingly popular with visiting jazz musicians. Although Shanghai's rock scene can't hold a candle to Beijing's, the local hip-hop scene and the DJ culture is strong.

CLUBS

Amber

A touch of style on Maoming Lu's infamous bar strip. Sophisticated patrons enjoy drink deals and being in the right place.

✉ 184 Maoming South Road, by YongjiaRoad 茂名南路 184 号，近永嘉路
☎ 6466 5224
🕒 6pm to 2am

Shanghai's city center, a mix of new and old.

ARK Live House

Open-space music bar format offers a variety of bands and welcome relief from cover band purgatory. Check Music Events for details. Free entry.

✉ House 15, North Block Xintiandi, Lane 181 Taicang Road, by Huang Pi South Road 太仓路 181 弄新天地广场北里 15 号，近黄陂南路

☎ 6326 8008

🕒 5:30pm to 1am

Bourbon Street

Three sprawling floors bustle with a hard-drinking, dice-cup slamming local crowd. Plenty of young ladies asking you to buy them a drink.

✉ 191 Hengshan Road, by Gao'an Road 衡山路 191 号，近高安路

☎ 6473 7911

🕒 7pm to 2am

Cotton Club

Modern Shanghai's first strong jazz club, Cotton Club draws a regular crowd as well as musicians on the Shanghai jazz circuit. Look for a mixture of jazz and blues with booming sound in a smoke filled room. Cotton Club is a bit cheaper than most of Shanghai's other jazz bars which is one reason for its' continuing popularity.

✉ 1428 Huaihai Middle Road 淮海中路 1428 号

☎ 6437 7110

🕒 7:30pm to 2am

Face

Set amongst the idyllic gardens of the Ruijin Guesthouse, Face combines sophisticated cool with ancient Chinese mystique. The terrace comes complete with opium beds upon which to sip your cocktails while heads of Buddhas and old stone statues gaze at you from the bar. Face has recently opened a branch in London. Long praised for having one of Shanghai's best happy hours and for knowing how to pour a good drink, Face attracts a wide variety of revelers both Chinese and foreign. In the summer, the gardens become a place for dancing and socializing while several fireplaces keep the winters warm. People often meet here for drinks after work and the pool table beside the bar is rarely empty.

✉ Building 4, Ruijin Guesthouse, 118 Ruijin Second Road
瑞金二路 118 号瑞金宾馆 4 号楼
☎ 6466 4328
🕒 6pm to late

Judy's Too
One of Shanghai's oldest watering holes has stood the test of time and is perpetually packed. The first floor is for drinking, dancing and jolly ogling. The upper area serves food.
✉ 176 Maoming South Road, by Yongjia Road 茂名南路 176 号,近永嘉路
☎ 6473 1417
🕒 8pm to late

Park 97
A complex consisting of a restaurant, two bars and a nightclub – Park 97, California Club and Upstairs draw Shanghai's fastest and hottest night after endless night. This is the place to see the corks on the Moet popping and sunglass clad hipsters shaking their heads away. A favorite of expats, wealthy Chinese and Shanghai's most stunning women, California Club has consistently good DJ's, a lively dance floor, and well-poured drinks.

Opened this past summer, Upstairs at Park 97 offers similar thrills at slightly lower prices in a significantly more low-key atmosphere. A Cuban band gets the dance floor going nightly while a backroom with a pool table offers welcome respite from the seething crowds.
✉ 2A Gaolan Road, inside Fuxing Park
皋兰路 2 号 A, 复兴公园内
☎ 5383 2328
🕒 6pm to late

Rojam Disco 罗杰舞台
A favorite of local hipsters and foreign students, Rojam's numerous specials and discounts draw a steady crowd throughout the week. The chill-out room in the back plays acid jazz and funk while the main dance floor is usually high-energy house. Ladies' night, foreigners' night, and students' night mean that cover charges are rarely of any consequence and the youthful crowd is friendly and warm. If you're ever looking to go out dancing on a Monday or Tuesday night, first try Rojam.

Shanghai's high-class nightlife at Xintiandi.

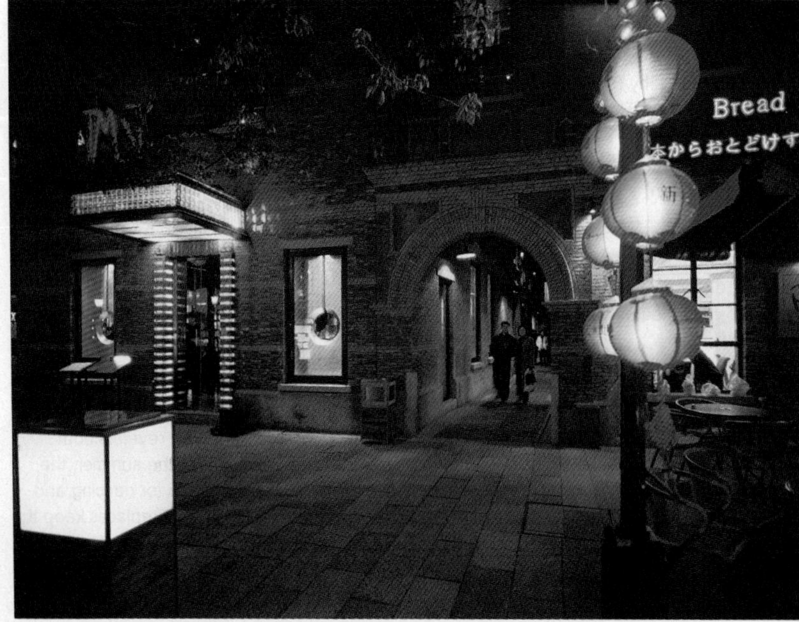

Memorable Experiences

Eating an exquisite candlelit dinner in the Jin Mao Tower at the Grand Hyatt and seeing the whole city spread before us.

Finishing off a dozen steamed dumplings after going on a shopping spree through the tiny antique shops in the Old City and buying tea sets and traditional Chinese paintings.

Going through all the sights along People's Square and Nanjing Road then heading across the river to Lujiazui and checking out the amazing aquarium and psychedelic Oriental Pearl TV Tower.

Every night eating cuisine from a different part of China or from a different part of the world.

✉ 4/F, Hong Kong Plaza, 283 Huaihai Middle Road 淮海中路 283 号香港大厦 4 层
☎ 6390 7181
🕒 8:30pm to 2am

BARS

Barbarossa 芭芭露莎
Built on a lake in Peoples Park, this beautifully decorated three story Moroccan lounge offers amazing skyline views and aromatic smells from the Sheesha pipes. Fantastic music, food and drinks selection, with indoor and outdoor seating Happy Hour 5-8pm, all drinks half price.
✉ 231 Nanjing Xi Lu, inside People's Park 南京西路 231 号,人民公园内
☎ 6318 0220
🕒 Sun-Thurs 11am-2am, Fri-Sat 11am-3am

Grand Hyatt
Various bars include the Piano Bar at the base of a soaring 33-storey atrium. Cloud 9 (87/F) is said to be the world's highest lounge with 360-degree views.
✉ Grand Hyatt Hotel, Jinmao Building, 88 Century Boulevard, Pudong 浦东世纪大道 88 号,金茂君悦酒店
☎ 5049 1234

House of Blues and Jazz
Housed in an old colonial villa, this spacious living room has been converted into one of Shanghai's best jazz and live music venues. Owner Li Dongfu parlayed his TV fame into nightclub notoriety when he opened in 2001. The stage is small but maintains a talented house band. Local and visiting musicians regularly stop by to sit in for a set and the talent frequently changes. Sturdy oak furnishing and a large, curving bar create the ideal atmosphere for sampling Shanghai's growing jazz scene. Soft, warm tones and sultry tunes float through the eclectic atmosphere and Li has been known to give noisemakers to audience members before pulling them up on stage. House of Jazz and Blues is truly a place to shine.
✉ 158 Maoming South Road, just south of Fuxing Road 茂名南路 158 号, 复兴路南
☎ 6437 5280
🕒 4pm to 2:30am

Long Bar 长廊酒吧
This bar and grill, named after the legendary "world's longest bar" that once stood in the Shanghai Club on the Bund, the Long Bar is a favorite for foreigners in Shanghai. With quality pub food, large-screen TV's, and a regularly updated jukebox, Long Bar is a good place to meet people after work. Their daily, 5 to 8pm happy hour features half-price pints of Guinness, one of the best deals in Shanghai.
✉ 2/F, Shanghai Center, 1376 Nanjing West Road 南京西路 1376 号上海商城 2 楼
☎ 6279 8268
🕒 11am to 2am

Noah's Bar 诺雅
Another locally treasured watering hole, Noah's has the views of M on the Bund without the frightening prices. Sitting atop one of Shanghai's more reasonably priced hostels, Noah's makes good bar food, pours nice drinks, and looks directly out over Pudong's magnificent skyline. The bar and restaurant is glassed in, giving the

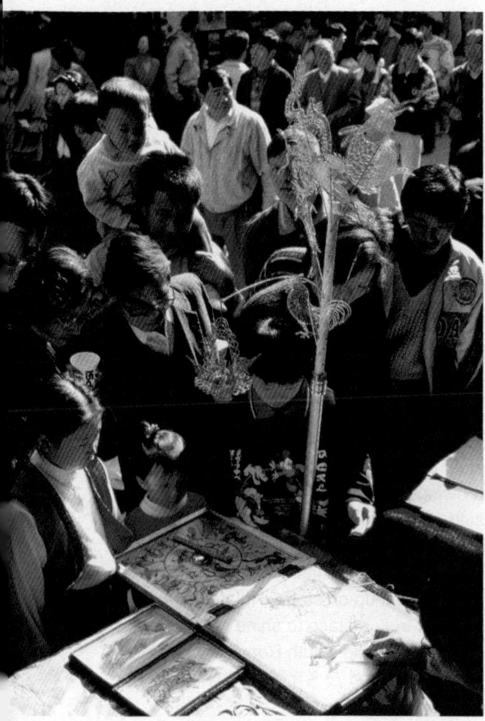

A sugar figure artist in Chenghuang Temple.

impression of a ship at sea while the patio looks like the ship's bow stuck out over the water. After entering Captain's Hostel, take the elevator to the top floor and continue up the stairs.

✉ 6/F, 37 Fuzhou Road 福州路 37 号 6 楼
☎ 6323 7869
🕒 11am to 2am

O'Malley's Bar 欧玛莉

Built in honor of Irish pirate queen Maggie O'Malley, O'Malley's enjoys a long tradition as Shanghai's premier Irish pub. With Guiness and Kilkenny's on tap, as well as their own home brew, O'Malley's is an expat favorite. Situated on the large compound of an old colonial villa, O'Malley's beer garden is packed all summer long. Entertainment at O'Malley's regularly fluctuates between large sporting events televised regularly and the weekend antics of their house Irish band. Designed with the feel of an old pirate ship, the decor is intimate and warm while large tables and booths welcome Shanghai's hardest working and hardest drinking expats.

✉ 42 Taojiang Road, Xuhui District
徐汇区桃江路 42 号
☎ 6474 4533
🕒 11am to 1am

Red Room 鼎红

With all drinks priced at a reasonable RMB 20 and a soundtrack that covers all musical genres while offending no one, this place is as comfortable as the proverbial girl-next-door.

✉ 2F 139 Rui Jin Yi Lu, by Changle Lu
瑞金一路 139 号 2 楼,近长乐路
☎ 1300 3170 171
🕒 8:00pm-late No cards

Room with View 顶层画廊/酒吧

✉ 479 Nanjing East Road 南京东路 479 号
☎ 6352 0256
🕒 3pm to 11pm

Time Passage 昨天・今天・明天

Tucked away on a small lane of the meandering Huashan Road, Time Passage is one of Shanghai's best-kept secrets. Drawing from a diverse selection of jazz, blues, rock, reggae and funk, Time Passage is decidedly laid-back. A long time favorite, local musicians jam frequently on the makeshift stage and audience participation is a must. Prices are reasonable and though it may be hard to find, Time Passage is well worth seeking out.

✉ No. 183, Lane 1038, Huashan Road, by Fuxing West Road
华山路 1038 弄 183 号,近复兴西路
☎ 6240 2588
🕒 5pm to late

Souvenirs

In Shanghai, nothing approaches the status of shopping. The Shanghainese are consummate shoppers with some of the best eyes for fashion and bargains in all of Asia. The city is literally filled with places where you can spend your money.

The major shopping districts are found in the Old French Concession near the Shaanxi South Road metro station, the Huangpi South Road metro station (including Xintiandi), in the Old International

Settlement on Nanjing West Road, and near the Bund along the Nanjing East Road Pedestrian Mall.

The most distinctive of all these places follows Shaanxi South Road between Yan'an Road to the north and Fuxing Road to the south. This strip and most of the roads branching off it are filled with stores selling shoes, famous label clothing at discount prices, antiques and curios.

A major highlight is just south of Huaihai Road where the Xiangyang Market buzzes with stands selling everything from imitation North Face and Louis Vuitton to Chinese silks and painted fans. The pace of this market is frenetic and on the weekends it often surges to near capacity. All prices are negotiable and hard bargaining pays off. If you know how much you want to pay, stick to your price and try walking away if they won't come down. Repeat visits often yield good friendships with the local merchants, though it's always wise to beware of shoddy merchandise – the old adage "you get what you pay for" often holds true.

The area around Huangpi South Road is filled with large department stores and clothing shops. Heading south from here brings you to Xintiandi, Shanghai's newest European-style arcade filled with high-end boutiques, restaurants and bars. Xintiandi draws large crowds whether by day or night. Shops featuring everything from haute couture to designer home furnishings buzz alongside Italian, Mexican and German restaurants as well as jazz and cigar bars.

The old International Settlement along Nanjing West Road is home to some of China's most exclusive shopping, including Cartier, Hermes and Louis Vuitton. Spread throughout several high-end shopping centers, it's a place where money is on display and many without come to gawk at those with.

At the other end of Nanjing Road, approaching the Bund along the pedestrian street, you come to what may be Shanghai's largest concentration of mid to low priced shops featuring everything from clothes to kitchen knives. Also being one of Shanghai's largest tourist areas, this part of Nanjing Road is always filled with people, many visiting Shanghai from other parts of China. It's a place to shop, to eat and drink, to people-watch and to stroll.

Angel Pearls 天使珍珠

Shanghai's finest selection of high-quality pearls. Angel's features a wide selection of freshwater, South Sea pearls, and Japanese cultured pearls.

✉ Room 104, 1/F Maosheng Mansion, 1051 Xinzha Road, Jing'an District
静安区新闸路 1051 号茂盛大厦一楼 104 室

☎ 6215 5031

Annly's Antique Warehouse
安丽家具有限公司

The best in custom-made Chinese-style sofas, chairs, draperies, and cushions.

✉ No. 68, Lane 7611, Zhongchun Road, Minhang District
闵行区中春路 7611 弄 68 号

☎ 6406 0242

🕒 9am to 6pm

Anthony Chao 朝安东尼丝绸

Domestic and overseas designers offer a wide selection of handmade silk pillows, rugs, handbags, bedding and trimmings in many styles. They can help you match items

An elegant tea set featuring China's most popular drink.

to your furniture as well. Silk pillow RMB 700, silk-covered photo album with jade decoration RMB 600, silk curtains RMB 5,000 per square meter (about 1.2 square yards).

✉ 4/F, Tianshan Building, 30 Tianshan Road, Changning District
长宁区天山路 30 号天山大厦 4 楼
☎ 6259 3060
🕒 9:30am to 6:30pm

Carpenter Tan 谭木匠
Focuses on wooden combs with some made from imported Brazilian timber. Some are dyed with the essence of herbs and some have even attained patents for their designs. Check out the folding combs. Combs are RMB 10 to 128.

✉ 75 Xiangyang South Road, by Huaihai Middle Road, Xuhui District
徐汇区襄阳南路 75 号，近淮海中路
☎ 139 0195 8718

Feel 金粉世家
Chinese traditional costume shop that sells its own designs and can make to order. Small selection of different types of traditional Chinese clothing with modern touches. Hemp jackets RMB 500, silk *qipao* RMB 400.

✉ No. 2, Lane 210, Taikang Road, by Sinan Road, Luwan District
卢湾区泰康路 210 弄 2 号，近思南路
☎ 5465 4519
🕒 10am to 10pm

Hong De Tang 鸿德堂
Located in a municipally-preserved building that was formerly a church. Offers Chinese and Western paintings, calligraphy works, antiques, curios and traditional embroidered items. Suzhou embroidery RMB 600-1,500, Chinese paintings RMB 1,480-28,500.

✉ 59 Duolun Road, by Sichuan North Road, Hongkou District
虹口区多伦路 59 号，近四川北路
☎ 5666 5518
🕒 9:30am to 6pm

Isetan 上海华亭伊势丹有限公司
This Japanese department store features high quality clothing, goods and furnishing at equally high prices. Located in the heart of Huaihai Road's shopping district, Isetan has an exceptional variety of goods from Japan and the world over.

✉ 527 Huaihai Middle Road, Luwan District
卢湾区淮海中路 527 号
☎ 5306 1111

Liuli Gongfang 琉璃工坊
Every piece of Liuli work on display tells a story, with most of them representing lessons from traditional Chinese ethics. The beautiful, peaceful works include Buddhist statues, tableware, ritual vessels and Chinese horoscope. Auspicious Kwan Yin RMB 9,000, Soaring High Above (a Liuli horse) RMB 30,000.

✉ 1/F, Central Plaza, 381 Huaihai Middle Road, by Madang Road, Luwan District
卢湾区淮海中路 381 号，近马当路，中环广场 1 楼
☎ 6273 7745
🕒 10am to 10pm

Maison Mode 上海美美百货
Modern Shanghai's first upscale department store, Maison Mode is filled with European designer boutiques. At the base of their stunning glass atrium, there's a charming café to rest in after a hard day's shopping.

✉ 1312 Huaihai Middle Road, Xuhui District
徐汇区淮海中路 1312 号⓫
☎ 6437 5970, 6431 0100

New World Department Store 新世界
Located where Nanjing Road's neon-lit pedestrian street begins, New World features a wide variety of Western clothing and cosmetics at more reasonable prices than many other high-end boutiques.

Quotes

"Shanghai is so full of energy it's like one big nuclear power station. This is a city that never sleeps. Walk down any street and you'll find a small restaurant or shop or convenience store. People go to sleep late and wake early here."

"This city is changing so unbelievably quickly. I came back after going back home for a month and I got lost trying to find my apartment."

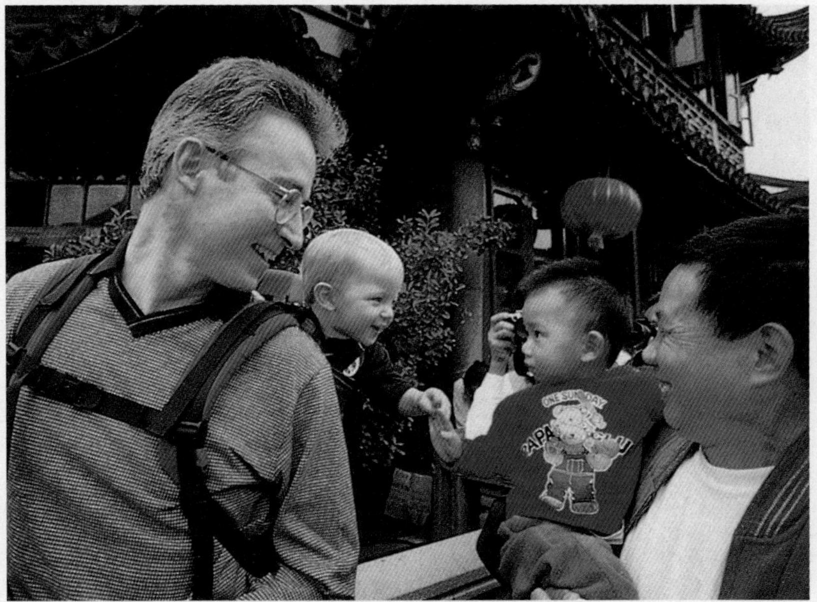

With each generation, China is becoming more and more multicultural.

✉ 2-68 Nanjing West Road, Huangpu District 黄浦区南京西路 2-68 号⑫
☎ 6358 8888

Nisar Antique Carpets 上海尼沙贸易商行
Shanghai's widest selection of high quality woven dreams from Xinjiang, Tibet, Mongolia and Central Asia. For the past 20 years, proprietor Ahmad Nisar has been scouring the earth to bring the high quality antique carpets to Shanghai. The gallery also regularly features the works of local artists.
✉ Room 315, Pujiang Hotel, 15 Huangpu Road 黄浦路 15 号浦江饭店 315 房⑬
☎ 6324 5974

Old Zhou Huchen Writing Brush Shop
老周虎臣笔墨庄
The old store presents a collection of tools for traditional Chinese calligraphy and painting arts, such as writing brushes and seals. Writing brushes RMB 3-1,320, yantai (ink slab) RMB 150-14,000.
✉ 179 Henan Middle Road, by Fuzhou Road, Huangpu District
黄浦区河南中路 179 号，近福州路
☎ 6329 7959
🕒 8:30am to 4:30pm

Shanghai Arts and Crafts Shopping Center 上海工艺美术商厦
A virtual supermarket for jewelry, clothing, chops and furniture – this arts and crafts emporium has been wooing visitors for years. Prices are not low but hard bargaining may yield some good deals.
✉ 190 Nanjing West Road, Huangpu District
黄浦区南京西路 190 号
☎ 6327 5299

Shanghai Jingdezhen Porcelain Artware
上海景德镇艺术陶瓷公司
Occupying prime real estate, this porcelain boutique features some of the finest crafts to be made and sold in China. Vases, plates, cups and artware are expensive here, but the quality is guaranteed.
✉ 1185 Nanjing West Road, Jing'an District
静安区南京西路 1185 号
☎ 6253 3178, 6253 8865

Shanghai Jade Caving Factory
上海玉石雕刻厂
A chance to combine a factory tour with shopping – some of Shanghai's finest jade ornaments, furnishings and jewelry are featured here.

Lu Xun is one of China's most revered writers.

✉ 33 Caobao Road, Xuhui District
徐汇区漕宝路 33 号
☎ 6436 0126

Silk Fabrics King Silk King
上海真丝商厦有限公司
A favorite stop for visiting diplomats, with silk available by the yard and in a good selection of clothing.
✉ 819 Nanjing West Road, Jing'an District
静安区南京西路 819 号
☎ 6215 3114

Art Galleries

Art50 旋宫 *xuán gōng*
✉ 50/F, 728 Pudong Boulevard
浦东大道 728 号 50 楼
☎ 5036 6666 ext 1688
🕒 11am to 11pm

Art Scene China
艺术景画廊 *yìshùjǐng huàláng*
✉ No. 8, Lane 37, Fuxing West Road
复兴西路 37 弄 8 号
☎ 6437 0631
🕒 11am to 9pm
@ www.artscenechina.com

Art Scene Warehouse
艺术景仓库 *yìshùjǐng cāngkù*
✉ 2/F, Building 4, 50 Mogan Shan Road
莫干山路 50 号 4 幢 2 楼
☎ 6437 0631
@ www.artscenechina.com

Aura Gallery 亦安画廊 *yì'àn huàláng*
✉ 5/F, 713 Dong Daming Road
东大名路 713 号 5 楼
☎ 6595 0901
🕒 10am to 5pm

Cang Bo Gallery 藏博堂 *cángbó táng*
✉ 9 North Block Xintiandi 新天地北里 9 号
☎ 6336 5862
🕒 11am to 1pm

D&D Coffee Gallery 达达艺苑 *dádá yìyuàn*
✉ No. 1, Lane 229, Huaihai West Road
淮海西路 229 弄 1 号
☎ 6281 5877
🕒 10am to 9pm

Highlight Gallery 海莱画廊 *hǎilái huàláng*
✉ 86 Wulumuqi Middle Road
乌鲁木齐中路 86 号
☎ 5404 5511
🕒 9am to 9pm

Madame Mao's Dowry
毛太设计 *máotài shèjì*
✉ 70 Fuxing West Road 复兴西路 70 号
☎ 6437 1255
🕒 10am to 6pm

The Room With a View
顶层画廊 *dǐngcéng huàláng*
✉ 12/F, 479 Nanjing West Road
南京西路 479 号 12 楼
☎ 6352 0256

ShangART 香格纳画廊 *xiānggénà huàláng*
✉ 2A Gaolan Road, inside Fuxing Park
皋兰路 2 号 A，复兴公园内
☎ 6359 3923
🕒 10am to 7pm

Shanghai Eye Level Gallery
上海视平线画廊 *shànghǎi shìpíngxiàn huàláng*
✉ Building 16, 50 Moganshan Lu 莫干山路 50 号 16 号楼

☎ 6234 0599
🕒 9am to 6pm

Other Information

POST OFFICES

Huangpu Post Office 黄浦邮电局
✉ 414 Fujian Middle Road 福建中路 414 号
☎ 6322 3152

Shanghai General Post Office
上海邮政总局
✉ 276 North Suzhou Road 北苏州路 276 号⑭
☎ 6393 6666

Xuhui Post Office 徐汇邮电局
✉ 105 Tianyao Qiao Road 天钥桥路 105 号⑮
☎ 6464 8177

HOSPITALS

Shanghai has one of the highest standards of living anywhere in China and there are at least five excellent hospitals where the staff speaks English and have foreign trained doctors that offer Western standards of healthcare. Most offer onsite pharmacies. All are open 24 hours for walk-in services, but appointments are advised. Prices can be quite high – around US $100 for a simple problem.

Huadong Hospital 华东医院
✉ 221 Yan'an West Road, Changning District 长宁区延安西路 221 号⑯
☎ 6248 3180

Huashan Hospital Foreigner's Clinic
华山医院
✉ 19/F, 12 Wulumuqi Middle Road 乌鲁木齐中路 12 号 19 层⑰
☎ 6248 9999

International Medical Care Centre of Shanghai, First People's Hospital
上海市第一人民医院国际医疗保健中心
✉ 585 Jiulong Road 九龙路 585 号⑲
☎ 6324 3852

International beauties pose in China's international city.

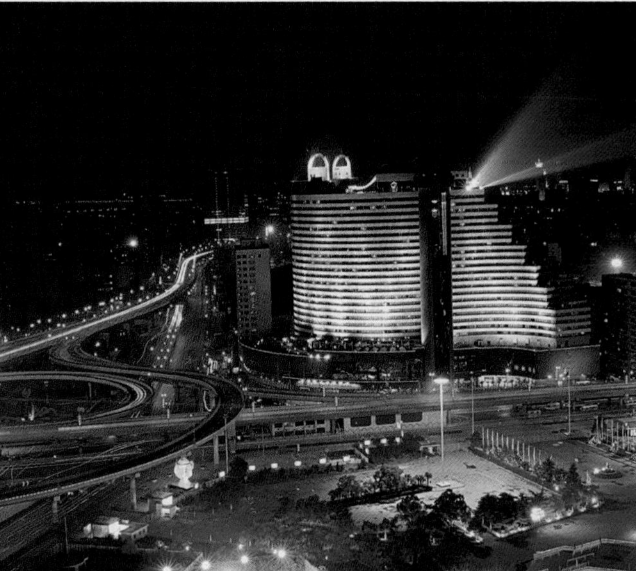

Huating Hotel's opulence is typical of Shanghai's modern style.

Ruijin Hospital 瑞金医院

Building 2, 197 Ruijin Road, Luwan District 卢湾区瑞金路 197 号 2 幢⑱

6437 0045

World Link 瑞新医疗中心

1376 Nanjing West Road 南京西路 1376 号

6279 7688

www.worldlink-shanghai.com

CONSULATES

Most of the foreign consulates are found at the Shanghai Centre on Nanjing Road and along Huaihai Road. The following consulates can assist with any problems or emergencies that might arise and connect you with embassies in Beijing if necessary.

Australia 澳大利亚

22/F, CITIC Square, 1168 Nanjing West Road 南京西路 1168 号中信泰福广场 22 楼

5292 5500

5292 5511 (Fax)

Canada 加拿大

Room 604, West Tower, Shanghai Center, 1376 Nanjing West Road 南京西路 1376 号上海商城西塔 604 室

6279 8400

6279 8401 (Fax)

France 法国

23B, Qihua Building, 1375 Huaihai Middle Road 淮海中路 1375 号启华大厦 23B

6289 7414

6279 2249 (Fax)

Germany 德国

Shimen First Road, 188 Wujiang Road 吴江路 188 号石门一路

6217 2884

6271 4650 (Fax)

Ireland 爱尔兰

Suite 700A, West Tower, Shanghai Center,1376 Nanjing West Road 南京西路 1376 号上海商城西塔 700A 房间

6279 8729

6279 8739 (Fax)

Malaysia 马来西亚

11F, 1168 Nanjing West Road 南京西路 1168 号 11 楼

5292 5424

5292 5951 (Fax)

New Zealand 新西兰

15A, Qihua Building, 1375 Huaihai Middle Road 淮海中路 1375 号启华大厦 15A

6471 1108

6431 4970 (Fax)

United Kingdom 英国

Room 301, West Tower, Shanghai Center, 1376 Nanjing West Road 南京西路 1376 号上海商城西塔 301 室

6279 7650

6279 8254 (Fax)

United States 美国

1469 Huaihai Middle Road 淮海中路 1469 号

6433 6880

6433 4122 (Fax)

Tai Shan, the Mountain of the Gods

Area Code 0538

Heritage: Tai Shan

Tai Shan's importance to Chinese mythology cannot be overstated. Visiting the mountain is more than a mountain-climbing excursion; it's a pilgrimage to China's most sacred mountain.

Centuries ago Confucius stood at the summit of Tai Shan and declared: "The world is small." Though you may feel a little small riding the cable car as it dangles between heaven and earth, it quickly transports visitors to the summit. Tai Shan has long been known as the sacred haven that links Heaven and Earth, and it's the most significant of the five Taoist mountains in China. According to Chinese mythology, the five sacred mountains were formed by the body of Pangu, the creator of the universe. Tai Shan sprouted from his head when his body broke apart.

Tai Shan itself has become more than a mountain – it has been given noble titles, elevated to divine status and given honors equal to emperor. Tai Shan has a long history of receiving awards: the first emperor of China made a tree an officer after he sought refuge under it during a storm. The mountain has been revered for eons and is central to Chinese mythological beliefs. Because Tai Shan is the highest point in eastern China, and the east was once thought to be where heaven and earth were linked, Tai Shan become a dominant symbol. Throughout China, symbols of Tai Shan abound, whether used as a good luck charm to invoke the powers of the earth or in the numerous temples dedicated to the mountain.

The mountain was originally where the emperors made offerings to Heaven and Earth (*fēng shàn* 封禅), but this practice was discontinued when the Temple of Heaven (*tiān tán* 天坛) and the Temple of Earth (*dì tán* 地坛) were built in Beijing during the Ming dynasty. Prior to that, for thousands of years, kings and emperors would climb Tai Shan to make their offerings; this was the most important of their imperial duties – to insure the mandate of heaven was maintained.

Standing a majestic 5,068 feet (1,545 m) above sea level, Tai Shan evokes both awe

Poetry and calligraphy add a literary side to Tai Shan's natural scenery.

and contemplation for all who stand atop gazing outward. It's inspiring to wander around Tai Shan imagining great poets carving their works into the stone walls and steles that speckle the mountainside; the area around **Jingshiyu** (*jīngshíyù* 经石峪) is the best place to see these great works. Your daydreams of beauty, however, may be interrupted by the shouts and beckoning of local vendors selling everything from incense to Halloween skeletons with chattering teeth.

From the city of Tai'an, at the base of the mountain, there are two ways to get to the top; you can brave the steps or you can take a combination of bus and cable car. A RMB 10 taxi ride from Tai'an will take you to **First Gate of Heaven** (*yītiān mén* 一天门), the starting point of the **central route**, which is also the most popular and dotted with historic sights. From there, buses depart regularly for **Middle Gate of Heaven** (*zhōngtiān mén* 中天门) and you can start your ascent. Be prepared for a throng of vendors that may very well surround your bus as it waits; during the low season they'll be particularly aggressive.

The Middle Gate of Heaven is the half-way point from the base to the summit and many unburden themselves of heavier luggage by checking into a guesthouse. There's a cable car that will whisk you to **Moon Viewing Peak** (*yuèguān fēng* 月观峰) just a short walk from **South Gate of Heaven** (*nántiān mén* 南天门) which is close to the summit. Here, you'll witness the compelling draw of the sacred mountain when meeting the legions of senior citizens climbing the 6,660 stone steps, a mere 4.3 miles (7 km). One climber, a woman in her seventies, made it clear

Tai Shan's rugged peak is the spectacular reward after a grueling climb.

through a series of gestures that the gods look more fondly on those who actually scale Tai Shan step by step than folks who opt for the luxury of the 8-minute cable car ride. These senior devotees were not the only ones on the imposing stone steps. The residents and shopkeepers of the Tai Shan temple complex still carry all their water and supplies up the mountain, shaking their heads at the extravagance of the cable car.

For those who actually climb Tai Shan, the central route, **Hongmen Route** (*hóngmén lù* 红门路), is lined with sights that have been graced with imperial presence and are commemorated with much calligraphy. Poets have long been drawn to the beauty and mystique of Tai Shan, many have waxed lyrical over Tai Shan and had their musings eternalized in stone. There are also numerous religious carvings, such as Buddhist sutras carved into the mountain face.

Tai Shan is home to a large group of temples and generously sprinkled with ornate entryways and cobbled paths. There are teahouses where you can sit outside sipping fragrant tea and admire the graceful peaks opposite. Wandering around will bring little surprises such as intricately carved archways, spectacular vistas and temples that have seen pilgrims for centuries. Photos are easily the best souvenir Tai Shan has to offer any visitor – the views are breathtaking.

The highlight of the mountain is the Song dynasty **Azure Cloud Temple** (*bìxiá cí* 碧霞祠). According to legend, Bixia is the local deity of Tai Shan and revered particularly by women. Her temple sees many women burning incense and praying for good fortune and a happy future for their progeny – or praying to have children if they haven't been so blessed. Tranquility mixes with transcendence when strolling around the large temple – the incense wafts through the

halls and turning a corner reveals the vastness of the peaks and open views.

While on the mountain be sure to visit the **Jade Emperor's Peak** (*yùhuáng dǐng* 玉皇顶). Perched on this summit is a temple dedicated to the Jade Emperor, ruler of the Chinese celestial world, which is an eclectic mixture of popular Confucian, Taoist and Buddhist beliefs. **Sun Viewing Peak** (*rìguān fēng* 日观峰) is the best vantage point for the sunrise visits that Tai Shan is so famous for – it's also where the hordes of other visitors will come to see the sunrise. When you're ready to head back down the mountain, you can catch the six-passenger cable car from Nantian Gate to **Peach Blossom Garden** (*táohuā yuán* 桃花源) and continue along the western route. You'll find yourself at the back of the mountain strolling downward through green and ambling scenery with smooth roads and lots of arborous sections to explore. There are clean public bathrooms as well as food and souvenir shops along the way, and buses transport you the rest of the way for RMB 15. They're often full, but at the end of a long day of climbing you'll be happy to board the bus and take a break, sitting or standing. The journey down the mountain is scenic, if a little cramped.

At the foot of Tai Shan is **Dai Temple** (*dài miào* 岱庙), where emperors would perform their sacrificial ceremonies in honor of the mountain. These ceremonies were held as early as the Qin dynasty by the first emperor. A Han dynasty palace was later built on the grounds. It saw constant expansion by later dynasties and was given the same form as the imperial palace. Today it's a sprawling million square feet (96,000 m^2). Because of the importance of the Dai Temple, the best materials were put into its construction and maintenance. The main structure in this complex is **Tiankuang Hall** (*tiānkuàng diàn* 天贶殿), which was built in 1009 on orders from the Song emperor The massive hall, which stands on a rectangular stone base, is 160 feet (48.7 m) long, 65 feet (19.7 m) wide, and reaches 73 feet (22.3 m) high. Inside stands a statue of the god of Tai Shan. On the east, west and north walls are large paintings of the Tai Shan deity on an inspection of his domain with a large entourage of 691. Put together the three paintings measure 203 feet (62 m) long and 10.8 feet (3.3 m) high. ■

Making Your Trip Easy

Practical Tips

High season is from May to October when the weather is warmest, with spring and autumn being the busiest – especially during the national holidays. During the off-season things will be more relaxed and the skies are clearer, but you'll be digging into your backpack for more layers. Wool sweaters, socks, hats and windbreakers will prove a godsend in this heavenly venue as the weather can change rapidly – and being so close to heaven, the summit is quite chilly. Carry lots of layers, a flashlight, a small first aid kit, a pocket knife, lots of snacks and a pack of disposable wipes for dirty hands and tables.

If you're lucky you might be able to catch a reenactment of the ancient and elaborate ceremonial offerings to Heaven and Earth.

Transportation

Airport – The closest airport is the Ji'nan

The sun rises over a sea of clouds at Tai Shan.

International Airport. From the airport to Tai'an by taxi is about 90 minutes. If you take the bus, it'll first go to Ji'nan Long Distance Bus Station, about 40 minutes. From the bus station to Tai'an is about 50 minutes.

Taxi – Flag-fall is RMB 5 during the day and RMB 5.8 from 10pm to 5am.

The Best of Tai Shan

Dai Temple 岱庙 *dài miào*
- ✉ Zhongduan, Shengping Jie 升平街中段
- ☎ 828 6392
- 🕒 8am to 6pm
- ¥ 20

Two recommended routes to climb Tai Shan are:

Hongmen Route 红门路 *hóngmén lù*
Begins from the First Gate of Heaven to the South Gate of Heaven, passes most of the scenic spots, 5.6 miles (9 km).
- ✉ Hongmen Lu 红门路
- ☎ 621 3702
- 🕒 24 hours
- ¥ 82 peak-season
  67 off-season

Tianwai Cun Route 天外村路 *tiānwài cūn lù*
(For those who want the quick and easy path to the top, from Tiandi Guangchang get a ride to the Middle Gate of Heaven then jump onto a cable car to the South Gate of Heaven.
- ✉ Longtan Lu 龙潭路
- ☎ 621 5441
- 🕒 6am to 6pm, peak-season
  7am to 5pm, off-season
- ¥ 102 peak-season
  82 off-season
  45 (cable car, one-way)

Hotels

Huaqiao Hotel 泰山华侨大厦 *tài shān huáqiáo dàshà* ★★★★
- ✉ 15 Zhongduan, Dongyue Da Jie
  东岳大街中段 15 号❶
- ☎ 822 8112
- ¥ 480 – double room, peak-season
  288 – double room, off -season
- @ www.huaqiaohotel.com

Memorable Experiences

Finally reaching the summit after a long hard climb and seeing the sun rise above the clouds.

Meandering down the mountain's western route amidst the ancient pine trees, temples and sneaking away from the crowds of pilgrims.

An ancient ceremony honoring Tai Shan.

Shenqi Hotel
神憩宾馆 *shénqì bīnguǎn* ★★★
✉ 10 Tian Jie, Top of Tai Shan
泰山极顶天街 10 号
☎ 822 3866, 833 7025
¥ 540 – double room
@ www.shenqihotel.com

Tai Shan Great Hotel
泰山大酒店 *tài shān dàjiǔdiàn* ★★★
✉ 210 Daizong Da Jie 岱宗大街 210 号❸
☎ 829 1216
¥ 180 – double room, peak season
144 – double room, off-season
@ sjt68@263.net, sjt66880718@sina.com

Tai Shan Hotel
泰山宾馆 *tài shān bīnguǎn* ★★★
✉ 26 Hongmen Lu 红门路 26 号❷
☎ 822 4678
¥ 210 – double room
@ www.tsguestandhotel.com

Yuzuo Hotel
御座宾馆 *yùzuò bīnguǎn* ★★★
✉ 50 Daimiao Bei Lu 岱庙北路 50 号❹
☎ 822 3852
¥ 300 – double room, peak-season
240 – double room, off-season

Food & Restaurants

Food on Tai Shan is simple – all that stuff needs to be hauled up by porters – and it gets more expensive the higher you go. Food stalls and vendors are available at various sections along the paths. Bringing your own munchies and drinks is a good idea for the long climb.

Shandong is well known for its fantastic and cheap roast duck. Look around Hongmen Route and the Dai Temple and you'll find many local eateries. Beware of the large Tai'an hotels that offer numerous restaurants with a variety of Western dishes – it's mediocre fare at not so reasonable prices. Tai Shan is also known for its tofu banquet which offers 150 different tofu dishes – even the most ardent carnivore is sure to find a tofu dish that'll bring them back for seconds. Definitely check out the sliced tofu and cabbage (*sānměi dòufu* 三美豆腐) – it's made from Tai Shan spring water and is renowned throughout China. If you've had enough tofu, *chilin yu* (赤鳞鱼) will delight the palate. This is a kind of fish, found only in the area around Tai Shan. For a quick snack, grab some *tai shan jianbing* (泰山煎饼), a corn based cookie – crispy and tasty.

RESTAURANTS

Jing Fuhua Feiniu 京福华肥牛
Famous hot pot restaurant with specially selected beef; dinner will cost about RMB 30 to 40 per person.
✉ 86 Dongyue Da Jie 东岳大街 86 号
☎ 827 0688
◷ 10:30am to 10pm

Jingya Dajiudian 净雅大酒店
Shandong and Cantonese dishes.
✉ Dongyue Da Jie 东岳大街
☎ 862 9888
◷ 11am to 2pm, 5pm to 9pm

Tai Shan Caiguan 泰山菜馆
Traditional Shandong cuisine such as stir-fried pork with sea-cucumber (*ròumò shāo*

Quotes

"The sunrise over the clouds and peak was exquisite."

"Despite a tough climb, the feeling of satisfaction and smugness over those who took the cable car."

cìshēn 肉沫烧刺参), a tasty tofu dish called *baodou babao doufu* (鲍斗八宝豆腐), pumpkin dipped in egg-yolk (*dànhuáng jū nánguā* 蛋黄焗南瓜) and the meat filled *jiangrou bao* (酱肉包) are highly recommended.

✉ 26 Hongmen Lu, north to Daizong Fang 岱宗坊北红门路 26 号

☎ 626 7888, 626 7777

🕒 10am to 10pm

Souvenirs

Souvenirs made from stone are popular in Tai Shan – they're like taking a part of the legend home with you. Popular items are stone vases and pen holders made from *yanzi shi* (燕子石), a type of rock with fossils. Locals like to buy *shi gandang* (石敢当); these pieces of rock are inscribed with the names of legendary heroes and it's believed they ward away evil spirits and bring good luck. Head towards Tai Shan Wenhua Plaza (*tài shān wénhuà guǎngchǎng* 泰山文化广场) near the First Gate of Heaven. Lots of small shops selling all sorts of souvenir items are located here. If you're looking to stock up on some basic goods, the Yichu Lianhua Supermarket (*yìchū liánhuā chāoshì* 易初莲花超市❺, Xiduan Dongyue Da Jie 东岳大街西段) is a good bet. The Yinzuo shopping center (*yínzuò shāngchéng* 银座商城❻), near the train station on Dongyue Da Jie, is also a good place to do some shopping.

Other Information

POST OFFICES

Qingnian Lu Post Office 青年路邮局

✉ 3 Dongyue Da Jie 东岳大街 3 号

☎ 853 8707

Tai Shan Post Office 泰山邮局

✉ 240 Daizong Da Jie 岱宗大街 240 号❼

☎ 853 8701

HOSPITALS

Tai Shan Medical School Hospital
泰山医学院附属医院

✉ 706 Tai Shan Da Jie 泰山大街 706 号❽

☎ 842 3120

Tai'an City Central Hospital
泰安市中心医院

✉ 29 Longtan Lu 龙潭路 29 号❾

☎ 822 4161

COMPLAINT HOTLINES

☎ General: 828 5462

☎ Taxi: 822 9769

A visitor takes a photo of the ancient ceremonies of Tai Shan.

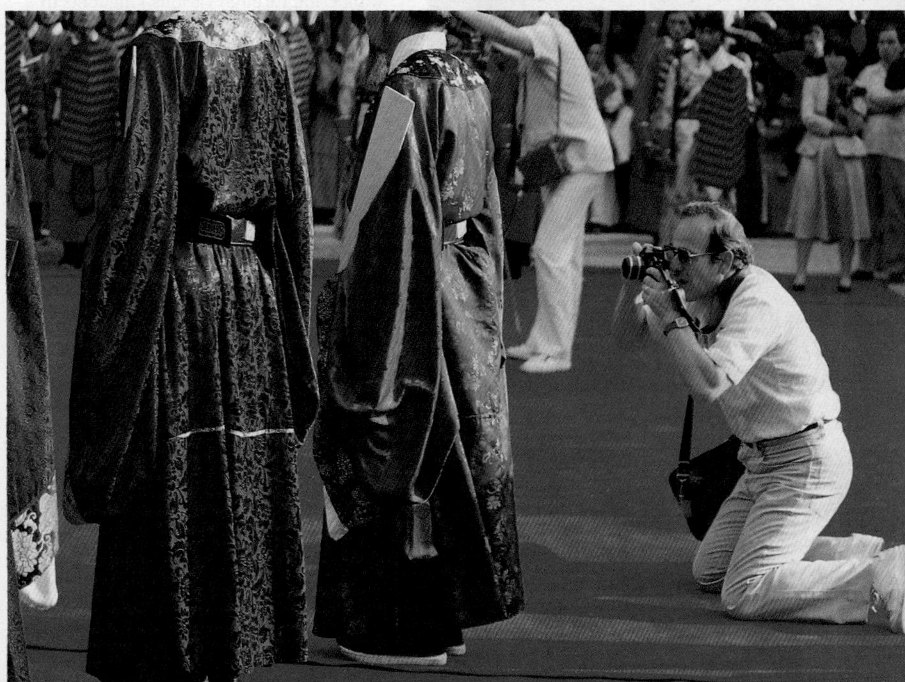

Qufu, Step into History

Area Code 0537

Heritage: Confucius Temple, Confucius Mansions, Confucius Cemetery

Qufu is legendary for the Chinese as the birthplace of Confucius, that ancient sage and teacher whose impact continues to influence Chinese education, politics, and thought.

Pleasant street markets and an air of historic importance mark Qufu as a great introduction to Chinese culture and one of China's most endearing legacies. It's easy to spend a few days in Qufu exploring the three major sights related to **Confucius** (*Kǒngzǐ* 孔子): the **Confucius Mansions** (*kǒng fǔ* 孔府) where the Sage and some 70 generations of his descendants once lived; the **Confucius Temple** (*kǒng miào* 孔庙) and the **Confucius Cemetery** (*kǒng lín* 孔林), a forest cemetery where Confucius and many of his deceased clan members rest.

The intricate dragon columns in the Confucius Temple.

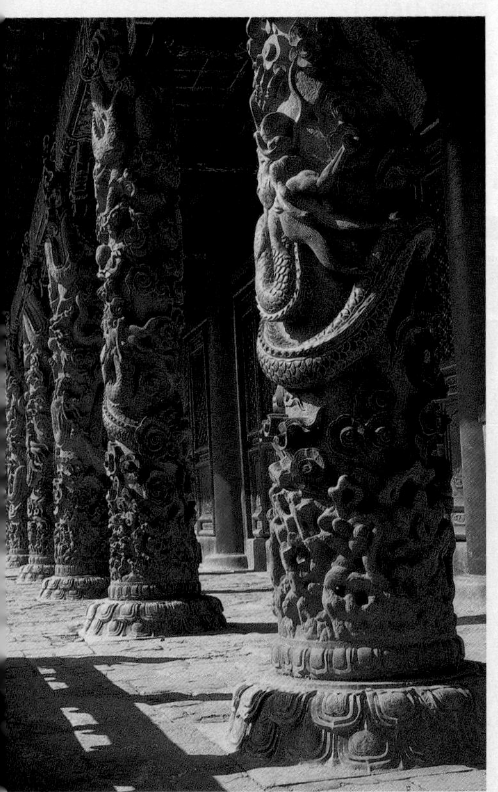

Qufu's history is directly linked to Confucius. Legend states that he was born in a cave 37 miles (60 km) to the east of Qufu in 551 BC, during the Spring and Autumn Period. Confucius settled in modern day Qufu, a pauper, after years of unsuccessfully wandering through various kingdoms in hopes of influencing rulers to adopt his teachings. It was only after his death in 479 BC that his ideas gained prominence.

The mansion and temple areas were only open to the Confucius family (Kong family) and visiting emperors; it was forbidden ground for commoners. As a measure of how much prestige the Kong family held, they were given the right to make laws and pass ordinances in Qufu. Over time the Kong family's statue grew to the point where they were considered equal to the imperial family.

Over the years, the mansion and temple saw substantial expansions, turning the complex into a sprawling spectacle that occupies nearly 20% of modern Qufu. Song, Ming and Qing dynasties architecture abound throughout the city, making strolls along Qufu's clean streets ascetically pleasing, as well as adding to the historic charm of the city. The architecture will transport you to another time. Buildings with beautiful red and yellow tiled roofs and striking pointed eaves greet the eye.

The **main south gate** (*wànrèn gōngqiáng* 万仞宫墙) marks the beginning of the temple. The gate is reminiscent of an old castle wall and passing through the gate's large iron studded red doors foreshadow the grandeur held within. The square just beyond the gate features a bustling market packed with vendors hawking vegetable pancakes and various trinkets. It makes you wonder how good of a bargainer Confucius was.

Upon entering the temple grounds, the noise of the market subsides and the tranquility of the temple brings out the scholar in us all. Quiet courtyards are home to withered pines so old they require support from metal poles. Numerous steles, honoring Confucius and his disciples, are found through the temple. Many of the steles, bearing dedications carved into the stone face, were dedicated by past emperors. Most of the steles are in the south and central portion of the temple. The steles are supported by a fabled creature akin to a tortoise. If you can't read Chinese, a highly recommended booklet introducing the most important steles and buildings is available throughout the temple.

In the center of the temple is the **Kuiwen Pavilion** (*kuíwén gé* 奎文阁), the tallest and most prominent building in the temple. This ornately decorated three-story hall is topped with a three-tiered tiled roof and gives some idea of the wealth and influence of the Kong family. The current pavilion dates to 1504; it was originally a library to store *The Analects* (*lúnyǔ* 论语), a collection of Confucius' sayings, known popularly in the West as "Confucius says…."

In this area of the temple is a cluster of 13 pavilions housing more steles honoring the Sage and his disciples – these steles were sponsored by important personages, such as emperors and nobles. Standing here is the **Pavilion of Gold Tablet** (*jīnbēi tíng* 金碑亭), the oldest building in the temple.

Passing through **Dacheng Gate** (*dàchéng mén* 大成门) brings you into the northern section of the temple, which leads into three courtyards. Just inside the gate is where a juniper tree was allegedly planted by Confucius, though the current tree was planted by a Qing dynasty emperor. In the

Dressed up to take part in a ceremony honoring Confucius.

same courtyard is the **Apricot Altar** (*xìngtán* 杏坛), where it's said Confucius gave his erudite lectures to his disciples. The altar is one of the most important places in the Chinese cultural world. Chinese tourists will wait for up to 30 minutes to have their picture taken next to the famous sight.

Behind the altar is the **Dacheng Hall** (*dàchéng diàn* 大成殿), the main hall of the temple. The hall was originally higher than those in the Forbidden City and had to be lowered to avoid offending the emperor. This Qing dynasty hall boasts a double roof of glazed tiles and 28 magnificently carved 19.7-foot-tall (6 m) stone pillars on the southern side. According to legend, when emperors dropped by, the stone pillars had to be covered with red silk to prevent the emperor from becoming jealous of the quality of work. Inside is a brightly painted statue of Confucius where people continue to pay their respects to the ancient Sage. The solemn faces and deep bows are evidence of

▶▶ Confucius

Confucius, who lived from 551 to 479 BC, was also known as Master Kong or Kongzi. Born in the late-Zhou dynasty, his social philosophy has remained central to Chinese and Asian thinking for over 2,500 years. Parents still teach children Confucian virtues and the Five Confucian Classics remain among the most widely read books in the world.

The end of the Zhou dynasty was a period of constant small-scale warfare between rival landlords and these disputes left much of the population in poverty. To those who lived in this time of chaos, public morals seemed in decline and grim prophets warned that the country would soon fall into total anarchy.

Enter one mild-mannered man from the state of Lu, present day Shandong, whose ideas had a clarity and simplicity that would cement Chinese morality for over two millennia.

In order to preserve harmony, the social hierarchy, he said, should be respected: fathers should love sons and sons should respect fathers, the people should listen to their leaders and the leaders should act benevolently. The best government would rule by example of virtue, not by strict law and retributive punishment.

Then there were three kinds of behavior: *li*, *yi*, and *ren*. *Li* was the essential desire for profit or advantage and was usually, but not exclusively, bad. *Yi* was "righteousness," and encouraged helping others and acting for the greater good. *Ren* was the best quality to strive for – love, charity and sympathy.

He was in his thirties when he began to lecture on these ideas. Prior to that, feudal officials had monopolized education and schooling had been confined to the children of nobles. Confucius, however, took in students from various social classes and personally taught more than 3,000 young men. He believed that teaching should be tailored to the individual student and would often give differing replies to the same question – students were instructed to "carpe diem" if they were shy and mull things over if too headstrong.

Confucius held government posts for some years, but the turmoil of the period and the constant squabbling for power frustrated him. Later in life, he traveled extensively and returned home only a few years before his death. His disciples collected his philosophy into *The Analects*, each section of the book begins with "*Kongzi yue*" (Master Kong said), known in the West as "Confucius says."

Years after his death, later emperors came to highly revere *The Analects*. Confucian teachings provided the basis for the civil service examinations, thousands of temples were built and the Confucian rituals were practiced as a religion. The Confucius Temple in Qufu survives today and is listed by UNESCO as one of the most important cultural and historical sites in the world.

his continued influence; even in modern times his teachings remain relevant.

Emerging from the temple via the east exit is a quaint square where hawkers ply their wares. To the south is the ancient **Bell Tower** (*zhōng lóu* 钟楼) and to the east is the **Drum Tower** (*gǔ lóu* 鼓楼). South of the Bell Tower, with its delicate and painstaking artwork, is the **Queli Arch** (*quèlǐ fāng* 阙里坊), where emperors once went for after-dinner strolls.

To the northeast of the temple is the maze-like Confucius Mansion where Confucius and his descendants once lived, the present complex built during the Ming dynasty and expanded during the Qing dynasty. The temple's ornate decorations and grand scale is toned down in the mansion complex. The real charm of the mansion is in its beautifully d0ecorated living quarters that offer a glimpse into the daily life of ancient Chinese aristocrats.

The southern part of the mansion is the administrative area. This is where guests were greeted and official business conducted. Follow one of the three main paths that meander through various halls and work areas. Along the eastern path is a tower that served as a final place of refuge in case unruly peasants staged an uprising. The Kongs, being practical folk, also used it as the Kong family treasury.

The central area of the mansion is where the family once lived. While strolling through the narrow grey lanes, it's easy to imagine the voice of young Kongs reciting the words of their influential ancestor and the footsteps of hundreds of servants, who once served this privileged family, echoing off the walls.

The rearmost part of the mansion is a pleasant garden and pool, which must have inspired many descendants of the Sage while they contemplated his ancient wisdom. There's no need to rush through the temple and mansion – a half-day is more than enough.

A short 10-minute taxi ride or 20-minute walk to the north of the mansion will bring you to the Confucius Cemetery, which is both park and cemetery. The walled cemetery is expansive, about 500 acres (2 km^2) – a good half day will be required to see all of the tombs in this ancient forest. Even today Confucius' descendants are buried here to rest alongside the illustrious teacher.

The quiet forest is sprinkled with pavilions, ceremonial archways and assorted trees. According to tradition, each of Confucius' disciples planted a tree from his native province. Shady trails lined with stern stone guardians allow for quiet strolls. It's in this forest where you really get a sense of timelessness. Confucius' tomb and those of his son and grandson lie near the main gate of the forest in the southern section. Near the Sage's tomb is a hut where one of

Confucius, China's most influential philospher.

Confucius' disciples lived guarding his teacher's tomb. The rest of the Kong graves lie in a separate section of the forest. It's possible to rent a bike for around RMB 10. Bargaining is advised. A quick bus tour that stops at some of the better-known tombs is also available, though Confucius' tomb is not included in the tour. The bus tour is RMB 10 and will take 15 to 20 minutes. For a slower pace, going by foot or bike is a better option. This way you can get away from the crowds and enjoy the tranquility at your own speed.

Also of interest in Qufu is the **Six Arts City** (*liùyì chéng* 六艺城) in the southern part of Qufu. Here they have re-creations of life in Confucius' day and there's a mockup of ancient Qufu. The Six Arts City is approximately a 5-minute taxi ride south from the temple and mansion complex. ■

Memorable Experiences

Taking a horse drawn carriage through Qufu.

Riding a horse at a little ranch on the way to the Confucius cemetery and almost losing my life when it decided to run as fast as it can.

Having a conversation with a member of the 74th generation of Confucius' descendants at the Confucius Mansion.

Making Your Trip Easy

Practical Tips

Qufu is quite small and easy to navigate. Upon entering the city, the temple and mansion complexes are easily recognizable by the pavilions and pagodas that rise above the rest of the city's skyline.

The winters are bitterly cold, though a heavy coat and gloves should do the trick. The summers are brutally hot, with temperatures often soaring to about 95°F (35°C). The best times to visit are either during the spring or fall. There's a festival commemorating Confucius' birthday on September 28 that takes over the entire city; the celebrations last until October 10. From April to October, there's an outdoor performance of traditional Confucian dances and music at the Xingtan Theater (*xìngtán jùchǎng* 杏坛剧场). The show begins at 8pm and tickets are RMB 40 per person.

Transportation

Airport – The closest airport is at Jinan, the provincial capital, about 112 miles (180 km) away. The trip will take about 90 minutes. Shuttle buses to Qufu are available at the airport.

Taxi – Taxis in Qufu come in two varieties, cars and vans. Both start at RMB 5. Vans are RMB 1 per kilometer (.62 mile) while cars are RMB 1.5 per kilometer. Some of the taxis don't have meters, so it's necessary to negotiate a price with the driver. Pedi-cabs charge anywhere from RMB 3 to 5 depending on the destination. Unique to Qufu are horse drawn carriages that charge RMB 20 per person.

The Best of Qufu

Confucius Cemetery 孔林 *kǒng lín*

- 0.9 mile (1.5 km) north of Qufu City 曲阜城北约 1500 米
- 8am to 5pm
- 102 (combo ticket for Confucius Cemetery, Confucius Mansion and Confucius Temple)

Confucius Mansion 孔府 *kǒng fǔ*

- near Confucius Temple 紧临孔庙
- 8am to 5pm
- 102 (combo ticket for Confucius Cemetery, Confucius Mansion and Confucius Temple)

Confucius Temple 孔庙 *kǒng miào*

- in the middle of Qufu 曲阜市中心
- 8am to 5pm
- 102 (combo ticket for Confucius Cemetery, Confucius Mansion and Confucius Temple)

Hotels

Kong's West Garden Hotel
孔府西苑 *kǒngfǔ xī yuàn* ★★★★★

- west of Confucius Temple 孔庙西侧
- 442 3666
- 960 – double room
  1360 – single room

Queli Hotel 阙里宾舍 *quèlǐ bīnshè* ★★★

- 1 Queli Jie 阙里街 1 号

An aerial view of the Confucius Temple from the main gate.

☎ 486 6818, 486 6402
¥ 398 – double room
298 – single room

Food & Restaurants

Graduates from the school of Confucius' philosophy.

The food in Qufu is Shandong cuisine; hearty meals of potatoes, meat and noodles. Traditional Confucius family cuisine is worth a try. Apparently Confucius was a picky eater and stipulated in great detail how each dish should be made. His descendants developed Confucian cuisine which tends to be light and clear. Good samples of this cuisine are *kongmen doufu* (孔门豆腐), a type of tofu; *yangguan sandie* (阳关三叠) and *shili yinxing* (诗礼银杏). Mutton kebabs are found throughout the streets and the night markets – 20 of them should be no more than RMB 5. Wumaci Jie and Zhonglou Jie are all food streets where tasty snacks can be found.

RESTAURANTS

Queli Hotel Restaurants 阙里宾舍餐厅

Ornately decorated, try the boiled chicken in a clay pot with vegetables.

✉ 1 Queli Jie 阙里街 1 号
☎ 486 6818

Souvenirs

Name seals, ink stones and dragonhead canes are popular items in Qufu. The best places to buy these are at the entrances to the three major sights. Expect to pay about RMB 20 for the seals, though with a little bargaining you can talk the seller down to RMB 10. If you want an ivory name stamp, expect to pay anywhere from RMB 300 to 500. Ink stones from nearby Mount Ni (*ní shān yàn* 尼山砚) are famous throughout China. They vary in size and detail, but will cost from RMB 100 to over RMB 1,000, less if you bargain. Books of calligraphy (*bìētiè* 碑贴) copied from the different steles also make unique souvenirs. Other interesting items include canes with a carving of a dragon's head on the handle. They range from the extremely ornate and expensive to the simple and cheap. A typical cane will cost RMB 30, but the expensive varieties may go up to RMB 100. Be sure to bargain hard.

Other Information

POST OFFICES

Gulou Post Office 鼓楼邮局

✉ 8 Gulou Da Jie 鼓楼大街 8 号
☎ 441 2214

HOSPITALS

Qufu People's Hospital 曲阜市人民医院

✉ Zhong Duan Tianguandi Jie 天官第街中段
☎ 442 0130

COMPLAINT HOTLINES

☎ General: 449 0788

TOURISM INFORMATION WEBSITE

www.confuciusta.com

Quotes

"If you read and studied everything that Confucius said, you'd be the next President of the United States."

"Everyone in Qufu knows something about the history of the city. If you want a history lesson, buy something from me and I'll give you one."

Qingdao, Beer and Beaches

Area Code 0532

Qingdao's clean beaches, European architecture and great beer made from Lao Shan's crisp spring water make this city an idyllic getaway spot to spend a few relaxing days strolling along the boardwalk while watching the sunrise over the ocean.

Despite having no island, Qingdao is deceptively named "Green Island" in Chinese. This doesn't deter locals from referring to this laidback city as the "island city." In southern Shandong, this city was only a small scenic fishing village until the might of international politics thrust it upon the world stage. In 1897, two German missionaries in Shandong Province were killed. Using this as a pretext, in 1898 Kaiser Wilhelm II forced the Qing government to lease Qingdao to Germany for 99 years.

The Kaiser intended to keep Qingdao for those 99 years and built a typical German-styled city. The Germans expanded Qingdao's infrastructure, enlarging its excellent harbor, building a rail connection to the provincial capital and piping in spring water from Lao Shan. Taking advantage of Lao Shan's spring water, a beer brewery was built in 1903 and today Qingdao is a center of Chinese beer production.

The city remained in German possession until the First World War when the Japanese, with British aid, took the city. As a member of the Allied Powers, the Chinese government demanded the return of Qingdao to Chinese sovereignty, but under the Treaty of Versailles, Qingdao and all German possessions in Asia were given to Japan. Bowing to widespread protests, the Chinese delegation refused to sign the treaty and in 1919, pent-up resentment and anger unleashed itself as the **May Fourth Movement**. The movement was a decisive point in the creation of a national Chinese consciousness. In 1922, control of Qingdao was finally transferred back to China.

Qingdao is a mixture of old world European villas and modern architecture.

The skilled German engineers built Qingdao into a small Bavarian town. Today, fresh air and crowd-free streets help complete the transformation. The area around **Bada Guan** (*bādà guān* 八大关), close to the No. 2 Bathing Beach (*dì'èr hǎishuǐ yùchǎng* 第二海水浴场), is the former German residential area, meaning " eight passes." Bada Guan now sports ten streets lined with 100 Western villas. Spacious and blessed with

The 2008 Olympic Sailing Regatta will take place in Qingdao.

greenery, each street is planted with a single type of tree; locals can tell what street they're on just by looking at the trees. Close to the ocean and bathed with a yearlong sea breeze, it's easy to understand why many choose this area for their home. Summers here are breathtaking and some of the historic villas are available for rent.

Next to Bada Guan and east of the beach is a giant outcropping of stone with a Russian-styled villa built on top. Built in 1932, this grandiose villa combines an interesting mix of Greek, Roman and Gothic influences. The five-story structure is made of stone and also features a large turret that adds a Gothic touch. Because of the colorful rocks used in building the villa, the locals have nicknamed the structure "the colourful rock building" (*huāshí lóu* 花石楼). There's also a bit of intrigue surrounding the villa – a secret passage used by Chiang Kai-shek leads from the building directly to the seashore.

In 1891, Qing soldiers began building a dock that extended some 650 feet (200 m) into the ocean. The dock was named **Zhan Qiao** (*zhànqiáo* 栈桥) and was extended to 1,150 feet (350 m) by the Germans who laid railroad tracks beside it and in 1931 the city government rebuilt the dock using concrete. At the end of the dock is the **Huilan Pavilion** (*huílán gé* 回澜阁), which offers an unrestricted view of the ocean. Locals like to head to the beach when the tide is out to collect seashells. Watch out for bombarding seagulls when they congregate in Qingdao during the winter.

Zhongshan Lu is Qingdao's major shopping thoroughfare. With a wealth of stores and restaurants, a leisurely stroll will end up with lots of shopping or eating, or both.

A 20-minute drive east on Zhongshan Lu is a commanding Catholic church on top of a hill. The majesty of the church is easily conveyed by two 66-foot-tall (20 m) bell towers, each housing four bells and topped with a 14.8-foot-wide (4.5 m) cross. The c hurch remains an active place of worship and holds regular mass. Entry for churchgoers is free during mass; outside of mass, a RMB 5 ticket is required from 8:30am to 4pm.

A few minutes southeast is the Protestant church. Built in 1910, it was the first German church in Qingdao. This elegant structure features a red-tiled roof and green clock tower with a clock that's still in use. Just north of this church is Signal Hill(*xìnhào shān* 信号山); flags were once raised here to signal ships in the harbor. Climbers are rewarded with a great view of the coast and the two churches.

On the south slope of the hill is a massive German villa. The magnificently built mansion was the former residence of the German governor and the entire estate covers 6.4 acres (26,000 m²). No extravagance was spared in its construction, and much of the construction material was shipped from Europe – the governor felt he deserved the utmost in luxury. Unfortunately for him, when the Kaiser saw the construction bill, the hapless governor was immediately recalled.

There's more to Qingdao than beaches and villas: the city is also dotted with free parks. Some of the particularly nice ones are **Lu Xun Park** (*Lǔ Xùn gōngyuán* 鲁迅公园), **Sea World** (*hǎidǐ shìjiè* 海底世界), **May Fourth Square** (*wǔsì guǎngchǎng* 五四广场) and **the Sculpture Garden** (*hǎibīn diāosùyuán* 海滨雕塑园), which has free displays of modern art. For a city that's famous for beer, the **Qingdao International Beer Festival** (*qīngdǎo guójì píjiǔjié* 青岛国际啤酒节) is an event that'll whet any beer lover's thirst. Every late August the city turns into a carnival of beer and sun. Live performances, parades and lots of beers add to the excitement. Just watch where you step, as some drink a little too much.

The city is now building a boardwalk that will stretch the entire length of the shore for those looking for a quiet walk along the

An aerial view of May Fourth Square.

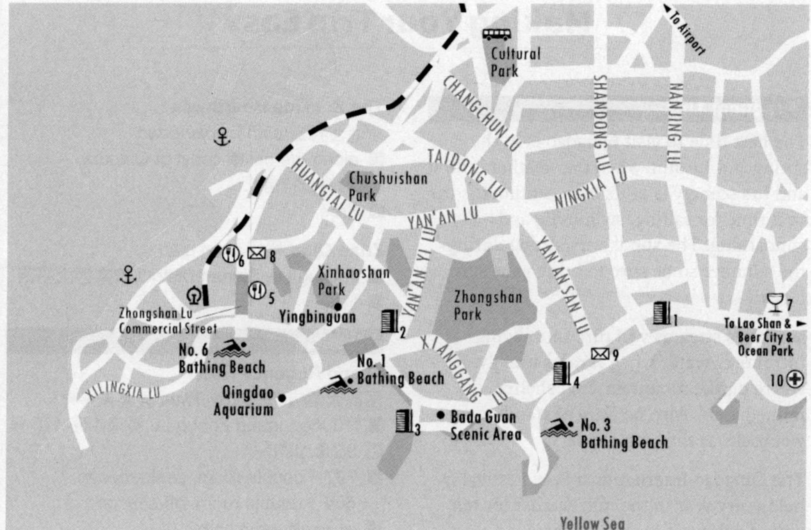

seaside. The boardwalk at the No.1 and No.2 beaches has already been built, construction will be completed by the 2008 Summer Olympics in Beijing.

LAO SHAN

Lao Shan (*láo shān* 崂山) is one of the places where Taoism first originated. About 4.3 miles (7 km) east of the **Old Stone Man** (*shí lǎorén* 石老人) beach; the mountain is one of Taoism's most important pilgrimage destinations. In the past, Taoist priests living on the mountain were conferred with special privileges. The mountain saw the most development during the late-Song and early-Yuan dynasties and was home to over 100 temples, each searching for "the Way" in solitude. Ancient travelers thought immortals lived on this scenic mountain and many legends grew out of that belief.

Lao Shan is now best known for its spring water, which is considered the best in China. It's also this spring water that made Qingdao famous for its beer. Not only is this water good for making people drunk, but vegetables grown using this water are reputedly much tastier, something local fruit and vegetable peddlers will all point out.

There are many routes up the mountain and many hidden trails make it a joy to explore. Oddly, palm trees are abundant on Lao Shan despite being in the north; note the varying vegetation at different elevations. At the end of Lao Shan Lu is the **Palace of Great Purity** (*tàiqīng gōng* 太清宫), which is made of three pavilions. The main pavilion is **Sanqing Pavilion** (*sānqīng diàn* 三清殿), which houses a statue of Laozi (*Lǎozǐ* 老子), the founder of Taoism, and the mythical Jade Emperor. To the left of this pavilion is the **Pavilion of the Three Emperors** (*sānhuáng diàn* 三皇殿) and to the right is the **Pavilion of the Three Officials** (*sānguān diàn* 三官殿). These buildings were constructed during the Song dynasty to perform Taoist ceremonies. **Beijiu Shui** (*běijiǔ shuǐ* 北九水) is just north of the Palace of Great Purity and is a wild area laced by rivers, streams and cascading waterfalls.

A cable car close to the Palace of Great Purity whisks visitors to **Shangqing Gong** (*shàngqīng gōng* 上清宫) at the peak of Lao Shan. Great views abound on Lao Shan, but make sure the strong ocean wind doesn't blow you off the mountain. South of the peak is the **Dragon Pool Falls** (*lóngtán pù* 龙潭瀑). Because of the high winds, the water is blown into spray that resembles a thundershower more than a curtain of water. Be careful in this area and stay on the high ground away from slippery surfaces. Visitors have been blown off the mountain and into the sea. ■

Making Your Trip Easy

Practical Tips

The best time to visit Qingdao is in the spring and autumn when the weather is mild and the scenery is at its best. Summer is the best time for sailing, swimming and sunbathing. The sun is very strong during the summer so be sure to bring your sun block.

ao Shan's streams will turn into raging torrents of water when it rains heavily. If you're on the mountain, find shelter immediately. Also be wary of standing on wet rocks as they can slippery.

The Qingdao International Beer Festival is held every year in the mid-August for ten days. Look for it at the Qingdao International Beer City (*qīngdǎo guójì píjiǔchéng* 青岛国际啤酒城) on Xianggang Dong Lu (香港东路). During the beer festival, there's lots of live entertainment and beer drinking. Tickets are about RMB 20, not including beer.

Transportation

Airport – The airport is about 19 miles (30 km) north of the city center and takes about an hour to get to by taxi.

Bicycle – You can rent bikes from McDonald's in Qingdao and return them at any McDonald's outlet.

Taxi – Flag-fall is RMB 7.

The Best of Qingdao

Palace of Great Purity 太清宫 *tàiqīng gōng*

✉ Lao Shan, Lao Shan District 崂山区崂山
🕒 24 hours
¥ 15

The Seaside Boardwalk
滨海步行道 *bīnhǎi bùxíngdào*

✉ along the entire coast of Qingdao 滨海步行道
¥ Free

Zhan Qiao 栈桥 *zhàn qiáo*

✉ Taiping Lu, Shinan District 市南区太平路
¥ Free

Hotels

Grand Regency Hotel
丽晶大酒店 *lìjīng dàjiǔdiàn* ★★★★★

✉ 110 Xianggang Zhong Lu 香港中路 110 号
☎ 8588 1818
¥ 797 – double room, peak-season
664 – double room, off-season
@ www.grh-ohm.com

Hai Tian Hotel, Qingdao 青岛海天大酒店
qīngdǎo hǎitiān dàjiǔdiàn ★★★★★

✉ 48 Xianggang Xi Lu 香港西路 48 号❹
☎ 8387 1888
¥ 828 – double room, peak-season
560 – double room, off-season
@ www.hai-tian-hotel.com

Huiquan Dynasty Hotel 汇泉王朝大酒店
huìquán wángcháo dàjiǔdiàn ★★★★★

✉ 9 Nanhai Lu 南海路 9 号❸
☎ 8288 6688
¥ 913 – double room, peak-season
564 – double room, off-season
@ qdhqdntl@qd-public.sd.cninfo.net

Equaporial Hotel
贵都大饭店 *guìdū dàfàndiàn* ★★★★

✉ 28 Xianggang Zhong Lu, near May Fourth Square 香港中路 28 号，五四广场附近❶
☎ 8572 1688
¥ 598 – double room, peak-season

Memorable Experiences

Strolling along the seaside boardwalk and watching the sun slowly creep above the horizon over the ocean.

Gorging on all the fresh seafood that's available throughout the city.

Taking languid walks through the old German residential areas then heading over to the many plazas that dot the city while letting the sea breeze choose where we go next.

A small fishing harbor in Qingdao.

458 – double room, off-season
www.equaporial.com

Huanghai Hotel
黄海饭店 *huánghǎi fàndiàn* ★★★★
75 Yan'an Yi Lu 延安一路 75 号❷
8287 0215
480 – double room, peak-season
280 – double room, off-season
www.huanghaihotel.com

Food & Restaurants

Qingdao is a seaside city so seafood is abundant. *Yingzhou bayu* (瀛洲鲅鱼), a local fish, is equally delicious fried, baked or smoked. *Jinhai sanxian danbing chuan* (金海三鲜单饼串) is made of shrimps, scallops and shell-fish and is wrapped in a pancake. Seafood tofu (*hǎixiān xiǎodòufu* 海鲜小豆腐) is made from stir-fried seafood and eaten with green onion pancakes (*cōngyóu bǐng* 葱油饼). A fish casserole (*shāguō quányú* 砂锅全鱼) is made with fresh fish and cooked in a clay pot.

RESTAURANTS

Beidahuang Ren Jiudian 北大荒人酒店
3 – 7 Haixian Meishijie, Laoshan District
崂山区海鲜美食街 3 – 7 号
8543 8888

Chunhe Lou 春和楼
Specializes in seafood, dumplings and local snacks.
146 Zhongshan Lu 中山路 146 号❻
8282 4346

Haidao Yucun 海岛渔村
Specializes in steamed buns.
46 Yunxiao Lu, Shinan District
市南区云霄路 46 号
8573 5588

Haimingwei Dafandian 海明威大饭店
7 Shandong Lu, Shinan District
市南区山东路 7 号❺
8581 1799

Qingdao Guotie 青岛锅贴
Specializes in potstickers.
161C Zhenhua Lu, Licang District
李沧区振华路 161 号丙
8461 8899

Qingdao Restaurant 青岛菜馆
Specializes in exotic seafood dishes.
inside Huiquan Dynasty Hotel
青岛汇泉王朝大酒店内
8288 6688, 8288 3888

Qingdao Yaoyao Meishi Yule
青岛瑶瑶美食娱乐
Beef, mutton, and seafood are on the menu here.
55 Furong Lu 芙蓉路 55 号
8363 8118

Yuehai Chinese Restaurant 粤海中餐厅
1/F Haijing Huayuan Dajiudian, 2 Yinghua Lu, Shinan District
市南区影化路 2 号海景花园大酒店 1 楼
8587 5777

Quotes

"This is a sea lover's paradise. The beaches are clean and the air is fresh. Seafood restaurants are everywhere. Qingdao is definitely one of the nicest cities we've visited."

"The beer festival was great. Lots of beer from all over the world, plus great entertainment throughout the city."

BARS

New York Bar 纽约吧
✉ 2/F Huaqiao Hotel, 41 Xianggang Zhonglu, Shinan District
市南区香港中路 41 号华侨饭店 2 楼❼
☎ 8388 1728

Langyuan Bar 朗园酒吧
✉ 6 Zhanshan 5th Rood 湛山五路 6 号
☎ 8387 5734

Souvenirs

Qingdao shell carvings (*qīngdǎo bèidiāo* 青岛贝雕) made from seashells have different designs carved into them. Lao Shan Yunfeng tea (*láoshān yúnfēngchá* 崂山云峰茶) is a type of green tea that's grown on Lao Shan. Lace (*jīxiù huābiān zhìpǐn* 机绣花边制品) made into curtains, table clothes and pillowcases is a local specialty. A local handicraft uses straw (*cǎo zhìpǐn* 草制品) woven into a variety of goods like handbags and hats.

Some stores to do your shopping at include the Crafts and Arts Company (*gōngyì měishù yǒuxiàn gōngsī* 工艺美术有限公司) at 212 Zhongshan Lu (中山路 212 号, ☎ 8282 8627) and the Wanglijiang Tea Center (*wànlǐjiāng cháchǎng cháyì zhōngxīn* 万里江茶场茶艺中心) on 289 Lao Shan Zhong Lu (崂山中路 289 号 ☎ 8880 2889).

Zhongshan Lu is the main shopping strip and is lined with many souvenir stores, boutiques and restaurants, making it an ideal place to spend a breezy afternoon window-shopping and sipping tea.

Other Information

POST OFFICES

Zhongshan Lu Post Office 中山路邮局
✉ 51 Zhongshan Lu 中山路 51 号❽
☎ 8286 4223

Zhanshan Post Office 湛山邮局
✉ 79 Xianggang Xi Lu 香港西路 79 号❾
☎ 8386 3088

HOSPITALS

Outpatient Department, East Area of Qingdao Municipal Hospital
青岛市市立医院东院区国际门诊
✉ 5 Donghai Zhong Lu, Shinan District 市南区东海中路 5 号❿
☎ 8596 8906, 8596 9688 ext 8662

CONSULATES

Republic of Korea 韩国
✉ 6/F, Korea-China Business Center, 8 Qinling Lu
秦岭路 8 号韩中商务中心 6 楼
☎ 8897 6001, 8897 6002

COMPLAINT HOTLINES

☎ General: 8591 2000
☎ Taxi: 8383 5074

TOURISM INFORMATION WEBSITE

@ www.qdta.cn/qden/enindex.htm

Residents of Qingdao remain loyal to the brew that carries their city's name.

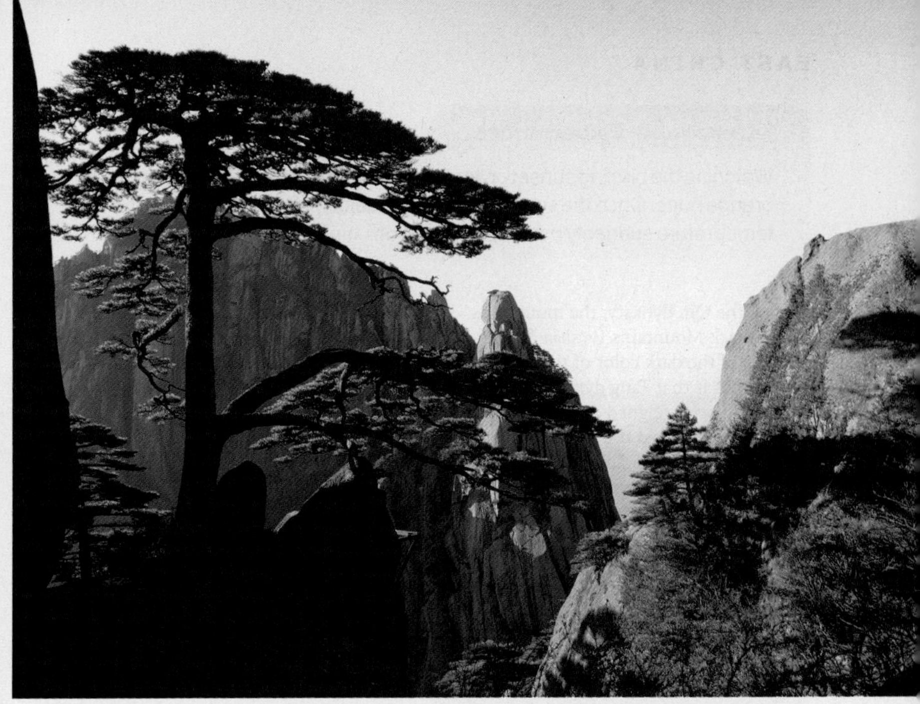

One of the many gnarled pines that grow on Huang Shan.

Huang Shan, the Mountain of Dreams

Area Code 0559

Heritage: Huang Shan, Xidi & Hong Villages

Huang Shan has been a major tourist destination since ancient times and still captures the imagination of those who have glimpsed its jade mountains protruding through the frosty mists.

Huang Shan, which means Yellow Mountains, has been a well-known destination for scholars, poets and the occasional recluse, all seeking personal inspiration and enlightenment – when you visit you will easily appreciate why.

Situated in the southern portion of the agriculturally rich Anhui Province and bordering Jiangxi and Zhejiang provinces, the picturesque Huang Shan has long been effusively described as "awesome," "a wonderland" and "Heaven on Earth." The formation of the remarkable peaks and breathtakingly sharp precipices has been attributed to the many thousands of years of geological activity on the imposing granite mountains, creating the astounding natural wonder visible today.

Memorable Experiences

Watching the blazing sunset on top of the mountain with its magnificent red and orange hues. Once the sun sets, darkness quickly enveloped us and the temperature suddenly became much colder - unforgettable.

During the Qin dynasty, the mountains called Black Mountains (*yī shān* 黟山) because of the dark color of their cliffs. Legend has it that Tang dynasty emperor Xuanzong, who reigned during the Tang's golden age, changed the name of the mountains to Huang Shan because the legendary Huang Emperor was thought to have made his pills of immortality here.

The **Huang Shan Scenic Area** (*huáng shān jǐngqū* 黄山景区) extends about 25 miles (40 km) from north to south and 19 miles (30 km) from east to west. As an important national scenic area, Huang Shan was listed as a UNESCO World Heritage Site in 1990 and as a result, the park is very well kept and amazingly enough in China, a no-smoking zone is strictly enforced.

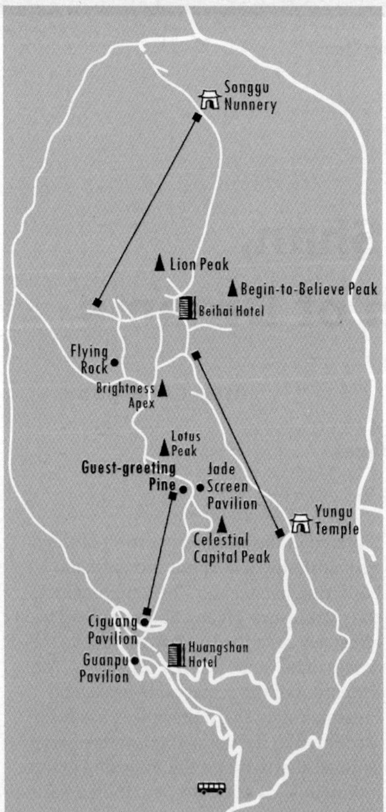

There are 72 peaks in total with **Lotus Peak** (*liánhuā fēng* 莲花峰), **Brightness Apex** (*guāngmíng dǐng* 光明顶) and the **Celestial Capital Peak** (*tiāndū fēng* 天都峰) being the three major ones, all towering above 5,900 feet (1,800 m). Although that might not seem too awe-inspiring at first, the sheer steepness of the peaks and sense of remotèness one gets when in Huang Shan coupled with frequent "weak knees" will make you think otherwise.

As you initially ascend the mountains, you'll come across stunted pine trees contorted into curious shapes. What's more amazing is that these gnarled trees sprout from rocks that are just as oddly shaped. Eroded by wind and time, the rock formations, together with the stunted pines growing off them, have long been the muse of many painters and poets. The gnarled trees and craggy rocks are the subject of numerous traditional Chinese paintings and poems and have become a recognized symbol of Huang Shan. If you see such a painting, chances are Huang Shan was the inspiration for the work.

Ever wondered what it would be like to float on a sea of clouds? At Huang Shan you can – or at least get a close approximation. The sea of clouds in the **Beihai Scenic Area** (*běihǎi jǐngqū* 北海景区) is ever-changing and unpredictable; one moment you've got the picture-perfect shot of a twisted pine on the next peak and in the next, it has disappeared, engulfed in a swirl of mist and clouds. The "now you see it, now you don't" effect lends a certain surreal quality to the experience that can make you feel rather like an immortal.

There are hot springs at the foot of Huang Shan, at **Purple Cloud Peak** (*zǐxiá fēng* 紫霞峰). For those aching after a strenuous but unforgettable climb, this opportunity should

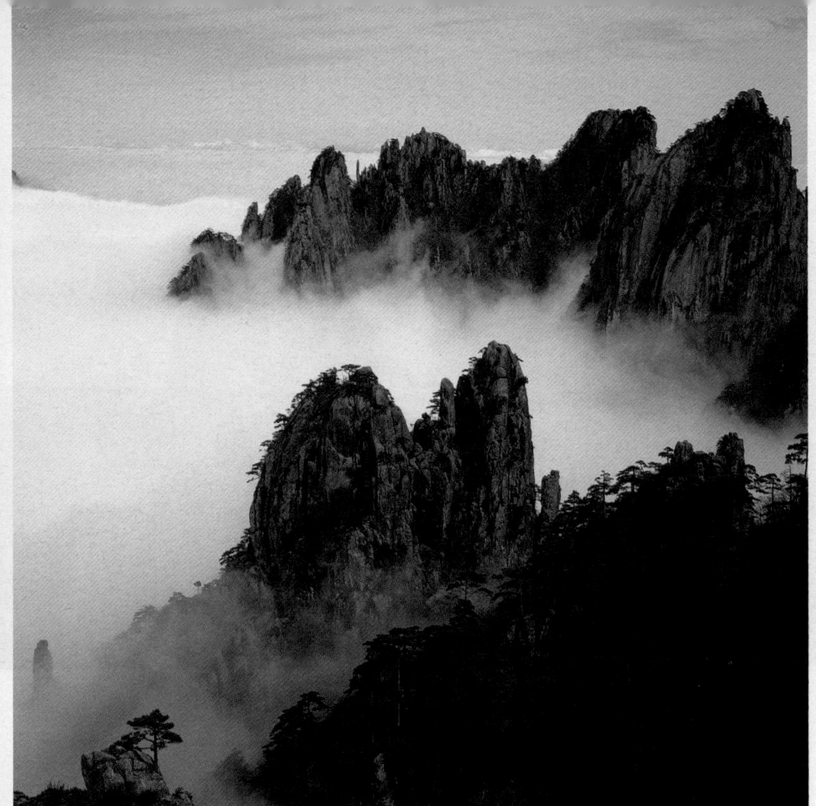

The clouds float between the jagged peaks of Huang Shan.

be utilized to pamper those tired and aching legs and feet. First tapped over a thousand years ago, the clear waters remain at a constant 104°F (40°C) year round and can be used for drinking and bathing, though not at the same time and from different pools. Special therapeutic baths and swimming pools have been built around the natural springs.

RECOMMENDED ROUTE

There are two main ways of getting to the top of Huang Shan, by foot or by cable car. A recommended route is to take the cable car up, ascending from the east side of the mountain to reach the **Beihai** (*běihǎi* 北海), stay overnight at the summit and catch the magical sunrise, then descend by foot down the western side. The western side is a lot steeper and isn't for the faint of heart. Although the scenery serves as a good distraction, don't be too distracted and lose your footing. If you do decide to climb the mountain, it's a 3-hour, 4.7-mile (7.5 km) climb from the east and a hefty 9.3 miles (15 km) from the western approach, which will take at least twice as much time.

On the eastern side of Huang Shan close to the summit, is the **Begin-to-Believe Peak** (*shǐxìn fēng* 始信峰). It's probably the most visited peak in Huang Shan due to its deep chasms and classic Huang Shan scenery. Along the way you might notice many locks clasped around the chain railings – these locks are meant to represent everlasting love. Couples romantically fasten their locks and throw the key off the peak, thereby cementing their relationship.

The Beihai Scenic Area is at the summit of Huang Shan. Paths are newly paved and well kept. This is the best place to view the sunrise above the eternal sea of clouds and pine tree-studded peaks.

Flying Rock (*fēilái shí* 飞来石) in the western part of the summit area is a huge pear-shaped rock 33 feet (10 m) high perched precariously on top of the peak. Steps leading to the top of the peak have one dubious looking handrail allowing the brave

The sun's orange glow reflects off a sea of clouds.

to really experience being on top of the world – if your eyes dare to stay open.

Along the central axis of the mountain range is the **Brightness Apex** (*guāngmíng dǐng* 光明顶). At 6,035 feet (1,840 m) this is the second highest peak on Huang Shan, and it separates the physically challenging western side from the more gentle eastern side. This is a good place to contrast the two faces.

Jade Screen Pavilion (*yùpíng lóu* 玉屏楼) is also known as the Jade Screen of Heaven. These fantastic sheer cliff faces feature unique rock formations with green pines. It looks like a giant Chinese landscape painting brought to life.

On the western side **Lotus Peak** (*liánhuā fēng* 莲花峰) is Huang Shan's highest peak. Surrounded by a group of lower peaks, Lotus Peak looks like a lotus flower in full bloom. The top of the peak offers panoramic views of Huang Shan though sore and wobbly legs are also inevitably part of the deal.

The **Celestial Capital Peak** (*tiāndū fēng* 天都峰) faces Lotus Peak in the west. At 6,000 feet (1,829 m), it's the steepest peak, but a stone stairway is cut into the near vertical cliff face and those wanting to venture up, much of it on all fours, are aided by heavy chains hammered into the rock face. This stone stairway can easily be spotted from afar as a thin white line creeping up to the summit. It should be noted that during winter this peak may be closed. Even so, just looking at the peak is mind-blowing enough to give anyone vertigo.

After leaving the Huang Shan Scenic Area, in Tunxi there is an old trading street known as **Tunxi Ancient Street** (*túnxī lǎojiē* 屯溪老街). This nearly mile-long (1.5 km) street has been a bustling center of trade since the Southern Song dynasty, taking its present-day form during the Ming and Qing dynasties. Paved with bluestone, the street is lined on both sides with old shops in an unmistakable Huizhou architectural style characterized by fine woodcarvings on lattice windows and doors. The shops retain the essence of traditional stores of yesteryear, selling wares such as traditional medicines and local specialties including Shexian ink stones, Huang Shan Maofeng tea and Huizhou ink sticks.

In **Yixian County** (*yī xiàn* 黟县), not far from Huang Shan, there are two very interesting villages worth visiting. The first is **Hong Village** (*hóngcūn* 宏村) where the movie "*Crouching Tiger, Hidden Dragon*" was partly shot. Hong Village was first built during the Southern Song dynasty, approximately 900 years ago, by the Wang clan. During the Ming dynasty, Wang Siqi, a

powerful retired government official, hired a famous *fengshui* expert to come and review the layout of the village which resulted in the addition of a lake and water channels flowing through nearly every household within the village.

In the center of the village is a beautiful pond surrounded by houses and the **Wang Clan Hall** (*wāngshì cítáng* 汪氏祠堂) where banquets and important clan gatherings were held. Today, many artists can be seen sitting beside the pond putting the tranquil setting onto canvas. The scenery and village itself is so inspiring that many young artists rent rooms and extend their stay.

Close to Hong Village is **Xidi** (*xīdì* 西递), which is notable for the many archways that line the road to the village. In the past, it was a status symbol of wealth and distinction to build grand archways, so the bigger the better. Because many rich merchants once lived here, there are scores of archways in this hidden area. Each archway is made of local marble and is carved in typical Anhui style, decorated with multiple reliefs.

The houses in Xidi are also remarkable because the local merchants, in order to protect their families and belongings from bandits, built their dwellings with very high walls and small, if any, windows. As a result, strolling through Xidi, one can feel the insular atmosphere that must have permeated throughout the village, especially when walking down the narrow alleyways between the walls of two dwellings. Within the walls, the exquisite woodcarvings and delicately created reliefs throughout the entire dwelling confirm the wealth of its owner and the opulence the family once enjoyed. ■

Making Your Trip Easy

Practical Tips

April to November is the best time to visit Huang Shan. Hiking boots or good sneakers are advised for climbing the mountain. Pay careful attention while walking the trails though – the scenery can be a dangerous distraction, especially at Celestial Capital Peak. Evenings are chilly, especially near the peak, and coat rentals are available on the mountain. Many people have visited Huang Shan more than once because the scenery is distinct in each season.

Make sure you take your camera and plenty of film and batteries. The shops on the summit area are limited in what they stock and prices are a lot higher than back on Earth.

A travel permit is required to visit Yixian County. The permit can be arranged through the local CITS and the application may take a few days. You can apply for the travel permit yourself at the Public Security Bureau in Huang Shan City (黄山市公安局出入境管理科) for a RMB 50 fee, but be sure to bring your passport. They're located at Changgan Lu (长干路, ☎ 231 5429, 1680 0789). Foreigners are forbidden to stay overnight in Xidi or Hong Village, making it an enforced daytrip.

Huang Shan's scenery has inspired countless painters and poets.

Transportation

Airport – Huang Shan Airport is in Tunxi, about 43 miles (70 km) from the mountain area. It takes about 10 minutes from the airport to the city by shuttle bus. A bus ride from the city to the Huang Shan Scenic Area costs RMB 10 and takes about an hour.

Bus – There is one daily bus that travels to Huang Shan directly from Shanghai. It leaves in the afternoon and arrives at Huang Shan around midnight. For the return trip there are two departing buses available at the Huang Shan Railway Station. One departs early in the morning and one in the evening.

Cable Car – Taking the cable car to get up Huang Shan is an easy way. It's open from 7:30am to 4pm during the winter and 8am to 4pm all other seasons. There are three cable car lines:

The Yungu Cable Car (*yúngǔ suǒdào* 云谷索道) goes from Yungu Temple (*yúngǔ sì* 云谷寺) to Bai'e Ridge (*bái'é lǐng* 白鹅岭).

The Songgu Cable Car (*sōnggǔ suǒdào* 松谷索道) goes from the Songgu Nunnery (*sōnggǔ ān* 松谷庵) to Songlin Peak (*sōnglín fēng* 松林峰).

The Yuping Cable Car (*yùpíng suǒdào* 玉屏索道) goes from Ciguang Pavillion (*cíguāng gé* 慈光阁) to Yuping Pavilion (*yùpíng lóu* 玉屏楼). All routes are RMB 56 for a one-way ticket.

Taxi – From Tunxi to Huang Shan is about 43 miles (70 km) and taking a taxi will cost approximately RMB 100. Passengers may need to switch cabs halfway for the drivers to avoid paying extra registration fees. Within Tunxi City limits, transportation is cheap and quick. The city isn't very big and zippy tricycle motorbikes cost only RMB 2 to 3. Taxis are RMB 5 at flag-fall.

Train – There are daily trains shuttling between Huang Shan and Shanghai.

The Best of Huang Shan

Huang Shan Scenic Area
黄山景区 *huáng shān jǐngqū*
✉ 43 miles (69 km) from Tunxi 距屯溪69公里
¥ 202

Five recommended sights are:

Begin-to-Believe Peak 始信峰 *shǐxìn fēng*
Brightness Apex 光明顶 *guāngmíng dǐng*

Rustic village life continues in Hong Village.

Celestial Capital Peak 天都峰 *tiāndū fēng*
Jade Screen Pavilion 玉屏楼 *yùpíng lóu*
Lion Peak 狮子峰 *shīzi fēng*

Hong Village 宏村 *hóng cūn*
✉ 37 miles (60 km) northwest of Tunxi, Yixian County 距屯溪西北 60 多公里，黟县境内
¥ 40

Xidi 西递 *xīdì*
✉ 34 miles (55 km) northwest of Tunxi, Yixian County 距屯溪西北 55 公里，黟县境内
¥ 40

Hotels

Golf Hotel 黄山高尔夫酒店 *huángshān gāo'ěrfū jiǔdiàn* ★★★★★
✉ 78 Longjing, Jichang Da Dao, Tunxi District 屯溪区机场大道龙井 78 号
☎ 256 8000
¥ 880 – double room, peak-season
704 – double room, off-season
@ www.hsgolf.com

Huang Shan Hongta Hotel 黄山红塔酒店 *huángshān hóngtǎ jiǔdiàn* ★★★★
✉ in the Huangkou Scenic Area, Tunxi District 屯溪区黄口度假区内
☎ 231 2888
¥ 680 – double room, peak-season
300 – double room, off-season

Huang Shan International Hotel 黄山国际大酒店 *huángshān guójì dàjiǔdiàn* ★★★★
✉ 31 Huashan Lu, Tunxi District 屯溪区华山路 31 号
☎ 256 5678
¥ 300 – double room
@ www.huangshaninterhotel.com

Huang Shan Shilin Hotel 黄山狮林大酒店 *huángshān shīlín dàjiǔdiàn* ★★★★
✉ in the Beihai Scenic Area, Huangshan Scenic Area 黄山风景区北海景区
☎ 558 4040
¥ 1080 – double room, peak-season
620 – double room, off-season
@ www.shilin.com

Huang Shan Xihai Hotel 黄山西海饭店 *huángshān xīhǎi fàndiàn* ★★★★
✉ in the Xihai Scenic Area, Huang Shan Scenic Area 黄山风景区西海景区
☎ 558 8888
¥ 1080 – double room, peak-season
720 – double room, off-season
@ www.hsxihaihotel.com

Quotes

"Don't look at the scenery when you are walking, and don't walk when you're looking at the scenery."

Taoyuan Hotel 黄山桃源宾馆 *huángshān táoyuán bīnguǎn* ★★★

✉ Wenquan Scenic Area, Huang Shan Scenic Area 黄山风景区温泉景区

☎ 558 5666

¥ 600 – double room, peak-season
300 – double room, off-season

@ www.huangshantaoyuanhotel.com

Food & Restaurants

For obvious reasons, food isn't one of the main reasons people flock to Huang Shan. All the food on the mountain has to be carried up by foot, which means food is expensive and variety is limited.

Once you've descended the mountain, Anhui cuisine is readily available and delicious. A unique characteristic of Anhui cuisine is the extensive use of mushrooms, bayberries and bamboo, which are all found in the mountainous areas of the province. In general, Anhui dishes tend to be slightly spicy and salty, while preserving most of the original flavor of the ingredients.

Anhui cuisine is also known for its use of wild game (*yěwèi* 野味), such as wild chickens (*yějī* 野鸡) and wild rabbits (*yětù* 野兔). Huang Shan's bounty includes exotic fruits such as Huang Shan kiwi (*huángshān míhóutáo* 黄山猕猴桃), Santan loquats (*sāntán pípá* 三檀枇杷) and Huizhou snow pears (*huīzhōu xuělí* 徽州雪梨).

A centuries old Huizhou tradition involves serving *bawanba* (*bā wǎn bā* 八碗八), made of 16 dishes to mark important occasions.

Some well-known Huizhou dishes includes stinky mandarin fish (*chòu guìyú* 臭鳜鱼) which is baked with a salted meat, steamed frog with mushrooms and ham (*qīngzhēng shíjī* 清蒸石鸡), Huizhou hairy tofu (*huīzhōu máodòufu* 徽州毛豆腐), made from a special recipe passed down from generation to generation and rolls (*xièkéhuáng shāobǐng* 蟹壳黄烧饼) that are delightfully flaky with a vegetable or meat filling.

RESTAURANTS

Diyilou Restaurant 屯溪老街第一楼

Large restaurant serving delicious *sanhuang* chicken(*sānhuáng jī* 三黄鸡). Exceptionally tender and tasty.

✉ 247 Lao Jie, Tunxi 屯溪老街 247 号

☎ 253 9797

Huang Shan Huicaiguan 黄山徽菜馆

Specializes in traditional Anhui cuisine like pickled mandarin fish and tofu (*hǔpí chòudòufu* 虎皮臭豆腐).

✉ 59 Huang Shan Xi Lu 黄山西路 59 号

☎ 251 7828

Laoshanghai Dajiudian 老上海大酒店

Specializes in seafood dishes.

✉ 266 Tunxi Laojie, 屯溪老街 266 号

☎ 251 3636

Souvenirs

Buying a walking stick for Huang Shan might seem an unnecessary purchase, but after the first day of climbing, the usefulness of such an aid will quickly become obvious. These walking sticks are cheap at less than RMB 10. Three kinds of tea are cultivated on Huang Shan, *Maofeng* (毛峰), *Houkui* (猴魁) and *Qihong* (祁红). Maofeng is particularly known for its flowery fragrance. Anhui is a major production center for the "Scholar's Four Treasures" (*wénfáng sìbǎo* 文房四宝) which consists of high quality Xuan paper (*xuānzhǐ* 宣纸), Shexian ink stones (*shèyàn* 歙砚), Huizhou ink sticks (*huīmò* 徽墨) and Xuancheng calligraphy brushes (*xuānchéng máobǐ* 宣城毛笔).

Other Information

POST OFFICES

Huang Shan City Post Office 黄山市邮政局

✉ Changgan Lu, Tunxi District 屯溪区长干路

☎ 251 2912

HOSPITALS

Huang Shan General Hospital
黄山市人民医院

✉ Liyuan Lu, Tunxi District 屯溪区栗园路

☎ 251 3763

COMPLAINT HOTLINES

☎ General: 251 7464

☎ Taxi: 235 3410

Lu Shan, the Mountain Retreat

Area Code 0792

Heritage: Lu Shan

Historic villas, forest trails and cool mountain peaks have been drawing people to this mountain hideaway for more than 100 years. The misty clouds blanket the lush forests and provide a mystical scene.

The peaks of **Lu Shan** in northern Jiangxi Province have long been a magnet for the spiritual, the rich and famous, the learned and powerful. Although wet, cold and misty for more than 200 day a year, Lu Shan's wooded slopes offer cool repose for those escaping the summer heat in the ancient city of **Jiujiang** in the south and the lowland valley areas of **Yangtze River** in the north.

Once you set eyes on the scenic landscape of Lu Shan, you will understand why people keep coming back. Of the some 99 peaks, **Dahanyang Peak** (*dàhànyáng fēng* 大汉阳峰) stands tallest at 4,835 feet (1,474 m). Peaks aside, there are gorges, waterfalls, overhanging cliffs, lakes, verdant forests and amazing bird life. No wonder eminent poets of every dynasty have eulogized the natural beauty of Lu Shan.

Lu Shan's famous summer resort boasts beautiful late 19th century colonial villas, the private retreats of European merchants and Christian missionaries who made the mountain their summer home. At one time there were about 2,000 such residences, and some of China's most powerful landowners and political figures, including Chiang Kai-shek, made Lu Shan their summer abode.

The mansions are concentrated in the

The Brocade Valley's gorgeous scenery is sure to impress.

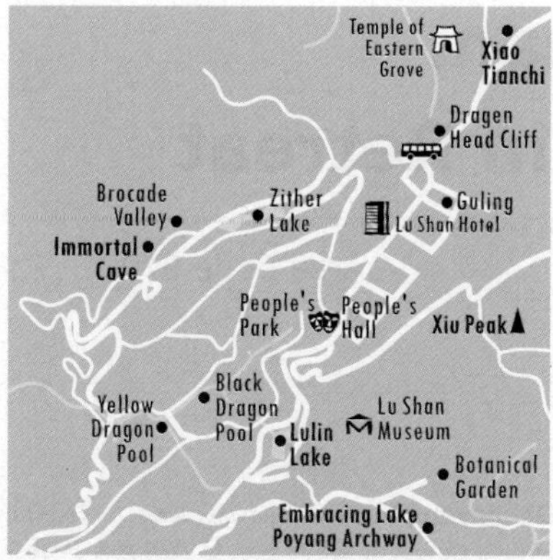

mountain town of Guling, located in **Lu Shan Park** (*lú shān gōngyuán* 庐山公园). From June through September, thousands of tourists flock to these architectural abodes to catch a glimpse of a bygone era.

One picturesque route is the **Brocade Valley's** (*jǐnxiù gǔ* 锦绣谷) mile-long (1.6 km) trail on the southeast bank of **Zither Lake** (*rúqín hú* 如琴湖), which is shaped like the harp-like musical instrument. This steep, narrow path, no more than shoulder wide, is hugged by peaks and valleys, all of which paints such moving scenery that it inspired the brushes of landscape artists for centuries.

This trail, famed for its 99 bends, boasts the **Immortal Cave** (*xiānrén dòng* 仙人洞) – a rock chamber on the edge of a precipice, within which bubbles a natural spring. Taoist priests transformed this remote cave into their temple, replete with a huge stone shrine, altars and scriptures carved onto the rocky walls. Legend has it that Lü Dongbin, one of the eight Taoist immortals, was granted a sword by a fire-breathing dragon here. With this celestial weapon, he vanquished all demons and became immortal.

Apart from Taoism, Buddhism also left its mark on Lu Shan, which became the epicenter of Buddhism in China at the time of the Eastern Han dynasty. A major temple that survived the Cultural Revolution is the **Temple of Eastern Grove** (*dōnglín sì* 东林寺) founded by Huiyuan in AD 391. His influential teachings eventually spread to Japan. Over 300 Buddhist and Taoist temples remain scattered on Lu Shan's slopes, as well as several churches and mosques. These flourished as a result of the steady influx of foreigners and missionaries.

During the Song dynasty, a prolific Neo-Confucian scholar founded the **Bailu Dong Academy** (*báilùdòng shūyuàn* 白鹿洞书院) at Wulao Peak on top the ground of an older complex. Here students listened to lectures given by the master who introduced metaphysical aspects to the Confucian ethical discourse.

Guling is where most people base themselves when exploring Lu Shan.

At Lu Shan, each manmade pagoda, temple, pavilion or monument has rich historical and cultural resonance, but nature has also left a beautiful gift at the foot of the mountain, **Poyang Lake** (*póyáng hú* 鄱阳湖). The biggest freshwater lake in China, Poyang's extensive surface is littered with thousands of boats and hosts one of the most notable migratory bird reserves in China. Since 1996, Lu Shan has ranked amongst UNESCO's prestigious list of World Heritage Sites.

COOLING GULING

Perched at 3,838 feet (1,167 m) and ringed by mountains, **Guling Town** (*gǔlǐng zhèn* 牯岭镇), better known to Westerners as "Kuling" for its "cooling" climate, is a convenient place to start any excursion.

Exploring by foot is easy within Guling. Start off with the European-styled villas, which used to be summer rest-stations for the large foreign summer community. Englishman E. L. Little was the first to set up the summer resort in 1895, and though the inhabitants are long gone, the colonial houses are architectural, cultural and historical repositories. Some have evolved into museums and others into guesthouses.

Meilu Villa (*měilú biéshù* 美庐别墅) is a must-see cultural relic. Built in 1903, the summer home was a gift to China's power couple: Chiang Kai-shek and his wife Song Meiling. The now-crumbling villa, named after her, is on the main sightseeing stretch of road along Hexi Lu on Hedong Lu, just southwest of central Guling. The paint is peeled and the garden grounds are in disarray, but several historical mementos still pepper the mansion's interiors. Decorated by paintings done by the former First Lady herself, her lavish bedroom remains unchanged and also contains pictures of the couple.

A stone's throw away is **People's Hall** (*rénmín jùyuàn* 人民剧院) now converted into a museum. Also known as **Lu Shan Conference Site** (*lúshān huìyì huìzhǐ* 庐山会议会址), it was at meetings here in 1959 and 1970 that Chairman Mao changed the course of China's history.

Between Guling and Embracing Lake Poyang Archway is **Lulin Lake** (*lúlín hú* 芦林湖), which is a good place to start excursions to

Cascading waterfalls are a common sight on the Lu Shan.

Three Ancient Trees (*sānbǎo shù* 三宝树) and the **Yellow and Black Dragon Pools** (*huánglóng tán* 黄龙潭, *wūlóng tán* 乌龙潭) and its five gorgeous waterfalls. Follow the cement paths for a pleasant daylong hike.

Beside the lake is the **Former Residence of Mao Zedong** (*Máo Zédōng gùjū* 毛泽东故居), which houses the **Lu Shan Museum** (*lúshān bówùguǎn* 庐山博物馆). Religion, geography, Communist and natural history can all be found under one roof. You can find archival pictures of visiting dignitaries as well as an educational collection of insect specimens. East of the museum is the **Monument of Mao Zedong's Poems** (*Máo Zédōng shībēi yuán* 毛泽东诗碑园), where Mao's own composition and favorite verses are

One of the many old villas that dot Lu Shan's mountain scenery.

inscribed on huge slabs of granite.

East of the museum is the **Botanical Gardens** (*zhíwù yuán* 植物园), which have a staggering 3,000 native alpine and tropical flora specimens on exhibit. South of the Botanical Gardens, a short taxi ride away, is **Embracing Lake Poyang Archway** (*hánpókǒu* 含鄱口), where you can catch the sun rising over Poyang Lake and southern Yangtze Valley. The sun rises at 5am in the summer and 7am in the winter.

You can also strike out on your own for a 3-hour hike towards **Sandiequan Falls** (*sāndiéquán pùbù* 三叠泉瀑布), where savage rapids literally cascade into clouds of mists. These famous falls are on the southeastern slope of the mountain and are considered one of Lu Shan's most majestic sights. The falls measure 705 feet (215 m) high and cascade down three levels. The falls have attracted their share of ancient poets, some of whom have left their poems carved into the rock. Like stepping into a landscape painting, the gnarled pine trees, craggy rocks and perilous peaks have all served as a natural Muse, especially during the sunrise and sunsets. Due to the popularity of the falls, be prepared to jostle enthusiastic tour groups along steep paths for a piece of the fantastic view.

Xiu Peak (*xiùfēng* 秀峰) is located in an area of Lu Shan called "shan nan." During the 10th century the Kaixian Temple was built here. In 1707, Qing emperor Kangxi gave the temple a visit and gave the temple its present name, **Xiufeng Temple** (*xiùfēng sì* 秀峰寺). The scenery around the temple, like throughout Lu Shan, is gorgeous. ■

Memorable Experiences

Trekking along the narrow trail to Sandiequan Falls early in the morning.

Enjoying a leisurely picnic near Lulin Lake, where Mao used to swim.

Savoring Lu Shan's specialty Cloud and Mist tea, brewed with natural spring water from the mountain.

Making Your Trip Easy

Practical Tips

May to November is the best time to visit Lu Shan. Make sure you bring enough clothes as it can get quite chilly at the high elevations.

Transportation

Airport – The closest airport is at Changbei in Xinjian County, but there are no shuttle buses to Lu Shan from there. Taking a taxi from Changbei to Lu Shan will take an hour.

Bus – Get tickets to Jiujiang from a booth off Guling Jie, then take the tunnel and make a left turn. The Nanchang Bus Depot is opposite this tunnel on Hexi Lu. Buses to Lu Shan from Jiujiang depart from the Yangtze River Ferry Terminal and the long-distance bus station. It takes about 30 minutes to get to Jiujiang and there are many buses everyday, tickets are around RMB 7. Going to Nanchang will take 2.5 hours and tickets are about RMB 35.

Scenic stopoffs abound at Lu Shan, but there's a lot of ground to cover. Take a minibus for a daylong tour of some of the spectacular sites further away from Guling. There are two tour options to choose from; both cost RMB 100. They'll head to the main scenic sights like Zither Lake, Immortal Cave, Dragon Head Cliff, Poyang Lake and the Sandiequan Falls.

Taxi – Taxis are very convenient at Lu Shan; full-size taxis are RMB 7 at flag-fall and compact taxis are RMB 5.

Train – From the Lushan Train Station there are shuttle buses to the mountains for RMB 7. Many trains don't stopover at the Lushan Train Station, so passengers get off at Nanchang or Jiujiang Stations where they take a long-distance bus into Lu Shan. There are trains from Lu Shan to Beijing, Chongqing, Nanchang, Shanghai and Wuhan.

The Best of Lu Shan

Lu Shan Scenic Area
庐山风景区 *lúshān fēngjǐngqū*
☎ 255 1796
¥ 135

Four recommended sights are:

Brocade Valley 锦绣谷 *jǐnxiù gǔ*
Meilu Villa 美庐别墅 *měilú biéshù*
Sandiequan Falls 三叠泉 *sāndiéquán*
Xiu Peak 秀峰 *xiùfēng*

Birds abound at Poyang Lake, close to Lu Shan.

Quotes

"Brilliant natural scenery all around. I'm not gifted in poetry but even I was inspired to write an ode in praise of nature."

"I walked the suspension bridge at Stone Gorge Valley. Awesome experience - just like everything else here."

"There are so many religious, cultural, historical, ecological things of value here, that I can spend weeks to fully enjoy Lu Shan's multifaceted treasures."

Hotels

Jiujiang Audit Hotel 九江欧迪大酒店 *jiǔjiāng ōudí dàjiǔdiàn* ★★★
- 28 Shili Da Dao 十里大道 28 号
- 898 7701, 8987702
- 358 – double room, peak-season
  268 – double room, off-season
- www.audit-hotel.com

Jiujiang Hotel
九江宾馆 *jiǔjiāng bīnguǎn* ★★★
- 118 Nanhu Lu 南湖路 118 号
- 898 1888
- 300 – double room
- www.jjhotel.cn

Lushan Hotel
庐山宾馆 *lúshān bīnguǎn* ★★★
- 446 Lushan Hexi Lu 庐山河西路 446 号
- 828 2060
- 580 – double room

White Deer Hotel
九江白鹿宾馆 *jiǔjiāng báilù bīnguǎn* ★★★
- 113 Xunyang Lu 浔阳路 113 号
- 898 0866, 898 0888
- 285 – double room

Wufeng Hotel
五丰宾馆 *wǔfēng bīnguǎn* ★★★
- 129 Xunyang Lu 浔阳路 129 号
- 898 7001, 898 7018
- 198 – double room, peak-season
  154 – double room, off-season
- www.wfhotel.jj.jx.cn

Food and Restaurants

Jiujiang and Lu Shan are famous for their fish dishes. *Xunyang yuyan* (浔阳鱼宴) is a set of dishes all made from fish and shrimp; they're not only delicious but also works of art. *Baijiao yongyutou* (白浇鳙鱼头) is a traditional Jiujiang stew that's made with 11 pounds (5 kg) of fish heads. Give Lu Shan's "three stones" (*lúshān sānshí* 庐山三石) a try. It's made with "stone ears," a type of mushroom; "stone fish," a fish that's only found in Lu Shan's springs; and "stone chicken," a kind of frog. Other local delicacies include *xiushui shaozi* (修水哨子), a big steamed bun shaped like a peach and filled with meat and vegetables, and *luobo ba* (萝卜粑), which is made from radishes.

RESTAURANTS

0792 Restaurant 0792 大酒店
- 50 Lushan Nan Lu 庐山南路 50 号
- 815 7777
- 11am to 9pm

Red Dog Restaurant 红狗酒屋
- beside Xindi Hotel, Lushan
  庐山新地宾馆旁边
- 820 7705

Wusong Restaurant 雾松酒楼
- 1 Guling Zheng Jie, Lushan
  庐山牯岭正街 1 号
- 828 1648
- 11am to 9pm

Xinhua Restaurant 信华大酒店
- 88 Lushan Nan Lu 庐山南路 88 号
- 818 8888, 818 9999
- 11am to 9pm

Xiuyu Hongchafang 秀玉红茶坊
Offers local cuisine and Western food.
- 310 Xunyang Lu 浔阳路 310 号
- 823 8617, 823 8618
- 9:20am to 2am

Zuishi Restaurant 醉石酒家
- 9 Lushan Hexi Lu 庐山河西路 9 号
- 828 1531
- 11am to 9pm

Souvenirs

All you need can be found on two streets in Guling. Hexi Lu and Guling Jie are full of

The mist sweeps off Poyang Lake into the scenic areas of Lu Shan's Hanpokou.

souvenir shops, thirsting for your tourist dollar. Worth the money are the daintily embroidered pouches and Lu Shan's famous Cloud and Mist tea (*yúnwù chá* 云雾茶), a famous Chinese green tea with a sweet taste.

Other interesting souvenirs include ink stones (*jīnxīng yàn* 金星砚) that cost from under RMB 100 to 3,000. Get these at the Yuanming Jinxing Yan Gongyichang (渊明金星砚工艺厂) at Ziyang Bei Lu (紫阳北路, 266 5982) in Jiujiang.

For general shopping in Jiujiang head over to 9-23 Xunyang Lu (浔阳路 9-23 号) for the Liansheng Shopping Center (*liánshèng gòuwù guǎngchǎng* 联盛购物广场), which offers shopping, food and lodging. Jiujiang Hualian Shangsha (九江华联商厦) is another general shopping center with a little of everything; it's over at Bajiaoshi Square (*bājiǎoshí guǎngchǎng* 八角石广场).

Other Information

POST OFFICES

Jiujiang City Post Office 九江市邮政局

✉ 12 Jiaotong Lu 交通路 12 号

☎ 822 5448

🕒 8am to 6pm

HOSPITALS

Lushan People's Hospital 庐山人民医院

✉ 39 Lushan Dalin Lu 庐山大林路 39 号

☎ 828 2958

The First Jiujiang People's Hospital 九江市第一人民医院

✉ 48 Taling Nan Lu, Xunyang District 浔阳区塔岭南路 48 号

☎ 858 2052

COMPLAINT HOTLINES

☎ General: 822 5571

☎ Taxi: 858 6853, 855 5003

TOURISM INFORMATION WEBSITE

@ www.china-lushan.com

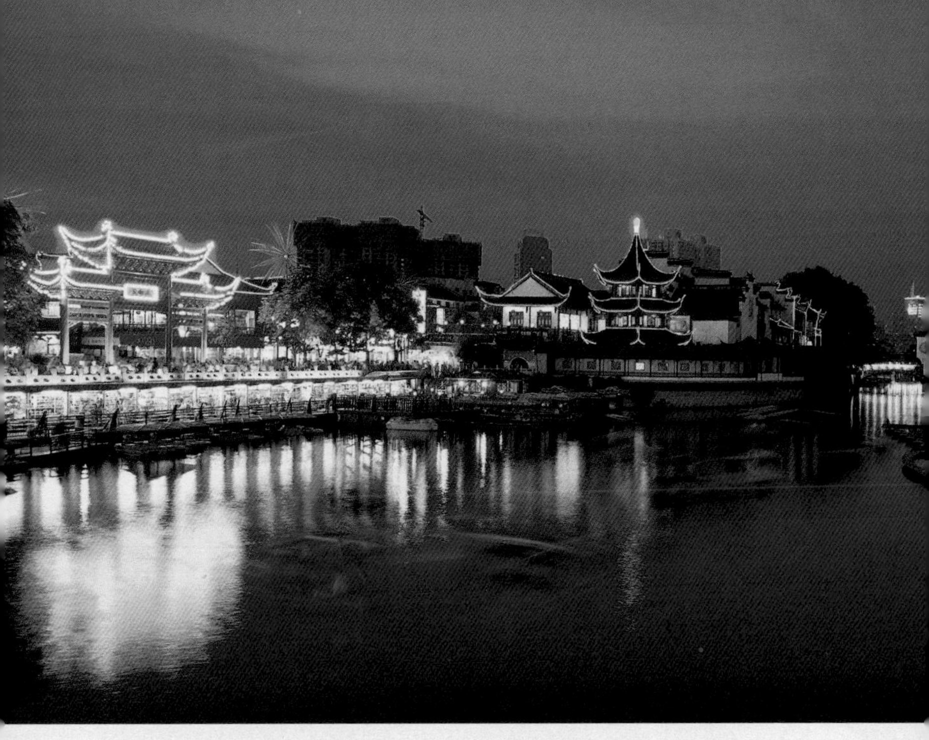

The old architecture lining the banks of the Qinhuai River is best viewed by boat.

Nanjing, the Eye of the Storm

Area Code 025

Nanjing has seen its capital moments – it was once an imperial capital, then the capital of the Taiping Rebellion and later the capital of the Republic of China. Sights telling the story of China's past and memorials to the events that shaped modern China are strewn across this pleasant city.

The city has certainly seen its fair share of crucial historical events. Once, with the **Yangtze River** on one side, surrounded by the **Purple Mountain** and shielded by massive city walls, Nanjing was perceived as impenetrable – but in fact the city has been destroyed and rebuilt on several occasions. Today Nanjing is the capital of **Jiangsu Province**, one of China's most economically vibrant provinces, receiving a big chunk of the foreign investments in China.

Nanjing, meaning "southern capital," was the seat of six dynasties and more recently, the Republic of China when under Nationalist leadership. In the context of Chinese politics, Nanjing came into the spotlight when a peasant revolt ousted the Yuan dynasty from the city in 1356. The rebel leader later became the first emperor of

the Ming dynasty. Nanjing was bombarded by the British during the First Opium War, which lasted from 1840 to 1842, and the subsequent Treaty of Nanjing, the first of the "unequal treaties" that China was forced to sign after its defeat, gave foreign powers privileges over China that would cripple the nation. During the Taiping Rebellion, from 1850 to 1864, Nanjing was made capital by rebels who controlled most of southern and central China. The city was renamed "The Heavenly Capital" and only with the help of foreign powers and after untold carnage, was the Qing dynasty able to retake Nanjing. In the **Taiping Heavenly Kingdom History Museum** (*tàipíng tiānguó lìshǐ bówùguǎn* 太平天国历史博物馆), the tale of one of the most astounding rebellions in Chinese history is told. The leader of the rebels, Hong Xiuquan was the self-professed little brother of Jesus and ruled under the name of Heavenly King. He was able to gather an army strong enough to nearly topple the Qing dynasty. Another museum, newly renovated and well-equipped, is the **Nanjing Museum** (*nánjīng bówùguǎn* 南京博物馆) exhibiting bronze vessels, jade, ceramics and calligraphy.

Sun Yat-sen (*Sūn Zhōngshān* 孙中山), who became president of the Republic of China after the Qing dynasty fell in 1911, also made Nanjing the national capital, until the Japanese attacked the city in 1937, an event that remains a sensitive issue between China and Japan. The Japanese soldiers, frustrated by a surprisingly dogged defense by Chinese troops, unleashed their frustrations on Nanjing's civilian populace when the Nationalist forces were eventually routed. When Japanese forces entered the city on December 13, 1937, an estimated 300,000 Nanjing residents were killed by marauding Japanese in a condoned and orchestrated orgy of rape and murder that lasted six weeks terrorizing the residents of Nanjing. The soldiers conducted bayonet practice on live victims, forced captives to dig their own graves before being buried alive, indiscriminately slaughtered and raped children and the elderly. A grotesque competition between two Japanese officers to see who could behead the most victims was eventually called a tie after both claimed over a hundred heads. The victims of the massacre are commemorated at the somber **Nanjing Massacre Memorial Hall** (*nánjīng dàtúshā jìniànguǎn* 南京大屠杀纪念馆), which is built over the site of a mass grave. Documents, videos and graphic pictures documenting the violence are exhibited, as is the site of the mass grave itself. Sadly, like the Holocaust, revisionists continue to refute the events that occurred, and the lack of a formal apology and scant coverage in Japanese history texts remains a point of contention for many in Asia.

Surrounding Nanjing is a 20.8-mile-long (33.5 km) **city wall** with an average height of 39 feet (12 m) and width of 26 feet (8 m), but unfortunately the wall is no longer complete. Built from 1366 to 1386, it was one of the longest city walls ever constructed. **Zhonghua Men** (*zhōnghuá mén* 中华门), the most imposing gate, still stands and is open for visits into its cavernous hall. Within the city wall, there are few older buildings, and most major historical sights are on the Purple Mountain on the eastern side of the city. The exceptions are the14th century **Drum Tower** (*gǔ lóu* 鼓楼) and the **Bell Tower** (*zhōng lóu* 钟楼) in the center of the city. However, along the **Qinhuai River** (*qínhuái hé* 秦淮河) an old neighborhood in typical southern Chinese style has been rebuilt as a pedestrian thoroughfare. The atmosphere is authentic Chinese market – loud and bustling, even if the buildings are

Memorable Experiences

Immersing ourselves in China's ancient and not so ancient history on the Purple Mountain.

Strolling around the Confucius Temple and Qinhuai River area, tasting the snacks and watching romantic couples sailing around in boats.

Learning more about Nanjing and Chinese history in one of the city's museums.

new. The area has many shops, teahouses and restaurants which make for a good way to pass a couple hours. Also in the area is the **Confucius Temple** (*fūzǐ miào* 夫子庙), once a center of learning, with an imperial examination hall nearby. The present buildings are Qing era or new reconstructions.

The **Yangtze River Bridge** (*nánjīng chángjiāng dàqiáo* 南京长江大桥) is the pride of modern Nanjing. The 2.8-mile-long (4.5 km) bridge is a key point for traffic between north and south China. Work on this double-decker bridge commenced in 1961 and was finished in 1968. A ferry link was used to cross the mighty river prior its construction.

History aside, Nanjing is a very pleasant city with almost every street flanked by trees and there are plenty of parks and lakes. The **Xuanwu Lake** (*xuánwǔ hú* 玄武湖) is a popular spot for an outing with pavilions and small pagodas and Chinese families splashing around in boats. Another enjoyable park, though once an execution ground, is also the **Martyr's Cemetery** (*lièshì língyuán* 烈士陵园), a memorial to the Communists who lost their lives battling the Nationalists.

PURPLE MOUNTAIN

The **Purple Mountain** (*zǐjīn shān* 紫金山), at the eastern edge of the city, is home to many of Nanjing's historical sights. A full day is

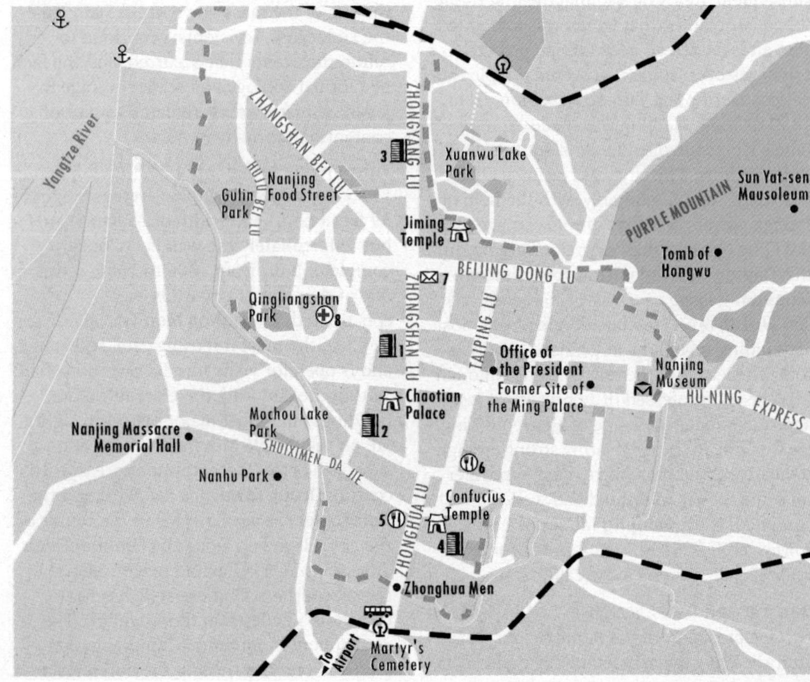

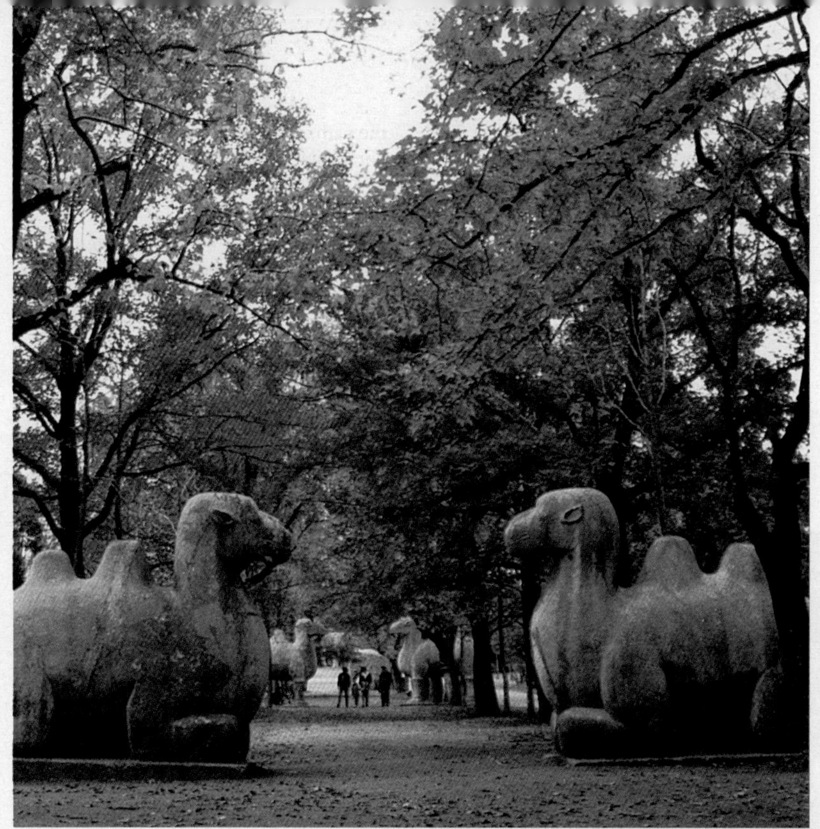

Statues line the Spirit Way to the tomb of the Ming dynasty's first emperor, Zhu Yuanzhang.

needed to explore all the sights. The newest addition to the field is the **Sun Yat-sen Mausoleum** (*zhōngshān líng* 中山陵). After Sun Yat-sen, revered as the leading force in bringing down the Qing dynasty, died in 1925, a tomb fit for an emperor was built for him. Pass through massive gates and climb 392 marble steps and you'll arrive in front of the mausoleum with white walls and a bright blue-tiled roof. A larger than life statue of Sun Yat-sen, appropriate for a man whose adventures included being kidnapped by Qing agents in London, greets you in the entrance to the main hall. Inscribed on the wall are his three principles for national salvation – nationalism, democracy and people's livelihood. In the round crypt is Sun Yat-sen's casket with a carved statue of him reclining. Behind the tomb is a small garden and a photographic exhibition from the early years of the Chinese republic. There's a great view over the lush green Purple Mountain from the top steps that lead up to the mausoleum – that is, when the weather permits it. The hills are often obscured by clouds and mist that lends the area an enchanting atmosphere.

The **Linggu Temple** (*línggǔ sì* 灵谷寺), a short walk from the mausoleum, rents bicycles, an ideal way to go from sight to sight around Purple Mountain. The centerpiece of the Linggu Temple is the 197-foot-tall (60 m) **Linggu Pagoda** (*línggǔ tǎ* 灵谷塔). Moved here from the Tomb of Hongwu in 1381, it was destroyed during the Taiping Rebellion and rebuilt again in 1911 to commemorate those who died fighting to overthrow the Qing dynasty. The only remaining building on the premises is the **Beamless Hall** (*wúliáng diàn* 无梁殿), 72 feet (22 m) high and 177 feet (54 m) wide, and built solely with bricks.

East of Sun Yat-sen's mausoleum is another mausoleum, the **Tomb of Hongwu** (*míngxiào líng* 明孝陵), the rebel turned emperor. Originally named Zhu Yuanzhang, he was born a peasant, did a stint as a monk, turned rebel and eventually became the first emperor of the Ming dynasty under the title Hongwu. The 13 other emperors of the Ming dynasty are buried in Beijing's Ming Tombs – the capital was moved from Nanjing to Beijing after one of his sons usurped power from the chosen heir. The mausoleum was built between 1381 and 1383 and required over 100,000 laborers. Of most interest here is the "spirit way" leading up to the mausoleum: 12 pairs of stone animals flank the path, among them elephants, camels, horses and mythical beasts, a style also used at the better known Ming Tombs north of Beijing.

If time allows for it the **Purple Mountain Observatory** (*zǐjīn shān tiānwéntái* 紫金山天文台) is worth a visit – if for nothing else than the view. It was built in 1929 and there's a cable car ride to the top, 1,148 feet (350 m) above sea level. ■

Making Your Trip Easy

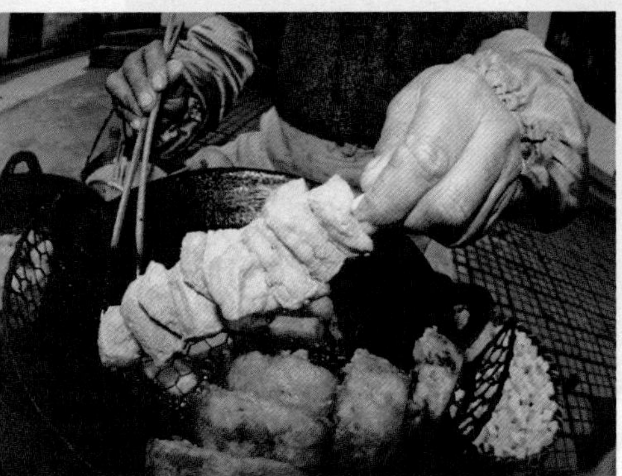

Nanjing's delicious snacks can be bought from street vendors.

Practical Tips

Nanjing is one of China's "four furnaces," a title well deserved, as it gets very hot and humid in the summer. Winters are cold with lots of rain and fog – the city actually seems to be constantly surrounded by fog. On the Purple Mountain it can get incredibly humid; though the temperature may not be high you'll still find yourself drenched in sweat. For some relief there are many trees, parks and lakes that make the heat more tolerable. Temperature-wise, spring and autumn are the best times to visit. However, spring sees a lot more rain than autumn. If you come during Chinese New Year, make sure you check out the Jinling Lantern Show that's held on the streets near the Confucius Temple.

Transportation

Airport – The airport is 22 miles (36 km) and about 40 minutes from the city center. Taking a taxi will cost as much as RMB 150.

Bus – Buses leaving for Shanghai take about 4 hours, and to Suzhou is about 2.5 hours. The Zhongyang Men Bus Station is close to the train station in the north of the city.

Taxi – Taxis in Nanjing are very cheap. Within the city walls it should cost under RMB 10; going to the Sun Yat-sen Mausoleum from the city center is about RMB 20. Flag-fall is RMB 7.

Train – Nanjing is on the express route between Beijing and Shanghai. It's a 2-hour-ride to Shanghai while Beijing can be reached in 8~9 hours.

The Best of Nanjing

Confucius Temple 夫子庙 *fūzǐ miào*

✉ south of Nanjing 南京城南

☎ 8662 8639

🕒 8am to 9pm

¥ 20

Office of the President 总统府 *zǒngtǒng fǔ*

✉ 292 Changjiang Lu 长江路 292 号

☎ 8457 8718

🕒 8am to 5:50pm

¥ 40

Sun Yat-sen Mausoleum
中山陵 *zhōngshān líng*

✉ inside Zhong Shan Scenic Area
南京东郊钟山风景区内

☎ 8444 6111

🕒 7am to 6:00pm

¥ 40

Hotels

Jinling Hotel

Quotes

"Few cities in China can surpass Nanjing in its wealth of historical sights. Nanjing is a city busy getting modern but the atmosphere is still very much colored by the Nanjing's fascinating history. For somebody like me in love with Chinese history this city is a treasure box."

金陵饭店 *jīnlíng fàndiàn* ★★★★★
✉ 2 Hanzhong Lu, Xinjiekou Square 新街口广场汉中路 2 号❶
☏ 8471 6666
¥ 1,410 – double room
🌐 www.jinlinghotel.com

Nanjing Hilton International Hotel
南京希尔顿国际大酒店 *nánjīng xī'ěrdùn guójì dàjiǔdiàn* ★★★★★
✉ 319 Zhongshan Dong Lu 中山东路 319 号
☏ 8480 8888
¥ 1,718 – double room
🌐 www.hilton.com
@ Nanjing@Hilton.com

Sheraton Nanjing Kingsley Hotel & Towers 金丝利喜来登酒店 *jīnsīlì xǐláidēng jiǔdiàn* ★★★★★
✉ 169 Hanzhong Lu 汉中路 169 号❷
☏ 8666 8888
¥ 1,660 – double room
🌐 www.sheraton-nanjing.com

Xuanwu Hotel
玄武饭店 *xuánwǔ fàndiàn* ★★★★★
✉ 193 Zhongyang Lu 中央路 193 号❸
☏ 8335 8888
¥ 900 – double room
🌐 www.xuanwu.com

Egret Hotel 白鹭宾馆 *báilù bīnguǎn* ★★★
✉ 68 Dashiba Jie, Confucius Temple, Qinhuai District 秦淮区夫子庙大石坝街 68 号❹
☏ 8662 1999
¥ 520 – double room

Food & Restaurants

People in Nanjing boast that their rich cuisine preserves the natural flavors of the ingredients without being either overpowering or underwhelming. A specialty around here is salted duck (*yánshuǐ yā* 盐水鸭) – the meat is succulently tender with a crispy skin. The area around the Confucius Temple at Shiba Jie (石坝街夫子庙) is newly restored and where the locals go for a fun evening out. There are many good restaurants and snack stalls there. Try a kind of pudding made from tofu (*dòufu nǎor* 豆腐脑儿), green onion pancakes (*cōngyóu bǐng* 葱油饼) and dumpling soup (*jiǎozi tāng* 饺子汤). Another food street to check out is at Hunan Lu Shiziqiao Meishi Jie (湖南路狮子桥美食步行街).

If you're really hungry, order the Eight Qinhuai Specialties; the recipes for these dishes have been passed from generation to generation. The specialties are:

Paper lamps enthrall a young visitor to the Confucius Temple.

A Colonel Sander's look-a-like wishes for a cold one after visiting the Sun Yat-sen Mausoleum.

Yongheyuan's (永和园) Huangqiao sesame seed cake (*huángqiáo shāobǐng* 黄桥烧饼) and Kaiyang dried vermicelli (*kāiyáng gānsī* 开洋干丝); Jiangyouji's (蒋有记) beef soup (*niúròu tāng* 牛肉汤) and beef-stuffed potstickers (*niúròu guōtiē* 牛肉锅贴); Liufengju's (六凤居) tofu (*dòufulào* 豆腐涝) and green onion pancake (*cōngyóubǐng* 葱油饼); Qifangge's (奇芳阁) crispy seasame seed cake (*yāyóu sū shāobǐng* 鸭油酥烧饼), steamed vegetable buns (*shíjǐn càibāo* 什锦菜包), sesame oil vermicelli (*máyóu sùgānsī* 麻油素干丝) and shredded chicken noodles (*jīsī shāomiàn* 鸡丝烧面); rice dumpling (*guìhuāxiàn jiāxīn xiǎoyuánxiāo* 桂花馅夹心小元宵) and five-colored cakes (*wǔsè xiǎogāo* 五色小糕) from the Lianhu Cake and Dumpling Restaurant (莲湖糕团店); Zhanyuan Noodle Restaurant's (瞻园面馆) smoked fish noodles (*xūnyú yínsīmiàn* 熏鱼银丝面) and steamed dumplings (*báopí bāojiǎo* 薄皮包饺); Kuiguangge's (魁光阁) five-spice broad beans (*wǔxiāngdòu* 五香豆) and five-spice eggs (*wǔxiāngdàn* 五香蛋)

RESTAURANTS

Jiangsu Restaurant 江苏酒家

Traditional Jiangsu cuisine, their fragrant chicken (*xiangsūjī* 香酥鸡) and Nanjing duck (*nánjīng yāzhūn* 南京鸭肫) are particularly good.

✉ 16 Jiankang Lu 健康路 16 号❺

☎ 8662 5632

🕒 24 hours

The King of Lions Restaurant
狮王府大酒楼

Offers food and entertainment.

✉ 2 Shiziqiao, Hunan Lu 湖南路狮子桥 2 号

☎ 8330 6777

🕒 11am to 2pm, 5pm to 9pm

Lüliu Ju Restaurant 绿柳居素菜馆

One of the finest vegetarian restaurants in Nanjing, specailizes in tofu chicken (*sùjī* 素鸡) and fried tofu duck (*sùshāoyā* 素烧鸭).

✉ 248 Taiping Nan Lu 太平南路 248 号❻

☎ 8664 3644, 8664 4171

🕒 5:30am to 8:30am for dim sum
10:30am to 8:30pm for meals

Nanjing Jingcai Guan 南京精菜馆

✉ inside Jingli Hotel, 7 Beijing Xilu, Gulou District 鼓楼区北京西路 7 号晶丽酒店内

☎ 8331 0818

Shizi Lou 狮子楼

✉ 29 Shizi Qiao, Hunan Lu, Gulou District 鼓楼区湖南路狮子桥 29 号

☎ 8360 7888

Yuehonghe Jiulou 粤鸿和酒楼

✉ 19-3 Shengtai Xilu 胜太西路 19-3 号

☎ 5210 7117

BARS

Danny's Irish Pub "丹尼"爱尔兰酒吧

The only Irish bar in Nanjing.

✉ inside Sheraton Nanjing Kingsley Hotel & Towers 金丝利喜来登酒店内

☎ 8666 8888

🕒 6:30pm to 2am

Souvenirs

Nanjing souvenirs include colorful pebbles (*yǔhuā shí* 雨花石) from the Yuhuatai area in Nanjing, cloud pattern brocades (*yúnjǐn* 云

锦) which come in several types with the *zhuangjin* (妆锦) and *zhijin* (织锦) considered the best examples. Jinling fans (*jīnlíng zhéshàn* 金陵折扇) have been renowned since the Ming dynasty and they come in bamboo (*zhúzhì zhéshàn* 竹制折扇), silk (*juān gōngshàn* 绢宫扇) and bone varieties (*gǔshàn* 骨扇). Swan velvet (*tiān'é róng* 天鹅绒) is a traditional Nanjing silk product, featuring flower patterns, that's intricately woven with fine silk floss. It's also available in different products from cushions to wall hangings.

On Hunan Lu and the area around Conscious Temple are night markets where souvenirs and antiques can be bought. From Daxing Gong to Jiankang Lu is another street packed with stores selling jewelry and souvenirs. Taiping Nan Lu (*tàipíng nánlù míngpǐn yìtiáojiē* 太平南路名品一条街) is lined with stores selling gold, silver and jade jewelry. The Nanjing International Shopping Center (南京旅游国际购物中心) specializes in the "scholar's four treasures" (*wénfáng sìbǎo* 文房四宝), jade and replica antique furniture. It's located at 39 Tu Cheng Tou, Qinhuai District (秦淮区土城头 39 号, ☎ 5233 2455).

Other Information

POST OFFICES

Gulou Post Office 鼓楼邮政局

✉ 364 Zhongshan Lu 中山路 364 号❼
☎ 8379 6673
🕒 8am to 6:30pm

HOSPITALS

Jiangsu Provincial People's Hospital
江苏省人民医院
✉ 300 Guangzhou Lu 广州路 300 号❽
☎ 8371 4511

Nanjing International SOS Clinic
国际救援中心南京诊所
✉ Hillton Hotel, 319 Zhongshan Dong Lu 中山东路 319 号希尔顿酒店
☎ 8480 2842

COMPLAINT HOTLINES

☎ Genral: 8360 6085
☎ Taxi: 8665 5664

TOURISM INFORMATION WEBSITE

@ www.jltour.com

Entertainment

Ye Zhan Yuan 夜瞻园
Traditional Chinese setting along the river, has live entertainment.
✉ 128 Zhanyuan Lu 瞻园路 128 号
☎ 8220 1849
🕒 6pm to 10pm
¥ 30

AT THE RESTAURANT 在餐馆					
Do you have an English menu?		yǒu yīngwén càidān ma		有英文菜单吗?	
I'm vegetarian.		wǒ shì sùshí zhě		我是素食者。	
What is this/that?		zhè/nà shì shénme		这/那是什么?	
Can you recommend any dishes?		néng jièshào jǐgè cài ma		能介绍几个菜吗?	
I'd like a knife and fork.		qǐng gěiwǒ dāozi hé chāzi		请给我刀子和叉子。	
Not too….		qǐng búyào tài …		请不要太…	
	salty		xián		咸
	sour		suān		酸
	spicy		là		辣
	sweet		tián		甜
So delicious!		zhēn hǎo chī		真好吃!	
The bill please.		qǐng jiézhàng		请结账。	
Where's the nearest…?		zuìjìnde … zài nǎr		最近的…在哪儿?	
	KFC		kěndéjī		肯德基
	McDonald's		màidāngláo		麦当劳

Suzhou's Timeless Romance

Area Code 0512

Heritage: Classical Garden of Suzhou

There has always been a level of elegance, grace and romance in **Suzhou** that few cities can rival, and its many gardens and canals lend Suzhou air of unmatched sophistication.

For more than 2,500 years, old Suzhou's architecture and scenery has impressed visitors enchanting them with moonlit walks along the canals through the perfume of osmanthus flowers. Time and progress haven't erased that past. During the Tang dynasty, the **Grand Canal** (*dà yùnhé* 大运河) linked Suzhou to the rest of the empire. The canal continues to feed an enormous network of smaller canals that penetrate every part of the city.

Water physically and culturally defines Suzhou. The seemingly infinite maze of canals gave rise to an efficient transportation network, a wealth of picturesque scenery and architecture typical of the eastern Chinese Jiangnan style. Nearby rivers and lakes yielded a bounty of fish and shellfish that still dominate the local cuisine. Aquatic images abound in the city's art, and if you travel the canals by boat, your guide may treat you to a rowing song that has remained unchanged for centuries.

A large part of Suzhou's prosperity and renown comes from its beautiful and ingenious arts and handicrafts, especially the most prized of Chinese treasures, silk. Suzhou was an early center of silk production and remains so to this day. The city and surrounding countryside are still thick with the mulberry trees that feed the silkworms. The silk trade brought wealth, but Suzhou's real mark was made by its embroidery. Suzhou silk embroidery is a true

Suzhou's Tuisi Garden is where a former official came to retire and ponder life's deep inner meaning.

marvel – on a screen of sheer silk, artists using silk thread finer than a human hair create detailed images on both sides of the fabric, deftly hiding all the knots between the pictures. Visitors to Suzhou can see this painstaking work being done in many local shops. The **Suzhou Silk Museum** (*sūzhōu sīchóu bówùguǎn* 苏州丝绸博物馆) is also a good place to learn more about silk production and they have interesting displays detailing each step of the silk making process.

One of Suzhou's oldest sights, the ancient Yunyan Pagoda sits on top of Tiger Hill.

SUZHOU'S LEGENDARY GARDENS

The abundance of water made possible the development of one of Suzhou's crowning glories: its many magnificent gardens. Streams, waterfalls, pools and lakes provide the central design element in a style that came to be emulated across China. These gardens are not the arrays of closely ordered flowers and pruned shrubbery to which Westerners are accustomed; they're more like miniature parks than gardens in the Western sense. The gardens of Suzhou, exquisitely built, were created to harmonize with nature; the goal of designing a garden was to bring a piece of nature, in miniature form, into the home. Most gardens were built during the Ming and Qing dynasties, and even then, space was scarce. The gardens are ingeniously designed to maximize the feeling of a large space in confined quarters. Winding pathways and strategically placed walls with portrait windows provide legendary landscape views.

Suzhou has long been famed as a home of distinguished scholars. After retiring from imperial service, they returned to their home cities and used their wealth to build gardens in which they could shut out the world and devote themselves to study and contemplation. These gardens were places to worship nature and find inspiration for their calligraphy and paintings. Here the scholar-officials pursued their romances and dreamt their poems, passing the languid days, sipping delicate teas and fragrant wines while their companions played chess. This sublime atmosphere still pervades Suzhou, though at times it may be hard to find serenity when throngs of people are all searching for their own corner of inspiration.

The gardens of Suzhou have been designated a UNESCO World Heritage Site, recognized as major repositories of cultural achievement. Perhaps the lord of them all is the **Humble Administrator's Garden** (*zhuōzhèng yuán* 拙政园), the largest of Suzhou's gardens. If you can only see one garden while in Suzhou, this one is highly recommended. About 60% of its area is water and there is an extensive network of paths and bridges following streams that culminate in a magnificent scenic lake. There are many pavilions for resting and taking in the striking views and a lovely home that features the Mandarin Duck Hall (*yuānyāng guǎn* 鸳鸯馆). There is an excellent collection of bonsai trees (*pénjǐng* 盆景) at one end of the garden. The **Lingering Garden** (*liú yuán* 留园) is quite large and lovely. It excels in architecture and stunning views. The **Surging Waves Pavilion** (*cānglàng tíng* 沧浪亭) is smaller and less dramatic but boasts an abundance of fine stone and wood carvings. Similarly, The **Master of Nets Garden** (*wǎngshī yuán* 网师园) is quite small and relatively simple, but may appeal to those limited in time or mobility. Its major benefits include its

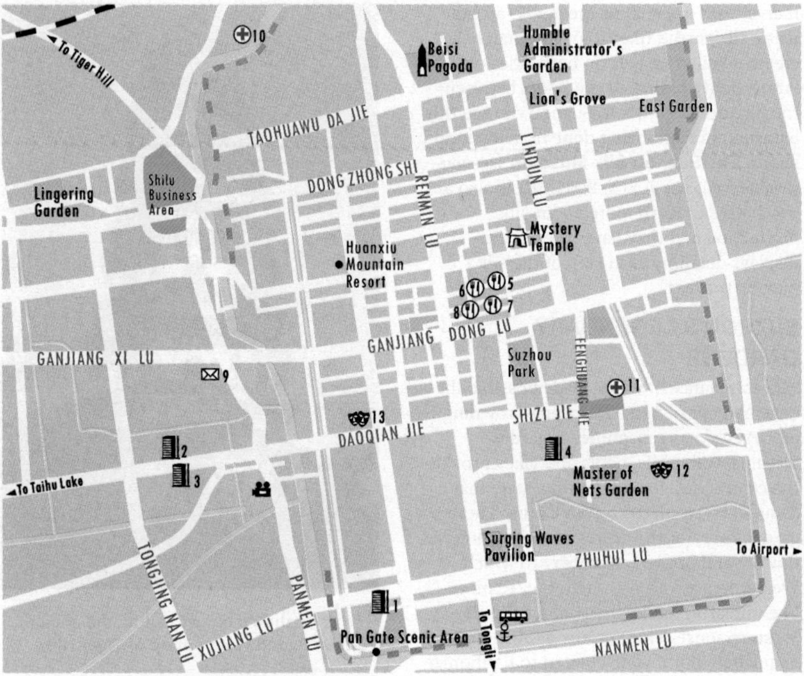

The intricate task of creating Suzhou's famed silk embroidery.

proximity to the major tourist area at Shiquan Jie and its evening musical, acrobatic and theatrical performances during the warmer months.

While not strictly a garden, **Tiger Hill** (*hǔ qiū* 虎丘) is another famed spot for historic natural and man-made scenery. Legend holds that some of its structures date back to He Lü the ruler of the ancient Wu Kingdom. He Lü was renowned for the quality of the swords he commissioned; supposedly, he was buried with 3,000 of them. Later rulers, not wanting to pass up on some freebies, excavated his tomb in search of the swords. In addition to a garden, Tiger Hill features a number of ancient tombs and historic sites. Its top is crowned by the ancient **Yunyan Pagoda** (*yúnyán sì tǎ* 云岩寺塔), which happens to be slightly off centered.

In Suzhou's southwest is **Pan Gate** (*pán mén* 盘门), the only remaining city gate. The gate dates back to the 12th century and is built over Suzhou's former moat. Good photo opportunities abound from the top of the gate.

Shiquan Jie (*shíquán jiē* 十全街) and **Guanqian Jie** (*guànqián jiē* 观前街) offers up

Memorable Experiences

Exploring the Bonsai garden in the Humble Administrator's Garden.

Sitting on an old stone bridge and watching the boats on the canals drift by.

Wandering the seemingly infinite labyrinths of small lanes in the old parts of town.

a lot of handicrafts, arts and antique shopping opportunities. Many fine restaurants can also be found here. This street has become very popular with resident foreigners in Suzhou as well as many of the more upscale locals. It's a bustling and busy place. At night it becomes something of a live-wire district with its many popular dance clubs booming techno music into the street. Shiquan Jie has a lot to offer for many different tastes, but do be sure to step back into one of the small lanes that intersect it during the daytime and head toward the canal. If you pick the right spots you will find some very picturesque scenes of the old houses fronting the canal.

About 12.4 miles (20 km) from Suzhou is the quiet village of Tongli (*tónglǐ* 同里). If Suzhou is too large for your tastes, Tongli is a great place to relax. A typical water village (*shuǐxiāng* 水乡), Tongli's architecture is a mix of Ming and Qing styles. Set on the rich Yangtze River basin, Tongli is the realization of pastoral Chinese poems and paintings of rustic villages criss-crossed with canals and bridges. This charming village features over 40 arched bridges and numerous temples and preserved homes.

Taihu (*tàihú* 太湖), one of China's largest freshwater lakes, is a short hop away from Suzhou. The lake has blessed the area around Suzhou with fertile land and water – agriculture and aquaculture have been major industries for centuries. Surrounding the lake are 72 statuesque peaks; the best place to see them up close is at **Xi Shan Scenic Area** (*xīshān fēngjǐngqū* 西山风景区). During the early spring the hills are covered with plum blossoms that cover the ground with their light pedals. Over at Shigong is where the craggy Taihu rocks are gathered. These rocks are featured in every self-respecting Chinese garden and have been exported as far as the Forbidden City in Beijing. ■

Making Your Trip Easy

Practical Tips

The best time to visit Suzhou is from April to October. The weather is good despite a tendency to be rainy and the osmanthus trees flower at this time, perfuming the entire city. Summers in Suzhou are hot and humid while springtime is pleasant but can be rainy. Winters are surprisingly cold, made worse by the poor heating and lack of insulation in most buildings. If you're in Suzhou during Chinese New Year, make sure to visit the Plum Blossom Festival in Xi Shan. There's also a Lantern Festival that takes place 15 days after the Lunar New Year at Pan Gate.

Transportation

Airport – Suzhou has no airport; the closest one is Shanghai's Hongqiao Airport, about 50 miles (80 km) away. Shuttle buses from the airport to Suzhou take about an hour.

Bus – Bus fares to or from Shanghai average around RMB 30. The Shanghai trip takes around an hour and a half.

Pedi-cab & Bicycle – Heavily traveled and toured areas will have bicycle pedi-cabs and drivers will take you to specific locations or take you on a tour. Rates are RMB 5 per person plus a charge depending on the distance traveled. The area by Shiquan Jie and the train station offers inexpensive bike rentals at around RMB 25 per day.

Ship – Boats traveling down the Grand Canal can be boarded at the northeast bank of Renmin Bridge. Boats leave at 5:30pm, but arrive at the dock 30 minutes before departure. Boats arrive in Hangzhou at 6am. Passage goes from RMB 30 to 95 depending on the boat and class. Cabins are either doubles or quads.

Taxi – Within Suzhou taxis are RMB 10 at flag-fall. Because Suzhou is relatively small, traveling to nearly any point in Suzhou will cost under RMB 40. (Suzhou Taxi Company, ☎ 6727 2200; Yong'an Taxi Company, ☎ 6822 4147)

Train – Suzhou is well connected by rail system and there are frequent trains to and from Shanghai. Travel times range from 45 to 80 minutes depending on the particular train taken. Train fares average around RMB 20. Trains fill up rapidly and buying tickets well in advance is recommended.

The Best of Suzhou

Taihu and Xi Shan 太湖西山 *tàihú xīshān*

✉ 25 miles (40 km) southwest of Suzhou 苏州西南四十公里

¥ 50 for Shigong Shan (*shígōng shān* 石公山)

50 for Linwu Cave (*línwū dòng* 林屋洞) and the Mei Garden (*méiyuán* 梅园)

The Humble Administrator's Garden 拙政园 *zhuōzhèng yuán*

✉ 178 Dongbei Jie 东北街 178 号

☎ 753 9869

🕒 8:15am to 4:15pm

¥ 70 – Peak season; 50 – off season

Tongli 同里 *tónglǐ*

✉ 12.4 miles (20 km) from Suzhou 距苏州 20 公里

☎ 6333 1140

¥ 80

Suzhou's quaint gardens are works of art.

Hotels

Crowne Plaza Suzhou
苏州中茵皇冠假日酒店 sūzhōu zhōngyīn huángguān jiàrì jiǔdiàn ★★★★★
✉ by Jinji Lake, Suzhou Industrial Area 苏州工业园区金鸡湖畔
☎ 6761 6688
¥ 697 – double room
@ www.nszihotel.com

Sheraton Suzhou Hotel and Tower
吴宫喜来登大酒店 *wúgōng xǐláidēng dàjiǔdiàn* ★★★★★
✉ 388 Xinshi Lu 新市路 388 号❶
☎ 6510 3388
¥ 1,660 – single room
1,760 – double room
@ www.sheraton.com

Aster Hotel 雅都大酒店
yǎdū dàjiǔdiàn ★★★★
✉ 156 Sanxiang Lu 三香路 156 号❷
☎ 6829 1888
¥ 830 – double room
@ www.aster.com.cn

Castle Hotel
胥城大厦 *xùchéng dàshà* ★★★★
✉ 120 Sanxiang Lu 三香路 120 号❸
☎ 6828 6688
¥ 799 – double Room
@ www.castlehotel.com.cn

Nanlin Hotel 南林饭店 *nánlín fàndiàn* ★★★
✉ 20 Gunxiufang, Shiquan Jie 十全街滚绣坊 20 号❹
☎ 6519 4641
¥ 450 – double room
@ www.nanlinhotel.com

Food & Restaurants

Suzhou's cuisine is very similar to that of Shanghai and is characterized by light flavors, sweet dishes and an abundance of

A bride and groom head to their wedding ceremony through one of Suzhou's many canals.

fish and shellfish. The signature Suzhou dish is the oddly named squirrel shaped mandarin fish (*sōngshǔ guiyú* 松鼠桂鱼). The fish is largely de-boned (a real blessing for travelers who are not fluent in the use of chopsticks) and sliced into pieces that remain attached to the fish then fried. When cooked, it looks a bit like a squirrel's tail and is garnished with shrimp, mixed vegetables and covered with a rich sweet sauce. *Biluo* shrimp (*biluó xiārén* 碧螺虾仁) is shrimp cooked with *Biluo* tea which adds a unique flavor. *Jiyou caixin* (鸡油菜心) is cabbage hearts cooked in a chicken broth. It's colorful and tasty. Watermelon chicken (*xīguā jī* 西瓜鸡) is chicken steamed in bowls made from watermelons. This dish is only available during the summer. If you've got a sweet-tooth, munch on *guihua wushu'ou* (桂花焐熟藕). It's made from lotus root steamed with sticky rice and white and brown sugar. Other favorites include snowflake crab, steamed hairy crabs (when they're in season around mid-autumn), freshwater shrimp, crayfish and river snails. Many of Suzhou's oldest and most famous restaurants can be found along Guanqian Jie. Go to Shiguan Jie if you've got a hankering for a steak or some sushi – lots of restaurants dishing up foreign food are there. Fenghuang Jie is packed with restaurants serving traditional Suzhou and Zhejiang dishes.

RESTAURANTS

Deyue Lou 得月楼

Specializes in Suzhou cuisine like the most famous Suzhou fish dish. *Songshu guiyu*, (松鼠桂鱼) *jiyou caixin* (鸡油菜心) and house creations like *deyue tongji* (得月童子鸡) and *zaoliu yupian* (糟溜鱼片).

✉ 25/27 Taijian Long, Guanqian Jie 观前街太监弄 25/27 号❺
☎ 6522 2230
🕒 10am to 10pm

Shijia Restaurant 石家饭店

Established during the Qing dynasty, known for their three-shrimp tofu (*sānxiā dòufu* 三虾豆腐), *jiyou caixin* (鸡油菜心) and *ba fei* soup (*bāfèi tāng* 鲃肺汤), a kind of fish soup.

✉ 15-1 Jinshan Lu, Mudu Town 木渎镇金山路 15-1 号
☎ 6626 2575
🕒 10am to 9:30pm

Song He Lou 松鹤楼

Visited by Emperor Qianlong, who provided the calligraphy for the restaurant's doorway tablet; restaurant specializes in the squirrel shaped mandarin fish (*sōngshǔ guìyú* 松鼠桂鱼), stir-fried prawns (*qīngchǎo xiārén* 清炒虾仁), meat and sticky rice steamed in a lotus leaf (*héyè fěn zhēngròu* 荷叶粉蒸肉) and *xiehuang doufu* (蟹黄豆腐).

✉ 141 Guanqian Jie 观前街 141 号❻
☎ 6727 7006
🕒 10:30am to 10pm

Suzhou Snack Restaurant 苏州小吃园

Specializes in Suzhou snacks such as *baitang wushu'ou* (白糖焐熟藕), osmanthus rice dumplings (*guìhuā tāngyuán* 桂花汤圆), sticky rice with duck's blood (*chǎo xuènuò* 炒血糯) and snails in soy sauce (*jiàng tiánluó* 酱田螺).

✉ 19 Taijian Long, Guanqian Jie 观前街太监弄 19 号❼
☎ 6523 7603
🕒 10:30am to 1:30pm, 4:45pm to 9:30pm

Wangsi Restaurant 王四酒家
Specializes in *sansi chuncai tang* (三丝莼菜汤), a succulent chicken dish – *jaohuaji* (叫化鸡), also try their homebrewed liquor (*zìzhì guìhuā báijiǔ* 自制桂花白酒) – it's strong stuff.
✉ 15 Taijian Long, Guanqian Jie
观前街太监弄 15 号❽
☎ 6522 7277
🕒 11am to 2pm, 4:30pm to 9:30pm

Yaba Shengjian 哑巴生煎
Famous for their noodle *yaba shengjian* (哑巴生煎), *popo huntun* (泡泡馄饨).
✉ opposite Building 24 Su'an Xincun, Donghuan Lu, Industrial Area
工业园区东环路苏安新村 24 幢对面
☎ 6741 0674

Souvenirs

As a major tourist center, Suzhou is naturally awash in souvenirs and handicrafts of every description. The most famous local products include Suzhou double-sided silk embroideries, which average RMB 300; silk and fragrant sandalwood fans – high quality sandalwood fans can cost up to RMB 400; woodcarvings, pearl jewelry, teapots and silk clothes of traditional and modern varieties.

The area centered on Guanqian Jie, sometimes referred to as "the walking street," is a famous shopping and entertainment area. It's a well renovated section of the old city converted to a shopping area. There are department stores and specialty shops of every description here, including a number of arts, handicrafts and antique centers. Perhaps more interesting is the profusion of market stalls clustered around the more formal shops. In the center of this district is the 1,700-year-old Mystery Temple (*xuánmiào guàn* 玄妙观), an old Taoist temple that was once the center of a large bazaar. It has recently been renovated and continues the market tradition. The area around Shi Lu is packed with specialty and department stores. Check out Shiquan Jie for souvenirs and antiques.

The old Confucian Temple (*kǒng miào* 孔庙) on Renmin Lu is a crumbling old complex with some fascinating antiquities strewn about. Hidden inside its walls is perhaps the most interesting informal crafts and antiques market in Suzhou. If you aren't an expert, be a bit more wary of imitations here.

Other Information

POST OFFICES

Suzhou Post Office 苏州邮局
✉ 36 Baita Xi Lu 白塔西路 36 号❾
☎ 6770 1138

HOSPITALS

The First Suzhou University Hospital
苏州大学附属第一医院
✉ 96 Shizi Jie 十梓街 96 号⓫
☎ 6522 3637

Guangji Hospital 广济医院
✉ 286 Guangji Lu 广济路 286 号❿
☎ 6533 1340

COMPLAINT HOTLINES

☎ General: 6522 3377
☎ Taxi: 6522 3377

TOURISM INFORMATION WEBSITE

@ www.sztravel.gov.cn

Entertainment

Meng Suzhou 梦苏州
Ballet and traditional Chinese acrobats.
✉ Convention Center, 100 Daoqian Jie
道前街 100 号会议中心.⓭
☎ 6522 8022, 6522 8055
¥ 300, 180, 120, 80

Wuyue Gong 吴乐宫
Traditional Jiangnan cuisine with a song and dance performance.
✉ inside Suzhou Hotel, 115 Shiquan Jie
十全街 115 号苏州饭店内⓬
☎ 6519 2556
¥ 200

Quotes

"Incredible. Suzhou really manages to give one the flavor of 'Old China.' It would take years to explore all the interesting things here!"

"The gardens must be experienced to be understood. The feeling of peace and tranquility they give is wonderful."

Yangzhou, the City Lost in Time

Area Code 0514

Awash in monuments of its former glory, **Yangzhou** is a great place to escape the urban grind and lose yourself in the relics of its cosmopolitan past.

For a small Chinese city, Yangzhou boasts an abundance of historic sites. In the past, Yangzhou was one of southern China's economic and culture centers. Located at the junctions of the **Grand Canal** (*dà yùnhé* 大运河) and the **Yangtze** and **Huaihe** rivers, its long history dates back to 500 BC.

It was these waterways, linking Yangzhou to China's interior and major city centers, that helped Yangzhou develop into a prosperous city. During the Tang dynasty, Yangzhou was home to many foreign communities, including a large group of Persian traders. But it was the revitalization of the Grand Canal and the massive influx of funds brought by the salt merchants and their monopolies during the Qing dynasty that allowed Yangzhou to truly flourish.

It was amongst such settings that Yangzhou developed its rich storytelling tradition (*píng huà* 评话), which frequently attracted the attention of the imperial court. In the wake of the imperial court flocked artists and their major patrons, mostly retired officials. The prosperity of the Tang dynasty gave scholars, painters, storytellers and poets the means to pursue their craft while the retiring officials, determined to live out their days in style, endowed temples, enclosed gardens and patronized the arts.

Though not completely able to stand the test of time, many relics of its past glory days still dot this languid city in Jiangsu Province. Its ancient joie de vivre, born of artists defying the painting conventions of their time, can still be felt while exploring the canals, tree-lined streets and arching bridges, which create charming scenes.

If hordes of visitors from Nanjing and other surrounding cities make the major sites feel overrun, Yangzhou is well situated for a lazy amble. In the north and northwest parts of the city are numerous gardens and temples. While smaller than the major sites they, provide a sense of the atmosphere and culture that made Yangzhou great.

Ge Garden (*gè yuán* 个园), a classic Chinese rock and water composition, is filled with curiously styled pavilions ideal for a midday picnic. Its landscaped rocks are meant to suggest the four seasons and can be sensed with a sprinkling of imagination. From here it's a short walk to the **Yangzhou City Museum** (*yángzhōu bówùguǎn* 扬州博物馆), which has incorporated a series of assorted old pavilions into its charming grounds. One of China's better provincial museums, it includes a 1,000-year-old wooden boat recovered from the Grand Canal. Even older is its centerpiece, a Han dynasty funeral suit made from 500 pieces of jade.

Right around the corner stands the **Shi Kefa Memorial** (*shǐgōng cí* 史公祠), a temple devoted to the memory of local hero Shi Kefa. Toward the end of the Ming dynasty, he gave his life fighting against the encroaching Qing armies. The victorious Qing supposedly raised this memorial to him in honor of his courage though it may as well have been to quiet their new subjects.

Moving towards the city center, students of China's Islamic past will be happy to find the **Crane Mosque** (*xiānhè sì* 仙鹤寺), the main surviving testament to the presence of Persian traders in Yangzhou during the Middle Ages. Simple, small and largely u

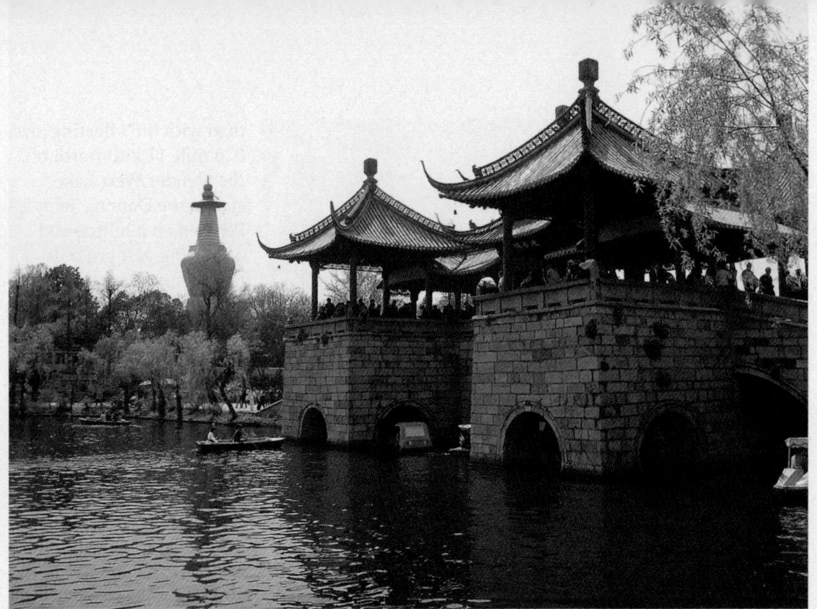

The tranquil Slender West Lake is ideal for peaceful strolls.

nadorned save for one wall covered entirely with Arabic script, it's a classic example of Islamic architecture in China. In a similar vein is the **Garden Tomb of Puhaddin** (*pǔhādīng mùyuán* 普哈丁墓园), dedicated to a descendant of the prophet Muhammad who came to China in the 13th century. He spent ten years in Yangzhou and made the city his adopted home, insisting on being buried within its walls. An adjacent hall contains paintings and artifacts depicting his life.

Yangzhou's southern half has its own share of attractions. A true diamond in the rough is the **He Garden** (*hé yuán* 何园). Built in the nineteenth century, this garden in miniature ingeniously employs trees, shrubs, and a raised walkway to give a sense of variety and depth. It's an ideal place for a sunny morning or sunset frolic. Several charming teahouses provide parched visitors with refreshment and ambiance.

A bit of a hike out of town but no less interesting is the **Wenfeng Pagoda** (*wénfēng tǎ* 文峰塔). Built in 1582, this large, seven-story pagoda is where Jian Zhen departed for Japan. Today it's more likely to be employed as a vista for viewing the intense activity on Yangzhou's canals and wharves.

IRREVERENCE & ENLIGHTENMENT IN YANGZHOU

Yangzhou's two major and most well-known tourist sites, **Slender West Lake** (*shòu xīhú* 瘦西湖) and **Daming Temple** (*dàmíng sì* 大明寺), are located mercifully close to each other and are best taken in one fell swoop. Providing most of Yangzhou's tourist draw, they can be unbearably crowded on weekends yet outside of the peak hours they provide a marvelous window into Yangzhou's fabled charms. It's easy to walk from one site to the other, but to do it in style (and pay for it) there are tourist boats linking the sites. Modeled after dragon boats and replete with plush yellow interiors, they will cruise you up the lake and drop you off at the temple entrance.

Modeled after the much larger and more famous West Lake in Hangzhou, the Slender West Lake makes up in charm what it lacks in size. Winding through a stretch of park area, it's filled with water scenes and weeping willows.

Whimsical structures, meticulously crafted bridges and replicas of historic sites will keep your hands full for at least a few hours. There's a white dagoba modeled after the one in Beijing's Beihai Park.

Better known are the park's bridges, the

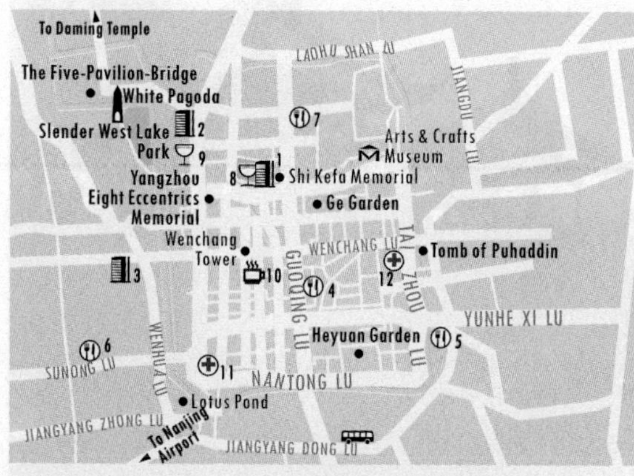

most famous of which is the **Five Pavilion Bridge** (*wǔtíng qiáo* 五亭桥) built in 1757. Its imposing triple arches and yellow tiled roofs are one of the most often photographed sites in the park. A short stroll along the north bank of the lake leads you to the dazzling, though relatively new, **Twenty-Four Bridges** (*èrshísì qiáo* 二十四桥), named after the 24 posts used in the bridge's design. These arches culminate in an apex so high that they nearly create a circle for boats to pass under. Though most of the ancient bridges are now replaced by new concrete ones, the bridge and canal atmosphere remain. A favorite spot for photo-ops is a replica of Emperor Qianlong's old fishing platform, which is located nearby. Local tales hold that Qianlong's servants would dive into the canal and hook fish on his line so that he, thinking Yangzhou had brought him luck, would allocate more funding to the town. Close by is the **Happiness Terrace** (*chuī tái* 吹台), with three moon gates each framing different scenes.

For those more concerned with eternity than with life's fleeting joys, 0 .6 mile (1 km) north of the Slender West Lake stands the Daming Temple. Perched on a hilltop and occupying vast grounds, this temple was originally built in the 5th century AD. Nowadays, it's experiencing a boom of patronage from Japanese Buddhists. Its centerpiece is a massive memorial built in 1973 to honor Chinese monk Jian Zhen, a famed Tang dynasty scholar who introduced Ritso Buddhism to Japan.

Jian Zhen was invited to teach in Japan and made five failed attempts at the crossing from China to Japan, each time being blown back to China by storms and gale force winds. On the sixth attempt, he successfully crossed, never to return. That he's still highly revered in Japan can be seen in the Japanese funding of two stone lamps.

If you find all this whetting your appetite, there's a wonderful Buddhist vegetarian restaurant on the temple grounds. Ask one of the monks to point you to it. The vast temple compound can be explored for the better part of a morning or afternoon. Not to be missed is the **Fifth Spring Under Heaven** (*tiānxià dìwǔquán* 天下第五泉), a series of parks and gardens built in 1751 and located to the north of the temple itself. Surrounding a natural spring, its clear waters run through the grounds, interlacing the sites. Here you can sample waters from the spring or opt for a cup of local tea brewed with the same ethereal waters. Airy teahouses dot the grounds, beneath which lie pools filled with brightly colored fish. ■

Making Your Trip Easy

Practical Tips

Though the canals lacing the city and the nearby rivers create a slight buffer, summers here can be extremely hot while winters can be cold. Dry, clear autumns and balmy springs with the gardens in full bloom are the ideal times to visit. Every April to May, the Yanhua Sanyue Festival (*yānhuā sānyuè jié* 烟花三月节) takes place in Yangzhou, celebrating the coming of spring. Make sure to check out the shows, exhibits and markets if you're visiting during this time. Yangzhou is now largely a modern city and many gems, unmarked on tourist maps, can be found

Memorable Experiences

Reading *Dream of the Red Mansion* in the pagodas of the He Garden.

Drinking tea in the gardens and parks outside the Daming Temple.

Enjoying Yangzhou fried rice at any of the late night street side stalls on the Ximen Jie Food Street.

through exploring its narrow lanes and old neighborhoods. Currently, it enjoys less fame than neighboring Nanjing and is therefore usually less crowded though by no means less interesting.

Transportation

Airport – The nearest airport is located in Nanjing. It normally takes airport shuttle buses two and a half hours from Nanjing to Yangzhou. Taxi drivers waiting by the arrivals exit will offer rides for around RMB 150 to 200.

Bicycle – Bicycle rentals are available from Giant Bicycle. They charge RMB 15 per hour, RMB 20 for 2 hours, RMB 50 for 4 hours and RMB 60 for a full day (57 Wenchang Zhong Lu, 文昌中路 57 号 ☎ 732 5087; 4 - 6 Ganquan Lu 甘泉路 4 -6 号, ☎ 710 5928).

Taxi –Taxis are cheap: flag-fall begins at RMB 6. Though useful for crossing large distances, many sites can be reached on foot.

The Best of Yangzhou

Daming Temple 大明寺 *dàmíng sì*

✉ Pingshantang Lu 平山堂路

☎ 734 0720

🕒 7:30am to 5:30pm, peak-season
7:45am to 4:45pm, off-season

¥ 45

Ornate rock formations decorate Ge Garden.

Ge Garden 个园 *gè yuán*

✉ 10 Yanfu Dong Lu 盐阜东路 10 号

☎ 734 7428

🕒 7:15am to 6pm, peak-season
7:30am to 5:30pm, off-season

¥ 40

Ancient buildings continue to see to new faces.

Slender West Lake Park
瘦西湖公园 *shòuxīhú gōngyuán*
✉ Dahongqiao Lu 大虹桥路
☎ 734 1324
🕒 7am to 6pm, peak-seaon
7am to 5pm winter hours
¥ 80, peak-season
60, off-season

Hotels

Yangzhou State Guesthouse
扬州迎宾馆 *yángzhōu yíngbīnguǎn*
✉ 1 Changchun Lu 长春路 1 号❷
☎ 780 9888
¥ 580 – double room

Garden International Hotel
扬州花园国际大酒店 *yángzhōu huāyuán guójì dàjiǔdiàn* ★★★★
✉ 56 Jiangyang Zhong Lu 江阳中路 56 号
☎ 780 3333
¥ 618 – double room

Grand Metropole Hotel 扬州京华大酒店 *yángzhōu jīnghuá dàjiǔdiàn* ★★★★
✉ 1 Wenchang Xi Lu 文昌西路 1 号❸
☎ 732 2888
¥ 700 – double room

New Century Hotel
新世纪大酒店 *xīnshìjì dàjiǔdiàn* ★★★★
✉ 2 Wenhui Nan Lu 文汇南路 2 号
☎ 787 8888
¥ 580 – double room

Xiyuan Hotel
西园大酒店 *xīyuán dàjiǔdiàn* ★★★★
✉ 1 Fengle Shang Jie 丰乐上街 1 号❶
☎ 780 7888
¥ 298 – double room

Yangzhou Hotel
扬州宾馆 *yángzhōu bīnguǎn* ★★★
✉ 5 Fengle Shang Jie 丰乐上街 5 号
☎ 780 5888
¥ 288 – double room

Food & Restaurants

Located on the fertile Yangtze delta, food has always been abundant in Yangzhou. In keeping with regional flavor, most dishes are lightly flavored, tending towards sweet, and emphasize the use of fresh ingredients cooked in their own juices. Nationwide, the most famous local specialty is Yangzhou fried rice (*yángzhōu chǎofàn* 扬州炒饭), which can be sampled at any number of restaurants or street side stalls. *Feicui shaomai* (翡翠烧麦) is a delicious steamed dumpling topped with ham and filled with vegetables. A good snack for those on the go is *sanding baozi* (三丁包子), buns filled with chicken, pork and bamboo shoots. A personal favorite of the Sui emperor was *qingdun shizi tou* (清炖狮子头), made of pork and supplemented with clams, mushrooms, crab meat or goose meat; this creation will give you a taste of imperial delight. Finally, for those with a sweet-tooth, the sweet 64 layered *qianceng yougao* (千层油糕) is a heavy treat.

Quotes

"The peace and tranquility of Yangzhou's gardens and parks made me feel like I'd entered a Chinese watercolor painting, never to emerge."

RESTAURANTS

Caigenxiang 菜根香

Specializes in Yangzhou fried rice (*yángzhōu chǎofàn* 扬州炒饭) and *shizitou* (狮子头).

✉ 115 Guoqing Lu, Guangling District 广陵区国庆路 115 号❺

☎ 734 2079

Chouxiaoya Jiulou 丑小鸭酒楼

Specializes in seafood and meat buns.

✉ 108 Wenhui Dong Lu 文汇东路 108 号❻

☎ 731 8528

🕒 11am to 2pm, 5pm to 9pm

Damingsi Suzhaiguan 大明寺素斋馆

A famous vegetarian restaurant in Daming Temple.

✉ in the Daming Temple,Pingshantang Lu 平山堂路大明寺内

☎ 734 0723

🕒 11am to 2pm, 5pm to 9pm

Fuchun Teahouse 百年富春

One of Yangzhou's oldest teahouses, specials include *dazhu gansi* (大煮干丝), *shousi feng'e* (手撕风鹅), which is made from goose, thousand-layer cake (*qiāncéng yóugāo* 千层油糕) and *sanding baozi* (三丁包子), a kind of bun.

✉ 35 Desheng Qiao, Guoqing lu 国庆路得胜桥 35 号❹

☎ 721 3289

🕒 6:30am to 1:30pm, 5pm to 8pm

Fumanlou Dajiudian 福满楼大酒店

Specializes in traditional dishes, including *shizitou* (狮子头), a fish head dish called *hongpa lianyutou* (红扒鲢鱼头) and stir-fried chicken with egg white (*fúróng jīpiàn* 芙蓉鸡片).

✉ 30 Wenhe Beilu 汶河北路 30 号

☎ 734 3777

🕒 11am to 2pm, 5pm to 9pm

The old doting on the young amidst Yangzhou's spring peach blossoms.

Riyueming Dachaguan 日月明大茶馆
Buffet-style teahouse, fruit and pastries with the purchase of any tea.
✉ Wenchang Square 文昌广场⑩
☎ 711 1777
🕒 9:30am to 2am

Shiweitian Jiudian 食为天酒店
Specializes in *maxiang yazhang* (麻香鸭掌) a tasty dish with duck's claws, *zhutong dufei* (竹筒肚肺), *liangban yupi* (凉拌鱼皮) which is made from fish's skin, and *dazhu gansi* (大煮干丝).
✉ 1 Hehuachi Lu 荷花池路 1 号⑦
☎ 786 9660
🕒 11am to 2pm, 5pm to 9pm

Yechun Teahouse 冶春茶社
Good for early morning dim sum as well as dinner, located in a serene garden.
✉ 1 Fengle Xia Jie 丰乐下街 1 号
☎ 736 8018
🕒 6:30am to 1:30pm, 5pm to 8pm

BARS

Cell Bar 塞乐酒吧
With snooker tables and darts; servers can speak English, west of the south entrance of the Xiyuan Hotel.
✉ Fengle Shang Jie 丰乐上街⑧
🕒 7pm to 2am

Taiji Bar 太极酒吧
One of the first bars in Yangzhou, popular place for foreigners living in Yangzhou.
✉ 38 Youyi Lu 友谊路 38 号⑨
🕒 7pm to 2am

Souvenirs

Yangzhou is an ideal place to shop for vases and birdcages. Near the Yangzhou Potted Plant Garden is an excellent bird and flower market filled with vendors selling both modern and classical items. Meticulously sculpted plants line their racks and are all for sale if you have the inclination to carry them with you. People throng the market from sun up to sun down and these two times are when you can usually get the best deals.

WELL WISHING 祝愿		
Congratulations!	gōngxǐ gōngxǐ	恭喜恭喜！
May you be happy and prosperous!	gōngxǐ fācái	恭喜发财！
Good luck!	zhù nǐ hǎoyùn	祝你好运！
Fantastic!	tàibàng le	太棒了！
Cheers!	gānbēi	干杯！

West of the city museum, lining the canal, are numerous stalls selling tourist knick-knacks and souvenirs. Jiangsu Province is known for its porcelain and it's also possible to find high quality embroidery and jade. Many of the jade artifacts displayed in the Forbidden City were made in Yangzhou; naturally jade goods made in Yangzhou still represent top quality craftsmanship. Jade jewelry and pendants range from RMB 100 to 300, while jade figurines cost RMB 300 to 500. Since the Han dynasty, Yangzhou has been known for its lacquerware; common lacquer products such as figurines sell for RMB 60 to 2,000 depending on the size and quality.

True antiques are hard to find anywhere and no matter what the vendors may claim, the trained eye is the best judge. These types of souvenir stands are popping up close to all the major sites and will more likely come to you before you have a chance to find them.

Other Information

POST OFFICES

Wenchang Post Office 扬州邮局文昌支局
✉ 162 Wenchang Zhong Lu 文昌中路 162 号
☎ 736 8186

Yangzhou City Post Office 扬州邮政局
✉ 51 Ximen Jie 西门街 51 号
☎ 736 6203

HOSPITALS

Subei People's Hospital 苏北人民医院
✉ 98 Nantong Xi Lu 南通西路 98 号⑪
☎ 793 7527

Yangzhou First People's Hospital
扬州市第一人民医院
✉ 45 Taizhou Lu 泰州路 45 号⑫
☎ 790 7373

COMPLAINT HOTLINES

☎ General: 732 5601
☎ Taxi: 787 1669

Leifeng Pagoda rises above West Lake's tranquil beauty.

Hangzhou, the City of the Lake

Area Code 0571

Hangzhou's legendary West Lake conjures images of sweeping willows and morning mist along the shores of China's most famous and revered of lakes.

Heralded as one of the most romantic cities in China, Hangzhou is ripe with historic and sensual sites to enchant the amorous and curious who make their way here. Just over 124 miles (200 km) southwest of Shanghai, Hangzhou requires only a short jaunt to sample its charming pagodas, the timeless West Lake and the city's modern amenities.

What really put Hangzhou on the proverbial map was the **Grand Canal** (*dà yùnhé* 大运河). Built during the Sui dynasty, the Grand Canal was a massive network of canals and waterways linking Hangzhou to the north. As food and goods were shipped from the agriculturally rich south to supply the comparatively desolate north, Hangzhou quickly developed into an important center of transportation and trade.

Hangzhou's height came when the Song dynasty court was driven from its capital at Kaifeng by northern invaders. The court resettled in Hangzhou and made it the imperial capital of the Southern Song dynasty. A population boom followed and the city flourished economically and culturally. Song influences still abound throughout the city – from the food to the language.

Qing emperor Kangxi was especially charmed by the **Lingyin Temple** (*língyǐn sì* 灵隐寺), and one of his couplets is inscribed on the **Hall of Four Heavenly Guardians**

▶▶ The Grand Canal

China's Grand Canal certainly lives up to its moniker: stretching over 1,054 miles (1,700 km), it's ten times longer than the Suez Canal and twenty times the length of the Panama Canal.

It took several dynasties to build the massive canal network. Work began as early as 506 BC, during the Spring and Autumn period, by King Wu, who had his people dig the first canals in a bid to control central China. Since most of China's major rivers flow from west to east, building a water link from north to south to connect the rivers would greatly facilitate transportation and this became the dream of many emperors.

Emperor Sui Yangdi of the Sui dynasty was noted for directing construction efforts. At the beginning of the 7th century the Sui united China and made its capital in Luoyang in north China. In order to move food and goods from the prosperous south to the north and to satisfy his personal sense of grandeur, he ordered the connection and expansion of the existing canals. In AD 603 over a million workers began connecting various rivers and existing canals into one Grand Canal linking Luoyang to Yangzhou. The emperor had a soft spot for luxury and travel. Taking advantage of his position as the "Son of Heaven," he took more than 200,000 attendants with him on his trips to Yangzhou on the Grand Canal. His massive barges were pulled by over 80,000 men while he partied into the night. After only 13 years on the throne, rebellions broke out and his dynasty was deposed.

In the 13th century, the emperor of the Yuan dynasty ordered the repair and expansion of the Grand Canal from Hangzhou to Beijing. This effort took ten years to complete. Today the Grand Canal has fallen out of use, but lengths of it, particularly in the Hangzhou and Suzhou area, continue to serve as an important waterway.

(*tiānwáng diàn* 天王殿) which stands at the front of the temple. This celebrated temple was originally built in AD 326; despite being destroyed and rebuilt 16 times over, it remains one of Hangzhou's main attractions. At the back of the temple is a giant 64.3-foot (19.6 m) camphor wood statue of Buddha. If it's not too crowded, the serenity of the grounds will let you feel as tranquil as Buddha. The **Lingyin Temple Scenic Area** (*língyǐn sì jǐngqū* 灵隐寺景区) is huge; the area includes the temple and the mini-mountain **Feilai Peak** (*fēilái fēng* 飞来峰). In one section of the park are large Buddhist rock carvings – explore the grounds and you'll discover many quaint photogenic scenes.

Other attractions are centered on Hangzhou's historic silk and tea production, both of which boomed after the city was connected to the Grand Canal at the end of the 6th century, a fact not lost on visitors who make their way to the **China Silk Museum** (*zhōngguó sīchóu bówùguǎn* 中国丝绸博物馆) to purchase choice fabrics or to the **Dragon Well Tea Village** (*lóngjǐng wènchá* 龙井问茶) to imbibe sweet drinks. If highbrow elbow rubbing is to your liking, follow the flocks to **Xihu Tiandi** (*xīhú tiāndì* 西湖天地). Located on the southern shore of West Lake, this trendy cluster of shops beckons with bamboo lined cobblestone walkways. It's quickly becoming the hottest place to be seen, but the **Six Harmonies Pagoda** (*liùhé tǎ* 六和塔) is still one of the coolest places to see. This 197-foot (60 m) octagonal giant once served as a lighthouse and rises in the southwest of the city overlooking the calm Qiantang River. Head behind the pagoda and follow the footpath that winds past sculptures and shrines.

For a dose of heroism, visit the **Mausoleum of General Yue Fei** (*yuè fēi mù* 岳飞墓). Inside a red brick chamber sits a stoic statue of the mighty general, the Southern Song dynasty's most talented defender against 12th century Jürchen hordes. This famed patriot was the Southern Song dynasty's greatest hope for survival in the face of a determined invader, but due to palace intrigue, he was stripped of his post and murdered in prison. He was posthumously rehabilitated and his tomb and that of his son now stand in the quiet temple grounds. Nearby are four iron statues of his tormentors kneeling in shame. Temple visitors used to spit at these statues, though this practice is now prohibited.

The lunar tidal bore phenomenon on the **Qiantang River** (*qiántáng jiāng* 钱塘江) is most spectacular around September or throughout the year at high tide. During these times, a massive wall of water is pulled inland to Qiantang's shallows. The best views are in the town of **Yanguan** (*yánguān* 盐官), 23.5 miles (38 km) northeast of Hangzhou, though it's also viewable in Hangzhou. A word of caution: this rushing wall of water has killed those who got sucked in, so don't get too close.

The main hall of Lingyin Temple is one of Hangzhou's best-known sights.

SECRETS OF WEST LAKE

There are 36 West Lakes throughout China, but Hangzhou's **West Lake** (*xī hú* 西湖) is the inspiration for them all. Originally a lagoon, it was dredged in the 8th century and later diked. Sidestepping the vacationing masses and trinket hawkers, there's plenty to do at this 1.9 by 1.9 mile (3 km by 3 km) lotus lined lake. Mist shrouds the jade-hued water as the sun rises and sets, while sentinel trees line the surrounding boulevards. The lake is bordered by three hills that hem it like a pillow cradling a liquid gem. Meandering paths lead visitors through graceful gardens to welcoming temples.

The **Baidi Causeway** (*báidī* 白堤), on the north shore of the lake, links up with **Solitary Hill** (*gū shān* 孤山), a large island brimming with plants and grassy parks. Wander past inviting park benches, cross bridges where old men fly kites, then enter a

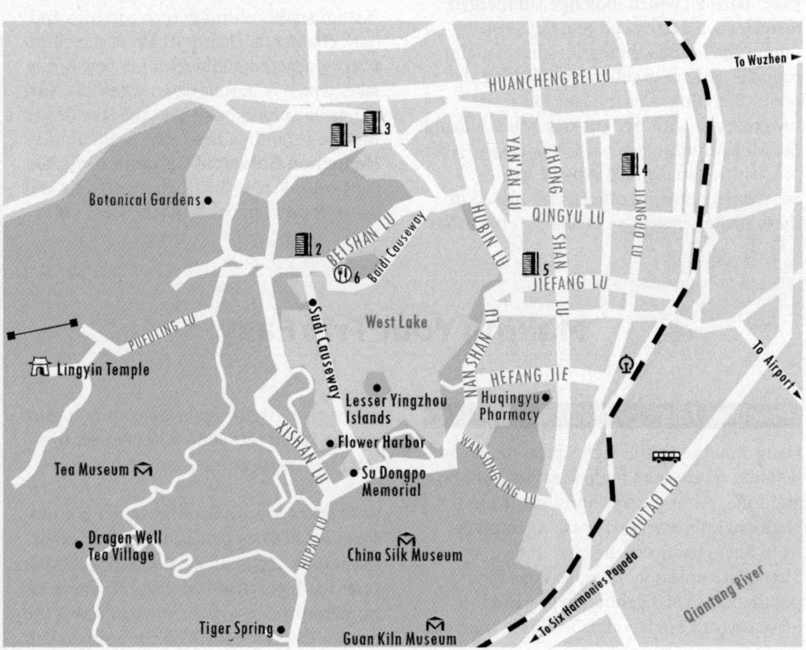

Memorable Experiences

Climbing the earth carved ascent up Baoshi Shan in early afternoon to view mist rise over West Lake.

Strolling along the lakefront with an iced coffee in one hand and camera in the other.

Renting a tandem bicycle from one of the many street vendors and pedaling past the different sights on the Baidi Causeway.

honeycomb of tree-shrouded pagodas where snacks and beverages are served. You can enjoy refreshments at several outdoor café or inside aged pagodas. A good way to get a better view of the lakeside scenery is to rent a pedal boat. Churn around the northern edge of the lake and take in the rich views. If the lake is calm, the reflection of **Baoshi Shan** (*bǎoshí shān* 宝石山) on the water is amazing. If you feel like watching things swim about, the **Flower Harbor** (*huāgǎng guānyú* 花港观鱼), home to thousands of obese carp, is a must-see.

Follow the **Sudi Causeway** (*sūdī* 苏堤) as it shoots across the lake like an arrow. From there you can spot the **Three Pools Mirroring the Moon** (*sāntān yìnyuè* 三潭印月) and the **Lesser Yingzhou** (*xiǎo yíngzhōu* 小瀛洲) islands, which look like submerged tortoises with trees and temples growing on them. The islands themselves have quaint pagodas and are excellent for viewing the pools. Standing over the lake are three towers, each with five cut-out holes. During the Mid-Autumn Festival (*zhōngqiū jié* 中秋节), which usually falls around late-September, glowing candles are placed in these niches creating a flickering effect that dances along the lakeshore. For this spectacle, it's best to rent or hire a boat – an old Mid-Autumn Festival tradition. Revelers would come to the lake to admire the moon while sipping tea and laughing with friends.

The **Zhejiang Provincial Museum** (*zhèjiāngshěng bówùguǎn* 浙江省博物馆) is on the Baidi Causeway and features displays of natural and regional history. Some of the more interesting exhibits include small figurines which were thrown into the lake to placate the lake spirits. The Qing emperor Qianlong once lived in part of the museum when vacationing in Hangzhou. Leaving the Baidi Causeway onto Beishan Lu, there's a splendid walkway to the top of Baoshi Shan where you can marvel at a 19th century tower that seems oddly Victorian. The path further snakes through rock carvings and dark chambers. Hearty trekkers can climb over weathered boulders for a view of the lake, which is best at dawn when the mist hangs like pipe smoke over the lake. If you're into flowers, then head east to the florid **Hangzhou Botanical Gardens** (*hángzhōu zhíwùyuán* 杭州植物园) where orchids and ferns flourish in balmy hothouses. ■

Making Your Trip Easy

Practical Tips

Hangzhou lies in the subtropical monsoon belt and receives its highest rainfall in May and June, but is partly sunny year round. National holidays are a crush as tourists from Shanghai flood the city. In fact, as Shanghai's economy rises, so does the population of Hangzhou; be prepared to leave early to catch your ride/flight/train out of the city – traffic jams are common. Also make sure to buy your tickets early; they tend to disappear fast.

Boat tours of are a fun way to get around West Lake. The boats can drop you off at numerous destinations along the lakeshore or at the little islands dotting it. There are numerous docks where you can board the boats; tickets are RMB 35 for a single trip.

Privately owned boats will usually charge about RMB 80 per hour for a tour, but you should be able to do some bargaining. The price of the boat tours doesn't include admission to the different sights.

Transportation

Airport – The airport is about 17 miles (27 km) east of Hangzhou. A taxi will take about 45 minutes and cost RMB 60 at most. Buses will take about an hour.

Bus – The East Bus Station is the main hub for luxury and long distance buses. It's 1.9 miles (3 km) northwest of the city. Lots of buses shuttle between Hangzhou, Shanghai and Suzhou.

Taxi – Hiring a taxi for tours around the lake can run between RMB 40 and 100, depending on your bargaining skills. You can get to most places for RMB 15 to 30; flag-fall is RMB 10.

Train – To the northwest is Hangzhou's new train station. Going to Shanghai takes about 2 hours on fast and comfortable trains.

The Best of Hangzhou

Lingyin Temple Scenic Spot
灵隐寺景区 *língyǐn sì jǐngqū*
✉ 1 Fayun Long 法云弄 1 号
🕒 8am to 4pm for the Lingyin Temple
8am to 6pm for the scenic area
¥ 30 for the Lingyin Temple's main hall
35 for Feilai Peak

Solitary Hill 孤山 *gū shān*
✉ north of West Lake 西湖北侧
¥ 5

West Lake 西湖 *xīhú*
¥ Free for the lake area, but boats tours and various sights will have their own admission charge

Hotels

Hangzhou Shangri-La Hotel
杭州香格里拉饭店 *hángzhōu xiānggélǐlā fàndiàn* ★★★★★
✉ 78 Beishan Lu 北山路 78 号❷
☎ 8797 7951
¥ 1,494 – double room, peak-season
830 – double room, off-season
@ www.shangri-la.com

Hangzhou Yellow Dragon Hotel 杭州黄龙饭店 *hángzhōu huánglóng fàndiàn* ★★★★★
✉ 7 Shuguang Lu 曙光路 7 号❸
☎ 8799 8833
¥ 664 – double room
@ www.dragon-hotel.com

Zhejiang World Trade Center
浙江世界贸易中心饭店 *zhèjiāng shìjiè màoyì zhōngxīn fàndiàn* ★★★★★
✉ 15 Shuguang Lu 曙光路 15 号❶
☎ 8799 0888
¥ 996 – double room, off-season
@ www.wtcgh.com

Going home after buying groceries at the morning market.

Hangzhou Xinqiao Hotel 杭州新侨饭店 *hángzhōu xīnqiáo fàndiàn* ★★★★
✉ 226 Jiefang Lu 解放路 226 号❺
☎ 8707 6688
¥ 782 – double room

Holiday-Inn Hangzhou 杭州国际假日酒店 *hángzhōu guójì jiàrì jiǔdiàn* ★★★★
✉ 298 Jianguo Bei Lu 建国北路 298 号❹
☎ 8527 1188
¥ 664 – double room, peak-season
540 – double room, off-season
@ www.holiday-inn.com

Food & Restaurants

Hangzhou cuisine is defined as being light, fresh and sweet – typical fare found south of the Yangtze River, an area called Jiangnan. Little oil, loads of fresh fruit and fish; carp, eel, shrimp and crabs – an extra teaspoon of sugar and bamboo shoots.

A nice snack is *xianrou xiaolong* (鲜肉小笼),

Quotes

"Every time I come to Hangzhou I feel relaxed. I really don't like living in Shanghai and want to move here, maybe get a small house with a view of the lake."

"It's such a relief to come and shop here without the crowds. The lake and the people give me a special feeling, impossible to put into words. I have visited Hangzhou since I was a child. I feel a deep connection. That's why I visit it often on the weekends."

mini-meat buns that are steamed in bamboo baskets; be careful eating them – they're juicy. A local specialty is sweet and sour West Lake carp (*xīhú cùyú* 西湖醋鱼); watch out for the bones though, A crispy tofu treat is *ganzha xiangling* (干炸响铃) which is similar to a spring roll – ground meat is wrapped with a slice of dried tofu then deep fried. Fresh river shrimp with Dragon Well tea (*lóngjǐng xiārén* 龙井虾仁) combines two local specialties into one very unique dish. A good dish for those who aren't afraid of their cholesterol count is Dongpo pork (*dōngpō ròu* 东坡肉). The dish is named after Su Dongpo, a poet and former governor of Hangzhou who created this dish for the laborers who expanded West Lake. A rich dark sauce, onions, ginger and chunks of succulent fatty meat defines the dish. Sister Song's fish broth (*sòngsǎo yúgēng* 宋嫂鱼羹)

Water villages dot the countryside in southern China.

is made from a recipe dating back to the Song dynasty, it calls for skinned fish with slivers of ham, dried mushrooms, scallion, egg yolk, ginger seasoned with rice wine and vinegar.

RESTAURANTS

Hao Yang Guang Dajiudian 好阳光大酒店

✉ 158 Tianmu shan Lu 天目山路 158 号

☎ 8821 1589

🕒 10am to 10:30pm

Jiangnan Honglou 江南红楼

✉ 53-4 Hefang Jie, Shangcheng District 上城区河坊街 53-4 号

☎ 8781 8799

Jiangnanyi 江南驿

Famous for its *ganshao yutou* (干烧鱼头) which made from fish head, and *jiaoma ji* (椒麻鸡) which made from chicken.

✉ 87 Siyanjing, Xiaman Juelong Lu, Xihu District 西湖区下满觉陇路四眼井 87 号

☎ 8715 3419

Louwailou Restaurant 楼外楼

Specializes in classic Hangzhou cuisine such as sweet and sour West Lake carp, shrimp with Dragon Well tea, Sister Song's fish broth.

✉ 30 Gushan Lu 孤山路 30 号❻

☎ 8796 9023

🕒 10am to 10:30pm

Waipojia Restaurant 外婆家

✉ 6-1 Macheng Lu 马胜路 6-1 号

☎ 8805 1987

🕒 10am to 10:30pm

Wang Runxing 王润兴

Established in 1940's, famous for its tofu with fish head (*yútóu dòufu* 鱼头豆腐).

✉ 101–103 Hefang Jie 河坊街 101–103 号

☎ 8780 7823
🕒 10am to 10:30pm

Zhangsheng Ji 张生记
Specializes in bamboo duck (*sŭngān lăoyā băo* 笋干老鸭煲).
✉ 33 Shuangling Lu 双菱路 33 号
☎ 8602 3333
🕒 10am to 10:30pm

Zhuang Yuan Guan 状元馆
Established during the Qing dynasty, famous for its Ningbo dishes.
✉ 85 Hefang Jie 河坊街 85 号
☎ 8702 5796
🕒 10am to 10:30pm

Souvenirs

As one of the top tourist draws in all of China, Hangzhou seems like one giant shopping haven, but a few venues stand out. Hit the Wulin Lu (*wŭlín lù nǚzhuāng jiē* 武林路女装街) in the heart of downtown if you want to shop till you drop – over 200 clothing stores line the square. Tiyuchang Lu offers big stores and nearby publishing houses. Fenqi Lu specializes in smaller stores for bags, shoes, suitcases and silk and satin. Qinghefang Old Street (*qīnghéfāng fănggŭjiē* 清河坊仿古街) was once a center of commerce during the Southern Song dynasty. Today it's been restored to its former glory and is a good place to load up on snacks. Xihutiandi is for those looking for something upscale. Wushan Lu is a good place to pick up some antique and replica pieces. Dragon Well tea (*lóngjĭng chá* 龙井茶) is a Hangzhou specialty, this green tea is famous throughout China and its fame is reflected in its price. The city is also known for its painted fans. Wangxingji (王星记) is one of the most famous stores selling these exquisite fans – they've been selling them for hundreds of years. Prices range from RMB 60 to 70 for paper fans, while silks ones can cost much more. Hangzhou's silk parasols are legendary for their artistry. Framed by bamboo and covered with silk, it was the sun-blocking device of choice for ancient beauties. Silk parasol costs around RMB 100.

Other Information

POST OFFICES

Yan'an Lu Post Office 延安路邮局
✉ 288 Yan'an Lu 延安路 288 号
☎ 8708 0365

HOSPITALS

Zhejiang Provincial People's Hospital
浙江省人民医院
✉ 158 Shangtang Lu 上塘路 158 号
☎ 8523 9988

COMPLAINT HOTLINES

☎ General: 96123
☎ Taxi: 96520

TOURISM INFORMATION WEBSITE

@ www.gotohz.com

A barge floats its way through modern Hangzhou.

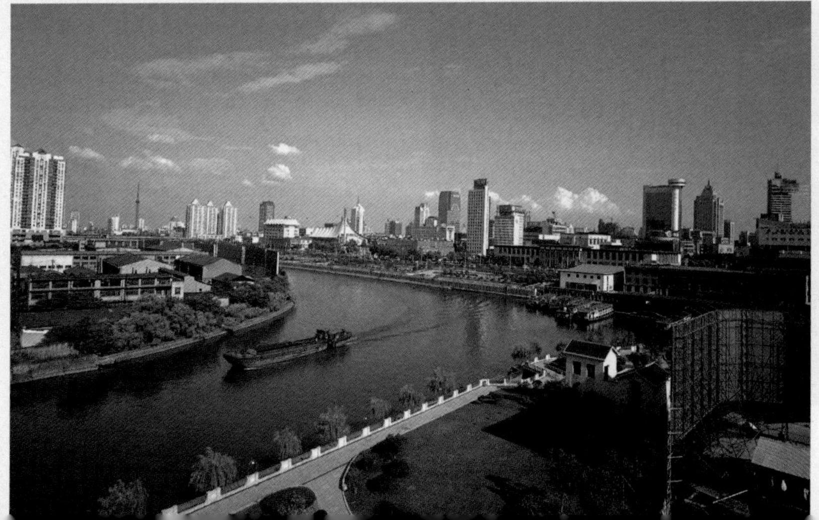

Shaoxing, the City of the Literati and History

Area Code 0575

Shaoxing's history is that of China's cultural heritage. The city has welcomed cultural heroes of all stripes, from social reformers like Lu Xun to wistful poets sipping Shaoxing's famed wine on the banks of a lazy stream.

Just 43 miles (70 km) away from Hangzhou, Shaoxing is sheltered by Kuaiji Shan and nestled in Zhejiang Province's rich Yangtze fed waterways. The architectural style and atmosphere is typical Jiangnan, which means south of the Yangtze. White walls punctuated with black tiles line narrow cobbled streets, and when harried city dwellers dream of an idyllic paradise and plan their retirement, they often picture Shaoxing. But more than a quiet city, Shaoxing is also home to many of China's most renowned scholars, writers and poets. The city draws learned tourists seeking to get a glimpse of China's rich cultural past.

It's easy to imagine what Shaoxing was like hundreds of years ago.

No city in China can claim to be the hometown of as many nationally known personalities as Shaoxing. **Yu the Great** (*Dà Yǔ* 大禹) was one of China's mythical early chiefs, whose reputation and reverence is on par with England's King Arthur. He's credited with teaching the Chinese people how to tame the rivers and control floods. His son followed his father's footsteps by founding the first Chinese dynasty in the 22nd century BC. Yu the Great's tomb lies in Shaoxing where visitors still come to pay their respects; the former Ming governor of Shaoxing wrote the memorial tablet at his tomb. During the Ming dynasty, a representative of the empire would come and perform ceremonial rituals in his honor.

Orchid Pavilion (*lántíng* 兰亭) is 7.8 miles (12.5 km) southwest of Shaoxing at the foot of Lanzhu Mountain. It's the site of China's most famous drinking party and spawned a drinking game that inspired men of letters all over China. In the 4th century AD, Wang Xizhi, a renowned calligrapher, organized a party at Orchid Pavilion. Since poets tend to be romantic souls, they found various ways to entertain themselves in style. Wang Xizhi devised a literary game where the poets

Ducks and farmers share the canals of Shaoxing in the early morning.

would sit on the banks of a small stream then float a small cup filled with wine downstream. The poet the cup stopped in front, of had to compose a poem or drink the wine as a penalty. A mixture of good wine and tranquil scenery inspired 37 poems that day. Wang Xizhi compiled the poems into an anthology and wrote its preface, which became the *Lanting Preface to the Orchid Pavilion* (*lántíngjí xù* 兰亭集序).

Today Orchid Pavilion is a pilgrimage site for those who daydream of holding their own drinking party. The **Goose Pool** (*é chí* 鹅池) is a major sight at Orchid Pavilion , so is the stream where the poets played their game. **Wang Xizhi's Memorial Temple** (*wáng yòujūn cí* 王右军祠) is also at this site. One of the pavilions features a memorial tablet written by an emperor in his honor. The **Lanting Calligraphy Museum** (*lántíng shūfǎ bówùguǎn* 兰亭书法博物馆) is a good place to check out Wang Xizhi's flowing calligraphic style.

On 393 Lu Xun Zhong Lu is the **Former Home of Lu Xun** (*Lǔ Xùn gùjū* 鲁迅故居), China's most influential modern writer and essayist. Born in 1881 in Shaoxing, Lu Xun went to Japan to study medicine. His life changed when one night he and other Chinese students were ordered to watch a slideshow of Chinese prisoners being executed by Japanese soldiers. His indignation and feeling of helplessness compelled him to become a writer in order to examine why China was so weak and to build a national consciousness. He felt that as a doctor, he could only help one person at a time, but as a writer, he could reach the whole nation. To this end, he became a leader of the New Culture Movement, which was a drive at cultural modernization. In 1918 he wrote the "*Diary of a Madman,*" a moral allegory condemning China's oppressive Confucian past. His most famous short story is "*The True Story of Ah Q.*" It's set in Shaoxing and is a morality tale about the shallowness of society.

Quotes

"Stinky tofu, what can I say? It's tofu and it stinks. Plug your nose and take a bite, you'll be surprised."

Wang Xizhi looks towards a pair of geese for his inspiration.

The **Lu Xun Memorial Hall** (*Lǔ Xùn jìniànguǎn* 鲁迅纪念馆) is across the street from his former home and is a great place to learn about Shaoxing's most famous son. Inside the bright museum are large exhibitions with photographs of Lu Xun, early editions of his works and some of his old possessions.

Lu Xun's family home is a large series of dark buildings grouped around courtyards characteristic of grander buildings of the region. Behind is a vegetable garden that he used as his playground when young. Lu Xun's old school is also nearby. Built in the manner of a typical private school of the period, it's reminiscent of the old one-room schools of the West.

A short walk north on Laodong Lu from the home of one of China's foremost writers is the ancestral home of one of China's greatest leaders, **Zhou Enlai**. A veteran revolutionary and a refined statesman, Zhou Enlai rose to become premier of the Chinese government. Because of his reputation for uprightness, he was China's most beloved politician when he passed away in 1976. Despite never living in Shaoxing himself, it's considered his ancestral home because it was where his grandfather lived. Inside his ancestral home is an exhibition of his life.

Other famed Shaoxing residents include Xi Shi, a famed beauty of the Warring States period, Song dynasty poet Lu You, revolutionary martyr Qiu Jin who was executed in 1907 for conspiring to topple the Qing dynasty, and Cai Yuanpei, dean of the prestigious Peking University during the New Culture Movement.

Shaoxing is known for more than its people, though Shaoxing wine is famed throughout China. From the lowliest farmer to the highest official, all take pleasure in imbibing this delight. The wine is made from glutinous rice and is distilled to a low alcohol content, which is a blessing for those who've had enough of fiery Chinese spirits. Perhaps only an excuse to drink more, **Shaoxing wine** is also claimed to have therapeutic effects like aiding digestion. The most famous brands today are Guyuelong Shan and Kuaiji Shan. The wine become famous during the Qing dynasty and one small restaurant has been immortalized because of it.

Lu Xun wrote a short story about the decline of the scholarly class. Once the elite of Chinese society, by the end of the Qing dynasty many intellectuals were reduced to mere paupers. In his story, Kong Yiji, a failed scholar and an alcoholic, visits a small restaurant called **Xianheng** (*xiánhēng* 咸亨) for a cup of wine and a dish of *huixiang*

▶▶ Chinese Wine and Spirits

It's easy to get drunk cheap in China and for some, it may be an opportunity worth taking. Cultural barriers disappear under the revelry and camaraderie of a shared drink. For every tale of Chinese history and tradition that are read through stodgy books, there are a thousand more fascinating stories about the country and its people that are told over the fifth glass of *baijiu* (白酒).

Inebriates often eulogize the inventor of alcohol, but in China it's unclear to whom the praise is due. Some say it was Yi Di, a daughter of one of the rulers of the Xia dynasty. According to legend, after one taste, dad immediately banned the fiery liquid fearing that a future ruler would overindulge himself and lose the throne. Others say it was a man named Du Kang, also from the Xia, while some date it even earlier to the mythic Huang Emperor. For still others, alcoholic drinking occurred in harmony with the creation of the universe.

Less speculatively, 5,000-year-old alcohol-drinking vessels were discovered in Shandong Province in 1987. An early milk-based drink called lilou was super ceded by liquor distilled from cereals. Those who first drank this liquor must have thoroughly enjoyed themselves because records are incomplete and scientists can't decide whether it was pioneered in the Eastern Han, Song, Tang or Yuan dynasties. The cereal based concoctions have evolved into modern Chinese spirits called *baijiu* (white alcohol).

There are a number of different kinds of *baijiu*, the most popular being the expensive *Maotai* (*máotái* 茅台) and the cheap and lethal *Erguotou* (*èrguōtóu* 二锅头). They are white, clear liquids with a strong and lasting aroma, and are drunk, to the consternation of those who have been offered a toast, in whole shots from small glasses. During meals, the Chinese toast almost continuously, glasses being clinked to shouts of *ganbei* (bottoms up 干杯 *gānbēi*). It should be noted that the lower you hold your glass the more respectful you are – this custom leads to glasses being scraped along tabletops in shows of excess humility.

Beer (*píjiǔ* 啤酒) was first brewed in the foreign concessions during the early-20th century by the Russians in Harbin and the Germans in Qingdao. Tsingtao (Qingdao) Beer is famous in China and abroad, but it was only in recent years that consumption of beer overtook that of *baijiu*.

Wine (*pútáojiǔ* 葡萄酒) production is limited, with the most famous vintages made from the grapes of the arid Xinjiang Uyghur Autonomous Region. Traditional Chinese wines are sweet and low in alcohol, while Western-style brands are passable with improving standards.

Appreciation of whisky, vodka and other foreign drinks remains limited. Keen to break into the market, Jack Daniel's has been steadily establishing a name for itself, as has Chivas Regal. They can cost over twenty-five times the price of their Chinese rivals.

beans (*huíxiāngdòu* 茴香豆) whenever he can scrounge up enough money. Lu Xun set his story in Shaoxing and based Xianheng on the restaurants near his home. A real Xianheng opened its doors not long after his story was published. Today the restaurant retains its turn-of-the-century atmosphere; from the furniture and décor to the recipes, everything has been preserved. Many visiting tourists have a small meal and a bottle of Shaoxing wine at this restaurant and locals claim that everyone in Shaoxing has eaten here at least once.

Being a water city it's natural that Shaoxing would have many bridges and waterways. Over 4,000 stone bridges crisscross the waterways connecting the city's roads. The waterways are filled with tiny sampans with black awnings, called *wupeng* (乌蓬), which are unique to Shaoxing. Despite being extremely narrow they can seat five to six people. Built low, these boats give passengers a feeling of sitting precariously on the water. The rowers wear traditional

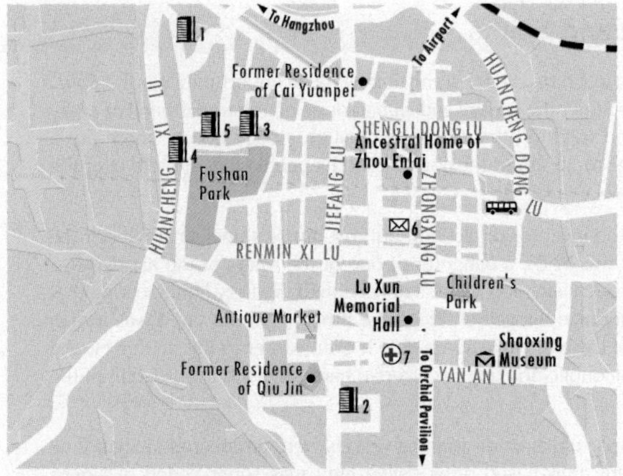

Shaoxing *wuzhan* hats (*wūzhān mào* 乌毡帽) and row using their feet and steer with their free hands. Sitting in a wupeng while watching the street scenes float by is a defining Shaoxing experience.

One peculiar bridge that connects the streets in Shaoxing is called the **Bazi Bridge** (*bāzi qiáo* 八字桥) because it looks like the number eight (*bā* 八) in Chinese. This exceptional bridge connects three streets over three waterways. It's over 16 feet (5 m) high, and uses large rocks for the walking surface. With the railings also made of stone, this 800-year-old bridge was made to last. The bridge and the surrounding area offer typical Shaoxing beauty with relaxed waterways crowded with wupengs and white painted buildings covered by black tiled roofs.

A visit to Shaoxing is more than escaping the frantic city to a quiet water-crossed city; it's taking a step into history and paying homage to some of China's most influential and prestigious movers and shakers. ■

Making Your Trip Easy

Tasty snacks can be bought on any street corner.

Practical Tips

Shaoxing is just south of the Yangtze River where the scenery is picturesque throughout the year. The best time to visit Shaoxing is in spring, summer and autumn. Every year around early-April, the China Lanting Calligraphy Festival (*zhōngguó lántíng shūfǎjié* 中国兰亭书法节) is held in Shaoxing. Calligraphers from all over the world gather in Orchid Pavilion, hold calligraphy symposiums, and write calligraphy. Shaoxing also holds an annual China Shaoxing Wupeng Boat Travel Festival (*zhōngguó shàoxīng wūpéngchuán lǚyóujié* 中国绍兴乌篷船旅游节).

There are several methods to get yourself onto one of the ubiquitous wupeng boats. The Luzhen Yacht Company (鲁镇游船公司) at Jishan Park (稽山园) on Huancheng Nan Lu (环城南路, ☎ 861 1527) offers two types of *wupengs* for hire at RMB 30 or RMB 50. The boats depart at 9:30am, 2:30pm and 7:30pm. The East Lake Wupeng (东湖乌篷船) in the East Lake Resort also offers wupeng rides. Entry to the resort is RMB 25 and hiring a *wupeng* is RMB 60 for up to three people in a boat. The resort is open from 7:30am to 5pm.

Transportation

Airport – Xiaoshan Airport is 25 miles (40 km) from the city. It takes about an hour to get to the airport by shuttle bus from the Dynasty Hotel on Shengli Lu (胜利路王朝大酒店门口, ☎ 513 5301). Shuttle buses depart hourly between 8:30am to 5:30pm.

Taxi – Shaoxing is a small city and RMB 5 will get you to most places in the city.

The Best of Shaoxing

East Lake 东湖 *dōnghú*

✉ Donghu Town, Yuecheng District 越城区东湖镇

☎ 864 9560

🕒 7:30am to 5pm

¥ 25

The Former Home of Lu Xun
鲁迅故居 *Lǔ Xùn gùjū*

✉ 393 Lu Xun Zhong Lu 鲁迅中路 393 号

☎ 512 4978

🕒 8am to 5pm

¥ 60

Orchid Pavilion 兰亭 *lántíng*

✉ Shaoxing County 绍兴县

☎ 460 6887

🕒 7am to 5pm

¥ 35

Hotels

Shaoxing International Hotel 绍兴国际大酒店 *shàoxīng guójì dàjiǔdiàn* ★★★★★

✉ 100 Fushan Xi Lu 府山西路 100 号❶

☎ 516 6788

¥ 966 – double room, peak-season
676 – double room, off-season

@ www.sxint.com

Xian Heng Hotel 咸亨大酒店
xiánhēng dàjiǔdiàn ★★★★★

✉ 680 Jiefang Nan Lu 解放南路 680 号❷

☎ 806 8688

¥ 1,127 – double room, peak-season
788 – double room, off-season

Shaoxing Hotel 绍兴饭店
shàoxīng fàndiàn ★★★★

✉ 9 Huanshan Lu 环山路 9 号❸

☎ 515 5888

¥ 605 – double room, peak-season
424 – double room, off-season

@ www.hotel-shaoxing,com

A grandmother dotes on her grandchild in a traditional Chinese home.

Fushan Hotel 府山饭店
fǔshān fàndiàn ★★★

✉ 341 Fushan Xi Lu 府山西路 341 号❹

☎ 515 5599

¥ 270 – double room

Longshan Hotel 龙山宾馆
lóngshān bīnguǎn ★★★

✉ 500 Shengli Xi Lu 胜利西路 500 号❺

☎ 515 5710

¥ 280 – double room

@ www.longshan.com

Food & Restaurants

Shaoxing's culinary delights reflect the agricultural richness of the Yangtze basin. Food in Shaoxing takes advantage of Shaoxing's famed wine and many of the dishes have a distinct aroma. Shaoxing *meigancai* (绍兴霉干菜) is made from preserved cabbage or mustard greens and served as a side dish or used as an ingredient for other dishes. Meat stew with preserved

Using legs to row one of Shaoxing's famous *wupeng* boats.

vegetables (*gāncài mènròu* 干菜焖肉) is one of Shaoxing's better-known traditional dishes. Shaoxing preserved tofu (*shàoxīng fǔrǔ* 绍兴腐乳) takes tofu and preserves it in Shaoxing wine, giving it a mellow flavor. Steamed mandarin fish (*qīngzhēng guìyú* 清蒸鳜鱼) with Shaoxing wine is a delicious local specialty. Shaoxing stinky tofu (*shàoxīng yóuzhá chòudòufu* 绍兴油炸臭豆腐) tastes better than it sounds or smells; it's particularly good deep-fried.

RESTAURANTS

Shaoxing Caiguan 绍兴菜馆
✉ Luxun Culture Square, Luxun Zhonglu 鲁迅中路鲁迅文化广场
☎ 513 1777

Shaoxing Fandian Chinese Restaurant
绍兴饭店中餐厅
✉ 9 Huanshan Lu 环山路 9 号
☎ 515 5888 ext 7776

Xianheng Jiudian 咸亨酒店
✉ 179 Luxun Zhonglu 鲁迅中路 179 号
☎ 511 6666

Souvenirs

Shaoxing has many souvenirs on offer. Shaoxing wine (*shàoxīng lǎojiǔ* 绍兴老酒) is one of the most popular products with four brands that stand out: *yuanhong* (元红), *jiafan* (加饭), *shanniang* (善酿) and *xiangxue* (香雪). Shaoxing tea (*shàoxīng cháyè* 绍兴茶叶) is an alternative for those who don't drink. Famous brands are *pingshui zhucha* (平水珠茶), *rizhu xuehua* (日铸雪花) and *qiangang huibai* (前岗辉白). Bamboo handicrafts (*shèngzhōu zhúbiān* 嵊州竹编) and Shaoxing paper fans (*shàoxīng zhǐshàn* 绍兴纸扇) are some local handicrafts; they're not only artistic but also practical. The local pottery, called *shengzhou zisha* (嵊州紫砂), is unique to Shaoxing. They come in a variety of shapes and uses such as vases, tea and wine sets and dishes. Shaoxing pearls are also a good buy. The antique market (*bùxíngjiē gǔwán shìchǎng* 步行街古玩市场) is stocked with curios and assorted souvenir stores. The Zhuji pearl market (*zhūjì zhēnzhū shìchǎng* 诸暨珍珠市场) in Shanxiahu Town (山下湖镇) is the biggest pearl market in China.

Other Information

POST OFFICES

Dongjie Zhongxing Post Office
东街中兴邮政局
✉ 1 Dong Jie 东街 1 号❻
☎ 513 2752

HOSPITALS

The Second Shaoxing Hospital
绍兴第二医院
✉ Yan'an Lu, Yuecheng District
越城区延安路❼
☎ 832 2299

COMPLAINT HOTLINES

☎ General: 96118
☎ Taxi: 515 7325

Memorable Experiences

Taking a ride in *wupeng* while drinking tea as the rower slowly guides the *wupeng* around the picturesque city.

Strolling along the quaint streets and crossing the many arched bridges that provide multitudes of photo opportunities then dropping into one of the many museums that line the streets.

Xiamen's International Convention & Exhibition Center.

Xiamen, Island of Music and Art of Living

Area Code 0592

Flowers bloom all year round in this subtropical climate. Just walk 20 minutes in any direction and you'll find a park with shady banyan trees and intoxicatingly sweet flowers.

Xiamen, known for centuries as **Amoy**, is an ancient island gateway to China. The city was part of the Maritime Silk Road and the heart of Chinese sea trade. Xiamen was founded in the 14th century as a Ming dynasty trade center and outpost to defend against Japanese pirates. Following the defeat of the Ming by Qing forces in 1644, Xiamen became a stronghold of resistance under the famous general Zheng Chenggong, better known in the West as **Koxinga**(*guóxìngyé* 国姓爷), his Ming title.

Geographically close to Taiwan, Xiamen shares similar cuisine, dialect and customs as many Taiwanese originally came from Minnan, an area of southern Fujian Province.

In 1841, the British forced Xiamen to open its port and it became one of the first treaty ports in China. People in Xiamen still cling to traditions that have long been discontinued in other parts of China – in almost every home can be found a shrine, where people light incense and give offerings of food and prayers. When meandering among the zigzagging old lanes in the evenings, you can often hear the gong and high-pitch singing of Minnan opera.

GULANGYU'S MUSIC

Across the Lujiang Channel, a 10-minute ferry ride from Xiamen is **Gulangyu** (*gǔlàngyǔ* 鼓浪屿), a 1.1 square mile (1.78 km^2) island. Gulangyu and Xiamen were once home to an indigenous species of egrets. Today these gorgeous birds are a protected species. Some egrets can still be seen lounging around the beaches and waters.

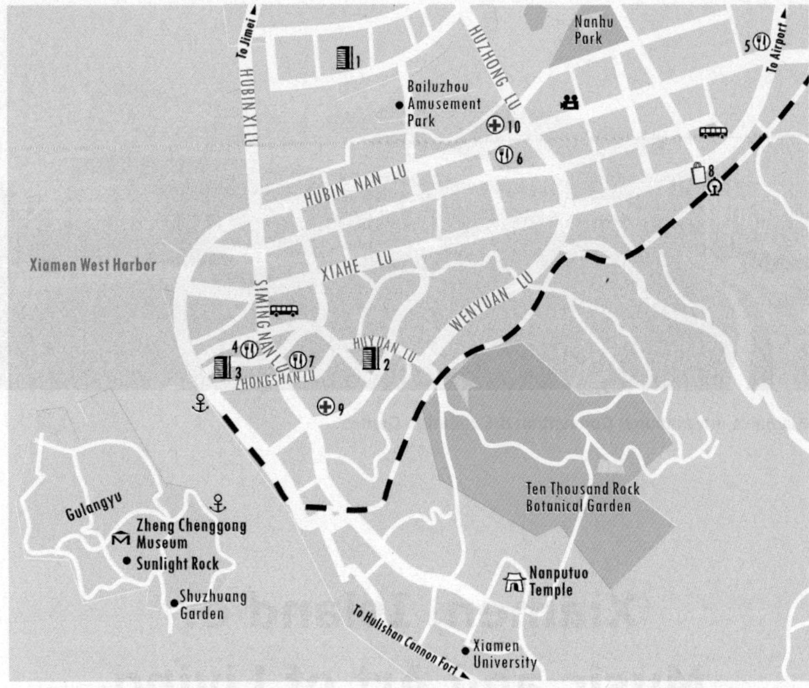

▶▶ Zheng He's Exploration of Discovery

Zheng He was a Muslim admiral of one of the greatest fleets in Chinese history and perhaps world history. Born to a poor family in southwest China, Zheng was captured by the Ming army as a young boy and who made a eunuch. Quickly rising up the ranks, he was eventually given command of the navy after Emperor Chengzu seized power. What followed were voyages of exploration that took Chinese "treasure ships" all over the globe.

From 1405, they visited Southeast Asia, Sumatra, Java, Ceylon, India, Persia, Arabia, the Red Sea as far as Egypt and parts of east Africa. Tributes and envoys were carried back to China from more than 30 countries and naval charts of unparalleled accuracy were drawn.

The size of the fleet was awesome. Around 30,000 men on up to 200 junks sailed with Zheng He, and his flagship was one and a half times the length of a football field, by far the biggest vessel in the world at that time. The fleet made seven separate expeditions and spread knowledge of Chinese silk and porcelain as well as nervous appreciation of the Ming dynasty's military might.

When the emperor died in 1424, Zheng He lost imperial sponsorship due to palace intrigue. When the succeeding emperor turned the Ming dynasty inwards, the days of Zheng He roaming the seas with the massive tribute fleet were finally over. The Chinese would never again dominate the sea as they did with Zheng He.

Recently Gavin Menzies in his book *1421,The Year China Discovered The World* claims that Zheng He's fleet also reached America and Australia years before Christopher Columbus or Captain Cook ever set sail. While many historians are skeptical about Menzies' claims, he has renewed public interest in this fascinating period of Chinese history.

Memorable Experiences

Sipping tea among lotus flowers in the Nanputuo Temple while monks chant in the background.

Strolling through Gulangyu's narrow streets while being serenaded by music drifting out of open windows.

A night cruise around Xiamen, Gulangyu and Jinmen Island while listening to musicians play traditional Chinese music.

The island became home to a group of non-native and unwelcome residents when it officially became a foreign concession in 1903. But in fact foreign settlement had already begun much earlier, when Xiamen became a treaty port in the 19th century. The foreigners who settled here, as in all concession areas, built the island in their own image. The island is an architectural museum of Victorian and Neo-Classical colonial buildings – churches, villas and Christian cemeteries all lend a Mediterranean feel. A ban on vehicles and bicycles and their accompanying horns helps maintain its quaint colonial charm and your peace of mind. For people dazed by horns, noise and pollution in big cities, this should be your first stop.

The 305-foot-high (93 m) **Sunlight Rock** (*riguāng yán* 日光岩), the highest point on this island, is the dominating landmark, making it a useful reference when strolling through the twisting streets. There's also the **Koxinga Museum** (*zhèng Chénggōng jiniànguǎn* 郑成功纪念馆), a tribute to the Ming trader turned patriot. Koxinga was born in Japan to a Japanese mother and a Chinese father who was a powerful maritime merchant. When the Qing dynasty overthrew the Ming dynasty, Koxinga found himself torn between supporting the Ming resistance or joining his father in support of the Qing forces. Ultimately, he chose to fight the Qing and at the height of his power he was able to resist the Qing forces, but slowly the Qing were able to encroach on his territory. He then moved his base to Taiwan where he evicted the Dutch and ended their 40-year presence on the island. The museum displays artifacts from the era and offers good views of the surrounding area; it's also close to the beach.

Once you enter the island's residential area, you'll begin to hear the soft echo of music. Gulangyu is also called "Piano Island" by locals; piano music drifts from the villas and lingers throughout the island's narrow street. Many a famous Chinese musician hails from Xiamen; perhaps the calm breeze from the ocean and the languid pace of life is conducive to musical genius. Every May there's an international music festival, and

Koxinga stands guard on Gulangyu.

A Buddhist worshipper places her incense in front of the Chinese character for Buddha painted in gold at the Nanputuo Temple.

piano competitions and music festivals are also frequently held. On Huangyan Lu, on the way to Sunlight Rock, there's a concert hall where classical concerts are regularly held on weekends. Along **Gangzaihou Beach** (*gǎngzǎihòu hǎitān* 港仔后海滩) is Shuzhuang Garden **Shuzhuang Garden** (*shūzhuāng huāyuán* 菽庄花园), where Asia's largest piano museum is located. There are also a couple of churches on Gulangyu, with the **Trinity Church** (*sānyī táng* 三一堂) on Anhai Lu being the largest. At night you can sometimes hear the choir singing hymns.

Back in Xiamen, the **Nanputuo Temple** (*nánpǔtuó sì* 南普陀寺) is a major destination for Buddhists. Situated at the foot of the **Five Old Men Peak** (*wǔlǎofēng* 五老峰) and next to **Xiamen University** (*xiàmén dàxué* 厦门大学), this peaceful temple is over 1,000 years old and is Xiamen's oldest sight. Look for the character *fo* (佛), which means Buddha in Chinese, carved into a rock - at 15 feet (4.6 m) it's hard to miss.

Next to Nanputuo Temple is Xiamen University, founded in 1921 by the wealthy Chen Jiageng, known as Tan Kah-kee in the local dialect, who made his fortune in Singapore. Chen's philanthropy was widespread, sponsoring many schools in his native Jimei, just east of Xiamen. The architecture of Xiamen University is a blend of Minnan and Western styles and the art college houses the **Chinese European Art Center**, where exhibitions of modern art by Chinese and European artists are regularly held.

On the southeast end of the campus and next to the beach is the **Hulishan Cannon Fort** (*húlǐshān pàotái* 胡里山炮台) where the biggest ancient cannon in Asia is on display. North of the university is the **Ten Thousand Rock Botanical Garden** (*wànshí zhíwùyuán* 万石植物园) which is full of subtropical plants and rocks of whimsical shapes.

Starting from the **Baicheng Beach** (*bái chéng hǎitān* 白城海滩) next to Xiamen University is the scenic **Island Ring Road** (*huándǎo lù* 环岛路). Rent a bicycle and tour along the most beautiful beach in Xiamen; you'll pass by strawberry fields, and be bathed in the soft sea breeze. If you're tired, sit down and grab some barbeque in Huangcuo or Ye Fengzhai and watch the kites sail through the cloudless sky while listening to the waves lap onto the sandy beach.

40 minutes southwest of Xiamen by bus is Changtai, where the Changtai River Club offers a range of activities such as whitewater rafting (*piāoliú* 漂流), parachuting, rock-climbing and other less-than-soothing activities. Contact them at www.fjdyp.com. Water lovers should head for Dongshan Island, a 4-hour bus ride from the Wucun bus station. Clean and clear beaches, swimming, water-skiing and

Making Your Trip Easy

Practical Tips

There is no real winter in Xiamen. Spring is unpleasant with heavy rain. Summer is hot with blue skies and cool breezes, though an occasional typhoon may storm in. Autumn is very pleasant. You can get a free map of Gulangyu Islet in the tourism booth not far from the ferry dock on Island Ring Road.

Transportation

Airport – Gaoqi Airport is only 7.4 miles (12 km) northeast of Xiamen. A taxi costs about RMB 30 from the airport to the city. Xiamen is well connected with domestic flights and has international flights, many to Southeast Asia.

Bicycle – Tandem bicycles are available for rent at RMB 20 for 30 minutes and RMB 5 for each additional 30 minutes. Bikes for three are also available. Bike rental stations can be found around Huandao Lu Taiyang Wan.

Ferry – The ferry from Xiamen to Gulangyu runs from 6am to 11pm. There's a ferry every few minutes, and it's RMB 3 for the return trip from Gulangyu (it's free to get there, but you have to pay to get back).

Taxi – Flag-fall is RMB 8.

The Best of Xiamen

Huli Shan Cannon Fort
胡里山炮台 *húlǐshān pàotái*
✉ Baicheng, Xiamen 厦门白城
☎ 209 9603
🕒 8am to 6pm
¥ 25

Sunlight Rock 日光岩 *rìguāng yán*
✉ Gulangyu Island 鼓浪屿岛
☎ 206 8251
🕒 8am to 6pm
¥ 60

Shuzhuang Garden
菽庄花园 *shūzhuāng huāyuán*
✉ 45 Huangyuan Lu, Gulangyu Island
鼓浪屿岛晃原路 45 号
☎ 206 3744
🕒 8am to 6pm
¥ 30

Hotels

Xiamen Mandarin Hotel 厦门悦华酒店
xiàmén yuèhuá jiǔdiàn ★★★★★
✉ 101 Yuehua Lu, Huli District
湖里区悦华路 101 号
☎ 602 3333
¥ 1,494 – double room
🌐 www.xmmandarin.com

Best Western Xiamen Central Hotel
厦门京闽中心酒店
xiàmén jīngmǐn zhōngxīn jiǔdiàn ★★★★
✉ Yuhou Nanli, Songbai Xiaoqu
松柏小区屿后南里
☎ 512 3333
¥ 1,242 – double room
🌐 www.bwxm.com

The Marco Polo Xiamen
厦门马哥孛罗东方大酒店 *xiàmén mǎgēbōluó dōngfāng dàjiǔdiàn* ★★★★
✉ 8 Jianye Lu, Hubin Bei Lu
湖滨北路建业路 8 号❸
☎ 509 1888
¥ 1,328 – double room
🌐 www.marcopolohotels.com

Xiamen Huaqiao Hotel 厦门华侨大厦大酒店
xiàmén huáqiáo dàshà dàjiǔdiàn ★★★★
✉ 70 – 74 Xinhua Lu 新华路 70 – 74 号❶
☎ 266 0888
¥ 540 – double room
🌐 www.xmhqhotel.com.cn

Quotes

"The students at Xiamen University must have a hard time studying. With the beach and such beautiful scenery nearby, who can sit all day in a classroom?"

"Walking through Gulangyu was like taking a stroll through time. Narrow streets and radiant atmosphere, graced with the occasional note from a piano, made this place hard to leave."

Lujiang Hotel
鹭江宾馆 *lùjiāng bīnguǎn* ★★★
✉ 54 Lujiang Dao 鹭江道 54 号❷
☎ 202 2922
¥ 616 – double room, peak-season
424 – double room, off-season
@ www.lujiang-hotel.com

Food & Restaurants

To say tea is popular in Xiamen is a slight understatement; with over 1,000 tea houses, it's a necessity. Kung fu tea (*gōngfu chá* 功夫茶) is as essential for the locals as coffee is for westerners – and has the same kick. Imagine a tea brewed like an espresso. A pot is stuffed with Oolong tea leaves and twice brewed; the tea is then poured into a thimble-sized cup and shot back. Kung fu tea is super strong and will literally have you doing high kicks all night if you drink too many of these mini-cups of caffeine. It'll take some time for you to get used to the strong taste, but it's something the locals savor like connoisseurs. Drinking tea, chatting with friends and loafing away their weekends on a hilltop park is a favorite pastime for the locals.

Xiamen dishes are usually fresh, light and sweet. Seafood restaurants usually have no menus – just point to the critter you want. Although ordering can be a little intimidating and chaotic, what eventually turns up on your plate is usually satisfyingly yummy.

Hakka food is something that shouldn't be missed. The Hakkas were a migratory group of ethnic Han who originated from central China and later settled in southern China. Hakka cuisine doesn't overpower the palate and retains the original flavors of the ingredients; their steam ribs and salted baked shrimp are worth a try.

Along with delicious main courses, Xiamen also offers a variety of tasty snacks. Sweet sticky rice with bamboo shoots, leeks and pork (*zházǎo* 炸枣), creamy and refreshing peanut soup (*huāshēng tāng* 花生汤) and sticky rice congee with crabmeat (*hǎixiè nuòmǐzhōu* 海蟹糯米粥) are all delicious.

In and near the Nanputuo Temple are quite a few vegetarian restaurants and you'll leave feeling good that no animals died in making your meal. For a cornucopia of snacks head to Ka Le Meishi Guangchang (卡乐美食广场, 5/F, Shimao Shangcheng, 世贸商城 5 楼, ☎ 398 8790) which is full of vendors and yummy delights.

RESTAURANTS

Haoqingxiang Dajiulou 好清香大酒楼
Sticky rice congee with crabmeat (*hǎixiè nuòmǐzhōu* 海蟹糯米粥), leek dumplings (*jiǔcài hé* 韭菜盒) and *shaorouzong* (烧肉粽) are the house specialties.
✉ 85 Hubin Zhong Lu 湖滨中路❻
☎ 220 9178

Huangzehe Peanut Soup Shop
黄则和花生汤店
Specializes in *zhazao* (炸枣) and peanut soup (*huāshēng tāng* 花生汤).
✉ 22 – 24 Zhongshan Lu
中山路 22 – 24 号❹
☎ 202 4670

Jiali Haixian Dajiulou 佳丽海鲜大酒楼
Seafood restaurant, with dishes like red-stewed abalone (*hóngshāo bàoyú* 红烧鲍鱼), swallow's nest soup (*wǔcǎi yànwō* 五彩燕窝).
✉ 4/F, Baofu Dasha, Hubin Nan Lu
湖滨南路宝福大厦 4 楼❺
☎ 516 5555

Shuyou Haixian Dajiulou 舒友海鲜大酒楼
Specializes in seafood, especially good is the *youlong chuang jinwo* (游龙闯金窝) and *youju hongxun* (油焗红鲟), which is made from sturgeon.
✉ Zhongyin Da Sha, Hubin Bei Lu
湖滨北路中银大厦
☎ 509 8888

Wuzaitian Snack Shop 吴再添小吃店
Especially recommended is *shacha mian* (沙茶面), *youcongke* (油葱粿) and *tusundong* (土笋冻).
✉ 49 Datong Lu 大同路 49 号
☎ 203 4820

Donghai Restaurant 东海大酒店
✉ 1 Zhongshan Lu 中山路 1 号❼
☎ 202 1111

Souvenirs

Longtou Lu, on Gulangyu, is full of souvenir shops where you can buy Chinese calligraphy and paintings, lovely teapots and tea sets, puppets and dried seafood.

A colorful ceremony honoring Mazu, an important Buddhist figure.

Souvenirs unique to Xiamen include gold-plated lacquerware (*qīxiàn diāo* 漆线雕), pearl embroidery (*zhūxiù* 珠绣) and Wenxing porcelain (wénxīng cí 文兴瓷).

Zhongshan Lu is the liveliest street in Xiamen; it's full of locals and tourists, shops and supermarkets. Most buildings date to the early 20th century, with buildings two or three stories high. The first floor is usually where the shops are located and the upper floors used as residences.

Next to the railway station is the World Trade Center (*shìmào shāngchéng* 世贸商城 ❽), a modern shopping mall with a strong international presence. Walmart, Printemps, McDonalds and KFC are all located here.

Trendy Xiamen residents go to Hexiang Xi Lu for their shopping forays. Traditional Chinese clothes, music stores featuring the latest hits and elegant furniture stores line the street and set the trend.

Other Information

POST OFFICES

Huli Post Office 湖里邮局

✉ 15 Huli Da Dao 湖里大道 15 号

☎ 602 1234

Lujiang Post Office 鹭江邮局

✉ 58 Haihou Lu 海后路 58 号

☎ 202 2580

HOSPITALS

The First Xiamen Hospital 厦门市第一医院

✉ 10 Shanggu Jie, Zhenhai Lu 镇海路上古街 10 号❾

☎ 207 6314, 213 7327

Zhongshan Hospital 中山医院

✉ 201 – 209 Hubin Nan Lu 湖滨南路 201 – 209 号❿

☎ 202 5468

CONSULATES

Philippines 菲律宾

✉ 2 Lingxiangli, Lianhua Xincun 莲花新村菱香里 2 号

☎ 513 0355

Singapore 新加坡

✉ Room 901, Dahua Bank Plaza, 19 Hubin Bei Lu 湖滨北路 19 号大华银行大厦 901 室

☎ 511 4695

COMPLAINT HOTLINES

☎ General: 531 8985, 800 858 2365

☎ Taxi: 202 2616

TOURISM INFORMATION WEBSITE

@ www.xmtravel.com.cn

The misty peaks of Wuyi Shan are straight out of a traditional Chinese painting.

Wuyi Shan

Area Code 0599

Heritage: Wuyi Shan

Located in northern Fujian Province close to the border with Jiangxi Province, the picturesque **Wuyi Shan** (*wǔyí shān* 武夷山) sits at 2,132 feet (650 m) above sea level. Once an ancient lake, Wuyi Shan came into being during the geological spasms of the dinosaur age. After many thousands of years, with nature shaping the landscape, Wuyi Shan has assumed its present form.

Wuyi Shan was inhabited thousands of years ago by a group anthropologists call the Yue. During the Han dynasty, emperors would visit the mountain to perform sacred ceremonies, offering sacrifices to Heaven and Earth. During the Tang dynasty, Wuyi Shan became elevated and was given honorific titles by the emperor. Later the mountain became an important center for Confucian learning, but Taoism and Buddhism also made the mountain their home, Taoists believe the mountain to be the abode of numerous immortals. An important Song dynasty Confucian scholar, Zhu Xi, founded an academy on the mountain in 1183, during the Song dynasty. He taught there for 10 years and his teachings would influence Confucian thought in China up to the 20th century.

The forests that carpet the mountain are subtropical and are home to many endangered species. In 1837 a French explorer discovered many new species of birds and animals hiding away on the mountain. Over the years more than 600 new species of animals have been found and the mountain is richly inhabited with insects. As early as the Qing dynasty, under Emperor Qianlong, the mountain was a protected nature reserve where fishing and logging was forbidden. In 1999 it became a UNESCO World Heritage Site.

One of the best ways to enjoy the mountain at a slow and languid pace is to hire a bamboo raft to take you on a 5.9-mile (9.5-km) cruise down the meandering **Nine Bends River** (*jiǔqū xī* 九曲溪). Board the rafts at the ninth bend, by **Xingcun Town** (*xīngcūn zhèn* 星村镇); there's also a market there that sells the very prized Yan tea (*yán chá* 岩茶), a type of red tea. While the raft slowly drifts along the river, steep cliffs and tree topped peaks jut out from the banks. The pristine waters sparkle with the reflection of trees and barren wind scraped rock faces.

With a long bamboo pole, a skilled oarsman gently guides the rickety looking bamboo raft as it leisurely floats down the river. The rafts have seats, so sit back and enjoy the scenery slowly drifting by.

After boarding the raft at the 9th bend for the 2-hour cruise, the first sight that'll come into view is the **Baiyun Yan** (*báiyún yán* 白云岩), a solitary peak which is also known as **Ling Peak** (*líng fēng* 灵峰). During the early morning, the river will be masked by lazy swirls of mist, which turn it into an ethereal fantasia. To the north of the Baiyun Yan is a cave hidden away in the middle of a steep cliff, for those who find the slow pace of the river overly lethargic, crawling up to the cave on all fours will give your heart a jump-start.

Wildlife abounds throughout Wuyi Shan; the pristine forest that lies at both banks of the river is home to a menagerie of rare butterflies, some of which are only found in this area. At the 8th bend, ancient tourists with vivid imaginations have dubbed a rock formation **Shuigui Shi** (*shuǐguī shí* 水龟石), which roughly translates as "water turtle rock." From certain angles, if the light is right, the two slabs of rock on top of each other just might look like two turtles, getting to know each other better.

Mother Nature is patient. She has to be for her to carve out the natural beauty of Wuyi Shan. At the 6th bend is **Shaibu Yan** (*shàibù yán* 晒布岩) which is a stark demonstration of nature's persistence. Over thousands of years, water flowing down the cliff has eroded small channels along the face. At some 1,300 feet (400 m) high and 650 feet (200 m) wide, this bare rocky cliff resembles a dried out meatloaf. If your boat stops and you're up to it, a climb to the top of **Tianyou Peak** (*tiānyóu fēng* 天游峰) will offer a grand view of the surrounding area.

The soothing sounds of water running over moss covered rocks amidst the gentle wind blowing through the trees, make the area an ideal place for reflection and contemplation. Zhu Xi, one of China's foremost Confucian scholars evidently thought so. At the 5th bend he founded an academy, the **Wuyi Jingshe** (*wǔyí jīngshè* 武夷精舍), during the Song dynasty. His academy saw vast expansion throughout the various dynasties.

Tea plantations abound throughout Wuyi Shan. Yan tea, a type of Oolong tea, grows especially well in this subtropical climate, something that has been known for centuries. During the Yuan dynasty, a tea

A stone Buddhist figure.

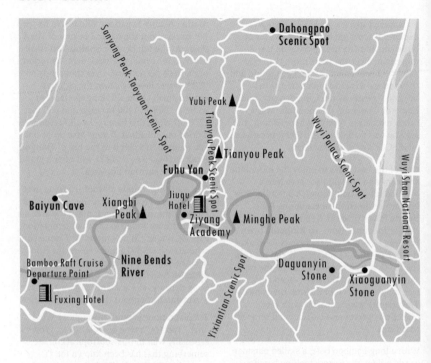

plantation was built at the 4th bend, which still has a working well that supposedly contains sweetish water. The tea trees here are the *dahongpao*(*dàhóngpáo* 大红袍) variety, a type that only grows on Wuyi Shan. Though the tea trees grow on Wuyi Shan, there are only 4 plants that grow on the side of a cliff that are considered worthy of their name. These plants produce only a small amount of tea per year, which reflects their high price.

At the 3rd bend are coffins hidden away up in the cliffs. 3,800 years ago, the Yue people inhabited this area. They placed their dead in niches high above the river a practice similar to ancient burial practices along the Yangtze River. In 1979 anthropologists excavated a coffin measuring 16 feet (4.89 m) long and carved from a complete tree. Inside the coffin they found a complete skeleton which was over 3,400 years old.

As final bend comes into view, so does the **Shuiguang Shi** (*shuǐguāng shí* 水光石), a rock face with calligraphy and poems carved into it. Once again the imagination takes over when viewing **Shizi Peak** (*shīzi fēng* 狮子峰), a peak that resembles a lion.

The raft finishes its journey at the 1st bend;

Wood carvings and root carvings in Fujian province are famous throughout China.

Memorable Experiences

Taking a slow paced raft down the lazy stream and catching sight of wild animals as they peek out of the underbrush.

Taking a sip of a highly prized tea that few people ever get to drink.

from here it's a quick walk to **Wuyi Palace** (*wǔyí gōng* 武夷宫), the older Taoist Temple on the mountain. Emperor Wudi of the Han dynasty offered sacrifices to the mountain here. During the Tang, from 742 to 755, the Tianbao Pavilion (*tiānbǎo diàn* 天宝殿) was added to the grounds. Outside the temple is a market street, **Song Jie** (*sòng jiē* 宋街), recreated in a traditional Song dynasty setting. The street is lined with teahouses, souvenir shops and restaurants. It's a good place to spend an hour or so browsing and relaxing with a cup of tea. There's also a small museum, the **Wuyi Shan Lishi Wenwu Bowuguan** (*wǔyíshān lìshǐ wénwù bówùguǎn* 武夷山历史文物博物馆); inside are exhibits of a coffin and the relics found within. ■

Making Your Trip Easy

Practical Tips

Any time of the year Wuyi Shan is a good place to visit, but summers and autumns are especially vibrant. If you want to go to Wuyi Shan during summer or fall you'll be going at its busiest, so make sure you make reservations. When taking the raft cruise, be sure to obey the guide's commands. Don't stand up on the raft unless you want to go for an unplanned swim.

Transportation

Airport – The airport is in the south of Wuyi Shan City, approximately 3 miles (5 km) from the Wuyi Shan Guojia Lüyou Dujiaqu (武夷山国家旅游度假区, ☎ 510 6513).

Taxi – Taxis are RMB 7 at flag-fall.

The Best of Wuyi Shan

Wuyi Shan Scenic Area
武夷山景区 wǔyí shān jǐngqū
Dahongpao-Waterfall Curtain Cave Scenic Spot 大红袍-水帘洞景区 dàhóngpáo-shuǐliándòng jǐngqū
Yunwo Tianyou Peak Scenic Spot
云窝天游峰风景区 yúnwō tiānyóufēng jǐngqū
¥ 110-one day, 120-two days, 130-three days

Nine Bends River Bamboo Raft Cruise
九曲竹筏 *jiǔqū zhúfá*
✉ Board – Xingcun Village Wharf No. 1 and No. 3 上船码头:星村镇 1 号码头和 3 号码头
☎ 526 2126, 526 2059
🕒 the cruise departs at either 7:30am or 8am; depending on the month, the last raft departs at 3:40pm with hours extended during the summer
¥ 100

Wuyi Shan's tea is prized throughout China.

▶▶ Chinese Tea

It's easy to tell tea is China's national drink, tea is consumed in restaurants, at home and carried around all day in transparent thermos flasks. It's a serious habit, and one that hasn't been broken by the introduction of coffee or the machinations of sugary soda companies.

Over 4,000 years ago, a legendary ruler of China named Shen Nong insisted his drinking water be boiled, while sitting under a tree a single leaf dropped into his cup and turn his purified water brown. When he braved a sip, he found the new drink refreshing and thus began the cultivation of the tea plant.

Scholars debate the historical veracity of this story and evidence of tea drinking only dates back to a slave's shopping list from around 50 BC. Research is made more difficult because the ancient character for tea also means "bitter vegetable." It's quite possible that tea has existed since the Xia dynasty and recent archaeological finds have found the Xia had a relatively advanced civilization.

It was during the Tang dynasty when tea really caught on. The modern Chinese word for tea (*chá* 茶) was adopted when Lu Yu wrote the *Cha Ching* around AD 780. His three-volume work covered tea from its growth to its brewing and the famous tea plantations throughout China. The book was influenced by Lu Yu's Buddhist beliefs and Japanese Buddhist missionaries brought the book to Japan along with tea plant seeds. Japan developed its own complicated tea ceremony and rich tea culture.

Tea slowly began to creep west, Indian legends tell of Bodhidharma's delight in the new drink and by AD 850 it had reached Arabia. It wouldn't be until Portuguese and Dutch traders took the sea route around Africa in the 16th century that tea would reach Europe. England's East India Company began its trade in the mid-17th century.

In 1773, British taxation on tea shipments to the Thirteen Colonies led to the Boston Tea Party where colonists dumped chests of tea into Boston Harbor. A trade imbalance unfavorable to West later led to the Opium War, as foreign governments fought for access to "all the tea in China."

Restaurants and supermarkets are stocked with assorted types of tea of varying quality. Black tea is called red tea (*hóng chá* 红茶) in China with green tea (*lǜ chá* 绿茶) being more popular. Standard brews are provided free in most restaurants, but if you are a connoisseur, then a trip to a specialized teahouse (*cháguǎn* 茶馆) – the best are found south of the Yangtze River. A new twist on an old drink is pearl milk tea (*zhēnzhū nǎichá* 珍珠奶茶), which is widely popular with the young.

Hotels

Fujian Province Wuyi Shan Post & Telecom Hotel
福建省武夷山邮电宾馆 *fújiànshěng wǔyíshān yóudiàn bīnguǎn* ★★★
✉ inside Wuyi Shan Lüyou Dujiaqu 武夷山旅游度假区内
☎ 525 2888, 525 0510
¥ 310 – double room, peak-season
260 – double room, off-season
@ www.wuyi-shan.com

Fujian Wuyi Tea Hotel 武夷茶苑大酒店 *wǔyí cháyuàn dàjiǔdiàn* ★★★
✉ inside Wuyi Shan Lüyou Dujiaqu 武夷山旅游度假区内
☎ 525 6777, 525 6710
¥ 480 – double room, peak-season
338 – double room, off-season

Wuyi Mountain Villa
武夷山庄 *wǔyí shānzhuāng* ★★★
✉ Wuyi Palace 武夷宫
☎ 525 1888, 525 5891
¥ 350 – double room
@ www.513villa.com

Wuyi Shan International Trade Hotel
国贸大酒店 *guómào dàjiǔdiàn* ★★★
✉ Wangfeng Lu, Wuyi Shan 武夷山望峰路
☎ 525 2521, 525 9328
¥ 288 – double room, peak-season

Travelers take a relaxing boat ride at Fujian's Wuyi Shan.

260 – double room, off-season
@ gmhotel.mycool.net

Food & Restaurants

The local cuisine makes use of the abundant herbs and spices that grow in the region. The mountainous region lends itself to a large selection of wild game that fill the menus. The snails stir-fried with chilies (*chǎo xiāngluó* 炒香螺) are popular during the summer and the fragrant dish goes well with a cold beer. *Wengong cai* (文公菜) may seem oily but it doesn't taste greasy. Its name literally means "great scholar dish" and was named after Zhu Xi, the Song dynasty Confucian scholar who is said to have frequently served this to his guests. A local smoked goose called *langu xun'e* (岚谷熏鹅) is mildly spicy and very popular. If you're looking for some serious dining, try the local banquet (*màntíng zhāoyàn* 幔亭招宴). This banquet features cold appetizers, hot courses, desserts and fruits.

RESTAURANTS

Juzhen Dajiudian 聚珍大酒店
Specializes in local snacks.
✉ 1 Liuyong Lu 柳永路 1 号
☎ 531 6970, 531 6568
🕒 7am to 10pm

Wuyi Shanzhuang Dawangge
武夷山庄大王阁
The largest and one of the best restaurants in the city, specializes in tea banquets (*cháyàn* 茶宴), mushrooms banquets (*gūyàn* 菇宴), and *manting zhaoyan* (幔亭招宴).
✉ Wuyi Gong 五夷宫
☎ 525 5900
🕒 7am to 9am, 11:30am to 2:30pm, 5pm to 8:30pm

Yunqing Dajiudian 云清大酒店
Specializes in local snacks.
✉ inside Wuyi Shan Lüyou Dujiaqu 武夷山旅游度假区内
☎ 523 0688
🕒 7am to 10pm

Quotes

"The cruise was definitely really cool. I thought it would be pretty boring, but the scenery was breathtaking and the ride was over before we knew, but not before I got some great shots."

Local opera performances continue Wuyi Shan's traditional culture.

Souvenirs

Craftsmen at Wuyi Shan are skilled carvers and carvings using bamboo with Wuyi Shan's scenery as a motif and bamboo tea tables are popular souvenirs. One of the best places to do your souvenir shopping is Sun City in Dujiaqu (武夷山度假区太阳城). It's a comprehensive shopping center. It's located on the second floor of the agricultural and trading market at the south end of the Sangu Shangye Jie (*sāngū shāngyèjiē* 三姑商业街,☎ 525 2526).

Tea culture is strong here and Yan tea is considered by connoisseurs as the elite of Oolong teas. Of the different types of *wuyi yan tea*(武夷岩茶), "*dahongpao*" is the reigning king. The Beiyuan Tea Center (*běiyuàn cháyì jiāoliú zhōngxīn* 北苑茶艺交流中心, ☎ 520 2629) is a good place to shop for Wuyi Shan's famous teas. You'll find an a ssortment of teas ranging from RMB 10 to 1,000 per 500g (about 1.1 pounds). The center is located on the main road to the Waterfall Curtain Cave Resort (*shuǐliándòng jǐngqū* 水帘洞景区) of the Wuyi Shan Scenic Spot.

Other Information

POST OFFICES

Holiday Inn Post Office 度假区邮局
✉ Sangu Jie, inside Wuyi Shan Lüyou Dujiaqu 武夷山旅游度假区内三姑街
☎ 525 2875

HOSPITALS

Wuyi Shan Municipal Hospital 武夷山市立医院
✉ 65 Wengong Lu 文公路 65 号
☎ 531 6255

COMPLAINT HOTLINES

☎ General: 525 0600, 525 0609
☎ Taxi: 511 6690

BARGAINING 讨价还价		
It's too expensive.	tài guì le	太贵了。
You're kidding!	kāiwánxiào	开玩笑!
Can you give me a discount?	néng dǎzhé ma	能打折吗?
Give me a discount on this.	ràng diǎnr jià ba	让点儿价吧。
Will I get a better price if I buy more?	duōmǎi néng piányi ma	多买能便宜吗?
I'll give you··· RMB.	wǒ gěi nǐ ··· yuán	我给你…元。
This cheaper at other places.	biéde dìfāng yǒu gèng piányi de	别的地方有更便宜的。
Can you give me this at a cheaper price?	néng piányì diǎnr ma	能便宜点儿吗?

CENTRAL CHINA

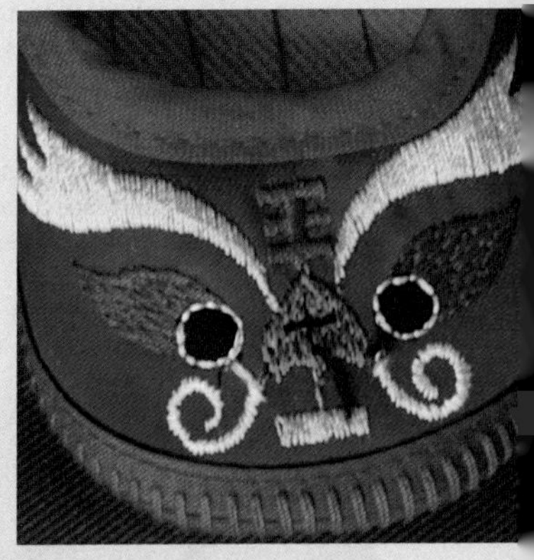

Shaolin Temple, Kicking It Up

Area Code 0371

Rounding hairpin turns on a winding mountain road, the **Shaolin Temple's** surrounding scenery is as rugged as the legendary fighting-monks themselves.

Both domestic and foreign travelers come from far and wide to the small village nestled away in Henan Province's **Song Shan** (*sōngshān* 嵩山), roughly an hour's drive from Luoyang or Zhengzhou, to visit the fabled birthplace of one of the world's most famous martial arts movements.

But Shaolin Temple (*shàolín sì* 少林寺) is more than that – thousands visit every year to pray and pay their respects at one of China's oldest Buddhist temples. The temple is believed to have been founded in AD 495 by Indian monk Ba Tuo, on land given to him by the Northern Wei emperor, so that monks could focus on the disciplines of their faith.

In AD 527, **Bodhidharma** (*dá mó* 达摩) visited and founded what became the Chan (Zen in Japanese) sect. According to popular lore, Bodhidharma crossed the Yellow River on a single reed then spent nine years meditating in a cave before entering the temple grounds. His shadow, it is said, can still be seen in a nearby cave to this day, aptly named **Bodhidharma's Cave** (*dá mó dòng* 达摩洞).

Because Chan Buddhism emphasizes

The fighting monks of Shaolin Temple show off their prowess.

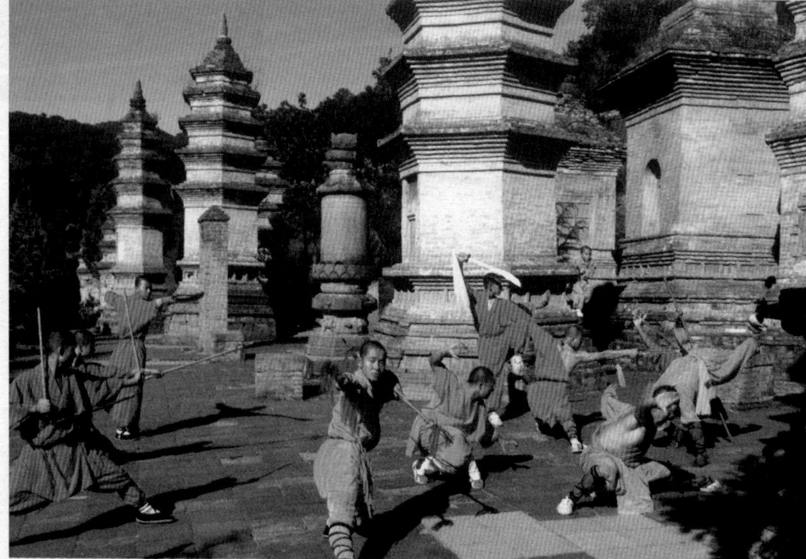

enlightenment through meditation, kung fu developed initially as stretching exercises between long hours sitting in a prone position, used to help the monks' concentration. Imitating animals and insects, the stretches eventually became fighting forms, which would make the name of the temple synonymous with kung fu.

The village at Shaolin is fully caught up in kung fu; stopping in the village around the temple affords visitors an opportunity to see youngsters training at the various schools nearby. Children of all ages can be seen spinning in mid-air, high-kicking, lunging with spears and sparring, with the sounds of hundreds of young voices barking in unison. Entry to the temple grounds includes access to all attractions within for RMB 40.

Strolling through the temple's main gate you can see the characters for Shaolin Temple written in calligraphy by the Qing emperor Kangxi. Among the highlights – apart from the main temple and its inherent shrines, hosts of contemplating Buddhas and monks roaming the area – are the pavilions on the grounds. A giant wok is also visible. It's said that it could cook 1,650 pounds (750 kg) of rice – and it's considered one of the smaller woks that once graced the grounds.

In front of the **Bell Tower** (*zhōnglóu* 钟楼) is a stele with three faces carved on one side. The faces of Buddha, Laozi (the founder of Taoism) and Confucius are grouped together to represent the harmonious unity of Buddhism, Taoism and Confucianism. Nearby another memorial stele provides a list of rewards given to the monks of Shaolin by the future Tang emperor Taizong. As the Sui dynasty disintegrated, Taizong rose up in rebellion. When he was cornered by a local warlord, 13 monks from the temple aided him in his escape. When he later ascended to the throne, he threw a huge banquet for the monks, with the finest dishes and wines available, to show his gratitude. To his chagrin the monks refused to eat due to their strict vegetarian diet – as emperors were likely to do, he simply issued a decree allowing the monks of Shaolin to drink wine and eat meat, though the monks today follow a vegetarian diet.

Many of the pavilions bear a number of wall murals devoted to Buddhist mythology, Shaolin legends and the different stances in

The main gate to the historic Shaolin Temple.

Shaolin kung fu – the most well-known depicting the rescue of the prince. Many of the murals were removed and re-painted when the building was rebuilt. The temple was destroyed by a warlord in 1928. It reputedly burned for 40 days. The floor in the **Thousand Buddha Hall** (*qiānfó diàn* 千佛殿) is sunken, supposedly due to the constant exercises held there.

For those seeking peaceful contemplation, the **Meditation Garden** is an ideal spot. A hallway wraps itself in a square around the quiet garden and there's a terrace to sit and meditate while swarms of tourists mill around outside. The hallway itself offers observers an insight into some of the colorful characters of Buddhist lore with statues of green-skinned arhats stretching their limbs and alternately scowling or smiling. Some eye you with joy while others stare you down with a sinister glare.

A must-see is the **Forest of Pagodas** (*shàolín tǎlín* 少林塔林), aptly named for the

A mural in the Shaolin Temple showing off the skills of past kung fu masters.

246 multi-tiered monuments to noted monks from years gone by. Many bear inscriptions detailing the lives and exploits of the monks for whom the pagodas were built. Each pagoda houses the ashes of a monk interred on the site from AD 791 to 1803. The pagodas take up a significant plot of land at the foot of breathtaking mountain scenery, although the views can be blanketed in a haze that obscure what would otherwise be a picturesque panorama.

Just outside of the Shaolin Temple grounds is the small town of Dengfeng which offers some good opportunities to get away from the crowds at the Shaolin Temple. Check out the **Zhong Yue Temple** (*zhōngyuè miào* 中岳庙), a Taoist temple which was originally built for the purpose of worshipping Song Shan – the mountain is one of the five sacred Taoist mountains, with each representing one of the five elements (earth, water, wood, fire, metal) that Taoists believe make up the world; Song Shan represents the earth element. Zhong Yue became a Taoist Temple during the Northern Wei period and was rebuilt during the Qing dynasty using Beijing's Forbidden City as a model. Just north of town is the **Songyang Academy** (*sōngyáng shūyuàn* 嵩阳书院) one of China's

Quotes

"It was amazing to see kids of all ages participating in such an ancient martial arts tradition."

four "great academies." Inside the academy grounds are two very old cypresses, over 2,100 years old, planted by Han emperor Wudi.

Apart from these obvious attractions, watch for demonstrations by martial arts practitioners held at various times throughout the day at the training center just inside the front gate to the compound. For those eager to get a shot of bald gentlemen in colorful robes striking kung fu poses, these types are plentiful around the grounds. ■

Making Your Trip Easy

Practical Tips

For a great kung fu fighting extravaganza check out the International Shaolin Martial Arts Festival that's held in Zhengzhou every two years from September 1 to 5.

Most visitors to the Shaolin Temple stay in either Zhengzhou or Luoyang and visit Song Shan as part of a day excursion. It's possible to stay at some of the schools in the village at varying rates, but the noise of young martial artists lunging and bellowing in the early morning may not provide a restful sleep.

Transportation

Airport – The airport is 19 miles (30 km) southeast of Zhengzhou and takes 30 minutes to reach the city center by taxi.

Bus – Buses and vans taking loads of visitors to and from Song Shan can be found with relative ease around the Luoyang train station. Bus fare can be bargained down to RMB 15, but be aware that most buses won't leave until they're full. Luoyang city buses also head to the temple, but they're not the most comfortable and take a long time.

Be wary of buses that stop at "attractions" like souvenir shops along the way. Once you've arrived at the village, touts may try to coax you into paying to watch kung fu demonstrations at the school.

Taxi – Taxis come in two types, the larger one is RMB 10 at flag-fall while the Volkswagens are RMB 7.

Students perform a mass demonstration of their Shaolin kung fu skills.

Memorable Experiences

Wandering through the Forest of Pagodas and imagining the lives of the past monks.

Sitting in the Meditation Garden and contemplating the meaning of life.

Visiting schools around Song Shan and watching the youngsters run through their drills.

Gazing at the various murals that fill the temple grounds and gaining insights into the legends of the monks.

The Best of Dengfeng

Shaolin Temple Scenic Spot, Song Shan
嵩山少林寺景区 *sōngshān shàolínsi jǐngqū*
✉ the north base of Song Shan, Shaoshi Shan, 8 miles (13 km) from Dengfeng
登封市嵩山少室山北麓
☎ 6287 2138, 6288 7139
🕒 6am to 7:30pm, peak-season
6:30am to 7pm, off-season
¥ 100

Songyang Academy
嵩阳书院 *sōngyáng shūyuàn*
✉ 1.5 miles (2.5 km) north of Dengfeng
登封城北 2.5 公里
☎ 6287 0409
🕒 7:30am to 6:30pm, peak-season
8am to 5:30pm, off-season
¥ 30

Zhong Yue Temple 中岳庙 *zhōngyuè miào*
✉ 1.9 miles (3 km) east of Dengfeng
登封城东 3 公里
☎ 6286 2577
🕒 8am to 5:30pm
¥ 25

Hotels

Crown Plaza Zhengzhou
河南中州皇冠假日酒店 *hénán zhōngzhōu huángguān jiàrì jiǔdiàn* ★★★★★
✉ 115 Jinshui Lu, Zhengzhou
郑州市金水路 115 号
☎ 6595 0055
¥ 699 – double room, peak-season
598 – double room, off- season
@ www.crowneplaza.com/hotels/cgcch

Sofitel Zhengzhou Hotel
郑州索菲特国际饭店 *zhèngzhōu suǒfēitè guójì fàndiàn* ★★★★★
✉ 289 Chengdong Lu, Zhengzhou
郑州市城东路 289 号
☎ 6595 0088
¥ 598 – double room
@ www.accorhotels.com/asia

Yuda Palace Hotel 郑州裕达国贸酒店
zhèngzhōu yùdá guómào jiǔdiàn ★★★★★
✉ 220 Zhongyuan Zhong Lu, Zhengzhou
郑州中原中路 220 号
☎ 6743 8888
¥ 698 – double room
@ yudaeo@public.zz.ha.cn

Huanghe Hotel
黄河饭店 *huánghé fàndiàn* ★★★
✉ 106 Zhongyuan Lu, Zhengzhou
郑州市中原路 106 号
☎ 6797 1005, 6797 6354
¥ 423 – double room
@ www.huanghehotel.net

Food & Restaurants

Most of the food found around Shaolin Temple is influenced by Buddhism – which means lots of vegetarian dishes. If you can't live without meat, you can fool your stomach into having a good time by ordering su zhai styled dishes. These dishes are vegetarian, but have the taste and texture of meat.

RESTAURANTS

He Ji Noodle Restaurant 合记烩面
Good noodles and Muslim dishes.
✉ 3 Renmin Lu 人民路 3 号
☎ 6622 8026
🕒 10am to 10:30pm

Lao Cai Ji Restautant 老蔡记
Lots of steamed dumplings (*zhēngjiǎo* 蒸饺) and wonton (*húntún* 馄饨).
✉ 4 Dehua Dong Jie 德化东街 4 号
☎ 6695 0885
🕒 9:30am to 10:30pm

Shaolin Restaurant 少林菜馆
Specializes in steamed dumplings and the vegetarian *shaolin luohan zhai* (少林罗汉斋).
✉ 89 Chengdong Lu 城东路 89 号
☎ 6631 8113
🕒 10am to 10:30pm

Shaolin Temple Vegetarian Restaurant 少林素斋馆
Specializes in various vegetarian dishes, all the waiters here are also Shaolin monks.
✉ inside of the Shaolin Temple 少林寺内

Xi Lan Pavilion Restaurant 西兰轩菜馆
Muslim and Henan cuisine – crispy leg of lamb (*xiāngsū yángtuǐ* 香酥羊腿) and sweet and sour fish on a bed of noodles (*tángcù liūyú bèimiàn* 糖醋熘鱼焙面) are particularly good.
✉ 49 Bei Shuncheng Jie 北顺城街 49 号
☎ 625 7841
🕒 10am to 9:30pm

Xue Yuan Restaurant 雪园酒家
Features Zhejiang dishes such as West Lake Fish (*xīhú cùyú* 西湖醋鱼) and curry beef (*gālí niúròu* 咖喱牛肉).
✉ 10 Datong Lu 大同路 10 号
☎ 695 1525
🕒 10am to 10pm

Little Bruce Lees in the making.

Souvenirs

Vendors hawking all manner of wares can be found near the schools outside the temple and in the temple itself. A large parking lot near the Forest of Pagodas features stands selling everything from incense for prayer and postcards to sinister swords and kitschy statuettes. Vendors are eager to make a sale, so any kind of bargaining ability will serve visitors well.

Yellow River ink stones (*huánghé chéngní yàn* 黄河澄泥砚) are gracefully shaped and make interesting souvenirs. Rub a white tissue against the stone; if the tissue remains white then it's genuine. Shaolin swords will definitely be an attention grabber if you take one home. They can be found at the Shaolin Sword Factory (*shàolín jiànchǎng zhǎnxiāobù* 少林剑厂展销部) at 1/F, Scientific Technique Committee, middle section of Songyang Lu Dengfeng (嵩阳路中段科学技术委员会 1 楼, ☎ 6287 1726).

Other Information

POST OFFICES

Huayuan Lu Post Office 花园路邮局
✉ 7 Huayuan Lu 花园路 7 号
☎ 6595 1347

Train Station Post Office 火车站邮局
✉ 80 Yima Lu 一马路 80 号
☎ 6698 2586

HOSPITALS

The Fifth Zhengzhou People's Hospital 郑州市第五人民医院
✉ 33, Huanghe Lu 黄河路 33 号
☎ 6385 8367, 6394 5120

COMPLAINT HOTLINES

☎ General: 6718 8061, 6718 1000
☎ Taxi: 6898 6439

Longmen Caves, Buddha's Caves

Area Code 0379

Heritage: Longmen Caves

Grandiose caves filled with immense Buddhas decorated with intricate designs are a testament to the skill and wealth of the people who inhabited **Luoyang** and their devotion to Buddhism.

Luoyang, once the capital of 13 dynasties, does not offer many historical reminders that it's more than 5,000 years old. Once the center of Chinese power and culture Luoyang is now best used as a base to explore the **Longmen Caves** (*lóngmén shíkū* 龙门石窟), 7.4 miles (12 km) from the city.

Originating in India, Buddhist cave carvings commemorate Sakyamuni, who used to teach his students in caves. Cave carvings became one of India's great artistic heritages and spread throughout Asia along with Buddhism. The Longmen Caves have been selected as an UNESCO World Cultural Heritage Site.

The site boasts not only the caves, but also lush mountains and ridges with springs and waterfalls. Two mountains on the east and west side of the Yi River are covered with green pines and cypresses, towers and pavilions dot each mountain. A hot spring near the entrance of the west mountain caves is a constant 75°F (24°C).

The caves got the name Longmen, which means "Dragon Gate," because the two mountains appear as a gate with the Yi River running through it, and when the Sui dynasty emperor built his palace in Luoyang, it faced the mountain "gates."

Many of the well-known caves are located on the western mountain. Work at the Longmen Caves started in AD 493 when the emperor of the Northern Wei dynasty moved his capital from Pingcheng (now Datong) to Luoyang. It continued up to the Qing dynasty with two thirds of the caves dating to the Song dynasty. According to the Longmen Caves Research Institute, there are 2,345 niches, over 2,840 inscribed tablets, more than 60 pagodas and some 100,000 stone statues.

Guyang Cave (*gǔyáng dòng* 古阳洞) is one of the oldest caves in Longmen, built from AD 428 to 488; it has comprehensive images of the royal family and the nobles of the Northern Wei period. Three tiers of Buddha statues in different sizes are carved on the north and the south walls. The statues, in typical Wei fashion, feature elongated necks and boxlike heads with stylistically rich patterns.

The **Three Binyang Caves** (*bīnyáng sān dòng* 宾阳三洞) were commissioned by Emperor Xuanwu of the Northern Wei to commemorate his parents, and later himself. The middle cave (*bīnyáng zhōng dòng* 宾阳中洞) took 802,326 workers 24 years to complete. Curtains and flower strings are carved on the ceilings of the caves with lotus patterns dominating the floor area. Inside the entrance on the two walls, there are large embossed carvings called "*Emperor as Donor with Attendants*" (*huángdì lǐfó tú* 皇帝礼佛图) and "*Empress as Donor with Attendants*" (*huánghòu lǐfó tú* 皇后礼佛图). The pictures vividly illustrate imperial Buddhist practices during the Northern Wei.

The Longmen Caves had two high periods of development. The devoutly Buddhist Northern Wei dynasty initiated the project as an expression of Buddhist devotion and built a large number of caves. But it was in the Tang dynasty when the real masterpieces were carved. The Tang carvings are lively and emotional, and they depict commoners, an oft-ignored subject matter. The statue of the

Losana Buddha in **Fengxian Temple** (*fèngxiān sì* 奉先寺) was built in the Tang dynasty by Emperor Gaozong. The statue is over 56 feet (17 m) tall with the head measuring 13 feet (4 m) and the ears almost 6.6 feet (2 m) long. Empress Wu Zetian, the first and only empress of China, donated a large portion of her cosmetics budget towards the construction of this statue and since she footed the bill for this statue, it's believed the face of the Buddha was carved in her likeness. This statue, together with the six accompanying statues, is considered the highest development of Buddhist carving art in China. With their lively expressions, lithe bodies, and elegantly detailed clothing, they are a strong contrast to the heavy and motionless Northern Wei statues.

Ten Thousand Buddha Cave (*wànfó dòng* 万佛洞) is another Tang masterpiece. It was built in AD 680 to honor the piety of Emperor Gaozong and Empress Wu. On the north and south walls of the cave, there are more than 15,000 carved small Buddha images. The central Buddha, with a plump serene face, sits on a lotus flower throne with his legs crossed; the vajras supporting the seat have a robust and forceful form. Beyond the halo of the main Buddha are 54 lotus flower bronze offering bodhisattvas. The north and south sides are covered with 15,000 diminutive Buddha figures. Below these tiny Buddhas are twelve apsareses, either dancing gracefully or playing musical instruments. Because the cave is protected behind a metal fence, binoculars are recommended to get a clear view of the small Buddhas.

Royal sponsorship was the main driving force in constructing the Longmen Caves. Although historical records and stone inscriptions reveal that the nobility, commoners and even foreign Buddhists all contributed towards the construction, only the emperor could summon the massive labor force and financial resources needed to fully realize such a massive project. The caves were built by the emperors as a tribute to their ancestors, but also out of vanity as the caves were a symbol of their own grandeur. In more practical terms, the emperors also saw themselves as living

An ancient wall carving of the empress off to worship Buddha.

On the follwing page: The largest statue at the Longmen Caves is that of Sakyamuni.

Memorable Experiences

Standing on the east mountain and looking at the western mountain gives you a panorama of the caves and the meandering Yi River that flows between the mountains.

Buddhas and the caves were a tool to impress upon the masses their divinity and gained their obedience.

Because Buddhism and its associated images came to China from India, all the statues have strong Indian influences. Over time, however, the carvings became a fusion of native Chinese and Indian styles. Statues built in the Northern Wei dynasty usually wear spacious clothes and wide belts while the bodies are slim with mild expressions that convey a strong spirit, whereas Tang dynasty statues tend to be plump with slim waists and more visually expressive features.

Most of the caves have survived the ravages of time and weather and the limestone at Longmen has proven especially durable. Sadly human nature is far more destructive than Mother Nature and many statues have been damaged in the last two centuries. Though most statues are complete, a large number had their heads lopped off, destined for a museum or a private collection. Now the niches and statues are protected by metal fence so visitors can only appreciate them from a distance.

The Longmen Caves not only showcase the development of Chinese Buddhism during the 5th and the 10th centuries, they also boast a huge collection of over 2,840 elegantly carved tablets on a variety of subjects.

While Luoyang itself isn't a cultural hotbed, there are some sights within the city that make it worth sticking around.

The peony is Luoyang's city flower, which naturally means there's an annual **Peony Festival** (*mǔdān huāhuì* 牡丹花会). According to legend, Empress Wu of the Tang dynasty once made a bet with an official that, on her orders, flowers would bloom during the winter. Acting upon her divine orders, all the flowers did, except for the peony. She became so enraged that she banished all peonies from Xi'an to Luoyang, which is why the city is synonymous with peonies. If you're not in Luoyang during the Peony Festival held in from April 10 to 25, the **White Horse Temple** (*báimǎ sì* 白马寺), China's first Buddhist temple, makes for an interesting visit. Han dynasty Emperor Mingdi dreamt of a golden man flying towards the west, and taking this as a sign, he sent two envoys to the west in search of Buddhist scriptures. His envoys met two eminent Indian monks who were invited to return with them to Luoyang. In AD 68, the emperor issued an edict to build a monastery to house the scriptures. The temple was renamed the White Horse Temple because the Buddhist scriptures were, according to legend, carried back by the monks on two white horses. ■

Making Your Trip Easy

Practical Tips

Spring and autumn are the best seasons to visit the Longmen Caves and Luoyang. Summers can be very hot and winters bitingly cold. The Luoyang Peony Festival (*luòyángshì mǔdān huāhuì* 洛阳市牡丹花会), from April 10 to 25, is the best time to see the blooming peonies. There may be some interesting activities during the festival.

A tour guide at the Longmen Caves is recommended to fully understand the significance and history of the statues and murals. A Chinese-speaking guide costs RMB 50 and an English-speaking guide is RMB 100.

Transportation

Airport – Luoyang's well-connected airport is about 6 miles (10 km) from downtown.

Taxi – Most taxis are RMB 6 at flag-fall.

The Best of Luoyang

Longmen Caves
龙门石窟 *lóngmén shíkū*
✉ Longmen Village, Longmen Town 龙门镇龙门村
☎ 6598 1299
🕒 6am to 6pm
¥ 80

White Horse Temple
白马寺 *báimǎ sì*
✉ 7.4 miles (12 km) east of Luoyang 洛阳市东 12 公里
¥ 35

Hotels

Luoyang Grand Hotel
洛阳大酒店
luòyáng dàjiǔdiàn ★★★★
✉ 1 Zhoushan Lu, Jianxi District 涧西区周山路 1 号
☎ 6432 4206, 6432 7606
¥ 456 – double room, peak-season
399 – double room, off-season
@ www.ly-grandhotel.com

Aviation Hotel
航空城酒店 *hángkōngchéng jiǔdiàn* ★★★
✉ 8 Tiyu Chang Lu, Xigong District 西工区体育场路 8 号
☎ 6338 5599
¥ 388 – double room

Peony Hotel
牡丹大酒店 *mǔdān dàjiǔdiàn* ★★★
✉ 15 Zhongzhou Xi Lu, Jianxi District 涧西区中州西路 15 号
☎ 6485 6699
¥ 600 – double room, peak-season
480 – double room, off-season

Food & Restaurants

Luoyang's famous "Water Banquet" (*shuǐ xí* 水席) is a must-try when visiting the city. The banquet gets its name because most of its dishes are soups; the dishes are also served continuously one after another like running water. The water banquet began as a feast for commoners, but it caught the eye (perhaps nose) of Tang dynasty Empress Wu Zetian who made it a royal delicacy. The banquet consists of 24 dishes. It starts with eight cold appetizers, four with meat and four vegetarian. Next come 16 hot dishes that are presented in groups of four, with each group based on a central flavor. Each dish usually costs around RMB 15 to 30. Noodles cooked in green soybean milk (*jiāng miàntiáo* (浆面条), topped with vegetables and hot pepper oil is a yummy snack. If you're craving dumplings then try *xin'anxian tangmianjiao* (新安县烫面饺); these pork dumplings are delicious with some vinegar. Mutton soup (*tiěxiè yángròu tāng* 铁榭羊肉汤) is a great way to fill up, and it's reputedly better than mom's chicken soup if you have a cold.

A tri-colored glazed sculpture from the Tang dynasty of musicians atop a camel.

RESTAURANTS

Donglaishun Restaurant 东来顺食府
Opened in 1916 and specializes in Muslim food.
✉ 11 Zhongzhou Dong Lu 中州东路 11 号

Quotes

"The Longmen Caves are magnificent work with incredible historical value. Without coming here in person, it is hard to appreciate the level of the skills that allowed humans to create such exquisite art on these rocks."

"The awesome Longmen Caves shows how marvelous a place can be made by pursuit of excellence and dedicated hard work."

☎ 6395 4705, 6398 2631
🕒 9am to 10pm

Longmen Diyijia Jiulou 龙门第一家酒楼
✉ south end of Longmen Zhong Jie, near Longmen Caves
龙门石窟附近龙门中街南端
☎ 6598 1719

Novelty Restaurant 新奇餐厅
American fast food restaurant in Luoyang.
✉ 10 Jinghua Lu, Jianxi District
涧西区景华路 10 号
☎ 6492 2888
🕒 9am to 9pm

Ya Xiang Lou Restaurant 雅香楼菜馆
Traditional Cantonese cuisine with dim sum and seafood.
✉ 4 Anhui Lu, Jianxi District
涧西区安徽路 4 号
☎ 6492 1666
🕒 10am to 10pm

Zhen Bu Tong 真不同
Has been serving banquets and snacks for over 100 years, dinner goes from RMB 50 to RMB 1,000.
✉ 359 Old City Area 老城 359 号
☎ 6395 5787, 6395 5788
🕒 7am to 11pm

Souvenirs

Apart from Chinese paintings of peonies that can be bought all over Luoyang, another local specialty is Tang dynasty tri-colored porcelain (*táng sāncǎi* 唐三彩). Traditionally,

The White Horse Temple, earliest Buddhist Temple in China.

most works are of horses, camels or people, but modern pieces have expanded into framed pictures of peonies or Chinese zodiac animals. Prices range from about RMB 100 and up for these exquisite pieces. Besides the color-glazed pieces, you can also find exquisite pottery replicas from Han and North Wei Dynasty tombs. For something that's less fragile, pick up some *heluo* stones (*héluò qíshí* 河洛奇石), which come in odd shapes and colors. Replicas of ancient bronzes (*fǎnggǔ qīngtóngqì* 仿古青铜器) are a local specialty – especially well made are the ancient wine vessels. Since the Tang dynasty, peonies have been a major theme in Luoyang and this is reflected in the paintings and calligraphy (*mǔdān zìhuà* 牡丹字画).

The Luoyang Tourist Shopping Center (*luòyángshì lǚyóu gòuwù zhōngxīn* 洛阳市旅游购物中心) on 1 Jiandong Lu (涧东路 1 号, ☎ 6393 5627) has a selection of nearly 3,000 different Tang tri-colored glazed pottery with prices starting at RMB 20. The Art Expo Garden (*yì bó yuán* 艺博园) at 43 Jinghua Lu (景华路 43 号, ☎ 6491 2921) has lots of replicas of the statues found at the Longmen Caves. They also have a big selection of paintings and calligraphy.

The Yinyixuan, Seal Art Co. (*yìnyìxuān* 印艺轩) at Shizi Jie in the old city (老城区十字街路口, 6396 5556) specializes in traditional paintings, the scholar's "four treasures" (Chinese Brush, Inkstone, Chinese ink and Xuan Paper) and Chinese seals.

Other Information

POST OFFICES

Xigong Qu Post Office 西工区邮局

✉ 216 Zhongzhou Zhong Lu 中州中路 216 号

☎ 6393 8683

HOSPITALS

Luoyang Central Hospital 洛阳市中心医院

✉ 288 Zhongzhou Zhong Lu 中州中路 288 号

☎ 6389 2257

COMPLAINT HOTLINES

☎ General: 6431 0882

☎ Taxi: 6394 7153

BY AIRPLANE 乘飞机		
Is there a flight to…?	yǒu qù … de hángbān ma	有去…的航班吗?
What time does the plane depart/arrive?	fēijī jǐdiǎn qǐfēi/dàodá	飞机几点起飞/到达?
I'd like to check-in my luggage.	wǒ xiǎng tuōyùn xíngli	我想托运行李。
Where do I board my plane?	wǒ zài nǎr dēngjī	我在哪儿登机?
What time will the plane land?	fēijī jǐdiǎn jiàngluò	飞机几点降落?
BY TRAIN 乘火车		
What time does the train depart/arrive?	huǒchē jǐdiǎn kāi/dào	火车几点开/到?
Where are we?	wǒmén dào nǎr le	我们到哪儿了?
Please tell me when we arrive at….	dàole …, qǐng gàosu wǒ yīshēng	到了…，请告诉我一声。
I'd like a glass of water.	wǒ xiǎngyào bēi shuǐ	我想要杯水。
BY TAXI 乘出租车		
I'd like a taxi.	wǒ xiǎng jiào chūzūchē	我想叫出租车。
Please take me to….	qǐng sòng wǒ dào …	请送我到…。
To….	qù …	去…
Please turn on the meter.	qǐng dǎ lǐchéngbiǎo	请打里程表。
Please slow down.	qǐng kāi màndiǎnr	请开慢点儿。
Please hurry.	qǐng kāi kuàidiǎnr	请开快点儿。
Stop here. Thanks.	tíng zhèr ba, xièxie	停这儿吧，谢谢。
How much?	duōshǎo qián	多少钱?

Kaifeng, the Forgotten Capital

Area Code 0378

On the southern bank of the Yellow River, the ancient city of **Kaifeng** has withstood natural disasters, invasions and time.

Since 361 BC Kaifeng's city walls have shielded early kingdoms and dynasties from northern invaders. The city's fortunes reached a zenith during the cosmopolitan Song dynasty – this period distinguished Kaifeng as one of China's most historically important cities.

For 168 years, the Eastern Capital, as Kaifeng was then known, flourished as a political, economic and cultural hub of the Middle Kingdom. Its streets bustled with people, animals and lively commerce. Resplendent temples and even synagogues drew crowds of the faithful. Through its gilded city gates, camel caravans and Silk Road merchants sauntered in with bags full of goods.

Culture blossomed through poetry, calligraphy, philosophy and the arts. Ceramic art reached its peak; no subsequent dynasty was able to replicate the exquisitely refined work of the Song ceramic masters. Today, only very few pieces of priceless porcelain from the famous **Guan Kiln** (*guānyáo* 官窑) exist.

Kaifeng, home to 1.5 million people in its heyday, is a city of "firsts." In 1041, printer Bi Sheng invented a revolutionary moveable type technology that accelerated the spread of ideas and culture throughout China. The first mechanical clock in the world was also produced here in 1092 and Kaifeng's astronomical clock tower ran on hydropower

Replica Song dynasty buildings in modern Kaifeng.

generated by a gigantic water wheel.

The Xiangguo Temple is lit up majestically at night.

The renowned Northern Song statesman and scientist Shen Kuo also came from Kaifeng. His 30-volume work called *Mengxi Bitan* (梦溪笔谈) is a priceless record of the learning and cultivation of his era, covering politics, economics, philosophy, history, military affairs, science and technology. In one article, Shen Kuo wrote about petroleum, which he called *shiyou* (rock oil), a term still used today. He recorded the properties of petroleum, its sources and uses such as how petroleum ashes could be made into ink sticks.

Even more fascinating is that Kaifeng is the earliest Chinese city to be home to a sizeable Jewish community. The first Jews arrived at Kaifeng having traveled the arduous Silk Road from Persia. Their first synagogue was built as far back as 1163, but never rebuilt after the flood of 1852. Three stone tablets in **Kaifeng Museum** (*kāifēng bówùguǎn* 开封博物馆) record their arrival.

Kaifeng's golden days are etched onto a 17.3-foot-long (5.28 m) long masterpiece called *The Riverside Scene in Pure Brightness* (*qīngmíng shànghé tú* 清明上河图). This valuable scroll painting was the handiwork of artist Zhang Zeduan of the Northern Song dynasty, depicts Kaifeng in amazing detail, offering an insight into the social milieu of the day – one can see the goods on sale along the market streets, the gentleman scholar interacting with his servants. It now rests with other national relics in the Palace Museum of Beijing's Forbidden City (*gùgōng bówùyuàn* 故宫博物院).

For 3,000 years, the city endured various manmade and natural disasters. It was subjected to incursions from the north and relentless flooding by the Yellow River – a catastrophic combination that has left precious few reminders of its forgotten splendor. Yet modern Kaifeng retains a character and sleepy charm lost to other ancient capitals touched by modernity. Song dynasty architecture, for one, still lives on in pockets of Kaifeng.

Archers' towers and watch stations have long vanished from the city fortifications but the city walls remain. They run for 8.9 miles (14.4 km) and are 23 feet (7 m) thick at the base tapering to 16.4 feet (5 m) at the top and rise an impressive 26.2 feet (8 m) high. Forget high-rise buildings, fancy hotels and shopping malls – the tallest structure here is the **Iron Pagoda** (*tiě tǎ* 铁塔), 180 feet (55 m) high and located northeast of the city at Beimen Da Jie – a slender 13-story octagonal temple with its current incarnation built in 1049.

Constructed in brick, the pagoda is wrapped in glazed tiles that give off a metallic gleam. Observe the tiles closely and you might catch a glimpse of celestial beings, dragons, Chinese unicorns (*qílín* 麒麟), lions and lotuses. RMB 20 entrance fee aside, you'll have to cough up another few yuan to get a bird's-eye view of the city from the top of the pagoda. If you look to the west, there's a tiny pavilion housing a 16.9-foot-tall (5.14 m) tall bronze Buddha from the Song dynasty.

In the city center is the **Xiangguo Temple** (*xiàngguó sì* 相国寺). Built in AD 555, it was the foremost Buddhist center and commercial hub of the city during the Song

Kaifeng was a bustling trade center during the Northern Song dynasty.

dynasty. Underlining Kaifeng's vulnerability to floods, it was destroyed several times and last restored in 1766. The temple was given its name in AD 712 by the Tang emperor to commemorate his ascension to the Dragon's Throne. Head for the **Octagonal Ceramic Palace** (*bājiǎo liúlídiàn* 八角琉璃殿), which houses a statue of the Buddhist Goddess of Mercy (*guānyīn* 观音). The 19.7-foot-tall (6 m) tall idol, with four faces and 1,000 arms and eyes, was carved from a single gingko tree.

About a miles (1.5 km) north of the Xiangguo Temple stands the **Dragon Pavilion** (*lóngtíng* 龙亭) in **Dragon Pavilion Park** (*lóngtíng gōngyuán* 龙亭公园). At this site once stood the ruins of Song, Jin and Ming buildings. In 1642 a catastrophic wiped out the Ming structures that once stood in the park. Dragon motifs are everywhere – on the staircase and the stone bench inside the pavilion. The park overlooks two lakes and the view the surrounding landscape from the top of the pavilion is extremely pretty.

BEYOND THE CITY WALLS

Southeast of the city, some 2 miles (3 km) from the Xiangguo Temple is the **Terrace of King Yu** (*yǔwáng tái* 禹王台), named after Yu the Great (Dà Yǔ 大禹), the tamer of floods. According to legend, this sage-king sought shelter here while battling the Yellow River and several steles commemorate his feats. There's a temple on the terrace called the **Temple of King Yu** (*yǔwáng miào* 禹王庙). The terrace was also previously known as **Ancient Music-Playing Terrace** (*gǔchuī tái* 古吹台) after a famous blind musician Shi Kuang who performed there frequently.

Memorable Experiences

Playing chess with an elderly man at Dragon Pavilion Park while a large crowd of spectators build up around us, giving advice and a running commentary.

Shopping for souvenirs in a hyperactive market and getting a vendor to lower the price by 60%.

Pottering around the city center's old streets and drinking in the frenzied street activities.

To the west stands Kaifeng's oldest structure – the **Po Pagoda** (*pó tǎ* 繁塔). The hexagonal temple was built in AD 974 and isn't easy to find – it's often mistakenly referred to as the Fan Pagoda. Of the original nine stories, there were just three left in the 14th century after floods damaged the structure and buried it in silt. Restoration work has added a six-story structure on top of the remaining base. Altogether the structure comprises 7,000 bricks with 178 exquisite patterns. Inside are Buddhist sutras engraved on stone. Get a grip on the railings as you scale to the top.

5.6 miles (9 km) north of Kaifeng is an impressive yet intimidating sight: **Heigangkou** (*hēigǎngkǒu* 黑岗口), where the 5-mile-wide (8 km) Yellow River rises above the surrounding land by 33 feet (10 m), making it obvious why the city suffered continual flooding. The riverbed rises continuously because the water is filled with so much silt and requires ever-larger dykes to hold back the water. It's also the silt that gives the Yellow River its color and name. ■

Making Your Trip Easy

Practical Tips

The busy season is from May through October, so you might want to skip the crowds. It's the coldest in January, around -16°F (-9°C), while July is the hottest at 100°F (38°C).

Around April there's a Temple Festival in the Temple of King Yu, which is held to commemorate the brave feats of the legendary sage-king Da Yu. The celebration is lively with tightrope walkers edging their way precariously on a wooden beam, boisterous lion dancers and cacophonic Henan and Beijing Opera performances. This festival is held at the Terrace of King Yu.

Beginning every October 18, Kaifeng celebrates the month-long Chrysanthemum Festival at Dragon Pavilion Park. Though it can get a little chilly, it's a beautiful time to soak in the atmosphere and join in the festivities and take a look at the gorgeous flowers.

Transportation

Airport – The airport is located 37 miles (60 km) west of the city, about 50 minutes to the city by taxi.

Taxi – It'll cost about RMB 10 to get anywhere within the city; flag-fall is RMB 5.

The Best of Kaifeng

Dragon Pavillion 龙亭 *lóngtíng*
✉ Beiduan Zhongshan Lu 中山路北段
☎ 566 0316

🕒 6am to 6:30pm, peak-season
7am to 6pm, off-season
¥ 35

The Former Kaifeng City Hall
开封府 *kāifēngfǔ*
✉ on the north bank of Baogong Lake
包公湖北岸
☎ 398 3319
🕒 7am to 7pm
¥ 35

Heigangkou 黑岗口 *hēigǎngkǒu*
✉ 5.6 miles (9 km) north of Kaifeng
开封城北 9 公里

Millennium City 清明上河园 *qīngmíng shànghé yuán*
✉ 5 Longting Xilu 龙亭西路 5 号
☎ 566 4874
🕒 9am to 6pm
¥ 60

Xiangguo Temple 相国寺 *xiàngguó sì*
✉ 36 Xiduan, Ziyou Lu 自由路西段 36 号
☎ 566 5090
🕒 8am to 6:30pm
¥ 30

Zhuxianzhen's famous Chinese New Year paintings.

Hotels

Dongjing Hotel
东京大饭店 *dōngjīng dàfàndiàn* ★★★
✉ 99 Yingbin Lu 迎宾路 99 号
☎ 398 9388
¥ 288 – double room

Grand Tianzhong Hotel
天中大酒店 *tiānzhōng dàjiǔdiàn* ★★★
✉ 41 Gulou Jie 鼓楼街 41 号
☎ 595 8888
¥ 318 – double room, peak-season
255 – double room, off-season

Kaifeng Guesthouse
开封宾馆 *kāifēng bīngguǎn* ★★★
✉ 64 Zhongduan, Ziyou Lu 自由路中段 64 号
☎ 595 5589
¥ 298 – double room

Food & Restaurants

Succumb to your midnight cravings. Everyone else you've met earlier today when you toured the city is probably at Drum Tower Square (*gǔlóu guǎngchǎng* 鼓楼广场) having supper. This is also the site of Kaifeng's famed Drum Tower night market. Several wooden restaurants and shops line the people-packed walkways. Any street stall crammed onto the sidewalk is a good bet for a tasty treat. Recommended are the fragrant skewers of succulent lamb. Soaking in the hive of nocturnal activity over delicious food and ice-cool beer packs a heady gastronomic punch that'll knock you into blissful sleep after the feast.

Carp with noodles (*lǐyú bèimiàn* 鲤鱼焙面), combining tender fish with thin noodles, are a local specialty. Deep fried pork (*zhá zǐsūròu* 炸紫酥肉) is also worth a try, its golden skin crispy and crunchy. Tube chicken (*mǎyùxīng tǒngzi jī* 马豫兴桶子鸡), which gets its odd name because the slices of chicken curl into the shape of a tube after they're cooked, is tasty. Kaifeng's meat-filled buns (*guàntāng bāozi* 灌汤包子) are famed throughout China. Finish off dinner with a sweet and crispy peanut cake (*huāshēng gāo* 花生糕) for desert.

RESTAURANTS

Caojia Guantang Baozi 曹家灌汤包子

Quotes

"Kaifeng has the weight of history about it; not just in the ruins, but in the atmosphere."

"Very compact city, yet so many treasures– big and small – pop up around the corners. There is a lot of the old, a bit of the new, all of which adds up to a visual potpourri."

✉ Dongdajie, Beiduang 东大街北段

Kaifeng No. 1 Restaurant 开封第一楼
Specializes in inexpensive deliciously juicy meat buns (*guàntāng bāozi* 灌汤包子), RMB 6 for a plate of them.
✉ 8 Sihou Jie 寺后街 8 号
☎ 565 0780
🕒 9am to 10pm

Mayuxing Jiya Dian 马豫兴鸡鸭店
With over 100 years of history, it is famous for the tube chicken (*mǎyùxīng tǒngzi jī* 马豫兴桶子鸡).
✉ Drum Tower Square 鼓楼广场
☎ 595 4233
🕒 9am to 7pm

Youyixin Fandian 又一新饭店
Established in 1906, it's famous for its *liyu beimian* (鲤鱼焙面) and *zha zisurou* (炸紫酥肉).
✉ 22 Gulou Jie 鼓楼街 22 号
☎ 595 6677
🕒 7am to 9pm

Souvenirs

Market time is fantastic fun and the visual spectacle includes lingerie strung on clothes lines between trees and belts cut to measure from a sheet of leather on the spot. Try to find samples of Kaifeng embroidery, called *bian xiu* (汴绣). If you're lucky, you'll find pieces depicting legendary personalities and assorted paintings. Prices range from a few yuan to over RMB 10,000 depending on the size and quality.

If you have time to spare, head for nearby Zhuxianzhen (朱仙镇), an ancient town known for its fine paintings. They sell specialty Spring Festival (Chinese New Year) paintings, called *zhuxianzhen muban nianhua* (朱仙镇木版年画). These paintings feature characters with exaggerated features and symbols representing good fortune and happiness for the New Year. It costs around RMB 150 to 400 for one booklet.

If you care for porcelain, you may be interested in buying imitation pieces inspired from the famous Guan Kiln porcelain (*guānyáo cíqì* 官窑瓷器) – a type of fine china found in the city. Guan Kiln was one of the imperial kilns of the Northern Song dynasty. The price varies from a few hundred RMB to over a thousand.

Jinggu Zhai (京古斋) is a good place to find traditional paintings, and if you feel like doing your own calligraphy, they also sell supplies. Find them at 43 Sihou Jie (寺后街 43 号, 595 6058). The Kaifeng Bian Embroidery Factory (*kāifēng biànxiù chǎng* 开封汴绣厂) has lots of embroidery on offer. They're located at 88 Mujiaqiao Jie (穆家桥街 88 号, 595 1780). Antiques in a store setting are at Wenwu Shangdian (文物商店) over at 108 Beiduan Shizhongxin (市中心北段 108 号, 596 1375). If you're looking for everyday items, then Sam's Time Square (*sānmáo shídài guǎngchǎng* 三毛时代广场☎ 398 6660) at 66 Zhongduan Zhongshan Lu(中山路中段 66 号) will cover your basic needs.

Other Information

POST OFFICES

Kaifeng Post Office 开封邮局
✉ 33 Xiduan Ziyou Lu 自由路西段 33 号
☎ 595 9338

HOSPITALS

The First Kaifeng People's Hospital
开封市第一人民医院
✉ 85 Hedao Jie 河道街 85 号
☎ 567 1288

COMPLAINT HOTLINES

☎ General: 387 0100
☎ Taxi: 397 2220

Wudang Shan's ancient architecture is nestled throughout the mountain.

Wudang Shan, the Mountain of Tao

Area Code 0719

Heritage: The Ancient Building Complex in Wudang Shan

A legendary mountain, immortalized in countless sword-fighting novels, **Wudang Shan** has been the cradle of Taoism for over 1,000 years.

The Wudang Mountain range joins the Qinling Mountains in the west and Shennongjia in the south. Wudang Shan itself is situated in Danjiangkou in Hubei Province, not far from Wuhan and comprises 72 peaks, 36 cliffs and 24 valleys. Its main peak, called **Heavenly Pillar Peak** (*tiānzhù fēng* 天柱峰), stands at a statuesque 5,287 feet (1,612 m) and together with the other mist-shrouded peaks, creates a spectacular vision. However physically daunting Wudang Shan may seem, its natural beauty and exquisite architecture, its rich history mixed with Taoist culture and lore, make it a worthwhile detour from Wuhan.

Hugging the terrain of Wudang Shan are pockets of architectural delights. Whether atop precipitous peaks, reclining on sloping terraces or tucked into ravines and caves, these exquisite pagodas, nunneries, prayer halls and cave temples have drawn pilgrims and tourists for centuries.

The oldest temple on Wudang Shan is the **Five Dragon Ancestral Temple** (*wǔlóng gōng* 五龙宫) which dates back to the 7th century AD. Like this temple, the 72 temples, 39 bridges, 36 nunneries and 12 pavilions on Wudang Shan reflect some of the best architectural styles of the Tang, Song, Yuan, Ming and Qing dynasties.

Although construction begun in the Tang dynasty and expanded through the Song and Yuan dynasties, it was during the Ming dynasty that an architectural building frenzy really took hold of Wudang Shan. The pivotal time for Wudang Shan's popularity as a center for Taoism, which spurred the construction, came with the ascension of Emperor Zhudi to the throne in 1403.

Emperor Zhudi, fourth son of the founder of the Ming dynasty, overthrew the appointed heir and pronounced himself emperor. To win the people over and justify his usurpation, the new emperor claimed that he had acted on celestial orders. He attributed his success to the widely revered Taoist deity Zhenwu of Wudang Shan, who had attained immortality atop the mountain. The new emperor initiated extensive construction projects to give thanks to the gods for his victory, but also to affirm his power in the eyes of his court. He commissioned the Forbidden City in Beijing as well as the huge temple complex on Wudang Shan, which he dedicated to his patron god Zhenwu, who is also known as the "Perfect Warrior."

Each structure became part of the elaborate Taoist architectural complex, comprising some 8,000 rooms. Countless imperial decrees commandeered the services of laborers, designers and craftsmen. Old temples were renovated and grand new ones were built from the toil of 300,000 workers over 12 years. The **Golden Hall, Taihe Temple, Southern Crag Palace, Purple Cloud Palace** and **Yuzhen Temple** were all built during this time.

Every aspect was planned to fine detail, from guidelines of construction to the treatment of surplus building materials. The result was that this ancient complex, which was surrounded by flora, foliage, springs and rocky outcrops, blended seamlessly with the landscape. In its synergy with the natural environment, the complex remains true to Taoist principles of respecting nature, maintaining balance and being one with "the Way."

Steadily Wudang Shan became home to the grandest temples and held the largest Taoist population in the country. It was honored across China with the sobriquet as "the first famous mountain under heaven." Today, it's recognized as an architectural achievement and in 1994, UNESCO bestowed Wudang Shan World Cultural Heritage status.

Wudang Shan is also world-famous for its

An incense holder for the brave and devout at Tianyi Zhenqing Stone Palace.

distinctive style of martial arts called *Wudang Wushu*. This form of martial arts is highly regarded in China on a par with the skills of the better known Shaolin monks. Created by martial arts exponent Zhang Sanfeng, it's still practiced by Taoist priests as part of their routine fitness and self-defense exercises. This kung fu style has been honed to a fine art through the centuries, evolving into variations like Tai Chi and Ba Gua. The technique is centered on one principle: to conquer toughness by gentleness, mainly using the opponent's force to gain mastery – this is considered soft or internal kung fu while the Shaolin style is hard or external. Today, kung fu enthusiasts still flock to Wudang Shan's martial arts schools to meditate and refine their skills.

About 0.6 mile (1 km) from Wudang Village is the entrance gate to begin the pilgrimage up the mountain. From this gate to the mountain is a good 6-mile (10 km) walk. By taking a minivan taxi for RMB 20 to the parking lot you can conveniently circumvent most of the pre-mountain hike, but while this 20 minute ride on a narrow, sharply curving road may be exhilarating for some, it could be stomach churning for others.

One of the first temples you'll see is the **Southern Crag Palace** (*nányán gōng* 南岩宫) – it's a 15-minute walk from the parking lot. Behind the main altar of Southern Crag Palace is the **Tianyi Zhenqing Stone Palace** (*tiānyǐ zhēnqing gōng* 天乙真庆宫), surrounded by craggy outcrops. A 9.5-foot-long (2.9 m) stone beam resembling a dragon's head protrudes out over a cliff with an incense burner at its end. Modern day visitors continue to be impressed by the ancient craftsmen who built this without any high-tech gadgets and worshippers test their faith by crawling onto the dragon's head to place their incense sticks, despite it being extremely dangerous.

Purple Cloud Palace (*zǐxiāo gōng* 紫霄宫), also close to the parking lot, reclines prettily on the mountainside as it has for 600 years. It has one of the largest and best-preserved Taoist halls of worship this side of the mountain known as **Nanyan Scenic Area** (*nányán jǐngqū* 南岩景区). It was built during the Song dynasty but received a makeover during the Ming dynasty. It consists of several halls, including the **Dragon and Tiger Hall** (*lónghǔ diàn* 龙虎殿), the **Purple Sky Hall** (*zǐxiāo diàn* 紫霄殿), the **East Hall** (*dōngdào yuàn* 东道院) and **West Hall** (*xīdào yuàn* 西道院). It was an important ancestral shrine of the imperial court and the monks here used to offer prayers for the emperor. There are 28 life-sized statues of Perfect Warrior Zhenwu. Look for two Chinese treasures: the "iron tree blossoms" lanterns, decorated with patterns of phoenixes, dragons, blossoms.

From the parking lot, a 2-hour hike to the **Golden Hall** (*jīndiàn* 金殿) awaits you. Alternatively, take a minivan around to the other side of the mountain where you can hop onto a cable car to reach the summit.

The Golden Hall is a copper wonder. Built in AD 1416, the gold-gilded hall is 18 feet (5.5 m) high, 14.4 feet (4.4 m) wide and 10.3 feet (3.15 m) deep and is completely copper-cast, save for its base. It houses a 10-ton life-size statue of Zhenwu. At the base is his symbol of a tortoise and a snake, the latter's body wound around the former and the two heads raised towards each other.

In the past, before lightning rods were installed, lightning struck the hall whenever there was a thunderstorm, which meant a spectacular visual treat of flashing lights and

Memorable Experiences

Reaching the summit after taking the endless stairs up, and drinking in the fantastic view.

Deciphering the poems, scriptures engraved on banners and rock walls.

Attending a martial arts camp, and getting first-hand experience of the tough training of *wushu* exponents.

Sitting with the monks for an early morning drink of tea. Stories unfold.

Priest climbing Wudang Shan on their way to a Taoist ceremony.

sparks of fire. Fortunately, despite numerous strikes, the hall has remained unscathed.

Another Taoist temple with a fascinating story is **Yuanhe Guan** (*yuánhé guàn* 元和观). Taoist monks who turned power-hungry and challenged the authority of the emperor were banished to lifelong repentance here. It was the only such jail for Taoist monks in China in the Ming dynasty.

Some notable sights include the five-story tall **Truth Returning Nunnery** (*fùzhēn guàn* 复真观), where there is a single column supporting 12 roof beams. If you've been to Beijing's Temple of Heaven, there is similar echo wall at Wudang Shan called **Nine-bend Yellow River Wall**(*jiǔqū huánghéqiáng* 九曲黄河墙). Then there is the special bell at **Turning Round Hall** (*zhuǎnshēn diàn* 转身殿). If you ring it, the sound lingers for a long time outside the hall, while hardly any sound can be heard inside the hall. Over at **Taizi Po** (*tàizǐ pō* 太子坡) is a gorgeous waterfall. It's a bit out of the way, but if you have an extra day or so, it's definitely worth the side trip. ■

Making Your Trip Easy

Practical Tips

Spring, summer and autumn are the best seasons to visit Wudang Shan. The mountain can be chilly near the top and be sure to have enough clothes for the nights.

You can stay on the mountain, but most prefer the convenience of staying closer to the town (called Laoying in the past), which is some 15.5 miles (25 km) from the main peak.

In early-April and early-October there are dragon boat races at Wudang Shan on the Han River. Every October, the weeklong Wudang International Tourism Festival takes place on the mountain with kung fu displays, photography exhibitions, and calligraphy and art exhibitions.

The Wudang Shan Scenic Area is quite large so most people spend a few days seeing the sights. A good itinerary is to spend one day checking out the sights at the foot of the mountain, then spend the night in one of the hotels surrounding the parking lot. On the second day, either hike or take the cable car up the mountain then spend the day exploring.

Transportation

Airport – Wudang Airport is 68 miles (110 km) southwest of Shiyan City and 43 miles (70 km) from Wudang Shan.

Bus – Direct sleeper buses are available from Wuhan's Wuchang long distance bus station. Tickets are about RMB 90 and it takes up to 12 hours to reach Wudang Shan. If you're leaving Wudang Shan by bus, the sleeper bus station is diagonally opposite the Xuanwu Dajiudian along Hanshi Gonglu.

Cable Car – A round trip ticket for the Wudang Shan cable car is RMB 70.

Taxi – Taxis in Shiyan City are RMB 6 at flag-fall.

Train – The Wudang Shan Train station is located south of the main road. There are daily trains from Wuhan to Wudang Shan, the trip takes about 6 hours and costs about RMB 40. Alternatively, you can disembark at Shiyan or Liuliping and take a bus to Wudang Shan. Both bus routes take an hour and cost RMB 5.

A ritual Taoist ceremony on the sacred Wudang Shan.

The Best of Wundang Shan

Wudang Shan Scenic Area
武当山风景区 *wǔdāng shān fēngjǐngqū*
✉ 22 miles (35 km) from Shiyan
十堰市城区 35 公里
☎ 566 5571, 566 8567
🕒 7am to 7pm
¥ 182 (includes Tianyi zhenqing Stone Palace)

The Golden Hall 金殿 *jīndiàn*
✉ Inside Wudang Shan Scenic Area
武当山风景区内
¥ 20

Purple Cloud Palace 紫霄宫 *zǐxiāo gōng*
✉ Inside Wudang Shan Scenic Area
武当山风景区内
¥ 15

Hotels

Huazhong Hotel 十堰市华中大酒店
shíyànshì huázhōng dàjiǔdiàn ★★★
✉ 5 Renmin Nan Lu 人民南路 5 号
☎ 889 1899
¥ 207 – double room, peak-season
196 – double room, off-season
@ www.huazhonghotel.com

Lingxiao Hotel 十堰市凌霄大酒店 *shíyànshì língxiāo dàjiǔdiàn* ★★★

Quotes

"I won't climb the stairs again, but for sure I'll come back to sample the temple treats on Wudang Shan."

"I have never seen so many monks on one mountain. A Taoist nun was practicing *wushu* – fascinating to watch her agile moves."

"So much history and folklore wrapped up with the structures, statues, pavilions, and even the natural landscape. One notebook isn't enough to capture the sights."

"Bring lots of film. You don't want to run out when a martial arts *shifu* (teacher) is demonstrating."

✉ 1 Renmin Bei Lu
人民北路 1 号
☎ 810 0000
¥ 224 – double room, peak-season
174 – double room, off-season

Wudang Shan Tianlu Holiday Hotel
武当山天禄度假村 *wǔdāng shān tiānlù dùjiàcūn* ★★★
✉ east slope of Purple Cloud Palace, Wudang Shan
武当山紫霄宫东侧
☎ 568 9115
¥ 290 – double room, peak-season
249 – double room, off-season

Yanliang Hotel 十堰市燕良大酒店 *shíyànshì yànliáng dàjiǔdiàn* ★★★
✉ 38 Renmin Lu 人民路 38 号
☎ 866 8888
¥ 249 – double room, peak-season
232 – double room, off-season

Food & Restaurants

The local cuisine is light with subtle flavors. Some of the local delicacies include Han River fish (*hànjiāng héyú* 汉江河鱼), *baiyu wuji* (白羽乌鸡) and different kinds of noodles like *moyu guamian* (磨芋挂面), *duzhong guamian* (杜仲挂面) and corn noodles (*yùmǐ guàmiàn* 玉米挂面).

The food offered in the hotels on the mountain isn't as tasty and costs at least three times more than in the city. Head to Yongle Lu where many family restaurants offer cheap and good eats. The Xuanwu Hotel's restaurant offers a great selection of Chinese cuisine-try the scallion pancakes and deep-fried dough cakes.

For street food in Shiyan, head over to the Shiyan Fengwei Snack Street (十堰风味小吃一条街) on Dongyue Lu (东岳路). You'll find cheap Sichuan, Muslim and local fare.

RESTAURANTS

Sanhetang Xiaochi Dian 三河汤小吃店
Lots of local snacks, with sanhe soup as the house special.
✉ Xianggang Jie, Shiyan 十堰香港街
🕒 9am to 11pm

Taoists performing ancient rites in honor of their ancestors.

Souvenirs

Jewels are abundant in Shiyan; silver jewelry, intricate swords and carved stones called tortoise jewels (*lǜ sōng shí* 绿松石) await souvenir hunters. A mine on the north slope of Wudang Shan produces a treasure trove of jewelry, from silver bracelets and necklaces to silver wine goblets and jade. Head to the Xinyin Jewelry Store (*xīnyín zhūbǎo háng* 鑫银珠宝行, ☎ 867 5918) or the Yiboyuan Gongyipin Guangchang (艺博源工艺品广场, 811 5337) to take a look at these goods. They don't come cheap though-prices range from RMB 2,000 to 4,000. Wudang Shan is also known for its swords (*wǔdāng jiàn* 武当剑). Swords are about RMB 45 to 500.

Other Information

POST OFFICES

Shiyan City Post Office 十堰市邮局
✉ 38 Chezhan Lu 车站路 38 号
☎ 889 5282

HOSPITALS

Shiyan People's Hospital 十堰市人民医院
✉ 23 Chaoyang Lu 朝阳路 23 号
☎ 865 2119

Taihe Hospital 十堰市太和医院
✉ 29 Renmin Nan Lu 人民南路 29 号
☎ 880 1533

COMPLAINT HOTLINES

☎ General: 868 3356
☎ Taxi: 888 2271

Wulingyuan, Nature's Playground

Area Code 0744

Heritage: Wulingyuan Scenic and Historic Interest Area

With primeval forests, rocky crags and rushing streams, **Zhangjiajie** is a sublimely beautiful place to explore nature's bounty. Be sure to bring lots of film and a good pair of shoes.

An ethnic Miao girl makes sweet music by blowing on a leafy flute.

Stashed away in a remote northwestern corner of Hunan Province, bordering Guizhou and Chongqing, is the **Wulingyuan Scenic Reserve** (*wǔlíngyuán fēngjǐngqū* 武陵源风景区), better known as Zhangjiajie. Wisely set aside in 1982 as one of China's first nature reserves, Wulingyuan protects an astounding variety of flora, fauna and minority tribes. The area has been given a UNESCO World Heritage listing, so extensive protection is in place, such as a complete fire ban (including smoking), conveniently placed rubbish bins and flagged erosion-resistance paths.

The reserve is home to three of China's minority groups, the **Tujia**, **Miao**, and **Bai** who continue to carry on their traditional ways. In **Zhangjiajie Village** (*zhāngjiājiè cūn* 张家界村), there is a **Museum of Tujia Culture** (*tǔjiā wénhuà bówùguǎn* 土家文化博物馆) focusing on traditional handicrafts. Traditional song and dance performances are held here and are a great way to get a taste of the local color. This is not simply a show to make the tourists happy, but is a family run center with aims of cultural preservation. The Tujia are suspected by some to be the last remaining descendants of western China's mysterious prehistoric Ba Kingdom.

Low cloud coverage and an endless array of streams often leave the reserve covered in a primordial mist. Original vegetation still covers 60% of the park and includes some 550 different species of trees. Some highlights include rare dove trees, ginkos and dawn redwoods, which were, until 1948, believed to be extinct. Highly prized medicinal herbs used in Chinese traditional medicine spring from the valley floor and grow on the high peaks.

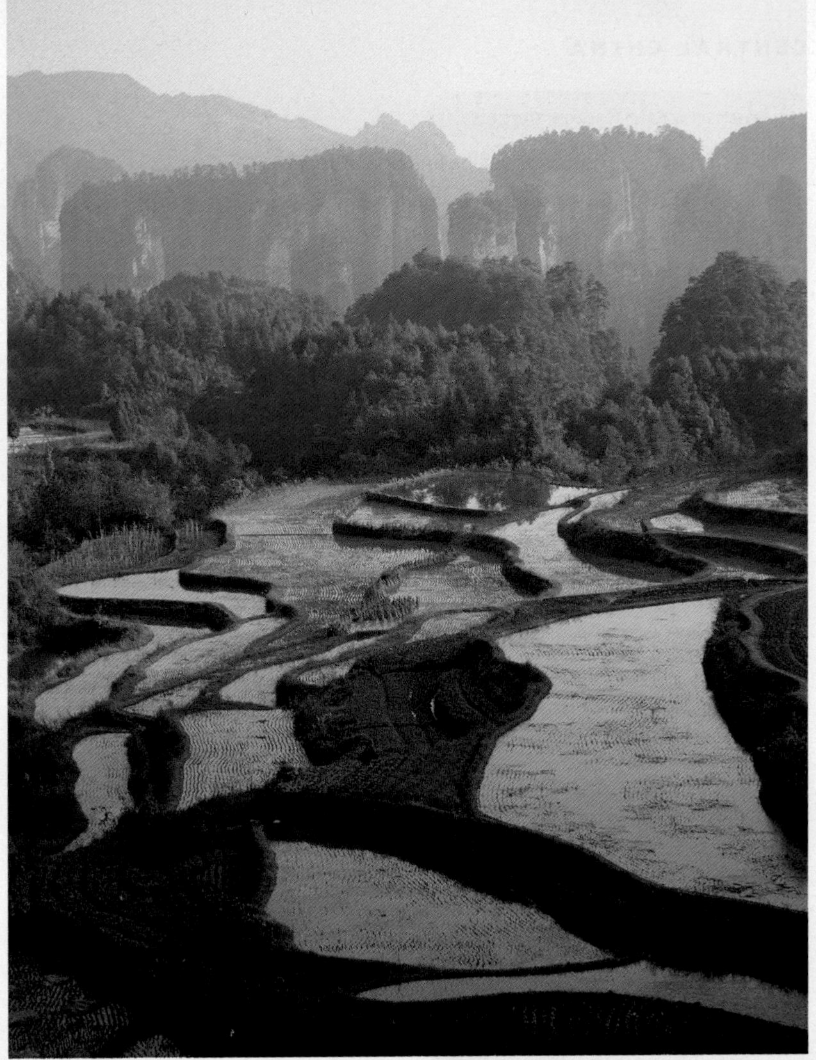

Rice paddies are carved out of the land, even amongst sheer cliffs and haunting scenery of Wulingyuan.

In the less crowded parts live wild animals and many species of rare bird. Rhesus monkeys, giant salamanders, civets, golden pheasants and tragopans populate the vast expanse of forest. It's a fairytale land of sandstone cliffs and fractured limestone pinnacles and lush subtropical foliage laced with clear, fast green streams covers the forest floor.

As would be expected from a nature reserve, most of the highlights are scenic spots. Atop a mountain peak, one of the most popular is **Huangshi Village** (*huángshí zhài* 黄石寨). For those inclined to hike, it'll take around 2 hours to get up the 3,878 stone steps, or for those who prefer to watch, a cable car whips you up to the top for RMB 48.

Located in the northern section of the reserve, the highest point, **Tianzi Peak** (*tiānzǐ shān* 天子山), at 4,100 feet (1,250 m), provides stunning views of the park and a top-of-the-world feeling for those who make the climb. As in most Chinese parks, poets and artists have been visiting for thousands

Memorable Experiences

Watching the sun go down over the Immortals' Bridge.

Hiking up to Huangshi Village as the early morning mist burns off in the rising sun.

Rafting on the Mengdong River while the guides sing local songs and monkeys scramble through the trees.

A dip in any one of Zhangjiajie's clear streams on a hot summer's day.

of years and have given imaginative names to many lookouts, gorges and peaks.

For fans of caves, Zhangjiajie has enough to please. **Jiutian Cave** (*jiǔtiān dòng* 九天洞), featuring Asia's largest chamber, is a massive limestone affair. Somewhat more accessible and located on the main trail in from **Tianzi Shan Village** (*tiānzǐshān cūn* 天子山村) is **Shuanghe Cave** (*shuānghé dòng* 双合洞). **Suoxi Valley** (*suǒxī yù* 索溪峪) features the

Stark and beautiful, the daunting peaks are an unforgettable sight.

Yellow Dragon Cave (*huánglóng dòng* 黄龙洞), a series of limestone caverns interconnected by a subterranean river.

Another option growing more popular by the year is whitewater rafting. Although Zhangjiajie's rivers have not earned much renown, the neighboring **Mengdong River** (*měngdòng hé* 猛洞河) is one of China's most popular stretches for river rafting. While the rapids are nothing death-defying, the clarity of the water and solitude of the high mountains and lush forests continue to draw visitors. In these sparsely populated cliffs and gorges, it is not uncommon to see monkeys swinging through the treetops and reaching into the water for fish.

ZHANGJIAJIE'S HEAVENLY TRAILS

For sheer highlights and a chance to more fully take in the awesome splendor of Wulingyuan, few options surpass hiking along the numerous trails interlacing the mountains, gullies and forests.

The high plateau surrounding the reserve only serves to accentuate the dramatic pinnacles and crags of Zhangjiajie. It creates the illusion that the ground is opening up at the valley floor, shattering the earth into forested towers of rock.

For hiking and exploring Zhangjiajie, there are numerous trails waiting to be traversed. From Zhangjiajie Village, the road leads down to the park entrance where single and multi-day passes can be purchased. Sedan chairs can also be hired to carry you along the trails for around RMB 100.

Branching left after the main gate, on the trail to Huangshi Village is a 4-hour circuit winding through a lush, forested valley. The crisp, clear **Pipa Stream** (*pípa xī* 琵琶溪)

Ethnic Miao men serenade their sweethearts in a courtship dance.

gurgles along to the left of the path, crossed by several bridges. Along the way, there are numerous pagodas and viewing platforms ideal for a rest stop or a picnic lunch beneath the shadows of the mighty **Double Pagoda Peak** (*shuāngtǎ fēng* 双塔峰).

To the right of the entrance are several different paths. The shortest, also taking around 4 hours, follows the **Golden Whipple Stream** (*jīnbiān xī* 金鞭溪). Filled with colorful fish and the occasional turtle, this stream also makes a great bathing spot in the warmer summer months. Following a heavenly valley for a couple of miles, the path then branches off and returns to the entrance beneath the **Yearning Couple** (*fūqī yán* 夫妻岩). These two rock pinnacles face each other in a longing gaze telling the story of forbidden lovers who chose to be frozen as rocks rather than face a life apart.

Another option, bearing left from the main trail, crosses the **Bewitching Terrace** (*míhún tái* 迷魂台), named after vistas so stunning that they are haunting to behold. The Shandao Valley is a lesser-visited section of the park and though it's physically more challenging, it reveals Zhangjiajie in its scenic splendor and silence. Tracing the western edge of the plateau, the trail continues through marvelous scenery to the **Black Dragon Village** (*hēilóng cūn* 黑龙村), a small mountain hamlet of wood and stone homes, before returning to the park gates. Possibly because it's a full day's walk, this route is less popular and you should have it more or less to yourself.

To explore the north and east of the Wulingyuan reserve, it's best to base yourself at Suoxi Valley. Though it has many of the food and lodging options as Wulingyuan Village, being off the tourist track has helped to better preserve its idyllic feel. Although it's only 6 miles (10 km) to the park entrance, the walk takes several hours. Set amidst river-filled gorges, there are opportunities here to raft in between the numerous rocky peaks. It's also possible to hike up a precipitous staircase to the mile-long **Baofeng Lake** (*bǎofēng hú* 宝峰湖) where, in the early morning hours, giant salamanders occasionally bask on the

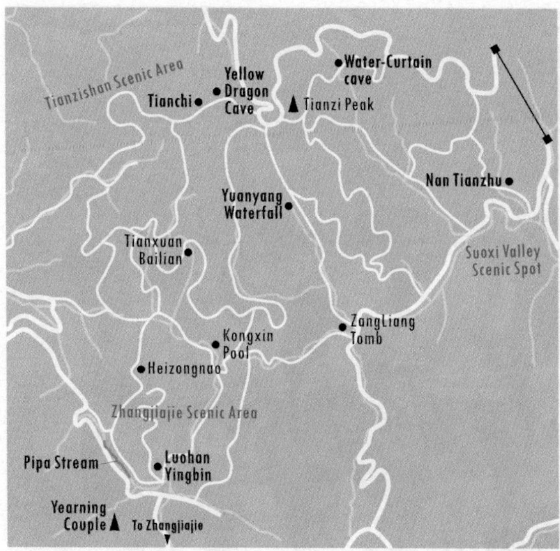

Next to the actual Tianzi Peak is the **Immortals' Bridge** (*xiānrén qiáo* 仙人桥), a narrow rock ledge bridging a cavernous gorge. Trying to cross the bridge is ill-advised but it's a stunning scene combining Zhangjiajie's grotesque rock formations, spiny pinnacles, valley floors and swirling streams. From here continue on to Tianzi Village where lodging can be had for the night. Hike out of the village the following morning and return to Zhangjiajie by foot or catch a bus back to civilization.

lakeshore.

From Suoxi Valley, a 19-mile (30 km) trail in the Tianzi Shan region takes travelers to the highest peak in the reserve. Following the **Ten Li Corridor** (*shílǐ huàláng* 十里画廊), the trail leads past the **Spirit Palace Bay** (*shéntáng wān* 神堂湾), where dagger-like rocks point up from the valley floor.

Hiking options in Zhangjiajie are numerous and many unmarked paths also lead to fantastic scenes. For those who prefer less strenuous activity but still want to explore the park, pick up a map and watch for trail signs. The trails are generally well-marked. Take them at your own pace and don't forget to stop every now and again to take in the majestic scenery that awaits. ■

Making Your Trip Easy

Practical Tips

Almost any time of the year is good for visiting Zhangjiajie. Though winter can be cold, snowfall turns the reserve into a winter wonderland. The dense foliage and high elevation make the hot Chinese summers tolerable. As with any temperate zone, spring is filled with blossoms and fresh scents while autumn's riot of color is borne through the changing colors of the leaves. Although the trails are well marked, the reserve is huge and it's possible to get lost especially if you leave the main paths. It's best to take a map and a flashlight and when in doubt, ask a local.

Though the entire reserve covers some 143 square miles (370 km²), most people base themselves at either Zhangjiajie City near

Quotes

"Zhangjiajie's beauty is such that it humbles even the proudest man. The primal forces at work here make him go back to examine his own fragile roots."

"That such natural diversity could be successfully protected here lends strong support to the case for environmental conservation. Coming here makes me realize that this thought must be extended to broader realms."

the train station or at Zhangjiajie Village on the reserve's southern edge in the Wuling foothills. For reasons of convenience and beauty, most notably the surrounding rock walls and towering peaks, the latter is preferable. Although both areas are filled with noisy karaoke joints and overpriced restaurants, the natural paradise of Zhangjiajie is close by.

One thing to note: there are no overnight facilities in the Wulingyuan Scenic Area, so you'll have to leave the park to find a hotel. The RMB 248 entrance fee gives you two days to visit, and includes all transportation within the park.

Transportation

Airport – The airport is about 6 miles (10 km) west of Zhangjiajie city, which is still 20.5 miles (33 km) from the park entrance, but there are shuttle buses into the city. Zhangjiajie airport has connections to most major Chinese cities.

Bus – Minibuses stop in front of the city's train and bus stations and take about one hour to reach the village. There are also buses to Tianzi Shan and Suoxi Valley. Long distance buses connect Zhangjiajie to Changsha.

Taxi – Taxis run between Zhangjiajie City, Zhangjiajie Village and the park entrance. When visiting other sights, it's best to negotiate a price first – distances are often difficult to judge in this mountainous region.

Train – Train service has greatly improved cutting the trip from Changsha to a mere 5 hours. There are also trains to Zhengzhou, Guangzhou and other regional centers.

The Best of Wulingyuan

Baofeng Lake
宝峰湖 *bǎofēng hú*
✉ inside the Suoxi Valley Scenic Spot 索溪峪风景区内
☎ 562 9888, 561 6609
¥ 74

Huangshi Village
黄石寨 *huángshí zhài*
✉ inside the Wulingyuan Scenic Area 武陵源风景区内
☎ 561 1098

Tianzi Shan 天子山 *tiānzǐ shān*
✉ inside the Wulingyuan Scenic Area 武陵源风景区内
☎ 561 1098

Hotels

Zhangjiajie International Hotel 张家界国际大酒店 *zhāngjiājiè guójì dàjiǔdiàn* ★★★★
✉ 42 Sanjiaoping, Yongding District 永定区三角坪 42 号
☎ 822 2888, 823 0966, 830 3019
¥ 480 – double room, peak-season
320 – double room, off-season
🌐 www.zjj-hotel.com
@ zjjhotel@sohu.com

Zhangjiajie Minnan International Hotel 张家界闽南国际酒店 *zhāngjiājiè mǐnnán guójì jiǔdiàn* ★★★★

An artistic rendition of market day in a village nearby Wulingyuan.

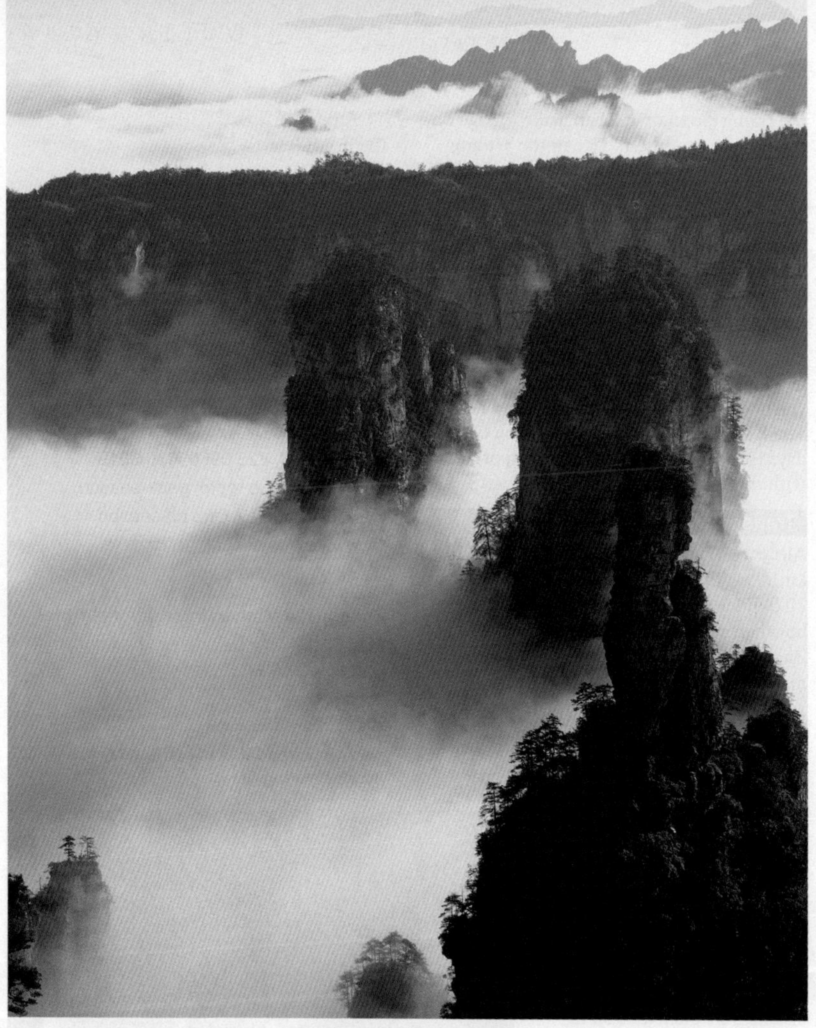

Clouds and mist swirl around the jagged jade peaks of Wulingyuan.

✉ 18 Ziwu Xi Lu 紫舞西路 18 号
☎ 822 8888
¥ 789 – double room
@ www.mn-hotel.com

Jianghan Mountain Villa
江汉山庄 *jiānghàn shānzhuāng* ★★★
✉ Wulingyuan District 武陵源区
☎ 561 8122
¥ 240 – double room, peak-season
180 – double room, off-season
@ www.zjjtour.com/jh

Wulingyuan Hotel
武陵源宾馆 *wǔlíngyuán bīnguǎn* ★★★
✉ 192 Wuling Dadao, Wulingyuan District 武陵源区武陵大道 192 号
☎ 561 5888
¥ 280 – double room, peak-season
180 – double room, off-season

Zhangjiajie Genli International Hotel
张家界亘立国际酒店 *zhāngjiājiè gènlì guójì jiǔdiàn* ★★★
✉ Zhongduan, Wuling Dadao, Wulingyuan District 武陵源区武陵大道中段
☎ 562 5999
¥ 330 – double room, peak-season
198 – double room, off-season
@ www.genlihotel.com

Food & Restaurants

Residents of China's mountainous regions are known for eating strange things and the Hunanese are known for loving spicy food. Zhangjiajie comes through on both counts. The mountain's wide variety of mushrooms often work their way into the cuisine as do other ingredients known for their healing or health boosting properties. As Zhangjiajie is a heavily toured area, many standard Chinese favorites are available as well. Most of the food is quite good but beware of the ubiquitous tourist trap. Enquire about the price before you order and beware of eating any expensive dishes that may contain endangered species.

Tujia flavors predominate with dishes like Tujia hotpot (*tǔjiā huǒguō* 土家火锅); deep-fried bee eggs (*yóuzhá yěfēngluǎn* 油炸野蜂卵) and *tuanniancai* (团年菜) are typical dishes. Tujia snacks such as *ge fen* (葛粉), rice wine (*mǐ jiǔ* 米酒), cold noodles (*liáng fěn* 凉粉), and *baba* (粑粑) are tasty diversions. Tuan niancai, which means something like "yearly reunion," is traditionally eaten by the Tujia during the New Year, a time when they would reflect on and pay tribute to their ancestors. Other local specialties include wild rabbit (*yětù* 野兔), snake soup (*shé tāng* 蛇汤) and dog meat hotpot (*gǒuròu huǒguō* 狗肉火锅). For lovers of spicy food, try the wild mountain pepper beef (*yěshānjiāo niúròu* 野山椒牛肉). Breakfast generally consists of steamed meat buns (*bāozi* 包子), noodles (*miàn tiáo* 面条) and wonton (*húntún* 馄饨).

RESTAURANTS

Jinfuli Jiudian 金富丽酒店
Specialized in Tujia cuisine.
✉ 89 Ziwu Lu, Zhangjiajie
张家界市紫舞路 89 号
☎ 830 0278
◷ 8am to 10pm

Minzu Shanzhuang 民族山庄
A Tujia managed lodge with dining room.
✉ inside Zhangjiajie National Forest Park
张家界国家森林公园内
☎ 571 2516, 571 9188
◷ 24 hours

Sanxiaguo 三下锅
Serves a kind of hot pot.
✉ Fengwan Bridge, Lingyuan Bei Lu
陵园北路凤湾大桥
◷ 9am to 9pm

Shanguizhai Restaurant 山鬼寨
✉ Fengwan Lu 张家界市凤湾路口
☎ 211 9339

Souvenirs

Zhangjiajie is located in the heart of the wilds of western Hunan in a region that most outsiders have only begun to explore. Local tribes, however, have lived here for hundreds and thousands of years and continue to make many of the handicrafts that were passed on to them through the generations. Minority handicrafts include finely woven baskets with black line patterns and intricately embroidered shoe insteps. Weavings and embroideries make up the bulk of the handicrafts. Wooden buckets and bamboo cradles are some of the other local specialties.

Also plentiful in this region are Chinese medicinal plants and herbs. Many different kinds of mushrooms are for sale and locals often display their goods along the trails. Ask for advice from local experts before buying or consuming anything that has medicinal properties – they can be dangerous if used improperly.

The Junsheng Gallery (*jūnshēng huàyuàn* 军声画院) on Ziwu Lu (子午路, ☎ 830 1239) is where artist Li Junsheng displays his sandstone art (*jūnshēng shāshíhuà* 军声砂石画). Using different plants, his creations infuse the natural colors of the sandstones with the artist's imagination. Prices range from RMB 200 to 5,000. Tujia embroidery (*tǔjiā zhījǐn* 土家织锦) is a popular buy here. You can get some good samples at the Museum of Tujia Culture.

Other Information

POST OFFICES

Zhangjiajie City Post Office
张家界市邮政局
✉ Daqiao Lu 大桥路
☎ 822 6898

HOSPITALS

Zhangjiajie People's Hospital
张家界市人民医院
✉ Tianmen Lu 天门路
☎ 822 2270

COMPLAINT HOTLINES

☎ General: 838 0188, 823 3754

▶▶ The Chinese Zodiac

In traditional Chinese culture 12 is an important number when calculating time. Ancient observers noted that there are 12 full moons in a year, with the length of time between the full moons being relatively constant. They also observed the day could be divided into 12 equal parts. These observations led to the development of the 12 month lunar year and the 12 watch day.

The Chinese began grouping years into a twelve year cycle, assigning each year an animal symbol. Legend has it that Buddha called a meeting of all the world's animals to determine how to restore order to the world, but only 12 heeded his call. They came to represent the 12-year-cycle, with each presiding over a year in the order they arrived at the meeting. As they traveled to the meeting, the strong ox was in the lead and only had a river to cross to come in first. Little did he know, however, that the cunning rat had hitched a ride on his back and became the first to arrive.

The twelve animals are: rat, ox, tiger, rabbit, dragon, snake, horse, sheep, monkey, rooster, dog and pig. The 12 animals associated with the years can be used to judge a person's character. A person born in the year of a particular animal is said to have the traits of that animal.

Rat (*shǔ* 鼠)

Rats are considered aggressive, suspicious, and power-hungry but are also honest, generous, and have a sense of fair play.

Ox (*niú* 牛)

Oxen are stubborn, but are natural leaders who strive for success.

Tiger (*hǔ* 虎)

Tigers are carefree and happy-go-lucky personalities. They're great to party with, but can be undependable and tend to take risks.

Rabbit (*tù* 兔)

Rabbits aren't risk takers and value security and tranquility. These people avoid conflict and emotional involvement.

Dragon (*lóng* 龙)

Those born in the year of the dragon are bossy, loud and garish, but also popular and successful.

Snake (*shé* 蛇)

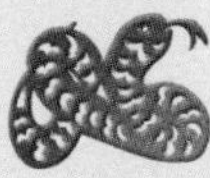

Chinese mythology's icon for cleverness, snakes are known for their abstract thought and idealism.

Horse (*mǎ* 马)

Those born in the year of the horse are thought to be hard working and considerate, though arrogant.

Sheep (*yáng* 羊)

Sheep are warm-hearted but disorganized and don't respond well to pressure.

Monkey (*hóu* 猴)

Monkeys are intelligent and entertaining, but have a flare for deception. They make close friends, but can't be trusted.

Rooster (*jī* 鸡)

Roosters are courageous, but arrogant and reckless. They're skilled at their work and are attentive to details.

Dog (*gǒu* 狗)

Dogs are quiet but intelligent; they're introverted listeners, dedicated and honest but also cynical and prone to letting their anxieties get the better of them.

Pig (*zhū* 猪)

Pigs are honest and reliable with a thirst for knowledge. They're often successful in financial affairs and are dedicated to good causes.

SOUTHWEST CHINA

Chongqing is one of western China's major commercial centers.

Chongqing, the Mountain City

Area Code 023

Heritage: Dazu Rock Carvings

Chongqing has long been a staging post for river journeys and a gateway to China's wild west. With its steep hills, raging rivers and spicy food, there's something for everyone.

Overlooking the confluence of the **Yangtze** and the **Jialing Rivers**, Chongqing is known throughout China as the "Mountain City." Many of city's hills are so precipitous that bicycles are scarce and motorcycles a far more common sight. Largely determined by its mountainous topography, Chongqing's districts are spread over a series of hilltops and separated by major rivers. As your taxi or bus zips across the overpasses linking the areas, check out the precariously stacked apartment buildings clinging to the hillsides. It's possible for one of these buildings to have both the first floor and the fifth floor at ground level.

Although Chongqing's major tourist destination, the **Three Gorges** (*sān xiá* 三峡), is now being inundated by waters from the Three Gorges Dam, the city has its own inherent charm and the region is worth exploring. Known for its spicy food and hot-tempered people, Chongqing, with its mountains and fog and its bubbling hotpots has secured a place in the Chinese imagination.

While the entire Chongqing municipality contains over 30 million people and like Beijing, Tianjin and Shanghai, reports directly to the Central Government and is no longer a part of Sichuan Province, the actual city itself has a population of only 5.8 million.

Due to its strategic location on the Yangtze River, for over 4,000 years every dynasty has had a provincial capital there. This climaxed during the Second World War when Chongqing, then known as Chunking, was made the wartime capital of the Republic of China. Its population exploded, filling the city with refugees and government officials. During the war, the city endured severe air raids by the Japanese and what followed was an intense period of poverty.

Since then, it has rebounded with fervor. Chongqing became southwest China's key industrial center and a focal point for China's "Go West" program to bring investment to China's underdeveloped west. Its rapid modernization can be felt most clearly around the **Liberation Monument** (*jiěfàng bēi* 解放碑), Chongqing's commercial and entertainment center. The actual monument, originally made of wood and dedicated to Sun Yat-sen, was rebuilt in 1945 to celebrate the end of the war with Japan. The monument is within walking distance of most of Chongqing's major hotels and shops.

If you want a taste of old Chongqing, the best place to begin is **Chaotian Gate** (*cháotiān mén* 朝天门), the only remaining city gate and Chongqing's chief wharf on the Jialing River. Traffic is intense with freight and passenger ships docking day and night. From Chaotian Gate, there are great views of the green waters of the Jialing meeting the murky brown currents of the Yangtze. Within walking distance are the two cable cars crossing the Jialing and the Yangtze and providing stunning views of Chongqing's surroundings.

Though Chongqing's modern historical sites are plentiful, ancient ones are sparse. A short walk from the main commercial center is the **Arhat Temple** (*luóhàn sì* 罗汉寺). Occupying the same site for over a thousand years, the temple has since undergone reconstruction. Inside are some 500 sculpted arhats (beings that have reached Nirvana) and a large golden Buddha. If you want to know your future, in the temple there's a specific route to follow based on your date of birth to find an arhat whose life course yours will closely follow.

A 45-minute bus ride outside the city takes you to the **SACO Prisons** (Sino- American Cooperation Organization 中美合作所). Developed in secret by the US in conjunction with Chiang Kai-shek, this was a training camp for Nationalist agents and a prison camp for captured Communists. Although the Nationalists and the Communists briefly formed a united front against the Japanese, civilian Communists suffered severe crackdowns under Nationalist hands and hundreds were kept captive.

Rather unique amongst Chinese historical sites is the **Stillwell Museum** (*shǐdíwēi jìniànguǎn* 史迪威纪念馆), honoring the US

Sichuan Bamboo covered porcelain used to be made exclusively for the Qing Royal family.

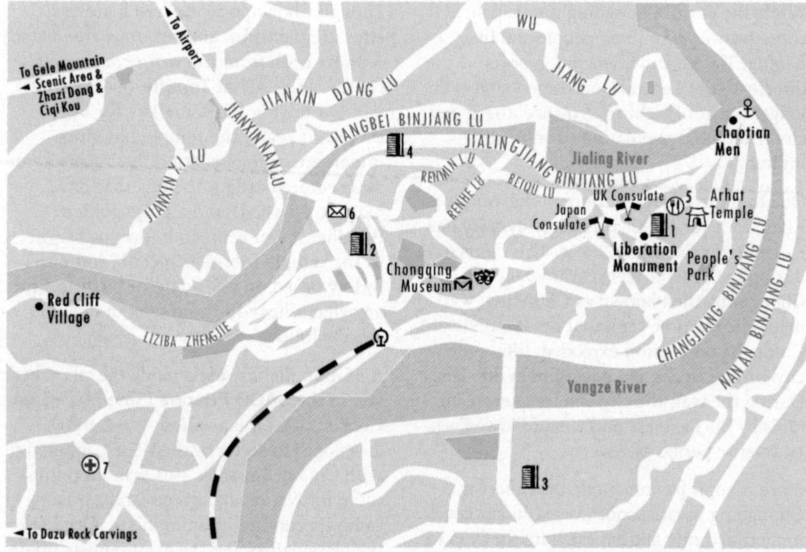

involvement in the Second World War. Located in the former Nationalist VIP guesthouse and the private residence of General Stillwell, the commander of the China-Burma-India Theater, it displays the wartime heroics of the Flying Tigers. These volunteer American pilots fought the Japanese over China, India and Burma in late 1941 for seven months, racking up an impressive kill ratio at a time when Japanese air supremacy was unrivaled.

If the urban congestion has gotten you down, try a stroll through the **People's Park** (*rénmín gōngyuán* 人民公园). Featuring a palatial conference and concert hall modeled after the Temple of Heaven, the park is large enough for an afternoon stroll and its trees and gardens are a welcome change of pace from Chongqing's urban development.

Ciqi Kou (*cíqì kǒu* 瓷器口) was Chongqing's old harbor and was once the home of many of Chongqing's rich merchants. Ming and Qing dynasty architecture abound throughout the town. Tea houses, dragon dances and temple fairs all make this a great place to really soak up the atmosphere of old Chongqing.

DAZU ROCK CARVINGS

More than a thousand years ago, Buddhist and Taoist sects fiercely competed for ascendancy and imperial endorsement. As power changed hands and religious orders came in and out of favor, the victors would create new monuments to their gods and destroy the old ones. One result was that significantly stronger materials were employed to build religious monuments, being hard to destroy, and the monuments got bigger. The monumental Dazu art testifies to this trend.

Memorable Experiences

Standing by Chaotian Gate on a foggy morning and watching the ships sail in and out.

A cable car ride across the Yangtze River.

Dazu when the setting sun turns the cliff carvings golden.

Chongqing hotpot with cold beer and sampling the numerous food stalls by the Liberation Monument.

The cliff carvings at Dazu.

The **Dazu Rock Carvings** (*dàzú shíkè* 大足石刻) and statues are scattered over some 70 sites in Chongqing's Dazu County. The statues here are stylistically different from those at Yungang and Dunhuang, both of which were much earlier projects. Dating back to the Tang and Song dynasties, the carvings at Dazu are purely Chinese in style, whereas earlier caves at Longmen, Dunhuang and Yungang have very obvious foreign influences. Revealing Buddhist, Taoist, and Confucian influences, the Dazu carvings range from small, intimate statues dedicated by pious families to massive reclining Buddhas, requiring hundreds of artisans. A welcome break from Chongqing's urban sprawl, the sites unfold over the idyllic scenery of rolling hills, placid farms and the red earth of the Sichuan basin.

Of the two major sites, **North Mountain** (*běi shān* 北山) is smaller and requires less time. It's believed that this was originally a military camp and that a general, perhaps hoping for good fortune in battle, commissioned the earliest statues. Although many of the statues have deteriorated over the centuries, there are a few that still remain in good condition. Among the most notable is **Niche 136**, which depicts Puxian the patron saint of Emei Mountain riding a white elephant and the goddess of mercy, Guanyin. The Peacock King can be found in **Niche 155**.

Fortunately, this site is 1.2 miles (2 km) from Dazu County and can be reached by a 30-minute walk from the bus station. Atop the site, good views can be had of the surrounding countryside.

The sculptures at **Baoding Mountain** (*bǎodǐng shān* 宝顶山), though further out of town, are far superior. Constructed from 1179 to 1249, the works range from near miniature to massive. Whether enjoying the artwork, the religious zeal or the beauty of the area, it's well worth spending half a day.

Although still somewhat shrouded in mystery, Tantric monk Zhao Zhifeng is credited with founding this site. Built on a mountainside with a monastery perched on top, the lower section is filled with sculpted figures carved into a cliff. Unlike Dazu's other sites with Buddhist carvings, Baoding was carefully planned out, utilizing the natural features of the rock to accentuate the work.

At the center is the giant, **Reclining Buddha** (*shuìfó* 睡佛) some 102 feet (31 m) long and 16.4 feet (5 m) high. Entering Nirvana, the expression on his face is one of peace and happiness. Flanking him is a 1,007-armed, gold Avalokitesvara. In each hand is an eye symbolizing all encompassing wisdom.

The sheer variety and volume of statues here

Buddha right before his enlightenment.

dazzles – there are heroes of the Buddhist faith, historical figures and scenes and depictions of daily life in the countryside.

While nearly 800 years have past since these grottos were made, many of the statues have held up remarkably well, though wind has eroded some and paint has pealed off others. About 9 miles (15 km) outside of town, reached by a 30 to 45-minute bus ride, the ride out to Baoding takes in solo sculptures carved along the winding road. ■

Making Your Trip Easy

Practical Tips

As one of China's "three furnace cities", Chongqing broils all summer with temperatures reaching 110°F to 120°F (high 40s°C). Although the winters rarely get very cold, the fog can be quite heavy at times. Spring is comfortable; it's also when the orange blossoms bloom. Autumn, when the oranges are ripe, create a riot of colors along the riverbanks. The best time for travel is from March to June and from September to November. It's usually around 42°F to 43°F (6°C) during winter and there's no snow, which makes it a good time to visit.

Chongqing's only real tourist area is down by the dock where touts sell maps and offer guided tours or cruise tickets. Although they can be aggressive, they won't follow you for long. The porters or "*bang bangs*" carry things from the docks to the ships and are notorious for aggressive behavior. Be sure to set a clear price before they pick up your bags. RMB 5 per piece of luggage is more than enough.

Transportation

Airport – Located 13 miles (21 km) north of the city is Chongqing's Jiangbei Airport. There are shuttle buses to and from the city and it's about 45 minutes from the airport to Shangqing Temple (*shàngqīng sì* 上清寺). Taking a taxi from the airport to Chongqing costs around RMB 100 and takes about 30 minutes.

Boat – Cruises to the Three Gorges are boarded at the Chaotianmen Dock in Yuzhong District (☎ 6310 0659); tickets require advanced booking. First-class cabins are RMB 1,022 for a double room, second-class cabins are RMB 578 with four people to a cabin, third-class cabins are RMB 270 with six to eight people and fourth-class cabins are RMB 212 with eight to 12 people.

Bus – Buses to Dazu take around 3 hours and depart daily from 6am to 6pm. Bus service between Chengdu and Chongqing takes about 4 hours and costs a bit over RMB 100.

Taxi – Taxis start at RMB 5 at flag-fall and rides around the city center rarely cost over RMB 12. Many of Chongqing's outlying districts are spread over hilltops so the meter can add up fast; expect to pay a minimum of RMB 30 when visiting these areas.

Train – Chongqing has good train connections though routes tend to be circuitous because of the mountainous terrain. There are connections to most major cities and the train station is located across from the bus station.

The Best of Chongqing

Arhat Temple 罗汉寺 *luóhàn sì*
- 🕒 8am to 5pm
- ¥ 5

Ciqi Kou 瓷器口古镇 *cíqì kǒu gǔzhèn*
- ✉ Ciqi Kou Town, Shapingba 沙坪坝区瓷器口古镇
- ☎ 6540 1002
- 🕒 24 hours
- ¥ Free

Dazu Rock Carvings 大足石刻 *dàzú shíkè*
- ✉ Baoding Shan, Dazu County 大足县宝顶山
- ☎ 4372 7651
- 🕒 8am to 5:30pm
- ¥ 80

Hotels

Harbour Plaza Chongqing 重庆海逸酒店 *chóngqìng hǎiyì jiǔdiàn* ★★★★★
- ✉ Wuyi Lu, Jiefang Bei, Yuzhong District 渝中区解放碑五一路❶
- ☎ 6370 0888 ext. 8686, 8618 or 8619
- ¥ 623 – double room
- @ www.Harbour-Plaza.com

Hilton Chongqing 重庆希尔顿酒店 *chóngqìng xī'ěrdùn jiǔdiàn* ★★★★★
- ✉ 139 Zhongshan Sanlu, Yuzhong District 渝中区中山三路 139 号❷
- ☎ 8903 8888
- ¥ 623 – double room, peak-season
580 – double room, off-season
- @ www.hilton.com

Holiday Inn Yangtze Chongqing 重庆扬子江假日饭店 *chóngqìng yángzǐjiāng jiàrì fàndiàn* ★★★★
- ✉ 15 Nanping Bei Lu 南坪北路 15 号❸
- ☎ 6280 8888, 800 830 1123
- ¥ 498 – double room, peak-season
390 – double room, off-season
- @ www.yangtzefocus.com

Wudu Hotel 重庆雾都宾馆 *chóngqìng wùdū bīnguǎn* ★★★★
- ✉ 24 Shangzengjiayan, Yuzhong District 渝中区上曾家岩 24 号❹
- ☎ 6385 1788
- ¥ 498 – double room
- @ www.wdhotel.com

Food & Restaurants

Sichuan cuisine's history can be traced back to the Qin and Han dynasties, and became a major school of cooking during the Tang dynasty. When chili peppers were

Quotes

"The green hills and fast rivers remind me that I am in China's wild west."

"The food here made my tongue go numb and set my mouth on fire. Now I know why the people here have so much energy."

▶▶ General Chennault and the "Flying Tigers"

Born in Texas in 1893, Claire Lee Chennault was to play a crucial part in China's struggle against Japanese occupation during the 1940's. His successes would not only win him the respect of the Chinese people, but also change the history of air warfare.

Originally a captain in the U.S. Army Reserve, he was forced to retire when he was 44 years old because of poor health and a stubborn insistence that fighter planes should be used to intercept incoming bombers – something that ran counter to the military wisdom of the day. Madame Chiang Kai-shek, however, had faith in Chennault, and in 1937 she recruited him to train and advise the newly formed Chinese Air Force.

Not long after he arrived in China, war against the Japanese broke out and Chennault's theories were put to the test. In early missions his planes performed well against unescorted Japanese bombers, but the Japanese responded quickly by sending out cutting-edge fighters. Chennault's rickety biplanes were no match for the agile Mitsubishi A5M; and so together with the rest of Chiang Kai-shek's Nationalist forces, they were forced to retreat 2,000 miles up the Yangtze River from Nanjing to Chongqing.

They could do nothing but wait: China needed modern aircraft. Negotiations with Washington eventually led to the purchase of 100 P-40B fighter planes; the final consignment would reach Burma, where Chennault had established his "American Volunteer Group," in November 1941. The volunteers were drawn from the American military or were former military flyers. The pilots were paid between US $250 and 750 a month, plus a US $500 bounty for each plane they destroyed.

December would see the beginning of a remarkable series of victories for the American pilots forming the AVG. In one of their first battles over Kunming they shot down at least three enemy bombers and gave hope to the beleaguered residents of the city. Time magazine, celebrating this first victory of the Pacific War, dubbed the volunteers "Flying Tigers."

There was more to come. Chiang needed to keep supplies moving along the Burma Road, and dispatched Chennault's Third Squadron to defend Rangoon. Over Christmas 1941, the "Flying Tigers" shot down 23 of Japan's best combat planes without a single loss. The elite Japanese 64th Sentai had never before been matched, and the psychological impact of the defeat was tremendous – three small squadrons were slowing the Japanese advance and challenging hitherto undisputed air superiority.

Chennault's AVG was disbanded in July 1942, but he was quickly appointed commander of the U.S. Army's 14th Air Force. He fought on until the end of the war, leading his group to destroy an estimated 2,600 planes and 44 warships by July 1945. When he left China in August, hundreds of thousands of Chinese rallied on the streets of Chongqing to pay their tributes.

Succumbing to lung cancer on July 27, 1958, he was laid to rest in Arlington National Cemetery in Virginia. The Chennault International Airport in Louisiana commemorates his exceptional contributions to aviation.

introduced to China during the Qing dynasty, Sichuan cooking developed into the modern spicy feast.

As Chongqing lies in the heart of China's chili belt, local dishes are not for the timid tongue. Chongqing's specialty is the addition of the Sichuan peppercorn, which produces a numbing heat, hence many dishes have the prefix *mala*, meaning numb and spicy. Many restaurants will tone down the spice count for tongues that have yet to be initiated.

The most famous Chongqing dish is a spicy hotpot called *mala huoguo* (麻辣火锅), a cauldron of red, bubbling soup in which diners cook raw meats and vegetables. The longer it simmers the spicier it gets and the custom is to save the leafy vegetables for last. Watch out – they pick up all the spices.

If this sounds a bit too much, many restaurants also serve a *yuan-yang* hotpot (*yuānyāng huǒguō* 鸳鸯火锅) with one side red and the other a clear chicken broth. Many street vendors sell a cold noodle (*liáng fěn* 凉粉) topped with cucumbers and drenched in a spicy sauce then sprinkled with chopped garlic. Barbecue (*shāo kǎo* 烧烤) is a popular way of cooking and can be less spicy. Small rice dumplings in a hot soup (*shānchéng xiǎotāngyuán* 山城小汤圆) are usually filled with sweet sesame paste.

Chicken is cooked in a variety of ways and two popular dishes are spicy chicken (*làzi jī* 辣子鸡) and a spicy chicken appetizer (*kǒushuǐ jī* 口水鸡) that's served cold. Chongqing's spring chicken (mineral water spring, not the season) is a local specialty. It's so good there's a whole street (*nánshān quánshuǐjī yītiáojiē* 南山泉水鸡一条街) dedicated to serving it. The chickens can be found by Nanshan Park at Huangjueya in the Nan'an District (南岸区黄桷垭南山公园).

Other goodies to look for include simple noodles (*dāndān miàn* 担担面), Sichuan five-spiced beef jerky (*lǎosìchuān wǔxiāng niúròugān* 老四川五香牛肉干) and huge pomelos (*liángpíng yòu* 梁平柚).

Wuyi Lu is locally known as hotpot road and has numerous options. Along Bayi Lu by the Liberation Monument is a food market (*jiěfàngbēi hǎochī yītiáojiē* 解放碑好吃一条街) that teems with vendors selling everything from noodles to barbecue.

RESTAURANTS

Chongqing Hotel 重庆宾馆
Specializes in southern cuisine like barbecue (*jùdéxiāng kǎoròu* 聚德香烤肉) and tofu with egg yolk (*dànhuáng dòufu bǎo* 蛋黄豆腐煲), they have monthly specials like *guoba yuzai* (锅巴芋仔) and *qingsun xiangla zaitu* (青笋香辣仔兔).
✉ 235 Minsheng Lu, Yuzhong District
渝中区民生路 235 号
☎ 6384 5888
🕒 24 hours

Chongqing Little Swan Bayu Restaurant
重庆小天鹅巴渝食府
Great all-you-can-eat hotpot spot, and especially good is their "son and mother" hotpot (*zǐmǔ guō* 子母锅); also has medicinal soups made from soft-shelled turtles (*jiǎyú* 甲鱼), tortoises (*guī* 龟), black chickens (*wūjī* 乌鸡) and spring pigeons (*rǔgē* 乳鸽). Lunch is RMB 48, dinner is RMB 58 not including alcoholic beverages or dipping sauce; there's also a 10% service charge.
✉ 6/F, New Chongqing Square, 22 Minzu Lu, Yuzhong District
渝中区民族路 22 号新重庆广场六楼❺

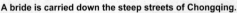

A bride is carried down the steep streets of Chongqing.

☎ 6378 8811, 6378 8934

🕒 11am to 9:30pm

Fuling Laozihao Feichangguan
涪陵老字号肥肠馆
Tasty Sichuan treats.

✉ 1 Gaosuntang 高笋塘 1 号

☎ 7224 7839

🕒 8am to 2pm, 5pm to 9pm

Lao Sichuan Restaurant 老四川餐厅
All kinds of beef, including a very thinly sliced spicy *dengying niurou* (灯影牛肉) *mala* shredded beef (*málà niúròusī* 麻辣牛肉丝) and ox-tail soup (*niúwěi tāng* 牛尾汤).

✉ 186 Minzu Lu, Yuzhong District
渝中区民族路 186 号

☎ 6382 6644

🕒 10am to 2pm, 4:30pm to 9:30pm

Waipoqiao 外婆桥

✉ 7/F Daduhui Guangchang, 68 Zourong Lu, Yuzhong District
渝中区邹容路 68 号大都会广场 7 楼

☎ 6383 5988, 6383 5188

Souvenirs

Inspired by the mountains and rivers surrounding Chongqing, numerous great artists come here, making Chongqing a great place to shop for watercolors and calligraphy. The scenery of the Yangtze and the Three Gorges has long been the subject matter of Chinese paintings. The area around the Liberation Monument has numerous galleries selling everything from large scrolls to painted fans and screens; many of these stores take credit cards.

For those who seek more assurance before making a purchase, there are several large department stores also near the Liberation Monument as well as high-end hotel gift shops. The galleries tend to be much cheaper and unlike the department stores, prices are negotiable. Paying half the offered price is reasonable, though this rule doesn't always apply.

Sichuan handicrafts are also good buys, check out the local brocade (*shǔjǐn* 蜀锦); common motifs include flowers, turtle shells and animals. Other local specialties include folding fans (*róngchāng zhéshàn* 荣昌折扇), lacquerware (*qīqì* 漆器) and painted bamboo curtains (*zhúlián huà* 竹帘画).

A good place to start your browsing is the Wanzi Qianhong Shangchang (*wànzǐqiānhóng shāngchǎng* 万紫千红商场) at the Chaotianmen dock (朝天门码头, ☎ 6310 0789).

Other Information

POST OFFICES

Jiulongpo Post Office 九龙坡邮局

✉ 18 Yanjiapingzhen Jie, Jiulongpo District
九龙坡区杨家坪镇街 18 号

☎ 6885 5383

🕒 8:30am to 7pm

Yuzhong District Post Office 渝中区邮政局

✉ 28 Nanping Xi Lu, Nan'an District
南岸区南坪西路 28 号❻

☎ 6291 5204

🕒 8:30am to 7pm

HOSPITALS

The First Chongqing Medical University Hospital 重庆医科大学附属第一医院

✉ 1 Youyi Lu, Yuanjiagang, Yuzhong District
渝中区袁家岗友谊路 1 号❼

☎ 6881 1360

The Second Chongqing Medical University Hospital
重庆医科大学附属第二医院

✉ 74 Linjiang Lu, Yuzhong District
渝中区临江路 74 号

☎ 6383 2133

CONSULATES

Canada 加拿大

✉ Room 1705, Daduhui Shangsha, Wuyi Lu, Yuzhong District
渝中区五一路大都会商厦 1705 室

☎ 6373 8007

Japan 日本

✉ 14/F, Business Tower, Chongqing Hotel, 283 Minsheng Lu,Yuzhong District 渝中区民生路 283 号重庆宾馆商务大厦 14 楼

☎ 6373 3585

United Kingdom 英国

✉ 28/F, Daduhui Shangsha, 68 Zourong Lu, Yuzhong District
渝中区邹容路 68 号大都会商厦 28 楼

☎ 6381 0321

COMPLAINT HOTLINES

☎ General: 6370 5525

☎ Taxi: 8908 3201

Chengdu, Teahouse-hopping and Chilies

Chengdu Area Code 028
Le Shan Area Code 0833

Heritage: Qingcheng Shan & the Dujiangyan Irrigation System, Emei Shan & Le Shan Giant Buddha

Get comfortable in a bamboo chair and watch life go by in one of **Chengdu's** countless teahouses. Feast on the famously spicy Sichuan cuisine, and don't forget to visit the pandas.

A giant statue of Chairman Mao marks the center of Chengdu. Surrounded by flashy advertisements, the chairman oversees the movements in the capital of Sichuan Province from atop his podium. The **Sichuan** is endowed with fertile land and its nickname, "China's breadbasket," is fitting. It is also diverse, with more than 40 ethnic minorities living in the province.

Chengdu is over 2,500 years old; paper money was first used here during the Song dynasty. But despite its antiquity and its laidback feel, the city is rapidly developing as an important commercial center in western China. In the drive to modernization, many of Chengdu's traditional areas have been torn down, but there are still enough traditional areas and historical sights to keep visitors entertained.

A bustling pedestrian overpass in Chengdu.

8th century poet Du Fu once called this bamboo forest home.

The best way to get a good feel for Chengdu is to find a spot in the shade at a teahouse and relax. Teahouses and the local cuisine vie for the top spot as the defining characteristic of Chengdu. There are few places in China where traditional teahouses can still be found – this is the place to sit back, order a cup of tea and forget about your troubles. Mahjong (*májiàng* 麻将), a domino-type game, is played everywhere. The click-clack of the mahjong pieces being shuffled fill the air, along with the whistles from songbirds that old men carry in bamboo cages. In some teahouses you can even enjoy your tea with a live performance of acrobatics or Sichuan opera while getting a head massage or your ears cleaned with long metal picks. In the area just north of the Jin River, which traverses the city from west to east, there's an excellent teahouse in the People's Park (*rénmín gōngyuán* 人民公园), aptly named the People's Teahouse (*rénmín cháguǎn* 人民茶馆).

Besides teahouses, there are many other attractions in Chengdu. One of the most pleasant experiences is to stroll around, or even better, to bike around the city and see the old residential areas and the food markets. Chengdu is a manageable size on a bike and most hotels will rent one for about RMB 10 to 20 per day. Most streets have a separate lane for bikes, making biking a far safer venture here than in many other Chinese cities. For travelers who have seen many of China's other cities, the abundance of greenery along the roads is a welcome change. A good area to explore is south of Renmin Dong Lu and east of Renmin Nan Lu. While over there, check out the **Qingshiqiao Market** (*qīnshíqiáo shìchǎng* 青石桥市场), the most dynamic market in Chengdu.

What can't be missed when coming to Chengdu is a visit to see the **pandas** (*dàxióngmāo* 大熊猫). Sichuan Province is the home of these celebrated creatures. There are only an estimated 500 to 1,000 pandas left in the wild and most of them live in northwestern Sichuan. The **Wolong Nature Reserve** (*wòlóng zìrán bǎohùqū* 卧龙自然保护区) is a 3-hour drive from Chengdu. This 772 square mile (20,000 ha) reserve was created in 1974 to protect the pandas, but is also home to thousands of plant species and 230 different species of birds. Even though the beauty of the area is justification enough for the trip, there is no guarantee that you will get lucky and run into a panda here. However, some 6 miles (10 km) north of the city center is the **Giant Panda Breeding Research Base** (*dàxióngmāo fánzhí yánjiū zhōngxīn* 大熊猫繁殖研究中心) where seeing a panda is guaranteed. There are around a dozen pandas here, and it's best to get here

Memorable Experiences

Exploring the city on bike or foot. Dive into the smaller alleys of the city and experience the local markets and traditional architecture.

Treating the taste buds to the exquisite Sichuan cuisine.

Taking in Chengdu in slow motion at a teahouse.

Visiting the pandas in the Giant Panda Breeding Research Base.

in the morning between 8am and 10am when the pandas are fed and at their liveliest. There is a museum with exhibits explaining everything there is to know about pandas.

There are some interesting temples in the city and if you only have time to visit one, it should be the **Wenshu Monastery** (*wénshū yuàn* 文殊院). In the **Wenhua Park** (*wénhuà gōngyuán* 文化公园) is the smaller **Qingyang Temple** (*qīngyáng gōng* 青羊宫), which is worth a visit as it's the oldest Taoist temple in town. The temple also has an eight-sided pagoda made without any nails. The bustling market surrounding the temple is a major leisure area for the locals – at times it may seem like the whole city is shopping. Just east of the temple is the **Qingtai Da Jie**, where the old architectural Chengdu has been recreated. Close to the Qingyang Temple is **Du Fu's Cottage** (*dùfǔ cǎotáng* 杜甫草堂), home of one of China's more revered poets of the Tang dynasty who wrote over 200 poems while living in this simple cottage.

A bronze sculpture from the Sanxingdui archeological site.

For some local flavor in the evening, 200-year-old **Sichuan Opera** (*chuānjù* 川剧) is an entertaining option. Ear-splitting Sichuan Opera is definitely an acquired taste and can be seen at the **Jinjiang Theater** (*jǐnjiāng jùyùan* 锦江剧院) or the **Shufeng Yayun** (蜀风雅韵). The contents of shows vary, but the most important elements are high-pitch singing, acrobatics, slapstick and unique to Sichuan Opera, "changing faces," in which the performer very quickly changes colorful masks. The whole atmosphere, from the show with tea and snacks to the enthusiasm of the audience and performers make it a memorable experience.

For history buffs with a little more time on their hands, a visit to **Sanxingdui** (*sānxīngduī* 三星堆), the site of the ancient Shu capital will be rewarding. Centered on Sichuan's Yangtze River valley more than 4,000 years ago, Sanxingdui holds the largest surviving ruins of the Shu Kingdom. Since the discovery of the ruins, more than 10,000 relics including bronze, gold, jade and marble artifacts, pottery, bone tools and ivory objects have been uncovered. The site's museum is in Guanghan City, about 25 miles (40 km) from Chengdu. Sanxingdui is considered the most important site for ancient Sichuan culture due to its sheer size and the number of artifacts found.

THE WENSHU MONASTERY

Arguably the most beautiful and well preserved temple in Chengdu is the very active **Wenshu Monastery**. Worshippers light candles and incense, constantly wrapping the temple in a thick perfumed smoke. The young manage to hold incense sticks in one hand and their mobile phone in the other while older visitors burn "ghost" paper money hoping it'll reach deceased ancestors, and touch iron figures of animals for good luck. During holidays, worshippers struggle through throngs of people to offer their incense. So much is being burned that monks frequently pull out fire hoses to extinguish the flames.

The monastery, situated north of the central square on Renmin Zhong Lu, was founded all the way back in the Tang dynasty but the buildings here today were built in 1691. It's the main temple for the province's *Chan* (Zen) Buddhist sect. The most stunning features of the temple are the White Jade Buddha (*báiyù fó* 白玉佛) and the Thousand Buddha Pagoda (*qiānfó tǎ* 千佛塔). Aside from beautiful carvings, there are peaceful green areas around the temple grounds and many locals take a nap under a tree or perform their daily exercises in the quiet shade. You might see seniors hugging trees and rubbing their backs against them to improve blood circulation.

There's a teahouse on the premises, probably the best one in town and also one of the biggest. There are also vegetarian restaurants around the teahouse specializing mainly in tofu dishes.

In Guan County, about 37 miles (60 km) from Chengdu, is **Qingcheng Shan** (*qīngchéng shān* 青城山), a mountain that can be visited as a day trip. During the Han dynasty it became a center of Taoism when a Taoist master made the mountain his home. The **Shangqing Hall** (*shàngqīng gōng* 上清宫) sits over 5,250 (1,600 m) above sea level and is the highest temple on the mountain. Halfway up the mountain is the **Tianshi Cave** (*tiānshī dòng* 天师洞) where the old master used to give his lectures and is now home to the Taoist Association. Most of the buildings have histories going back to the Han dynasty or earlier, but the actual structures are mainly Qing dynasty or later. Many of the buildings, in accordance to Taoist beliefs, blend into the

The Giant Buddha statue at Le Shan overlooks the Minjiang River.

natural surroundings without disturbing nature's grace.

On the edges of Guan County is **Dujiangyan** (*dūjiāngyàn* 都江堰), one of China's earliest irrigation systems. Begun over 2,200 years ago by Li Bing and his son, the system irrigates the area around the Minjiang River and has been continually expanded. It's still in use today, though with modern equipment instead of stones and bamboo.

The best place to see the system is at **Fulong Temple** (*fúlóng sì* 伏龙寺), built in AD 168 during the Han dynasty in honor of Li Bing and his son. The Guanlan Bridge is the highest point in the temple complex and overlooks the river. In the buildings are artifacts related to Li Bing and in the main hall is a nearly 10-foot-tall (3 m) 5-ton (4.5-metric ton) statue of him that was thrown into the river as a sacrifice.

EMEI SHAN

Emei Shan (*éméi shān* 峨眉山) is the highest of China's four holy Buddhist mountains, rising 10,167 feet (3,099 m) above sea level about 105 miles (170 km) from Chengdu.

Buddhists believe the mountain is home to Samantabhadra – patron of the Lotus Sutra and Bodhisattva of Pervading Goodness.

The route to the summit crosses a lush and diverse landscape with enchanted rock formations, waterfalls and narrow gorges. Climbing upwards you'll encounter countless temples and pavilions. Thousands of pilgrims walk the way to the top – many of them elderly and sporting canes with their pockets filled with incense and ghost money to be burned.

The first temple erected on the mountain was built during the Han dynasty, and during the Ming and Qing dynasties, Emei Shan became one of China's most important centers for Buddhism. Many of its 100 temples fell into disrepair after the fall of the Qing dynasty, but since 1976, much has been done to restore past glory.

By far the most beautiful path to the top follows the southern route, which is also the longest. However, you'll be rewarded with marvelous landscapes and pass by colonies of monkeys. A word of warning: don't monkey around with the monkeys – they can be aggressive and they'll steal right out of your bag if you happen to open it in front of them. But if you act humble and show them your empty hands, they're also smart enough to go look for wealthier prey. Either that or buy a strong walking stick for self-defense.

At 1,804 (550 m) is the **Baoguo Temple** (*bàoguó sì* 报国寺) with a 25-ton bronze bell dating from 1564. The **Qingyin Pavilion** (*qīngyīn gé* 清音阁) offers some of the best views on the mountain. The **Wannian Temple** (*wànnián sì* 万年寺), built in the Jin dynasty houses a a 23-foot-high (7m) bronze figure of Samantabhadra sitting on a six-tusked white elephant weighing 68 tons (62 metric tons). Between **Hongchunping** (*hóngchūnpíng* 洪椿坪), at 3,674 feet (1,120 m), and the **Xianfeng Temple** (*xiānfēng sì* 仙峰寺) you pass by the 99 Curves and the thousands of steps will start to make themselves felt in your muscles – but the splendid views here should reinvigorate even the exhausted. At the **Leidongping Temple** (*léidòngpíng si* 雷洞坪寺) there is a cable car going to the top of the mountain. Continuing on foot from here takes another 2 hours. If the weather cooperates, the vista is divine at the 10,095-foot-high (3,077 m) **Golden Peak** (*jīn dǐng* 金顶). This is the place to relax, meditate and enjoy the sunset. The sunrise is also one of China's legendary experiences, but enjoying this means hiking up at night to be at the peak by sunrise. On Golden Peak, the **Golden Peak Temple** (*jīndǐng huázàng sì* 金顶华藏寺) is a very active place of worship – so transcendence might be lost among the hubbub of pilgrims. The highest point of Emei Shan is the **Ten Thousand Buddha Summit** (*wànfó dǐng* 万佛顶) at 10,167 feet (3,099 m); a monorail can take you there from Golden Peak.

LE SHAN

Le Shan (*lè shān* 乐山) is about 19 miles (30 km) east of Emei Shan. The city's relaxed atmosphere is just the right prescription for sore muscles after some tough hiking. The giant attraction of the city is the world's largest Buddha statue. It's 233 feet (71 m) high and you'll feel infinitely small just compared with one of the Buddha's toenails. The statue is carved out from the rocks at the confluence of the Dadu, Minjiang and Qingyi Rivers. Legend has it the swift currents created by the clash of these rivers sunk innumerable ships and drowned their passengers. In AD 713 the monk Haitong began building the Buddha in the hope this would prevent further disasters. Construction finished 90 years later and the waste rocks from the carving succeeded in calming the waters.

The scale of the Buddha is amazing: his head is 49 feet (15 m) high, the nose is 20 feet (6 m) long and the index fingers are 26 feet (8 m) long. The best views of the Buddha are onboard a boat on the river or from the hills that flank its head. Admission to the Buddha is RMB 40 and opening hours are from 8am to 6pm.

The **Dongfang Fodu Museum** (*dōngfāng fódū* 东方佛都) specializes in copying some of China's most famous Buddhist sites in large size – some even bigger than the original. Here is the world's largest reclining Buddha with a length of 568 feet (173 m). There is also a section of foreign Buddhas from places including Japan, Nepal and India.

The **Mahao Museum** (*máhào yánmù* 麻浩岩墓) offers a glimpse of life during the Han dynasty. These cave tombs were dug high into the cliff over 2,000 years ago and are valuable for their insights into Han society, architecture, religion and politics. The tombs were furnished as typical Han dynasty dwellings for the spirit of the deceased to use in the afterlife and a treasure of relics have survived to this day. ■

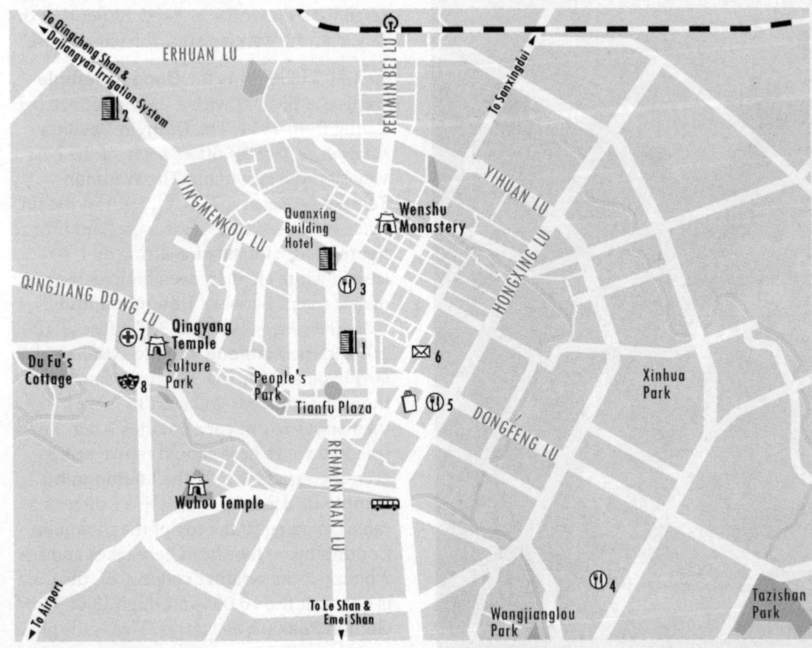

China's first Taoist temple at Qingcheng Shan.

Making Your Trip Easy

Practical Tips

Though Chengdu's weather is temperate, it's also very humid. During the winter, it feels colder than the actual temperature may lead you to believe and in the summer, the humidity can feel overwhelming when combined with the heat – don't forget to bring your sun block and sunglasses.

The temperature at the peak of Emei Shan will be a lot cooler than at the bottom. In the summer, the peak is cool and breezy compared to the blistering heat below. In the winter the temperature can go well below freezing at the peak. If you stay the night on the mountain, it's definitely recommended to bring warm clothing, be sure to bring enough if you're going in the winter.

The admission ticket to the Emei Shan is RMB 120 and some of the temples extra admission tickets are charged. On the mountain, places to go for food are the monasteries, they also offer basic shelter if you plan on spending a night on the mountain.

Transportation

Airport – The airport is approximately 10 miles (16 km) southwest of Chengdu. There are shuttle buses, about RMB 10 and taxis, about RMB 40, to the center of the city. Le Shan is about 75 miles (120 km) from Chengdu and will take about 80 minutes by taxi.

Bus – There are lots of buses from Chengdu to Emei Shan and Le Shan, tickets are from RMB 20 to 38 depending on the kind of bus. Buses from Emei Shan to Le Shan depart every 15 minutes, tickets are RMB 5.

Ferry – From 8am to 5pm there are ferries every ten minutes from the Giant Buddha in Le Shan to Wuyou Temple. Tickets for the tour boat are RMB 30 while the regular ferry is RMB 1.

Quotes

"Enjoying Chengdu is all about enjoying the atmosphere here. The Sichuanese seem to be people who understand how to slow down and enjoy life, whether it be in a teahouse where time suddenly moves slower or at the table feasting on the fantastic food."

Pedi-cab – Pedi-cabs can be flagged down in Chengdu; make sure the driver is properly licensed. Flag-fall is RMB 5, but you'll have to negotiate the price based on distance traveled. There are also many pedi-cabs at Le Shan and Emei Shan; flag-fall is RMB 2 and getting around shouldn't cost more than RMB 10.

Taxi – Taxis in Chengdu are cheap – flag-fall is RMB 5 and moving from one end of the city to the other shouldn't exceed RMB 20. In Emei Shan and Le Shan flag-fall is RMB 3, and fares to most places should be around RMB 10. Taking a taxi from Emei Shan to Le Shan will cost from RMB 50 to 60. Two numbers for taxis at Emei Shan are: ☎ 0833 – 553 4222 or 0833 – 553 1555.

The Best of Chengdu

Du Fu's Cottage 杜甫草堂 *dùfǔ cǎotáng*

✉ southwest of Chengdu City 成都市区内西南
☎ 028 – 8734 5202
🕒 8am to 6pm
¥ 60

Emei Shan Scenic Spot
峨眉山风景区 *éméi shān fēngjǐngqū*

✉ 3.7 miles (6 km) southwest of Emei Shan City 峨眉山市城西南 6 公里处
☎ 0833 – 552 8065, 552 8028
¥ 120
70 – Golden Peak cable car, round trip

Le Shan Giant Buddha
乐山大佛 *lè shān dàfó*

✉ Bizi Jie, Le Shan 乐山市篦子街
☎ 0833 – 230 2131
🕒 7am to 7pm, peak-season
7:30am to 6pm, off-season

Qingcheng Shan & Dujiangyan Irrigation System
青城山都江堰 *qīngchéng shān dūjiāngyàn*

✉ Dujiangyan City, 60km northwest of Chengdu City
成都西北面都江堰市,距成都约 60 千米
¥ 60

Hotels

Sheraton Chengdu Lido Hotel
天府丽都喜来登酒店 *tiānfǔ lìdū xǐláidēng jiǔdiàn* ★★★★★

✉ 15 Yiduan, Renmin Zhong Lu, near the Chengdu City Physical Center
人民中路一段 15 号, 成都市体育中心旁❶
☎ 028 – 8676 8999
¥ 664 – double room
@ www.sheraton-chengdu.com

California Garden Hotel 加州花园酒店 *jiāzhōu huāyuán jiǔdiàn* ★★★★

✉ 258 Shawan Lu, Chengdu International Exhibition Center, Chengdu
成都沙湾路 258 号成都国际会展中心❷
☎ 028 – 8764 9999
¥ 415 – double room
@ www.ecccn.com

Emei Shan Grand Hotel
峨眉山大酒店 *éméi shān dàjiǔdiàn* ★★★★

✉ located inside the Baoguo Temple Scenic Area, Emei Shan 峨眉山报国寺景区
☎ 0833 – 552 6888
¥ 300 – double room, peak-season
216 – double room, off-season

Jinhaitang Grand Hotel
金海棠大酒店 *jīnhǎitáng dàjiǔdiàn* ★★★★

✉ 99 Haitang Lu, Le Shan
乐山市海棠路 99 号
☎ 0833 – 212 2666
¥ 418 – double room
@ www.jht-hotel.com

Emei Shan Jinding Hotel 峨眉山金顶大酒店 *éméi shān jīndǐng dàjiǔdiàn* ★★★

✉ located in Golden Peak Scenic Area, Emei Shan 峨眉山金顶景区
☎ 0833 – 509 8088
¥ 464 – double room, peak-season
348 – double room, off-season

Food & Restaurants

Sichuan cuisine is in a league of its own; the food seems so much in contrast to the slow ambience of the teahouses. Sichuan is the center of spicy hot dishes – eating here is a passionate affair, even more so than in the rest of China. Almost every dish is mixed up with a ferocious package of burning chilies and the special Sichuan pepper that leaves your mouth numb. Some of the most famous Chinese dishes have their origin here: kung pao chicken (*gōngbǎo jīdīng* 宫保鸡丁), stir-fried chicken with peanuts and chili added with a heavy hand, is world famous but there's nothing like eating it in a Sichuan restaurant. Mapo tofu (*mápó dòufu* 麻婆豆腐), stewed tofu with minced pork and of course chili, is another favorite. The curiously named dish "ants climbing up a tree" (*máyǐ shàng shù* 蚂蚁上树) is vermicelli with ground pork and, guess what, chili. When you see the dish you'll understand. It might not be the most appetizing name for a dish but it still tastes great.

What is really going to test your threshold for pain is another local specialty: hot pot (*huǒguō* 火锅), literally "fire pot." Imagine fondue but with a serious kick to it. All kinds of thinly sliced meats and vegetables are put into a fiery soup, shiny red from chilies, garlic, onions and Sichuan peppers. This is what the Sichuanese treat themselves to, especially in the winter as it's bound to warm you up. Hot pot restaurants are normally very lively places – probably because of all the beer that's downed to keep the pain from the chili at bay. It's a shock to the senses and your taste buds will be tingling long after the meal, but don't worry. Other delightfully spicy dishes include the meaty *fuqi feipian* (夫妻肺片), *dandan mian* (担担面) a spicy noodle, *huiguo rou* (回锅肉) a spicy dish of fried pork slices and beef stewed in a spicy broth (*shuǐzhǔ niúròu* 水煮牛肉). You can always head back to a teahouse and relax again after the ordeal and soothe your tongue with green tea. The spices seem to have affected the temperament of the Sichuan people. More emotion is displayed openly here than in any other place in China.

Pearl dumplings (*zhēnzhū yuán* 珍珠圆) are Le Shan's most famous snack. When Emperor Kangxi visited Le Shan, he downed five plates of them in one sitting and dubbed them "Pearl Dumplings." Also try Zhou's chicken (*zhōu jīròu* 周鸡肉), a yummy cold chicken dish invented by a Mr. Zhou. A good place to eat is He Jie Xiaochi

Monks perform their religious ceremonies in a temple on Emei Shan.

Jie, a food street that features many restaurants and food vendors.

RESTAURANTS

Baguo Buyi 巴国布衣
Sichuan dishes with a modern twist.
✉ 20 Siduan, Renmin Nan Lu, Chengdu 成都人民南路四段 20 号
☎ 028 – 8553 1688
◷ 10am to 10:30pm

Chen Mapo Tofu 陈麻婆豆腐
Specializes in *mapo tofu*.
✉ 81 Kehua Lu, Wuhou District, Chengdu 成都武侯区科华路 81 号❸
☎ 028 – 8523 3655

Gongshi Xiba Doufu Dajiudian 龚氏西霸豆腐大酒店
Great tofu dishes.
✉ 121 Dong Da Jie, Zhongqu, Le Shan 乐山市中区东大街 121 号
☎ 0833 – 210 0848
◷ 10am to 10pm

Honglilai Jiulou 红利来酒楼
Traditional Sichuan dishes, specializes in Zhou's chicken.
✉ 268 Jiading Zhong Lu, Zhongqu, Le Shan 乐山市中区嘉定中路 268 号
☎ 0833 – 213 7988
◷ 10am to 10pm

Hongxing Jiujia 红杏酒家
✉ 289 Shuhan Lu, Jinniu District, Chengdu 成都金牛区蜀汉路 289 号

☎ 028 – 8752 6846

Long Chaoshou 龙抄手
Specializes in wonton, RMB 15 to 25 for a set meal.
✉ Chun Xi Lu, Chengdu 成都春熙路❺
🕒 8am to 10:30pm

Nanguo Yuzhou 南国渔舟
Specializes in fish hot pot.
✉ Binjiang Lu, Le Shan 乐山市滨江路
☎ 0833 – 298 6355
🕒 10am to 10pm

Rongle Yuan 荣乐园
Specializes in traditional Sichuan dishes.
✉ 169 Liangui Nan Lu, Chengdu 成都莲桂南路 169 号❹
☎ 028 – 453 5800
🕒 10am to 10:30pm

Souvenirs

The most famous local handicrafts include Sichuan brocade, lacquerware, embroidery and bamboo covered porcelain. Where hair-fine bamboo strands are plaited around ceramic ware to form an outer covering, encasing the ceramic vessel in a bamboo sheath. The pottery and bamboo seem to be all of a piece, an effect that is quite striking. Prices for brocade pieces vary from RMB 80 to 200 depending on the size and design. Small bamboo covered porcelain vases are RMB 30 to 50 while bigger ones go for RMB 500 to 600. Lacquerware is anywhere from RMB 120 to 400 depending on quality. You can find these crafts at Songxianqiao Art City (*sòngxiānqiáo yìshù chéng* 送仙桥艺术城 ❽, ☎ 8734 6051) – one of the biggest handicrafts market in town, it's across from Qingyang Temple. In the evening on Renmin Nan Lu, opposite the Jingjiang Hotel, is an antique market. Just don't expect the items to be genuine antiques – even if the seller insists. But there are beautiful things to be bought – woodcarvings and calligraphy.

The area just east of the central plaza around Dong Da Jie you'll find Chengdu's fanciest shops. There are big malls and clothing shops. In the same area, around Chunxi Lu, is a night market.

If Chengdu is as close as you will get to Tibet, which borders Sichuan on the west, then head for the Tibetan Market. All kinds of Tibetan trinkets are sold at this market in front of the Wuhou Temple (*wǔhóu cí* 武侯祠) in the southwestern part of the city.

Other Information

POST OFFICES

Chengdu Shuwa Jie Post Office
成都暑袜街邮局
✉ Shuwa Jie, Chengdu 成都市暑袜街❻
☎ 028 – 8674 2685

HOSPITALS

Emei Shan City First People's Hospital
峨眉山市第一人民医院
✉ Santai Shan Jie, Emei Shan 峨眉山市三台山街
☎ 0833 – 554 3819

Le Shan City People's Hosptial
乐山市人民医院
✉ 76 Baita Jie, Zhongqu, Le Shan 乐山市中区白塔街 76 号
☎ 0833 – 211 9328

Sichuan Province People's Hospital
四川省人民医院
✉ 2 Dongduan, Chunxi Lu, Chengdu 成都春煦路东段 2 号❼
☎ 028 – 8666 7223, 8665 0186

COMPLAINT HOTLINES

☎ General: 028 – 8662 2065 in Chengdu
0833 – 553 3355 in Emei Shan
0833 – 211 0226 in Le Shan
☎ Taxi: 028 – 8663 6630 in Chengdu
0833 – 553 4222, 553 1555 in Emei Shan
0833 – 243 0017 in Le Shan

TOURISM INFORMATION WEBSITE

@ www.ems517.com

Entertainment

Shufeng Yayun 蜀风雅韵
Sichuan Opera and acrobatics.
✉ inside Wenhua Park, 23 Qintai Lu, Chengdu 成都市琴台路 23 号,文化公园内
☎ 028 – 8776 4530
🕒 8pm to 9:30pm
¥ 150, 180, 220

Shunxing Old Teahouse 顺兴老茶馆
This teahouse features Sichuan cuisine and traditional shows.
✉ 3/F International Exhibition Center, 258 Shawan Lu Chengdu 成都沙湾路 258 号国际会展中心三楼
☎ 028 – 8769 3202
🕒 8pm
¥ 48

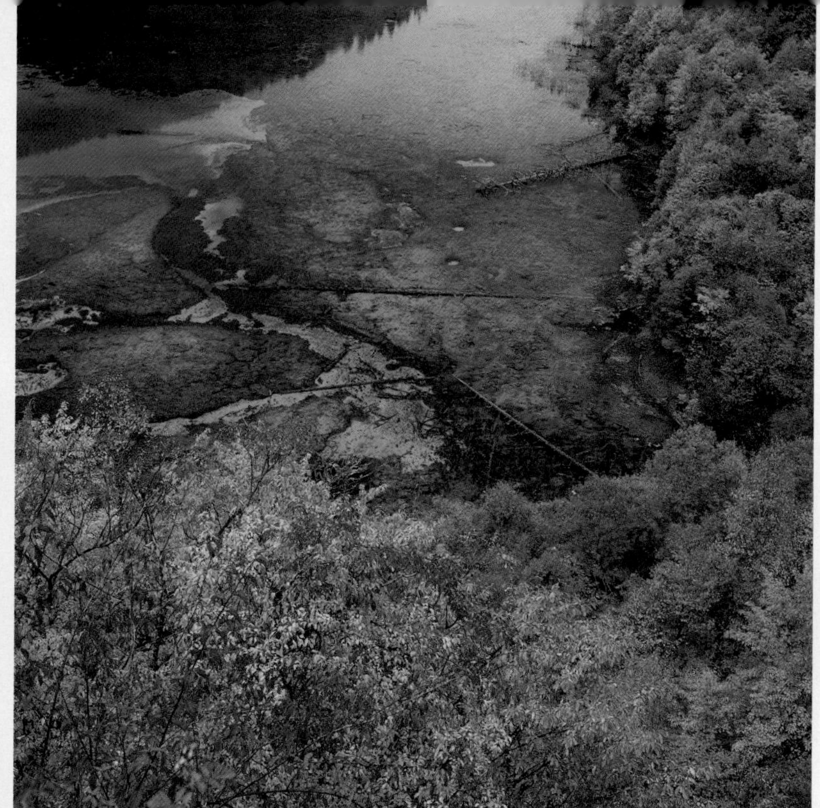

Jiuzhaigou's scenery is Mother Nature at her best.

Jiuzhaigou & Huanglong's Picturesque Parklands

Area Code 0837

Heritage: Jiuzhaigou, Huanglong

Sprinkled with an incredible palette of natural colors, Sichuan's UNESCO listed nature reserves are home to rare animals and plants as well as the Baima Tibetan minority.

Jiuzhaigou's patchwork of shimmering lakes was discovered when scientists trailing some pandas, observing their habitat and migratory patterns, followed the pandas into this scenic wonderland. Scientists believe the lakes were formed at a time when the earth was between ice ages. As the global climate warmed up, calcium carbonate in the water – the compound is the stuff of chalk and limestone – aggregated around other existing objects and eventually formed the milky white, lunar shapes we see today in Jiuzhaigou's lakes. But in fact the sheer

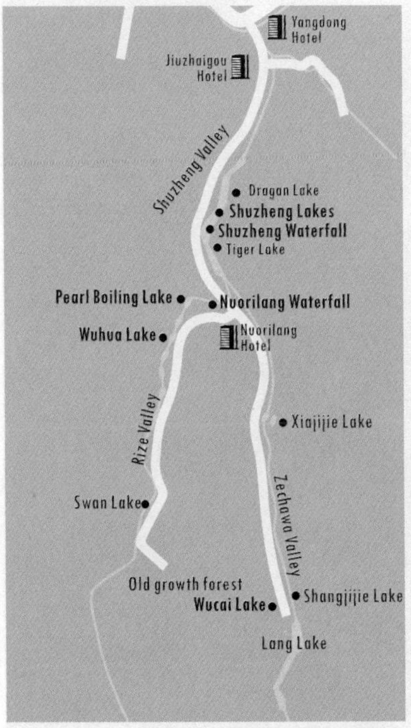

beauty of the lakes and the vibrancy of the colors defy explanation, and the scenery leaves most breathless.

Cut into the mountains in the shape of a "Y," three valleys, Shuzheng, Rize and Zechawa, extend over 30 miles (50 km) into three main zones. Pathways and roads have been laid in the valley areas and buses ferry tourists from one section of the park to another. The average height of the hills overlooking the valley is around 5,900 feet (1,800 m), but the elevations here are gentle, making for easy strolls as well as strenuous, longer hikes. Nearest to the park's entrance lies the **Shuzheng Lakes** (*shùzhèng qúnhǎi* 树正群海). Of the 114 lakes in Jiuzhaigou, only **Shuzheng**, **Rize Valley**, **Zechawa** and **Zharu Valley** are open to tourism. Shuzheng is the largest of the lake areas, so if time is limited, this is where you should spend it.

Legend says that the lake water is colored by the substance of fairy maidens. The amazing hues of the lakes vary from blue and green to light brown, dark gray and light purple. According to science, the dazzling colors come from the aquatic plants in the lakes, the different temperatures of the water and how it refracts light and the amount of calcium carbonate in the water. Whatever the reason, there's no doubting that the gods and nature have been exceptionally kind to Jiuzhaigou.

Jiuzhaigou is indeed all about color. Set in the **Aba Autonomous Region** (*ābà zàngzúqiāngzú zìzhìzhōu* 阿坝藏族羌族自治州), it may take more effort to see than most of Sichuan's other sights – but understatement is impossible when it comes to natural scenery. Listed by UNESCO as a World Natural Heritage, there is an airport in nearby Songpan, cutting to less than an hour the 280-mile (450 km) from the provincial capital of Chengdu. The rising number of tourists at the site may be expected to rise much faster with the direct air connection but Jiuzhaigou is large enough to allow for introspective hikes off the more-beaten paths.

The name Jiuzhaigou refers to the nine Tibetan villages scattered throughout the valley. The **Baima** tribe of Tibetans live here – farmers and hunters, they grow corn on terraced mountainsides and farm bison. The Baima are distinct from other Tibetans in that they have their own script for their language. They have their own religious writings too and worship mountain gods as opposed to being part of broader spectrum of the Tibetan Buddhism.

Quotes

"It's like visiting an art gallery of nature. There are so many bright, natural colors – that's the most awe-striking feature of the place."

"To really appreciate the serenity of the forests and the higher hills and mountains, you need to walk out on your own, and that's something you can't really do in a day."

RAMBLING THE SHUZHENG LAKESIDE PATHS

It's impossible to pick a favorite among the many lakes, considering the natural beauty of Jiuzhaigou. Shuzheng, the largest and most accessible of the three lake-specked valleys, is an ideal place to begin your exploration. Spread out over hundreds of acres, the main attractions in Shuzheng Valley are the **Shuzheng** and **Nuorilang Lakes** (*nuòrìlǎng qúnhǎi* 诺日朗群海), **Dragon Lake** (*wòlóng hǎi* 卧龙海) and **Spark Lake** (*huǒhuā hǎi* 火花海). The first two are stepped lakes, dropping in stages over mountain ledges with crystal clear water cascading from one tier to the next. Water music rarely sounds as sweet.

The milky yellow dike at the center of Shuzheng lake is clearly visible through the clear water, looking like a dragon crouching below the lake. **Shuzheng Waterfall** meanwhile bangs and crashes its way down the hillside before plummeting into the lake.

All around, forests of many colors are reflected in the water. Many endangered animals such as the giant panda live in those woodlands, out of the reach of all but the most energetic tourists. Tastefully created wooden paths cut through the lower slopes of the valley and comfortable pavilions offer a respite to weary legs. On less crowded days they're also perfect picnic points.

Calcium carbonate coatings on dead trees on the bed of the lake resemble abstract art creations in their twisted, yellow shapes. Add to the color mix the turquoise, saffron and crimson colors of vegetation in the lake and the tree leaves reflected on its surface and you've got an image more colorful and pretty than a George Seurat painting. Sketch pads can often be spotted here, mostly on the knees of foreign visitors – there's plenty of justification for taking an easel and box of paints up here

Worthy of at least a photo are the small pockets of wildflowers, mostly

Crystal clear waters reflect the autumn trees.

rhododendrons, which cluster in Jiuzhaigou's forests. There's also an abundance of wild fruit: apples, hawthorn berries, apricots, strawberries and other, exotic-looking berries. The plentiful bamboo shoots feed a precious resident, the panda. Walking through the lower forest areas jealousy is a reasonable reaction to the idyll enjoyed by the panda and his hundreds of neighbors who live on protected ground here.

Leaving the lakes, follow the trails leading to the Shuzheng stockade or village, home to a settlement of Baima. The paths are lined with prayer flags of variously colored cloth with Buddhist religious scripture printed on them. At the end of a day's walking, a bowl of noodles and several cups of Tibetan buttered tea, made with yak milk, will give you a shot of energy, enough to view the setting sun as the day draws to a close.

Top: One of Chengdu's most famous loveable citizens, the giant panda.
Bottom: A small jade pool at Huanglong.

HUANGLONG

Praised for its colorful limestone ponds, **Huanglong** (*huáng lóng* 黄龙), which means Yellow Dragon Mountain, lies in the south part of Min Shan in Songpan County. Situated in the northwest of Sichuan Province and 79 miles (128 km) south of Jiuzhaigou, the Huanglong Valley is edged by snow-capped peaks and glaciers. An incredible biodiversity of flora and fauna thrives here alongside spectacular limestone formations, waterfalls and hot springs. The area also has a population of endangered animals, including the giant panda and the Sichuan golden snub-nosed monkey.

Making it onto the UNESCO World Heritage Site listings in 1992, Huanglong is sectored into two gorges, Huanglong and **Muni** (*mùní* 牟尼). The Huanglong part of the park is watered by tributaries of the **Fujiang River**, which run down Snow Mountain Ridge, feeding hundreds of small lakes and ponds. The rocks on the valley's sides have been twisted into weird shapes by snow and rain, as have the rocks lying beneath the clear lake water. Most visitors first concentrate on the Huanglong section of the park. Dotted with ponds and patterned like a dragon, Huanglong Valley cuts its way through Min Shan.

More than half of the Huanglong zone is forested, with mountain pines mixing with broadleaf trees, flowers, shrubbery and meadow grasslands. Sitting atop the parkland, **Snow Mountain Peak** (*xuěbǎodǐng* 雪宝鼎) is permanently snow-covered and looks a daunting climb. Equally daunting are

▶▶ The Giant Panda

The giant panda is an endangered animal found only in western China. Because of human encroachment, the panda's habitat is now reduced to six isolated patches, mainly in Sichuan. Pandas are related to bears, though they are significantly different in many ways.

Bamboo is the main source of food for pandas and they spend at least 12 hours a day eating. They have to – bamboo is a poor source of nutrition for pandas, so they eat as much as 40 pounds (18 kg) of it a day. One reason the habitat range of the panda is limited is because they only eat specific species of bamboo found within their home range, and the areas are becoming progressively smaller.

The lifespan of pandas in the wild is unknown, but pandas in captivity live 14 to 20 years. The female panda begins to breed when it's around six or seven years old and usually delivers only one or two cubs. The average weight of a newborn panda is only 3.5 ounces (100 g) compared to the 330 pounds (150 kg) of its mother. The newborn cub is completely helpless; it has no fur and can't open its eyes and will be completely dependent on its mother for the next few months.

Today the number of pandas in the wild is uncertain, but estimates put the number at no more than a thousand. The Chinese government has enacted laws and funded conservation efforts to protect the pandas. Breeding centers and research stations have been set up and studies continue to explore ways to protect the species. In 1961, the World Wildlife Fund adopted the panda as its emblem to highlight the issues of world wildlife conservation.

the spectacular cliffs overhanging the Fujiang River's drive through the **Danyun Gorge** (*dānyún xiá* 丹云峡). Algae and growth in the little lakes below turn the water a rainbow of colors: orange, yellow, green and blue. Other karst features include long limestone shoals, fan-shaped slopes of limestone deposited and covered by a thin layer of flowing water.

The **Muni Gully** (*mùní gōu* 牟尼沟) subdivision consists of two parallel small gullies, **Zhaga** (*zhāgǎ* 扎嘎) and **Erdaohai** (*èrdàohǎi* 二道海). The hot springs in **Pearl Boiling Lake** (*zhǔzhū hú* 煮珠湖) simmer at 70°F (21°C) in what amounts to a massively sized swimming pool. The waters of both springs have high mineral contents and are said to have important medicinal properties. Muni Gully also contains a number of very attractive lakes and the **Zhaga Waterfall** (*zhāgǎ pùbù* 扎嘎瀑布).

Because of its relatively pristine state, the forests at Huanglong are home to hundreds of bird species. On a walk into the higher reaches of the hills, away from the hordes of tourists below, one hears a cacophony of different birdcalls. Pandas meanwhile are found at four to five specific locations within the site, though visitors should tread carefully and slowly if they're hoping to catch a glimpse. Much harder to spot is Sichuan golden snub-nosed monkey, an endangered species that hides out in Huanglong's more undisturbed woodlands.

As in Jiuzhaigou, but perhaps with their presence even more low key, there are also plenty of indicators of Tibetan religion, culture and folklore in Huanglong. A pair of small stone pagodas stand near the entrance to the park that date from the Ming dynasty. Nearby the **Huanglong Temple** (*huánglóng sì* 黄龙寺) and the ruins of a much older temple still draw plenty of worshippers. Also in the vicinity, **Body Washing Waterfall** (*xǐshēn pùbù* 洗身瀑布) is said to have healing properties for those who bathe in its waters.

Huanglong Town is a medium sized Tibetan village close to the center of the main Huanglong subdivision. Local Tibetan herdsmen grazing their livestock and cultivating the land nearby make for great subjects if you're slinging a camera. The larger town of **Songpan** (*sōngpān* 松潘) cuts Huanglong off from the Muni gully subdivision and is worth exploring in its own right if only for its stout town walls, Tibetan architecture and colorful vitality. It's also a good spot for souvenir hunting. ■

Making Your Trip Easy

Practical Tips

Like the scenery, the climate at Jiuzhaigou and Huanglong is alpine. Think damp and cold in the high mountains and cool and dry in the river valleys. Autumn begins in early-October and is the best time to visit because the scenery is at its most colorful. It's important to be prepared when up in the mountainous areas, be sure to bring plenty of food, water and enough clothing.

Around mid-July is the Huanglong Temple Fair (*huánglóng miàohui* 黄龙庙会) in the Huanglong Scenic Area. Ethnic Qiang and Tibetans dress in their traditional clothes in honor of the god of Huanglong (*huánglóng shénrén* 黄龙神人).

Get your picture taken at the ticket office when you buy your ticket – this will allow you to buy the next day's ticket for RMB 40.

Transportation

Airport – Jiuzhaigou's airport has connections to Chengdu and China's major cities.

Bus – New and refurbished roads have made Jiuzhaigou more accessible, but bus service isn't comprehensive. It's best to arrange bus tickets through your hotel or travel agent.

Taxi – Taking a taxi from Jiuzhaigou County to the scenic area is about RMB 10.

The Best of Jiuzhaigou & Huanglong

All scenic spots in Jiuzhaigou and Huanglong should not be missed. Try your best to enjoy every one of them if you have enough time and energy.

Huanglong 黄龙 *huánglóng*

✉ Se'ercuozhai, Songpan County 松潘县瑟尔嵯寨

☎ 724 9108, 724 9012

🕒 8am to 7pm

¥ 200, peak-season
80, off-season

The interconnected pools of Huanglong.

Jiuzhaigou 九寨沟 *jiǔzhàigōu*

✉ Zhangzha Town 漳扎镇

☎ 773 9444, 773 9777-292

🕒 6:30am to 7pm

¥ 220, peak-season
80, off-season
90, shuttle bus pass within the park

Hotels

Sheraton Jiuzhaigou Resort
九寨沟喜来登国际大酒店 *jiǔzhàigōu xǐláidēng guójì dàjiǔdiàn* ★★★★★

✉ Zhangzha Town,Jiuzhaigou 九寨沟漳扎镇

☎ 773 9988

¥ 1,000 – double room, peak-season
500 – double room, off-season

@ www.sheraton.com

Jiulong Hotel
九龙宾馆 *jiǔlóng bīnguǎn* ★★★

✉ Pengfeng Village, Zhangzha Town, Jiuzhaigou 九寨沟漳扎镇彭丰村

☎ 773 4155

¥ 780 – double room, peak-season
280 – double room, off-season

Jiuxin Hotel
九鑫山庄 *jiǔxīn shānzhuāng* ★★★

✉ Zhangzha Town, Jiuzhaigou 九寨沟漳扎镇

☎ 773 9588

¥ 680 – double room, peak-season
380 – double room, off-season

Jiuzhaigou Hotel
九寨沟宾馆 *jiǔzhàigōu bīnguǎn* ★★★

✉ Zhangzha Town, Jiuzhaigou 九寨沟漳扎镇

☎ 773 4859

¥ 400 – double room, peak-season
200 – double room, off-season

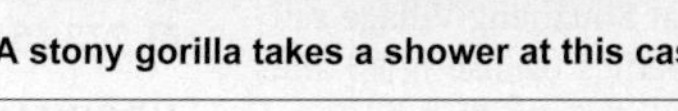

A stony gorilla takes a shower at this cascading waterfall.

Xingyu International Hotel
星宇国际大酒店 *xīngyǔ guójì dàjiǔdiàn*

✉ Huodiba, Longkang Village, Zhangzha Town, Jiuzhaigou 九寨沟漳扎镇龙康村火地坝

☎ 773 9222

¥ 410 – double room, peak-season

Memorable Experiences

Getting into the fresh mountain air, gazing at snowcapped peaks.

Gazing down on the amazing colors in the lakes, surrounded by a thousand differently colored plants and leaves.

Strolling through the Tibetan villages, experiencing Tibetan architecture and religious imagery.

Taking care of the yaks is a yearlong chore.

288 – double room, off-season

Food & Restaurants

Culinary variety isn't great and prices are steeper than in the city, and serious nature lover's intent on staying a few days at the park should stock up at a supermarket before setting out. Food in this area is mainly Sichuan, with variations on the theme. The food inside the park is simple comfort cooking; the China Travel Hotel is a good choice and features comfortable dining rooms offering local fare. Outside the park are hotel restaurants offering more choices. Tibetan restaurants at Shuzheng Village sell the local staple of noodles (*lāmiàn* 拉面) and Tibetan buttered tea (*sūyóuchá* 酥油茶), a local favorite.

Songpan's twisting alleys are jammed throughout the day with food stalls, many of them selling meat kebabs. Sichuan hotpots and rice dishes are found in nearly every restaurant. Other local specialties include *ci ba* (*tǔdòu cíbā* 土豆糍粑) a potato snack, shredded potato pancakes with vegetable (*càibǐng* 菜饼). Yak steaks (*gāoyuán máoniúròu* 高原牦牛肉) also make good eating.

Souvenirs

The most common souvenirs at Jiuzhaigou are Tibetan trinkets, but be aware of the quality, and also be prepared to bargain. Necklaces and bracelets usually bear religious symbols or local script and make unique gifts. Musical instruments and traditional Tibetan clothing are also available; yak jackets are perhaps the most fetching item.

At all of the villages in Jiuzhaigou, vendors sell the scarf-like *Hada*, a symbol of friendship given to guests on entering a Tibetan home. Usually white, more colorful versions can be purchased. Wait until you're in Songpan for a wider range of traditional Tibetan products in one of the many stalls lining the streets there.

Other Information

POST OFFICES

Zhangzha County Post Office 漳扎镇邮局
✉ Zhangzha Town 漳扎镇
☎ 773 4546

HOSPITALS

There are patrols through the park in case of emergencies.
☎ 773 9309

The closest hospital to Jiuzhaigou is 25 miles (40 km) away. Ask park or hotel staff if you need aid.

COMPLAINT HOTLINES

☎ General: 96927

TOURISM INFORMATION WEBSITE

@ www.jiuzhaigouvalley.com

Entertainment

Traditional Tibetan Dance and Song Performance 藏羌歌舞表演
✉ Sheraton Jiuzhaigou Resort, Zhangzha Town, Jiuzhaigou County
九寨沟漳扎镇九寨沟喜来登国际大酒店内
☎ 773 9988
¥ 180

Guiyang's Karst and Waterfalls

Area Code 0851

Hidden amongst jagged karst (limestone) mountains, misty waterfalls and undulating hills, **Guiyang** is a gem hidden under layers of gorgeous scenery, and with each step, a new vista emerges.

Guizhou Province is in China's southwest on the Yunnan-Guizhou Plateau over 3,280 feet (1,000 m) above sea level. The mountainous terrain has diligently kept much of the province's early history a mystery. This mystique is heightened by the province's misshapen land. Craggy rock formations poke out of the rough earth, rivers are squeezed by narrow mountains and form swift rapids. One of China's most spectacular waterfalls can be found in Anshun, a small city not far from Guiyang.

A local saying goes, "It doesn't go more than three days without raining and you won't find more than a square meter of flat land," and despite being agriculturally poor because of the mountainous terrain, it's the same mountains that make the province so appealing for the visitor. The rugged landscape is constantly changing: one moment there are expansive mountains that stretch to the clouds then around the next bend are waterfalls splashing down sheer

Jiaxiu Tower, Guiyang's former center of study.

cliffs with rivers that spill into raging rapids past old growth forests and into underground caverns. After a day of exploring, chances are you'll be tired, but the visual spectacle will keep your eyes begging for more.

To emphasize Guizhou's former isolation, a legend goes that the emperor of the Han dynasty, one of China's most celebrated periods of development, sent an envoy to Yelang, the largest of the many small kingdoms that inhabited the area. The king, in his ignorance, asked the envoy of the mighty Han, "Which kingdom is larger?"

Bulls going head to head.

Today Guizhou remains off the radar of most tourists to China despite having extensive transportation links that make traveling to this relatively unspoiled beauty no harder than to other destinations in China.

Guizhou is now home to 48 ethnic minorities out of China's 56 ethnic groups. The Miao, Dong, Yi, Zhuang, Yao, and Buyi all inhabit the land. Their bright festivals and villages offer plenty of scope for exploration.

The provincial capital is Guiyang, which also serves as the province's transportation center. In Chinese, Guiyang means "precious sunshine" and it's an appropriate name for a city that rests 3,514 feet (1,071 m) above sea level. Even though the city sits amongst the clouds, it's protected from harsh weather by surrounding mountains.

The city may seem like any developing Chinese city, but spend an afternoon exploring the narrow lanes set with large stone steps, upturned eaves at every corner, gray tiles framing weathered wooden doors on aged homes and it becomes clear that the city is a boon for those who seek a city that remains true to its past.

A short 10.5 miles (17 km) from Guiyang is **Huaxi Park** (*huāxī gōngyuán* 花溪公园), whose softly rolling hills, vivid flowers, crystal clear pools and silent pavilions have made it one of the city's star attractions. The centerpiece is a small clear stream that runs through the park, allowing visitors to indulge in rowing their boats gently down a stream.

Various ethnic minority festivals fill the year. During these times of celebration people put on their most colorful clothing and gather for a big party. Many of these festivals are musical affairs featuring an intricate instrument made of many reed tubes glued together. Dancing and singing are also prevalent, with many of the numbers originating in ancient courtship rituals that formed the local version of Valentine's Day.

The wonderfully large **Qianling Park** (*qiánlíng gōngyuán* 黔灵公园) immediately captures the visitor's imagination. Once you

Memorable Experiences

Strolling through the Water-Curtain Cave and touching the wall of water as it roars down the falls.

Spending a day wandering through Guiyang's many parks during a festival day and chatting with the locals dressed in their best.

Sightseeing through Guiyang's many ethnic villages and getting a close up look of real village life that has continued undisturbed through the centuries.

go through its main gate, a hypnotic weave of green mountains refuses to release its grip. Old growth trees continue to cast their shadows over clear springs and distorted rocks as they have been doing for thousands of years. More than 1,500 species of trees, flowers and medicinal herbs grow in the mountains. Groups of monkeys and birds perch themselves on swaying branches as visitors climb the **Nine Bend Trail** (*jiǔqū jìng* 九曲径) to the **Hongfu Temple** (*hóngfú sì* 弘福寺). Built in 1672, the temple is one of Guizhou's most important Buddhist temples. Thousands of images of Buddha can be seen on the cliffs not far from the temple and the peak of **Qianling Shan** (*qiánlíng shān* 黔灵山) offers a panoramic view of Guiyang. One unique feature is the **Chuiluo Wall** (*chuīluó bì* 吹螺壁), which is pocked with many small holes. Blowing on the holes creates a sound and the locals claim that the louder that sound, the longer you'll live.

On the Fuyu Bridge that crosses the Nanming River is the **Jiaxiu Tower** (*jiǎxiù lóu* 甲秀楼). A local official built this tower in 1598 to encourage local scholars succeed in the imperial examinations. The three-story tower rises 66 feet (20 m) high and is decorated with green tiles, red pillars, engraved windows and white stone parapets, which is more than enough to inspire any would-be scholar to academic heights.

In Anshun, 56 miles (90 km) from Guiyang, is the **Huangguoshu Waterfalls** (*huángguǒshù pùbù* 黄果树瀑布), which have been deservedly called Guizhou's most impressive scenic sight. Only recently discovered, the area consist features 18 waterfalls, caves, karst mountains and deep pools. The Huangguoshu Waterfalls is the best known of the 18 waterfalls and depending on the season, the water flow can be spectacular. This 3.7-mile-long (6 km) stretch makes a great day trip and the roaring water can be heard long before actually reaching the falls. The falls plunge 243 feet (74 m) into the **Rhinoceros Pool** (*xīniú tán* 犀牛潭), and standing beside the pool is the **Wangshui Pavilion** (*wàngshuǐ tíng* 望水亭), which is a great place to get an up-close view of the crashing water. The **Guanpu Pavilion** (*guānpù tíng* 观瀑亭) offers a panorama view of the falls. The 440-foot-long (134 m) **Water-Curtain Cave** offers a unique view of the falls from behind. The power of the falls is best viewed during the rainy season when the mist from the cascading water envelopes the Huangguoshu Village.

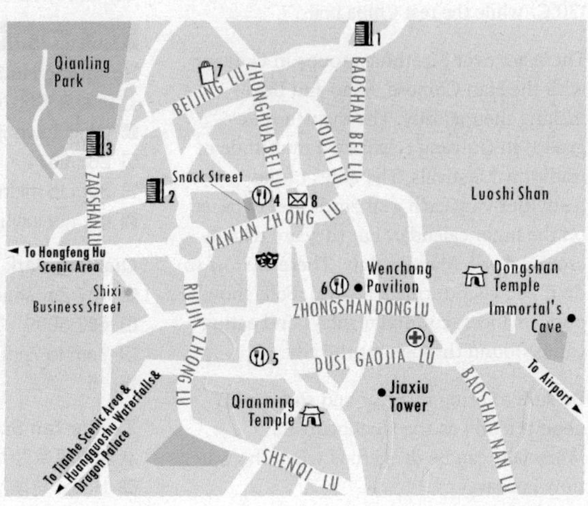

A typical Miao village.

About 17 miles (27 km) from Anshun and conveniently located on the way to the Huangguoshu Waterfalls is China's longest karst river cave complex,coupled with the 3-mile-long (5 km) **Dragon Palace** (*lónggōng* 龙宫). A boat ride into the cave takes visitors past an underground landscape of spiky stalactites and stalagmites. Underground falls and imaginatively named sights await within the cave and the surrounding scenic area.

The traditional villages also offer a relaxed getaway from the city life. Some tour packages will include these villages with various performances and handicrafts demonstrations, but for a true glimpse of village life head to one of the villages on your own. Here visitors will see stone houses, water buffalos at work and farmers in their fields. Friendly villagers are accustomed to tourists and will offer toothy smiles and handicrafts for sale. ■

Making Your Trip Easy

Practical Tips

Guiyang's weather is mild throughout the year and the average temperature is a balmy 59°F (15°C) with winter temperatures dipping to 39°F (4°C) and summers rarely exceeding 86°F (30°C) while the rest China boils.

There are over 30 ethnic groups in Guiyang with the Han Chinese, Miao and Buyi making the majority. The many ethnic groups in Guiyang celebrate a multitude of traditional festivals. The dates of the festivities vary each year since they're based on the lunar calendar, but they are usually around April, May and July. There are lots to do if you visit during a festival. Folk show performances, cultural displays and eating can be found throughout the city.

Be sure to bring raingear and shoes with good traction as the Huangguoshu Waterfalls can be dangerous when the water flow is heavy.

Transportation

Airport – The airport is about 7.5 miles (12 km) east of the city and is 17 minutes away.

Taxi – Taxis are RMB 8 at flag-fall during the day and RMB 10 after 10pm.

The Best of Guiyang

Hongfeng Hu Scenic Area
红枫湖风景区 *hóngfēnghú fēngjǐngqū*
✉ Qing Town 清镇
☎ 262 0671
🕒 8am to midnight
¥ 40, not including boat rides

Qianling Park 黔灵公园 *qiánlíng gōngyuán*
✉ 187 Zaoshan Lu 枣山路 187 号
☎ 682 3039
🕒 7am to 7pm
¥ 15

Tianhe Tan Scenic Area
天河潭风景区 *tiānhétán fēngjǐngqū*
✉ Huaxi 花溪

Quotes

"The scenery here is really cool, it's so diverse. Mountains, trees and waterfalls with these tiny villages. I'm glad we came here before it becomes all touristy."

☎ 330 8014
🕒 8am to 7pm
¥ 50, includes a water cave cruise

Hotels

Miracle Hotel Guiyang 贵阳神奇大酒店
guìyáng shénqí dàjiǔdiàn ★★★★
✉ 1 Beijing Lu, Yunyan District
云岩区北京路 1 号❶
☎ 677 1888
¥ 473 – double room, peak-season
415 – double room, off-season
@ www.miraclehotels.com

Qianling Hotel
黔灵大酒店 *qiánlíng dàjiǔdiàn* ★★★
✉ 255 Beijing Lu, Yunyan District
云岩区北京路 255 号❸
☎ 827 1888
¥ 390 – double room, peak-season
258 – double room, off-season

Shanlin Hotel
山林大酒店 *shānlín dàjiǔdiàn* ★★★
✉ 118 Shanlin Lu, Yunyan District
云岩区山林路 118 号❷
☎ 652 3000
¥ 382 – double room, peak-season
315 – double room, off-season

Food & Restaurants

Southwest China's cuisine is spicy with a tinge of sour. Most of the cuisine comes from the mountain bounty. Exotic fruits are plentiful; try the local pears (*cìlí* 刺梨) and Chinese gooseberries (*míhóutáo* 猕猴桃).

Tofu balls (*léijiā dòufu yuánzi* 雷家豆腐圆子) are deep-fried flavorful egg-sized balls of tofu, crispy on the outside and tender on the inside, they're usually served as an appetizer. Spicy chicken (*làzi jī* 辣子鸡), is colorfully covered in dried chili peppers, but it's not as spicy as it looks. China doesn't have many salads, so take the opportunity to try the refreshing *zhe'ergen* (*liángbàn zhé'ěrgēn* 凉拌折耳根).

Head over to the snack street (*xiǎochī jiē* 小吃街) and eat your way up and down the street. The vendors here sell all kinds of local delicacies. The street is only open in the evenings, but it's open until late.

RESTAURANTS

Baijiyan 百鸡宴
✉ 24 Xinhua Lu 新华路 24 号
☎ 551 2646

Daya Yuan 大雅园
One of the most famous restaurants in the city, specializes in seafood and wild game.
✉ 102 Wenchang Bei Lu 文昌北路 102 号
☎ 560 2918
🕒 9am to midnight

Ethnic Miao women showing off their intricate headwear.

Dingguan Cheng 鼎罐城
Miao's Sour Broth Fish (*suāntāngyú* 酸汤鱼) is their house specialty, also offers live entertainment.
✉ Longdong Bao 龙洞堡
☎ 540 2632
🕒 9am to midnight

Huaxi Wang's Niuroufen Dian
花溪王记牛肉粉店

Spectacular waterfalls give Guizhou some of China's best scenery.

Offers delicious beef noodle soup for only RMB 3.5.

✉ Dusi Lu 都司路❺

◷ 7am to 7pm

Laokaili Suantangyu
老凯里酸汤鱼

✉ 55 Shengfu Lu 省府路 55 号❻

◷ 584 3665

Sihe Yuan 四合院

Traditional Guiyang cuisine, especially good is their broiled beef (*huǒyàn niúròu* 火焰牛肉) and red stewed croaker (*hóngshāo huánghuāyú* 红烧黄花鱼).

✉ 79 Qianling Xi Lu 黔灵西路 79 号❹

☎ 682 5419

◷ 9am to midnight

Souvenirs

Guiyang offers great souvenirs for visitors. Wax-dyed fabrics (*làrǎn* 蜡染) are a local handicraft using nature and animal motifs. Designs are drawn onto the fabric with wax then dipped in dye and a beautiful pattern is revealed when the wax is removed. They cost from RMB 50 to 100, framed pieces are around RMB 200 each. The Miao people love silver jewelry and accessories. Make sure you check out the elaborate silver headdresses and delicate silver bracelets. Traditional Miao embroideries (*miáozú cìxiù* 苗族刺绣) that come in geometric patterns are a bargain at RMB 150 to 200. Unique pieces of art made entirely of plants ranges a few RMB to a few thousand.

You can do all your souvenir shopping at Qiancui Hang (*guìzhōu qiáncuìháng* 贵州黔粹行❼) at 48 Beijing Lu (北京路 48 号, ☎ 685 3718), the Dachanglong Shopping Center (*dàchānglóng gòuwù zhōngxīn* 大昌隆购物中心) at 26 Jiefang Lu (解放路 26 号, 575 9822). The Shixi Trade Street (*shìxī shāngyè jiē* 市西商业街) is a good place to go browsing.

A colorful Nuo mask of Zhang Fei.

Other Information

POST OFFICES

Guiyang City Post Office 贵阳市邮政局

✉ 2 Zhonghua Bei Lu 中华北路 2 号❽

☎ 686 0891

HOSPITALS

Guizhou Provincial People's Hospital
贵州省人民医院

✉ 83 Zhongshan Dong Lu 中山东路 83 号❾

☎ 592 5503

COMPLAINT HOTLINES

☎ General: 586 4583, 586 4091

☎ Taxi: 528 0719

THANK / REPLY 道谢		
Thank you.	xièxie	谢谢。
Thank you very much.	fēicháng gǎnxiè	非常感谢。
I really appreciate it.	wǒ zhēnde hěn gǎnjī	我真的很感激。
Don't mention it.	méiguānxi	没关系。
No problem.	méiwèntí	没问题。
APOLOGY / REPLY 道歉		
I'm sorry.	duìbùqǐ	对不起。
It's ok.	méiguānxì	没关系。

Kunming's mild weather attracts migrating seagulls who spend their winters here.

Kunming, the Spring and Flower City

Area Code 0871

The "Spring City" is one of the most beautiful places in China, cradled in the foothills of the Himalayas and decorated with diverse flora and fauna – all wrapped up with a culturally rich history.

Marco Polo may have been the first Westerner to be captivated by Yunnan's awesome natural beauty, cultural diversity and food. Wandering the city, one sees minority peoples in embroidered garb selling fruit and a huge variety of beautiful tropical flowers from baskets carried on bamboo poles slung across their shoulders, the towering mountains and clean fresh air contrast with a rapidly modernizing Chinese city bustling with large scale construction projects.

Kunming's history goes back thousands of years. The city became known during the Ming dynasty because of Kunming's ready supply of metals, the main source for Ming coins. Although a large center of trade, the city nonetheless remained relatively isolated from the rest of China. In fact, it was considered a form of semi-banishment for imperial officials to be posted here. Upon the completion of the Indochina railroad in 1910, Kunming rapidly opened up and became more accessible to the rest of the world, but still remains a nice contrast to the bustling chaos of other Chinese cities. Kunming is also a major exporter of flowers – it's impossible for their presence to go unnoticed because their scent wafts through the streets.

Nowadays Kunming is a jumping-off point for tourists to the western regions of Yunnan and Tibet. 25 of China's 55 ethnic minorities live in Yunnan, making up 30% of the province's population. With mountains to the north, east and west, and located on a mile high plateau, the city's temperate climate year-round serves to make it a great place to visit.

Dianchi Lake (*diānchí hú* 滇池湖) or the "Pearl of the Plateau" is situated to the south of the city. It's the largest lake in Yunnan, and offers many things to do and see. **West Mountain's Dragon Gate** (*xīshān lóngmén* 西山龙门), known as "Sleeping Beauty," has cliffs bordering the western side of the lake that are perfect for hiking. On the way to the top you'll pass by both forgotten and refurbished temples, expansive vistas of the lake, gardens and the tomb of the musician Nie Er (*niè'ěr mù* 聂耳墓), the composer of the Chinese national anthem. There's a chairlift if you get too tired. More than a hike, this is a journey into China's history. The notable **Huating Temple** (*huátíng sì* 华亭寺), dates to the 11th century and offers a quiet repose from the strains of hiking. Along the way, make sure to stop at the numerous view-points to soak in the beauty of the scenery: blue skies, green water with slow sailing fishing boats, the chirping of birds, and the grey peaks in the distance with the coastline dotted with fishing villages.

On the opposite side of the lake is **Grand View Park** (*dàguān gōngyuán* 大观公园), which features a Buddhist temple and the **Grand View Tower** (*dàguān lóu* 大观楼). From here you can rent a boat to West Mountain or just to tour the lake while the rower serenades you with traditional Naxi songs.

Set in a national forest preserve, the **Golden Temple** (*jīn diàn* 金殿) has the largest bronze temple in China. The 23-foot-high (6m) Taoist temple was built in 1671 after the original Ming temple was taken to Dali, but this one is not threatened by the same fate: weighing an estimated 250 tons, it sits on a marble foundation.

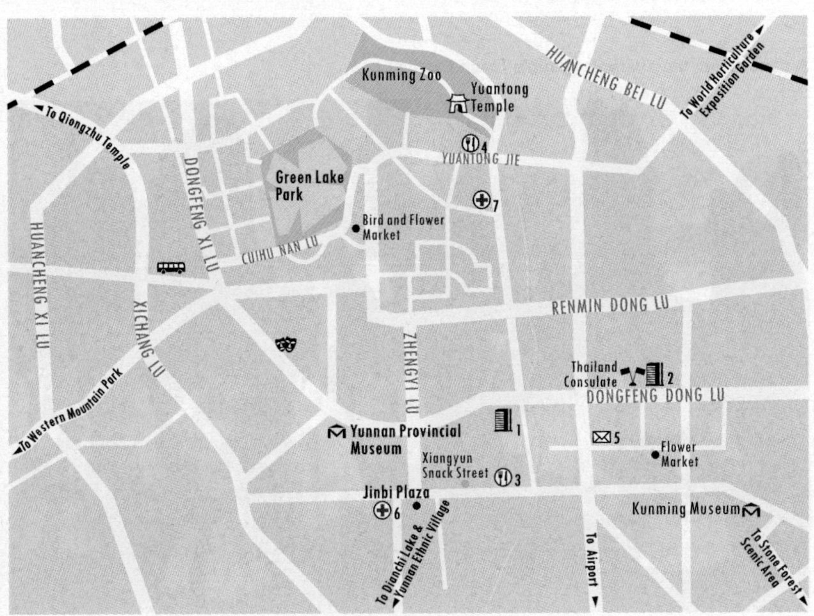

Memorable Experiences

Eating scoops of jackfruit, mango and pineapple flavored ice cream while strolling down Renmin Zhong Lu in downtown on a sunny Saturday.

Strolling around Green Lake Park and shopping in the ethnic minority shops along the southern side.

Not far from the Golden Temple is the **World Horticultural Exposition Garden** (*shìjiè yuányì bólǎnyuán* 世界园艺博览园), a major attraction for those with green thumbs. Flora and fauna are arranged in small gardens according to China's provinces and 34 different countries.

One can't help but feel awed by the **Stone Forest** (*shí lín* 石林), a natural wonder 51 miles (83 km) southeast of Kunming. Spending the day there is a perfect way to see some of Yunnan's amazingly stark landscape. This place is breathtaking – a lake, caves, gorgeous vistas of the surrounding countryside and stone formations projecting from the ground provide the feeling of being in a primeval forest. Joining a tour is worthwhile as it provides historical and cultural context to the natural beauty of the place – just get there early be sure to find a group with an English-speaking guide. There are numerous different areas where one can see the rock formations, including **Long Lake** (*chánghú* 长湖) which has underwater stalactites and an island in the middle.

The forests come in all sizes, large and small, but some of the more interesting ones are the **Major Stone Forest** (*dà shílín* 大石林), **Minor Stone Forest** (*xiǎo shílín* 小石林) and **Naigu Stone Forest** (*nǎigǔ shílín* 乃古石林). The stone formations are imaginatively likened to all kinds of animals, plants, people and other earthly creations. The stalactite studded **Zhiyun Cave** (*zhīyún dòng* 芝云洞) offers an underground version of the stone forests. Although not providing the same contrast of the sky against the stone, its containment within a cave gives it a surreal, awe-inspiring feeling. This bizarre natural wonder formed around 270 million years ago when the area was underwater. The movements of the earth's plates caused the limestone formations to rise then rain

A dance from the Yi ethnic group's Torch Festival.

gradually wore down the limestone to make the peaks. There are many folk tales and customs surrounding the individual stone peaks – every year the Sani people gather here to celebrate the Torch Festival, which involves traditional performances, wrestling, bullfighting and a ceremony where young men propose to women by moonlight.

A legend surrounding **Bamboo Temple** (*qióngzhú sì* 筇竹寺) stems from the surrounding bamboo forest: two brothers saw an unusual rhinoceros, which they followed deep into the forest where they spied odd monks performing an unknown ritual. When the monks saw the two brothers, they vanished, leaving only their walking sticks as evidence that they had ever existed. The following day the sticks had magically grown into a bamboo forest. The brothers then built the temple there as a sign of piety. Dating to the Song dynasty, the temple was rebuilt in the 1880's. The most noted feature of the temple is the 500 Buddhist arhats sculptures by Li Guangxiu. These sculptures are amazing, not just in their quantity, but also in the craftsmanship of each individual arhat. Taking seven years from concept to realization, each of these life-size sculptures is a reflection of the human personality and soul. The meticulous work that went into each is clearly visible in the sculptures' faces, stances and expressions.

For a low-key afternoon or evening in the city, spend some time in **Green Lake Park** (*cuìhú gōngyuán* 翠湖公园) in the university district, which is surrounded by teahouses and shops selling minority clothes and other goods. This is a relaxing place to go for a leisurely stroll; get up early enough and you can watch, and participate, in early morning Tai Chi exercises.

Throwing a gift to your would-be beau, an ethnic courtship game in Yunnan Province.

Yunnan Provincial Museum (*yúnnánshěng bówùguǎn* 云南省博物馆) has three exhibits displaying ethnic clothes, bronze drums and Buddhist art. The museum provides a quiet and relaxed way to learn more about the city's history and culture. ■

Making Your Trip Easy

Practical Tips

It's beautiful all year round, no extreme temperatures, but not exactly balmy – the summer average is 66°F (19°C) so it's important to bring warm clothes and a jacket. Mornings and evenings can be chilly with the temperature becoming quite warm by noon.

Transportation

Airport – The airport is less than 2 miles (3 km) south of the city. From the airport to pretty much anywhere downtown by taxi shouldn't exceed RMB 20.

Taxis – Full-sized taxis are RMB 8 at flag-fall while compact taxis are RMB 7.

The Best of Kunming

Golden Temple 金殿 *jīn diàn*

✉ 4.3 miles (7 km) northeast of Kunming 昆明东北郊,距市中心 7 公里

☎ 501 8306

🕒 7am to 7pm

¥ 30

Stone Forest 石林 *shílín*

✉ 51 miles (83 km) from Kunming 距昆明市 83 公里

Quotes

"Kunming is a laid back place away from the larger, hustle bustle markets in the south of China."

"Flowers are everywhere, a real delight to the cyes and senses… Folk culture is real here."

☎ 771 1439
🕒 24 hours
¥ 140

West Mountain's Dragon Gate
西山龙门 *xī shān lóngmén*
✉ west bank of Dianchi Lake 滇池西岸
☎ 842 6288
🕒 7:30am to 7pm
¥ 30

World Horticultural Exposition Garden
世界园艺博览园 *shìjiè yuányì bólǎnyuán*
✉ 2.5 miles (4 km) northeast of Kunming
昆明市东北 4 公里
☎ 501 2367
🕒 8am to 6pm
¥ 100

Hotels

Horizon Hotel
天恒大酒店 *tiānhéng dàjiǔdiàn* ★★★★★
✉ 432 Qingnian Lu, west of Central Square
市中心广场西侧,青年路 432 号❶
☎ 318 6666
¥ 1,137 – double room
@ www.horizonhotel.com.cn

Kai Wah Plaza International Hotel 佳华广场酒店 *jiāhuá guǎngchǎng jiǔdiàn* ★★★★★
✉ 577 Beijing Lu 北京路 577 号
☎ 356 2828
¥ 1,162 – double room
@ www.kaiwahplaza.com

Dianchi Garden Hotel Kunming
昆明滇池温泉酒店 *kūnmíng diānchí wēnquán jiǔdiàn* ★★★★
✉ Dianchi Lu 滇池路
☎ 431 2888
¥ 830 – double room
@ www.spangardenhotel.com

Jinjiang Hotel, Kunming 昆明锦江大酒店
kūnmíng jǐnjiāng dàjiǔdiàn ★★★★
✉ 98 Bejing Lu, beside the train station
火车站旁,北京路 98 号
☎ 313 8888
¥ 423 – double room
@ www.kingworld.com.cn

Kunming Hotel
昆明饭店 *kūnmíng fàndiàn* ★★★★
✉ 52 Dongfeng Dong Lu 东风东路 52 号❷
☎ 316 2063
¥ 772 – double room
@ www.kmhotel.com

Food & Restaurants

Food in Yunnan, as everywhere in China, is as varied as the local ingredients. Yunnan's diverse environment, from mountains in the west to subtropical forests in the south, inspires an extremely palatable, although strange range of dishes. True to Chinese style, the thousands of varieties of plants and animals are well represented in cooking.

Cross-the-bridge noodles (*guòqiáo mǐxiàn* 过桥米线) are prepared at the table by adding raw ingredients into a hot broth. The ingredients in the soup are seemingly unlimited, except by what your palate can handle. These include an assortment of meats, mushrooms, tofu (also available in many varieties, including dry tofu, tofu strips, and tofu skin to name a few), eggs, cheese, potatoes, pumpkins, melons and green vegetables. The story of the soup is famous – a woman preparing food for her scholar-husband realized that if she put a thin layer of oil on top of the broth and carried the raw ingredients separately, the hot broth would cook the food once she arrived at her husband's study – providing him a hot meal.

Definitely try street food, which allows you to sample many different kinds without making a large financial commitment. There is a choice of almost anything skewered and barbecued, coated in hot pepper and oil. Although not a meal, definitely a worthy side trip for a post-museum or late night snack. Check out the food street on Shuncheng Lu, which mainly offers Muslim fare. Another street to check out is Xiangyun Xiaochi Jie.

There is also an abundance of chestnuts which are served roasted shell-on, sautéed, prepared with meat, made into savory and sweet pastes or as dessert, including mouth-watering caramelized chestnuts. For those who are looking for the comforts of chicken soup, *qiguo ji* (汽锅鸡), a steamed chicken in broth, is delicious. If you want something to chew on, pick up some beef jerky (*niúgān bā* 牛干巴) or some ham (*xuānwēi huǒtuǐ* 宣威火腿). An exotic variation of hotpot, try the wild mushroom hotpot (*yěshēngjūn huǒguō* 野生菌火锅). Different varieties of mushrooms are slow cooked in the broth before you add your own chosen goodies. Each mushroom has its own medicinal properties – tasty and good for you. Some varieties of mushrooms are only available from May to December.

From the southern region of Xishuangbanna, fruit is delicious and available year round. Apples, grapes, peaches and oranges to pomelos, jackfruits and mangosteens – the queen of the fruits are available.

Don't forget the cuisine of Yunnan's numerous ethnic minorities, which includes Naxi cheese (made of goat's milk and deep-fried, somewhat reminiscent of a potato chip) as well as Bai local specialties such as spicy and sour fish and sweet deep-fried goat cheese.

RESTAURANTS

Fuzhao Lou 福照楼

Famous for its *qiguoji* (汽锅鸡) and *liang mifen* (凉米粉).

✉ 393 Lianmeng Lu, Panlong District
盘龙区联盟路 393 号

☎ 571 0158

Kunming Xinshijie Meishi Yule Guangchang 昆明新世界美食娱乐广场

Seafood and Yunnan cuisine with live entertainment.

✉ 16 Yuantong Jie 圆通街 16 号❹

☎ 514 0891, 514 0862

🕒 10am to 9pm

Xiangyun Huiguan 祥云荟馆

Famous for its *tianyuan tuji geng* (田园土鸡羹), which made from chicken.

✉ 43 Xiangyun Lu, Xihua District
西华区祥云路 43 号

☎ 362 2929

Xinyunyuan Jiulou 新云园酒楼

Specializes in Yunnan cuisine.

✉ 452 Qingnian Lu 青年路 452 号❸

☎ 315 9668

🕒 11am to 9:30pm

Yejun Yuan 野菌园

Specializes in over 50 kinds of wild mushroom

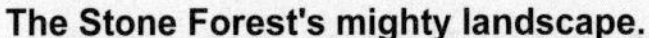

The Stone Forest's mighty landscape.

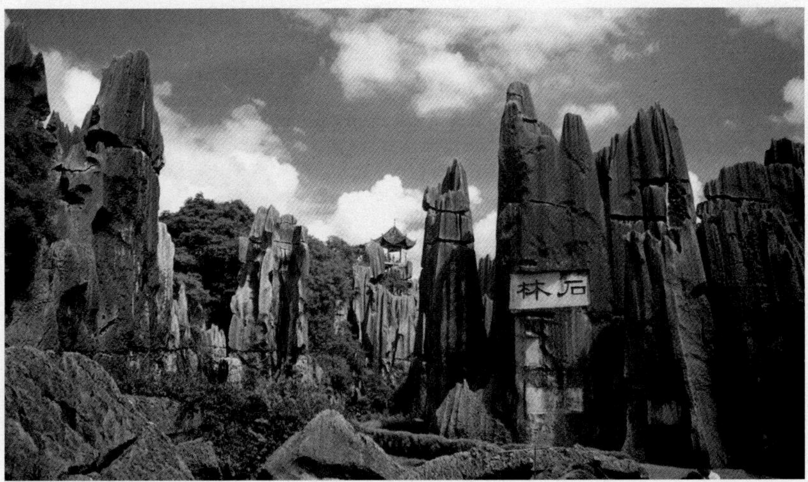

in a chicken or fish broth hotpot.

✉ 173 Guanxing, Guanshang Lu
关上路,关兴 173 号

☎ 716 7476

🕒 10am to 10pm

Yixin Yuan 怡心园

A spacious and classy venue.

✉ Dianchi Lu 滇池路

☎ 464 9926

🕒 10am to 10pm

Souvenirs

Local specialties include embroidery, cloth (cotton and hemp) clothing and decorative pieces; ethnic minority handicrafts are available most places. Beautiful goods include embroidered clothing and home decorations such as tablecloths, pillow covers and large embroidered batik blue and white cloths that can be made into bed covers or used as wall hangings. There are also many different kinds of clothing if the loose and casual hemp clothes don't match your style.

There are also the standard silver rings, bracelets and necklaces – be sure to bargain. Many kinds of tea are grown here and tea shops are a great Chinese experience. Pressed cakes of tea are a great gift to bring home.

Jade from Myanmar is plentiful and of good quality. It can be found as bracelets, pendants and assorted types of jewellery. To see if your jade is of good quality, look at it carefully under a light and look for imperfections – it's best not to spend too much money on jade unless you're a jade expert.

Behind the Kunming Department Store (*kūnmíng bǎihuò dàlóu* 昆明百货大楼) is a bird and flower market which lives up to the expectations one would have for such a market in the Spring City. Go early to avoid the crowds. The Jixin Antique Market (*jíxīn gǔwán shìchǎng* 吉鑫古玩市场, 102 Dongfeng Lu 东风路 102 号, ☎ 317 8379) has numerous shops under one roof selling every antique imaginable.

Other Information

POST OFFICES

Dongfeng Dong Lu Post Office
东风东路邮政局

✉ Dongfeng Dong Lu 东风东路❺

☎ 316 3375

HOSPITALS

Yunnan Province First People's Hospital
云南省第一人民医院

✉ 157 Jinbi Lu 金碧路 157 号❻

☎ 363 4031

Yunnan Province Red Cross Hospital
云南省红十字会医院

✉ 176 Qingnian Lu 青年路 176 号❼

☎ 515 6650

CONSULATES

Thailand 泰王国昆明总领事馆

✉ 1/F, South Tower, Kunming Hotel, 52 Dongfeng Dong Lu
昆明市东风东路 52 号昆明饭店东楼 1 层

☎ 316 6626

COMPLAINT HOTLINES

☎ General: 353 7361

☎ Taxi: 331 2533

EMERGENCIES 紧急情况		
Help!	jiùmìng	救命!
Police.	jǐngchá	警察!
Thief!	xiǎotōu	小偷!
Be careful.	xiǎoxīn	小心!
Go away.	zǒukāi	走开!
I'm lost.	wǒ mílù le	我迷路了。
Where is the toilet?	nǎ yǒu cèsuǒ	哪有厕所?
I don't understand.	wǒ bù míngbái	我不明白。
I understand.	wǒ míngbái le	我明白了。

Dali's Bai ethnic group celebrate one of their many festivals.

Dali, the Jewel of the Southwest

Area Code 0872

Dali is a little present waiting for you after a strenuous journey by road. It offers a lake shore dotted with rustic villages, mountains cut with waterfalls and the relaxed atmosphere of a backpacker's retreat.

While tourists choke its streets today, centuries ago Dali was visited by flocks of foreign invaders, who coveted this little town for its favorable location near the Silk Road. Legend goes that Piluoge, an 8th century prince from Yunnan, invited his rivals to a feast, burnt them alive, then set out to merge six small Dai kingdoms into the powerful Nanzhao Kingdom. Dali, called Taihe at the time, became the capital of this powerful kingdom, which dominated northern Yunnan and upper Myanmar. From here, the ruler of Nanzhao controlled the trade route to India until the kingdom fell in the 13th century under the attack of the Mongol armies of Kublai Khan.

Set against the stunning mountain backdrop of Cang Shan in northwest Yunnan Province, lackadaisical Dali holds very little to remind the visitor of its turbulent past. In the revitalized town of **Old Dali** (*dàlǐ gǔchéng* 大理古城), a backpacker's paradise of cappuccinos and pizza joints alternate with traditional shops selling tea, Chinese medicine and handicrafts. The cobbled streets of the old town are filled with the patter of feet as tourists and locals alike take leisurely jaunts through the small town. Be aware that the nearby town of Xiaguan is also called Dali City. Don't end up in the middle of Xiaguan wondering why the small town has suddenly turned into a midsized gray city.

While a modern brush has touched Dali, this quaint town perched 1,900m above sea level

Dali's famous three pagodas reflect off a still lake while mountains rise in the background.

still retains much of its charm. Architecture is often Bai-inspired. The Bais, an ethnic minority, form the majority in Dali vis-à-vis the Han, Hui, Yi and Tibetan ethnic groups. The indigenous Bai community has grown long roots here. They number over a million today.

Their cultural influences are found in Dali Town, and in surrounding villages, especially around the Erhai Lake region, just east of Dali. Their homes are often two-story stone and wood abodes, topped by double-tiered roofs with wooden folding doors and ornamental windowpanes. Being artistically inclined, Bais love to decorate their walls with elegant wash paintings. Courtyards are very popular and well-tended. Bai women adore flowers and camellia and bougainvillea plants are a common feature at home. It also gives the Bai women, clothed in ethnic hues, their nickname "Golden Flowers."

To fully appreciate Bai-style architecture, cuisine, their fragrant tea and distinctive culture, head for **Xizhou** (*xǐzhōu* 喜洲) and **Zhoucheng. The Yan**, **Hou** and **Zhou Compounds** in Xizhou, a photogenic village 12 miles (20 km) north of Dali, are good examples of the Bai flair for architecture and elegant living. Zhoucheng Village, some 19 miles (30 km) north of Dali, has made a specialty of "tie-dying". Bai women are masters of this folk art. Using a special dye called *banlangen*, the women paint designs of animals and flowers on fabric tied with threads. The threads are cut, and these colorful handkerchiefs, blouses, and scarves flutter like flaming banners in the courtyards as they dry in the sun.

AROUND DALI

Several superb natural and cultural sights are outside "old" Dali's walled city gates. Be adventurous and be ready to move distances. A 10-minute bicycle ride from Dali takes you to the shores of the breathtaking **Erhai Lake** (*ěrhǎi hú* 洱海湖). On its eastern banks is **Wase Village** (*wāsè cūn* 挖色村) where souvenir hunters thrive every five days. You can ride around the lake and meander through Xizhou, Zhoucheng and Shaping villages. The isle in the center is rocky **Putuo Island** (*pǔtuó dǎo* 普陀岛), which retains a Buddhist population and several ruins, including the **Lesser Putuo Temple** (*xiǎopǔtuó sì* 小普陀寺). For a short island trip, hop onto a boat from Caicun dock some 3 miles (5 km) east of Dali and watch trained cormorants with nooses around their necks pick the day's catch.

Board a passenger ferry at 9am from Xiaguan **Erhai Lake Docks** (*ěrhǎi mǎtóu* 洱海码头). Skim along the eastern side of Erhai Lake and catch a glimpse of **Golden Spindle Island** (*jīnsuō dǎo* 金梭岛), Putuo Island, **Guanyin Ge** (*guānyīn gé* 观音阁) and **Nanzhao Fengqing Island** (*nánzhāo fēngqíngdǎo* 南诏风情岛). The ferry finally rests on the west bank of Erhai Lake near **Butterfly Springs** (*húdié quán* 蝴蝶泉), where thousands of butterflies congregate in springtime. From here, hop onto a bus to tour Butterfly Springs, the old city of Dali and the **Temple of the Three Pagodas** (*sāntǎ sì* 三塔寺), then head back to Xiaguan at 4:30pm. Several travel agencies in Xiaguan offer this tour, which costs around RMB 180. The price includes boat fare, admission, bus fare, lunch, a Bai "three courses of tea" on the boat and a Chinese-speaking guide. A half-day tour, which doesn't include lunch, is also available. This tour stops at the west bank and costs about RMB 90.

For an aerial view of the lake, head to the top of **Zhonghe Temple** (*zhōnghé sì* 中和寺). The 20-minute cable car ride to the temple gates is RMB 35 and the cobalt Erhai Lake sprawls below. As your cable car skims the canopies of pine forests, you'll pass over old cemeteries.

An obvious landmark is the Temple of the Three Pagodas, situated northwest of Dali. The original structures were built in the 9th century but destroyed by a fire in the 19th century. While being rebuilt in 1978, 600 relics dating from the Nanzhao period were discovered in the pagodas, adding to their prestige. The tallest, called **Pagoda of the Thousand Searches** (*qiānxún tǎ* 千寻塔), stands 230 feet (70 m) high and is comprised of 16 levels, and flanked by two ten-story octagonal pagodas. These structures not only store the ashes and bones of saints, scriptures and precious objects, they also invoked Buddha's protection against natural disasters. The marble stele in front of the Pagoda of the Thousand Searches bears the characters "*Yong Zhen Shan Chuan*" which means, "Forever subdue the mountains and rivers." Just behind them is the **Temple of the Exalted One** (*chóngshèng sì* 崇圣寺), which is a museum detailing the history and construction of the pagodas.

Follow the trail near the pagodas if you want to do some hiking. At the end of the 6-mile (10 km) trail through pine forests are several natural pools and a waterfall waiting to soothe tired feet. If that hike gets your adrenaline pumping, and you're looking out for more adventure, trek around stunning **Cang Shan's** 19 peaks, soaring 13,120 feet (4,000 m) high. Your meanderings may take you to the forgotten **Yita Temple** (*yītǎ sì* 一塔寺). Within the temple walls is a mysterious 10th century pagoda completely sealed in the quiet landscape.

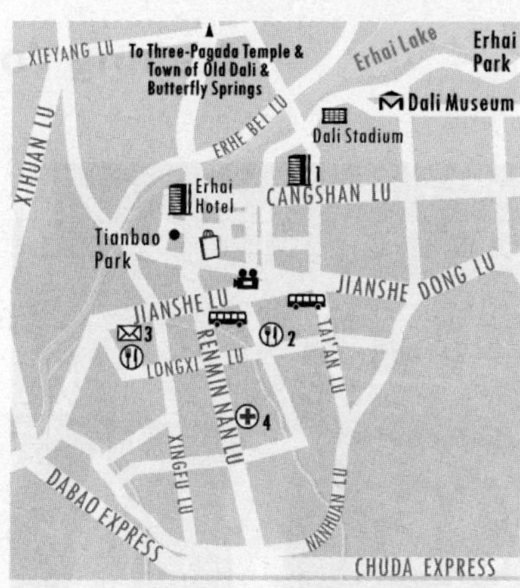

Two major remnants of ancient Dali are its **North Gate** (*běi mén* 北门) and **South Gate** (*nán mén* 南门), with their Qing-styled towers rising above the gateway in vibrant hues. Leading from the North Gate is the main thoroughfare, Fuxing Lu, along which lies the **Tower of the Five Glories** (*wǔhuā lóu* 五花楼). This central bell tower was once the south gate of the original town. Huguo Lu, known to locals as **Foreigner's Street** (*yángrén jiē* 洋人街), is another Dali attraction. This stretch pulses with souvenir shops, guesthouses, internet and food cafés – this backpackers' haven that has spilled into neighboring streets like Bo'ai Lu and Fuxing Lu. ■

Taking a break in one of Dali's many cafés.

Making Your Trip Easy

Dali tie-dyed tapestries have complex and beautiful designs.

Practical Tips

The weather in Dali is mild every season. Summers are comfortably warm and winters are only slightly chilly.

A festive spirit spreads throughout the streets during special occasions. The Sanyue Jie (*sānyuè jiē* 三月街), beginning in April, lasts a week and commemorates a visit by Guanyin, the Buddhist Goddess of Mercy, to the Nanzhao monarch, and is also known as the Guanyin Festival (*guānyīn jiē* 观音街). The markets go into overdrive as people trade wares and smiles. The three-day Three Temples Festival (*ràosān líng* 绕三灵) is another vibrant event in May. A procession starts from Dali's South Gate (*nán mén* 南门), to Xizhou's Sacred Fountain Temple (*shèngyuán si* 圣源寺), where merrymaking rocks the village until dawn. The troupe heads to Jingui Temple (*jīnguī si* 金圭寺) near Erhai Lake before going back to Dali. If you spot torches and firework displays through the night in July then you've come during the Torch Festival (*huǒbǎ jié* 火把节). Held usually in July or August, celebrations include dragon boat racing, an event that has spread all over Asia.

Transportation

Airport – The airport is about 9 miles (15 km) from Xiaguan, and there are daily flights to Kunming. From the airport to Xiaguan by shuttle bus is RMB 5 and by taxi is RMB 50.

Bicycle – Bicycles are cheap and easy to rent from guesthouses or any bicycle shop along Bo'ai Lu. Mountain bikes cost around RMB 10 per day, Chinese models cost RMB 5 per day.

Bus – When taking express buses from Xiaguan or Lijiang to Dali; some buses will drop you off at the eastern end of Dali along the highway. You'll have to flag down a passing car to take you into Dali, RMB 5 for the ride is reasonable. Express bus tickets out of Dali can be purchased from the Dali Passenger Service Ticket Office on Bao'ai Lu or any travel agency on Huguo Lu. You can also purchase tickets for the Xiaguan long-distance bus station in Dali; buses to Kunming are about 8 hours and cost RMB 55.

Taxi – Taxis are RMB 6 at flag-fall.

Train – A leisurely train ride can be pleasant and overnight sleeper trains from Kunming to Dali are popular. Tickets can be arranged through your hotel or travel agent.

Quotes

"Great food, relaxed streets and souvenirs galore. What more can you ask for?"

"The cultural experience of Dali is great. The colorful dress of the minorities, the hectic village markets and imposing mountains make this place a blitz of colors and flavor."

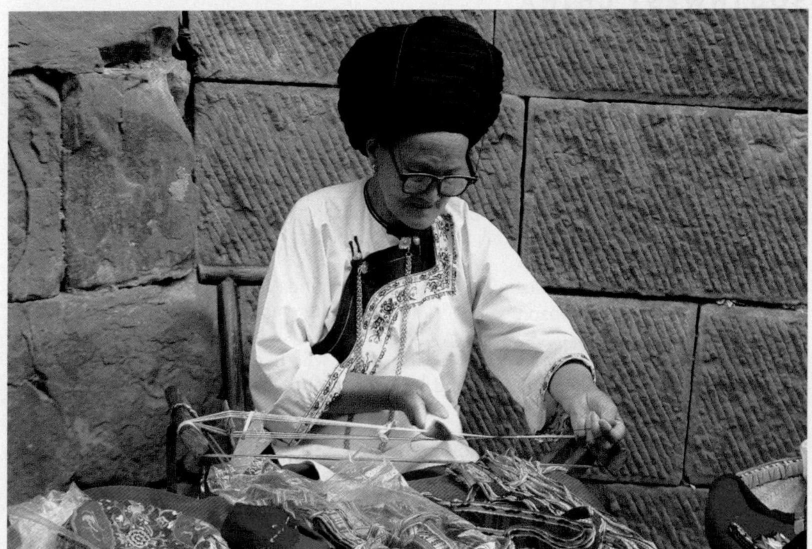

A Bai ethnic grandma is weaving a belt.

The Best of Dali

Butterfly Springs 蝴蝶泉 húdié quán
✉ about 2 miles (3 km) from Erhai Lake Docks 在洱海码头下船，乘车约3公里
☎ 243 1125
🕒 8am to 6:30pm
¥ 30

Cang Shan 苍山 *cāng shān*
✉ on the bank of Erhai Lake 大理洱海畔
¥ 40, two-way ticket, for cable car to view Dali and Erhai Lake
80, two-way ticket, for cable car to view Cang Shan Valley

Erhai Lake 洱海 *ěrhǎi*
✉ Erhai Nan Lu, by Dali Port
大理港码头洱海南路
🕒 9am to 5:30pm
¥ 10

Old Dali 大理古城 *dàlǐ gǔchéng*
✉ 8 miles (13 km) from Xiaguan 下关北13公里

Hotels

Manwan Hotel
漫湾大酒店 *mànwān dàjiǔdiàn* ★★★★
✉ Canglang Lu, Dali Economic Development Zone 大理经济开发区沧浪路
☎ 218 8188
¥ 580 – double room, peak-season
464 – double room, off-season

Meideng Hotel
美登大酒店 *měidēng dàjiǔdiàn* ★★★★
✉ Dongduan, Cangshan Lu, Dali Economic Development Zone
大理经济开发区苍山路东段
☎ 213 8999
¥ 690 – double room, peak-season
414 – double room, off-season

Cangshan Hotel
苍山饭店 *cāngshān fàndiàn* ★★★
✉ 118 Cangshan Lu, Xiaguan
下关苍山路118号❶
☎ 217 1999
¥ 480 – double room, peak-season
180 – double room, off-season

Golden Dali Hotel
金达酒店 *jīndá jiǔdiàn* ★★★
✉ Canglang Lu, Dali Economic Development Zone 大理经济开发区沧浪路
☎ 219 1888
¥ 560 – double room, peak-season
392 – double room, off-season
@ www.goldendalihotel.com.cn

Mingzhu Hotel
明珠宾馆 *míngzhū bīnguǎn* ★★★
✉ next to Mingzhu Square, Yunling Da Dao, Dali Economic Development Zone
明珠广场旁，大理经济开发区云岭大道
☎ 232 3566

Memorable Experiences

Sampling local Bai cuisine at a modest hillside village while entertained by traditional song and dance.

Chilling at a sidewalk café in old Dali's main street, people watching with chocolate cake topped with ice cream for company.

¥ 460 – double room, peak-season
280 – double room, off-season

Food & Restaurants

Diversity is the catchword on Bao'ai Lu and Huguo Lu. There's something for every mood: Western, rustic country and ethnic Bai cuisine to name a few. Modern Bai cuisine is a mixture of southern Chinese and the Bai flavors. *Barou ersi* (巴肉饵丝), one of Dali's local specialties, is made from pig's knuckle and a vegetable unique to Dali called *er cai*. The Erhai Lake area is famous for its fresh and plentiful fish. Try some Dali plums called *diaomei* (雕梅). The plums are preserved for months in brown sugar and honey; the sweetness of the sugar and honey contrast with the sour plum to make it a yummy treat.

A unique tea is the "Three Courses of Tea" (*sāndào chá* 三道茶), which symbolically mirrors life's progress – first bitter then sweet. The first course is slightly bitter; the second course a trifle sweet (walnuts and candy are added to the tea), and the third course is unforgettably satisfying. If you feel like a martini or a beer, head to Yangren Jie where there are Western bars and menus written in English. Go to the restaurant-lined Jinxing Mingshi Jie (锦兴名食街) at Shangduan Canglang Lu in the Dali Economic Development Zone (大理经济开发区沧浪路上段) for a local atmosphere.

RESTAURANTS

Dali Renjia 大理人家

✉ Canglang Lu Nanduan, Xiaguan 下关沧浪路南段

☎ 310 3997

Sifang Xiaochi 四方小吃

Specializes in Bai cuisine, their house specialty is clay pot fish (*shāguō yú* 砂锅鱼).

✉ Yu'er Lu, Old Dali 大理古城玉洱路

Souvenirs

There's a lot of kitsch in the streets, but with it rare finds as well. For the light traveler, there are embroidered clothing, tie-dyed scarves, Dali batik and jade jewelry. For those who like to lug around large slabs of stone, authentic Dali marble (*dàlǐshí* 大理石) can be found everywhere. This quality marble is usually set into wood furniture, tabletops and table screens. Dali's Gantong tea (*gǎntōng chá* 感通茶), Cangshan snow tea (*cāngshān xuěchá* 苍山雪茶) and Xiaguantuo tea (*xiàguān tuóchá* 下关沱茶) make good gifts.

Monday is market day in Shaping Village, some 19 miles (30 km) north of Dali. Whether you're buying or just browsing, the market is great fun. From 10am to 2pm, it's a shopping frenzy on a hill near the highway. Traders peddle anything from pots to clothes. To get there from Dali, hop onto a minibus organized by the local hotels or café, which usually costs RMB 15.

On the eastern shore of Erhai Lake is the Wase Village market the fifth day of each month; rural women in colorful jackets, long tunics and sequined chapeaus pack the market square. Locals arrive on horses and donkeys, and amidst wandering pigs, trade wares ranging from rice and nuts to horses and squawking chickens. Forget proper stalls, most items are displayed out of woven baskets.

Other Information

POST OFFICES

Dali Post Office 大理州邮政局

✉ Jianshe Lu, opposite People's Park 建设路人民公园对面

☎ 212 4442

HOSPITALS

Dali Hospital 大理州医院

✉ Renmin Nan Lu, Xiaguan 下关人民南路

☎ 212 7094

COMPLAINT HOTLINES

☎ General: 267 0384, 96927

☎ Taxi: 212 5512

Lijiang, the Jade Dragon's Abode

Area Code 0888

Heritage: the Old Town of Lijiang

Exploring **Lijiang** is like opening a Chinese jewel chest – each exquisitely crafted compartment leads to richer more dazzling sights.

Perched at bottom of the Himalayas and the Qinghai-Tibet Plateau, this remote town in southwest China's Yunnan Province is a show-stealer for its amazing landscape and rich culture. Nestled in a valley ringed with snow-capped mountains, springs, lakes and frothy rivers, nature's touch extends into Lijiang County. The **Old Town** (*gǔchéng* 古城) is full of cobbled streets, crisscrossing canals, swaying willow trees and gaily-hued blossoms. Every so often, a bridge – stone, wooden, flat, arched, roofed – pops up and along it trundles local folk in traditional dress.

Over 22 different ethnic minorities have made Lijiang their home. Among them are the Lisu, Pumi, Bai, Yi, Tibetan, Miao and Naxi. People of Lijiang are like vibrant butterflies: cheerful, busy and visually stunning. The market squares and alleys are peppered with locals in their individual ethnic fashions, ornaments and hairstyles. Local customs, architecture, spiritual beliefs, language, arts and craft are influenced by ethnic diversity and are rich with symbolism and creativity.

Lijiang's ancient old city has preserved its charming antiquity despite the modern changes sweeping through China. Old-style architecture and pathways were rebuilt along the original model after an earthquake

Tea break by the gushing water of Lijiang's Old Town.

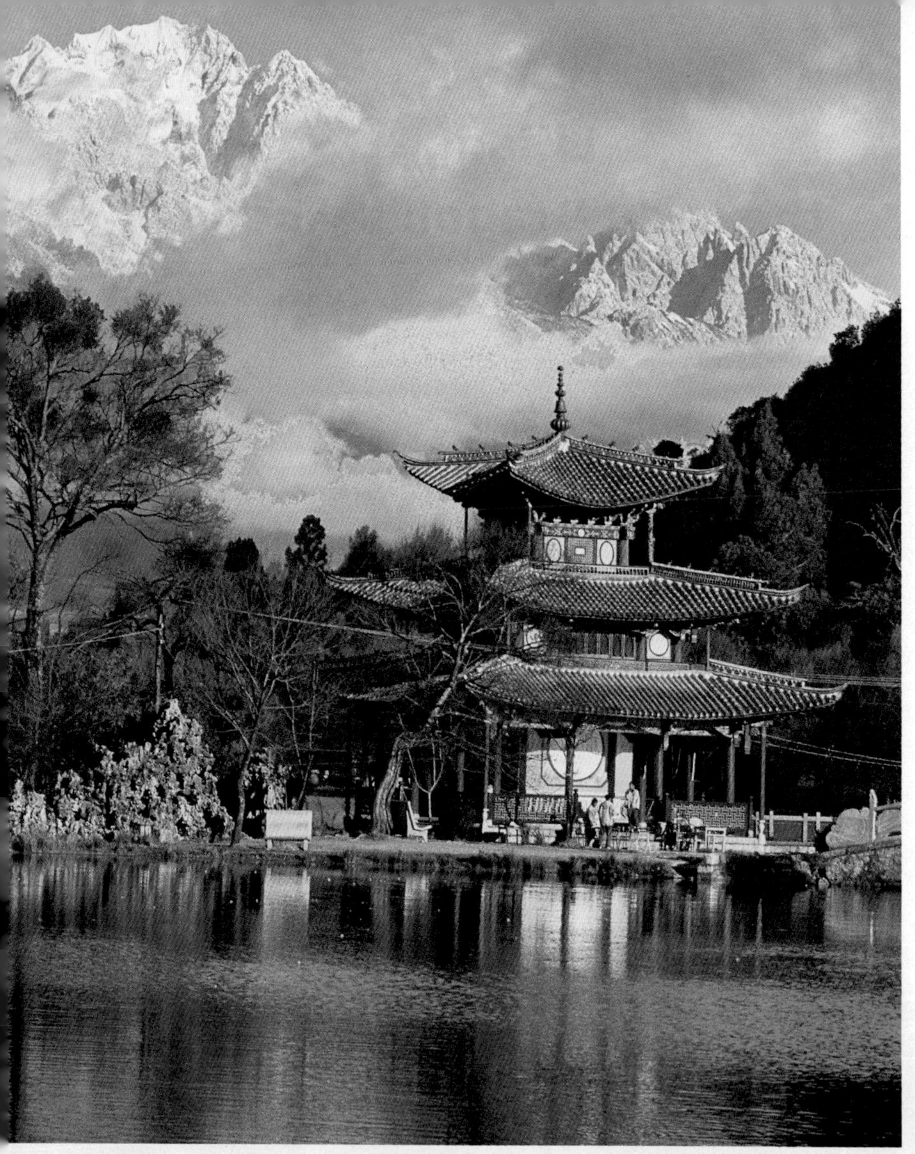

Jade Dragon Snow Mountain serves as the backdrop to the Black Dragon Pool.

in 1996 damaged sections of the town. In individual enclaves, pebbles and smashed tiles are arranged symbolically to denote happiness or good fortune. Rooms are built beside running water for a soothing effect. Doors and windows sport decorative woodcarvings of phoenixes, legends and nature. Pathways, barely two-shoulders wide, are crammed by two-story shop-houses, inns or private residences all built in the traditional style. Cobblestone streets are free of vehicular nuisances and the maze of back alleys offers innumerable possibilities for shortcuts and scenic surprises.

Although the town grew from humble nomadic origins, there's little that's transitory or mercurial about Lijiang. Several houses, streets, monasteries and bridges have been there since the Tang, Song, Ming and Qing dynasties. At the heart of the Old Town is **Square Street** (*sìfāng jiē* 四方街).

Centuries ago, it was the central bazaar where mountain tribes, Tibetan and Han traders and farmers briskly bartered yak butter, poultry, grain and linen. Today, this ancient crossroads for trade continues to hum with mercantile activities; business is open every day. On sale are a variety of handicrafts, from homemade griddlecakes to handpicked tea leaves from Yunnan's hills.

Lijiang's people adore learning and the arts. They're the bookkeepers of the ancient Dongba scripts. Called "*sijiulujiu*" in the Naxi language, meaning "signs on rock and wood," these eloquent drawings depict the history of Naxi culture, their religious rites, folktales and legends. Over 20,000 volumes of Dongba sutra, painted on wooden tablets, are scattered around the world, but many are still lovingly preserved in Lijiang's sacred monasteries. Amazingly, this one-of-its-kind pictographic language has not been simply locked away and forgotten. The Naxis deep appreciation for culture and their roots ensure that it is still used within the community today.

In 1997, Lijiang became the first Chinese hill town to earn a World Cultural Heritage status from UNESCO.

FOOTLOOSE IN & AROUND LIJIANG

Forget your Ferragamo shoes. Lijiang's sights are best appreciated by strolling through the Old Town. That could mean a whole day pottering through the enclaves of handicraft shops and back lanes and sampling steaming Lijiang cakes from a hot grill. Start off the day with a sumptuous breakfast at the hodgepodge of café along **West Canal** (*xīhé* 西河) and **Xinhua Street** (*xīnhuá jiē* 新华街).

First thing you notice is the town gurgles with water. Everywhere, canals bubble with the crystal clear waters of **Lashi Lake** (*lāshì hǎi* 拉市海) and **Black Dragon Pool**(*hēilóng tán* 黑龙潭), located at the foot of Jade Dragon Snow Mountain. The locals practice a sensible three-part system to manage water use. Water is diverted from canals into three ponds. The uppermost pond supplies drinking water. The middle one is for rinsing vegetables and the last pond downstream is used for laundry. On either side of the canals, local children splash their feet in cool

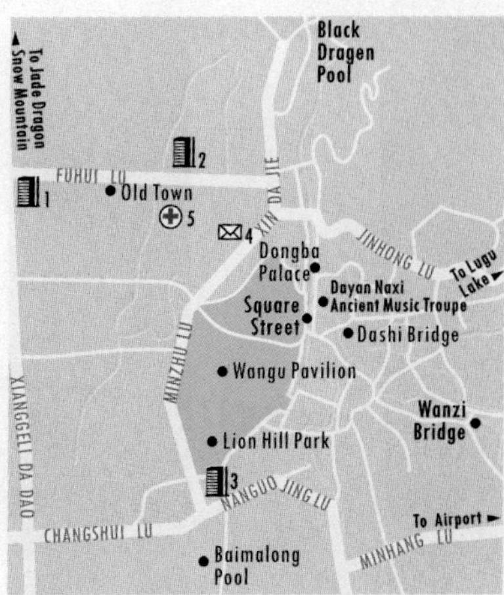

water and women rinse the morning laundry. All of which adds to the restful, homely atmosphere in Lijiang.

There are as many bridges as there are waterways. Over 350 bridges of stone or chestnut wood span the canals of Lijiang, creating a poetic and idyllic setting. One of the most scenic bridges is double-arched and found at the eastern end of Square Street. Built in the Ming dynasty, it's known as the **Bridge That Mirrors Snow** (*yìngxuě qiáo* 映雪桥) because its waters reflect the mystic peaks of Jade Dragon Snow Mountain. The largest stone bridge is 92 feet (28 m) long. Also built during the Ming dynasty, it was once the conduit for the village chief to travel from his Lijiang home to the nearby Buddhist grounds. Lion-head sculptures, one of which lost its head during the Cultural Revolution, adorn the stone railings. Each bridge has a story to tell. **Baisuifang Bridge** (*bǎisuìfāng qiáo* 百岁坊桥) was named after father and son centenarians who once lived in that lane, while a rich man who desired a son built **Wanzi Bridge** (*wànzǐ qiáo* 万子桥).

You will see lots more local women than men in the street. That is because Lijiang consists mostly of the Naxi tribe. In Naxi tradition, women are the pillars of Naxi family life. They raise farm animals, brew wine, weave cloth and grind beans to make tofu and noodles. If they're not on their way to the markets or running errands, local residents adore sitting by the bridge to chat, knit, play chess or baby-sit grandchildren.

A modern advertisement using ancient Naxi pictographs.

The Naxis traditionally live in matrilineal families – a system that survives particularly in the **Yongning** (*yǒngníng* 永宁) area, north of Lijiang. Any children born of romantic liaisons belong to the woman, as does all property.

Buildings in Lijiang are a salve for eyes that have had enough of modern towns. Architecture here is elegant and practical, yet blends with the surroundings – townsfolk will be happy to point out the Han, Bai and Tibetan influences visible in each building. Each compound consists of three houses. A screen wall, painted with floral patterns or auspicious poems, completes the square. Ornately carved wooden windows and doors stand out against clean, plain walls. Long corridors link each house to the main courtyard, where families socialize in open-air comfort.

Peek past the main entrance of a residential home to catch a glimpse of the tasteful interiors. Homes are spacious and airy. Courtyards are landscaped with rocks and p

▶▶ Naxi Script

The Naxi tribe is one of China's most interesting ethnic minorities. Scattered mainly around Yunnan Province, with small settlements in Sichuan and Tibet, they were first visited by Western ethnologists in the early part of the 20th century and have been studied and written about ever since. There are about 280,000 Naxi and most live in Lijiang Autonomous County in northwest Yunnan.

The Naxi have a culture that's rich and diverse with their own music, art and most unique of all, their thousand-year-old pictographic writing system which is similar to hieroglyphics. The Naxi language is also the only remaining pictographic written language in use.

The Naxi priests are called Dongba and they play an important part in keeping the language alive. The Naxi are Buddhists and their ancient Buddhist texts are passed down through generations of priests who are the caretakers of the texts. Only priests are allowed to learn the written script and begin studying the pictographs when young, only becoming fluent after many years of study. Because of the complexity of the written language and the role of the priests its preserving it, the Naxi language is named Dongba.

The language has approximately 2,200 pictographs. When put together, some sentences appear as a series of pictures that have many possible interpretations without any fixed meaning. This highly symbolic language requires years of study to fully understand.

The religious scriptures are also a record of Naxi life, recording everything from politics to poetry to Naxi legends in about 20,000 encyclopedic volumes. In 1957, the Naxi adopted a writing system based on Latin characters in order to promote literacy. Sadly, only a few Naxi today can read the Donga pictographs, though there are efforts to encourage its study.

Memorable Experiences

Buying a custom-made window frame, with its intricate designs carved from wood.

Watching wizened elderly ladies as they embroider patterns that later go onto their traditional dress.

Enjoying a mud-pie while watching the locals at their daily activities.

otted plants. The artistic decor reels with religious, cultural significance. If you spot a roof eave in a fish design, that's Taoist for "Supreme Being." Even the tiles on the ground are arranged to denote longevity, good fortune or peace.

Local homes sometimes double as workshops. During the harvest season, entrances are transformed into golden gateways as the women harvest yellow-colored millet, maize, melons and pumpkins.

Not only do locals have a close relationship with nature, but also with education. Naxi Chief Ahja Ahde was legendary for his love for learning and sophistication, as reflected in his beautiful abode. Famed as a cultural relic, his palatial compound holds Buddhist and Taoist halls, a meeting hall, a pavilion of the Jade Emperor, a family ancestral temple, as well as a library containing a complete collection of Buddhist teachings.

Streets in Lijiang are rich in history. **May 1st Street** (*wǔyī jiē* 五一街), site of the famous over-270-year-old **Snow Mountain Academy** (*xuěshān shūyuàn* 雪山书院), was frequented by scholars and politicians during the Qing dynasty. Naxis call this street "**Gaoken**," meaning "Street of Private Schools." The town's first young scholar, who successfully passed the imperial examination, sponsored the three-story building beside **Bean Market Bridge** (*wāndòu qiáo* 豌豆桥).

At **Xianwen Lane** (*xiànwén xiàng* 现文巷) on **Guangyi Street** stands a famous bookshop visited by dignitaries and learned men. Above its entrance reads an inscription made by the Naxi chieftian in the Ming dynasty, which reads "*tianyu liufang*," meaning "Go to Read Books." Galleries, arts and crafts shops also line the narrow lane. In the past, merchants from Dali rented houses along here, so the Naxis call Xianwen Lane "**Jianlogo**" (*jiànluòguò* 建洛过), meaning "Street of Dali."

Mishi Lane (*mìshi xiàng* 密士巷) on **Xinyi Street** (*xīnyi jiē* 新义街) has always been a lane of commerce. Tibetan merchants from Sichuan and Yunnan provinces used to stay here, but now tourists rest their tired feet in its many teahouses and café. At night, hover around Square Street, a favorite Naxi venue for merrymaking, song and dance. Operas are staged here during festivals. But you can catch ancient Naxi tunes by the Dayan Naxi Ancient Music Troupe nightly at the **Naxi Music Research Institute** on **East Street** ,

Some of the many souvenirs that await visitors in Lijiang.

just north of the market square.

The musicians, some of whom seem as old as the ancient instruments they use, play a repertoire of ancient Taoist music dating back to the Han dynasty. This unique music has been long lost in the rest of China, but has been passed on through the generations in Lijiang. Using original instruments and playing authentic compositions, the musicians give you an opportunity to listen to history.

Several cultural and religious relics are found in Lijiang's neighborhood. Only 55 of Lijiang's 200 famous murals, perfected by ethnic artists of Dongba, Tibetan lama and Han heritage, remain in the county. They are found in **Great Treasure Palace** (*dàbǎojī gōng* 大宝积宫), **Dadingge Pavilion** (*dàdìng gé* 大定阁), **Dajue Palace** (*dàjué gōng* 大觉宫) and the **Colored Glaze Hall** (*liúlí diàn* 琉璃殿) in Baisha Town. Above the Old Town is the beautiful **Lion Hill** (shīzi shān 狮子山), from which you can enjoy views of the town coming to life in the mornings, or slowing down to rest at the end of the day. There's also the unique pagoda **Wan Gou Lou**, which is worth a visit – it's relatively new, but the spectacular workmanship and detailed carvings make it a wonder in its own right.

North of the town is **Black Dragon Pool Park** (*hēilóngtán gōngyuán* 黑龙潭公园), where you find scrolls and artifacts at the **Dongba Research Institute** (*dōngbā wénhuà bówùguǎn* 东巴文化博物馆). The park also has stunning views. Not far away is **Wufeng Temple** (*wǔfèng lóu* 五凤楼). If you follow the winding trail upwards, you are headed for **Elephant Hill** (*xiàng shān* 象山). It takes about an hour to make your way up and back down again. Other monasteries around are the **Puji, Fuguo, Yufeng and Wenbi** Monasteries. If you have time, head for **Tiger Leaping Gorge** (*hǔtiào xiá* 虎跳峡) for some serious trekking and **Lugu Lake** (*lúgū hú* 泸沽湖) – cradle of the **Yongning Mosuo tribe** (*yǒngníng mósuōrén bùluò* 永宁摩梭人部落).

A visit to the **Yulong Xue Shan** (*yùlóng xuěshān* 玉龙雪山), which means "jade dragon and snow mountain," offers expansive mountains views and snowy scenery. Local travel guides offer tour packages, though they're quite pricey. You can scale the 18,045 feet (5,500 m) mountain on your own without much trouble. There are two chairlifts – the first one goes up halfway the mountain, while the second, the highest chairlift in Asia, lifts you up to 14,783 feet (4,506 m). Don't let the stunning views of glaciers and peaks distract you too much – be aware of signs of altitude sickness; symptoms include dizziness, headaches and a feeling of sluggishness. Hiring a van for about RMB 130 is the easiest way to get out to the mountain on your own. ■

Quotes

"It's amazing that the locals have adapted so well to time, yet preserved so much of their culture."

"These are people who have long roots and love their history."

Making Your Trip Easy

Practical Tips

At an altitude of over 6,560 feet (2,000 m), the weather is pleasant all year round. But bring something warm in case you climb the highlands or feel chilly at night. Winters are a little chilly while summers bring the most visitors; this means spring and autumn are the best times to visit. Many of the café also provide tour and ticket buying services.

Lijiang is an area clustered with 12 different ethnic groups who account for 57.4% of the total population. The San Duo Festival (*sānduǒ jié* 三朵节), usually in early-March, is a traditional Naxi festival when the Naxi go

Old music played on old instruments by old men.

horseracing, perform the *alili* dance and have a good time. People flood to the Yufeng Temple to take in the famous *wanduo chahua* (万朵茶花), a Camellia tree – related to tea trees – that's reputedly over 500 years old and blooms with over 10,000 blossoms. The Bangbang Festival (*bàngbàng jié* 棒棒节), usually in mid-February, sees horseracing and market fairs.

It's a good idea to hire a guide when hiking at Jade Dragon Snow Mountain (*yùlóng xuěshān* 玉龙雪山). Proper hiking equipment, enough food and water, sunglasses to prevent snow blindness and warm clothes are necessary. Be aware that night temperatures are extremely low. Binoculars are useful to view the snowy scenery.

Transportation

Airport – Flights from Kunming to Lijiang take about 45 minutes. The Lijiang Airport is about 17 miles (27 km) from south of the city and takes 25 to 30 minutes to reach by car.

Bicycle – Bikes are usually RMB 4 per hour to rent.

Taxi – Flag-fall is RMB 6, and rides within town shouldn't go over that.

The Best of Lijiang

Lugu Lake 泸沽湖 *lúgū hú*
✉ 45 miles (72 km) from Ninglang County 距宁蒗县 72 公里

The Old Town of Lijiang
丽江古城 *lìjiānggǔchéng*
✉ inside Lijiang City 丽江市内

Jade Dragon Snow Mountain
玉龙雪山 *yùlóng xuěshān*
✉ 9 miles (15 km) north of Lijiang Old Town 丽江古城北 15 公里
☎ 516 1501
🕒 8am to 6pm
¥ 80

The two recommended sights are:

Glacier Park 冰川公园 *bīngchuān gōngyuán*
Can only be reached from Ganhaizi (甘海子) by cable car.
¥ 160 one-way ticket for the cable car

Yunshan Ping 云杉坪 *yúnshān píng*
Can be reached by cable car from Baishui River.
¥ 45 one-way ticket for the cable car

Hotels

Guanfang Hotel Lijiang 丽江官房大酒店

On their way to the market to buy and sell.

lijiāng guānfáng dàjiǔdiàn ★★★★★
✉ Shangri-La Road Lijiang
丽江市香格里拉大道❶
☎ 518 8888
¥ 1,328 – double room
@ www.gfhotel-lijiang.com

Lijiang Golden Spring Hotel
丽江金泉酒店 *lijiāng jīnquán jiǔdiàn* ★★★★
✉ Zhongduan, Shangri-La Road
香格里拉大道中段
☎ 515 2888
¥ 336 – double room, peak-season
320 – double room, off-season
@ www.jghotel.net

Senlong Hotel
森龙大酒店 *sēnlóng dàjiǔdiàn* ★★★★
✉ Minzhu Lu 民主路❸
☎ 512 0666
¥ 688 – double room
@ www.senlonghotel.com

Lijiang Binguan
丽江宾馆 *lijiāng bīnguǎn* ★★★
✉ Fuhui Lu 福慧路❷
☎ 517 5018
¥ 384 – double room, 320 – single room

Food & Restaurants

Lijiang cuisine is a blend of Han Chinese and Tibetan styles. Charming hole-in-the-wall street outlets offer delicious *baba* (粑粑) any time of the day. Best eaten in the mornings, this thick flatbread of wheat – served plain or stuffed with vegetables, meat, lard, extracted ham cubes or condiments such as sugar mixed with pure mountain water, heated over a slow fire on a flat frying pan – is a Lijiang specialty. For local fare, a "Naxi sandwich" will have goat cheese and tomato slices between *baba* slices. For the more adventurous, deep-fried grasshoppers, dragonflies and other insects are also offered. Gulp them down with a selection of wine.

Zhubiao rou (猪膘肉) is a traditional Mosuo preserved pork. A whole pig is de-boned, stuffed with salt and spices, then shaped into a pipa and then air-dried. Because of its unique shape, it's also called *pipa rou* (*pípa ròu* 琵琶肉). If you haven't had enough pork, Lijiang is also known for its three-river ham (*sānjiāng huǒtuǐ* 三江火腿). For those who want something stronger than tea to wash down all that meat, cellar wine (*jiàojiǔ* 窖酒) fits the bill. Butter tea (*sūyóu chá* 酥油茶) is a common drink in the area and a favorite of the ethnic Naxi and Tibetans. Jade Dragon Snow Mountain tea (*yùlóng xuěshān chá* 玉龙雪山茶) is made from tea plants grown high on the mountain, approximately 9,850 feet (3,000 m) high.

The Cuiwen section of Xinhua Jie (新华街翠文段) is a popular bar street. Wandering singers will serenade you for RMB 10 a song. The night market (*yèshì* 夜市) outside the old town on Xin Da Jie (古城外新大街三岔路口一带) is great for barbeque and beer. Enjoy rice noodles (*xiǎoguō mǐxiàn* 小锅米线), rice casseroles (*shāguō fàn* 砂锅饭) and fried rice with ham (*huǒtuǐ chǎofàn* 火腿炒饭) at the Square Street Snack Street (*sìfāng xiǎochī yìtiáojiē* 四方小吃一条街). Yangren Jie (洋人街) hosts loads of bars and is located on the border of Xinyi Street and the new town (新义街与新城区交界地区).

RESTAURANTS

Mosuo Customs Garden 摩梭风情园
Great accommodation and delicious Mosuo dishes.
✉ Luoshui Village, on the bank of Lugu Lake
泸沽湖畔落水村
☎ 588 1268

Naxi Food and Beverage Culture City
纳西饮食文化城
The only live entertainment and food venue in Lijiang, its Jade Dragon Snow Mountain banquet (*yùlóng xuěshān yàn* 玉龙雪山宴) and *sandieshui* (三叠水) are renowned.
✉ Zhongduan Fuhui Lu 福慧路中段
☎ 518 7300

Naxi Ge 纳西阁
Specializes in Naxi dishes and Western food.
✉ SChangshui Lu 长水路
☎ 517 7719
🕒 10am to 1:30pm, 4:30pm to 8:30pm

Lüxuezhai Bahao Restanrant
绿雪斋8号餐馆
✉ 8 Yuhezhongcun, Gucheng District
古城区玉河中村8号
☎ 581 8098

Souvenirs

Much of the souvenirs available in Lijiang are related to the ethnic groups that populate the area. Hot items include copperware, leather and fur goods, carpets and rugs, and painted scrolls with poems written in calligraphy. Yunnan is also known for its flora and fauna, many of which are used in teas or medicines. The cryptic Yunnan White Power (*yúnnán báiyào* 云南白药), also known as "Hundred Treasures Drug," purportedly treats anti-inflammation and gynecological ailments. There are also many varieties of Yunnan teas available: white orchid, jasmine, smoked tea, Xuanchun, Hongbao and Yinzhen. Yongsheng porcelain (*yǒngshèng cíqì* 永胜瓷器) is transparent and the colors are light and elegant. Carved wooden plates (*diāokè mùpán* 雕刻木盘) are tastefully simple. Handmade tie-dying cloths are another local specialty (*dōngbā zhārǎn* 东巴扎染).

Some places to do your shopping include the Baixin Department Store (*bǎixìn shāngchǎng* 百信商场) on Minzhu Lu (民主路) and Fuzihao (*fúzìhào* 福字号) for Chinese knots at 28 Mishi Xiang, Xinyi Street (新义街密士巷28号). Artist Tang Xingsheng, who specializes in Naxi art, manages Juyiyuan Wenhua Shangdian (*jǔyìyuàn wénhuà shāngdiàn* 聚艺苑文化商店); it's over at 74 Mishi Yuan, Xinyi Jie (新义街密土苑74号, ☎ 518 3529). If you prefer market browsing, then head to Guangchang Jie (广场街) for a lively market.

Other Information

POST OFFICES

Lijiang City Post Office 丽江市邮局
✉ Minzhu Lu, Xin Dajie, Gucheng District
古城区新大街民主路❹
☎ 512 2711

Square Street Branch Post Office
四方区支局
✉ Square Street 四方街
☎ 512 1012

HOSPITALS

Lijiang People's Hospital 丽江市人民医院
✉ Fuhui Lu, Gucheng District 古城区福慧路❺
☎ 518 5181, 512 2335, 512 2392

COMPLAINT HOTLINES

☎ General: 96927, 512 3432
☎ Taxi: 518 2908

TOURISM INFORMATION WEBSITE

@ www.chinalijiangtravel.com

AT THE DOCTOR 看病		
I'm sick.	wǒ bìng le	我病了。
I feel…	wǒ gǎnjué …	我感觉…
dizzy	tóuyūn	头晕
weak	sìzhī wúlì	四肢无力
I have a cold/cough.	wǒ gǎnmào/ késou le	我感冒/咳嗽了。
My… hurts.	wǒ … téng	我…疼。
head	tóu	头
stomach	wèi	胃
teeth	yáchǐ	牙齿

Lhasa's Ocean of Culture

Area Code 0891

Heritage: Potala Palace, Jokhang Temple, Norbu Lingka

Surrounded by jagged mountains and steeped in mysticism, **Lhasa** continues to be defined by Buddhism. Busy markets, sweet incense and flowing yellow robes all greet you as you take your first step into the city.

After spending hours gazing out of your airplane window at snow peaked mountains, the clouds finally open up to reveal a vast plain surrounded by mountains. It's as if you have arrived in another world of clouds, mountains and color. Lhasa is the heart of this Buddhist land hidden away in the mightiest mountain range in the world, the Himalayas.

In Lhasa you'll find religion blended into every aspect of life – the city is the spiritual anchor of Tibet. Lhasa literally means "holy land" and it's a well-deserved name. With many holy sites, Lhasa is an important place of pilgrimage for people from all over Tibet who stream into the city from far-flung villages. They're easily identifiable with their prayer flags and prayer wheels; the signs of devotion abound throughout the land.

It's easy to forget that you're already at an altitude of nearly 12,000 feet (3,650 m) as you look at the towering mountains that surround Lhasa, but that's why Tibet is also known as the "rooftop of the world." The 58-mile (93 km) trip from the airport to the city follows the winding path of the scenic Lhasa River, past families working in fields of barley and yellow canolo flowers and young monks walking along the roadside. Vivid colors are set against the mountains, surrounded by ever-changing clouds and the deep blue sky.

Lhasa itself is a noisy vibrant city, a mixture of old and modern. The city has an eclectic mix of people, Tibetans with their colorful clothes, Sichuan migrants with their spicy cuisine, as well as explorers, mountaineers and tourists from all over the world. There's a saying describing Tibetans, "that if a Tibetan can talk, he can sing; if he can walk, he can dance." This aptly describes their lively and vibrant culture.

The newly completed Qinghai-Tibet railroad is the world's highest railway.

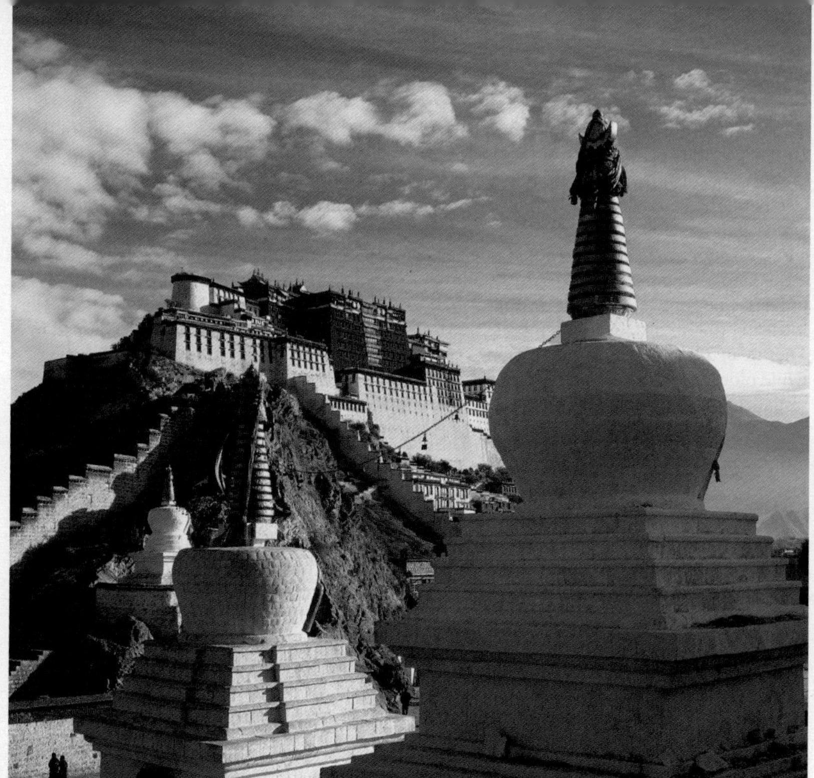

The Potala Palace is Lhasa's best-known landmark.

Over 1,300 years old, Lhasa dates back to the 7th century AD when the colorful Tibetan figure Songtsen Gampo built his palace in Lhasa. In 1642, the 5th Dalai Lama also made Lhasa his capital and rebuilt the architectural wonder, the **Potala Palace** (*bùdálā gōng* 布达拉宫), on top of the ruins of Songtsen's old abode. Today the Potala Palace continues to dominate the Lhasa skyline and is the most visible of all of the city's sights. It offers one of the best views of Lhasa and the surrounding area, especially in the early morning. The Potala Palace is comprised of the **White Palace** (*báigōng* 白宫), which was the living quarters of the Dalai Lama and the central religious **Red Palace** (*hónggōng* 红宫). It's in the Red Palace that you can move through narrow corridors, dimly lit by many small butter lamps, to see the jewel-encrusted tomb stupas of the 5th and the 7th to 13th Dalai Lamas. The many chapels and former apartments give an insight to what life must have been like centuries ago in this theocratic sanctuary.

Some of Tibet's richest treasures are held in the Potala Palace, particularly in the western part of the Red Palace. One especially dramatic sight is the jewel-encrusted tomb of **Lobsang Gyatso** (*luósāngjiācuò* 罗桑嘉措), the 5th Dalai Lama. His gilded 48.7-foot-tall (14.85 m) tomb stupa contains

Memorable Experiences

Spending a day taking photos of people in the Lhasa market – all the various peoples and goods makes for a collage of colors.

Watching dawn from the mountain above the Drepung Temple.

Looking out at the starlit sky and silhouetted mountains from the top of one of the open rooftop restaurants in Lhasa.

8,203 pounds (3,721 kg) of gold as well as 10,000 precious pearls and stones. One of the most beautiful works of Buddhist art is also here, the mandala of the **Wheel of Time** which contains 200,000 pearls as well as coral, turquoise and gold thread. Mandalas are a pictorial representation of the Buddhist universe; not only are they beautifully intricate, they're also deeply symbolic. They're an aid in teaching young monks while older monks use them as a visualization tool for meditation.

The **Norbu Lingka** (*luóbùlínkǎ* 罗布林卡), built in 1751 as the summer residence of the Dalai Lama, lies 1.9 miles (3 km) west of the Potala Palace. As harsh winters gave way to spring, a grand procession of Lamas and officials accompanied the Dalai Lama from the Potala Palace to his summer home. Norbu Lingka, which means "jeweled garden," is a fitting title for the large compound of buildings and extensive gardens. Successive Dalai Lamas continually expanded the palace and up until 1959, commoners weren't allowed within its walls. Today this once forbidden palace is ideal for quiet strolls and lazy afternoons. The palace contains some fabulous murals fusing Tibetan history and myth. Some of the finest murals are found at the back of the woods in the **Golden Lingka** (*jīnsè línkǎ* 金色林卡) and **Chensal Potrang** (*jīnsè pōzhāng* 金色颇章).

One of the best places to view modern day Lhasa and its diversity of culture is in the bustling **Barkhor** (*bākuò jiē* 八廓街), a section of the old city. Here, the **Barkhor Market** (*bākuòjiē shìchǎng* 八廓街市场) has all manner of goods from turquoise jewelry to meditation beads, colorful traditional Tibetan clothes and yak wool sweaters. Here you can watch groups of monks draped in their maroon and saffron robes mingling with Tibetans from remote areas wearing long boots, sporting daggers and large turquoise necklaces.

Long streams of pious Tibetan pilgrims walk clockwise in Barkhor chanting prayers with their meditation beads, spinning their prayer wheels or performing full prostrations as they circle the **Jokhang Temple** (*dàzhāo sì* 大昭寺), one of Tibet's holiest temples. These devout pilgrims wear yak leather gloves and aprons to protect their hands as they slide over the rocky ground, their reverent prostrations atoning for bad deeds performed in the past. Prostrating pilgrims journey from all over Tibet to worship here.

The Jokhang Temple, situated in **Barkhor Square** (*bākuòjiē guǎngchǎng* 八廓街广场), is the noisy and colorful heart of Lhasa. It was built in the 7th century when King Songtsen Gampo wanted to build a temple to house two famous statues brought by his brides from Tang dynasty and Nepal. Being unable

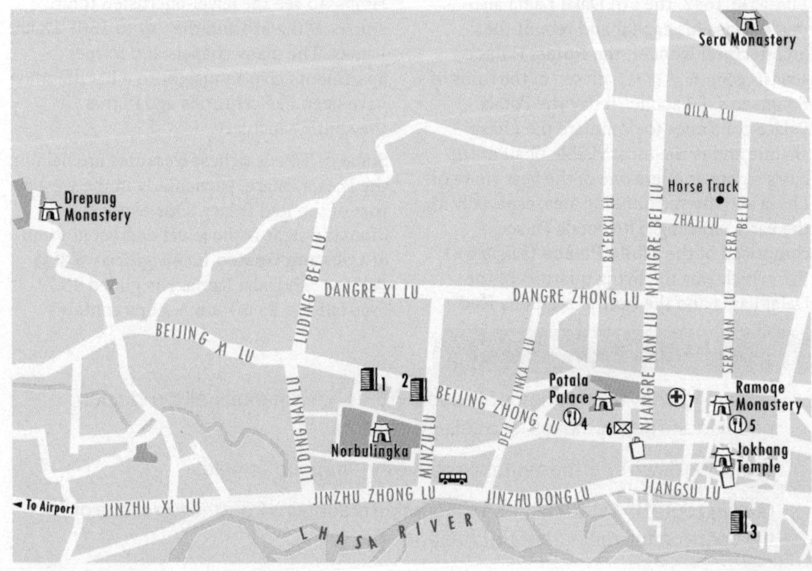

The unfurling of a massive Buddha tapestry is a time for celebration.

to decide where to build the structure, he left it up to fate and threw his ring in the air and promised to build a temple wherever it landed. It landed in a lake, striking a rock where a white stupa miraculously emerged; the lake was filled with rocks and here the Jokhang Temple was constructed. The main entrance to the Jokhang is marked by a large golden, eight-spoke Dharma wheel flanked by two deer. The spokes of the wheel represent the Buddhist eightfold path to enlightenment and the deer serve as a reminder that Buddha gave his first sermon in a deer park.

Dim corridors lined with statues of fierce and benign guardians lead to the innermost shrine. This is the home of the oldest and most precious object in Tibet – the gold statue of **Sakyamuni Buddha** (*shìjiāmóuní jīnxiàng* 释迦牟尼金像) brought by Princess Wencheng of the Tang dynasty to Tibet 1,300 years ago as part of her dowry. Inside the inner chamber, mellow butter lamps create shadows that dance across his features. Also in the innermost shrine is a 19.7-foot-tall (6 m) tall statue of Padmasambhava, the Buddha of compassion and the half-seated figure of Maitreya, Buddha of the future. If you find the narrow corridors stifling then head to the roof. Monks often lead prayers here and it's a great spot to watch modern Lhasa life in Barkhor Square or just sit in the afternoon sun.

About 5 miles (8 km) west of Lhasa, just outside the city, is the **Drepung Monastery** (*zhébàng sì* 哲蚌寺). This jumble of white buildings stands out against the majestic **Mount Gambo Utse** (*gēnpéiwūzī shān* 根培乌

▶▶ Princess Wencheng

Princess Wencheng is the most beloved queen in Tibetan history. A beautiful and intelligent woman, she brought the Tibetans many of the scientific and agricultural advances of the Tang dynasty and is also credited with the introduction of Buddhism into the region. Born the daughter of a courtier, Wencheng became royal only later in life. Emperor Taizong of the Tang dynasty needed to find a bride for King Songtsen Gampo, the new ruler of the Tubo Kingdom (Tibet), and smart and pretty Wencheng seemed an ideal match. She was conferred the title of princess and sent west.

In AD 641, she set out from Chang'an, capital of the Tang dynasty, accompanied by envoys from both sides. They met King Songtsen Gampo in Baihai (Qinghai Province), where the delighted king ordered the construction of a nuptial palace by the Zhaling and E-ling lakes. They were married and honeymooned in the mountain valleys further towards Tibet.

On their way to Tibet, Princess Wencheng taught the locals how to cultivate vegetables, grind wheat flour and distill wine. Grateful villagers carved her footprints into rocks and by the early 8th century, a temple was constructed in her honor in Yushu.

When she finally arrived in Tibet, she was surprised to find Buddhism hadn't yet reached her husband's kingdom. She set about introducing the religion, and had her husband build the first Potala Palace; it later burned down and was rebuilt in the 17th century.

She was also responsible for the Jokhang Temple, one of the oldest examples of Tibetan architecture still standing. Having decided from her knowledge of Tang astrology and geomancy that a particular large pool upset the balance of the elements, she insisted a flock of special white goats fill it in. The spot was given the name "goat-earth," which in Tibetan is "rasa." Later generations modified the sound and the city around the temple came to be known as Lhasa.

Frescoes on the wall of the temple and the Potala Palace record many of her other achievements. Tibetan people learned how to cultivate corn, soybeans and wheat in the highland environment, and horses, donkeys and camels were bred to assist the yaks.

As far as political marriages go, Princess Wencheng's was a great success. Relations between the Tang dynasty and the Tubo steadily improved, and when Emperor Taizong died in AD 649, the new emperor promoted King Songtsen Gampo to the position of "treasured Prince."

Around AD 710, Jincheng, another princess from the Tang court was married to another Tubo king, one of King Songtsen Gampo's descendants.

孜山). The monastery was once the largest in Tibet and where each reincarnation of the Dalai Lama received his training. Built during the 15th century, it's now home to about 700 monks.

Another important temple to the north of Lhasa is the **Sera Monastery** (*sèlā sì* 色拉寺). It continues as a training center set at the foot of Tatipu Hill where young monks train in the debating garden and prepare for scholastic examinations by holding mock debates. In Lama Buddhism, the debating garden is a whetstone where the mind is sharpened. After the garden, climb the wall and walk up the hill to see the beautiful rock art, depicting life-size blue bodhisattvas. A short climb is rewarded with a landscape view of Lhasa and the expansive mountains that ring the city. Here you'll see the sky stretching from the tallest mountains to the heavens.

Wherever you are in Lhasa, you're always surrounded by colorful people, striking natural scenery, humbling mountains, flowing rivers and fields of green, gold and yellow. Although some of the main temples can be busy, just turn the corner or wander off for a few minutes and you'll quickly find yourself in a picturesque rural Tibetan scene out of a postcard.

FESTIVALS IN TIBET

Tibet has many colorful festivals that take place throughout the year and if your trip coincides with one of them, it shouldn't be missed. The festivals are fantastic opportunities to feel, see and taste living Tibetan culture – this is when all of Lhasa comes out.

A Dharma wheel and two golden deer on top of the Jokhang Temple.

One particularly impressive festival around Lhasa is the **Shötun Festival** (*xuědùn jié* 雪顿节), which is held from mid-August to early September depending on the Tibetan lunar calendar. During the festival, giant tapestries of Buddha hang from the mountainside and the Potala Palace. Monks from different monasteries spend an entire year constructing the tapestry as a form of meditation.

In order to see the unfurling, you'll have to stumble up a narrow mountain path in the pre-dawn darkness as incense lights the many small shrines along the path. Only when first light arrives does it become apparent that you're amongst thousands of pilgrims who are also making their way along this circuit.

Senior Lamas and monks stand a large stage on the side of the mountain chanting sutras; flanking the stage are two giant horns held by two monks. The deep piercing bellow from these horns accompanied with the low guttural chants of the monks vibrates the entire mountain and the anticipation is contagious. Once the tapestry is unfurled, thousands of brightly colored pieces of prayer paper envelop the air while taras run down the side of the tapestry launched by pilgrims hopeful for Buddha's blessing. ■

Making Your Trip Easy

Practical Tips

Visiting Tibet requires a special travel permit that can arranged through many offices throughout China. Some of the offices are: Beijing (☎ 010 6228 8845), Shanghai (☎ 021 6228 8845) and Guangzhou (☎ 020 8667 8356). To apply for the travel you'll need to provide some basic information like: passport number, purpose of travel, route. The easiest way to get this permit is apply for it through a travel agent.

The main hazard in Lhasa is the high altitude. Although Lhasa is situated on a plain it is already some 12,000 feet (3,650 m) above sea level. It will take a few days to a week to acclimatize so factor this time into

Quotes

"Instead of an ocean, Tibet has an 'Ocean of culture.'"

"The images that stand out at the end of the day are the children; colorful beautiful kids that approach you everywhere and can't resist the curiosity."

your trip. On arrival don't try to carry your own bags at the airport – go slow, rest and drink plenty of water. The key is not to become out of breath. Some symptoms of altitude sickness include: headaches, loss of appetite or nausea, shortness of breath and lightheadedness or dizziness.

The weather in Lhasa is milder than other places in Tibet and April to October is the best time to go. Expect snow outside these months. In July and August be prepared for temperatures of around 32°F (0°C) at night and up to 86°F (30°C) during the day. Lhasa can also be rainy in August.

Having an ethnic Tibetan guide is an excellent way to see Lhasa. Sights are spread out and except for the city center, public transportation is inconvenient. Guides also have detailed information on the sights, which allows you to see more in a day and they often have detailed knowledge of the sites or of the different festivals or events that are taking place.

Transportation

Airport – Gankhor Airport is 56 miles (90 km) from the city center. It takes about 1.5 hours to Lhasa by shuttle bus, an hour by taxi. Transportation from the airport to Lhasa is inconvenient; it's best to have your travel agent or guide arrange a pick-up.

Pedi-cab – If you only have a short distance you might want to try a rickshaw – they're usually RMB 3.

Taxi – Within Lhasa taxis are a convenient way to get around and most rides will be RMB 10.

The Best of Lhasa

Jokhang Temple 大昭寺 *dàzhāo sì*
✉ in the middle of Barkhor Jie 八廓街中央
🕒 9:30am to 7pm
¥ 70

Norbu Lingka 罗布林卡 *luóbùlínkǎ*
✉ located in the west of Lhasa 拉萨城西
☎ 682 2896
🕒 9:30am to 7pm
¥ 80

Potala Palace 布达拉宫 *bùdálā gōng*
✉ Beijing Zhong Lu 北京中路
☎ 682 2896
🕒 9am to 5pm
¥ 100

Hotels

Lhasa Hotel 拉萨饭店 *lāsà fàndiàn* ★★★★
✉ 1 Minzu Lu 拉萨市民族路 1 号❷
☎ 683 2221, 683 2145
¥ 1,020 – double room, peak-season
714 – double room, off-season

Himalaya Hotel 喜马拉雅饭店
xǐmǎlāyǎ fàndiàn ★★★
✉ 6 Linkuo Dong Lu 拉萨市林廓东路 6 号❸

▶▶ Taboo in Tibet

Some basic etiquette rules that should be followed when in Tibet include:

Never touch the head of a Tibetan, the head is considered a sacred part of the body.
Show proper respect in the temples, don't wear noisy shoes, drink alcohol, smoke or make unnecessary noise.
Don't put your arms around someone's shoulders.
When visiting a temple, follow the pilgrims and circle the temple clockwise, never counter-clockwise.
Never touch, sit on or walk over any religious items such as prayer flags or texts.
Don't kill any animals or insects in monasteries.
Don't be intrusive during religious ceremonies, this means be respectful when taking photos.
Don't harm animals wearing red, yellow or green cloth.
Don't step on the threshold of Tibetan homes.
Don't spit in front of people.
Don't throw garbage into a fire.
Don't engage in strong displays of public affection.
Dress modestly.

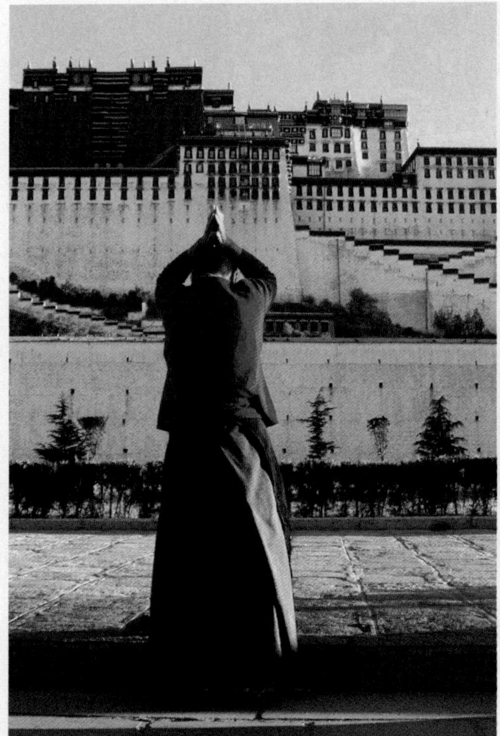

A Tibetan Buddhist monk praying in front of the Potala Palace.

☎ 632 1111, 633 9043
¥ 747 – double room, peak-season
280 – double room, off-season

Post Hotel 西藏邮政酒店 *xīzàng yóuzhèng jiǔdiàn* ★★★
✉ 33 Beijing Zhong Lu 拉萨市北京中路 33 号
☎ 699 8018
¥ 568 – double room, peak-season
380 – double room, off-season

Tibet Hotel 西藏宾馆 *xīzàng bīnguǎn* ★★★
✉ 21 Beijing Xi Lu 拉萨市北京西路 21 号❶
☎ 683 4966
¥ 780 – double room, peak-season
300 – double room, off-season

Xiangbala Hotel
香巴拉酒店 *xiāngbālā jiǔdiàn* ★★★
✉ 1 Danjielin Lu 拉萨市丹杰林路 1 号
☎ 632 3888
¥ 580 – double room, peak-season
160 – double room, off-season

Food & Restaurants

Tibetan cuisine is basic and hardy and most dishes derive from yak milk and meat as well as barley flour. Because of the harsh climate, vegetables and fruits are scarce. Tsamba (*zānba* 糌粑) is made of barley flour and is a local staple. It's often mixed into porridge and eaten with butter tea for breakfast.

Yak steaks are commonly eaten. *Maoniu rou jiang* (*máoniú ròu jiàng* 牦牛肉酱) is made from ground yak steaks in a meaty sauce. Dried yak (*fēnggānròu* 风干肉) is made by mixing cuts of yak meat with salt and chilies then hanging them to dry. Any time is good for a cup of butter tea (*sūyóu chá* 酥油茶) made from a mixture of yak butter, tea and salt; occasionally milk and eggs will also be mixed in. Tasty yak yogurt (*suānnǎi* 酸奶) is a refreshing treat. Another popular drink is barley wine (*qīngkē jiǔ* 青稞酒); it's a little sweet.

Reflecting Tibet's accessibility, an international medley of cuisines is now readily available. Lhasa to is close Nepal and northern India so representative restaurants are particularly good. Thanks to the many Sichuan migrants to Tibet, many restaurants serve up spicy Sichuan cuisine.

RESTAURANTS

Maji'ami 玛吉阿米餐厅
✉ Barkhor 八廊街
☎ 632 4455

Ganglameiduo 冈拉梅朵餐厅
Eclectic mix of Tibetan, Chinese, Nepali food and Western food.
✉ 127 Beijing Dong Lu 北京东路 127 号❺
☎ 633 3657

Snow Palace Restaurant of Tibetan Style
雪神宫藏式餐厅
Specializes in Tibetan local snacks.
✉ west of Potala Palace Square
布达拉宫广场西侧❹
☎ 682 5866

A sounenirs shop in the Barkhor Market area.

Souvenirs

Lhasa has a fantastic array of exotic items and there are a number of truly unique items to buy. *Pulu* (氆氇) is a hand-woven cloth made from wool and most clothing in Tibet is made from this material. Tibetan joss sticks (*zàngxiāng* 藏香) are made from local plants and are seen everywhere. Tibetan knives (*zàngdāo* 藏刀) are both decorative and practical, most Tibetans carry one. The knives are inlaid with gold or silver with bone or wood handles. The scabbards are commonly carved with lion, dragon, tiger or flower designs and inlaid with gemstones. *Kadian* (*kǎdiàn* 卡垫) are often woven into carpets or tapestries.

The Barkhor Market area is the most colorful and cheapest place to shop, items such as traditional turquoise jewelry, clothing, meditation beads, prayer wheels and white and colored prayer scarves (taras) are available. Bargaining in the market is a must and beware of fakes.

Another place to purchase souvenirs such as beautiful Buddhist protection amulets is in the temples. Here you'll find less hassle, there's no need to haggle. Also if you purchase an item inside the temple, it'll have been blessed by a Lama and the funds support the monks of the monastery.

Another item that should be on the shopping list is the splendid Tibetan tankas which are Buddhist paintings. They're a part of Tibetan history and can be seen hanging from walls, often beautifully intricate and bold in color. A great place to purchase them is the Lhasa Carpet Factory located south of the city government and west of Tibet University. All the tankas sold here are handmade and use traditional vertical looms. Here you can see them being made, it's also a nice break from the temples.

Other Information

POST OFFICES

Autonomous Region Post Office
自治区邮局
✉ 64 Beijing Zhong Lu 北京中路 64 号❻

HOSPITALS

Autonomous Region First People's Hospital 自治区第一人民医院
✉ Linkuo Bei Lu 林廓北路❼
☎ 633 2462

COMPLAINT HOTLINES

☎ General: 683 4193
☎ Taxi: 683 4105

TOURISM INFORMATION WEBSITE

@ www.tibettour.com.cn

SOUTH CHINA

Nanning, the Green City

Area Code 0771

Nanning's mixture of natural beauty and ethnic flavor is a great for travelers who want to get away from bustling cities, but still want their conveniences. Full of colorful sights and lush parks, Nanning is a park city that will dazzle any visitor.

Towering buildings and chaotic traffic are all too common in modern China, which makes a trip to Nanning all the more pleasant. Given that Nanning is capital of the Guangxi Zhuang Autonomous Region, the same region that's home to legendary Guilin and Yangshuo, you can bet Nanning has some spectacular scenery. Set in a subtropical climate with palm trees lining the streets and parks, the city enjoys year-round sun and with 40% of the city covered in green space, the locals boast with pride that their city is half-park and half-city.

The city's long history begins with the Bai Yue, a group who were the first inhabitants of the area. Development began in earnest

Nanning is contrast of modern buildings and green parks.

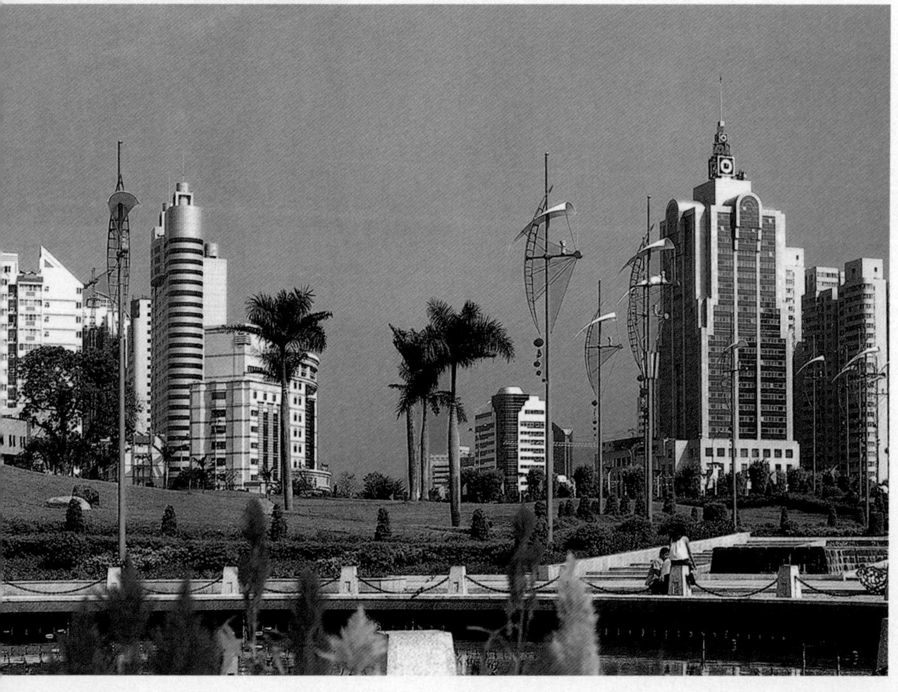

when Qin Shihuang, the first emperor of a united China, incorporated the region into his empire. The Zhuang ethnic minority makes up the bulk of the population, but with over 30 ethnic groups, the city is an eclectic mix of colors and cultures.

Ornate roofs cover this timeworn bridge.

The **Guangxi Minzu Wenwu Yuan** (*guǎngxī mínzú wénwù yuàn* 广西民族文物苑), inside the **Guangxi Museum** (*guǎngxī bówùguǎn* 广西博物馆), is the best place to get a quick introduction to the cultural richness of these groups without leaving the comforts of the city. In front of the main gate stands a replica of a large bronze drum. The earliest bronze drums date back over 2,700 years and were used by the ancestors of the Zhuang as instruments for their elaborate dances, religious ceremonies, ancestral worship rituals and during times of war. There are 320 beautifully cast drums inside the compound, with the largest one about 65 inches (165 cm) in diameter, 26 inches (67.5 cm)-high and weighing over 660 pounds (300 kg).

A variety of artifacts are held within the Wenwu Yuan, such as raised huts built on stakes belonging to the Yao ethnic minority, and drum towers and roofed bridges built by the Dong ethnic minority. There are also workshops where visitors can really get a hands-on experience in the day-to-day life of these people. Give making cooking oil a try or spend some time de-husking rice. After a day of insights into the lives of the various ethnic groups, stop by the various restaurants in the Wenwu Yuan and try out their delicious snacks.

White Dragon Park (*báilóng gōngyuán* 白龙公园), which is also called People's Park (*rénmín gōngyuán* 人民公园), is a nice getaway not far from the city center. About a 10-minute walk from Minzu Square (*mínzú guǎngchǎng* 民族广场), this park is situated on the side of **Wangxian Po** (*wàngxiān pō* 望仙坡), a small hill that's the highest point in Nanning. From the main gate, there's a 33-foot-wide (10 m), 141-step stairway leading to the top of the hill and what's left of an old fort and cannon. The base is made of qing shi and was built in 1917 and the cannon was built in 1890 by Krups, the famous German armaments maker.

South of the hill is **White Dragon Lake** (*báilóng hú* 白龙湖), a small lake surrounded by lush palms and sweeping trees. A small island sits in the middle of the jade green lake and is connected to the shore by two charming bridges. The colorful bridge on the west side of the island features nine bends and on the north end of the island is a bridge with three elegant moon arches.

Yilingyan (*yīlǐngyán* 伊岭岩) is about 19 miles (30 km) north of Nanning and is surrounded by the same karst mountains that made Guilin and Yangshuo famous. The main attraction at Yilingyan is the massive cave complex, which was originally an underground river. The shell shaped cave has three levels and burrows 148 feet (45 m) below ground at its deepest. With an assortment of rock formations that were formed over thousands of years, the stalactites and stalagmites are eerily lit up and make for a unique visual treat. The whole cave site has an area of 1.5 square miles (4 km^2) and is over 0.6 mile (1 km) long. You won't need to worry about getting lost, though, the cave pathways are clearly marked.

Following the Zuo River (*zuǒ jiāng* 左江) downstream, about 19 miles (30 km) from Nanning, is the village of **Yangmei** (*yángměi*

Quotes

"Going to Nanning was a great idea, we didn't plan on it, but this city definitely has a relaxed pace to it. There was a lot of good exploring and we didn't have to deal with huge crowds."

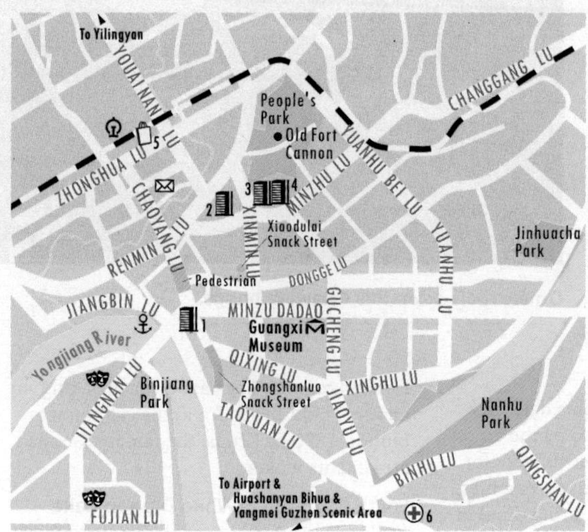

a tourist attraction; it's a living set for many films that use it as a backdrop for period architecture.

For those with some extra time, a trip to the cliff paintings at **Huashanyan Bihua** (*huāshānyán bìhuà* 花山岩壁画) in the Zuojiang Scenic Area (*zuǒjiāng fēngjǐngqū* 左江风景区) offers a glimpse into Guangxi's distant past. About 100 miles (160 km) away from Nanning in Ningming County, there are over 1,800 paintings on an 853-foot-high (260 m)-high cliff. The paintings stretch over 130 feet (40 m) and were painted by the ancestors of the Zhuang over 2,000 years ago. The largest figure is a 10-foot-tall (3 m) mounted chief wearing ceremonial feathers and waving a dagger; he's surrounded by dancers, riders on mystical beasts and a bronze drum and drummers. These paintings are significant, not only because of their age, but also because there are very few paintings of this type in China. The composition of the ink used in these paintings continues to baffle researchers because they have remained bright and vibrant despite 2,000 years of weathering from the sun and rain. How the painters were able to scale the cliff to do their art also remains a mystery. ■

gǔzhèn 扬美古镇), a perfectly preserved Qing dynasty village. The village was once prosperous thanks to its convenient location for trade: three sides of it are fronted by the river. Over 700 years old, the buildings reflect the wealth that once flowed through the streets and onto the waiting boats at the river's edge. The preserved **Qing Dynasty Street** (*qīngdài yītiáojiē* 清代一条街) showcases Guangxi's best remaining architecture from that period. Ornate roofs and eaves decorated with dragons and phoenixes jut out at every corner. More than just the buildings have been preserved; the village retains its rustic turn of the century atmosphere. The rustic village is more than

Making Your Trip Easy

Practical Tips

Subtropical Nanning is blessed with year round temperate weather and a balmy 72°F (22°C) average. Winters will dip to 55°F (13°C) and summers will see the mercury rising to 82°F (28°C).

The Nanning International Folk Music Festival is held every November and features many performances of the local folk culture. Chinese and foreign performers display their skills and exhibitions are displayed. This festival is held mainly at the Nanning Minge Guangchang, but the whole city gets involved and smaller venues dot the city.

Fishing along the lakeshore is a popular pastime in the parks.

Be aware that also in November, Nanning holds the annual ASEAN summit, this means hotel rooms may be scarce.

Transportation

Airport – Nanning's airport is about 19 miles (30 km) southeast of downtown and takes about 40 minutes to reach by taxi. Convenient airport shuttle buses are also available and most go to Nanning's high-end hotels.

Boat – At the Linjiang Lu Port, Xingdao Cruise Lines offers various one-day cruises and night cruises. Call them at 283 1320 or 282 1266 for more information.

Taxi – Taxis are RMB 7 at flag-fall.

The Best of Nanning

Huashanyan Bihua 花山岩壁画
huāshānyán bìhuà
✉ 116 miles (187 km) from Nanning, Ningming County, Chongzuo
崇左市宁明县,距南宁市 187 公里
☎ 862 8915
🕒 8am to 5:30pm
¥ 13

Yangmei Guzhen Scenic Area
扬美古镇风景区 *yángměi gǔzhèn fēngjǐngqū*
✉ 24 miles (38 km) from Nanning
南宁市郊, 距南宁市区 38 公里
☎ 263 2375
🕒 8am to 5pm
¥ 10

Yilingyan Scenic Area
伊岭岩风景区 *yīlǐngyán fēngjǐngqū*
✉ in Wuming County 武鸣县内
☎ 626 0381
🕒 8am to 5pm
¥ 40, entrance to the cave and snacks
25, entrance to the cave
15, not including entrance to the cave

Memorable Experiences

Taking an underground journey through the underground cave complex at Yilingyan and exploring the karst formations that rise high above the ground.

Strolling through the ancient stone cobbled lanes of Yangmei Village and getting a sense of what life was like centuries ago in a village that has stopped in time.

Hotels

Mingyuan Xindu Hotel 明园新都酒店
míngyuán xīndū jiǔdiàn ★★★★★
✉ 38 Xinmin Lu 新民路 38 号❹
☎ 211 8668
¥ 600 – double room, above the 5th floor
380 – double room, below the 5th floor
@ www.nn-myxd.com

Mingyuan Hotel
明园饭店 *míngyuán fàndiàn* ★★★★
✉ 38 Xinmin Lu 新民路 38 号❸
☎ 211 8668
¥ 460 – double room, building 1
303 – double room, building 2
@ pmyhtl@public.nn.gx.cn

Yongjiang Hotel 邕江宾馆
yōngjiāng bīnguǎn ★★★★
✉ 41 Jiangbin Dong Lu 江滨东路 41 号❶
☎ 218 0888
¥ 363 – double room
@ www.yongjianghotel.com.cn

Xiangyun Hotel 翔云大酒店
xiángyún dàjiǔdiàn ★★★
✉ 59 Xinmin Lu 新民路 59 号❷
☎ 210 1999
¥ 278 – double room
@ www.nnxyhltel.com

Food & Restaurants

Nanning cuisine is generally light with dishes placing an emphasis on the freshness of the ingredients. For lovers of spicy food, try old friend noodles (*lǎoyǒu miàn* 老友面); according to legend, this dish was created to cure a friend's cold. Although its curative properties may be suspect, its spice factor will make you sweat. A thin crepe filled with green onions (*juǎntǒng fěn* 卷筒粉) is a delicious local snack. Another local favorite is a crescent shaped dumpling (*nánníng fěnjiǎo huáng* 南宁粉饺皇) filled with pork and a tasty seafood sauce. Over at Minsheng Lu (民生路) is Xiaodulai Shijie (南宁饭店小嘟来食街, ☎ 210 3980), a great food street where you can eat your way up and down the street. Another street to check out is Zhongshan Lu Meishi Jie (中山路美食街), which is lined with traditional restaurants serving local favorites.

RESTAURANTS

Jindalu Seafood World 金大陆海鲜世界
One of the best seafood restaurants in Nanning.
✉ 2 Hengyang Donglu 衡阳东路 2 号
☎ 390 0682
🕒 9am to 11:30pm

Ethnic Zhuang men during one of the year's many festivals.

Yongjiang Hotel Yangguang Cheng 邕江宾馆阳光城
Famous for Guangxi cuisine, house specialties include sticky rice wrapped in lotus leafs (*héyè xiāng nuògǔ* 荷叶香糯骨) and fried whole fish (*yōngjiāng tèsè zhá quányú* 邕江特色炸全鱼).
✉ 41 Jiangbin Dong Lu 江滨东路 41 号
☎ 218 0998
🕒 9am to 10pm

Zhuliba Fenweizhuang 竹篱笆风味庄
Specializes in dishes using bamboo shoots, try their dried bamboo and red stewed beef (*sǔngān hóngshāoròu* 笋干红烧肉).
✉ 5/F Xiangyang Department Store, 110 Mingsheng Lu 民生路向阳百货 5 楼
☎ 283 2903
🕒 9am to 10pm

Souvenirs

Unique Nanning souvenirs are mostly ethnic Zhuang handicrafts. Handmade cloth balls in a variety of colors are traditional Zhuang engagement gifts, they go for RMB 8 to 15. If weight isn't a factor, then get a beautifully cast bronze drum for RMB 100 to 200. Dyed brocades made by the Zhuang women can be used as curtains or wall hangings and cost from RMB 80 to RMB 200.

The intersection of Xingning Lu (兴宁路) and Minsheng Lu (民生路) is a fashionable pedestrian mall where modern amenities can be found. The Fuye Tiandi Specialty Supermarket (*fùyètiāndì lǚyóu tǔtèchǎn shāngpǐn chāoshì* 富业天地旅游土特产商品超市❺) sells various souvenirs and is a good place to browse.

The ancient cliff paintings at Hua Shan.

Other Information

POST OFFICES
Xincheng Post Office 新城邮局
✉ Macun, Minzu Da Dao 民族大道麻村路口
☎ 585 4368

HOSPITALS
Guangxi Medical University Hospital
广西医科大学附属医院
✉ 6 Shuangyong Lu 双拥路 6 号❻
☎ 535 9339

COMPLAINT HOTLINES
☎ General: 551 6551
☎ Taxi: 321 2015

TOURISM INFORMATION WBSITE
🌐 www.nn-tourism.gov.cn

BY BUS 乘公共汽车		
Does this bus go to…?	zhè liàng chē qù … ma	这辆车去…吗?
Which bus goes to…?	nǎ liàng chē qù …	哪辆车去…?
Please tell me when we arrive at….	dàole … qǐng gàosu wǒ xiàchē	到了…,请告诉我下车
What stop is this?	zhèzhàn shi nǎr	这站是哪儿?
I want to get off.	wǒ yào xiàchē	我要下车!
AT THE BANK 在银行		
I want to make a withdrawal.	wǒ xiǎng qǔqián	我想取钱。
I'd like to exchange some money.	wǒ xiǎng huànqián	我想换钱。
I want to cash this check.	wǒ xiǎng yòng zhīpiào huàn xiànjīn	我想用支票换现金。

Guilin's Karst Castles

Area Code 0773

Elephant Trunk Hill is one of Guilin's most recognizable landmarks.

Guilin's limestone karst mountains and Yangshuo's laidback setting have long drawn backpackers and nature enthusiasts. With the Li River serving as a backdrop, the surrounding area is an emerald waiting to be explored.

"Guilin's scenery is the most beautiful under heaven," goes a Chinese saying describing the immortal beauty of Guangxi Zhuang Autonomous Region's Guilin. Boats float down the charming **Li River** (*líjiāng* 漓江) as limestone karst mountains jut from the ground like dragon's teeth. This immortal scenery can be seen on the back of the RMB 20 notes.

While Guilin is far from the crush of other Chinese cities, it is becoming developed and is a major tourist destination. Like many places in China, its history can be traced further back than many nations in the West. During the Han dynasty, Guilin became the political and economic center of Guangxi and continues to thrive today.

Although Guilin is a city, many sights are located within the town or a short distance away. The **Solitary Beauty Peak** (*dúxiù fēng* 独秀峰), located on the campus of the Guangxi Normal University, projects out from the ground like giant spike. The climb to the peak is steep, but the view from the top is worth the effort as you'll be able to take in the surrounding countryside and the Li River. At the bottom of the peak is the **Wang Cheng** (*wáng chéng* 王城), which was a Ming dynasty palace where the regional imperial exams were held.

With half its base sticking out into the Li River, **Wave-Subduing Hill** (*fúbō shān* 伏波山) is located in the northeast of Guilin, near Solitary Beauty Peak. The hill is dotted with many interesting caves; one called **Returned Pearl Cave** (*huánzhū dòng* 还珠洞) has a thousand-year-old image of Buddha etched into the wall along with many others from the Tang and Song dynasties. Among the best carvings is a self-portrait by painter Mi Fu, and a poem by Fan Chengda, both from the Song dynasty.

Folded Brocade Hill (*diécǎi shān* 叠彩山), another well-known peak, offers cool relief with the aptly named Wind Cave. **Reed Flute Cave** (*lúdí yán* 芦笛岩) has some of the best scenery in Guilin with stalactites and stalagmites casting distorted shadows that contort to the shifting multi-colored lights. **Seven Star Park** (*qīxīng gōngyuán* 七星公园) is a large park with many attractive trails that wind around seven peaks in the shape of the Big Dipper. To the south of town is **Elephant Trunk Hill** (*xiàngbí shān* 象鼻山),

Guilin's best known sight.

Finally, there is the **Ling Canal** (*língqú* 灵渠), in Xing'an County 43 miles (70 km) north of Guilin. Built from 219 to 214 BC, it's considered one of China's three engineering marvels beside the Great Wall and the Dujiangyan irrigation system in Sichuan. The canal can be seen in the market town of Xing'an.

TRAVELING ALONG THE LI RIVER

The charming Li River, one of the major attractions of the Guilin/Yangshuo region, has been described as "a green silk ribbon with hills like jade hairpins" and is ideal for exploration on a boat. The meandering 40 mile (65 km) cruise lasts 5 hours and takes you past a panorama of bamboo groves, sleepy villages, karst peaks and fisherman on rickety bamboo rafts fishing with cormorants. Most cruises go down river to Yangshuo and then bus it back to Guilin, though some cruises begin from Yangshuo and go upriver to Guilin. The best times are spring and autumn; the summers can be overwhelmingly hot and muggy while the winters have low water levels.

A river cruise, which includes lunch, can be expensive. If you're willing to forgo an English-speaking tour guide, going with a Chinese group is cheaper at RMB 160. A cheaper, though just as stunning way of experiencing the serenity of Yangshuo is by taking the bus and exploring the surrounding area by bike. Due to seasonal fluctuations in the river's water level, all cruises now begin at **Millstone Hill** (*mòpán shān* 磨盘山), just outside of Guilin.

Along the cruise, you'll pass by whimsically named formations given by tourists of old, though a strong imagination may be needed to fully visualize their namesake. South of **Millstone Hill** and the gray-bricked riverside village of Daxu is **Bat Peak** (*biānfú shān* 蝙蝠

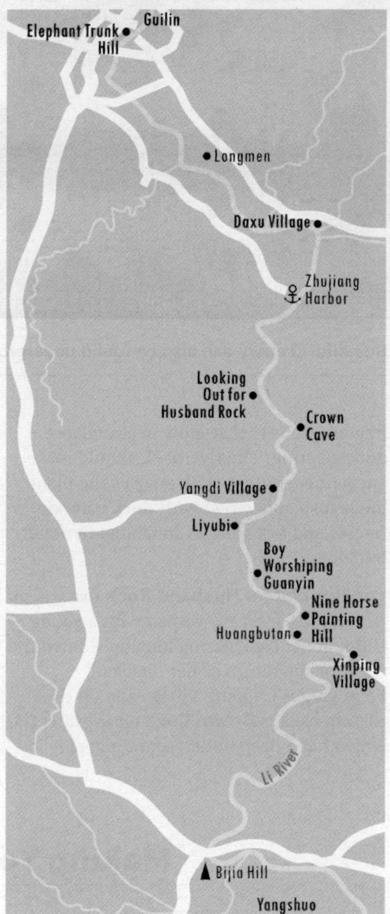

山) with cliffs resembling bats. Unlike in the west, bats are symbols of good fortune in China as the word for bat and good fortune are homonyms. Further along is **Dragons Play in the Water** (*qúnlóng xìshuǐ* 群龙戏水), the rocky outcroppings dive into the water, inspiring a legend that dragons were sent here by the Jade Emperor to retrieve the

Memorable Experiences

Exploring Elephant Trunk Hill Park in the evening while listening to the birds.

Doing Tai Chi in Mulong Pagoda in the early morning as the mist slowly gives way to the gorgeous surrounding scenery.

Eating local dishes from food stalls in the Zhengyang Pedestrian Mall then soaking up the culture at the various arts and crafts stalls.

Beautiful scenery can also be found underground in Guilin.

Continuing on is the village of Yangdi, the small villages along the river are typical of the architecture found in this region. Next is the village of Daxu, which features gray brick buildings covered with gray tiles and upturned eaves.

Before reaching the village of **Xingping** (*xīngpíng* 兴坪), you'll meet the **Boy Worshipping Guanyin** (*tóngzǐ bài guānyīn* 童子拜观音), which resembles a toddler kneeling in prayer, giving his respects to the Buddhist goddess of

fragrant flowers that grow in abundance during spring. The riverbank should make any gardener green with envy as the plant life is lush and varied with thick bamboo forests and rice paddies inhabited by water buffaloes.

Looking Out for Husband Rock (*wàngfū shí* 望夫石) resembles a woman with a young child on her back gazing longingly down the river for the return of her husband. Following is Caoping Village and on the eastern bank is **Crown Cave** (*guān yán* 冠岩), which has a deep underground river.

mercy. After that is the **Nine Horses Painting Hill** (*jiǔmǎ huà shān* 九马画山), a jagged outcropping with the imprint of a wild herd of horses, though these horses can be elusive – most people can only see seven.

As you reach the area surrounding Xingping, some of the most striking scenery along the river comes into view. If you decide to stay in Yangshuo, you can readily return to the area for a second close-up visit. Local travel agents can arrange personalized tours that include visits to the various picturesque villages in the area. ■

Making Your Trip Easy

Practical Tips

Summers can be unpleasantly hot, and the winters can get a bit chilly. The best time to visit is autumn as the weather is a bit cooler and dryer. You won't have to look far for an English map in Guilin, by the way – somebody will offer to sell you one. While the touts and souvenir sellers are generally tolerable, the situation can get unbearable in certain areas with sellers refusing to leave you alone unless you buy something.

If crowds aren't a worry then head to Guilin during some of the traditional ethnic minority festivals. The Longsheng Red Dress Fair (*lóngshèng hóngyījié* 龙胜红衣节) is a time of celebration for the ethnic Hongyao in Longsheng County. Every early April people gather for a colorful market dressed in their traditional best and the young perform songs and dances as part of lively courtship rituals.

The Ziyuan Water Lantern Festival (*zīyuán hédēngjié* 资源河灯节), which takes place around mid-August, is a time when locals float water lanterns down the river in remembrance of past relatives and perform songs hoping for a fruitful harvest.

Transportation

Airport – The airport is approximately 20 miles (32 km) west of Guilin. There are airport shuttle buses to the city and a taxi should cost about RMB 80. The city has many domestic connections and some international flights.

Bicycle – Bikes can be rented from hotels and the many bike shops lining the streets.

Bus – Short distance buses, such as to Yangshuo or Xing'an, depart from the front of the train station and the main bus station, which is north of the train station.

Taxi – Full-size taxis are RMB 7 at flag-fall. Most taxi rides around Guilin will be around RMB 20. Motorcycle taxis are around RMB 5 per trip. (282 0099, 383 5909, 261 5983)

Train – Guilin isn't as well connected as Nanning, the capital of Guangxi, but has connections to most major cities. The station is located to the southwest of the city.

The Best of Guilin

Li River Cruise 漓江一日游 *lijiāng yíriyóu*
- ✉ Zhujiang Wharf 竹江码头
- ☎ 282 5502
- ¥ 270 – luxury cruise, peak-season
- ⏲ 7am to 6:30pm

Reed Flute Cave 芦笛岩 *lúdí yán*
- ✉ northwest from Guilin, Ludi Scenic Area 桂林市区西北部芦笛风景区
- ☎ 269 5075
- ⏲ 8am to 6pm, peak-season, 8:30am to 5:30pm, off-season
- ¥ 60

Seven Star Scenic Area
七星景区 *qīxīng jǐngqū*
- ✉ east bank of the Li River, Seven Star Scenic Area 漓江东岸七星景区
- ☎ 581 4342
- ⏲ 6am to 10:30pm
- ¥ 35

Hotels

Guilin Lijiang Waterfall Hotel 漓江大瀑布饭店 *lijiāng dàpùbù fàndiàn* ★★★★★
- ✉ 1 Shanhu Bei Lu 杉湖北路 1 号
- ☎ 282 2881, 282 3050
- ¥ 1,534 – double room
- @ www.waterfallguilin.com

Guilin Royal Garden Hotel
帝苑酒店 *dìyuàn jiǔdiàn* ★★★★★
- ✉ 186-1 Linjiang Lu 临江路 186-1 号
- ☎ 581 2411
- ¥ 730 – double room

Sheraton Guilin Hotel 大宇大饭店 *dàyǔ dàfàndiàn* ★★★★★
- ✉ Binjiang Nan Lu 滨江南路
- ☎ 282 5588
- ¥ 1,245 – double room
- @ www.sheraton.com/guilin

Gui Shan (JasPer) Hotel
桂山大酒店 *guishān dàjiǔdiàn* ★★★★
- ✉ 1 Chuanshan Lu 穿山路 1 号
- ☎ 581 3388
- ¥ 860 – double room

Preparing for a day of dragon boat racing.

Ronghu Hotel
榕湖饭店 *rónghú fàndiàn* ★★★★
✉ 17 Ronghu Bei Lu 榕湖北路 17 号
☎ 289 3811
¥ 668 – double room
@ www.ronghuhotel.com

Food & Restaurants

Sightseeing, cultural illumination and thrill seeking are all excellent reasons to travel, but the real plum in exploring China is to experience local cuisine. Gourmand tourists won't be disappointed with the Guilin region. Southern cuisine reigns supreme here with Guilin's cuisine a mixture of Guangdong and Hunan styles. While regional favorites include such exotic fare as snakes and dogs, special emphasis is placed on critters drawn from the Li River and assorted types of seafood may be the most unusual you wish to encounter.

Well-known area specialties include stuffed snails and *pijiu yu* (啤酒鱼), a local catfish simmered in a delicious beer broth. Dog hotpot (*gǒuròu huǒguō* 狗肉火锅) and horsemeat with rice noodles (*mǎròu mǐfěn* 马肉米粉) are local specialties. Other favorites include steamed meat buns with water chestnuts (*mǎtí zhēngròu bǐng* 马蹄蒸肉饼), fruit and duck stew (*báiguǒ dùnlǎoyā* 白果炖老鸭), chicken stir fry with mushrooms (*mǎtí chǎo jīqiú* 马蹄炒鸡球) and *heye fen zhengrou* (荷叶粉蒸肉), a pork and rice powder mixture wrapped in lotus leaves then steamed, which infuses the rice powder with the flavor of the pork and the subtle aroma of the lotus leaves. For vegetarians, there's the nun's vegetarian noodles (*nígū sùmiàn* 尼姑素面) served with assorted local veggies. All of these dishes go down better with a few bottles of *LiQ* , the locally brewed beer.

Fans of lighter fare can rejoice in an abundance of fruit. Nearly every street has at least one stall selling freshly cut pineapple chunks, oranges, sugarcane, mangosteen, tangerines, bananas and even durians – those "stink fruit" can be found nearly everywhere. If you have a hankering for Western food, there are many opportunities to indulge in some of the area's newer culinary standards, including pizzas, salads, burgers and banana pancakes. Some streets to check out for good eats include Binjiang Lu, Jiefang Lu and Zhishan Lu.

RESTAURANTS

Jufulin 聚福林
Offers traditional Guilin cuisine.
✉ 10 Zhengyang Lu 正阳路 10 号
☎ 282 9542
🕒 10am to10pm

Tonglai Guang 同来馆
Food court specializes in Guilin snacks.
✉ 2/F, 4 Zhongshan Zhonglu
中山中路 4 号 2 楼
☎ 282 5496

Yiyuan Restaurant 怡园饭店
Specializes in rice noodle dishes.
✉ Nanhuan Lu 南环路
☎ 583 7566

Yueya Lou 月牙楼
Vegetarian restaurant, their nun's vegetarian noodle is very tasty.
✉ inside Seven Star Park 七星公园内
🕒 10am to 10pm

BARS

Red Star Express 红星特快
✉ 56 Guihua Lu 桂花路 56 号
☎ 882 2699
🕒 1pm to 2am

Souvenirs

Being a major tourism nexus, Guilin is filled with souvenir buying opportunities though bargaining is a must since overcharging is

Quotes

"The beauty of the area is astonishing. I came from the gray concrete jungles of Beijing and to see all the green makes me wonder why I didn't come here sooner."

"The attractiveness of Guilin lies not only with the scenery, but also with the people. They are open and friendly, as if the scenery is a reflection of its people."

common. Popular items include combs made from buffalo horns, scrolls, painted fans and paper umbrellas, ethnic Zhuang clothing, bamboo carvings, jewelry and replica antiques. Several local artists maintain booths along the Yangshuo riverfront, including local hero Meng Hui, an artist missing two limbs who does calligraphy quite skillfully using a brush strapped to a stump. Scrolls and huge painted fans are available all over Yangshuo and Guilin, but the best prices are actually available in the little town of Fuli. If you buy anything from any of the hotel gift shops in Guilin, prepare to pay up to ten times as much as you might by shopping around on the streets. Another good market for shopping is the Guilin International Commodity Market (*guójì lǚyóu shāngpǐn pīfā shìchǎng* 国际旅游商品批发市场) in the southern section of the city featuring a big selection of handicrafts. Zhongshan Zhong Lu (中山中路商业街) is lined with souvenir stores and is a good place to browse. The Porcelain Arts Factory (*guìlín měishù táocíchǎng* 桂林美术陶瓷厂) at 74 Qixing Lu (七星路 74 号, ☎ 581 5440) is a good place to look for porcelain vases and the Museum Calligraphy and Painting Store (*zhǎnlǎnguǎn shūhuàtīng* 展览馆书画厅, ☎ 581 2887) is the place to start your Chinese calligraphy and painting collection.

A fisherman and his comorants set out for the morning's catch.

Other Information

POST OFFICES

Guilin City Post Office 桂林市邮政局

✉ 75 Zhongshan Zhong Lu 中山中路 75 号

☎ 281 4339

HOSPITALS

Guilin City Bo'ai Hospital 桂林市博爱医院

✉ 20 Fengbei Lu 凤北路 20 号

☎ 283 6100

Guilin City People's Hospital
桂林市人民医院

✉ 12 Wenming Lu 文明路 12 号

☎ 282 2218

COMPLAINT HOTLINES

☎ General: 280 0315

☎ Taxi: 282 4692

TOURISM INFORMATION WEBSITE

@ www.guilin.com.cn

Entertainment

Impression · Liu Sanjie 印象・刘三姐

China's largest outdoor performance. Guilin's mountains and the Li River form a 500 acre (2 km²) natural stage. Old folktales are combined with modern effects to create a spectacle for the eyes and ears.

✉ Shutong Shan, Yangshuo County
阳朔县书童山

☎ 285 4698, 881 1982

🕒 8pm

¥ 680, 320, 188

Li River Dreamworld 梦幻漓江

Performance in an outdoor setting with ballet and acrobatics.

✉ 95 Qixing Lu, Menghuan Theater
七星路 95 号梦幻剧场

☎ 585 0998, 585 8018

🕒 8pm

¥ 120, 150, 180

Following the cows home after a hard day in the fields.

Yangshuo's Charmed Existence

Area Code 0773

Just over an hour south of Guilin, **Yangshuo**, with its natural scenery and laid back air, is a great escape from the gray and pollution of China's big cities.

The town of Yangshuo is a backpacker's paradise. Quirky souvenir shops and essential services like internet café, telecom services, food guzzling corners and pharmacies abound. Yangshuo town has flourished so swiftly that it is practically unrecognizable from the latest edition of whichever guidebook you own – new streets have sprouted up with shops offering all sorts of comfort foods, and the main thoroughfare has been widened to accommodate the growing volume of traffic. Clusters of shops selling herbs, teas and daily provisions line the inner alleyways.

A lively buzz hums throughout the cobbled streets. Young and old gravitate towards the new hot spots, especially along **West Street** (*xījiē* 西街), a 1.2 mile (2 km) stretch crammed with shops, pubs, café and hotels. Here's where flickering neon lights have replaced red lanterns and the air is rich with band music and banter.

Yangshuo's subtropical weather, characterized by temperate summers and winters, encourage the travel-weary to lounge by numerous street-front café, enjoy a banana pancake and sip an ice-cold beer or two.

The western face of the remodeled town is juxtaposed with the eastern charm of the postcard-perfect natural scenery. Dotting the horizon are craggy tree-covered mounds ranging from more than 300 to 1,000 feet (100 m to 300 m) high.

This little county of some 300,000 inhabitants, comprised of various ethnic groups such as the Zhuang, Yao, Miao and Han, has blossomed since the Sui dynasty some 1,400 years ago. Glimpses of the rich cultural background can be seen in the many shops selling local products such as talcum, silk, huge wall fans, scrolls and exquisite pottery pieces.

Enriching the land are the pristine waters of the **Jinbao** (*jīnbǎo* 金宝) and **Li rivers** (*líjiāng* 漓江), the latter winding some 35 miles (56 km) through Yangshuo, connecting it with Guilin. The river is central to Yangshuo's prosperity; river water is funneled to irrigate the lush fields. Most locals still work the land on the paddy fields and in the orchards punctuating Yangshuo's many peaks, though a growing number of locals are involved in the more profitable tourism industry.

Walking, biking, rafting or swimming are several ways to appreciate Yangshuo's charms. To beat the noonday heat, take a leaf from the village children frolicking in the clear river waters, often seen watching over a herd of buffaloes or wielding homemade fishing rods fashioned from bamboo.

Bamboo groves and willow trees line both banks of the waterfront, and locals use the light but hardy plant to build wafer-thin rafts to fish, rinse vegetables or ferry tourists from one embankment to the next. When visiting the water caves, these bamboo river taxis will bring you close up to stalactites as they slide effortlessly beneath dipping limestone canopies.

UNRAVELING YANGSHUO

There is plenty au naturel to see in Yangshuo: karst peaks, plains and villages. Fortunately, Yangshuo's many pretty sights are incredibly well-connected. Rent a bike for a day from one of the many bicycle rental shops in Yangshuo and drink in the sights as you pedal.

A leisurely 30-minute ride from Yangshuo, and to the west of the highway, is **Moon Hill** (*yuèliang shān* 月亮山), a limestone pinnacle with a moon-shaped hole square in the middle. It cost RMB 9 to access Moon Hill's superb view. Although there are stairs that lead from the bottom of Moon Hill to its windy, arched peak, be prepared for a good workout as you haul yourself to the top. The path gets narrower, rougher and more slippery as you near the peak, but the panoramic view is worth the sweat. If you start at 5:30am, you can make it in good time for the electrifying sunrise. On a clear day, you get a rewarding 360-degree-view of karst topography and Jinbao River unfurling in the distant horizon.

Karst mountains and rustic views along the Li River's breathtaking scenery.

If you're hungry from your climb, head for Moon Hill Village **Moon Hill Village** (*yuèliàng shān cūn* 月亮山村), just across the road from Moon Hill. Mama Moon (*yuèliang māma* 月亮妈妈) is a sprightly tour guide who speaks a smattering of eight foreign languages and whips up a delicious spread of village fare for the famished including tomato and egg omelets, fresh fish, steamed

Souvenir hunting is easy and laidback.

chicken, and tasty winter melon soup.

Climbing enthusiasts will be thrilled with the thousands of natural peaks to test their rock-climbing skills. Climbing equipment is easily available from Mountain Retreat, Lizard Lounge and Karst Café all located in Yangshuo. Suggested peaks include **Copper Door** (opposite Mountain Retreat), **Gold Cat Hill** (*jīnmāo dòng* 金猫洞) and **Thumb Peak** (*mǔzhǐ fēng* 拇指峰). Or try scaling slippery **Green Lotus Hill** (*bìlián fēng* 碧莲峰), **Upper** and **Lower Antenna Hills.**

Just a stone's throw away is a series of newly opened caves: **Black Buddha Caves** (*hēifó dòng* 黑佛洞), **Water Caves** (*shuǐyán* 水岩) and **Dragon Cave** (*jùlóng tán* 巨龙潭). Entrance fee ranges from RMB 100 to a steep RMB 120 per person. The Water Caves have garnered rave reviews, but be prepared to leave damp and slightly dirty from your splashing about. The boat ride into the dark cave seems foreboding – the limestone canopy dips so low at certain points, passage between rock and water seems impossible, but somehow the master oarsman gets the crew through. The tour inside the cave can take up to 5 hours, after which you can rest your feet at the Water Cave Café.

The Black Buddha Caves, located at the back of Moon Hill Village boast rich mineral clays with purported medicinal qualities. You can buy a bathing suit from the equipment shop near the cave entrance and your exploration can last up to 3 hours. There are no toilets in the cave, but it's discreetly dark. A popular cave activity is the muddy mudslides. All hell breaks loose on this sludgy playground as adults are transformed to gleeful seven years old rolling in dollops of thick gooey mud.

Famous for its exquisite Ming dynasty architecture and centuries-old wood carvings, **Xingping Village** (*xīngpíng* 兴坪)is also noteworthy for its superior *fengshui*. Seven mountains form a protective shield around the village and two stone guardians stand erect at the village entrance. Together, they keep the temptations of the modern world at bay, but these relics also tend to discourage proper sanitation and sanitary habits. Odors of the natural kind abound in this rural backwater albeit culturally rich village.

Ornamental eaves, elegant sloping roofs and ancient homes have long drawn scholars and dignitaries to walk the quaint back alleys. It's said that Sun Yat-sen visited the village when he was preparing to tackle the warlords of the north. In 1998, former American President Bill Clinton also popped by. Xingping can be reached from Yangshuo via a RMB 2.50 minibus, but picture-perfect Xingping is best appreciated if you bike or walk along the country roads.

The scenery along the Li River, which snakes all the way from Guilin, will knock you senseless – it's got the Chinese ideal of water and mountains. Farmers, children and water

Quotes

"Two days weren't enough. I extended my stay to a week to enjoy the beauty of Yangshuo at a leisurely pace."

"The mud-slides at the Black Buddha Caves were better than any expensive mud treatment at a spa!"

"Lots of film is needed. There is so much to capture: children at play, ancient waterways and bridges, never-ending peaks."

Terraced hills abound in Longsheng.

buffaloes are visible along the many river bends playing, washing, collecting water or transporting their day's catch. Fishermen come in the feathered coat of cormorants, birds perching on their master's bamboo boats waiting for prey. The metal clasped around their neck stops them from swallowing their catch.

A recently opened **Lotus Cave** (*liánhuā dòng* 莲花洞) in Xingping showcases more than a hundred different types of lotus flower; the entrance fee is about RMB 50 and it takes a good 4 hours to enjoy.

The enormous **Banyan of a Thousand Years** (*qiānnián gǔróng* 千年古榕) is 1,400 years old. Located just 4.6 miles (7.5 km) south of Yangshuo, is a major tourist attraction. Measuring 55.7 feet (17 m) high, 23.3 feet (7.1 m) wide and spanning nearly a quarter-acre (more than 1,000 m^2) – the ancient tree lies on the western bank of the Jinbao River. Entrance to the park is RMB 18. ■

Making Your Trip Easy

Practical Tips

Bring plenty of RMB in small denominations to pay for minibus rides and bike rental. As it's hot in summer and easy to get sunburned, wear a cap and pour on the sun block.

Fire fishing began as a night fishing technique where fishermen use torches to attract fish. Now the Yangshuo Fire Fishing Festival (*yángshuò yúhuǒjié* 阳朔渔火节), held in late autumn, is a time for shows, food and riverside bonfires.

Café and restaurants compete with travel agencies to sell bus, train and plane tickets. Train tickets, especially to Kunming, should be bought early.

Transportation

Bicycle – Bikes can be rented from many of the rental shops in Yangshuo. Bikes for two and three people are also available. Rentals should be about RMB 10 per day.

Bus – The main bus station is prominently in Yangshuo. From Yangshuo to Guilin by bus takes just over an hour; tickets are RMB 5 for a bus without air-conditioning and RMB 6 for an air-conditioned bus.

Luxury buses via CITS and China Southern Airlines (☎ 2723 2923) from Guilin to Kowloon are RMB 350, from Yangshuo to Kowloon, RMB 340.

The Best of Yangshuo

Moon Hill 大榕树月亮山景区 *dàróngshù yuèliangshān jǐngqū*

✉ Fenglouchuanyan Village, Gaotian Town 高田镇凤楼穿岩村

☎ 882 2481, 882 2125

¥ 18 – Darongshu Scenic Spot 大榕树景区
9 – Moon Hill Scenic Spot 月亮山景区

Nice View Garden 阳朔文化古迹山水园 *yángshuò wénhuà gǔjì shānshuǐyuán*

✉ 2 Binjiang Lu, Yangshuo Town 阳朔镇滨江路 2 号

☎ 882 3486

¥ 40

Shangri-La 世外桃源 *shìwài táoyuán*

✉ Wuli Dian, Baisha Town 白沙镇五里店

☎ 877 5666

¥ 50

Hotels

Paradise Hotel 阳朔百乐来度假饭店 *yángshuò bǎilèlái dùjià fàndiàn* ★★★★

✉ 116 Xi Jie, Yangshou County 阳朔县西街 116 号

☎ 882 2109

¥ 664 – double room

@ www.paradiseyangshuo.com

Imperial City Hotel 阳朔帝都大酒店 *yángshuò dìdū dàjiǔdiàn* ★★★

✉ 9 Binjiang Lu, Yangshuo County 阳朔县滨江路 9 号

☎ 881 2568

¥ 280 – double room

@ www.imperialcityhotel.com

New Century Hotel 阳朔新世纪酒店 *yángshuò xīnshìjì jiǔdiàn* ★★★

✉ Pantao Lu, Yangshuo County; near Yangshuo Park 阳朔县蟠桃路，阳朔公园旁

☎ 882 9891, 882 9821, 882 9701, 882 9702

¥ 498 – double room

@ www.yangshuo.com/htls/newhtl.htm

New West Street Hotel 阳朔县新西街大酒店 *yángshuòxiàn xīnxījiē dàjiǔdiàn* ★★★

✉ 68 Pantao Lu, Yangshuo County 阳朔县蟠桃路 68 号

☎ 881 8888

¥ 688 – double room

@ www.nwshotel.com

Baofeng Hotel 阳朔宝峰大酒店 *yángshuò bǎofēng dàjiǔdiàn*

✉ Da Cun Men Developing Area 大村门开发区

☎ 881 3888

¥ 368 – double room

@ www.baofenghotel.net

Memorable Experiences

Watching cormorants lift their prey skillfully from the river and deposit the day's pickings into the fishing boat.

Biking 19 miles (30 km) on bumpy dirt tracks to visit surrounding villages like Baisha Town, which is peppered with ancient bridges.

Sunning on the boat's deck as it cruises along the Li River and trying to make out the unintelligible garble of the boatman as he identifies each rocky wonder.

Riding the bicycle along the highway from Yangshuo Town to Moon Hill Village on a moonlit night and enjoying the phosphorescent outline of karst peaks.

Food & Restaurants

Ethnic Yao girls showing off their finest clothes.

Local cuisine is delightfully varied and delicious. The rivers are well stocked with tench, a type of fish that tastes great when deep-fried and cooked with beer (*píjiǔ yú* 啤酒鱼), green peppers and tomatoes – it's slightly spicy. Pomelos (*shātián yòu* 沙田柚) abound in Yangshuo, and are best eaten in October when they're ripe and pomelos stuffed with pork (*yòupí niàng* 柚皮酿) is a Yangshuo specialty. Horse chestnuts, an October delicacy, are often found stuffed into a juicy duck's breast. Yangshuo's snails are famed for their succulence, but be sure they have been thoroughly scrubbed. They're great stir-fried with pickled bamboo shoots, chilies, ginger and peppermint. Spicy Guilin rice noodles (*guìlín mǐfěn* 桂林米粉) can be found just about anywhere.

Anywhere along West Street (*xī jiē* 西街) is a good place to start looking for lip-smacking grub: Minnie Mao's, Planet Yangshuo, Under the Moon, Nonance, Green Lotus and Lisa's Café are recommended. Menus are in both Chinese and English and the food is as authentic as it can get in China with very reasonable prices. The nearby Front Street (*qián jiē* 前街) is another well-known foreigner's hangout with the same kinds of offerings as West Street.

RESTAURANTS

Ding Ding Restaurant 丁丁饭店

✉ 62 Yangshuo Xi Jie, Guilin
桂林市阳朔西街 62 号

☎ 882 7873

Elder Sister Peng's Beer Fish Dapaidang Vendor 彭大姐啤酒鱼大排档

✉ 1 Rongyin Lu, Yangshuo Town, Guilin
桂林市阳朔镇蓉阴路 1 号

☎ 886 6818

Twin Peaks Café 李萍咖啡屋

A pleasant place to sample Chinese and Western cuisine, plus well made Italian coffee and pizza.

✉ 81 Xi Jie, Yangshuo County 阳朔县西街 81 号

☎ 882 2663

Yangshuo Yikuaiwa Beer Fish Restaurant
阳朔一块瓦啤酒鱼店

Don't leave without ordering a dish of beer fish, their signature dish.

✉ Huashan Lu, Yangshuo County
阳朔县画山路

☎ 881 9123

Souvenirs

Yang Shuo has an interesting variety of painted folding fans. Fans are painted with traditional Chinese ink and wash paintings by the local artisans. The sizes vary from 30 center meters to 1– 2 meters.

Several stores along West Street make custom silk clothing and musical instruments, though they're a little pricey. A good tip is to head to the larger stores and check out their prices and quality then go to the markets and buy there. West Street is an ancient walking street with Western, simple and sophisticated styles. The street is lined with arts and crafts shops selling trinkets from traditional Chinese clothes to ethnic handicrafts.

Other Information

POST OFFICES

Yangshuo County Post Office 阳朔县邮局

✉ 28 Pantao Lu 蟠桃路 28 号

☎ Phone: 882 2461

HOSPITALS

Yangshuo County Hospital 阳朔县医院

✉ 26 Chengzhong Lu, Yangshuo County
阳朔县城中路 26 号

☎ Phone: 882 2472

COMPLAINT HOTLINES

☎ General: 882 7944

☎ Taxi: 882 2301

The Pearl River winds its way through Guangzhou.

Guangzhou, China's Commercial Powerhouse

Area Code 020

Few cities have developed as quickly as **Guangzhou** and while many guides may treat its metropolitan atmosphere with disdain, the city has many attractions for those who seek them out.

During the Tang dynasty, thousands of trade ships visited Guangzhou annually; a large community of Arab traders lived in the old Muslim quarter, now Liwan, dealing in exotic commodities such as pearls, rhino horns and hawksbill turtles.

Situated on the **Pearl River** (*zhūjiāng* 珠江), Guangzhou is the capital of Guangdong Province and was the epicenter of the West's semi-colonization of China, which began in the 19th century. The two Opium Wars both began here and following years of often violent and turbulent relations with the West, foreigners have now returned under the auspices of China's economic reforms. Under Deng Xiaoping's reforms, the first Special Economic Zones (SEZ) were created in the south, and when these economic experiments flourished, Guangzhou quickly adopted the same economic reforms. The city soon became an economic role model for the rest of China. The surrounding province continues to be by far the most developed and wealthy in the country.

During Guangzhou's transformation into a city of commerce, many of the area's

▶▶ The Opium War

The 18th century saw international trade with China blossom, but there was one problem: Western countries had little that pre-industrial China wanted. This trade imbalance frustrated British merchants, who needed to supply an increasing demand for a new drink – tea, which was rapidly becoming popular. They found their answer in the poppy fields of colonial India.

Opium-smoking had been banned by the imperial Chinese government in 1729, but British traders bribed the local officials, who turned a blind eye to their activities, and started shipping large quantities of the drug from British India to the southern Chinese port. Their intention was to create a nation of addicts and thus, an endless market.

2,330 chests of opium were imported in 1788, but that number had risen to 17,257 by 1830. Opium dens spread throughout the country. Officials, often addicts themselves, found it impossible to refuse the sweeteners offered by the now-wealthy British companies.

In 1839, the Qing government appointed Lin Zexu as Imperial Commissioner at Guangzhou. Stubbornly resistant to bribery, in two months he had shut down the trade and destroyed more than 20,000 chests of the drug. He also wrote a moral appeal to Queen Victoria, pointing out that while her government had made opium illegal in Britain, it continued to export it to other countries.

When Chinese junks turned back English merchant vessels in November 1839, China received its answer. The Royal Navy was dispatched and sailed along the coast attacking forts and landing troops who would win victories over the technologically inferior Chinese. It was a complete disaster for the Qing government, and they were forced to sign the humiliating Treaty of Nanking (Nanjing) in 1842.

Five ports were to be opened to British trade, a huge indemnity paid and Hong Kong was to be ceded to Her Majesty's Empire. In the end, this would not be enough, however, and in 1856 the British joined with the French to wage a second Opium War. After occupying Beijing and seeing the imperial court flee to northwest China, the European powers secured the legalization of opium, as well as a provision that allowed the free passage of Christian missionaries throughout the whole country.

Ultimately these conflicts finally convinced China that it needed to modernize if it was to hold its own against Western nations. Within the Qing dynasty, a protracted power struggle between reformers and the ultra-conservatives would lead to the ultimate demise of the dynasty.

In 1997 Hong Kong was returned to China, thus finally ending an ignominious era of British imperialism in China that began more than 160 years ago over opium.

traditional arts and crafts have suffered. Skills requiring years of apprenticeship, such as embroidery, gem cutting and carving have all declined as the enterprising businessman and their factories, keen to exploit this geographically important gateway replace the traditional craftsman. Fortunately, jade polishers and silversmiths are still at work in the old-quarter surrounding **Changshou Lu** (*chángshòu lù* 长寿路).

The march of time has not been so kind to local music styles. Yue, Chaozhou and Guangdong Han operas have all but dwindled into obscurity and there are fewer opportunities to see performances of the traditional music as the young and hip are more interested in modern pop. Just a handful of stores still stock the intricately embroidered costumes of Guangzhou's opera stars of yesteryear, though performances are still given at various venues.

The central shopping street **Shang Xia Jiu** (*shàngxiàjiǔ* 上下九) sports glossy department stores and fashionable boutiques line the main pedestrian street. Every alleyway leads back in time to reveal classic Liwan architecture. Take a shortcut through the modern shopping mall that is

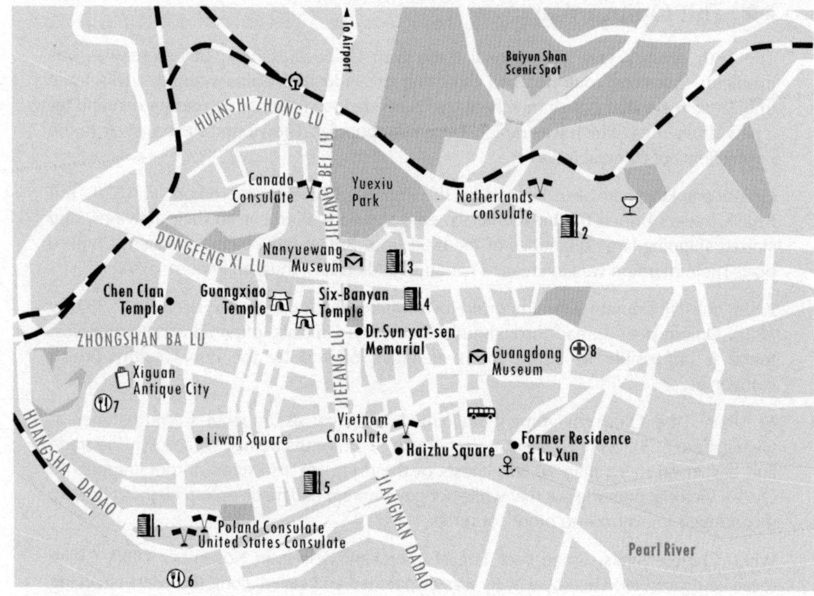

Liwan Plaza (*lìwān guǎngchǎng* 荔湾广场), to discover the jade market and literally hundreds of antiques dealers.

The recently opened subway means that the bird market at **Huadiwan** (*huādì wān* 花地湾) is now easily accessible. Animals of all shapes and sizes fill the stores but it may well be the inanimate objects such as viewing stones and bonsai landscapes (called *penjing* in Chinese), that many international visitors will find most fascinating. Huadiwan has its own stop on subway line 1 and is located in the Fangcun District just south of the river from Shamian Island.

Perhaps the most representative wholesale area in this vast city of markets is the one found at **Haizhu Square** (*hǎizhū guǎngchǎng* 海珠广场). Anything and everything that bears the ubiquitous "Made in China" tag can be found here. More colorful than any Arab souk and certainly to have more bargains, this is a fantastic display of the export machine that feeds the rest of the world.

Baiyun Shan (*báiyún shān* 白云山), which is a small mountain that dominates the town, is approximately 9 miles (15 km) north of the town centre. Hardly a mountain at only 1,253 feet (382 m), it's part of the **Kun Shan** (*kūn shān* 昆山) mountain range. Pagodas, monasteries and teahouses are dotted about its base and when the weather is clear and the pollution isn't too bad, views from the top can be gorgeous. However, it is often difficult to get away from other tourists. Some cramped cable cars ascend to the peak – known as the "**Ridge that Scrapes the Stars**" (*móxīng lǐng* 摩星岭), but be aware that it's a good 3-hour trek back down to the base. Recently, bungee jumping, grass skiing and tobogganing facilities have opened.

For a more relaxed stroll, the former British Concession area, **Shamian Island** (*shāmiàn dǎo* 沙面岛), offers peaceful surroundings. Here you can see the old British and

Quotes

"Guangzhou is the opposite of the rest of China. There is not much to see but there is loads to eat."

"Whoever said that Hong Kong was a Mecca for shopping had obviously never been to Guangzhou!"

American consulates and buildings of colonial foreign powers such as Jardine & Matheson and Butterfield & Swire. Heading eastward is the old French concession, which includes the former French Consul's garden, now a public park, and Our Lady of Lourdes Catholic Church. At one time, overseas traders were restricted to this small island, the bridges were closed at 10pm and merchants were forbidden to learn Chinese. These days it's home to some of the priciest shopping in the city. Many visitors are also attracted to the tranquility of the Overseas Chinese Village (*huáqiáo xīncūn* 华侨新村) on Huanshi Lu.

A little outside of town is the **Chen Clan Temple** (*chénjiā cí* 陈家祠), the former academy and ancestral shrine for the large Chen family. Built at the end of the 19th century from funds given by Chens throughout the province, this compound was built in a broad and open classic southern Chinese style. The lavishly decorated compound was where the family ran their private school and maintained their ancestral shrine; today it exhibits local crafts such as potteries and carvings. ■

Making Your Trip Easy

Practical Tips

Early spring or late autumn is by far the best time to visit Guangzhou and avoid the sweltering summer temperatures. English remains a rarity outside the larger hotels, while Mandarin is spoken by most, with only the older generation limiting themselves to the singsong tones of Cantonese.

Transportation

Airport – Flights from Hong Kong land in Guangzhou's Baiyun International Airport almost as soon as they've taken off. It's a 20 minute hop, hardly worth the effort of getting out to the airport – which takes twice as long as the flight itself and then through the hassle of customs. The Guangzhou International Airport is about 28km to the city center. The high-speed extension of Guangzhou's subway line to the airport isn't completed yet – until then the only access is via the freeway. When you arrive at the airport, go directly to a hotel, it's cheaper than making your arrangements at the airport.

Bus – Buses to Hong Kong take anywhere from 3 to 5 hours depending on traffic and customs. Luxury coaches leave for Shenzhen from the Guanghua Lu bus station every few minutes for RMB 60. At the terminus, simply cross the border on foot and jump on the KCR train headed to Hung Hom or the metro interchange at Mongkok for another HK $32. Obviously this works equally well in reverse. If you're really stuck, in a mad rush or have some friends to share the cost with, there are always Guangzhou taxis in Shenzhen looking for a fare back to the city. You can get them down to around RMB 400 one way.

Subway – Now that the second subway line has opened up, getting around the city is much easier. Line 2 goes from north to south, while the line 1 goes from mostly east to west. Recorded announcements and signs are in English and Chinese.

Taxi – Taxis are RMB 7 at flag-fall. A typical ride across town will rarely be more than RMB 30. Air-conditioned taxis are slightly

Intricate carvings line the walls in the Chen Clan Temple.

Memorable Experiences

Exploring Huadiwan Bird Market and buying gifts for friends back home.

Hiking up Baiyun Shan, watching the visitors collect local spring water.

Bargain hunting in Haizhu Square Wholesale Market.

Discovering hidden Buddhist temples on the way from the Jade Market to the antiques market on Dai He Lu.

A typical busy street in Guangzhou.

more expensive than those that aren't. (Baiyun Taxi Company, ☎ 8360 0000)

Train – As demand grows, so does the frequency of express trains from Hong Kong to Guangzhou. Prices range from HK $190 to HK $260 for the Special First Class. The commuter train is the newest and cleanest. It's operated by the KCR (Kowloon-Canton Railway, www.kcrc.com), rather than by China Railways. It has airplane-style seats and only takes 2 hours. On the return journey from Guangzhou, check luggage on the second floor and then check in on the fourth floor with your passport and ticket. All formalities including customs are taken care of there.

The Best of Guangzhou

Baiyun Shan Scenic Spot
白云山风景区 *báiyún shān fēngjǐngqū*
✉ 9 miles (15 km) north of the Guangzhou City 广州市北部 15 公里
☎ 8770 6871
🕒 24 hours
¥ 5

Chen Clan Temple 陈家祠 *chénjiā cí*
✉ 34 Enlongli, Zhongshan Qi Lu 中山七路恩龙里 34 号
☎ 8181 7371
🕒 8:30am to 5:30pm
¥ 10

Night Cruise on the Pearl River
珠江夜游 *zhūjiāng yèyóu*
✉ Dashatou wharf, Yanjiang Lu 沿江路大沙头码头
☎ 8760 9937, 3760 5513

Hotels

Garden Hotel
花园酒店 *huāyuán jiǔdiàn* ★★★★★
✉ 368 Huanshi Dong Lu 环市东路 368 号❷
☎ 8333 8989
¥ 1,162 – double room
@ www.gardenhotel.com.cn

White Swan Hotel
白天鹅宾馆 *báitiān'é bīnguǎn* ★★★★★
✉ 1 Shamian Nan Jie 沙面南街 1 号❶
☎ 8188 6968
¥ 1,228 – double room
@ www.whiteswanhotel.com

Canton Hotel
广州大厦 *guǎngzhōu dàshà* ★★★★
✉ 374 Beijing Lu, Yuexiu District 越秀区北京路 374 号❹
☎ 8318 9888
¥ 734 – double room
@ www.hotel-canton.com.cn

Guangdong Hotel
广东大厦 *guǎngdōng dàshà* ★★★★
✉ 309 Dongfeng Zhonglu 东风中路 309 号❸
☎ 8333 9933
¥ 396 – double room
@ sales@guangdong-hotel.com

Aiqun Hotel
爱群大酒店 *àiqún dàjiǔdiàn* ★★★
✉ 113 Yanjiang Xi Lu 沿江西路 113 号❺

☎ 8186 6668, 8103 8220
¥ 350 – double room
@ www.aiqunhotel.com

Food & Restaurants

Visitors to Guangzhou never fail to be amazed at the size and scope of the city's restaurants, some large enough to seat literally thousands of diners on each of their multiple floors. Nowhere in the world do people eat out as much as they do here. Every self-respecting establishment has a full array of live fish and fowl on display for patrons to inspect before eating. Freshness, a major factor in Cantonese cuisine, is deemed to be so important that everything is kept alive, either in huge water tanks or tightly grilled cages. For an overseas visitor this can all be rather daunting. Requests for "chop suey" and "chow mein" will be received with blank stares; menus are overflowing with bizarre delicacies such as stir-fried giblets and all manner of chicken's feet.

Recently, statistics showed that there were almost 20,000 restaurants in Guangzhou and that locals spent more per capita on dining out than in any other city in China. Particularly renowned are Cantonese soups; often they include ingredients that claim to have therapeutic properties. Soups in the south are served first in the meal while in the north they're served last. Another local specialty is *baizhan ji* (白斩鸡), a boiled chicken chopped into bite size pieces and served with soy sauce or a dipping paste of ginger and green onions. Beijing may have its duck, but the quack doesn't stop there. Guangzhou's barbequed duck is equally famous – it's served in small pieces with a plum sauce or a light gravy dip.

The Cantonese love affair with all that's edible goes beyond the three daily meals all of us are familiar with – the Cantonese gourmand also partakes in *yum cha* or *zao cha* (早茶), *ham cha* and *xiao ye* (宵夜) (which could literally be translated as morning tea, afternoon tea and late night snack). *Yum cha*, literally meaning to drink tea, is more commonly known in the West as dim sum, which roughly translates as "heart's delight." It's usually eaten in the morning – and can be as early as 6 or 7 am – or in the afternoon and consists of small steamed or deep fried dishes served in round bamboo containers. Dishes are diverse, from steamed buns with meat fillings to shrimp dumplings to marinated tripe. *Yum cha* is more than an eating excursion, but rather a social event – the restaurants tend to be loud and boisterous places with families and friends gathered around large tables with restaurants wheeling out endless trolleys of freshly made dim sum dishes to accompany piping hot cups of tea. Ordering is easy, just point to what's on the trolley.

The bright colors of a busy flower market.

If you want to do some restaurant browsing, head over to Xi Guan at Shangxia Jiu Lu; you'll find a street packed with traditional restaurants there.

Bars in Guangzhou are clustered on three streets: Huanshi Lu (*huánshì lù* 环市路), Yanjiang Lu (*yánjiāng lù* 沿江路) and Bai'e Tan (*bái'é tān* 白鹅滩). Bars on Huanshi Lu tend to be less crowed. The Bai'e Tan bar street is only 10 minutes away from Fangcun subway station by foot. Many of the bars here cater to the large expat population and feature live entertainment.

RESTAURANTS

Dongjiang Seafood Restaurant 东江海鲜城

Branches all over town, go to the aquarium and choose the aquatic critter you want to eat.

✉ 2 Qiaoguang Lu 侨光路 2 号

☎ 8318 4901

◷ 24 hours

Guangzhou Restaurant 广州酒家

A tasty chicken dish they serve here is called *wenchang ji* (文昌鸡), the chicken is first boiled, then steamed then fried; lobster is also available here (*sānsè lóngxiā* 三色龙虾).

✉ 2 Wenchang Nan Lu 文昌南路 2 号❻

☎ 8138 0985, 8108 8388

◷ 7am to 3pm, 5:30pm to 10pm

Huacheng Haixian Jiujia 花城海鲜酒家

Seafood and Cantonese food, delicious.

✉ 3/F, Dongshan Lou, Dongshan Plaza, 65 Xianlie Zhong Lu
先列中路 65 号东山广场东山楼 3 层

☎ 8732 0428

◷ 10:30am to 3pm, 5pm to 10:30pm Monday to Friday,
8:30am to 3pm, 5pm to 10:30pm Saturday and Sunday

Ke Jia Restaurant 客家食府

Hakka food.

✉ 1/F Meizhou Dasha, 338 Hengfu Lu
恒福路 338 号梅州大厦一楼

☎ 8359 2881

◷ 6:30am to 10pm

Liyuan Jiujia 利苑酒家

✉ 2/F Baifu Square, 112 Tiyu Donglu, Tianhe District
天河区体育东路 112 号百福广场 2 楼

☎ 3880 6788, 8757 6788

Panxi Jiujia 泮溪酒家

Dozens of dim sum trolleys, just point and choose what you want.

✉ 151 Longjin Xi Lu 龙津西路 151 号❼

☎ 8181 5955

◷ 6:30am to 11:30pm

South Fish Village 南海渔村

Classy Cantonese seafood.

✉ 903 Renmin Beilu 人民北路 903 号

☎ 8666 8668

◷ 7:30am to 3am

BARS

Mooncarol 蒙地卡罗西餐厅

✉ 2/F, 77 Tiyu Xilu 体育西路 77 号 2 楼

☎ 8559 6048

◷ 11am to midnight

Souvenirs

Keepsake shopping can be a difficult proposition in a city that acts as a conduit for mass-produced factory goods that pass through to nearly every corner of the world. The latest wave of mega-malls with their supermarkets and fashion outlets aren't really suited for souvenir hunting, although they're often very good for regular shopping sprees. One option is the bird market down at Huadiwan. Viewing stones and bonsai trees of the Lingnan variety along with ornately carved bird cages and accessories make wonderful keepsakes.

While Guangzhou not traditionally a center of silk production, the fabric plays an important role in local textile industries and a wide range of goods, from suits and *qipaos* to dressing gowns and phone covers can be purchased at the brightly colored Haiyin Market.

If you're looking for antiques, stop by Xi Guan Guwan Cheng (*xīguān gǔwán chéng* 西关古玩城) near Fengyuan Lu (逢源路) and Longjin Xi Lu (龙津西路). Jewelry can be found at the historical Jade and Jewelry Street on Changshou Lu.

For the best selection of herbs and spices, head for the newly renovated market on Liu Er San Lu which is situated conveniently close to the White Swan Hotel. A seeming endless assortment of bugs, mushrooms and other assorted fungi spill out of bursting sacks, alongside every possible kind of dried herbs and flowers. Most of the bizarre botanical offerings are difficult to identify

The Pearl River lights up at night.

with even the largest of translation dictionaries, but the sights and sounds and above all the smells of this strange place make it an essential visit.

For an eye-opening alternative, try the wholesale markets around Haizhu Square, where the combined production of so many local factories is on display. Look for unusual items such as New Year decorations that represent the liveliness of local culture. Don't be afraid to bargain for items that can be found at many times the price at high-end department stores such as Xin Da Xin and the Friendship Chain.

Other Information

POST OFFICES

Beijing Lu Post Office 北京路邮局

✉ 987 Beijing Lu 北京路 987 号

☎ 8333 3983

HOSPITALS

The First Zhongshan University Hospital
中山大学第一附属医院

✉ 58 Zhongshan Er Lu 中山二路 58 号

☎ 8775 5766

Guangdong Province People's Hospital
广东省人民医院

✉ 106 Zhongshan Er Lu 中山二路 106 号❽

☎ 8382 7812

CONSULATES

Australia 澳大利亚

✉ Room 1401, Main Tower, Guangdong International Hotel, 339 Huanshi Dong Lu
环市东路 339 号广东国际大厦主楼 1401 号

☎ 8335 0909, 8335 5911

Cambodia 柬埔寨

✉ Room 804, East Tower, Garden Hotel, 368 Huanshi Dong Lu
环市东路 368 号广州花园酒店东楼 804 房

☎ 8333 8999, 8666 0569

Canada 加拿大

✉ Room 801, Office Tower, China Hotel, Liuhua Lu 流花路中国大酒店商务楼801 号

☎ 8666 0569

Denmark 丹麦

✉ Room 1578, Officer Tower, China Hotel, Liuhua Lu
流花路中国大酒店商务楼 1578 号

☎ 8666 0795

France 法国

✉ 8/F, Main Tower, Guangdong International Hotel, 339 Huanshi Dong Lu
环市东路 339 号广东国际大酒店主楼 8 楼

☎ 8330 3405

Germany 德国
✉ 19/F, Guangdong International Hotel, 339 Huanshi Dong Lu
环市东路 339 号广东国际大酒店 19 楼
☎ 8330 6533

Indonesia 印度尼西亚
✉ 2/F, West Building, Dong Fang Hotel, 120 Liuhua Lu 流花路东方宾馆西楼 2 层
☎ 8601 8772

Italy 意大利
✉ Room 5207-8, CITIC Plaza, 233 Tianhe Bei Lu, Tianhe District
天河区天河北路 233 号中信广场 5207-8 房
☎ 3877 0556

Japan 日本
✉ 1/F, Garden Hotel, 368 Huanshi Dong Lu
环市东路 368 号花园酒店 1 层
☎ 8333 8999

Malaysia 马来西亚
✉ Room 1915-18, 19/F, CITIC Plaza, 233 Tianhe Bei Lu, Tianhe District 天河区天河北路 233 号中信广场 19 层 1915-18 房
☎ 8739 5660, 3877 0766, 3877 0765

From the tank straight to your plate.

Netherlands 荷兰
✉ Room 905, Main Tower, Guangdong International Hotel, 339 Huanshi Dong Lu
环市东路339号广东国际大酒店主楼905室
☎ 8330 2067
@ www.cgguangzhou.org

Philippines 菲律宾
✉ Room 710, Main Building, Guangdong International Hotel, 339 Huanshi Dong Lu
环市东路339号广东国际大酒店主楼710室
☎ 8331 1461, 8331 0996

Poland 波兰
✉ 63 Shamian Da Jie 沙面大街 63 号
☎ 8121 9993, 8121 8991

Republic of Korea 韩国
✉ 18/F, West Tower, International Trade Centre, Tiyu Dong Lu
体育东路羊城国际商贸中心西塔 18 楼
☎ 3887 0555

Singapore 新加坡
✉ Unit 3318, CITIC Plaza, 233 Tianhe Bei Lu, Tianhe District
天河区天河北路 233 号中信广场 3318 房
☎ 3891 2345

Sweden 瑞典
✉ Room 1205, Main Tower, Guangdong International Hotel, 339 Huanshi Dong Lu
环市东路339号广东国际大酒店主楼1205室
☎ 8331 0976

Thailand 泰国
✉ Room 207, Garden Hotel, 368 Huanshi Dong Lu 环市东路 368 号花园酒店 207 室
☎ 8333 8989

United Kingdom 英国
✉ 2/F, Main Tower, Guangdong International Hotel, 339 Huanshi Dong Lu
环市东路 339 号国际大酒店主楼 2 楼
☎ 8335 1354

United States 美国
✉ 1 Shamian Nan Jie 沙面南街 1 号
☎ 8121 8000

Vietnam 越南
✉ 2/F, Building13 Hua Xia Hotel,Qiaoguang Lu Haizhu Square
海珠广场侨光路华夏大酒店 13 座 2 楼
☎ 8330 5910 for visas,
8330 5911 for cultural & economic matters

COMPLAINT HOTLINES
☎ General: 8666 6666
☎ Taxi: 96900, 8601 0314

The man who made it all happen, Deng Xiaoping.

Shenzhen, the Spirit of Speed

Area Code 0755

Few talk about **Shenzhen** without making reference to its modest origins as a tiny fishing village. While much of its obscure 6,000-year history has been lost, its present incarnation as one of the fastest growing cities in China is nothing less than miraculous. The area consists of three parts, **Shenzhen City**, **Shenzhen County** and the **Special Economic Zone** (SEZ), which is the business and financial center of the city. As one of the first cities to "open" with economic reforms in 1979, and situated next to Hong Kong, sleepy Shenzhen went from village to metropolis in just over 20 years, and is now a magnet for fortune-seekers.

Many people are drawn to Shenzhen by a certain energy, what locals call "Shenzhen speed." Speed is the catchphrase here in a city that sees the opening of one supermarket per day and an unmatched prosperity in trade. Efficient and courteous service is a merit of Shenzhen. In this highly commercial and competitive society, 24-hour-a-day delivery is offered by your neighborhood stores for any purchase down to a lump of soap.

A spirit of pragmatism pervades Shenzhen's unusually young population of migrant workers. They're an interesting mix of

Shenzhen remains busy late into the night.

graduates of prestigious universities as well as villagers from rural areas – but they're all attracted by the possibilities that lie in Shenzhen. Because Shenzhen is a city of migrants, there's no Shenzhen dialect. The locals speak a peculiar mix of Cantonese and Mandarin flavored with a mish-mash of regional accents. While Shenzhen still holds a reputation as a newly formed city, two decades of development has shown signs of a maturing metropolis, from well-developed residential and commercial districts to an efficient public transportation system. Many young settlers have not only started a career in the city, but also started their families here; buying their first house and car, thus establishing Shenzhen as more than an office city, they have made it their home.

There's more to Shenzhen than what meets the eyes. On the surface, it appears to only feature blocks after blocks of high-rises and factories. Under its subtropical climate, Shenzhen enjoys year-round warmth and days filled with sunshine punctured with tropical rains. The city planners, seeing an opportunity to create a modern livable environment, placed great emphasis on the city's greenery. An exceptional model is **Shennan Da Dao** running through Shenzhen from east to west for 25 miles (40 km). The broad avenue features a wide green belt down the middle

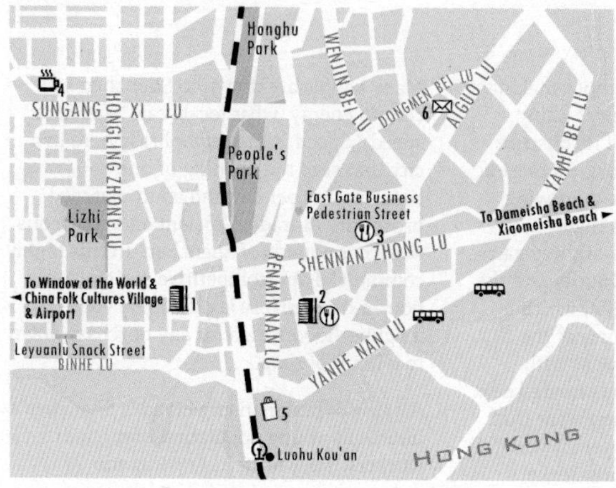

Quotes

"People say Shenzhen is like a pretty lady without much depth or soul but Shenzhen is full of opportunities and challenges for those who are willing to try. It's stimulating."

"There are many amazing things to see in the Overseas Chinese city. I can't get enough of it."

which makes up 40% of its width. While Shenzhen is still used as a transit point to Hong Kong, the city is fast becoming a popular travel destination in south China thanks to its assortment of parks, beaches, shopping centers, as well as plenty of dining and drinking options.

Geography and architecture-loving tourists in Shenzhen shouldn't pass up the three large theme parks of replicated landscape and architecture located inside the **Overseas Chinese City** (*huáqiáo chéng* 华侨城), a full-fledge community of tourist attractions and residences. The attractions there include Splendid China, China Folk Culture Villages and Window of the World, all must-sees in Shenzhen. **Splendid China** (*jǐnxiù zhōnghuá* 锦绣中华) recreates 100 or so tourist attractions from all corners of China in miniature, including such sights as: the Great Wall, the Terracotta Warriors, Tai Shan, the Three Gorges, Hangzhou's West Lake, Suzhou's Gardens, Lijiang's landscape as well as numerous pagodas and temples. Continuing the shrinking trend, **Window of the World** (*shìjiè zhī chuāng* 世界之窗) packs in 118 world famous scenic spots and architectural wonders from the Great Pyramids to the Sydney Opera House, allowing visitors to traverse the world at one site. The **China Folk Cultures Village** (*zhōnghuá mínsú wénhuà cūn* 中华民俗文化村) weaves into one tapestry the customs and traditional lifestyles of 24 Chinese ethnic groups. The site also includes mock-ups of their native villages, from Beijing courtyard houses to Shaanbei cave-dwellings. Minority performers regularly stage variety shows and artists make handicrafts on site. True to Shenzhen speed, all three theme parks are next to each other and allow you to take in not only the whole of China but also the world in a few days. During summer, there are many evening entertainment programs to partake in.

Lianhua Shan (*liánhuā shān* 莲花山), in the northern tip of central Shenzhen, is a hit with residents and tourists alike. It's a readily accessible park that contains extensive areas of greenery. There is no admission charge and the fields of grass come to life at night with young couples and families. Many visitors take the easy-going trail for a 20-minute stroll to the top of the mountain that offers a splendid view of downtown Shenzhen.

Two favorite weekend destinations for locals are **Dameisha** (*dàméishā* 大梅沙) and **Xiaomeisha** (*xiǎoméishā* 小梅沙), two seaside resorts about an hour's drive from downtown and easily reached by bus. Both beaches lean against a hill and are surrounded by lush tropical forests. Dameisha is heaving with swimmers and surfers on weekends; there are also some colorful sculptures. All this and no admission charge. Xiaomeisha is Shenzhen's

Fast food Shenzhen style.

largest resort and it boasts an extensive white sand beach lying to the east of Dapeng Bay. It's well-equipped with beach and aquatic toys as well as accommodations and catering facilities. The RMB 10 admission charge makes Xiaomeisha slightly more exclusive than Dameisha.

All the shopping and theme parks may make for aching muscles, but it should come as no surprise that this city, which moves at a breakneck speed, is also full of massage salons. Literally any massage salon you visit, whether at a street corner or inside a shopping mall, will be clean, professional, affordable and above all, immensely relaxing. Many complain that Shenzhen is all about money – but money, not necessarily a lot of it, can indeed buy you a lot of satisfaction in this land of material temptations. ■

Making Your Trip Easy

Practical Tips

Be sure to bring sun block when exploring Shenzhen, especially at the beaches and theme parks where there isn't a lot of shade. The temperature is high all year and averages – 86°F (30°C) into late November.

A great way to cool off during the hot summers is to head to the Beer Festival that's held from July 8 to August 15 at Window of the World. Art connoisseurs will appreciate the Art Festival that's held in October at the Shenzhen Grand Theater.

There are many options for entering Hong Kong from Shenzhen. Many who travel to Hong Kong choose to fly to Shenzhen then cross the border on foot as it's significantly cheaper than going directly to Hong Kong. In Shenzhen, head over to the customs building at the Luohu Train Station; once through, it's a quick and easy ride on the KCR into Hong Kong. If you're taking a bus into Hong Kong then you'll go through customs at Huanggang Port (皇岗口岸). Those who land at the Shenzhen Airport can take a ferry that goes to Hong Kong Island or Kowloon. The ferry takes about an hour and tickets are RMB 180. It's a quick 10-minute bus ride to the port from the airport.

Transportation

Airport – Shenzhen Bao'an International Airport is 22 miles (35 km) from downtown. Airport shuttles buses make the 40-minute trip into the city run 24 hours a day and cost RMB 20. The airport is well connected with international and domestic flights.

Bus – Shenzhen is well connected by buses. Buses between Shenzhen and Guangzhou run as frequently as every 20 minutes.

Taxi – There are three kinds of taxis in Shenzhen, each with their own price structure and destination limits. Red taxis are RMB 12.5 at flag-fall and can access Shenzhen and the SEZ. Green taxis are RMB 7 at flag-fall and can only run outside the SEZ. Yellow taxis start at RMB 10.5 and only service the SEZ. For convenience's sake it's best to hop into a red taxi.

Train – Luohu Train Station is on the east side of the city and connects Shenzhen to most southern Chinese cities. Trains to Guangzhou take only 45 minutes and run every 30 minutes.

Memorable Experiences

Sunbathing on the beaches of Dameisha or Xiaomeisha.

Having midnight snacks a hole-in-the-wall restaurant on Badeng Lu.

Shopping in the area around Tongbao Secondhand Market in Huaqiang Bei Lu.

Getting a body rubdown in a local massage salon.

The Best of Shenzhen

Shenzhen Dameisha Travel Development Co. Ltd 深圳市大梅沙旅游发展有限公司 *shēnzhèn dàméishā lǚyóu fāzhǎn yǒuxiàn gōngsī*
✉ 94 Dameisha, Yantian District
盐田区大梅沙 94 号
☎ 2506 0927

Window of the World
深圳世界之窗有限公司
shēnzhèn shijièzhīchuāng yǒuxiàn gōngsī
✉ Huaqiao Cheng, Nanshan District
南山区华侨城
☎ 2660 8000
🕒 9am to 10pm
¥ 120
@ www.szwwco.com

Waterlands Resort
深圳西部海上田园旅游区生态馆 *shēnzhèn xībù hǎishàng tiányuán lǚyóuqū shēngtàiguǎn*
✉ Shajing Town, Bao'an District
宝安区沙井镇
☎ 2725 9888
🕒 9am to 7pm
¥ 60

Hotels

Nanhai Hotel
南海酒店 *nánhǎi jiǔdiàn* ★★★★★
✉ Gongye Lu, Shekou, Nanshan District
南山区蛇口工业路
☎ 2669 2888
¥ 715 – double room, peak-season
625 – double room, off-season
@ www.nanhai-hotel.com

Sunshine Hotel
阳光酒店 *yángguāng jiǔdiàn* ★★★★★
✉ 1 Jiabin Lu, Luohu District
罗湖区嘉宾路 1 号❷
☎ 8223 3888
¥ 1,800 – double room
@ www.sunshinehotel.com

Hotel Oriental Regent
晶都酒店 *jīngdū jiǔdiàn* ★★★★
✉ Finance Center Tower, Shennan Zhong Lu
深南中路金融中心大厦❶
☎ 8224 7000
¥ 880 – double room
@ www.jingdow.com

Shenzhen Bay Hotel 深圳湾大酒店 *shēnzhènwān dàjiǔdiàn* ★★★★
✉ Huaqiao Cheng, Nanshan District
南山区华侨城
☎ 2660 0111
¥ 688 – double room, peak-season
430 – double room, off-season

East Lake Hotel
东湖宾馆 *dōnghú bīnguǎn* ★★★
✉ 4006 Aiguo Lu, Luohu District
罗湖区爱国路 4006 号
☎ 2540 0088
¥ 358 – double room, peak-season
298 – double room, off-season

Food & Restaurants

There's an impressive selection of cuisines including Cantonese, Chaozhou, Sichuan, Hunan and seafood – the cuisines available are just as diverse as the make-up of its residents. Morning and afternoon dim sum is just as good as in Hong Kong for a fraction of the price. Restaurants are in abundance but for a unique dining experience head for Badeng Jie (八登街) opposite the Municipal Government building or Leyuan Lu (乐园路食街) in Dong Men. Both are lined up with Da Paidang (大排档), hole-in-the-wall restaurants ling the street. Even at 3am, Badeng Jie is teeming with hungry bar-hoppers, goldfish hawkers and fruit sellers. Leyuan Lu is especially worth going for its seafood, though hygiene is often second to flavor; business hours extends to the wee hours. Zhenhua Lu Food Street (振华路食街) offers a potpourri of dishes from every region in China in addition to Indian, Japanese and Western offerings. Shenzhen has great tropical fruits – try the deliciously nanshan lychee (*nánshān lìzhī* 南山荔枝).

RESTAURANTS

Beihai Yucun 北海渔村
It's spicy snake (*xiānglà shélù* 香辣蛇碌) will get your mouth tingling.
✉ 79 Zhenhua Lu, Futian District
福田区振华路 79 号
☎ 8322 1852

Chang'an Dasha Jingdu Jiulou
长安大厦京都酒楼
Green onions with sea cumber (*cōngshāo hǎishēn* 葱烧海参) are flavorful and crunchy.
✉ 1/F Chang'an Dasha, Shennan Dong Lu, Luohu District
罗湖区深南东路长安大厦一楼
☎ 2511 2500

Staying in the shade at a busy plaza.

Qinxianglou 沁香楼
✉ 128 Fenghuang Lu, Luohu District 罗湖区凤凰路 128 号❸
☎ 2552 3229

Nangang Yucun 南岗渔村
Specializes in Guangdong cuisine.
✉ 1105 Nanshan Da Dao, Nanshan District 南山区南山大道 1105 号
☎ 2605 1578

Nanshan Xintaoyuan Dajiulou 南山新桃园大酒楼
Great goosefeet in abalone sauce (*bàozhī ézhǎng* 鲍汁鹅掌).
✉ 1 Taoyuan Dong Lu, Nanshan District 南山区桃园东路 1 号
☎ 2649 3388

Shenzhen Fuhua Seafood Restaurant 深圳富华海鲜酒家
Delicious abalone in a rich sauce (*háohuáng dà'àobào* 蚝皇大澳鲍).
✉ Bingang Xincun, Dongyuan Lu, Futian District 福田区东圆路宾岗新村
☎ 8224 6446

Xinquansheng Seafood Restaurant 新全盛海鲜酒楼
Its king lobster (*lóngxiā dàwáng* 龙虾大王) takes the crown.
✉ Building C, Sea Food Street, Yantian 盐田海鲜食街 C 栋
☎ 2520 1222

TEAHOUSES

Mingmeng Xuan Teahouse 明梦轩茶艺馆
Lush plants, flowing water and swimming fish accompanied by ancient music with a huge assortment of teas and other beverages on offer.
✉ 2/F Yihua Tower, Building 617, Bagua Yi Lu, Futian District 福田区八卦一路 617 栋艺华大厦 2 楼❹
☎ 8247 0191

Ziyuan Teahouse 紫苑茶馆
A peaceful retreat in a noisy city.
✉ 1/F Guanshanyue Art Museum, 6026 Hongli Lu 红荔路 6026 号关山月美术馆一楼
☎ 8306 5494

Souvenirs

Shenzhen doesn't have much to offer in terms of homegrown specialties or tourist shopping, but the theme parks in the Overseas Chinese City sell minority souvenirs, such as food, clothes and eclectic products that show strong local characteristics and culture. Migrants from all over China bring products from their hometowns so there are a great variety of things to buy.

Many visitors from Hong Kong go to Shenzhen on a regular basis to do their shopping. Starting from the train station: Luohu (罗湖) is a bustling port of restaurants, shops and massage salons. The Luohu Business Center (*luóhú shāngyè chéng* 罗湖商业城❺) is teeming with cheap clothing, footwear and accessories booths interspersed with massage and manicure salons. Hard bargaining is the rule here and don't hesitate to slice the price to one third of what's offered. Dong Men (东门) is packed with shopping malls and individual booths flaunting an inexhaustible array of the latest Cantopop, Korean and Japanese fashions as well as a kaleidoscope of knick-knacks at bargain prices.

The Tongbao Secondhand Market (*tōngbǎo jiùhuò shìchǎng* 通宝旧货市场) is reminiscent of a giant flea market where furniture, computers and electronic products are up for grabs, but the real gem is the area adjoining the market which is jam-packed with booths selling clothes and toys left over from export orders as well as CDs and DVDs. CITIC City Plaza (*zhōngxìn chéngshì guǎngchǎng* 中信城市广场) is a first class shopping arcade. The flashy glass structure is opposite the Municipal Government building and has an expansive piazza with fountains. High-end name brand products are on offer and the various shop displays are eye-catching. You can finish your shopping spree with a coffee in Starbucks on the ground floor.

Other Information

POST OFFICES

The Branch Post Office of Aiguo Lu
爱国路邮政支局
✉ 1/F, 1033 Aiguo Lu 爱国路 1033 号一层❻
☎ 8223 8679
🕒 8:30am to 6:30pm

The Branch Post Office of Jianshe Lu
建设路邮政支局
✉ 1-2/F, Postal Tower,.3040 Shennan Dong Lu 深南东路 3040 号邮政大厦一至二楼
☎ 2516 8331
🕒 8:30am to 6:30pm

HOSPITALS

Peking University Shenzhen Hospital
北京大学深圳医院
✉ Lianhua Bei Lu, Futian District 福田区莲花北路
☎ 8306 1341

The Second People's Hospital
第二人民医院
✉ Huaqiang Bei Lu and Sungang Lu 笋岗路与华强北路交汇处
☎ 8336 7449

COMPLAINT HOTLINES

☎ General: 8322 1397
☎ Taxi: 8322 8000

TOURISM INFORMATION WEBSITE

@ www.shenzhentour.com

SOUVENIRS 纪念品		
antiques	gǔdǒng	古董
calligraphy	shūfǎ	书法
Chinese brush	máobǐ	毛笔
ink stone	yàntái	砚台
carpet	dìtǎn	地毯
clay figurines	nísù	泥塑
cloisonné	jǐngtàilán	景泰蓝
porcelain	cíqì	瓷器
chopsticks	kuàizi	筷子
earrings	ěrhuán	耳环
embroidery	cìxiù	刺绣
fabrics	bùliào	布料
fans	shànzi	扇子
handmade	shǒugōngzhì de	手工制的
jadeware	yùqì	玉器
jewellery	zhūbǎo	珠宝
lacquerware	qīqì	漆器
musical instruments	yuèqì	乐器
paintings	huà	画
paper cuttings	jiǎnzhǐ	剪纸
pottery	táoqì	陶器
silk products	sīzhīpǐn	丝织品

Sanya, China's Tropical Playground

Area Code 0898

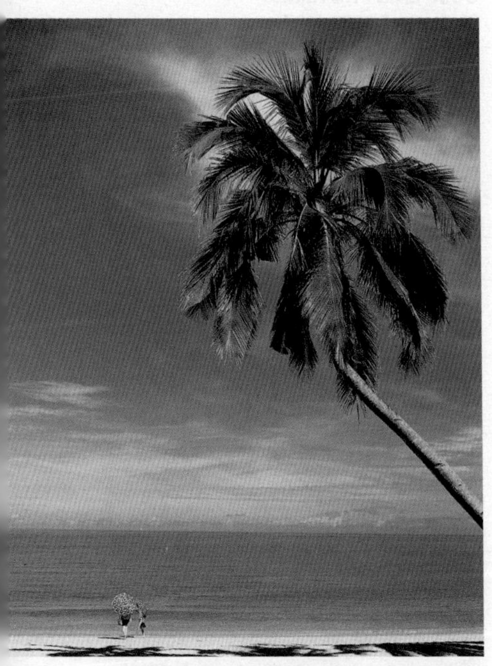

White sand, blue water and palm trees make Sanya a great destination for sun worshippers.

Pearl-white beaches and swaying palms greet visitors to China's tropical paradise. Whether sipping coconut milk as the clean ocean water laps at your feet or floating through a coral jungle, you'll find **Sanya** is the place to go for "beach, sun and fun."

When southerners head to China's frozen northeast to catch the snow sculptures and ice lanterns in the winter, the northerners stream south to **Hainan** Province for Sanya's sun drenched beaches and luxuriant jungles. On the southernmost point of China's southernmost province, when the rest of China freezes in frigid winters, Sanya remains balmy and sun worshippers strut down the beach in Speedos and bikinis, digging their toes into the white sand. It's hard to imagine that this holiday paradise was once considered a place of exile. Disgraced officials were sent as far away as possible and this steamy island on the edge of imperial China represented the end of the world.

One of the best beaches in Hainan is 17 miles (28 km) southeast of Sanya at **Yalong Bay** (*yàlóng wān* 亚龙湾). This 4.3-mile-long (7 km) crescent shaped beach is one long strip of clean white sand bordered by rolling blue waters and luxury hotels. The pristine waters off this beach are amazingly clear with underwater visibility up to 33 feet (10 m). This lends itself to great scuba diving and snorkelling, two of the most popular activities. For those who aren't inclined to get wet, boats with glass bottoms sail the waters off the beach allowing an equally impressive view of life under the sea. Speed demons can go for rides on motorboats or rent jet skis and zip over the waves. For something not involving water, take to the air for a seagull-eye-view of the beach by going parasailing.

The **Central Square** (*zhōngxīn guǎngchǎng* 中心广场) at the resort has all the amenities for an unhurried stay – open air café, souvenir stores selling handicrafts made from seashells – and overlooking the whole expanse is a 95-foot-high (29 m) totem pole carved with images of animals and Chinese deities.

Dadonghai (*dàdōnghǎi* 大东海) is a 1.2-mile-long (2 km) beach that's one of the most popular and is only 1.8 miles (3 km) southeast of Sanya. Its main draw is the abundance of activities available for both the adventurous and timid. All the excitement found at Yalong Bay is readily available here at better prices. Although not exactly 20,000 leagues unde the sea, a submarine tour offers great views of the vibrant corals and reefs.

Between Dadonghai and Sanya is the **Luhuitou Park** (*lùhuítóu gōngyuán* 鹿回头公园), where a large cliff shaped like a deer extends into the sea. According to legend, an ancient hunter stalked his prey for two days. When he was finally overcome by exhaustion, the deer turned its head and looked back at the hunter and suddenly turned into a beautiful maiden. One thing led to another and their descendants are now the Li ethnic minority that inhabits this part of the island. Today a large 39-foot-high (12 m) stone statue of a deer commemorates this event. Climbing the cliff also gives a spectacular view of the surrounding area, especially as the sun sets over the ocean and the city lights up.

About 16 miles (26 km) west of Sanya at Maling Shan is **Tianya-Haijiao** (*tiānyá hǎijiǎo* 天涯海角). The beach here is peppered with rounded water-worn boulders. Two large boulders, about 66 feet (20 m)-high and over198 feet (60 m)-long, have the characters *tianya-haijiao*, meaning "edge of the sky, rim of the sea," carved into them. This site is of special significance to Chinese tourists because this was once considered the end of the known world. Many melancholic poems have been written by disgraced officials, with one official decrying that it would take a bird six months to fly here.

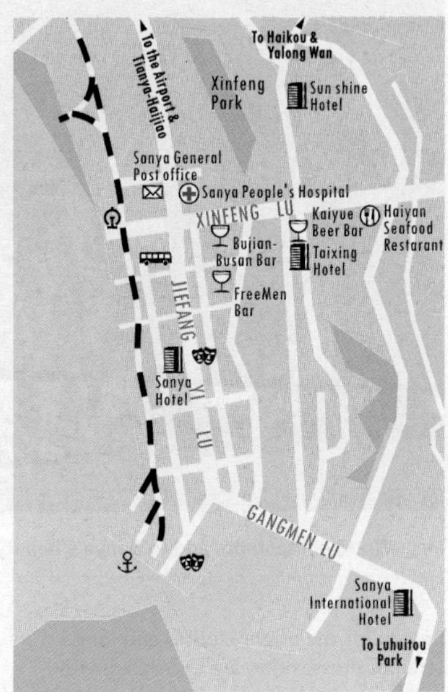

More than beaches and sun, Hainan's mountainous terrain is home to clusters of sleepy villages. About 55 miles (89 km) from Sanya is Tongshi City, which is close to traditional Miao and Li villages. The Li are the original inhabitants of Hainan and are

At Hainan's southernmost point – Tianya-Haijiao.

Miss World contestants add to Sanya's beauty.

known for the bright clothes and long straight dresses that are decorated with seashells, coral, small bells and pearls. The Miao were originally from Guangxi and many moved to Hainan during the Ming dynasty as part of the Ming army. Many settled on the island and moved into the rugged mountains where most of their villages are now. Two traditional courtship festivals are held usually in early-April and display the vibrant culture of Hainan's inhabitants.

Not far from these villages is the **Wuzhi Shan** (*wǔzhǐ shān* 五指山). At 6,125 feet (1,867 m) above sea level, it's Hainan's highest point and the symbol of the province. The five peaks of the mountain are covered with lush tropical jungles and misty clouds. Climbing up the peak, with the mist rolling in, gives visitors a sense of what it's like to walk on clouds. There are rapids on the mountain and white-water rafting is a popular sport.

It's best to make arrangements with your hotel to go white water-rafting. You can head out yourself by taking a 2-hour bus ride to Wuzhi Shan City from Sanya. Buses begin at 7am and depart every 30 minutes; tickets are RMB 13. From Wuzhi Shan City you'll need to take another bus to Wuzhi Shan Town, then a motorcycle to the rapids. The rapids are at their best from July to October and safety gear is a must. ■

Making Your Trip Easy

Practical Tips

Sanya has great weather all year, though summers can be very hot and humid. It's the hottest in July when it is arenage at 82°F (28°C), during winters it's still a warm 70°F (21°C). Be aware that Hainan is prone to typhoons from May to November.

Sanya is a tropical paradise so much sure you're prepared for it, bring your sunglasses, use plenty of sun block and remember the sun is a lot stronger than it feels when by the beach. Around early April is the Coconut Festival, a traditional ethnic Li and Miao holiday that's celebrated with dragon boat races and dances around a bonfire.

Unlike the rest of China, which requires visas for entry, visas can be applied for upon arrival in Hainan.

Transportation

Airport – Sanya's Fenghuang Airport is 11 miles (18 km) from downtown Sanya. Shuttle buses cost RMB 15. Taxis cost around RMB 40 from airport to downtown.

Memorable Experiences

Sipping on a coconut cocktail while sitting under a palm tree as the sun slowly sets and the waves serenade us.

Scuba diving in the warm clear waters off Sanya's beaches and getting a close up look at the diverse colors of a living coral reef.

Munching on sea critters taken straight out of the nets.

Bicycle – Bikes can be rented from most hotels; rentals are from RMB 20 to 50 per hour. Bikes for two or three people are also available.

Taxi – Taxi costs around RMB 5 to 10 within the city.

The Best of Sanya

Nanshan Cultural Tourism Zone
南山文化旅游区 *nánshān wénhuà lǚyóuqū*
✉ Nanshan 南山
☎ 8883 7888
🕒 7:30am to 6pm
¥ 65

Yalong Bay Seaside Park 亚龙湾滨海公园
yànlóngwān bīnhǎi gōngyuán
✉ Yalong Bay 亚龙湾
☎ 8856 8899
🕒 7:30am to 6:30pm
¥ 60

Tianya-Haijiao Scenic Area
天涯海角风景区 *tiānyá-hǎijiǎo fēngjǐngqū*
✉ 14 miles (23 km) southwest of downtown Sanya 位于三亚西南 23 公里处
☎ 8891 0131
🕒 7am to 7pm
¥ 65

Hotels

Gloria Resort Sanya
凯莱酒店 *kǎilái Jiǔdiàn* ★★★★★
✉ inside the Yalong Bay National Resort District 亚龙湾国家旅游度假区内
☎ 8856 8855
¥ 838 – double room
@ www.gloriaresort.com

Sanya Shanhaitian Hotel 三亚山海天大酒店
sānyà shānhǎitiān dàjiǔdiàn ★★★★★
✉ Luling Lu, Dadonghai Beach 大东海旅游风景区鹿领路
☎ 8821 1688
¥ 1,298 – double room
@ www.shthotel.com

Sheraton Sanya Hotel
喜来登酒店 *xǐláidēng Jiǔdiàn* ★★★★★
✉ inside the Yalong Bay National Resort District 亚龙湾国家旅游度假区内
☎ 8855 8855
¥ 1,370 – double room
@ www.sheraton.com/sanya

Landscape Beach Hotel Sanya 三亚丽景海湾酒店 *sānyà lìjǐng hǎiwān jiǔdiàn* ★★★★
✉ Dadonghai Beach 大东海旅游风景区
☎ 8822 8666 8822 8556
¥ 388 – double room
458 – double room (seascape)
@ www.sanyaliking.com

Sanya Guoxi Hotel
三亚果喜酒店 *sānyà guǒxǐ jiǔdiàn* ★★★★
✉ 13 Jiefang Si Lu 解放四路 13 号
☎ 8825 4888
¥ 298 – double room, peak-season
268 – double room, off-season
@ www.guoxihotel.com

Crafts made with coconut shells are great novelty gifts.

Quotes

"Sanya was definitely a blast. The beaches, the water and the great weather, can't forget the bikinis too."

"Nothing beats getting a tan on the beach while my friends back in Beijing freeze."

Food & Restaurants

Fresh seafood and tropical fruit can be found everywhere in Sanya. Hainan's four most famous dishes are tender chicken (*wénchāng jī* 文昌鸡), tasty goat (*dōngshān yáng* 东山羊), yummy duck (*jiājī yā* 加积鸭) and fresh crab (*hélè xiè* 和乐蟹).

RESTAURANTS

Babaoji Restaurant 阿宝鸡饭店
✉ Yingbin Lu, Sanya 三亚迎宾路
☎ 8866 0660

Chunyuan Haixian Guanchang
春园海鲜广场
✉ Jixiang Lu 吉祥路

Dongjiao-Yelin Seafood Restaurant
东郊椰林海鲜城
Offers seafood and Cantonese cuisine.
✉ 109 Yuya Da Dao 榆亚大道 109 号
☎ 8821 0999

Haiyun Restaurant 海运海鲜大排挡
Specializes in seafood and Hainan delicacies.
✉ Sanyawan Lu 三亚湾路国际码头
☎ 8826 2099

Two newlyweds are urged by friends to show some affection.

Mingrun Seafood
明润海鲜排档
Specializes in seafood.
✉ 11 Sanyawan Lu 三亚湾路 11 号
☎ 8827 9868

Yuanqi Restaurant 缘起楼
Great vegetarian food.
✉ Nanshan Tourism Area 南山旅游区内
☎ 8883 7921

Souvenirs

Pearls are in abundance in Sanya. Anything and everything made from pearls can be found at the Jinrun Pearl Store (京润珍珠馆) at Hengxin Da Dao in Tiandu Town (田独镇亨新大道, ☎ 8871 0611). Rub two pearls together to see if they're real – genuine pearls will feel rough and fakes will be smooth. Crystal souvenirs are also a popular item and can be found at the Changyuan Crystal Store (昌源水晶) at Fenghuang Town (凤凰镇, ☎ 8833 1111). Traditional brocade works and seashell carvings can be found throughout Sanya and they make great gifts. Bracelet, necklace, and handbags made from coconut shells are also popular unique souvenirs in Sanya.

Other Information

POST OFFICES

Sanya General Post Office 三亚邮政总局
✉ 2/F, Youdian Dasha, Jiefang San Lu 解放三路邮电大厦二层
☎ 8826 0555

HOSPITALS

Sanya People's Hospital
三亚市人民医院
✉ 004 Jiefang San Lu 解放三路 004 号
☎ 8825 8748

COMPLAINT HOTLINES

☎ General: 8826 8454
☎ Taxi: 8827 2336

TOURISM INFORMATION WEBSITE

www.sanyatour.com

HONG KONG MACAU TAIWAN

One of the many small boats that shuttle through the bustling Victoria Harbour.

Hong Kong, Playing Amongst Skyscrapers

Area Code 00852

Hong Kong will draw you in, dazzle your senses and have you begging for more. It's fast, vibrant and cutting edge.

Hong Kong is a metropolis in the truest sense of the word. Of the 7 million people inhabiting this city most are Chinese but many Pakistanis, Indians, Filipinos, Europeans and many other nationalities call Hong Kong their home – and they've all managed to add their own flavor to the Hong Kong milieu.

In 1997 the British returned Hong Kong to China under the "One Country, Two Systems" framework in which Hong Kong is guaranteed a high level of autonomy for 50 years. Hong Kong's history – that of an Asian city ruled by Europeans – has given it a distinctive mix of East and West. The past and the present are side by side in the incense-filled temples and the towering skyscrapers, in the densely populated urban areas and in the outlying islands where nature continues her hold over a slower pace of life.

Hong Kong covers an area of a little more than 386 square miles (1,000 km²) and is divided into Hong Kong Island, Kowloon, the New Territories and the outlying islands. **Hong Kong Island** is home to one of the most impressive and recognizable skylines in the world. In **Central**, the buildings appear to stretch to the sky while on the ground below a seemingly infinite crowd of people bustle through their day. Hong Kong Island is actually very hilly and walking from Central to the residential mid levels area feels like mountain climbing. Luckily the world's longest escalator – 2,624 feet (800 m) – or nearly half a mile long – has been constructed here. The **Central Escalator** starts at the crossing of Queens Road Central and Queen Victoria Street and has its terminus all the way up at Conduit Road. Use it after 10am though, before then it heads down. The ride is free. On the way it passes the Soho area, with restaurants and food markets cramped in between high-rises. The frenetic pace of the north side of the island gives way to beaches and leisurely retreats further on.

Kowloon, which faces Hong Kong across the harbor at the tip of the peninsula, is one of the most densely populated areas in the world. The buildings here aren't as glitzy as on the island but nonetheless, it's a very dynamic commercial area. In the area of **Tsim Sha Tsui**, there are almost as many camera stores facing the street as there are people in Hong Kong. Inside the buildings, the shopping centers run continuously – check out **Harbour City** that has its southern entrance by the Star Ferry terminal. If shopping is your poison, then watch out for an overdose – it can't get more intense than Nathan Road and its restaurants, shops and bars. There are many lively markets in Kowloon. Some of the best, to name a few, are near the Prince Edward MTR station at the northern end of **Nathan Road**, the **Yuen Po Street Bird Market**, the **Flower Market** and **Temple Street Night Market**.

Amidst all the heady shopping it's easy to forget that Hong Kong is also rich in cultural experiences. As a reminder to explore beyond the malls and boutiques, the **Hong Kong Cultural Centre** is a good place to begin; it has a worthwhile historical section and contemporary art section. Also check the local listings for special performances at the center. The **Museum of History** on Chatham Road offers glimpses into pre-skyscraper Hong Kong – when it was still nothing but barren rock.

A nice respite from the busy streets is a visit to the **New Territories** and its outlying islands. Many visitors are surprised that there's more to Hong Kong than the island and Kowloon. The rural areas and nature reserves are a world away from the glam and glitter of urban Hong Kong. This is also Hong Kong's spiritual side; there are plenty of monasteries and temples to explore. Not far from Tsuen Wan is a beautiful Taoist temple, the **Yuen Yuen Institute**. Nearby is Hong Kong's highest mountain, the **Big Misty Mountain**. At 3,140 feet (957 m) it's a manageable climb and you're rewarded with a grand view. Another intriguing monastery is the **Po Lin Monastery** on Lantau Island. Next to the temple is the **Tian Tan Buddha** – this Buddha's claim to fame is its size: it's the world's largest outdoor bronze Buddha statue. There's a great view of the surrounding hills after climbing the stairs to reach the Buddha.

SKYSCRAPER SPOTTING

As in most major metropolises, people in Hong Kong seem to live in hyper-speed – they're always on the go and it's easy to get caught up in the rush. It's a good idea to slow down and remember you're on holiday. Relax and take it all in from a distance before you attack the streets of Central on Hong Kong Island. From the Kowloon side of the harbor the whole skyline is laid out before you, ready to be photographed. The **Opera Hall**, where the hand-over ceremony was held, is on the left; on the right is the brand new 1,362-foot-high (415 m) **International Finance Center**. It's easy to spot – it dwarfs every other building in sight, so far. In between, the buildings rise to the sky shoulder to shoulder. Some of the architectural wonders include the **Bank of China Tower**, designed by I.M. Pei. The building consists of four triangular glass and aluminum towers of varying heights that emerge from a granite podium. There is a small sky deck open to the public on the 42nd floor that gives a view of the northwest side of Hong Kong. Just next to the Bank of China Tower, by Statue Square, is the home of the HSBC. Designed by the famous architect Norman Foster, it's a glass and steel wonder with a 171-foot-high (52 m) atrium.

To view it all from a different angle, take the Star Ferry across the harbor and get on the **Peak Tram** on Garden Road to **Victoria Peak**. The tram makes its precarious way up the steep hills that form the backdrop to

Hong Kong's skyline. On a clear day the view from 1,811-foot-high (552 m) Victoria Peak is striking. And when you're ready, take the plunge into the streets and experience the glass and steel giants up close. If you're still up for more skyscraper spotting then do the whole trip one more time at night when the sky is illuminated by the many high-rises.

EXPERIENCING THE OTHER SIDE OF HONG KONG

In case you actually "shop 'til you drop," there are plenty of opportunities in Hong Kong to take time out – the serene beaches that hold their own against the best in Asia, the lush green mountains and the city parks all offer soothing respite – and they're all within easy reach. On the southern end of Hong Kong Island, the areas around **Aberdeen**, where 6,000 people live and work on junks anchored in the harbor, **Stanley** and **Repulse Bay** offer a more relaxed holiday atmosphere with beaches and small markets. Only half an hour by boat, **Lamma Island** offers a complete escape from the urban jungle. It's a relaxed retreat with good beaches and seafood.

If you've got time on your hands, then venture out and explore the rural side of Hong Kong in the New Territories. There are fantastic beaches and amazing treks to be made in the green mountains. The **Shek O Big Wave Bay**, dotted with beautiful beaches, on the eastern side of the New Territories is a great place for sun worshippers. It's possible to reach this area by taxi or bus from **Sai Kung** to the **Sai Kung East Country Park**, but that leaves an hour of tough walking. A better option is to rent a boat in Sai Kung – it's a beautiful sail, which passes stunning views of white beaches, red rocks and soaring hills.

There are more than 200 smaller islands around Hong Kong. Going to **Tap Mun Chau Island** will transport you to another age – you won't believe that one of the world's busiest cities is right around the corner. Stepping off the ferry you arrive in a small fishing village with scenery reminiscent of a Norwegian fjord, though quite a bit warmer. All about the island, deeply tanned fisherman lay their catch out in the sun to dry – their clothes a far cry from the business suits seen in Central. Walks around the small island are quite tranquil.

While getting to these outlying areas isn't as fast as taking the metro from Central to Kowloon, the ferry connections are frequent. For more convenience, though, you can rent a fast speedboat or a leisurely junk. ■

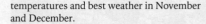

Making Your Trip Easy

Practical Tips

Nature still rules in Hong Kong even though it's hard to see it in Central or Kowloon. It can get incredibly hot and humid in Hong Kong and it'll rain endlessly during the monsoon season, which is usually from May to September. In Central it's possible to get almost anywhere via tunnels and covered walkways and you'll probably walk through air-conditioned buildings. However, take the heat and humidity into consideration if you're planning a hike in the New Territories. Hong Kong has the mildest temperatures and best weather in November and December.

Most people in Hong Kong can speak basic English and shopping will be a breeze whether in large department stores or bargaining in the markets. Not all stores accept RMB, so it'll be more convenient to convert your RMB into Hong Kong dollars. English newspapers and magazines are widely available in Hong Kong.

Hong Kong is home to many consulates so it's a good place to pick up visas. Apply for visas to China at the local CITS or any travel agent. Be aware that entering Hong Kong from the Chinese mainland invalidates your Chinese visa, unless it's a multiple entry visa, and you'll have to apply for a new visa to reenter the mainland. Hong Kong is a Special Administrative Region of China under the One Country, Two Systems policy so visa requirements are different from those on the mainland. Holders of passports from Canada, America, Australia, New Zealand and most Western European countries don't require visas.

Transportation

Airport – Hong Kong International Airport (2181 0000) is just north of Lantau Island on Chek Lap Kok Island. Be sure to drop by the Hong Kong Tourist Association (HKTA) and pick up a map of the city, sightseeing brochures and hotel information. The easiest way to get to Kowloon and Central is to take the Airport Express train; tickets are HK $100 and it's a quick trip to the heart of Hong Kong.

Hong Kong's busy roads thread around gleaming skyscrapers.

Hong Kong's financial sector is one of the world's most vibrant.

Bus – Hong Kong's bus system is extensive and well run, but unless you know Chinese, it'll be difficult to navigate. It's better to stick to the MTR.

Ferry – The famous Star Ferry goes between Hong Kong Island and Kowloon. Inexpensive and convenient, it's one of the best ways to get a close-up view of Victoria Harbour and the classic Hong Kong skyline.

Subway – Hong Kong's Mass Transit Railway (MTR) is a boon for visitors. It's fast, relatively cheap and will get you to most places in Hong Kong. The four lines are color-coded coded and buying tickets is a cinch using the bilingual machines.

Taxi – Taxis in Hong Kong are relatively expensive for all but the fare short jaunts. Flag-fall is HK $15, but quickly adds up on the meter. There's a KH $5 surcharge per piece of luggage and for calling taxis by phone. Crossing tunnels will also add surcharges: HK $20 for the Cross-Harbour Tunnel, HK $30 for the Eastern Harbour Crossing, HK $45 for the Western Harbour Tunnel and HK $5 for the Aberdeen Tunnel.

Train – The Kowloon-Canton Railway (KCR) is fast and cheap and signs are in both Chinese and English. It runs from the Hung Hom Station near Tsim Sha Tsui East to the Shueng Shui at the border with Shenzhen. Hung Hom station is also the place to board China-bound trains.

Tram – Tramlines are found only along the north side of Hong Kong Island, and the fare is HK $2. The tram to Victoria Peak crawls its way up the steep slope to one of Hong Kong's main attractions. Two-way tickets are HK $30 for adults and HK $9 for children.

The Best of Hong Kong

Hong Kong Space Museum 香港太空馆
✉ near the harbor in Tsim Sha Tsui
尖沙咀海旁
🕒 1pm to 9pm, Monday to Friday except Tuesday
10am to 9pm, weekends and public holidays
HK $: 25 for adults;
12.5 for children and seniors over 60

Ocean Park 海洋公园
✉ between Aberdeen and Repulse Bay
香湾仔与浅水湾之间
🕒 10am to 6pm
HK $: 150 for adults; 75 for children

The Po Lin (Precious Lotus) Monastery 宝莲寺
✉ located on western Lantau Island
位于大屿山西部的昂坪高原
🕒 10am to 6pm

Repulse Bay 浅水湾
✉ south of Stanley 香港岛的南端

Hotels

Conrad International Hong Kong Hotel 港丽酒店 ★★★★★
✉ Pacific Place, 88 Queensway
金钟道 88 号太古广场
☎ 2521 3838
HK $: 1,768 – superior

Grand Hyatt Hong Kong 君悦酒店 ★★★★★

🖂 1 Harbour Road, Wanchai
湾仔港湾道 1 号
☎ 2588 1234
HK $: 1,453 – standard

Kowloon Shangri-La Hong Kong
九龙香格里拉大酒店 ★★★★★
🖂 64 Mody Road, Tsim Sha Tsui East, Kowloon
九龙尖沙咀东部么地道 64 号
☎ 2721 2111
HK $: 2,067 – standard

Sheraton Hong Kong Hotel & Towers
香港喜来登酒店 ★★★★★
🖂 20 Nathan Road, Tsim Sha Tsui, Kowloon
九龙尖沙咀弥敦道 20 号
☎ 2369 1111
HK $: 1,403 – standard

Holiday Inn Golden Mile Hong Kong
香港金域假日酒店 ★★★★
🖂 50 Nathan Road, Tsim Sha Tsui, Kowloon
九龙尖沙咀弥敦道 50 号
☎ 2369 3111
HK $: 955 – standard

Regal Kowloon Hotel Hong Kong
富豪九龙酒店 ★★★★
🖂 71 Mody Road, Tsim Sha Tsui East, Kowloon 九龙尖沙咀东部么地道 71 号
☎ 2722 1818
HK $: 955 – standard

Bishop Lei International House Hong Kong 宏基国际宾馆 ★★★
🖂 4 Robinson Road, Mid-Levels
半山区罗便臣道 4 号
☎ 2868 0828
HK $: 730 – standard

The Marco Polo Gateway Hong Kong
马哥孛罗港威酒店 ★★★

Dolphin's leaping for joy at Ocean Park.

🖂 13 Harbour City, Canton Road, Tsim Sha Tsui, Kowloon
九龙尖沙咀广东道海港城 13 号
☎ 2113 0888
HK $: 813 – superior

Park Hotel Hong Kong 百乐酒店 ★★★
🖂 61-65 Chatham Road South, Tsim Sha Tsui, Kowloon
九龙尖沙咀漆咸道南 61-65 号
☎ 2366 1371
HK $: 739 – standard

Food & Restaurants

Hong Kong is one of Asia's most dynamic centers of dining. Enthusiasts of all levels of sensitivity can delight themselves with the newest in fusion cooking or dig down into a large bowl of noodles and soup with won ton. From ritzy restaurants and small family run café to the avant-garde and the

Memorable Experiences

Marveling at the skyline of Hong Kong Island from the Kowloon ferry pier and Victoria Peak.

Exploring the outlying islands with beautiful beaches and village life.

Experiencing commercial Hong Kong from the local food markets to Kowloon's countless shopping centers.

Eating dim sum in a typical busy Hong Kong restaurant.

traditional, everything can be found in Hong Kong.

Befitting its status as an international city, Hong Kong offers up cuisines from all over the world. Everything from greasy burger joints to understated Japanese restaurants to oases of European refinement are available in every part of the city.

Cantonese food is the most common. The cuisine emphasizes the freshness of the ingredients and most dishes are light and savory. But every type of Chinese cuisine can be found in Hong Kong; if you have a hankering for spicy Sichuan or heavy northern fare, it's all here. Hong Kong cuisine has also been strongly influenced by the British; café with finger sandwiches and milk tea are filled with office workers taking their afternoon tea break.

A Buddhist sanctuary in the midst of a busy city.

In Hong Kong, you won't have to search very long to find a good restaurant catering to your taste or budget.

RESTAURANTS

Café Deco

✉ Peak Galleria, Victoria Peak
☎ 2849 5111
🕒 10am to 11pm

The Chinese

✉ in the Hyatt Regency, 67 Nathan Road, Tsim Sha Tsui
☎ 2311 1234
🕒 11:30am to 3pm, 6:30pm to 11:30pm

City Chiuchow Restaurant

✉ East Ocean Centre, 98 Granville Road, Tsim Sha Tsui East
☎ 2723 6226
🕒 11am to 3pm and 5pm to midnight, Monday to Thursday
11am to midnight, Friday to Sunday

Food Lam Moon

✉ 53-59 Kimberley Road, Tsim Sha Tsui
☎ 2366 0286
🕒 11:30am to 2:30pm, 6pm to 11:30pm

Gaylord

✉ 23-25 Ashley Road, Tsim Sha Tsui
☎ 2376 1001
🕒 noon to 2:30pm, 6pm to 11pm

Golden Island Bird's Nest Chiu Chau Restaurant

✉ 2/F Star House, 3 Salisbury Road, Tsim Sha Tsui
☎ 2736 6228
🕒 11am to 3pm, 5:30pm to 11:30pm

Happy Garden Noodles & Congee Kitchen

✉ 76 Canton Road, Tsim Sha Tsui
☎ 2377 2604
🕒 7am to noon

Jumbo Floating Restaurant

✉ Aberdeen Harbour, Hong Kong Island
☎ 2553 9111
🕒 11am to 11pm, Monday to Saturday
8am to 11pm, Sunday

Open Kitchen

✉ 6/F Kong Kong Arts Centre, 2 Harbour Road, Wan Chai
☎ 2827 2923
🕒 11am to 11pm

Sammy's Kitchen

✉ 204-206 Queen's Road West, Sheung Wan
☎ 2548 8400
🕒 11:30am to 11:30pm

Stanley's French Restaurant

✉ 1-2/F Oriental Building, 90B Stanley Main Street, Stanley
☎ 2813 8873
🕒 noon to 3pm, 6:30pm to 10:30pm

Hong Kong's world famous skyline glitters at night.

Va Bene
✉ 58-62 D'Aguilar Street, Central
☎ 2845 5577
🕒 noon to 3pm, Monday to Friday
7pm to midnight, Saturday to Sunday

The Viceroy
✉ 2/F Sun Hung Kai Centre,
30 Harbour Road, Wan Chai
☎ 2827 7777
🕒 noon to 3pm, 6pm to 11pm

Yung Kee
✉ 32-40 Wellington Street, Central
☎ 2522 1624
🕒 11am to 11:30pm

Souvenirs

You might not have planned it before arriving in Hong Kong, but you'll end up doing some serious shopping. It's part of the Hong Kong psyche and seeing endless rows of shops and shopping centers will make you cave in. Most of the sales staff in shops speak English and do a great job of encouraging you to spend. The shopping spectrum of Hong Kong spans the high-end clothing stores in Central to the markets of cheap bargains in Kowloon. Tsim Sha Tsui has many stores and shopping arcades to choose from and upscale shopping can be found in Central and Causeway Bay. The Stanley Market on the southern end of Hong Kong island is the best known market in Hong Kong.

Nearly every kind of consumer good can be bought in Hong Kong from electronics to clothes to Chinese curios. Be sure to look around before you buy – many shops offer the same items and a quick comparison of prices and quality will earn big savings. Look for shops with the HKTA label to ensure the shop is reputable and be careful of buying secondhand electronic items. There's leeway for bargaining at the smaller stores or at the markets; make sure to ask what the lowest price is.

Quotes

"The contrasts in Hong Kong are extremely fascinating, even within one specific area of the city. There are places where you feel like you've landed right in a science fiction movie but then you turn the next street corner and you find yourself in a small alley with maybe a little temple with burning incense or an outdoor food market."

Other Information

POST OFFICES

General Post Office

✉ next to the Star Ferry Concourse, Central
☎ 2921 2222
🕒 8am to 6pm Monday to Friday, 8am to 2pm Saturday

The Kowloon Central Post Office

✉ G/F, Hermes House, 10 Middle Road, Tsim Sha Tsui, Kowloon
🕒 8am to 6pm Monday to Friday, 8am to 2pm Saturday

HOSPITALS

Grantham Hospital, Hong Kong West Cluster

✉ 125 Wong Chuk Hang Road, Aberdeen
☎ 2518 2111

Queen Elizabeth Hospital

✉ 30 Gascoigne Road, Kowloon
☎ 2958 8888

Queen Mary Hospital (QMH)

✉ 102 Pokfulam Road
☎ 2855 3111, 2855 3838, 2816 6366

Tang Shiu Kin Hospital, Hong Kong East Cluster

✉ 282 Queen's Road East, Wan Chai
☎ 2291 2000

COMPLAINT HOTLINES

☎ General: 2807 6177

Busy streets with busy stores.

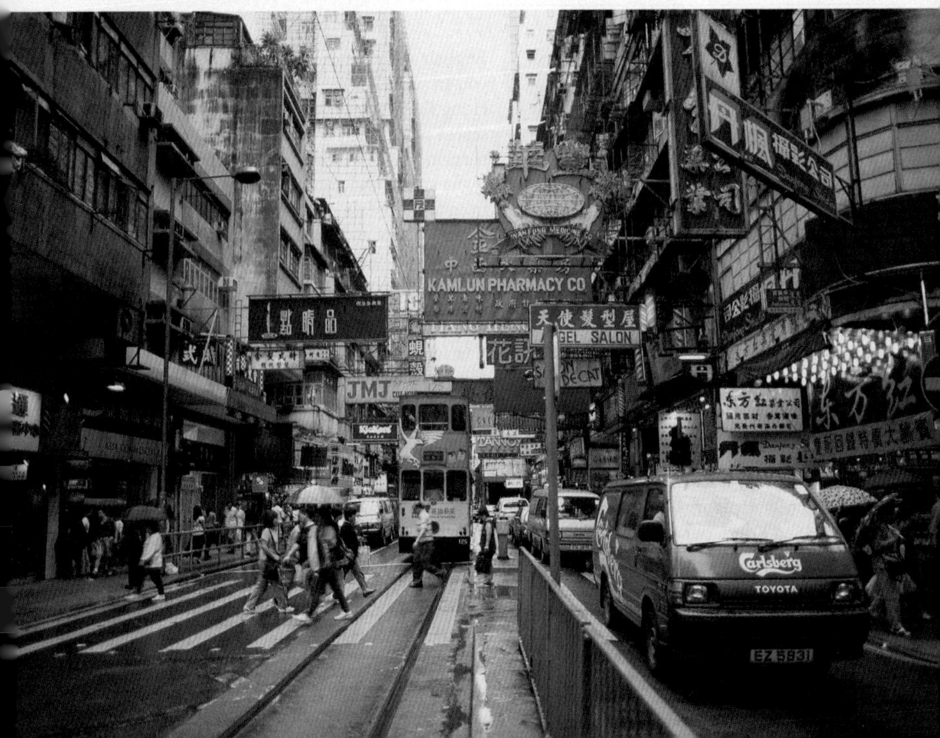

Macau, the Magnificent

Area Code 00853

Heritage: the Historic Centre of Macau

Macau's mixture of East and West brings together an eclectic mix of Old World Europe and Asia in one beautiful package.

Portuguese traders leased Macau from the Guangzhou Mandarins in 1557, and Portugal governed Macau for more than 440 years until returning it to China in 1999. Today, Macau still maintains its Portuguese style, and with its numerous Mediterranean buildings, it feels as European as it does Chinese.

Senado Square, surrounded by bright-colored Portuguese buildings and cobbled stone alleys, is the best place to get a feel for what Macau has to offer. Surrounding Senado Square you will find some of the best shopping in Macau, with everything from antique Chinese furniture to the latest in designer fashion. The beautiful **St. Dominic Church**, which has been standing for the past 400 years, east of Senado Square, holds mass on the weekends in Cantonese. Farther down the cobbled stone street is the **Ruins of the Church of St. Paul**. Built in the 1602 by Jesuit priests, the church was destroyed by fire in 1835, and only the massive stone façade survived. Today the ruins of St. Paul are the official symbol of Macau and offer great photo ops. Next to the ruins is **Monte Fortress**, the largest fortress remaining from Macau's imperial past. Inside the fort is the **Macau Museum**, an interesting museum with artifacts and a detailed history of Macau from the early days to the present.

Within walking distance of the museum is **St. Michaels Cemetery** to the east and **Camoes Grotto and Gardens**, to the north. South of Senado Square is the tallest point in Macau, the **Macau Sky Tower**, standing at 1,109 feet (338 m), it's hard to miss. Along the road leading to the tower you'll pass by

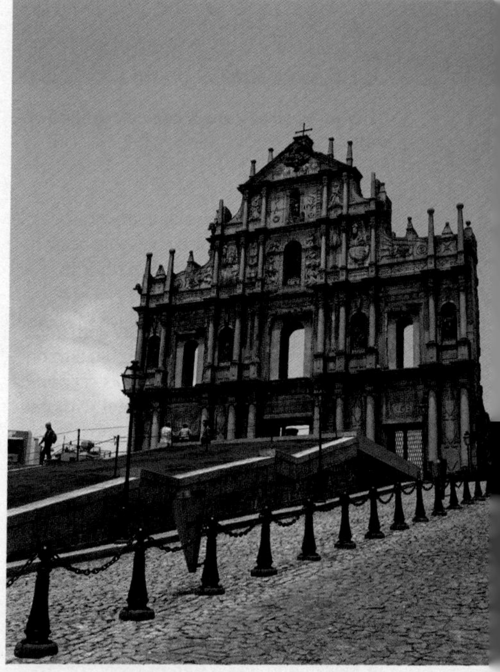

The ruins of the Church of St. Paul continue to stand majestically.

the brightly painted **Residence of the Portuguese Consul** and the **Chapel of Our Lady of Penha**. The gothic church sits on top of a small knoll overlooking the bay and glows eerily when lit up at night. Macau Sky Tower offers an unparalleled 360-degree-view of the ocean, Macau and the mainland border city of Zhuhai. For those who are a little more adventurous, there are tours available that allow visitors to walk around the outer rim of the observation deck

Senado Square is one Macau's best-known sights.

unimpeded by windows or even a rail. Harnesses with lines attached to a beam keep people from being blown off into oblivion.

If you prefer finding excitement with your feet firmly on the ground, then head to one of the many casinos or racetracks scattered throughout Macau. **Lisboa Hotel** with its birdcage shaped building is the most famous casino in town and is conveniently located between Senado Square and Macau Sky Tower. Across from the Lisboa Hotel is the **Cybernetic Fountain**, which provides a mesmerizing show of lights and water at night.

Guia Lighthouse, northwest of Senado Square, occupies the highest natural point in Macau and was a sign of relief for far-Eastern trade ships, signaling that their arduous voyage from Europe was finally over. Beside the lighthouse is a small chapel and **Flora Garden** sits at the base and offers gondola rides for those who would prefer not to walk.

North of Flora Park is **Kun Lam Temple**, one of the largest temples in Macau, where many important documents have been signed, including the treaty leasing Macau to Portugal. The **A-Ma Temple** is on the southwest corner of the peninsula and is another site worth visiting; it is located across from the **Maritime Museum** and **Barra Fort**. The fort was once a cannon battery, but it has since been turned into a Portuguese inn with amazing character and charm.

Along with the main peninsula, home to the majority of the 460,000 Macanese, there are two islands, Taipa and Coloane. Taipa was home to many of the wealthy Macanese whose row of impressive mansions has been restored and turned into the **Taipa House Museum**. This museum gives viewers a taste of what life was like for 18th and 19th century traders. **Taipa Village** has become a popular place with tourists and locals alike, known for having some of the best restaurants in Macau. Make your way up the small hill, located in the middle of the island, and you will find the **Chapel of Our Lady Carmel**, a quaint, quiet church built in 1885. Taipa Island is also home to the international airport, University of Macau, **Jockey Club** and **Four Faces Buddha**.

Coloane Island is the most remote part of Macau, a spot where it is still possible to get a glimpse of village life. **Hac SA Beach** with its black sand, gentle waves and barbeque pits is a favorite retreat for locals. Coloane Village is home to **St. Francis Xavier Church** and **Tin Hau Temple**. To the northeast is **Coloane Arboretum** and **Seac Pai Park**. Coloane also holds Macau's only golf course, located at the **Macau Golf and Country Club**.

High rollers, big and small, come to Macau for its many casinos. The largest is in the Lisboa Hotel, but there are many venues to choose from, and all of them offer a variety of ways for you to win or lose. The casinos here are world class and most are open 24 hours.

Quotes

"Macau is the real deal when it comes to East meets West style."

"The spas are incredible. I felt like an emperor getting a royal rubdown."

ZHUHAI BORDER JUMPING

Once you leave Macau, border jumping is as easy as jumping rope, with three-day to three-month tourist visas easily obtained in a few minutes from the Chinese Customs office. For three-day visas the cost is about HK $100; three-month visas go for HK $180.

As soon as you cross the border and enter **Zhuhai** you will be at the steps of the **Gongbei Underground Market**, a place that draws thousands of Macanese across the border each day for shopping. Taxis are readily available, but to avoid being ripped off, always insist that the driver use the meter.

With its wide roads and separate bicycle paths, Zhuhai is the model for modern Chinese city planning. The majority of the population lives in the three main districts of Gongbei, Jida and Xianzhou. Zhuhai was nothing more than a fishing village 20 years ago, but after Deng Xiaoping designated it a SEZ (Special Economic Zone) in 1980, the village soon became a city. Compared to cities with richer histories, such as Macau and Guangzhou, Zhuhai has few historical attractions. Instead the city makes up for this deficit by offering forms of recreation and entertainment that are difficult to find in more densely populated places.

In the northern section of **Gongbei**, next door to each other, are three venues that could keep you busy for days. **New Yuan Ming Palace** is a life size replica of the original in Beijing that was burnt down during the Opium Wars. Most of the buildings show painstaking detail and the sheer size of the grounds makes it easy to get lost for hours among the ponds, gardens and architecture. There are many plays and musical performances put on throughout the complex daily. For those who haven't been to Beijing it is worth a visit despite a steep RMB 100 entrance fee. Those who prefer wetter forms of entertainment should head next door to the **Lost World Water Park**. With its waterslides, tide-pools and play areas, there is something for all ages. Also on hand is a an 89-foot-high (27 m) bungee jump dangling above some of the pools, offering a great view of New Yuan Ming Palace before

The A-Ma Temple is Macau's oldest temple.

The Guia Lighthouse was once a beacon of sanctuary for weary mariners.

you leap. Conveniently located next door to the water park is a spa containing numerous mineral water and tea baths, deep tissue massages, acupuncture and other forms of traditional Chinese medicine. You may find it so relaxing you will wonder how you ever lived without such pampering before. Price depends on what you want but averages RMB 150. Larger spas like **Zhuhai Hot Springs** and the **Imperial Hot Springs** offer more amenities but are each 30-minute taxi rides into the countryside.

Lover's Road might not be as relaxing as a spa but with a cool sea breeze and a setting sun it can be a comfortable alternative. It runs the length of Zhuhai's coastline, stretching across all three major districts, with the best views along the Jida district section. Here you'll find **Hai Bing Park** and the Fisher Girl Statue, the latter being the city symbol. **Jiuzhou Port** is 10 minutes by taxi from the Fisher Girl and offers cruises around Macau that are spectacular at night. If time permits other forms of recreation can be found in the northern part of Zhuhai. **Lakewood Golf Course**, **Zhuhai F1 Race Track** and **Pearl Land** are a little over 15 minutes by taxi from Lover's Road.

Whatever it is that you find entertaining, Zhuhai most likely has it, and a one or two day visit is a perfect complement to your stay in Macau. ■

Making Your Trip Easy

Practical Tips

The best time to visit Macau is in the autumn when it's not as humid as the summer and the weather is still warm. Winter can be chilly and though springs is nice, it can be drizzly. The annual average temperature is about 68°F (20°C) with summers hovering around 86 °F (30°C). The monsoon season is from May to November.

The city is the busiest during Chinese New Year, the Macau Grand Prix in November and Hong Kong's public holidays. Hotel rooms may be difficult to find at these times.

The most common language is Cantonese although Mandarin, English, and Portuguese are spoken too.

Macau is now a Special Administrative Region of China under the One Country, Two Systems policy so the visa requirements are different from those on the Chinese mainland. Holders of passports from Canada, America, Australia, New Zealand and most Western European countries don't require visa for stays less than 20 days. Be aware that entering Macau from the Chinese mainland invalidates your Chinese visa, unless it's a multiple entry visa, and you'll have to apply for a new visa to reenter the mainland.

Currency in Macau is the pataca (MOP), which is pegged to the Kong Kong dollar.

▶▶ Matteo Ricci

Matteo Ricci, who lived from 1552 to 1610, was an Italian Jesuit priest who struggled for 30 years to bring Christianity to China. Few missionaries have ever managed to win the respect of Chinese officials, but Ricci managed to gain the confidence and admiration of the emperor himself.

In the 16th century all traces of earlier missions to China had vanished. The Nestorians of the 7th century and Catholic monks of the 13th and 14th centuries had been forgotten and the few priests who were admitted into the country were ignored, or worse, punished for their proselytizing.

Coming to Guangzhou through the Portuguese enclave of Macau, Ricci realized that he would have to study China's language and customs if he was to have any success spreading the gospel. He also shaved his head to appear similar to a Buddhist monk, hoping this would eliminate other obstructions to his preaching.

In 1589, after nearly ten years winning small acclaim for his knowledge and descriptions of the advances of the West – then believed to be largely barbaric compared to China – he headed slowly north to continue his work. Now appreciating the role of Confucius's teachings in Chinese society, he swapped his Buddhist robes for those of a Confucian and pragmatically suggested that the ancient rites were not incompatible with worship of the Christian God.

By 1599, he had established himself in Nanjing and introduced the Chinese to Western mathematics, astronomy and geography. Many found his descriptions of Euclid and other important figures baffling, but all were intrigued at what this (supposedly barbarian) foreigner knew and was trying to teach.

Perhaps his greatest achievement was in mapmaking. It was this that particularly astonished the Ming dynasty emperor, who finally agreed to see him in January 1601. Earlier maps from Zheng He's explorations hadn't illustrated to the same degree the size and number of the other kingdoms around the world or China's relative geographical position. The emperor immediately demanded Ricci make a copy of the *Great Map of Ten Thousand Countries* for the palace.

Now given a residence in Beijing, Ricci used his position to spread Christian teachings. The emperor was presented with images of Jesus, the Virgin Mary, and a crucifix, as well as a chiming clock to distract from the seriousness of the other gifts. Ricci wrote a number of short moral treatises, in Chinese and adapted to Chinese tastes, about Christian morality and the beliefs behind the faith. His *True Doctrine of God* became influential and was used by other missionaries for years after his death.

Hong Kong dollars are also widely accepted in Macau, but RMB should be exchanged as lots of stores won't accept them.

The Macanese festivals are colorful and loud affairs. Various festivals are held throughout the year showing off Macau's Portuguese and Chinese heritage. In March, July, October and December, the Kun Lam festival is held at the Kun Lam Temple. Worshippers head to the temple in droves and light incense and candles. Like everywhere else in China, Chinese New Year is a riot of colors and noise. In February head to the Pou Tai Un Temple on Taipa Island for the Fest of the Earth God. In March is the Procession of Our Lord of Passion. The temples dedicated to A-Ma are alive during her festival days. June sees dragon boats, and September and October have fireworks, with the Grand Prix in November.

Transportation

Airport – Macau's airport isn't very busy, so expect quick turnarounds. There are many links to Asian cities and there are helicopter shuttles to Hong Kong. Helicopter shuttles take about 20 minutes and cost around MOP 1,300 (☎ 790 7240). The airport tax is MOP 80 to China and MOP 130 to other destinations.

Bus – There are many buses to Zhuhai and Guangzhou via "Barrier Gate."

Ferry – There are numerous options for heading to Hong Kong and Shenzhen. The fastest boats will get you to Hong Kong in less than an hour. Ticket prices depend on date and time of travel, but are generally around MOP 150. The ferry dock is at the Macau Ferry Terminal in the Outer Harbor. Passengers should arrive at the dock 30 minutes before departure for customs procedures.

A winding dragon dances its way through Macau on Chinese New Year.

Taxi – Taxis are reasonably priced, MOP 20 to 30 for most destinations, but most drivers don't speak English. There's a MOP 5 surcharge to Taipa Island and MOP 10 to Coloane Island; flag-fall is MOP 9. Pedi-cabs (tricycles) are restricted to the waterfront area and can be more expensive than taxis, but they're slow and allow you to soak up the atmosphere. Pedi-cabs are MOP 25 per trip and about MOP 100 for an hour of touring.

The Best of Macau

A-ma Temple

✉ Situated at the base of Penha Hill

Kun Lam Temple

One of the most important temples in Macau.

Monte Fortress and Macau Museum

Offers an interesting peak into the life of Macau.

✉ Monte Fort, located close to the Ruins of St. Paul's

◷ 10am to 6pm, Tuesday to Sunday

Ruins of St. Paul's

Symbol of Macau.

Hotels

Hotel Royal Macau
澳门皇都酒店 ★★★★★
✉ 2-4 Estrada da Vitoria 得胜马路 2-4 号
☎ 552 222
US $: 68

Hyatt Regency Macau
澳门凯悦酒店 ★★★★★
✉ 2 Estrada Almirante Marques Esparteiro, Taipa Island 氹仔史伯泰海军将军马路 2 号
☎ 831 234
US $: 108

Mandarin Oriental Macau
澳门文华东方酒店 ★★★★★
✉ Avenida da Amizade
☎ 567 888
US $: 120

Holiday Inn Macau
澳门假日酒店 ★★★★
✉ 82-86 Rua de Pequim 新口岸北京街 82-86 号
☎ 783 333
US $: 75

Pousada Marina Infante Macau
澳门皇庭海景酒店 ★★★★

A Buddhist worshipper places her incense as fragrant smoke swirls around her.

✉ Aterro COTAI, Marina da Taipa Sul, Taipa 澳门氹仔南部，路氹填海区
☎ 838 333
US $: 55

Hotel Fortuna Macau 澳门财神酒店 ★★★
✉ 63 Rua De Cantao 新口岸广州街 63 号
☎ 786 333
US $: 72

Food & Restaurants

For a chic culinary fusion of East and West, few places in the world can compare to Macau, having had 400 years to perfect the blend. Food is the most famous handicraft in Macau and by the time your trip is over it's guaranteed you will bring some of it back with you, packed mostly in your belly and thighs. South China seafood with Portuguese seasoning is a favorite, along with chicken dishes. Traditional morning tea (dim sum or *yum cha*) is popular among local Cantonese and is worth a try. Carts of steamed buns, dumplings and sweets are pushed around to individual tables where dinners pick what they want straight off the

Memorable Experiences

Watching the fireworks explode over Macau Sky Tower during the annual international firework competition.

Soaking in a warm herbal tea bath.

Exploring the narrow side alleys of Macau.

Walking around the docked shipping boats as they unloaded fish.

cart. Most dim sum restaurants only offer this service before 11 am. Indian, Italian, Japanese, regional Chinese and just about any other cuisine you can think of are readily available at restaurants throughout the city.

Traditional dishes from Portugal include *bacalhau*, a cod that's served baked, grilled, stewed or boiled; oxtail and ox breast; rabbit prepared in various delicious ways and soups such as *caldo* verde that are rich with vegetables, meat, and olive oil. Portuguese cuisine has been strongly influenced by African and Indian spices so expect pungent and flavorful dishes.

RESTAURANTS

Dom Afonso III

✉ G/F, 11A Rua Central
☎ 586 272
🕒 noon to 3pm, 7pm to 11pm

Fat Siu Lau

✉ Rua de Felcidade 64
☎ 573 585

Fernando's Restaurant

Great Portuguese food.
✉ Praia Hac Sa 9 on Coloane Island
☎ 882 264

Restaurant Lei Hong Kei

Cantonese food, delicious selection of shellfish.
✉ Caldeira 33-37
☎ 376 670

Restaurant Sol Nascente

Specializing in Macanese seafood.
✉ Av. Dr. Sun Yat-sen,
29-37 R/C on Taipa Island
☎ 836 288

Souvenirs

Macau isn't known for its unique crafts or great shopping but clothes and Chinese furniture are cheap and worth browsing. Antiques can be found at reasonable prices around the Ruins of St. Paul's. Also worth checking out are gold and jade jewelry. Both benefit from low import taxes and many shops around Senado Square offer a wide variety of styles. Buying from licensed jewelers is recommended; otherwise, you could end up with a pricey, but worthless fake – be sure to get a warranty card. Gongbei Market in Zhuhai is where many Macanese shop and is a great place to find fake designer items to impress your friends with back home. Genuine name brand items can also be found but usually cost about the same as they do back home. Taipa Village has craft markets on Saturdays where you can find a number of traditional Chinese handiworks and trinkets like jade carvings, paper cuttings, wood engravings, pottery and knot decorations.

The main shopping areas are along the Avenida do Infante D. Henrique and Avenida Almeida Ribeiro, Sao Domingos Market, Rua da Palha, Rua do Campo, and Rua Pedro Nolasco da Silva. Antiques can be found in the stalls around the Ruins of the Church of St. Paul's – remember to bargain and don't expect any treasures.

Other Information

HOSPITALS

Conde S. Januario Hospital

✉ Estrada S. Francisco
☎ 313 731

Kiang Wu Hospital

✉ Rua Tomas Viera & Estrada Do Repouso
☎ 371 333

COMPLAINT HOTLINES

☎ General: 315 566, 313 355
☎ Taxi: 519 519

Taiwan, the Island Beauty

Area Code 00886

TAIPEI, ROOTED IN CHINESE CULTURE

From Towering Plazas to Taoist Temples, Taipei has much to offer to visitors of all stripes – from those seeking ultra-modern gadgets to those seeking a respite from the bustle of modern life.

If you're looking for the juxtaposition of old and new then you won't want to miss out on Taipei's many temples, where ancient ways live on beneath the shadows of skyscrapers. If the pursuit of the latest high-tech gadget is your cup of Oolong tea, then a visit to the **Kuanghua Computer Market** or indeed any one of the many computer markets that are popping up like mushrooms in the city may well be in order. Whether you're shopping for the latest fashion or just looking to see and be seen, then a trip to the ultra-fashionable **Hsimending** will be necessary.

From high-tech shopping areas to low-tech night markets to traditional Chinese art, music and culture, today's Taipei has a lot of enticements. Still, this is a modern metropolis surrounded on all sides by natural beauty, and getting out of town is as simple as catching a bus or train heading in nearly any direction.

Taipei is easy to get around, either by foot, bus or subway. A walking tour of the downtown area is a good place to start. Unsure of which direction to head? Try the observation deck of the **Landmark Taipei Shingong Tower** for a bird's-eye view of the city and pick a direction to walk – it's right across from **Taipei Main Station**. Heading west from there takes you into **Hsimending** where the young and beautiful shop. There are restaurants for all tastes in Hsimending, from coffee shops and steak houses to sushi bars of both the cheap and expensive variety. There are 24-hour dim sum restaurants where you can get stewed chicken feet and other Cantonese delicacies at any hour. Not surprisingly, Hsimending's main cash trade is in the field of corporeal

The bright lights of Taiwan's vibrant nightlife.

beautification it boasts at least one outlet of every trendy clothing place found in Taiwan, as well as hundreds of smaller stores. While you might not find them along the main drag, the smaller alleys boast no fewer than six storefront tattoo parlours, if jewellery just isn't permanent enough for you.

Lovers of Qing dynasty architecture won't want to miss **Hsiao Nanmen**, a beautiful old square fort with a northern Chinese "palace" style roof. A quick subway ride north will bring you to the **Confucius Temple** and the **Taipei Fine Art Museum**. Close to Shilin MRT Station you'll find **Chishan Park**, which has a genuine Song dynasty style garden, complete with pavilions, ponds and arched bridges.

If you'd like to skip the culture and shopping in favor of just chilling out, head to **Ta-an Forest Park** on Xin-yi Road Section Two, a great place to play frisbee, read or just relax.

The Dr. Sun Yat-sen Memorial Hall in the heart of Taipei.

If you really want to relax, head up to Yangming Shan, easily one of the most awe-inspiring parks to be located close to a major metropolitan area. From the southern slope of the mountain one can easily look over the whole of Taipei, all the while being surrounded by beautiful foliage as sulfuric volcanic steam rises from the ground around you. The park is loaded with plenty of trails, several hot springs resorts, temples, shrines, and other objects of Chinese beauty. It's easy to forget that you're anywhere near a major city from way up on Yangming Shan.

When night falls, head back down into the city and to the **Shihlin Night Market**, where traditional Taiwanese snacks can be bought. **The Huashi Street Night Market**, otherwise known as Snake Alley, is perhaps the most famous tourist street in Taipei. In addition to snake meat soup and strong liquor infused with snake bile (said to be an aphrodisiac), the area is noted for its fortune tellers, traditional Chinese herbalists and of course, excellent food. It's also a good place to buy small religious items, ornaments and other stuff to impress the folks back home.

For those who really want to stay up all night, the area around **Fushing** and **Chunghsiao Road** is well known for its many bars and clubs. After partying the night away, hungry night owls with a hankering for after-hours cuisine know to head south on Fushing to a stretch known collectively as "**breakfast row**," where excellent traditional Taiwanese eats like dumplings, fried fish and sweet potato rice porridge – that surefire hangover cure can be bought 24/7. Just look for the lights and the people eating.

For a hot night at the **hot springs**, the area directly around the New Peitou station is loaded with hotels and guesthouses that pipe sulfurous hot-spring water up from underneath the mountains. If you want to spend less, there are public hot springs located across from the oddly named "**Anti-Calamity Park**." **Wulai** also is renowned for its hot-spring resorts, though it's a bit harder to get to, requiring a subway ride to Hsintien Station and a 35-minute bus up to the mountain town of Wulai (signs from the subway station are clearly marked in English). Hotels will set you back NT $600 for three hours and considerably more for the night, but the public hot-springs charge a paltry admission fee of between NT $50 and 100.

TAIWAN'S RUGGED NORTHEAST

When most people think of Taiwan, they

Taipei Square is a major center in Taipei.

think of endless factories churning out textiles and computers and crowded streets filled with business-suit types rushing from business meeting to business meeting. While this may be true of the cities, the picture over in the northeast – Taiwan's vacation paradise – is far different and a whole lot prettier.

This is being a small island, you don't have to travel too far from the heart of Taipei to find yourself feeling as if you're a thousand miles away from the big city. The last stop on Taipei's MRT line is the old town of **Tamshui**, where the river of the same name meets the ocean. Here you can revisit the Qing dynasty on **Chongjian Street**, where narrow lanes and unevenly paved stones harkens back to ancient times, or **Yinshan Temple**, a house of worship that was built in 1822 with strict adherence to the principles of fengshui.

Whether you go by bike, motorcycle or bus, a drive along the north coast of Taiwan will tell you quickly why so many Taipei city dwellers head north on the weekends. Carved by the ocean from underwater rock, Shimen Cave (the name means stone gate) is a popular spot for exploration, fishing or ocean gazing. Another popular spot is the **Yeliou Scenic Area**, where visitors can check out strange rock formations like the famous "Queens Head" rock (really does look like an Egyptian Queen in profile) or reel in excellent fish meals at the nearby **Yeliou Harbor**. If you're interested in hang gliding, the hills nearby **Feicueiwan**, a nearly mile-long (1.5 km) beach of white sand, are popular. The beach itself is beautiful and great for swimming, sailing and windsurfing in all but the coldest months. You'll easily be able to find places to rent all needed equipment once you get there, so don't bother trying to put your windsurfing board in your carry-on.

The most famous of north Taiwan's "Old Towns" is the hillside village of **Jiufen**, where the three main streets have been designated historical landmarks. **Jishan Street** is the best place for traditional snacks and many tea shops are clustered along the stone steps of **Shuci Road**. Of course, Jiufen is also a good place for souvenir shopping.

Bitou Cape is a well maintained trail

The Palace Museum in Taipei is one of the best places see the treasures of China's past.

running along the edges of a small finger of land jutting out into the sea. The tip of the cape has a lighthouse, which is open to the public. Just south of the cape lies the **Taoyuan Valley Trail** which brings hikers to a gently sloping carpet of green grass from which you can view a 360 degree view of the Pacific. This area also offers other hiking opportunities, so comfortable footwear is a must.

Heading south along Route 2, you'll have the mountains to your right and the ocean to your left. In most spots, the ocean is pretty rocky and rough. **Yanliao Beach**, **Fulong Beach** and **Honeymoon Bay** are all popular with people who dig the beach, Fulong Beach is the spot of many all night parties on the weekend and all three places see some surfing action – apparently the best waves are right before the typhoons hit.

Central Taiwan's Sun-Moon Lake.

South of Honeymoon bay is the **Lion's Kingdom Museum / Leo Club**, a museum that doubles as a hotel, and a stunningly beautiful resort. The owner, Mr. Kao, also happens to be a man with a powerful affinity for stone lions. This obsession has resulted in his owning the largest collection of stone lions in the world, 6,000 pieces and rising – definitely worth a visit for fans of lions, sculpture or both. Just next door is the **Beiguan Tidal Park**, a series of trails that lead over the rocks and along the beach. There's a set of excellent food stalls next to the park where you can eat seafood caught fresh from the sea, or just hang out and snack on apple soda and peanut candy.

Until recently, **Kueishan Island** was off limits to the public. It's now possible to get a permit to visit, but it's still a bit of a hassle. However, the sunrise over the island is beautiful and for those who want to see the island closer or see the superheated water of underwater hot springs turn the ocean at the head of the island a strange shade of green, there are several boat tours leaving every day from nearby **Wushih Harbor**.

Even if the island doesn't interest you – it looks like a turtle, complete with a stony face and a long sandy tail – the boat trip is well worth it, as the ocean east of the island is rich with opportunities for dolphin and whale watching.

Though the entire road down the east coast is amazing and loaded with sightseeing opportunities, the northeast sector of Taiwan is the best of the best. Be sure to see the town of **Jiaosi**, just north of the city of **Ilan**. Jiaosi is best known as a hot spring resort and all of the hotels boast of having superheated water – reputed to cure a number of physical illnesses – pumped into their rooms. ■

Making Your Trip Easy

Practical Tips

Taipei is just north of the Tropic of Cancer. Expect hot and sticky summers, cool and damp winters and rain in the spring and fall. Typhoon season is generally in August and September.

Be aware that Taiwan has its own visa requirements separate from the Chinese mainland. Visitors from some nations can stay up to 14 days without a visa, while others will require a visa that allows up to a 30-day stay. Contact the Taiwan representative office for more information. The currency in Taiwan is the New Taiwan Dollar (NT) and money can be easily exchanged at banks and hotels. Taiwan uses a different system for romanizing Chinese words than on the Chinese mainland, and Taipei has its own unique system, which can cause lots of confusion.

Busy roads fill with people on the go.

Traditional Chinese culture is strong in Taiwan and festival days are celebrated with zest. Chinese New Year is the most important of these celebrations and the island will be decked out in its best. Other festivals to look for are the Lantern Festival, the Dragon Boat Festival, the Ghost Festival, the Mid-Autumn Festival and Double Ninth Day.

Transportation

Airport – Most international flights will arrive at the International Airport in Taoyuan, outside of Taipei. Plans for a high speed rail from the airport into downtown Taipei are in the works, but until that happens, your best bet is to take one of the many private buses that go from the airport to the train station for around NT $150. If you want to take a cab, it'll cost you around NT $1,000.

The Songshan Airport is Taipei's local airport

Quotes

"Northeast Taiwan has dramatic scenery – waves crashing against rocks, beautiful stretches of beach – combined with the ancient feeling of Chinese culture. Add to this some of the best seafood in the world and amazing hot springs."

"Taipei is a 24-hour city. The city combines the best of both worlds, from the old world charm of the Wanhua area to the 21st century energy of Chunghsiao East Road. I love the clubbing and love the fact that there are so many spots of natural splendor so close by. In Taipei, you can go to a beach in the morning, a mountain temple in the afternoon, a world-class restaurant for dinner, a cutting edge lounge for drinks then clubbing until dawn."

and there is an international airport at Kaohsiung. The airport tax in Taiwan is NT $300. There are no direct flights between Taiwan and the Chinese mainland – you'll have to transfer planes in Hong Kong.

Bus – Inter-city bus service in Taiwan is good with government and private buses to choose from. There are plenty of buses from Taipei to all points in the northeast and the most typical starting point for a day trip is Fulong Station.

Subway – Taipei is an extremely convenient city to travel through with a highly efficient subway system (MRT). Various MRT lines run throughout the city and announcements are made in Chinese and English.

Train – There are four train classes. The fourth class is cheap but very slow compared to buses.

The Best of Taiwan

TAIPEI

The city is *renao* (lively) – a sprawling mass of skyscrapers and people. With excellent food, entertainment, shopping and cultural sights, Taipei is the place to see the seamless blend of traditional Chinese culture and

A crowd gathers around a street artist in one of Taipei's many lively markets.

Food markets serve tasty snacks late into the night.

modern lifestyle.

The Palace Museum

With a collection of over 750,000 objects, this is the place to see China's historical legacy.

✉ 34 Chishan Road, Sec. 2, Shilin

☎ 2881 2021

🕒 9am to 5pm

NT $: 100 for regular admission,80 for groups of 20 or more, 50 for students

NORTHEAST TAIWAN

The natural highlights of the northeast contrast nicely with ultra-modern Taipei. Sights like the Taroko Gorge (just continue further down the coast), perhaps one of Taiwan's most majestic scenic spots, and the small quaint towns lined with hidden coves and rough beaches are thrown together with hot springs and beautiful scenery.

Jiufen

This strange little town is built right into the side of a hill, making it somewhat reminiscent of a surreal painting.

Kueishan Island

One of the most postcard perfect moments is that of the sun rising over Kueishan Island, which can be seen best from the area around the town of Toucheng.

THE REST OF TAIWAN

Ali Shan

Right in the middle of Taiwan is the Ali Shan resort and Taiwan's tallest mountain Yu Shan, which stands 12,966 feet (3,952 m) above the island. Try to get here on the weekdays when it's not so crowded and take a ride on the steam train.

Penghu Islands

Starkly beautiful, the 64 islands of Penghu are covered in brush and grassy plains. Beaches and tranquil villages await visitors. Makung, on Penghu Island is the only city and has a quant harbour, outdoor markets and Taiwan's oldest temple. Paisha and Hsiyu, two islands linked to Penghu by a bridge, have ancient trees and stark coves. On the south of Hsiyu is the Hsitai Fort. The weather on these islands is best from May to September, the rest of the year can be cold. There are flights from Taiwan to the islands and a ferry service from Kaohsiung.

Tainan

On Taiwan's southwest coast is Tainan, the ancient provincial capital of Taiwan. Loaded with temples that come alive during the many temple festivals and the remnants of the old town, Tainan offers a great historic getaway. It's also a great spot for eating and nightlife.

Hotels

Evergreen Laurel Keelung ★★★★★

✉ 62-1 Chung Cheng Road, Keelung 202, Taiwan

US $: 102

Rebar Crown Plaza ★★★★★

✉ 32 Nanking East Road, Sec. 5, Taipei

US $: 116

Sheraton Taipei Hotel ★★★★★

✉ 12 Chung Hsiao East Road Sec. 1, Taipei

US $: 130

United Taipei ★★★★★

✉ 200 Kwang Fu South Road, Taipei

US $: 123

Food & Restaurants

Culinary considerations are definitely one of the top reasons to visit Taipei. Some of the dishes most associated with Taipei are Taiwanese beef noodle soup, a beef stock with thick noodles and chunks of beef served piping hot with or without hot sauce; *chou doufu* – there's a reason why this stuff is called stinky tofu and you'll either love it or hate it, but finding it won't be a problem –

Bright clothes and big smiles as they prepare for an ethnic festival.

just follow your nose; oyster pancakes – an omelet made with fresh oysters, eggs and plenty of lard.

Taipei's international fare will satisfy the fussiest gourmand. Cuisine from all over the world can be found in Taipei's upscale dining rooms and in the populist McDonald's.

Vegetarians are in luck, as Taipei is one of the most vegetarian friendly cities to be found. Most neighborhoods boast at least one Buddhist buffet. The fruit in Taiwan can't be beat and many fruit stands sell pre-cut fruit, great for those steamy days. Look for the many markets in Taiwan that sell great food at low prices. The area south of Shita University between Hoping and Roosevelt Roads is great for cheap and delicious eats anytime.

When in the northeast, seafood tops the list as the coast abounds with seafood markets small, medium and large. You can buy hundreds of varieties of fish and shellfish at the markets and barbeque them yourself on the beach. Many of these markets have small food stall areas next to them, so you won't have to eat sashimi if you don't feel like cooking for yourself. Astute travelers will notice that many of the shops in the area have vacuum packed plastic bags with what looks like whole and half ducks that have been run over by steamrollers. This is a pressed and salted duck, sold in a ready to eat package; the method of preserving the meat is from the days before refrigeration – some find the taste too salty. Fried taro cakes are very popular around these parts, sometimes served with dried shrimp on the top. A surprisingly light oyster soup comes in a clear, delicately seasoned broth with a hint of ginger, served with a handful of plump, fresh oysters. Some of the hot spring resorts in Jiaosi have a local dish consisting of vegetables cooked in hot spring water. Jishan Street in Jiufen offers the best variety of traditional northern Taiwanese snacks.

RESTAURANTS

Celestial

Beijing cuisine.

✉ 2-4/F-1, Nanking West Road

☏ 563 2380

Elysee French

French food.

No. 20, Alley 33, Lane 351, Tunhua South Road
781 4270

Fukul
60 Fuhsing North Road
772 7738

Genghis Khan
The Mongolian Khan's own cooking.
176 Nanking East Road, Sec. 3
711 4412

Golden Royal Taiwan Restaurant
Yummy Cantonese food.
404 Fuhsing North Road
504 7699

Hsiang Garden
Sweet Shanghainese cuisine.
No. 6, Lane 27, Jenai Road, Sec. 4
771 2277

Hsing Yeh
Delicious local cuisine.
34-1 Shuangcheng Road
596 3255

Hui Liu
A swank vegetarian restaurant serving organic meals and tea.
No. 9, Lane 41, Yung-Kang Street
2392 6707

Italian Casa Mia
628 Linsen North Road
596 4636

La Cucina
8-2, Lane 198, Hsin 1 Road, Sec. 2
397 4176

Natori
No. 3, Lane 199, Hsinyi Road, Sec. 4
705 2288

Seoul
No. 4, Lane 33, Chungshan North Road, Sec. 1
511 2326

Special Shans Kitchen
Spicy Hunanese food.
136 Nanking East Road Sec. 3
781 5858

Souvenirs

Taipei sits squarely on the crossroads of the ancient and the modern, and whether you're looking for a gift reeking of antiquity or the latest timesaving electronic gadget, chances are that you can find it here. The city has everything from the ultra-expensive and chic to the kitschy and cheap.

The weekend jade market is a great place to buy jade; it's located under the Jiengguo

Memorable Experiences

Getting our fill of culture at Taipei's museums: the city has enough excellent museums to keep even the most discriminating purveyor of art and culture busy for days. If you see only one museum in Taipei, it must be the Palace Museum, a repository of traditional Chinese art.

Gorging at the night markets, Taipei is world renowned for its street cuisine and the best way to sample a wide variety of local delicacies is to wait until after dark and head over to a night market.

Hot-spring hopping at Yangming Shan and Wulai.

Hiking, bird watching and ocean gazing, the many trails of the northeast coast offer amazing opportunities for hiking and nature watching.

Camping on the beach: there are several good campsites along the NE coast, but you'll have to bring your own camp gear – we haven't found a place to rent tents yet.

Dolphin watching at Wuhshih Harbor, though none of the tours are in English. Still, no matter what language they speak, if there are dolphins to be seen, you'll see them.

A unique souvenir shop in Taipei.

Road overpass by Ren Ai Road and is open only on Friday and Saturday. The Kuanghua Computer Market is known as one of the best places in Asia to buy discount computer equipment. Though modern stores abound, a favorite place for cyberpunk shopping is one block north of the Chunghsiao Hsinsheng Station, where hundreds of small hole-in-the-wall shops compete for your computer business. West of Taipei Main Station on Hankou Street by Po Ai Road is an area called Camera Street – bargain hard and you can wind up getting a new digital camera for half what you might pay back home. The Chinese Handicraft Market is an excellent place to find jeweler, ceramics, calligraphy, sculpture and other traditional Chinese objects d'art; it's on the corner of Zhongshan North and Xuzhuo Road.

Asiaworld Department Store
✉ 50 Jungshiau West Road, Sec. 1, Taipei

Dayeh Takashimaya
✉ 55 Jungcheng Road, Sec. 2, Taipei

Everrich Duty Free Taipei Downtown Shop
✉ B1, 72, Minchiuan East Road, Sec. 3, Taipei

The Mall
✉ 203 Duenhua South Road, Sec. 2, Taipei
☎ 545 8888

Pacific Sogo Department
✉ 45 Jungshiau East Road, Sec. 4, Taipei

Shio Kong Mitsukoshi Department Store
✉ 12 Nanking West Road, Taipei

Other Information

HOSPITALS

Mackay Memorial Hospital Mail Branch
✉ 92 Chungshan North Road, Sec. 2 Taipei
☎ 543 3535

COMPLAINT HOTLINES

☎ General: 717 3737

DRINK 酒和饮料			FRUIT 水果		
beer	píjiǔ	啤酒	apple	píngguǒ	苹果
spirits	báijiǔ	白酒	banana	xiāngjiāo	香蕉
wine	pútaojiǔ	葡萄酒	cherries	yīngtáo	樱桃
fruit juice	guǒzhī	果汁	coconut	yēzi	椰子
milk	niúnǎi	牛奶	grapes	pútao	葡萄
mineral water	kuàngquánshuǐ	矿泉水	lemon	níngméng	柠檬
water	shuǐ	水	lychees	lìzhī	荔枝
coffee	kāfēi	咖啡	muskmelon	hāmìguā	哈密瓜
green tea	lǜchá	绿茶	orange	chéngzi/júzi	橙子/橘子
black tea	hóngchá	红茶	peach	táozi	桃子
jasmine tea	mòlihuāchá	茉莉花茶	pear	lí	梨
oolong tea	wūlóngchá	乌龙茶	watermelon	xīguā	西瓜

Index

Index

D

E

F

G

H

M

N

O

T

U

V

W

X

Y

Z

WRITERS

Abram Deyo, Adam Balbo, Adam Pillsbury, Benjamin McCall, Berek Ho, Booth Haley, Brandon Zatt, Brian Thomson, Carol Lu, Charles Vaske, Chris Cottrell, Chris Winnan, Deshu Yu, Eugene Law, Eve Bergazyn, Hu Juan, Jeff Wilson, Jiayang Yuan, Jiayi Yuan, Josh Brown, Juan Chaparro, Julian Suddaby, Julie Lindsay, Justin Hirschkorn,Katherine Zhao, Kuangwei Zhao, Lucy Chen, Mark Godfrey , Mark Harding, Martin Gottske, Michael Lin, Perri Dong, Phillip Stephens, Lei Shi, Su-Yin Yap, Vawn Himmelsbach, Ying Xiao, Yiling Chen, Li Zhang, Zhuoliang Mao

PHOTOGRAPHERS

An Dong(安东), Bao Kun(鲍昆), Bernard Teo Tiant How, Cai Rongzhang(蔡荣章), Chen Baosen(陈宝森), Chen Bixin(陈碧信), Chen Changsheng(陈长生), Chen Feng(陈锋), Chen Han(陈涵), Chen Jin(陈锦), Chen Jin (陈劲), Chen Qing(陈庆), Chen Sheng(陈盛), Chen Shichuan(陈仕川), Chen Xuefeng(陈学锋), Chen Xuewu(陈学武), Chen Zhenhua(陈震华), Cheng Yuyang(程玉杨), Cui Youli(崔友利), Da Tou(大头), Da Yu(大于), Deng Yongqing(邓永庆), Di Xianghua(狄祥华), Ding Wei (丁卫), Dong Yinchun(董引春), Du Feibao(杜飞豹), Du Zongjun(杜宗军), Enrico Bossan, Eric Lefeuvre, Fan Jiwen(范继文), Fu Jiangyang (傅江洋), Gao Ge(高戈), Gao He(高和), Gao Jianguo(高建国), Gao Tunzi(高屯子), Gu Yue (古月), Guo Xuesong(郭雪松), Guo Yan(郭燕), Guo Yijiang(郭一江), Hai Yun(海韵), Hei Feng(黑风), Hong Fang(洪芳), Hou Heliang (侯贺良), Hu Kebin(胡克斌), Hu Weibiao(胡维标), Huang Lisheng(黄力生), Huang Taoming (黄韬明), Huang Yiming(黄一鸣), Huang Yizhu(黄以注), Jack, Jiang Nan(江南), Jiang Xin(江心), Jiang Yubin(姜玉彬), Jin Jun(金俊), Jing Wei(井韦), John Hogg, Khong Miaw Leong, Kuang Long(匡龙), Lan Taixuan(兰太萱), Li Chengzhong(李承中), Li Jiangshu(李江树) ,Li Jiangsong(李江松), Li Jianquan(李健泉), Li Jun(李军), Li Liandi(李连娣), Li Ming(黎明), Li Quanju(李全举), Li Yashi(李亚石), Li Zhigang(李志纲), Liang Guanshan(梁冠山), Liang Hanchang(梁汉昌), Lim Kwong Ling, Ling'er(玲儿), Liu Haidong(刘海东), Liu Jianming(刘建明),Liu Nianhai(刘念海), Liu Qing(刘卿), Liu Weixiong(刘伟雄), Liu Xuezhong(刘学忠), Liu Yong(刘勇), Liu Zhankun(刘占坤), Liu Zhaoming(刘兆明), Long Hai(龙海), Lu Guangwei(吕光伟), Lu Qing(卢青), Lu Wenlong(陆文龙), Luo Keheng(罗克恒), Luo Wei(罗伟), Luo Xiaoyun (罗小韵), Luo Zhewen(罗哲文), Ma Jinghua (马经华), Ma Zixin(马自新), Miao Gangzhu (缪钢珠), Nagashima Yoshiaki, Nie Ming(聂明), Pan Guoji(潘国基), Qi Fengchen(齐凤臣), Qi Zhenlin(戚振林), Qin Jiangying(覃江英), Qin Ying(秦颖), Robert Gordon Henderson, Ru Suichu(茹遂初), Shao Hua(邵华), Shen Yantai(沈延太), Shui Xiaojie (税晓洁), Si Xiaojian(司小建), Su Huimin(苏惠民), Su Wan(苏皖), Sula Enbo(苏拉恩波), Sun Qing (孙清), Sun Weizhong(孙伟忠), Tai Qisen(台启森), Tan How Jwat, Tan Lip Seng, Tan Ming (谭明), Tian Songhu(田松沪), Tong Jiang(仝江), Tu Zhonghua(涂中华), Wang Fuchun(王福春), Wang Gangfeng(王刚锋), Wang Guiquan(王贵泉), Wang Jianjun(王建军), Wang Qiong(王琼), Wang Shunling(汪顺陵), Wang Xuefeng(王雪峰), Wang Yulin(王育林), Wang Zheng(王征), Wei Ye(韦晔), Wei Ying (韦应), Wen Danqing(闻丹青), Weng Guangjie(翁广解), Wu Dongjun(吴东俊), Xia Juxian (夏居宪), Xia Rili(夏日利), Xiao Bai(小白), Xiao Xiong(肖雄), Xie Mo(谢墨), Xie Tongzhou(谢统宙), Xie Xinfa(谢新发), Xiong Yuansheng(熊元生), Xu Meixia(徐美夏), Xu Xiaohua(许小华), Xu Xuezhe(徐学哲), Xue Ting(薛挺), Yan Xiangqun(严向群), Yan Zhongyi(严钟义), Yang E'nuo(杨婀娜), Yang Hua(杨桦), Yang Qitao(杨祺涛), Yang Xiuyun (杨秀云), Yao Keshen(姚克慎), Yao Tianxin (姚天新), Yin Nan(尹楠), Yong He(雍和), Yu Zhixin(于志新), Yuan Jun(袁军), Yuan Xinhua (员新华), Zeng Nian(曾年), Zeng Zhi(曾智), Zhang Bo(张波), Zhang Fang(张放), Zhang Fengqing(张奉清), Zhang Haiyan(张海雁), Zhang Hanzhong(张汉忠), Zhang Hengnian (张衡年), Zhang Heping(张和平), Zhang Jianxin(张建新), Zhang Liping(张力平), Zhang Quanyue(张全跃), Zhang Rendong (张仁东), Zhang Tongsheng(张桐胜), Zhang Yibing(张毅兵), Zhang Yongfu(张永富), Zhang Zhenguang(张振光), Zhao Dadu(赵大督), Zhao Yong(赵勇), Zhao Zuoci(赵作慈), Zheng Jie(郑杰), Zhong Guohua(钟国华), Zhou Jucheng(周巨成), Zhou Kang(周抗), Zhou Li(周利), Zhou Lilong(周礼龙), Zhou Qinjun(周沁军), Zhou Yongxiang(周永祥), Zhu Hu(朱琥), Zhu Yuanbin(朱元斌), Zuo Wei(左伟), Colphoto(中国图片网), Panorama Stock (全景视拓图片), Photocome(北京百联网图), Zhu Hongyu(朱洪宇)

Published by China Intercontinental Press
6 Beixiaomachang, Lianhuachi Donglu, Beijing, China

Yuan Bao'an, Editor
Hellen Wu, Associate Editor
Wang Xin, Associate Editor
Jiayang Yuan, Associate Editor
Du Jing, Assistant Editor
Sally Guo, Assistant Editor
Jin Jun, Photo Editor
Yan Zhijie, Art Editor
Hollan Zhang, Map Editor
Liu Na, Designer
Shen Zhenzhen, Designer

图书在版编目(CIP)数据

中国旅游指南 = Best of China ／五洲传播出版社编.—2 版
—北京:五洲传播出版社,2008.1
ISBN 978-7-5085-1203-7
Ⅰ.中… Ⅱ. 五… Ⅲ. 旅游指南 – 中国 – 英文 Ⅳ. K928.9

中国版本图书馆 CIP 数据核字 (2007) 第 171789 号

五洲传播出版社
电话:(8610) 58891281
地址:中国北京莲花池东路北小马厂 6 号
邮编:100038
字数: 420 千字
开本: 大 32 开
印张: 17
版次: 2008 年 1 月第二版　2008 年 1 月第五次印刷
印数:73001-83000 册
印刷:北京华联印刷有限公司
书号:ISBN 978-7-5085-1203-7
定价:168.00 元

Disclaimer

Although we've made every effort to ensure the information in *Best of China* is accurate, we cannot be held responsible for errors, omissions or details that have changed. Prices given in our guide are only for reference and are subject to change. Hotel prices are subject to change without notice and vary from season to season. All assessments of sites, hotels, restaurants, food, souvenirs and stores are the subjective opinions of the individual writers and do not reflect the publisher's opinion. We accept no responsibility for any consequences that may arise from using this *Best of China*.